A PEOPLE AND A NATION

A History of the United States

VOLUME ONE

To 1877

SIXTH EDITION

Mary Beth Norton
Cornell University

David M. Katzman
University of Kansas

David W. Blight
Amherst College

Howard P. Chudacoff
Brown University

Thomas G. Paterson
University of Connecticut

William M. Tuttle, Jr.
University of Kansas

Paul D. Escott
Wake Forest University

Houghton Mifflin Company   Boston   New York

The icons used throughout Chapters 1–16 are details from "Sampler Block Quilt" by Evelyn Derr. National Museum of American Art, Smithsonian Institution, Washington, D.C./Art Resource, N.Y.

Sponsoring Editor: Colleen S. Kyle
Development Editor: Ann Hofstra Grogg
Editorial Assistant: Michael Kerns
Senior Project Editor: Christina M. Horn
Senior Production/Design Coordinator: Carol Merrigan
Senior Designer: Henry Rachlin
Senior Manufacturing Coordinator: Sally Culler
Senior Marketing Manager: Sandra McGuire

Picture research by Pembroke Herbert and Sandi Rygiel, Picture Research Consultants & Archives.

Cover design: Diana Coe / ko Design Studio
Cover image: *Pat Lyon at the Forge*, 1829, by John Neagle. Oil on canvas. Courtesy of the Pennsylvania Academy of Fine Arts, Philadelphia. Gift of the Lyon family.

Printed in the U.S.A.

Library of Congress Catalog Card Number: 00-103884

ISBN: 0-618-00551-X

1 2 3 4 5 6 7 8 9-VH-04 03 02 01 00

BRIEF CONTENTS

CONTENTS

16   RECONSTRUCTION: AN UNFINISHED REVOLUTION, 1865–1877   427

APPENDIX

MAPS

CHARTS

PREFACE

"What? Another edition?" asked one of our friends. "History hasn't changed that much in the last few years!" Wrong. "History" *has* changed, in several ways. More of "history's" story has been told in new books and articles and revealed in newly released documents. Our interpretation of "history" has changed because new perspectives on familiar topics have continued to emerge from the prolific writings of historians, anthropologists, and other scholars. And, last, our understanding of "history" has changed as our engagement with current events reshapes how we remember the past.

Like other teachers and students, we are always recreating our past, restructuring our memory, rediscovering the personalities and events that have influenced us, inspired us, and bedeviled us. This book represents our rediscovery of America's history—its diverse people and the nation they created and have nurtured. As this book demonstrates, there are many different Americans and many different memories. We have sought to present all of them, in both triumph and tragedy, in both division and unity.

Although much is new in this Sixth Edition in coverage, interpretation, and organization, we have sustained the qualities that have marked *A People and a Nation* from the begin-

About *A People and a Nation*

ning: our approach of telling the story of all the people; our study of the interaction of the private sphere of everyday life with the public sphere of politics and government; our integration of political and social history; our spirited narrative based on diaries, letters, oral histories, and other sources; and our effort to challenge readers to think about the meaning of American history, not just to memorize facts. Students and instructors have commented on how enjoyable the book is to read. Scholars have commended the book for its up-to-date scholarship.

Readers have also told us that we have demonstrated, in section after section and in the "How Do Historians Know?" feature, how the historian's mind works asking questions and teasing conclusions out of vast and often conflicting evidence. Each chapter's highlighted "How Do Historians Know?" explains how historians go about using sources—such as arti-

facts, cartoons, census data, medical records, and popular art—to arrive at conclusions. This feature also helps students understand how scholars can claim knowledge about historical events and trends. Chapter-opening vignettes, dramatically recounting stories of people contending with their times, continue to define the key questions of each chapter. Succinct introductions and summaries still frame each chapter. As before, myriad illustrations, maps, tables, and graphs tied closely to the text encourage visual and statistical explorations. Readability, scholarship, critical thinking, clear structure, instructive illustrative material—these strengths have been sustained in this edition.

Guided by Houghton Mifflin's excellent editorial and design staffs, by instructors' thorough reviews, by

What's New in This Edition

the authors' ongoing research, and by our frank and friendly planning sessions and critical reading of one another's chapters, we worked to improve every aspect of the book. We added a distinguished new author, David W. Blight, whose expertise on the antebellum period, slavery, the Civil War, and historical memory has strengthened these topics in the book. To reflect new scholarship and to satisfy instructors' needs for improved chronological flow, we substantially reorganized the chapters that cover the antebellum and post-1945 periods. We have expanded our treatment of slavery, women, religion in America's social and political life, race theory and the social construction of racial identity, the West, the South's relationship to the nation, cultural expansion as a dimension of foreign relations, and the globalization of the U.S. economy. Throughout the book, we reexamined every sentence, interpretation, map, chart, illustration, and caption, refining the narrative, presenting new examples, and rethinking and labeling the Summary section for each chapter. More than half of the chapter-opening vignettes are new to this edition, as are more than one-third of the "How Do Historians Know?" entries. The "Important Events" tables have been trimmed for easier reference. The "Suggestions for Further Reading" have been revised to include new literature and conveniently consolidated at the end of the book.

Eager to help students link the past to the present, to identify the origins of issues of current interest, we have introduced in each chapter a new feature: "Legacy for a People and a Nation." Appearing after each chapter's Summary, the Legacy feature spotlights a specific contemporary topic; examples include Columbus Day, women's education, Bible Belt, revolutionary violence, Fourteenth Amendment, ethnic food, intercollegiate athletics, Peace Corps, atomic waste, and the Internet. After exploring the subject's beginnings, a few tightly focused paragraphs trace its important history to the present, inviting students to think about the historical roots of their world today and to understand the complexity of issues that on the surface seem so simple. For students who ask what history has to do with the immediate events and trends that swirl around them—or who wonder why we study history at all—these timely legacies provide telling answers.

New "Legacy for a People and a Nation"

As in previous editions, several themes and questions stand out in our concerted effort to incorporate the most recent scholarship that integrates political, social, and cultural history. We study the many ways Americans have defined themselves—gender, race, class, region, ethnicity, religion, sexual orientation—and the many subjects that have reflected their multidimensional experiences: social, political, economic, diplomatic, military, environmental, intellectual, cultural, technological, and more. We highlight the remarkably diverse everyday life of the American people—in cities and on farms and ranches, in factories and in corporate headquarters, in neighborhood meetings and in powerful political chambers, in love relationships and in hate groups, in recreation and in work, in the classroom and in military uniform, in secret national security conferences and in public foreign relations debates, in church and in prison, in polluted environments and in conservation areas. We pay particular attention to lifestyles, diet and dress, family life and structure, labor conditions, gender roles, and childbearing and child rearing. We explore how Americans have entertained and informed themselves by discussing their music, sports, theater, print media, film, radio, television, graphic arts, and literature, in both "high" culture and "low" culture. We study how technology has influenced Americans' lives, such as through the internal combustion engine and the computer.

Themes in This Book

The private sphere of everyday life always interacts with the public sphere of politics and government. To understand how Americans have sought to protect their different ways of life and to work out solutions to thorny problems, we emphasize their expectations of governments at the local, state, and federal levels; governments' role in providing answers; the lobbying of interest groups; the campaigns and outcomes of elections; and the hierarchy of power in any period. Because the United States has long been a major participant in world affairs, we explore America's descent into wars, interventions in other nations, empire-building, immigration patterns, images of foreign peoples, cross-national cultural ties, and international economic trends.

Mary Beth Norton, who had primary responsibility for Chapters 1–8, expanded and revised her coverage of the peopling of the Americas and early settlements, the Salem witchcraft crisis, and masculinity and public rituals in the colonial period. She reorganized Chapter 3 to highlight new scholarship identifying the 1670s as a crucial turning point in the relationships of Europeans and Indians in several regions of North America, and to emphasize the key role of the slave trade in the economy of all the colonies. In Chapter 4, she added a discussion of regional differences in African American family life. Chapters 3, 4, and 8, moreover, all incorporate recent scholarship on the complex relationship between the development of the slave system and the creation of racial categories.

Section-by-Section Changes in This Edition

David M. Katzman, who had primary responsibility for Chapters 9–12, substantially reorganized the early-nineteenth-century chapters. Chapters 9–11 now have a more focused chronological narrative, integrating political events with related social, economic, and cultural developments. The antebellum chapters give added emphasis to regional interconnections in the emerging market economy, Indian–white relations and Native American adaptations to the market economy, demographic changes, internal migration, popular culture, and the formation of racial ideas. Katzman also gives new attention to the Barbary captives, the Lewis and Clark expedition, early Texas settlement, and population movements. He also explores anew immigration, ethnicity and race, frontier communities in the West, and the links between reform politics and religion.

David W. Blight, who had primary responsibility for Chapters 13–16, brought fresh perspectives to the antebellum South and its relation to the nation's cultural life and market revolution. He added new material on slave culture and resistance, slavery's intersection with westward expansion, the War with Mexico, and the Underground Railroad. In his discussion of the South, he increased coverage of free blacks and social reform movements. In the Civil War and Reconstruction chapters, Blight has revised the history of military battles, women and nursing, emancipation, wartime reconstruction, the meanings of freedom for former slaves, and the Fourteenth Amendment. He has introduced the problem of memory—especially Americans' difficulty in confronting the Reconstruction period of their history. Replacing Paul D. Escott, who brought distinction to *A People and a Nation* for five editions and whose fine writing and scholarship remain evident throughout, Blight has worked with co-author Katzman to reorganize all the antebellum period chapters.

Howard P. Chudacoff, who had primary responsibility for Chapters 17–21 and 24, reconfigured material throughout these chapters. Chapter 17 now focuses solely on the West, with additions on Indian economic and cultural life, women in frontier communities, mining, irrigation, and transportation. In his other chapters, he has increased the coverage of southern industrialization, immigrants and migrants in southern cities, and southern Progressivism. He also presents new discussion of the characteristics of the industrial revolution, race and ethnicity in urban borderlands, Mexican American farmers, religion and science, technology, the clash between modernism and fundamentalism, women's political activities, and the causes of the Great Depression.

Thomas G. Paterson, who had primary responsibility for Chapters 22–23, 26, 29, and 31, and shared responsibility for 33, and who served as the book's coordinating author, offers new material throughout on cultural expansion and on the influence of ideology and images of foreign peoples on foreign policy decisions. He has augmented coverage of religious missionaries, Anglo-American cooperation, and navalism. Labor issues, Indian soldiers, weapons technology, and gas warfare receive new treatment for World War I. As part of the restructuring of the post-1945 chapters, Chapters 29 and 31 are newly designed to parallel chapters on domestic history. Paterson reexamines the Korean War, U.S. Information Agency activities, and popular fears of nuclear war. For the Vietnam War, he has revisited presidential leadership, the war's impact on domestic reform, and military experiences. The last

chapter newly explores environmental diplomacy, the globalization of U.S. culture, intrastate wars, and humanitarian intervention.

William M. Tuttle, Jr., had primary responsibility for Chapters 25, 27–28, 30, and 32, and shared responsibility for 33. In Chapter 25, he expanded treatment of New Deal cultural programs, unionism, and the question of "whiteness." For World War II, he added new material on the cultural history of the home front, the wartime economy, technological research, and homosexuals in the armed forces. In his post-1945 chapters, Tuttle has revised his coverage of McCarthyism, race relations, the New Left and counterculture, Indian protest, immigration legislation, the Reagan presidency, AIDS, and the anti-abortion movement. In the last chapter, Tuttle has expanded his discussion of political violence and public dissatisfaction with government, and he has included new material on school shootings and the presidential impeachment crisis.

The multidimensional Appendix, prepared by Thomas G. Paterson, has been brought up to date. Once again, the Appendix includes a guide to reference works on key subjects in American history. Students may wish to use this updated and enlarged list of encyclopedias, atlases, chronologies, and other books, for example, when they start to explore topics for research papers, when they seek precise definitions or dates, when they need biographical profiles, or when they chart territorial or demographic changes. The tables of statistics on key features of the American people and nation also have been updated, as have the tables on the states (and the District of Columbia and Puerto Rico), presidential elections, presidents and vice presidents, party strength in Congress, and the justices of the Supreme Court. Other information, including the Articles of Confederation and a complete table of the cabinets by administration, is available on the *A People and a Nation* web site.

A People and a Nation continues to be supported by an extensive supplements package. For this edition, many more resources will be available to students and instructors online and on CD-ROM. We have also revised and updated all elements of our existing package.

Study and Teaching Aids

A new version of *@history*, Houghton Mifflin's CD-ROM featuring nearly one thousand primary source materials, including video, audio, visual, and textual resources, has been keyed to the organization of the Sixth Edition of *A People and a Nation*. Available in both instructor's and student's versions, *@history* is an interactive multimedia tool that can improve the analytical skills of students and introduce them to historical sources.

American History GeoQuest is a CD-ROM designed to improve students' geographical literacy. The program consists of thirty interactive historical maps, each of which provides background information and a series of self-correcting quizzes so that students can master the information on their own.

The *A People and a Nation* web site has been redesigned, updated, and augmented for users of the Sixth Edition. An *Instructor's Web Site* includes the *Online Instructor's Resource Manual* (see below), downloadable PowerPoint lecture outline slides, interactive Legacy activities, online primary sources with teaching instructions, and annotated links to other sites. The *Student's Web Site* includes ACE reading self-quizzes; online primary sources, including text, photo, and audio resources; an annotated guide of the top historical research Web sites; and interactive Legacy activities.

The *Study Guide*, prepared by George Warren of Central Piedmont Community College, includes an introductory chapter on studying history that focuses on interpreting historical facts, test-taking hints, and critical analysis. The guide also includes learning objectives, a thematic guide, lists of terms, multiple choice and essay questions with answer keys, and map exercises.

A new *Online Instructor's Resource Manual*, also created by George Warren, will now be downloadable from Houghton Mifflin's web site. For each chapter, the manual includes a content overview, a brief list of learning objectives, a comprehensive chapter outline, ideas for classroom activities, discussion questions, and ideas for paper topics.

A *Test Bank*, also prepared by George Warren, provides approximately 1,700 new multiple choice questions, more than 1,000 identification questions, and approximately 500 essay questions. This content is also available in a *Computerized Test Bank* for both Windows and Macintosh platforms.

A set of *American History Map Transparencies* is also available to instructors upon adoption.

At each stage of this revision, a sizable panel of historian reviewers read drafts of our chapters. Their suggestions, corrections, and pleas helped guide us through this momentous revision. We could not include all of their recommendations, but the book is better for our having heeded most of their advice. We heartily thank

Acknowledgments

Patrick Allitt, *Emory University*
Cara Anzilotti, *Loyola Marymount University*
Felix Armfield, *Western Illinois University*
Robert Becker, *Louisiana State University*
Jules Benjamin, *Ithaca College*
Roger Bromert, *Southwestern Oklahoma State University*
Jonathan Chu, *University of Massachusetts at Boston*
Nathaniel Comfort, *George Washington University*
Mary DeCredico, *U.S. Naval Academy*
Judy DeMark, *Northern Michigan University*
Jonathan Earle, *University of Kansas*
Alice Fahs, *University of California, Irvine*
Neil Foley, *University of Texas*
Colin Gordon, *University of Iowa*
Robert Gough, *University of Wisconsin at Eau Claire*
Brian Greenberg, *Monmouth University*
Harland Hagler, *University of North Texas*
Elizabeth Haiken, *University of British Columbia*
Benjamin Harrison, *University of Louisville*
Elizabeth Cobbs Hoffman, *San Diego State University*
Marianne Holdzkom, *Ohio State University*
John Inscoe, *University of Georgia*
Frank Lambert, *Purdue University*
David Rich Lewis, *Utah State University*
Nancy Mitchell, *North Carolina State University*
Patricia Moore, *University of Utah*
John Neff, *University of Mississippi*
James Reed, *Rutgers University*
Joseph Rowe, *Sam Houston State University*
Sharon Salinger, *University of California, Riverside*
Richard Stott, *George Washington University*
Daniel B. Thorp, *Virginia Polytechnic Institute and State University*
Marilyn Westerkamp, *University of California, Santa Cruz*
John Wigger, *University of Missouri, Columbia*
John Scott Wilson, *University of South Carolina*

The authors once again thank the extraordinary Houghton Mifflin people who designed, edited, produced, and nourished this book. Their high standards and acute attention to both general structure and fine detail are cherished in the publishing industry. Many thanks, then, to Colleen Shanley Kyle, sponsoring editor; Ann Hofstra Grogg, freelance development editor; Christina Horn, senior project editor; Jean Woy, editor-in-chief; Sandra McGuire, senior marketing manager; Pembroke Herbert, photo researcher; Charlotte Miller, art editor; and Michael Kerns, editorial assistant.

The authors also extend their thanks to the following for helping us: Sandra Greene, Karin Beckett, Nancy Board, Frank Couvares, Jan D. Emerson, Alice Fahs, Jeffrey Ferguson, Irwin Hyatt, Steven Jacobson, Andrea Katzman, Eric Katzman, Henry W. Katzman, Julie Stephens Katzman, Sharyn Katzman, Ariela Katzman-Jacobson, Elizabeth Mahan, Terri Rockhold, Martha Sandweiss, Martha Saxton, Barry Shank, John David Smith, Kathryn Nemeth Tuttle, and Samuel Watkins Tuttle.

We welcome comments from instructors and students about this new edition of *A People and a Nation*, which can be communicated through its accompanying web site, found at **http://college.hmco.com.**

For the authors, THOMAS G. PATERSON

THE AUTHORS

Mary Beth Norton

Born in Ann Arbor, Michigan, Mary Beth Norton received her B.A. from the University of Michigan (1964) and her Ph.D. from Harvard University (1969). She is now Mary Donlon Alger Professor of American History at Cornell University. Her dissertation won the Allan Nevins Prize. She has written *The British-Americans* (1972), *Liberty's Daughters* (1980), and *Founding Mothers and Fathers* (1996), which was one of three finalists for the Pulitzer Prize in 1997. She has coedited *To Toil the Livelong Day* (1987), *Women of America* (1979), and *Major Problems in American Women's History* (1995). Her articles have appeared in such journals as the *William and Mary Quarterly*, *Signs*, and the *American Historical Review*. Mary Beth has served on the National Council on the Humanities, as president of the Berkshire Conference of Women Historians, as vice president for research of the American Historical Association, and as general editor of the *AHA Guide to Historical Literature* (1995). In 1999 she was elected a fellow of the American Academy of Arts and Sciences. The National Endowment for the Humanities, Guggenheim Foundation, and Rockefeller Foundation have assisted her scholarship.

David M. Katzman

Born in New York City and a graduate of Queens College (B.A., 1963) and the University of Michigan (Ph.D., 1969), David M. Katzman is professor of American studies and courtesy professor of history and African American studies at the University of Kansas. He has written *Before the Ghetto* (1973) and *Seven Days a Week* (1978), which won the Philip Taft Labor History Prize. He has coedited *Plain Folk* (1982) and *Technical Knowledge in American Culture* (1996). He has also coauthored *Three Generations in Twentieth-Century America* (1982). David has been a visiting professor at University College, Dublin, Ireland, the University of Birmingham, England, Hong Kong University, and the University of Tokushima, Japan. He has also directed National Endowment for the Humanities Summer Seminars for College Teachers. He has sat on the Board of Directors of the National Commission on Social Studies and is coeditor of *American Studies*. At the University of Kansas, he is a former director of the College Honors Program. The Guggenheim Foundation, National Endowment for the Humanities, Ford Foundation, and Rockefeller Foundation have supported his research.

David W. Blight

Born in Flint, Michigan, David W. Blight received his B.A. from Michigan State University (1971) and his Ph.D. from the University of Wisconsin (1985). He is now Class of 1959 Professor of History and Black Studies at Amherst College. For the first seven years of his career, David was a public high school teacher in Flint. He has written *Frederick Douglass's Civil War* (1989) and *Race and Reunion: The Civil War in American Memory, 1863–1915* (2000). His edited works include *When This Cruel War Is Over: The Civil War Letters of Charles Harvey Brewster* (1992), *Narrative of the Life of Frederick Douglass* (1993), W. E. B. Du Bois, *The Souls of Black Folk* (with Robert Gooding Williams, 1997), *Union and Emancipation* (with Brooks Simpson, 1997), and *Caleb Bingham, The Columbian Orator* (1997). David's essays have appeared in the *Journal of American History*, *Civil War History*, and Gabor Boritt, ed., *Why the Civil War Came* (1996), among others. In 1992–1993 he was senior Fulbright Professor in American Studies at the University of Munich, Germany. A consultant to several documentary films, David appeared in the 1998 PBS series, *Africans in America*. In 1999 he was elected to the Council of the American Historical Association. David also teaches summer seminars for secondary school teachers, as well as for park rangers and historians of the National Park Service.

Howard P. Chudacoff

A University Professor and professor of history at Brown University, Howard P. Chudacoff was born in Omaha, Nebraska. He earned his A.B. (1965) and Ph.D. (1969) from the University of Chicago. He has written *Mobile Americans* (1972), *The Evolution of American Urban Society* (with Judith Smith, 1999), *How Old Are You?* (1989), and *The Age of the Bachelor* (1999). He has also edited *Major Problems in American Urban History* (1993). His articles have appeared in such journals as the *Journal of Family History, Reviews in American History*, and *Journal of American History*. At Brown University, Howard has cochaired the American Civilization Program, chaired the Department of History, and since 1990 has been faculty adviser to the women's basketball team. He has also served on the board of directors of the Urban History Association. The National Endowment for the Humanities, Ford Foundation, and Rockefeller Foundation have given him awards to advance his scholarship.

Thomas G. Paterson

Born in Oregon City, Oregon, and graduated from the University of New Hampshire (B.A., 1963) and the University of California, Berkeley (Ph.D., 1968), Thomas G. Paterson is professor emeritus of history at the University of Connecticut. He has written *Soviet-American Confrontation* (1973), *Meeting the Communist Threat* (1988), *On Every Front* (1992), *Contesting Castro* (1994), *American Foreign Relations* (with J. Garry Clifford and Kenneth J. Hagan, 2000), and *America Ascendant* (with Clifford, 1995). Tom has also edited *Kennedy's Quest for Victory* (1989), *Explaining the History of American Foreign Relations* (with Michael J. Hogan, 1991), and *Major Problems in American Foreign Relations* (with Dennis Merrill, 2000). With Bruce Jentleson he was senior editor for the four-volume *Encyclopedia of U.S. Foreign Relations* (1997). He has served on the ed-

itorial boards of the *Journal of American History* and *Diplomatic History*. He has been president of the Society for Historians of American Foreign Relations and has directed National Endowment for the Humanities Summer Seminars for College Teachers. He has won fellowships from the Guggenheim Foundation, among others. In 2000 the New England History Teachers Association awarded him the Kidger Award for excellence in teaching and mentoring.

William M. Tuttle, Jr.

A native of Detroit, Michigan, William M. Tuttle, Jr., received his B.A. from Denison University (1959) and his Ph.D. from the University of Wisconsin (1967). A professor of history and American studies at the University of Kansas, Bill has written *Race Riot* (1996) and *"Daddy's Gone to War"* (1993). He has also edited *W. E. B. Du Bois* (1973) and coedited *Plain Folk* (1982). His articles have appeared in such journals as the *Journal of American History, American Studies*, and *Child Welfare*. He has been a research associate at the Institute of Human Development at the University of California, Berkeley. As a historical consultant, Bill has helped prepare several public television documentaries and docudramas, including *The Killing Floor*, which appeared on PBS's *American Playhouse*. Bill's scholarly work has been assisted by the American Council of Learned Societies, Institute of Southern History at Johns Hopkins University, Charles Warren Center, Guggenheim Foundation, Stanford Humanities Center, Radcliffe College, and National Endowment for the Humanities. In 1998 Bill was awarded the William T. Kemper Fellowship for Teaching Excellence.

A PEOPLE AND A NATION

Prom.Lupi

Portus Regalis, siue F. S. Helenæ.

5

As they neared the village called Cofitachequi on May 1, 1540, the band of Spanish explorers led by Hernán de Soto beheld a surprising scene. Villagers came to meet the Europeans, carrying their female chief, or *cacica*, "with much prestige on a litter covered in white (with thin linen)." The Lady of Cofitachequi, a Spanish chronicler recorded, was "young and of fine appearance." Speaking to Soto "with much grace and self-assurance," she welcomed the weary Spaniards to her domain in today's western South Carolina, giving Soto a string of pearls from her neck. Her people offered gifts of "well tanned hides and blankets, all very good, and a large amount of jerked venison and dry wafers, and much and very good salt." Later, she gave the hungry men huge quantities of corn and, seeing that they especially valued pearls, suggested they take the ones they would find in nearby burial chambers.

The Spanish explorers had landed at Tampa Bay, Florida, about a year earlier. They would wander through what is now the southeastern United States for three more years, encountering many different peoples, whom they often treated with great cruelty. Always they futilely sought the greatest riches of all—gold and silver. The people of Cofitachequi told the Spaniards they might find these treasures in another ruler's domain, about twelve days' travel away. When Soto left, he took the Lady with him as a captive. But the chronicler reported that she, "going one day with her slave women who were carrying her, stepped aside from the road and went into a wood saying that she had to attend to her necessities. Thus she deceived them and hid herself in the woods." Presumably, she then returned home.

Why had the Lady greeted Soto's force so kindly? Perhaps she did not have enough men to resist the Europeans. Her people had been devastated by an unknown "pestilence" two years earlier, the Spaniards observed, describing deserted settlements and reporting the residents' explanations. Or possibly messengers had informed the Lady about Soto's vicious

THREE OLD WORLDS CREATE A NEW 1492–1600

A 1591 print depicted what French adventurers saw in 1562 when they sailed into Port Royal River near today's Beaufort, South Carolina. From Theodor de Bry's *America,* the first book illustrating American scenes for a European audience. (John Carter Brown Library at Brown University)

treatment of villages he had previously encountered. Whatever her reasoning, the strategy worked: Soto and his men moved on, and although they destroyed other villages and peoples, Cofitachequi survived to be recorded by Spanish, French, and finally English visitors in the course of the next 130 years.

For thousands of years before 1492, human societies in the Americas had developed in isolation from the rest of the world. The era that began in the Christian fifteenth century brought that long-standing isolation to an end. As Europeans sought treasure and trade, peoples from different cultures came into regular contact for the first time. All were profoundly changed. The brief encounter of Soto and the Lady of Cofitachequi illustrated many of the elements of those contacts and changes: cruelty and kindness, greed and deception, trade and theft, surprise and sickness, captivity and enslavement. By the time Soto and his men landed in Florida in 1539, the age of European expansion and colonization was already well under way. Over the next 350 years, Europeans would spread their influence across the globe. The history of the tiny colonies that would become the United States must be seen in this broad context of European exploration and exploitation.

The continents that European sailors reached in the late fifteenth century had their own history, one the interlopers largely ignored. The residents of the Americas were the world's most skillful plant breeders; they had developed vegetable crops more nutritious and productive than those grown in Europe, Asia, or Africa. They had invented systems of writing and mathematics and created calendars as accurate as those used on the other side of the Atlantic. In the Americas, as in Europe, states rose and fell as leaders succeeded or failed in expanding their political and economic power. The arrival of Europeans immeasurably altered the Americans' struggles with one another.

After 1400, European nations not only warred on their own continent but also tried to acquire valuable colonies and trading posts elsewhere in the world. Initially interested primarily in Asia and Africa, many Europeans eventually focused their attention on the Americas. Their contests for trade and conquest changed the course of history on four continents. Even as Europeans slowly achieved dominance, their fates were shaped by the strategies of Americans and Africans, such as that of the Lady of Cofitachequi. In the Americas of the fifteenth and sixteenth centuries, three old worlds came together to produce a new. ■

American Societies

 Human beings originated on the continent of Africa, where humanlike remains about 3 million years old have been found in what is now Ethiopia. Over many millennia, the growing population slowly dispersed to the other continents. Because the climate was then far colder than it is now, much of the earth's water was concentrated in huge rivers of ice called glaciers. Sea levels were accordingly lower, and land masses covered a larger proportion of the earth's surface than they do today. Scholars have long believed that all the earliest inhabitants of the Americas crossed a land bridge known as Beringia (at the site of the Bering Strait) approximately 12,000 to 14,000 years ago. Yet striking new archaeological discoveries in both North and South America suggest that some parts of the Americas may have been settled much earlier, perhaps by seafarers crossing from northern Europe by island-hopping from Iceland to Greenland to Baffin Island, much as the Vikings did many millennia later (see Map 1.1 on page 8). When approximately 12,000 years ago the climate warmed and sea levels rose, Americans were separated from the peoples living on the connected continents of Asia, Africa, and Europe.

The first Americans are called Paleo-Indians. Nomadic hunters of game and gatherers of wild plants,

Paleo-Indians they spread throughout North and South America, probably moving as bands composed of extended families. By about 11,500 years ago the Paleo-Indians were making fine stone projectile points, which they attached to wooden spears and used to kill and butcher bison (buffalo), woolly mammoths, and other large mammals then living in the Americas. But as the Ice Age ended and the human population increased, all the large American mammals except the bison disappeared. Scholars cannot agree whether overhunting or the change in climate caused their demise. In either case, deprived of their primary source of meat, the Paleo-Indians found new ways to survive.

By approximately 9,000 years ago, the residents of what is now central Mexico began to cultivate food crops, especially maize (corn),

Importance of Agriculture squash, beans, and peppers. In the Andes Mountains of South America, people started to grow potatoes. As knowledge of agricultural techniques

IMPORTANT EVENTS

15,000–10,000 B.C.E.	Paleo-Indians begin migrating from Asia to North America across the Beringia land bridge
7000 B.C.E.	Cultivation of food crops begins in America
c. 1000 B.C.E.	Olmec civilization appears
c. 300–600 C.E.	Height of influence of Teotihuacán
c. 600–900 C.E.	Classic Mayan civilization
1000 C.E.	Anasazi settlements in modern states of Arizona and New Mexico flourish as trading centers
1001	Norse establish settlement in "Vinland"
1050–1250	Height of influence of Cahokia; prevalence of Mississippian culture in midwestern and southeastern United States
14th century	Aztec rise to power
1450s–80s	Portuguese explore and colonize islands in the Mediterranean Atlantic and São Tomé in Gulf of Guinea
1477	Publication of Marco Polo's *Travels*, describing China
1492	Columbus reaches Bahamas
1494	Treaty of Tordesillas divides land claims between Spain and Portugal in Africa, India, and South America
1496	Last Canary Island falls to Spain
1497	Cabot reaches North America
1513	León explores Florida
1518–30	Smallpox epidemic devastates Indian population of West Indies and Central and South America
1519	Cortés invades Mexico
1521	Tenochtitlán surrenders to Cortés; Aztec Empire falls to Spaniards
1524	Verrazzano sails along Atlantic coast of United States
1534–35	Cartier explores St. Lawrence River
1539–42	Soto explores southeastern United States
1540–42	Coronado explores southwestern United States
1587–90	Raleigh's Roanoke colony vanishes
1588	Harriot publishes *A Briefe and True Report of the New Found Land of Virginia*

improved and spread through the Americas, vegetables and maize proved a more reliable source of food than hunting and gathering. Except for those living in the harshest climates, most Americans started to adopt a more sedentary style of life so they could tend fields regularly. Some established permanent settlements; others moved several times a year among fixed sites. They became adept at clearing forests through the use of controlled burning. The fires not only created cultivable lands by killing trees and fertilizing the soil with ashes but also opened meadows that attracted deer and other wildlife. All the American cultures emphasized producing sufficient food to support themselves. Although they traded such items as shells, flint, salt, and copper, no society ever became dependent on another group for items vital to its survival.

Wherever agriculture dominated the economy, complex civilizations flourished. Such societies, as-sured of steady supplies of grains and vegetables, no longer had to devote all their energies to subsistence. Instead, they were able to accumulate wealth, produce ornamental objects, trade with other groups, and create elaborate rituals and ceremonies. In North America, the successful cultivation of nutritious crops such as maize, beans, and squash seems to have led to the growth and development of all the major civilizations: first the large city-states of Mesoamerica (modern Mexico and Guatemala), and then the urban clusters known collectively as the Mississippian culture and located in the present-day United States. Each of these societies, many historians and archaeologists now believe, reached its height of population and influence only after achieving success in agriculture. Each later declined and collapsed after reaching the limits of its food supply, with dire political and military consequences.

The earliest major Mesoamerican civilization was that of the Olmecs, who about 3,000 years ago lived near the Gulf of Mexico in large cities dominated by temple pyramids. More than 1,000 years later, the Mayan civilization developed on the Yucatán Peninsula, in today's eastern Mexico. The Mayas built large urban centers containing tall pyramids and temples with brightly painted stuccoed and carved façades. They studied astronomy, created the first writing system in the Americas, and developed a richly symbolic religious life in which rituals of bloodletting played a major role. By the fifth century C.E. (Common Era), or about 1,500 years ago, the kings of the Mayan city-states started to war with one another, attempting conquest on a grand scale. But no king or city could win total victory. Eventually, the constant fighting combined with an inadequate food supply to cause the collapse of the most powerful cities, ending the classic era of Mayan civilization by 900 C.E. By the time Spaniards arrived five hundred years later, only a few remnants of the once-mighty society remained intact.

Mesoamerican Civilizations

Some of the more than 100,000 residents of Teotihuacán, the largest Mesoamerican metropolis, traded regularly with the Mayas. That city, founded in the Valley of Mexico about 300 B.C.E. (Before the Common Era)—some 2,300 years ago—was one of the most heavily populated urban areas in the world in the fifth century C.E. (By contrast, Paris had only about 10,000 residents at the time.) The rulers of Teotihuacán gained their position chiefly through commerce; their trading network extended hundreds of miles in all directions. Thousands of craftspeople lived in the city, many especially skilled in working the green glass called obsidian, which was valued throughout the region as a source of fine knives and mirrors. Teotihuacán also served as a religious center; pilgrims must have come long distances to visit the impressive Pyramid of the Sun, Pyramid of the Moon, and the great temple of Quetzalcoatl—the feathered serpent, the primary god of central Mexico.

Teotihuacán's influence was felt so widely in Mesoamerica before its decline in the eighth century C.E. that some scholars have argued that this Mexican city-state also influenced societies farther north, in what is now the United States. The Moundbuilders of the Ohio River region, who flourished about 2,000

Moundbuilders, Anasazi, and Mississippians

years ago, just as Teotihuacán rose to prominence, constructed earthen mounds. But the Ohioan mounds were used as burial sites, not as bases for temple pyramids. Also, the Moundbuilders' economy, which was based on hunting and gathering, bore little resemblance to that of Mesoamerica. Trade goods from as far away as the Great Lakes and the Gulf of Mexico have been found in the mounds, but direct evidence of contact with Teotihuacán is lacking.

Nor is there evidence of contact with Teotihuacán in sites inhabited by the Anasazi peoples in the modern states of Arizona and New Mexico. Pueblo Bonito, one of nine "Great Houses" in Chaco Canyon, by 1100 C.E. consisted of a series of large adobe buildings constructed along the sides of the canyon. Chaco Canyon, with a population of perhaps two thousand, sat at the juncture of over 400 miles of roads and served as a major regional trading center for turquoise, used then as now to create beautiful ornamental objects. The Anasazi constructed extensive irrigation systems in order to cultivate maize and other Mesoamerican crops in an arid environment, but they did not construct temple pyramids, nor did their towns resemble those built by their contemporaries in what is now Mexico.

More likely, Teotihuacán had an impact on the development of the Mississippian culture, which included the village of Cofitachequi and which flourished around 1000 C.E. in what is now the midwestern and southeastern United States. (Indeed, the historian Francis Jennings has argued that some of the Mississippians were "colonists" dispatched from Teotihuacán.) This civilization, like those to the south, depended on the cultivation of maize, beans, and squash. Not until after 800 C.E. were these nutritious crops grown successfully in the present-day United States. That introduction of agriculture made possible the growth of large cities, many of which included plazas and earthen pyramids. The largest of the urban centers was the City of the Sun (now called Cahokia), near modern St. Louis. At its peak (in the twelfth century), the City of the Sun covered more than 5 square miles and had a population of about twenty thousand—small by Mesoamerican standards but larger than any other northern community. Like Teotihuacán and Chaco Canyon, Cahokia was a religious and trading center. Its main pyramid, today called Monks Mound, was at the time of its construction the third largest structure of any description in the Western Hemisphere; it remains the largest earthwork ever built anywhere in the Americas.

Pueblo Bonito in Chaco
Canyon in what is now the
state of New Mexico.
More than six hundred
buildings were present on
the well-defended site.
The circular structures
were kivas, used for food
storage and for religious
rituals.   (David Muench
photography)

The Aztecs' histories tell of the long migration of their people (who called themselves Mexica) into the Valley of Mexico during the twelfth century. The uninhabited ruins of Teotihuacán, which by then had been deserted for at least two hundred years, awed and mystified the migrants. The Aztecs' primary god, Huitzilopochtli, was a god of war represented by an eagle. The chronicles record that Huitzilopochtli directed the Aztecs to establish their capital at the spot on an island where they saw an eagle eating a serpent (thus symbolizing Huitzilopochtli's triumph over Quetzalcoatl). That island city became Tenochtitlán, the center of a rigidly stratified society composed of hereditary classes of warriors, merchants, priests, common folk, and slaves.

Aztecs

The Aztecs conquered their neighbors, forcing them to pay tribute in luxury items, raw materials, and human beings who could be sacrificed to Huitzilopochtli. They also engaged in ritual combat, known as "flowery wars," to obtain further sacrificial victims. The war god's taste for blood was not easily quenched. In the Aztec year Ten Rabbit (1502) at the coronation of Motecuhzoma II (the Spaniards could not pronounce his name correctly, so they called him Montezuma), five thousand people are thought to have been sacrificed by having their still-beating hearts torn from their bodies.

The Aztecs believed that they lived in the age of the Fifth Sun. Four times previously, they wrote, the earth and all the people who lived on it had been destroyed. They predicted that their own world would end in earthquakes and hunger. In the Aztec year Thirteen Flint, volcanoes erupted, sickness and hunger spread, wild beasts attacked children, and an eclipse of the sun darkened the sky. Did some priest wonder whether the Fifth Sun was approaching its end? In time, the Aztecs learned that Thirteen Flint was called 1492 by the Europeans.

North America in 1492

Over the centuries, the Americans who lived north of Mexico adapted their once-similar ways of life to very different climates and terrains, thus creating the diverse cultures that the Europeans encountered when they first arrived (see Map 1.1). Scholars often refer to such cultures by language group (such as Algonquian or Iroquoian), since neighboring Indian nations commonly spoke related languages. Bands that lived in environments not well suited to agriculture—because of

Map 1.1 Native Cultures of North America The natives of the North American continent effectively used the resources of the regions in which they lived. As this map shows, coastal groups relied on fishing, residents of fertile areas engaged in agriculture, and other peoples employed hunting (often combined with gathering) as a primary mode of subsistence.

inadequate rainfall or poor soil, for example—followed a nomadic lifestyle similar to that of the Paleo-Indians. Within the area of the present-day United States, these groups included the Paiutes and Shoshones, who inhabited the Great Basin (now Nevada and Utah). Because of the difficulty of finding sufficient food for more than a few people, such hunter-gatherer bands were small, usually composed of one or more related families. The men hunted small animals and women gathered seeds and berries. Where large game was more plentiful and food supplies therefore more certain, as in present-day central and western Canada and the Great Plains, bands of hunters were somewhat larger.

In more favorable environments, larger groups combined agriculture with gathering, hunting, and fishing. Those who lived near the seacoasts, like the Chinooks of present-day Washington and Oregon, consumed fish and shellfish in addition to growing crops and gathering seeds and berries. Residents of the interior (for example, the Arikaras of the Missouri River valley) hunted large animals while also cultivating maize, squash, and beans. The peoples of what is now eastern Canada and the northeastern United States also combined hunting and agriculture. They regularly used controlled fires both to open land for cultivation and to assist in hunting.

Societies that relied primarily on hunting large animals like deer and buffalo assigned that task to men and allotted food preparation, clothing production, and child rearing to women. Before such nomadic bands acquired horses from the Spaniards, women—occasionally assisted by dogs—also carried the family's belongings whenever the band relocated. Such a sexual division of labor was universal among hunting peoples, regardless of their location. Agricultural societies, by contrast, differed in their assignments of work to the sexes. In what is now the southwestern United States, the Pueblo peoples, who lived in sixty or seventy autonomous villages and spoke five different languages, defined agricultural labor as men's work. In the east, large clusters of peoples speaking Algonquian, Iroquoian, and Muskogean languages allocated most agricultural chores to women, although men cleared the land. In all the farming societies, women gathered wild foods, prepared food for consumption or storage, and cared for children, while men were responsible for hunting.

Sexual Division of Labor in North America

The southwestern and eastern agricultural peoples had similar social organizations. They lived in villages, sometimes sizable ones with a thousand or more inhabitants. The Pueblos, descendants of the Anasazi, lived in large, multistory buildings constructed on terraces along the sides of cliffs or other easily defended sites. Northern Iroquois villages (in modern New York State) were composed of large, rectangular, bark-covered structures, or long houses; the name Haudenosaunee (which the Iroquois called themselves) means "People of the Long House." In the present-day southeastern United States, Muskogeans and southern Algonquians lived in large houses made of thatch. Most of the eastern villages were surrounded by wood palisades and ditches to aid in fending off attackers.

Social Organization

In all the agricultural societies, each dwelling housed an extended family defined matrilineally (through a female line of descent). Mothers, their married daughters, and their daughters' husbands and children all lived together. Matrilineal descent did not imply matriarchy, or the wielding of power by women, but rather served as a means of reckoning kinship. Extended families were linked into clans defined by matrilineal ties. The nomadic bands of the Great Plains, by contrast, were most often related patrilineally (through the male line). They lacked settled villages and defended themselves from attack primarily through their ability to move to safer locations when necessary.

The defensive design of eastern and western villages discloses the significance of warfare in pre-Columbian America. Long before Europeans arrived, residents of the continent fought one another for control of the best hunting and fishing territories, the most fertile agricultural lands, or the sources of essential items like salt (for preserving meat) and flint (for making knives and arrowheads). Bands of Americans protected by wooden armor battled while standing in ranks facing each other, the better to employ their clubs and throwing spears, which were effective only at close quarters. (They began to shoot arrows from behind trees only when they confronted the more accurate and longer-range European guns, which also rendered their armor useless.) People captured by the enemy in such wars were sometimes enslaved and dishonored by losing their previous names and identities, but slavery was never an important source of labor in pre-Columbian America.

War and Politics

Jacques Le Moyne, an artist accompanying the French settlement in Florida in the 1560s (see page 34), produced some of the first European images of North American peoples. His depiction of native agricultural practices shows the sexual division of labor: men breaking up the ground with fish-bone hoes before women drop seeds into the holes. But Le Moyne's version of the scene cannot be accepted uncritically: unable to abandon a European view of proper farming methods, he erroneously drew plowed furrows in the soil.   (John Carter Brown Library at Brown University)

American political structures varied considerably. Among Pueblo and Muskogean peoples, the village council, composed of ten to thirty men, was the highest political authority; no government structure connected the villages. Nomadic hunters also lacked formal links among separate bands. The Iroquois, by contrast, had an elaborate political hierarchy incorporating villages into nations and nations into a confederation; a council comprising representatives from each nation made crucial decisions of war and peace for the entire confederacy. In all the North American cultures, political power was divided between civil and war leaders, who wielded authority only so long as they retained the confidence of the people. Autocratic rule of the sort common in Europe (see page 15) was unusual in these political systems. Women more often assumed leadership roles among agricultural peoples, especially those in which females were the primary cultivators, than among nomadic hunters. Female

sachems (rulers) led Algonquian villages in what is now Massachusetts, but women never became heads of Great Plains hunting bands. Iroquois women did not become chiefs, yet clan matrons nevertheless exercised political power. The older women of each village chose its chief and could both start wars (by calling for the capture of prisoners to replace dead relatives) and stop them (by refusing to supply warriors with necessary foodstuffs).

Americans' religious beliefs varied even more than did their political systems, but all the peoples were

Religion

polytheistic, worshiping a multitude of gods. Each group's most important beliefs and rituals were closely tied to its means of subsistence. The major deities of agricultural peoples like the Pueblos and Muskogeans were associated with cultivation, and their chief festivals centered on planting and harvest. The most important gods of hunters (such as those living on the Great Plains) were associated with animals, and their major festivals were related to hunting. A band's economy and women's role in it helped to determine women's potential as religious leaders. Women held the most prominent positions in those agricultural societies (like the Iroquois) in which they were also the chief food producers, whereas in hunting societies men took the lead in religious as well as political affairs.

A wide variety of cultures, comprising more than 5 million people, thus inhabited mainland North America when Europeans arrived. The hierarchical kingdoms of Mesoamerica bore little resemblance to the nomadic hunting societies of the Great Plains or to the agricultural societies that dominated a significant share of the continent. The diverse inhabitants of North America spoke well over one thousand different languages. For obvious reasons, they did not consider themselves one people, nor did they—for the most part—think of uniting to repel the European invaders.

African Societies

Fifteenth-century Africa, like fifteenth-century America, housed a variety of cultures adapted to different terrains and climates (see Map 1.2). Many of these cultures were of great antiquity. In the north, along the Mediterranean Sea, lived the Berbers, a Muslim people. (Muslims are adherents of Islam, founded by the prophet Mohammed in the seventh century C.E.) On the east coast of Africa, Muslim city-states engaged in extensive trade with India, the Moluccas (part of modern Indonesia), and China. In these ports, sustained contact and intermarriage among Arabs and Africans created the Swahili language and culture. Through the East African city-states passed waterborne commerce between the eastern Mediterranean and East Asia; the rest followed the long land route across Central Asia known as the Silk Road.

South of the Mediterranean coast in the African interior lie the great Saharan and Libyan deserts, vast expanses of nearly waterless terrain crisscrossed by trade routes passing through oases. The introduction of the camel in the fifth century C.E. made such long-distance travel possible, and as Islam expanded after the ninth century, commerce controlled by Muslim merchants helped to spread similar religious and cultural ideas throughout the region. Below the deserts, much of the continent is divided between tropical rain forests (along the coasts) and grassy plains (in the inte-

rior). People speaking a variety of languages and pursuing different subsistence strategies lived in a wide belt south of the deserts. South of the Gulf of Guinea, the grassy landscape came to be dominated by Bantu-speaking peoples, who left their homeland in modern Nigeria about 2,000 years ago and slowly migrated south and east across the continent.

West Africa was a land of tropical forests and savanna grasslands where fishing, cattle herding, and agriculture had supported the inhabitants for at least 10,000 years before

West Africa (Guinea)

Europeans set foot there in the fifteenth century. The northern region of West Africa, or Upper Guinea, was heavily influenced by the Islamic culture of the Mediterranean. As early as the eleventh century C.E., many of the region's inhabitants had become Muslims. Trade via camel caravans between Upper Guinea and the Muslim Mediterranean was sub-Saharan Africa's major connection to Europe and West Asia. In return for salt, dates, silk, and cotton cloth, Africans exchanged ivory, gold, and slaves with northern merchants. Most of the enslaved people carried to North America came from this region, which Europeans called Guinea.

Upper Guinea runs northeast-southwest from Cape Verde to Cape Palmas. The people of its northernmost region, the so-called Rice Coast (present-day Gambia, Senegal, and Guinea), fished and cultivated rice in coastal swamplands. The Grain Coast, the next region to the south, was thinly populated and not readily accessible from the sea because it had only one good harbor (modern Freetown, Sierra Leone). Its people concentrated on farming and raising livestock. Both the Rice and the Grain Coasts—especially the former—supplied slaves destined for sale in the Americas, but even more enslaved people came from Lower Guinea, known as the Gold and Slave Coasts, to the east of Cape Palmas, and from the Bight of Biafra (modern Nigeria) and Angola.

In the fifteenth century, most Africans in Lower Guinea were farmers who practiced traditional religions, not the precepts of Islam. Believing that spirits inhabited particular places, they invested those places with special significance. As did the agricultural peoples of the Americas, they developed rituals intended to ensure good harvests. Throughout the region, individual villages composed of kin groups were linked into hierarchical kingdoms. At the time of initial European contact, decentralized political and social authority characterized the region's polities.

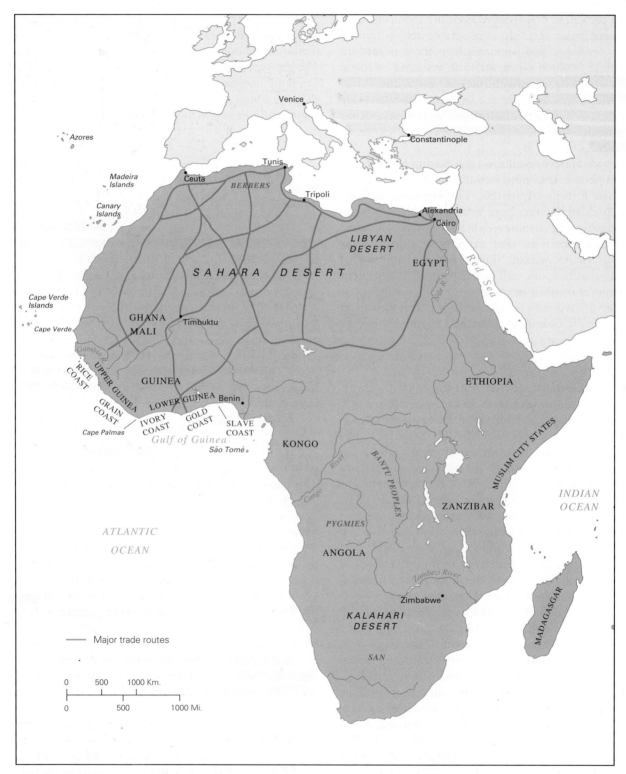

Map 1.2   Africa and Its Peoples, c. 1400   On the African continent resided many different peoples in a variety of ecological settings and political units. Even before Europeans began to explore Africa's coastlines, its northern regions were linked to the Mediterranean (and thus to Europe) by a network of trade routes.

West African law recognized both individual and communal land ownership, but men seeking to accumulate wealth needed access to labor—wives, older children, or slaves—who could work the land. Africans held in slavery on their own continent (primarily criminals, debtors, or wartime captives, and their descendants) were therefore essential components of the economy. An African who possessed slaves had a right to the products of their labor, although the degree to which slaves were exploited varied greatly. Some slaves were held as chattel; others could engage in trade, retaining a portion of their profits; and still others achieved prominent political or military positions. All, however, found it difficult to overcome the social stigma of enslavement.

Slavery in West Africa

Many of the first slaves destined for sale across the Atlantic came from the Gold Coast, composed of thirty little kingdoms known as the Akan States. By the eighteenth century, though, the area farther east and south—the modern nations of Togo, Benin, Nigeria, and Angola—supplied most of the slaves sold in the English colonies. The Adja kings of the Slave Coast encouraged the founding of slave-trading posts and served as middlemen in the trade. Access to valuable European trade goods enhanced their positions in their own societies and improved their kingdoms' standing relative to their neighbors. When Europeans in America increasingly demanded slave labor, Africans responded by selling male prisoners of war, instead of killing them. Europeans then transported the purchased captives to the colonies.

The societies of West Africa, like those of the Americas, assigned different tasks to men and women. In general, the sexes shared agricultural duties. Men also hunted, managed livestock, and did most of the fishing. Women were responsible for childcare, food preparation, and cloth manufacture. Everywhere in West Africa women were the primary local traders. They managed the extensive local and regional networks through which goods were exchanged among the various families, villages, and small kingdoms.

Sexual Division of Labor in West Africa

Despite their different economies and the rivalries among states, the peoples of Lower Guinea had similar social systems organized on the basis of what anthropologists have called the dual-sex principle. In Lower Guinea, each sex handled its own affairs, just as male political and religious leaders governed men, so

This decorative brass weight, created by the Asante peoples of Lower Guinea, was used for measuring gold dust. It depicts a family pounding fu-fu, a food made by mashing together plantains (a kind of banana), yams, and cassava. The paste was then shaped into balls to be eaten with soup. This weight, probably used in trading with Europeans, shows a scene combining foods of African origin (plantains and yams) with an import from the Americas (cassava), thus bringing the three continents together in ways both symbolic and real.　(Trustees of the British Museum. Photo by Michael Holford)

females ruled women. In the Dahomean kingdom, for example, every male official had his female counterpart; in the Akan States, chiefs inherited their status through the female line, and each male chief had a female assistant who supervised other women. Many West African societies practiced polygyny (one man having several wives, each of whom lived separately with her children). Thus few adults lived permanently in marital households, but the dual-sex system ensured that their actions were subject to scrutiny by members of their own sex, if not by a spouse.

Throughout Upper Guinea religious beliefs stressed complementary male and female roles. Both women and men served as heads of the cults and secret societies that directed the spiritual life of the villages. Young women were initiated into the Sandé cult, young men into Poro.

West African Religion

Neither cult was allowed to reveal its secrets to the opposite sex. Although West African women (unlike some of their Native American contemporaries) rarely held formal power over men, female religious leaders did govern other members of their sex within the Sandé cult, enforcing conformity to accepted norms of behavior and overseeing their spiritual well-being.

The West Africans carried to the Americas, then, were agricultural peoples, skilled at tending livestock, hunting, fishing, and manufacturing cloth from plant fibers and animal skins. Both men and women were accustomed to working communally, alongside other members of their own sex or in family groups. They were also accustomed to a relatively egalitarian relationship between the sexes, especially within the context of religion. In the Americas, they entered societies that used their labor but had little respect for their cultural traditions.

European Societies

In the fifteenth century, Europeans, too, were agricultural peoples. The daily lives of Europe's rural people had changed little for several hundred years. Split into numerous small, warring countries, Europe was divided linguistically, politically, and economically, yet in social terms Europeans' lives were more similar than different. European societies were hierarchical: a few families wielded autocratic power over the majority of the people. English society in particular was organized as a series of interlocking hierarchies; that is, each person (except those at the very top or bottom) was superior to some, inferior to others. At the base of such hierarchies were people held in a variety of forms of bondage. Although Europeans were not subjected to perpetual slavery, Christian doctrine permitted the enslavement of "heathens" (all non-Christians), and some Europeans' freedom was restricted by such conditions as serfdom, which tied them to the land if not to specific owners. In short, Europe's kingdoms resembled those of Africa or Mesoamerica but differed greatly from the more egalitarian societies found in America north of Mexico.

Most Europeans, like most Africans and Americans, lived in small villages. Only a few cities dotted the landscape, most of them political capitals. European farmers, who were called peasants, owned or leased separate landholdings, but they worked the fields communally. Because fields had to lie fallow (unplanted) every second or third year to regain fertility, a family could not ensure itself a regular food supply unless the work and the crops were shared annually by all the villagers. Men did most of the fieldwork; women helped out chiefly at planting and harvest. In some areas men concentrated on herding livestock. Women's duties consisted primarily of childcare and household tasks, including preserving food, milking cows, and caring for poultry. If a woman's husband was a city artisan or storekeeper, she might assist him in business. Since Europeans kept domesticated animals (pigs, goats, sheep, and cattle) for meat, hunting had little economic importance in their cultures. Instead, hunting was primarily a sport for male aristocrats.

Sexual Division of Labor in Europe

Unlike in African and American societies, in which women often played prominent roles in politics and religion, men dominated all areas of life in Europe. A few women—notably Queen Elizabeth I of England—achieved status or power by right of birth, but the vast majority were excluded from positions of political authority. In the Roman Catholic Church and later in the new Protestant denominations, leadership roles were reserved for men. Husbands and fathers likewise expected to control their families. European women generally held inferior social, economic, and political positions, yet within their own families they wielded power over children and servants.

When the fifteenth century began, European nations were slowly recovering from the devastating epidemic of plague known as the Black Death, which first struck them in 1346. Bubonic plague, spread by rats and fleas as well as by human contact, arrived in Europe from China, traveling with long-distance traders along the Silk Road to the eastern Mediterranean. The disease then recurred with particular severity in the 1360s and 1370s. Although no precise figures are available and the impact of the Black Death varied from region to region, the best estimate is that fully one-third of Europe's people died during those terrible years. That decimation led to a precipitous economic decline—in some regions more than half of the workers were lost—and to severe social, political, and religious disruption because of the deaths of clergymen and other leading figures.

Black Death

As plague ravaged the population, England and France waged the Hundred Years War (1337–1453), initiated because the English monarchy claimed the French throne. The war interrupted overland trade routes through France connecting England and the

Political, Economic, and Technological Change

Netherlands to the Italian city-states and thence to Central Asia. Merchants in the eastern Mediterranean thus had to find new ways of reaching their northern markets. They solved that dilemma by forging a regular maritime link with the Netherlands to replace the overland route. The use of a triangular, or lateen, sail (rather than the then-standard square rigging) improved the maneuverability of ships, enabling them to sail out of the Mediterranean and north around the European coast. Also of key importance was the perfection of navigational instruments like the astrolabe and the quadrant, which allowed oceangoing sailors to estimate their position (latitude) by measuring the relationship of the sun, moon, or certain stars to the horizon.

In the aftermath of the Hundred Years War, European monarchs forcefully consolidated their previously diffuse political power and raised new revenues through increased taxation of an already hard-pressed peasantry. The long military struggle led to new pride in national identity, which eclipsed the prevailing regional and dynastic loyalties, and to heightened hostility toward foreigners. In England, Henry VII in 1485 founded the Tudor dynasty and began uniting a previously divided land. In France, the successors of Charles VII unified the kingdom and levied new taxes. Most successful of all were Ferdinand of Aragón and Isabella of Castile. In 1469 they married and combined their kingdoms, thereby creating the foundation of a strongly Catholic Spain. In 1492 they defeated the Muslims, who had lived in Spain and Portugal for centuries, thereafter expelling all Jews and Muslims from their domain.

The fifteenth century also brought technological change to Europe. Movable type and the printing press, invented in Germany in the 1450s, made information more accessible than ever before. Printing stimulated the Europeans' curiosity about fabled lands across the seas, lands they could now read about in books. The most important such work was Marco Polo's *Travels,* first published in 1477, which recounted a Venetian merchant's adventures in thirteenth-century China and, most intriguing, described that nation as bordered on the east by an ocean. Polo's account circulated widely among Europe's educated elites, first in manuscript and later in print. The book led many Europeans to believe that they could trade directly with China in oceangoing vessels instead of relying on the Silk Road or the route through East Africa. A transoceanic route, if it existed, would allow northern Europeans to circumvent the Muslim and Mediterranean merchants who hitherto had controlled their access to Asian goods.

Technological advances and the growing strength of newly powerful national rulers made possible the European explorations of the fifteenth and sixteenth centuries. Each country craved easy access to desirable African and Asian goods—spices like pepper, cloves, cinnamon, and nutmeg (to season the bland European diet), silk, dyes, perfumes, jewels, sugar, and gold. Avoiding Muslim and Venetian middlemen and acquiring such valuable products directly would improve a nation's income and its standing relative to other countries.

Motives for Exploration

A secondary concern for spreading Christianity around the world supplemented the economic motive. The linking of materialist and spiritual goals might seem contradictory today, but fifteenth-century Europeans saw no necessary conflict between the two. Explorers and colonizers could honestly want to convert "heathen" peoples to Christianity. At the same time they could hope to increase their nation's wealth by establishing direct trade with Africa, China, India, and the Moluccas (also known as the Spice Islands).

Early European Explorations

Before European mariners could discover new lands, they had to explore the oceans. To reach Asia, seafarers needed not just the maneuverable vessels and navigational aids increasingly used in the fourteenth century, but also knowledge of the sea, its currents, and especially its winds. Wind would power their ships. But how did the winds run? Where would Atlantic breezes carry their square-rigged ships, which, even with the addition of a triangular sail, needed to run before the wind (that is, to have the wind directly behind the vessel)?

Europeans learned the answers to these questions in the region that has been called the Mediterranean Atlantic, the expanse of the Atlantic Ocean that is south and west of Spain and is bounded by the island groups of the Azores (on the west) and the Canaries (on the south), with the Madeiras in their midst (see Map 1.3). Europeans reached all three sets of islands during the fourteenth century—first the Canaries in the 1330s, then the Madeiras and the Azores. The

Sailing in the Mediterranean Atlantic

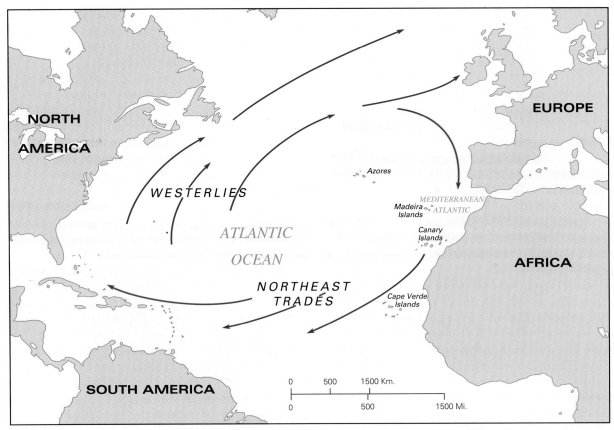

Map 1.3   **Atlantic Winds and Islands**   European mariners had to explore the oceans before they could find new lands. The first realm they discovered was that of Atlantic winds and islands.

Canaries proved a popular destination for mariners from Iberia, the peninsula that includes Spain and Portugal. Sailing to the Canaries from Europe was easy because strong winds known as the Northeast Trades blow southward along the Iberian and African coastlines. The voyage took about a week, and the volcanic peaks on the islands made them difficult to miss even with navigational instruments that were less than precise.

The problem was getting back. The Iberian sailor attempting to return home faced a major obstacle: the very winds that had brought him so quickly to the Canaries now blew directly at him. Early travelers to the islands sometimes used galleys powered by oarsmen as well as by sails, but even oarsmen had a difficult time fighting the contrary winds and currents. Another alternative was similarly tedious: tacking back and forth to the east and west, attempting each time to make more headway north. The problem seemed intractable, and in earlier eras European sailors had been

unable to solve it. When confronted with contrary winds, they simply waited for the wind to change. But for the most part, the Northeast Trades did not change. They blew steadily, shifting slightly with the seasons but never reversing course.

What could be done? Some unknown seafarer figured out the answer: sailing "around the wind." If a mariner could not sail against the trade winds, he had to sail as close as possible to the direction from which the wind was coming without being forced to tack. In the Mediterranean Atlantic, that meant pointing his vessel northwest into the open ocean, away from land, until—weeks later—he reached the winds that would carry him home, the so-called Westerlies. Those winds blow (we now know, though the mariners at first did not) northward along the coast of North America before heading east toward Europe.

This solution must at first have seemed to defy common sense, but it became the key to successful exploration of both the Atlantic and the Pacific Oceans.

In the fifteenth and sixteenth centuries, caravels ventured into the open oceans, thereby changing the contours of the known world. This illustration from a manuscript account of William Barents's 1594 expedition into the Arctic Ocean shows the combination of square rigging and lateen sails that gave ships greater maneuverability and allowed them to navigate along unfamiliar coastlines far from their home ports.   (Bridgeman Art Library)

Once a sailor understood the winds and their allied currents, he no longer feared leaving Europe without being able to return. Faced with a contrary wind, all he had to do was sail around it until he found a wind to carry him in the proper direction. This strategy might seem to take him hundreds of miles out of the way, but in the long run it was safer and surer than attempting the monumental task of tacking against the wind.

During the fifteenth century, armed with knowledge of the winds and currents of the Mediterranean Atlantic, Iberian seamen regularly visited the three island groups, all of which they could reach in two weeks or less. The uninhabited Azores were soon settled by Portuguese migrants who raised wheat for sale in Europe and sold livestock to passing sailors. The Madeiras also had no native peoples, and by the 1450s Portuguese colonists were employing slaves (probably Jews and Muslims brought from Iberia) to grow large quantities

Islands of the Mediterranean Atlantic

of sugar for export to the mainland. Madeira developed by the 1470s into the world's first colonial plantation economy.

The Canaries, by contrast, did have indigenous residents—the Guanche people, who began trading animal skins and dyes with their European visitors. In 1402 the French attacked one of the islands; thereafter, Portuguese and Spanish expeditions continued the sporadic assaults. The Guanches resisted vigorously, even though they were weakened by their susceptibility to alien European diseases. One by one the seven islands fell to Europeans, who then carried off Guanches as slaves to the Madeiras or the Iberian Peninsula. Spain conquered the last island in 1496 and subsequently devoted the land to sugar cultivation. Collectively, the Canaries and Madeira became known as the Wine Islands because much of their sugar production was directed to making sweet wines.

While some Europeans concentrated on exploiting the islands of the Mediterranean Atlantic, others used them as steppingstones to Africa. In 1415 Portugal seized control of Ceuta, a Muslim city in North Africa (see Map 1.2). Prince Henry the Navigator, son of King John I of Portugal, knew that vast wealth awaited the first European nation to tap the riches of Africa and Asia directly. Each year he dispatched ships southward along the African coast, attempting to discover an oceanic route to Asia. But not until after Prince Henry's death did Bartholomew Dias round the southern tip of Africa (1488) and Vasco da Gama finally reach India (1498).

Long before that, Portugal reaped the benefits of its seafarers' voyages. Although West African states

Portuguese Trading Posts in Africa

successfully resisted European penetration of the interior, they allowed the Portuguese to establish trading posts along their coasts. Charging the traders rent and levying duties on goods they imported, the African kingdoms set the terms of exchange and benefited considerably from their new, easier access to European manufactures. The Portuguese gained too, for they no longer had to rely on trans-Saharan camel caravans. Their vessels earned immense profits by swiftly transporting African gold, ivory, and slaves to Europe. When they carried previously enslaved Africans back to Iberia, the Portuguese introduced black slavery into Europe.

An island off the African coast, previously uninhabited, proved critical to Portuguese success. São Tomé, located in the Gulf of Guinea (see Map 1.2), was colonized in the 1480s. By that time Madeira had already reached the limit of its capacity to produce sugar. The soil of São Tomé proved ideal for raising that valuable crop, and plantation agriculture there expanded rapidly. Planters imported large numbers of slaves from the mainland to work in the cane fields, thus creating the first economy based primarily on the bondage of black Africans.

By the 1490s, even before Christopher Columbus set sail to the west, Europeans had learned three key lessons of colonization in the

Lessons of Early Colonization

Mediterranean Atlantic. First, they learned how to transplant their crops and livestock successfully to exotic locations. Second, they discovered that the native peoples of those lands could be either conquered (the Guanches) or exploited (the Africans). Third, they developed a viable model of plantation slavery—an exploitative economy based on the labor of large numbers of people held in perpetual bondage—

and a system for supplying nearly unlimited quantities of such workers. The stage was set for a pivotal moment in world history.

The Voyages of Columbus, Cabot, and Their Successors

Christopher Columbus was well schooled in the lessons of the Mediterranean Atlantic. Born in 1451 in the Italian city-state of Genoa, Columbus, the largely self-educated son of a wool merchant, was by the 1490s an experienced sailor and mapmaker. Like many mariners of the day, he was drawn to Portugal and its islands, especially Madeira, where he commanded a merchant vessel. At least once he voyaged to the Portuguese outpost on the Gold Coast. There he acquired an obsession with gold, and there he came to understand the economic potential of the slave trade.

Like all accomplished seafarers, Columbus knew the world was round. (So, indeed, did most educated people: the idea that his contemporaries believed the world to be flat is a myth dating from the nineteenth century.) But he differed from other cartographers in his estimate of the earth's size: he thought that China lay only 3,000 miles from the southern European coast. Thus, he argued, it would be easier to reach Asia by sailing west than by making the difficult voyage around the southern tip of Africa. Experts scoffed at this crackpot notion, accurately predicting that the two continents lay 12,000 miles apart. When Columbus in 1484 asked the Portuguese authorities to back his plan to sail west to Asia, they rejected the proposal. After all, why should they adopt such a crazy scheme just as their efforts to round the Cape of Good Hope promised success?

Ferdinand and Isabella of Spain, ruling a newly united kingdom and jealous of Portugal's successes in Africa, were more receptive to

Columbus's Voyage

Columbus's ideas. Urged on by some Spanish noblemen and a group of Italian merchants residing in Castile, the monarchs agreed to finance the risky voyage, in part because they hoped the profits would pay for an expedition to conquer Muslim-held Jerusalem. And so, on August 3, 1492, in command of three ships—the *Pinta*, the *Niña*, and the *Santa Maria*—Columbus set sail from the Spanish port of Palos.

The first part of the journey must have been very familiar, for the ships steered down the Northeast Trades to the Canary Islands. There Columbus refitted his square-rigged ships, adding triangular sails to make them more maneuverable. On September 6, the ships weighed anchor and headed out into the unknown ocean.

Just over a month later, pushed by favorable trade winds, the vessels found land approximately where Columbus had predicted (see Map 1.4). On October 12, he and his men landed on an island in the Bahamas, which its inhabitants called Guanahaní but which he renamed San Salvador. (Because Columbus's description of his landfall can be variously interpreted, three different places—Samana Cay, Plana Cays, and Mayaguana Cay—are today proposed as the most likely locations for his landing site.) Later he went on to explore the islands now known as Cuba and Hispaniola, which their residents, the Taíno people, called

Colba and Bohío. Because he thought he had reached the Indies, Columbus referred to the inhabitants of the region as Indians.

Three themes predominate in Columbus's log, the major source of information on this first encounter.

Columbus's Observations

First, he insistently asked the Taínos where he could find gold, pearls, and valuable spices. Each time, his informants replied (largely via signs) that such products could be obtained on other islands, on the mainland, or in cities in the interior. Eventually he came to mistrust such answers, noting, "I am beginning to believe . . . they will tell me anything I want to hear."

Second, Columbus wrote repeatedly of the strange and beautiful plants and animals. "Here the fishes are

This map, produced in 1489 by Henricus Marcellus, represents the world as Christopher Columbus knew it, for it incorporates information obtained after Bartholomew Dias, a Portuguese sailor, rounded the Cape of Good Hope at the southern tip of Africa in 1488. Marcellus did not try to estimate the extent of the ocean separating the west coast of Europe from the east coast of Asia.   (Trustees of the British Library)

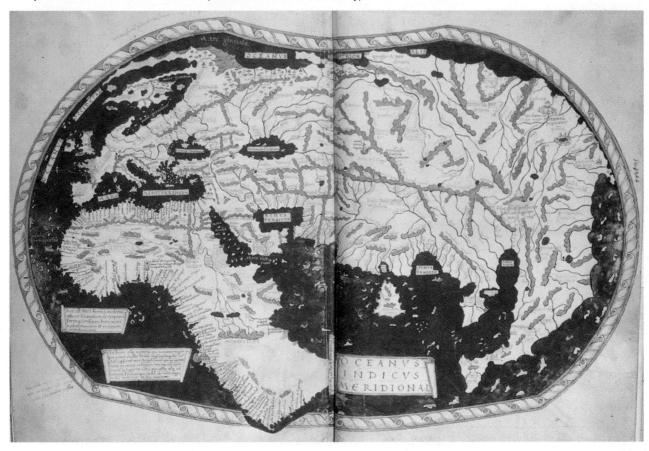

so unlike ours that it is amazing. . . . The colors are so bright that anyone would marvel," he noted, and again, "The song of the little birds might make a man wish never to leave here. I never tire from looking at such luxurious vegetation." Yet Columbus's interest was not only aesthetic. "I believe that there are many plants and trees here that could be worth a lot in Spain for use as dyes, spices, and medicines," he observed, adding that he was carrying home to Europe "a sample of everything I can," so that experts could examine them.

Third, Columbus also described the islands' human residents, and he seized some to take back to Spain. The Taínos were, he said, very handsome, gentle, and friendly, though they told him of fierce people who lived on other nearby islands and raided

The Taíno People

their villages. The Caniba (today called Caribs), from whose name the word *cannibal* is derived, were reported to eat their captives (today scholars disagree about whether the tales were true). Columbus believed the Taínos to be likely converts to Catholicism, remarking that "if devout religious persons knew the Indian language well, all these people would soon become Christians." But he had more in mind than conversion. The islanders "ought to make good and skilled servants," Columbus declared. It would be easy to "subject everyone and make them do what you wished."

Thus the records of the first encounter between Europeans and America and its residents revealed the themes that would be of enormous significance for

In 1507 Martin Waldseemüller, a German mapmaker, was the first person to designate the newly discovered southern continent as "America." He named the continent after Amerigo Vespucci, the Italian explorer who realized that he had reached a "new world" rather than islands off the coast of Asia.   (John Carter Brown Library at Brown University)

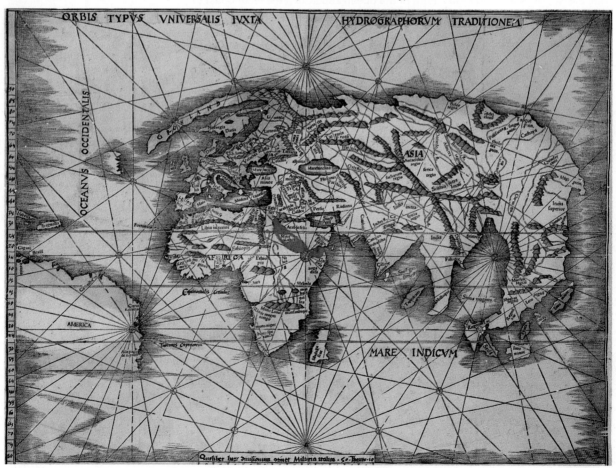

centuries to come, motivating such later explorers as Hernán de Soto as well. Above all, Europeans wanted to extract profits from North and South America by exploiting their natural resources, including plants, animals, and peoples alike.

Christopher Columbus made three more voyages to the west, exploring most of the major Caribbean islands and sailing along the coasts of

Naming of America

Central and South America. Until the day he died in 1506 at the age of fifty-five, Columbus believed that he had reached Asia. Even before his death, others knew better. Because the Florentine Amerigo Vespucci, who explored the South American coast in 1499, was the first to publish the idea that a new continent had been discovered, Martin Waldseemüller in 1507 labeled the land "America," as is evident in his map (reproduced on page 20). By then, Spain, Portugal, and Pope Alexander VI had signed the Treaty of Tordesillas (1494), confirming Portugal's dominance in Africa—and later Brazil—in exchange for Spanish preeminence in the rest of the Americas.

The mariners who explored the region of North America that was to become the United States and

Northern Voyages

Canada followed a very different route. Some historians argue that European sailors may have found the rich Newfoundland fishing grounds in the 1480s, even before Columbus's first voyage, but kept their discoveries a secret so that they alone could exploit the sea's bounty. Whether or not fishermen crossed the entire width of the Atlantic, they thoroughly explored its northern reaches. In the same way the Portuguese traveled regularly in the Mediterranean Atlantic, fifteenth-century seafarers voyaged among the European continent, England, Ireland, and Iceland.

The winds these sailors confronted posed problems on their outbound rather than homeward journeys. The same Westerlies that carried Columbus and other southern voyagers back to Europe blew in the faces of northerners looking west. But mariners soon learned that the strongest winds shifted southward during the winter and that, by departing from northern ports in the spring, they could make adequate headway if they steered northward to catch sporadic easterly breezes. Thus, whereas the first landfall of most sailors to the south was somewhere in the Caribbean, those taking the northern route usually reached America along the coast of what is now Maine or the Canadian maritime provinces.

Artifacts from L'Anse aux Meadows, Newfoundland, a site the Vikings called Straumond. These inconspicuous items reveal a great deal to archaeologists investigating the Norse settlements in North America. The small circular object, a spindle whorl for use in spinning yarn, discloses women's presence at Straumond; the nut comes from a tree that grows only south of the St. Lawrence River, thus indicating the extent of Viking travel along the coast.   (L'Anse aux Meadows, Canada)

Five hundred years before Columbus, about the year 1001, the Norseman Leif Ericsson and other

Norse Seafarers

Viking explorers sailed to North America across the Davis Strait, which separated their villages in Greenland from Baffin Island (located northeast of Hudson Bay; see Map 1.1) by just 200 nautical miles, settling at a site they named Vinland. Attacks by local residents forced them to depart hurriedly from Vinland after just a few years, the tale of their exploits subsequently being preserved in oral-history sagas. (In the 1960s, archaeologists determined that the Vikings had established an outpost at what is now L'Anse aux Meadows, Newfoundland, but Vinland itself was probably located farther south.) The European generally credited with "discovering" North America is John Cabot. More precisely, Cabot brought to Europe the first formal knowledge of the northern coastline of the continent.

Like Columbus, Cabot was a master mariner from the Italian city-state of Genoa. He is known to have

John Cabot's Explorations

been in Spain when Columbus returned from his first trip to America. Calculating that England—which traded with Asia only through a long series of middlemen stretching from Belgium to Venice to the Muslim world—would be eager to sponsor exploratory voyages, Cabot sought and

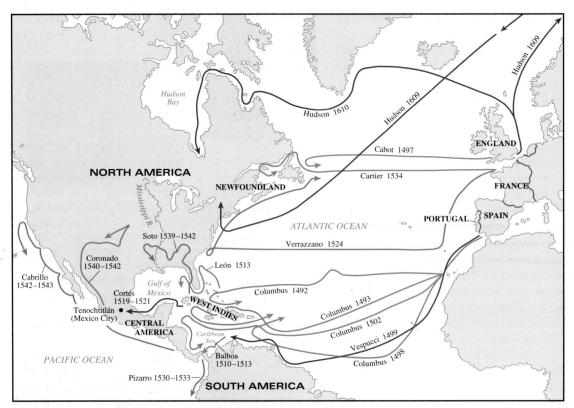

Map 1.4   European Explorations in America   In the century following Columbus's voyages, European adventurers explored the coasts and parts of the interior of North and South America.

won the support of King Henry VII. He set sail from Bristol in late May 1497 in the *Mathew*, reaching his destination on June 24. Scholars disagree about the location of his landfall (some say it was Cape Breton Island, others Newfoundland), but all recognize the importance of his month-long exploration of the coast. Having achieved his goal, Cabot rode the Westerlies back to England, arriving just fifteen days after he left North America.

The voyages of Columbus, Cabot, and their successors finally brought the Eastern and Western Hemispheres together. The Portuguese explorer Pedro Alvares Cabral reached Brazil in 1500; John Cabot's son Sebastian followed his father to North America in 1507; France financed Giovanni da Verrazzano in 1524 and Jacques Cartier in 1534; and in 1609 and 1610 Henry Hudson explored the North American coast for the Dutch West India Company (see Map 1.4). All these men were primarily searching for the legendary, nonexistent "Northwest Passage" through the Americas, hoping to find an easy route to the riches of Asia. Although they did not attempt to plant colonies in the Western Hemisphere, their discoveries interested European nations in exploring North and South America.

Spanish Exploration and Conquest

Only in the areas that Spain explored and claimed did colonization begin immediately. On his second voyage in 1493, Columbus brought to Hispaniola seventeen ships loaded with twelve hundred men, seeds, plants, livestock, chickens, and dogs—along with microbes, rats, and weeds. The settlement named Isabela (in the modern Dominican Republic) and its successors became the staging area for the Spanish invasion of America. On the islands of Cuba and Hispaniola the Europeans learned to adapt to the new environment, as did the horses, cattle, and hogs they imported. When the Spaniards moved on to explore the mainland, they rode island-bred horses and ate island-bred cattle and hogs.

At first, Spanish explorers fanned out around the Caribbean basin. In 1513 Juan Ponce de León reached Florida and Vasco Núñez de Balboa crossed the Isthmus of Panama to the Pacific Ocean. In the 1530s and 1540s, conquistadors traveled farther, exploring many regions claimed by the Spanish monarchs: Francisco Vásquez de Coronado journeyed through the southwestern portion of what is now the United States at approximately the same time as Hernán de Soto explored the southeast and encountered the Lady of Cofitachequi. Juan Rodriguez Cabrillo sailed along the California coast; and Francisco Pizarro, who ventured into western South America, acquired the richest silver mines in the world by conquering and enslaving the Incas. But the most important conquistador was Hernán Cortés, who in 1521 seized control of the Aztec Empire.

Hernán Cortés and Malinche

Cortés, an adventurer who first arrived in the West Indies in 1504, embarked for the mainland in 1519 in search of wealthy cities rumored to exist there. As he moved his force inland from the Gulf of Mexico, local Mayas presented him with a gift of twenty young female slaves. One of them, Malinche (soon baptized as a Christian and renamed Doña Marina by the Spaniards), who had been sold into slavery by the Aztecs and raised by the Mayas, became Cortés's translator and mistress. Did she do so willingly? No one knows, but perhaps she felt little loyalty to those who had enslaved her. Malinche bore Cortés a son, Martín—one of the first *mestizos*, or mixed-blood children—and eventually married one of his officers. When the Aztec capital Tenochtitlán fell to the Spaniards in 1521, Cortés and his men seized a fabulous treasure of gold and silver. Thus not long after Columbus's first voyage, the Spanish monarchs—who treated the American territories as their personal possessions—controlled the richest, most extensive empire Europe had known since ancient Rome.

Spanish Colonization

Spain established the model of colonization that other countries later attempted to imitate, a model with three major elements. First, the Crown maintained tight control over the colonies, imposing a hierarchical government that allowed little autonomy to New World jurisdictions. That control included, for example, limiting the number of people permitted to emigrate to America and insisting that the colonies import all their manufactured goods from Spain. Roman Catholic priests ensured the colonists' conformity with orthodox religious views. Second, most of the colonists sent from Spain were male. They took Indian—and later African—women as their sexual partners, thereby creating the racially mixed population that characterizes much of Latin America to the present day.

Third, the colonies' wealth was based on the exploitation of both the native population and slaves imported from Africa. The Mesoamerican peoples, many of whom lived in urban areas, were accustomed to autocratic rule. Spaniards simply took over roles once assumed by native leaders, who had also exacted labor and tribute from their subjects. The *encomienda* system, which granted tribute from Indian villages to

A European artist recorded this scene of a Carib war dance. The leaders in the middle of the circle blow tobacco smoke on the dancers to give them courage in the coming battles.   (1996 MAPes MONDe Ltd.)

How do historians know...

that Indians and Europeans interacted in complex ways as early as the sixteenth century? The study of artifacts such as this plate fragment (shown here, with a clearer drawing underneath) can reveal much about the early years of intercultural contact. Called the Coosawattee plate, it was discovered in 1984 on a farm in northwestern Georgia. The site was once an Indian village (abandoned before 1600), and the plate was found in the grave of a ten-year-old child.

Archaeologists believe that an Aztec artisan made the plate in Mexico before 1560. It probably represents the Annunciation of the Virgin Mary, with a rendering of the Virgin dominating the middle (her modesty shown by her torn and mended skirt, a common Aztec symbol), the angel, who announced that she would bear God's son, carrying a torch of illumination on the left, and an ox (more often seen in Nativity scenes) on the right. Originally manufactured as a cover for a Bible, it almost certainly belonged to a Franciscan friar attached to a Spanish expedition that traveled to northwest Georgia twenty years after the initial visit of Hernán de Soto. An Indian punched holes in the

plate (the small black circles in the drawing) to turn it into a ceremonial necklace, and it was eventually buried with the child, perhaps its last owner. The object not only reveals the Aztecs' syncretic Christianity but also illustrates how Indians creatively used items they obtained from Europeans. (Photos: Courtesy James B. Langford, Jr.)

individual conquistadors as a reward for their services to the Crown, in effect legalized Indian slavery. Yet in 1542 a new code of laws reformed the system, forbidding Spaniards from enslaving Indians while still allowing them to collect money and goods from their tributary villages. In response, the conquerors, familiar with slavery in Spain, began to import Africans in order to increase the labor force under their direct control. They employed Indians and Africans primarily in gold and silver mines, on sugar plantations, and on huge horse, cattle, and sheep ranches. Yet African slavery was far more common in the Greater Antilles (the major Caribbean islands) than on the mainland.

The New World's gold and silver, initially a boon, ultimately brought about the decline of Spain as a ma-

Gold, Silver, and Spain's Decline

jor power. The influx of unprecedented wealth led to rapid inflation, which (among other adverse effects) caused Spanish products to be overpriced in international markets and imported goods to become cheaper in Spain. The once-profitable Spanish textile-manufacturing industry collapsed, as did scores of other businesses. The seemingly endless income from American colonies emboldened successive Spanish monarchs to spend lavishly on wars against the Dutch and the English. Several times in the late sixteenth and early seventeenth centuries the monarchs repudiated the state debt, wreaking havoc on the nation's finances. When the South American gold and silver mines started to give out in the mid-seventeenth century, Spain's economy crumbled and the nation lost its international importance.

Spanish wealth derived from American suffering. The Spaniards deliberately leveled American cities, building cathedrals and monasteries on sites once occupied by Aztec, Incan, and Mayan temples. Some conquistadors sought to erase all vestiges of the great Indian cultures by burning the written records they found. With traditional ways of life in disarray, devastated by disease, and compelled to labor for their conquerors, many demoralized residents of Mesoamerica accepted the Christian religion brought to New Spain by friars of the Franciscan and Dominican orders.

The friars devoted their energies to persuading Mesoamerican people to move into new towns and to build Roman Catholic churches. In

Christianity in New Spain

such towns, Indians were exposed to European customs and religious rituals designed to assimilate Catholic and pagan beliefs. Friars deliberately juxtaposed the cult of the Virgin Mary with that of the corn goddess, and the Indians adeptly melded aspects of their traditional world-view with Christianity, in a process called syncretism. Thousands of Indians residing in Spanish territory embraced Catholicism, at least partly because it was the religion of their new rulers and they were accustomed to obedience.

The Columbian Exchange

A broad mutual transfer of diseases, plants, and animals (called the Columbian Exchange by the historian Alfred Crosby) resulted directly from the European voyages of the fifteenth and sixteenth centuries and from Spanish colonization. The two hemispheres had evolved separately for thousands of years, developing widely different forms of life. Many large mammals like cattle and horses were native to the connected continents of Europe, Asia, and Africa, but the Americas contained no domesticated beasts larger than dogs and llamas. The vegetable crops of the Americas—particularly corn, beans, squash, cassava, and potatoes—were more nutritious and produced higher yields than those of Europe and Africa, such as wheat, millet, and rye. In time, native peoples learned to raise and consume European livestock, and Europeans and Africans became accustomed to planting and eating American crops. The diets of all three peoples were consequently vastly enriched. Partly as a result, the world's population doubled over the next three hundred years.

Diseases carried from Europe and Africa, though, had a devastating impact on the Americas. Indians fell victim to microbes that had long infested the other continents and had repeatedly killed hundreds of thousands but had also left survivors with some measure of immunity. The

Smallpox and Other Diseases

A male effigy dating from 200–800 C.E., found in a burial site in Nayarit, Mexico. The lesions covering the figurine suggest that the person it represents is suffering from syphilis, which, untreated, produces these characteristic markings on the body in its later stages. Such evidence as this pre-Columbian effigy has now convinced most scholars that syphilis originated in the Americas—a hypothesis in dispute for many years. (Private Collection)

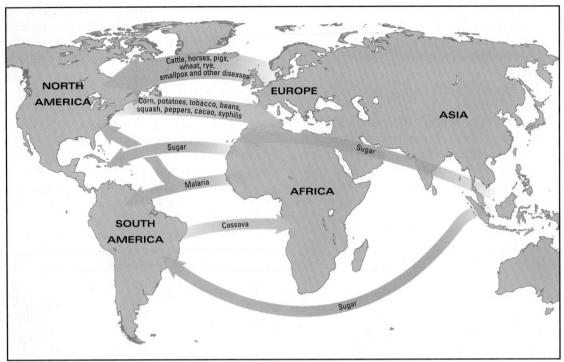

Figure 1.1   Major Items in the Columbian Exchange   As European adventurers traversed the world in the fifteenth and sixteenth centuries, they initiated the "Columbian Exchange" of plants, animals, and diseases. These events changed the lives of the peoples of the world forever, bringing new foods and new pestilence to both sides of the Atlantic.

statistics are staggering. When Columbus landed on Hispaniola in 1492, approximately half a million people resided there. Fifty years later, fewer than two thousand native inhabitants were still alive. Within thirty years of the first landfall at Guanahaní, not one Taíno survived in the Bahamas. Overall, historians estimate that the arrival of the alien microorganisms could have reduced the precontact American population by as much as 90 percent, especially because the epidemics continued to recur at twenty- to thirty-year intervals.

Although measles, typhus, influenza, malaria, and other illnesses severely afflicted the Native Americans, the greatest killer was smallpox, spread primarily by direct human contact. A Spanish priest recorded the vivid words of an old Aztec man who survived the first smallpox epidemic in Tenochtitlán. That epidemic, which began on Hispaniola in December 1518, was carried to the mainland by Spaniards in the spring of 1520. The epidemic peaked about six months later, fatally weakening Tenochtitlán's defenders. "It spread over the people as great destruction," the elderly Aztec remembered. "Some it quite covered [with pustules]

on all parts—their faces, their heads, their breasts. . . . There was great havoc. Very many died of it." Largely as a consequence, Tenochtitlán surrendered, and the Spaniards built Mexico City on its site.

Far to the north, where smaller American populations encountered only a few Europeans, disease also ravaged the countryside. A great epidemic, probably smallpox coupled with measles, swept through the villages along the coast north of Cape Cod from 1616 to 1618. Again the mortality rate may have been as high as 90 percent. An English traveler several years later commented that the people had "died on heapes, as they lay in their houses," and that bones and skulls covered the ruins of villages. Because of this dramatic depopulation of the area, just a few years later English colonists were able to establish settlements virtually unopposed.

The Americans, though, took a revenge of sorts. They gave the Europeans syphilis, a virulent venereal disease. The first recorded European case of the new ailment occurred in Barcelona, Spain, in 1493, shortly after Columbus's return from the

Syphilis

A Spanish map from 1519 showing the coast of Hispaniola, focusing on what is now the modern nation of Haiti. The decorative figures, shown with tools for hunting and cultivation, appear to be African slaves imported as laborers to replace the Indian population, already being rapidly depleted by disease and mistreatment.   (Bibliothèque Nationale)

Caribbean. Although less likely than smallpox to cause immediate death, syphilis was dangerous and debilitating. Carried by soldiers, sailors, and prostitutes, it spread quickly through Europe and Asia, reaching as far as China by 1505.

The exchange of three commodities had significant impacts on Europe and the Americas. Sugar, which was first domesticated in the East Indies, was being grown on the islands of the Mediterranean Atlantic by 1450 (see page 17). The insatiable European demand for sugar, which after initially being regarded as a medicine became a desirable luxury foodstuff, led Columbus to take Canary Island sugar canes to Hispaniola on his 1493 voyage. By the 1520s,

Sugar

plantations in the Greater Antilles worked by African slaves regularly shipped cargoes of sugar to Spain. Half a century later, the Portuguese colony in Brazil (founded 1532) was producing sugar on an even larger scale for the European market, and after 1640 (see pages 39–40), sugar cultivation became the crucial component of English and French colonization in the Caribbean.

Horses, which like sugar were brought to America by Columbus in 1493, fell into the hands of North American natives during the seventeenth century. Through trade and theft, horses spread among the peoples of the Great Plains, reaching most areas by 1750. Sioux, Comanches, and Crows,

Horses

among others, came to use horses for transportation and hunting, calculated their wealth in the number of horses owned, and waged wars primarily from horse-back. Women no longer had to carry the bands' belongings on their backs. Some groups that previously had cultivated crops abandoned agriculture altogether. Because of the acquisition of horses, a mode of subsistence that had been based on hunting several different animals, in combination with gathering and agriculture, became one focused almost wholly on hunting buffalo.

In America, Europeans encountered tobacco, which at first they believed to have beneficial medicinal effects. Smoking and chewing the

Tobacco

"Indian weed" became a fad in Europe after it was planted in Turkey in the sixteenth century. Despite the efforts of such skeptics as King James I of England, who in 1604 pronounced smoking "loathsome to the eye, hatefull to the Nose, harmfull to the brain, [and] dangerous to the Lungs," tobacco's popularity climbed. Its contribution to lung cancer was discovered only in the twentieth century.

The European and African invasion of the Americas therefore had a significant biological component, for the invaders carried plants and animals with them. Some creatures, such as livestock, they brought deliberately. Others, including rats (which infested their ships), weeds, and diseases, arrived unexpectedly. And the same process occurred in reverse. When the Europeans returned home, they deliberately took back such crops as corn, potatoes, and tobacco, along with that unanticipated stowaway, syphilis.

Europeans in North America

 Northern Europeans, denied access to the wealth of Mesoamerica by the Spanish and beaten to South America by the Portuguese, were initially more interested in exploiting North America's abundant natural resources than in the difficult task of establishing colonies on the mainland. John Cabot reported that fish were so plentiful along the North American coast that they could be caught merely by lowering baskets over the side of a vessel. Europeans rushed to take advantage of the abundance of fish, a product in great demand in their homelands as an inexpensive source of nourishment. By the 1570s, more than 350 ships, primarily from France and England, were capitalizing on the bounty of the Newfoundland Banks each year.

European fishermen soon learned that they could augment their profits by exchanging cloth and metal goods like pots and knives for the native trappers' beaver pelts, which Europeans used to make fashionable hats. At first the Europeans conducted their trading from ships sailing along the coast, but later they established permanent outposts on the mainland to centralize and control the traffic in furs (see page 36). All were inhabited chiefly by male adventurers, whose major aim was to send as many pelts as possible home to Europe.

Trade Among Indians and Europeans

The Europeans' demand for furs, especially beaver, was matched by the Indians' desire for European goods that could make their lives easier and establish their superiority over their neighbors. Some bands began to concentrate so completely on trapping for the European market that they abandoned their traditional economies. The Abenakis of Maine, for example, became partially dependent on food supplied by their neighbors to the south, the Massachusett tribe, because they devoted most of their energies to catching beaver to sell to French traders. The Massachusetts, in turn, intensified their production of foodstuffs, which they traded to the Abenakis in exchange for the European metal tools they preferred to their own handmade stone implements. The intensive trade in pelts also had serious ecological consequences. In some regions, beavers were completely wiped out. The disappearance of their dams led to soil erosion, especially when combined with the extensive clearing of forests by later European settlers.

Although their nation reaped handsome profits from fishing, English merchants and political leaders watched enviously as Spain's American possessions enriched Spain immeasurably. In the mid-sixteenth century, English "sea dogs" like John Hawkins and Sir Francis Drake began to raid Spanish treasure fleets sailing home from the West Indies. Their actions caused friction between the two countries and helped to foment a war that in 1588 culminated in the defeat of a huge invasion force—the Spanish Armada—off the English coast. As a part of the contest with Spain, English leaders started to think about planting colonies in the Western Hemisphere, thereby gaining better access to valuable trade

Contest of Spain and England

goods and simultaneously preventing their enemy from dominating the Americas.

The first English colonial planners saw Spain's possessions as both a model and a challenge. They hoped to reproduce Spanish successes by dispatching to America men who would similarly exploit the native peoples for their own and their nation's benefit. In the mid-1570s, a group that included Sir Humphrey Gilbert and his younger half-brother Sir Walter Raleigh began to promote a scheme to establish outposts that could trade with the Indians and provide bases for attacks on New Spain. Approving the idea, Queen Elizabeth I authorized first Gilbert, then Raleigh, to colonize North America.

Sir Walter Raleigh's Roanoke Colony

Gilbert failed to plant a colony in Newfoundland, dying in the attempt, and Raleigh was only briefly more successful. After two preliminary expeditions, in 1587 he sent 117 colonists to the territory he named Virginia, after Elizabeth, the "Virgin Queen." They established a settlement on Roanoke Island, in what is now North Carolina, but in 1590 a resupply ship—delayed in leaving England because of the Spanish Armada—could not find them. The colonists had vanished, leaving only the word Croatoan (the name of a nearby island) carved on a tree. Recent tree-ring studies have shown that the North Carolina coast experienced a severe drought between 1587 and 1589, which would have created a subsistence crisis for the settlers and which could well have led them to abandon the Roanoke site.

Thus England's first attempt to plant a permanent settlement on the North American coast failed, as had similar efforts by Portugal on Cape Breton Island (early 1520s) and France in northern Florida (mid-1560s). All three enterprises collapsed because of the hostility of their neighbors and their inability to be self-sustaining in foodstuffs. Spanish soldiers wiped out the French colony in 1565 (see page 34), and neither the Portuguese nor the English were able to maintain friendly relations with local Indians.

The explanation for such failings becomes clear in Thomas Harriot's *A Briefe and True Report of the New Found Land of Virginia,* published in 1588 to publicize Raleigh's colony. Harriot, a noted scientist who sailed with the second of the preliminary voyages to Roanoke, described the animals, plants, and people of the re-

Thomas Harriot's *Briefe and True Report*

John White, an artist with Raleigh's 1585 expedition (and later the governor of the ill-fated 1587 colony), illustrated three different fishing techniques used by Carolina Indians: to the left, the construction of weirs and traps; in the background, spearfishing in shallow water; in the foreground, fishing from dugout canoes. The fish are accurately drawn and can be identified today.   (Trustees of the British Museum)

gion for an English readership. His account revealed that although the explorers depended on nearby villagers for most of their food, they needlessly antagonized their neighbors by killing some of them for what Harriot himself admitted were unjustifiable reasons.

The scientist advised later colonizers to deal with the native peoples of America more humanely than his comrades had. But the content of his book suggested why that advice would rarely be followed. *A Briefe and True Report* examined the possibilities for economic development in America. Harriot stressed three points: the availability of commodities familiar to Europeans, like grapes, iron, copper, and fur-bearing animals; the potential profitability of exotic American products such as maize, cassava, and tobacco; and the relative ease of manipulating the native population to the Europeans' advantage. Should the Americans attempt to resist the English by force, Harriot asserted, the latter's advantages of disciplined soldiers and superior weaponry would quickly deliver victory.

Harriot's *Briefe and True Report* depicted for his English readers a bountiful land full of opportunities for quick profit. The people already residing there would, he thought, "in a short time be brought to civilitie" through conversion to Christianity, admiration for European superiority, or conquest—if they did not die from disease, the ravages of which he witnessed. Thomas Harriot understood the key elements of the story, but his prediction was far off the mark. European dominance of North America would be difficult to achieve. Indeed, some historians today argue that it never was fully achieved, in the sense Harriot and his compatriots intended, and that the societies that subsequently developed in North America owed as much to their native origins as to their immigrant ones.

Summary

 The process of initial contact between Europeans and Americans that ended with Thomas Harriot near the close of the sixteenth century began approximately 250 years earlier when Portuguese sailors first set out to explore the Mediterranean-Atlantic and to settle on its islands. That region of the Atlantic so close to European and African shores nurtured the mariners who, like Christopher Columbus, ventured into previously unknown waters—those who sailed to India and Brazil as well as to the Caribbean and the North American coast. When Columbus first reached the Americas, he thought he had found Asia, his intended destination. Later explorers knew better but, except for the Spanish, regarded the Americas primarily as a barrier that prevented them from reaching their long-sought goal of an oceanic route to the riches of China and the Moluccas. Ordinary European fishermen were the first to realize that the northern coasts had valuable products to offer: fish and furs, both much in demand in their homelands.

The wealth of the north could not compare to that of Mesoamerica. The Aztec Empire, heir to the trad-

ing networks of Teotihuacán as well as to the intellectual sophistication of the Mayas, dazzled the conquistadors with the magnificence of its buildings and its seemingly unlimited wealth. As an old man, Cortés's aide Bernal Diaz del Castillo recalled his first sight of Tenochtitlán, situated in the midst of Lake Texcoco: "We were amazed and said that it was like the enchantments . . . on account of the great towers and cues [temples] and buildings rising from the water, and all built of masonry." Some soldiers asked, he remembered, "whether the things that we saw were not a dream."

The Aztecs had predicted that their Fifth Sun would end in earthquakes and hunger. Hunger they surely experienced after Cortés's invasion; and, if there were no earthquakes, the great temples tumbled to the ground nevertheless, as the Spaniards used their stones (and Indian laborers) to construct cathedrals honoring their God and his son Jesus rather than Huitzilopochtli. The conquerors employed first American and later enslaved African workers to till the fields, mine the precious metals, and herd the livestock that earned immense profits for themselves and their mother country.

The initial impact of Europeans on the Americas proved devastating. Flourishing civilizations were, if not entirely destroyed, markedly altered in just a few short decades. The Europeans' diseases and livestock, along with a wide range of other imported animals and plants, irrevocably changed the American environment, affecting the lives of the Western Hemisphere's inhabitants. By the end of the sixteenth century, fewer people resided in North America than had lived there before Columbus's arrival, even taking into account the arrival of many Europeans and Africans. And the people who did live there—Indian, African, and European—resided in a world that was indeed new—a world engaged in the unprecedented process of combining foods, religions, economies, styles of life, and political systems that had developed separately for millennia. Understandably, conflict and dissension permeated that process.

LEGACY FOR A PEOPLE AND A NATION
Columbus Day

Each year, the United States celebrates the second Monday in October as a tribute to Christopher Columbus's landing in the Bahamas in 1492. When viewed in the context of other holidays that mark the birthdays of great Americans or key events in the nation's past, Columbus Day is an anomaly. After all, the Genoese mariner never set foot on North American soil.

The first known U.S. celebration of Columbus's voyage occurred in New York City on October 12, 1792, when a men's social club gave a dinner to mark its three hundredth anniversary. In the late 1860s, Italian American communities in New York City and San Francisco began to celebrate October 12, but not until the four hundredth anniversary in 1892 did a congressional resolution order a one-time national commemoration. Columbus Day was first observed as a national holiday in 1971, although a majority of the states already celebrated it (Colorado was the first, in 1907).

More than thirty years ago Congress proclaimed Columbus Day as a national holiday with little opposition, except from Americans of Scandinavian descent who would have preferred to honor the Norse explorers of 1001. Today, though, the annual observances can arouse strong emotions. The American Indian Movement (AIM), founded in 1968, has declared that "from an indigenous vantage point, Columbus' arrival was a disaster." Terming Columbus a "murderer," the AIM contends that he "deserves no recognition or acco-

lades"—certainly not a holiday. At the same time, as immigration has increased the Latino presence in the United States, people of Hispanic descent have claimed Columbus as their own, insisting that his voyage was "a thoroughly Spanish event." In some cities—most notably New York—their celebrations rival those long organized by Italian Americans; in others, such as Miami, Hispanics control the official commemorations. Still other Latinos, especially those of Mexican descent living in Los Angeles, call October 12 Día de la Raza and use it as an occasion to protest current U.S. immigration policy.

As ethnic diversity has increased in the nation, and as peoples of different origins have sought to claim a share of the American heritage, holidays have unsurprisingly become the occasion for heated contests. Each fall, the American people and nation therefore continue to confront the controversial legacy of Columbus's 1492 voyage.

For Further Reading, see page A-1 of the Appendix. For Web resources, go to http://college.hmco.com.

La V. M. Maria de Iesus de Agreda, Predicando á los Chichimecos del Nuebo-mexico. Antt.º de Castro f.

In August 1630, Fray Alonso de Benavides brought thrilling news to Madrid. Franciscan priests in the remote territory called New Mexico had successfully converted at least eighty thousand heathens to Roman Catholicism. In village after village and even among the nomadic Apaches and Navajos, Indians had eagerly embraced baptism in the new faith, had built beautiful churches and schools with their own hands, and had demonstrated their willing adherence to the true religion of Jesus Christ. Moreover, the priests' missionary activities had repeatedly benefited from God's "wonders and miracles." For example, when an old woman from Taos tried to convince four others to renounce their Christian marriages, "a bolt of lightning flashed from a clear untroubled sky, killing that infernal agent of the demon."

Fray Alonso, who was born in the Azores in the 1570s, supervised the New Mexico missions from 1626 to 1629. His account of the Franciscans' miraculous successes created a sensation in Europe. Alonso's *Memorial* not only was immediately published in Spanish but also was quickly translated into Latin, French, Dutch, and German. Fray Alonso undertook the arduous journey to Spain to convince the king to increase his financial and administrative support of the Franciscan missions. He achieved that goal: King Philip IV agreed to send additional priests to New Mexico at his own personal expense, and he ordered the colonial governor to assist the missionaries' efforts actively.

Yet even Fray Alonso de Benavides's enthusiastic and optimistic report contained a troubling undercurrent. Only about 250 Spaniards (along with another 750 Pueblos and *mestizos*) inhabited the colonial capital at Santa Fe. The soldiers were "few and poorly equipped," and the church had been "a miserable hut" before Fray Alonso ordered the construction of a new one. Furthermore, not all the local Indians had been receptive to the priests' message. The residents of Picurís, for one, were "treacherous" and "on various occasions" had tried to murder the priests stationed there. Many of the miracles Fray Alonso described

When Fray Alonso de Benavides arrived in Spain (see text above), he visited a Franciscan nun, Maria de Jesús de Agreda, who claimed to have traveled in spirit to preach to the Indians of New Mexico. In this 1631 woodcut, an artist depicted the missionizing revealed in her visions. The Indians, she declared, could see her, but Spaniards in the colony could not.   (University of Texas at Austin, Benson Latin Center for American History)

EUROPEANS COLONIZE NORTH AMERICA 1600–1640

(such as the one recounted above) had been occasioned by the Indians' rejection of Christianity. For example, some Hopis' skepticism about Christian teachings had led one priest to cause a boy blind from birth to see for the first time, and a Franciscan attempting to convert a group of Apaches had been saved from death only because at the last minute his attackers miraculously "did not dare shoot" the arrows they were aiming at him.

So, while praising the Spaniards' stunning successes in New Mexico, Fray Alonso revealed their equally striking weaknesses: many Native Americans resisted their proselytizing; both priests and soldiers lacked adequate financial resources; and the one tiny, impoverished European settlement was surrounded by tens of thousands of potentially troublesome Pueblos, Apaches, and Navajos. Fray Alonso furthermore failed to identify an additional problem: royal governors often clashed with the Franciscans in a struggle for control of the region. A half-century later, the Pueblo peoples capitalized on such Spanish weaknesses in a successful revolt.

By the time Fray Alonso arrived in Madrid in 1630, England, France, and the Netherlands had also founded permanent colonies in North America. No longer were the Spaniards the only Europeans on that vast continent. Just as Franciscans played a major role in the Spanish settlements, so too Jesuit priests were active in New France. The French and Dutch colonies, like the Spanish outposts, were settled largely by European men. Like the conquistadors, French and Dutch merchants (on the mainland) and planters (in the Caribbean islands) hoped to make a quick profit and then perhaps return to their homelands. The English, as Thomas Harriot made clear in the 1580s, were just as interested in profiting from North America. But they pursued those profits in a different way.

In contrast to other Europeans, most of the English settlers came to America intending to stay. Especially along the northeast Atlantic coast of the continent, in the area that came to be known as New England, they arrived in family groups, sometimes along with friends and relatives from neighboring villages back home. They recreated European society and family life to an extent not possible in the other colonies, where migrant men found their sexual partners within the Native American or African populations. Among the English colonies, those in the Chesapeake region and on the Caribbean islands most closely resembled colonies founded by other nations. Their economies, like those of Hispaniola or Brazil, soon came to be based on large-scale production for the international market by a labor force composed of bonded servants and slaves.

Wherever they settled, the English, like other Europeans, prospered only after they learned to adapt to the alien environment. The first permanent English colonies survived because nearby Indians assisted the newcomers. The settlers had to learn to grow unfamiliar American crops such as maize (corn) and tobacco. They also had to develop extensive trading relationships with Native Americans and with colonies established by other European countries. Needing laborers for their fields, they first used English indentured servants, then later began to import African slaves, copying the example of the Spanish in the Atlantic and Caribbean islands, and the Portuguese in São Tomé and Brazil. Thus the early history of the region that became the United States and the English Caribbean is best understood not as an isolated story of English colonization but rather as a series of complex interactions among a variety of European, African, and American peoples and environments. ■

New Spain, New France, and New Netherland

 Spaniards were the first Europeans to establish a permanent settlement within the boundaries of the modern United States, but they were not the first to attempt that feat. Twice in the 1560s groups of French Protestants (Huguenots) sought to escape from persecution in their homeland by planting colonies on the south Atlantic coast. The first colony, in present-day South Carolina, collapsed, and its starving inhabitants had to be rescued by a passing ship. The second, near modern Jacksonville, Florida, was destroyed in 1565 by a Spanish expedition under the command of Pedro Menéndez de Avilés. To ensure Spanish domination of the strategically important region (located near sea-lanes used by Spanish treasure ships bound for Europe), Menéndez set up a small fortified outpost, which he named St. Augustine—now the oldest continuously inhabited European settlement in the United States. Franciscan missionaries soon followed, but nearby Indians fiercely resisted the priests' efforts to Christianize them. Only after the native peoples were forcibly moved to mission towns did many assent to baptism. Even so, by the end of the sixteenth century a chain of Franciscan missions stretched across northern Florida.

IMPORTANT EVENTS

1533   Henry VIII divorces Catherine of Aragon; English Reformation begins

1558   Elizabeth I becomes queen

1565   Founding of St. Augustine (Florida), oldest permanent European settlement in present-day United States

1598   Oñate conquers Pueblos in New Mexico for Spain

1603   James I becomes king

1607   Jamestown founded, first permanent English settlement in North America

1608   Quebec founded by the French

1609   Hudson explores Hudson River for the Dutch

1610   Founding of Santa Fe, New Mexico

1611   First Virginia tobacco crop

1614   Fort Orange (Albany) founded by the Dutch

1619   Virginia House of Burgesses established, first representative assembly in the English colonies

1620   Plymouth colony founded, first permanent English settlement in New England

1622   Powhatan Confederacy attacks Virginia colony

1624   Dutch settle on Manhattan Island (New Amsterdam)
English colonize St. Kitts, first island in Lesser Antilles to be settled by Europeans
James I revokes Virginia Company's charter

1625   Charles I becomes king

1630   Massachusetts Bay colony founded

1634   Maryland founded

1636   Williams expelled from Massachusetts Bay; founds Providence, Rhode Island
Connecticut founded

1637   Pequot War in New England

1638   Hutchinson expelled from Massachusetts Bay colony; goes to Rhode Island

c. 1640   Sugar cultivation begins on Barbados

1642   Montreal founded by the French

1646   Treaty ends hostilities between Virginia and Powhatan Confederacy

---

More than thirty years passed after the founding of St. Augustine before conquistadors ventured anew into the present-day United States. In 1598, drawn northward by rumors of rich cities, Juan de Oñate, a Mexican-born adventurer, led a group of about five hundred soldiers and settlers to New Mexico. At first, the Pueblos greeted the newcomers cordially. When the Spaniards began to use torture, murder, and rape to extort food and clothing from the villagers, however, the residents of Acoma killed several soldiers. The invaders responded ferociously, killing more than eight hundred people and capturing the remainder. All the captives above the age of twelve were ordered enslaved for twenty years, and men older than twenty-five had one foot amputated. Not surprisingly, the other Pueblo villages surrendered.

New Mexico

Yet Oñate's bloody victory proved illusory, for New Mexico held little wealth. It also was too far from the Pacific coast to assist in protecting Spanish sea-lanes, which had been one of Oñate's aims (he, like others, initially believed the continent to be much nar-

The women of Acoma pueblo have long been accomplished potters. Before the arrival of Europeans with iron utensils, residents of the pueblo stored food and water in pots like this. The unusual shape derived from its function: the low center of gravity allowed a woman to balance the pot easily on her head as she carried water from a cistern to the top of the mesa.   (The Field Museum, #A109998c)

Table 2.1 The Founding of Permanent European Colonies in North America, 1565–1640

Colony	Founder(s)	Date	Basis of Economy
Florida	Pedro Menéndez de Avilés	1565	Farming
New Mexico	Juan de Oñate	1598	Livestock
Virginia	Virginia Company	1607	Tobacco
New France	France	1608	Fur trading
New Netherland	Dutch West India Company	1614	Fur trading
Plymouth	Pilgrims	1620	Farming, fishing
Maine	Sir Ferdinando Gorges	1622	Fishing
St. Kitts, Barbados, et al.	European immigrants	1624	Sugar
Massachusetts Bay	Massachusetts Bay Company	1630	Farming, fishing, fur trading
Maryland	Cecilius Calvert	1634	Tobacco
Rhode Island	Roger Williams	1636	Farming
Connecticut	Thomas Hooker	1636	Farming, fur trading
New Haven	Massachusetts migrants	1638	Farming
New Hampshire	Massachusetts migrants	1638	Farming, fishing

rower than it actually is). Many of the Spaniards returned to Mexico, and officials considered abandoning the isolated colony, which lay 800 miles north of the nearest Spanish settlement. Instead, in 1609, the authorities decided to maintain a small military outpost and a few Christian missions in the area, with the capital at Santa Fe (founded in 1610). This was the constricted world in which Fray Alonso de Benavides arrived in 1626 and on which he made his mark (see Map 3.3 on page 68).

After Spain's destruction of France's Florida settlement in 1565, the French turned their attention northward, to the area that Jacques Cartier had explored in the 1530s.

Quebec and Montreal

Several times they tried futilely to establish permanent bases along the Canadian coast, not succeeding until 1605, with the founding of Port Royal. Then in 1608 Samuel de Champlain set up a trading post at an interior site the local Iroquois had called Stadacona when Cartier spent the winter there seventy-five years earlier. Champlain renamed it Quebec. He had chosen well: Quebec was the most easily defended spot in the entire St. Lawrence River valley, a stronghold that controlled access to the heartland of the continent. In 1642 the French established a second post, Montreal, at the falls of the St. Lawrence (and thus at the end of navigation by oceangoing vessels), a place the Indians called Hochelaga.

Before the founding of these settlements, French fishermen served as the major transporters of North American beaver pelts to France, but the new posts quickly took over control of the lucrative trade in furs (see Table 2.1). Only a few Europeans resided in New France; most were men, some of whom married Indian women. The colony's leaders gave land grants along the river to wealthy seigneurs (nobles), who then imported tenants to work their farms. A small number of Frenchmen brought their wives and took up agriculture; even so, more than twenty-five years after Quebec's founding, it had just sixty-four resident families, along with traders and soldiers. With respect to territory occupied and farmed, northern New France never grew much beyond the confines of the river valley between Quebec and Montreal (see Map 2.1).

One other important group composed part of the population of New France: missionaries of the Society of Jesus (Jesuits), a Roman Catholic order dedicated to converting non-believers to Christianity. First arriving in Quebec in 1625, the Jesuits, whom the Indians called Black Robes, initially tried to persuade indigenous peoples to live near French settlements and to adopt European agricultural methods as well as the Europeans' religion. When that effort failed, the Jesuits concluded that they could introduce Roman Catholicism to their new charges without insisting that they fundamentally

Jesuit Missions in New France

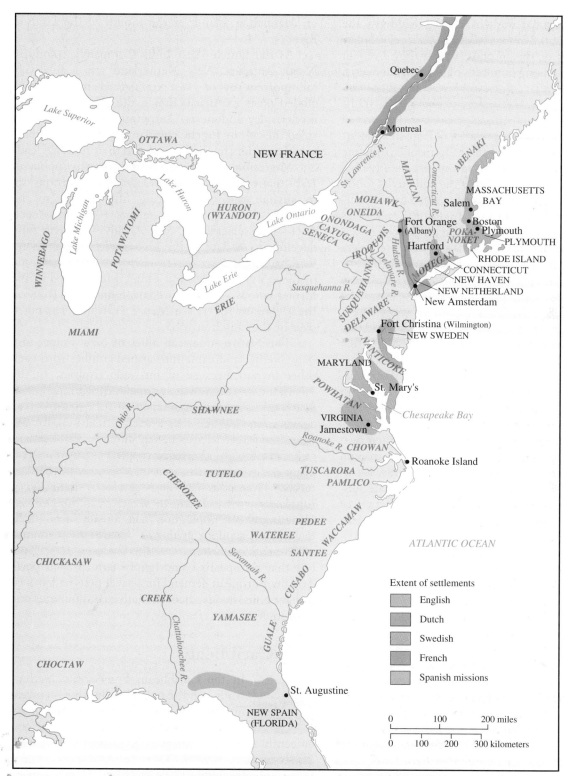

Map 2.1 European Settlements and Indian Tribes in Eastern North America, 1650
The few European settlements established in the east before 1650 were widely scattered, hugging the shores of the Atlantic Ocean and the banks of its major rivers. By contrast, America's native inhabitants controlled the vast interior expanse of the continent and Spaniards had begun to move into the West.

alter their traditional ways of life. Accordingly, the Black Robes learned Indian languages and traveled to remote regions of the interior, where they lived in twos and threes among hundreds of potential converts.

Using a variety of strategies, Jesuits sought to undermine the authority of village shamans (the traditional religious leaders) and to gain the confidence of leaders who could influence others. Trained in rhetoric, they won admirers by their eloquence. Immune to smallpox (for all had survived the disease already), they explained epidemics among the Indians as God's punishment for sin, their arguments aided by the ineffectiveness of the shamans' traditional remedies against the new pestilence. Drawing on European science, Jesuits predicted solar and lunar eclipses. Perhaps most important, they amazed the villagers by communicating with each other over long distances and periods of time by employing marks on paper. The Indians' desire to learn how to harness the extraordinary power of literacy was one of the critical factors making them receptive to the missionaries' spiritual message.

Although the process took many years, the Jesuits slowly gained thousands of converts, some of whom moved to reserves set aside for Christian Indians. In those communities they followed Catholic teachings with fervor and piety. The converts replaced their own culture's traditional equal treatment of men and women with notions more congenial to the Europeans' insistence on male dominance and female subordination. Further, they altered their practice of allowing premarital sexual relationships and easy divorce because Catholic doctrine prohibited both customs.

Jesuit missionaries faced little competition from other Europeans for Native Americans' souls, but

New Netherland

French fur traders had to confront a direct challenge. In 1614, only five years after Henry Hudson sailed up the river that now bears his name, his sponsor, the Dutch West India Company, established an outpost (Fort Orange) on that river at the site of present-day Albany, New York. Like the French, the Dutch sought beaver pelts, and their presence so close to Quebec posed a threat to French domination of the region. The Netherlands, at the time the world's dominant commercial power, was interested primarily in trade rather than colonization. Thus New Netherland, like New France, remained small, mostly confined to a river valley that offered easy access to its settlements. The colony's southern anchor was New Amsterdam, a town founded in 1624 on Manhattan Island, at the mouth of the Hudson River.

As the Dutch West India Company's colony in North America, New Netherland was a relatively unimportant part of a vast commercial empire that included posts in Africa, Brazil, the West Indies, and modern-day Indonesia. Autocratic directors-general ruled the colony for the company; with no elected assembly, settlers felt little loyalty to their nominal leaders. Migration was sparse. Even a company policy of 1629 that offered a large land grant, or patroonship, to anyone who would bring fifty settlers to the province failed to attract takers. (Only one such tract—Rensselaerswyck, near Albany—was ever fully developed.) As late as the mid-1660s, New Netherland had only about five thousand inhabitants. Some of those were Swedes and Finns, who resided in the former colony of New Sweden (founded in 1638 on the Delaware River; see Map 2.1), which was taken over by the Dutch in 1655.

The Native American allies of New France and New Netherland came into armed conflict with each other in part because of fur-trade rivalries. In the 1640s, the Iroquois, who traded chiefly with the Dutch and lived in modern upstate New York, went to war against the Hurons, who traded primarily with the French and lived in present-day Ontario. The Iroquois wanted to become the major supplier of pelts to Europeans and to ensure the security of their hunting territories. They achieved both goals by using guns supplied by the Dutch to largely exterminate the Hurons, whose population had already been decimated by a smallpox epidemic. The Iroquois thus established themselves as a major force in the region, one that Europeans could ignore only at their peril. And the European demand for beaver pelts had proved to have a disastrous effect on native communities and their interactions.

The Caribbean

In the Caribbean, France, the Netherlands, and England—the third entrant into the contest for North America—clashed openly in the first half of the seventeenth century. The Spanish concentrated their colonization efforts on the Greater Antilles—Cuba, Hispaniola, Jamaica, and Puerto Rico. They left many smaller islands alone, partly because of resistance by their Carib inhabitants, partly because the mainland offered greater wealth for less effort. But the tiny islands attracted other European powers: they could provide bases from which to attack Spanish vessels loaded with American gold and silver, and they could serve as sources of valuable tropical products such as spices, dyes, and fruits.

England was the first northern European nation to establish a permanent foothold in the smaller West Indian islands (the Lesser Antilles). English people settled on St. Christopher (St. Kitts) in 1624, then later on other islands such as Barbados (1627). France was able to colonize Guadeloupe and Martinique only by defeating the Caribs, whereas the Dutch more easily gained control of St. Eustatius (strategically located near St. Kitts). In addition to indigenous inhabitants, Europeans had to worry about conflicts with Spaniards and with one another. Most of the islands were attacked at least once during the course of the century, and some changed hands. For example, the English drove the Spanish out of Jamaica in 1655, and the French soon thereafter took over half of Hispaniola, creating the colony of St. Domingue (modern Haiti).

Why did other Europeans devote so much energy to gaining control of these tiny bits of land neglected by Spain? The primary answer to

The Importance of Sugar

that question is sugar. Early in the 1640s, English residents of Barbados discovered that the island's soil and climate were ideally suited for cultivating sugar cane, grown at the time primarily in the Wine Islands, São Tomé, and Brazil. Europeans loved sugar, which provided its users with both a sweet taste and a quick energy boost. Entering the European market in substantial quantities at approximately the same time as coffee and tea, the stimulating, addictive, and bitter Asian drinks improved by the addition of a sweetener, sugar quickly became a crucial element of Europeans' diet.

The Dutch helped to introduce sugar cane into the newly colonized Lesser Antilles. In 1630 they seized control of northeastern Brazil, holding the region until 1654. There the Dutch learned how to grow

In the 1660s, a French book illustrated the various phases of sugar processing for curious European readers. Teams of oxen (A) turned the mill, the rollers of which crushed the canes (C), producing the sap (D), which was collected in a vat (E), then boiled down into molasses (K). African slaves, with minimal supervision by a few Europeans (foreground), managed all phases of the process. (Library Company of Philadelphia)

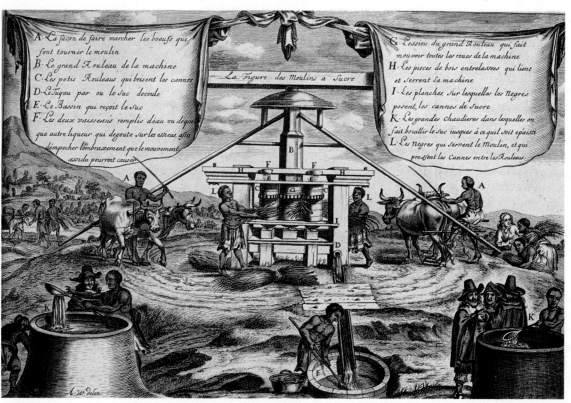

the canes and to process them into molasses and refined brown and white sugars. When they taught those skills to Barbadians, they were not being altruistic. The Dutch expected to sell African slaves to West Indian planters and to carry to Europe barrels of molasses and rum, which was distilled from sugar. The results must have exceeded their wildest dreams. The Barbados sugar boom in the 1640s was both explosive and lucrative. Planters, slave traders, and Dutch shipping interests alike earned immense profits.

As other Caribbean planters adopted sugar-cane cultivation, Barbadians' profits fell. Even so, sugar remained the most valuable American commodity for more than one hundred years. In the eighteenth century, sugar grown by slaves in British Jamaica and French St. Domingue dominated the world market. Yet, in the long run, the future economic importance of the Europeans' American colonies lay on the mainland rather than in the Caribbean.

English Interest in Colonization

The failure of Raleigh's Roanoke colony ended English efforts to settle in North America for nearly two decades. When the English decided in 1606 to try once more, they again planned colonies that imitated the Spanish model. Success came only when they abandoned that model and founded settlements very different from those of other European powers. Unlike Spain, France, or the Netherlands, England eventually sent large numbers of men and women to set up agriculturally based colonies on the mainland. Two major developments prompted approximately 200,000 ordinary English men and women to move to North America in the seventeenth century and led their government to encourage their emigration.

The first impetus that led English folk to move to North America was the onset of dramatic social and economic change caused by a population boom. In the 150-year period after 1530, largely as a result of the introduction of nutritious American crops into Europe, England's population doubled. All those additional people needed food, clothing, and other goods. The competition for goods led to high inflation, coupled with a fall in real wages as the number of workers increased. In these new economic and demographic circumstances, some English people—especially those with sizable landholdings that could produce food and clothing fibers for the

Social Change in England

growing population—substantially improved their lot. Others, particularly landless laborers and those with very small amounts of land, fell into unremitting poverty. When landowners raised rents, took over common lands previously open to use by peasants, or decided to combine small holdings into large units, they forced tenants off the land. As a result, geographical as well as social mobility increased, and the population of the cities swelled. London, for example, more than tripled in size between 1550 and 1650. By the latter year 375,000 residents were living on its crowded streets.

Well-to-do English people reacted with alarm to what they saw as the disappearance of traditional ways of life. Steady streams of the landless and homeless filled the streets and highways. Obsessed with the problem of maintaining order, officials came to believe that England was overcrowded. They concluded that colonies established in North America could siphon off England's "surplus population," thus easing social strains at home. For similar reasons, many English people decided that they could improve their circumstances by migrating from a small, land-scarce, apparently overpopulated island to a large, land-rich, apparently empty continent. Such economic considerations were rendered even more significant in light of the second development, a major change in English religious practice.

The sixteenth century witnessed a religious transformation that eventually led large numbers of English dissenters to leave their homeland. In 1533 Henry VIII, wanting a male heir and infatuated with Anne Boleyn, sought to annul his marriage to his Spanish-born queen, Catherine of Aragon, despite nearly twenty years of marriage and the birth of a daughter. When the pope refused to approve the annulment, Henry left the Roman Catholic Church. He founded the Church of England and—with Parliament's concurrence—proclaimed himself its head. In general, English people welcomed the schism. Many had little respect for the English Catholic Church, which at the time was filled with corrupt bishops and ignorant priests. At first the reformed Church of England differed little from Catholicism in its practices, but under Henry's daughter Elizabeth I (child of his marriage to Anne Boleyn), new currents of religious belief that had originated on the European continent early in the sixteenth century dramatically affected the English church.

The English Reformation

The leaders of the continental Protestant Reformation were Martin Luther, a German monk, and

John Calvin, a French cleric and lawyer. Combating the Catholic doctrine that priests must serve as intermediaries between laypeople and God, Luther and Calvin insisted that people could interpret the Bible for themselves. One result of that notion was the spread of literacy; to understand and interpret the Bible, people had to learn how to read. Both Luther and Calvin rejected Catholic rituals and denied the need for an elaborate church hierarchy. They also asserted that salvation rested on faith alone, rather than—as Catholic teaching had it—on a combination of faith and good works. Calvin, though, went further than Luther in stressing God's omnipotence and emphasizing the need for people to submit totally to God's will.

Elizabeth I tolerated religious diversity among her subjects as long as they generally acknowledged her authority as head of the Church of England. Accordingly, during her long reign (1558–1603) Calvin's ideas gained influence within the English church. By the late sixteenth century, many English

Puritans

Calvinists—those who came to be called Puritans because they wanted to purify the Church of England—believed that the English Reformation had not gone far enough. Henry had simplified the church hierarchy; they wanted to abolish it altogether. Henry had subordinated the church to the interests of the state; they wanted a church free from political interference. And the Church of England, like the Roman Catholic Church, continued to include all English people in its membership. The Puritans preferred a more restricted definition; they wanted to confine church membership to persons they believed to be "saved"—those God had selected for salvation before birth.

Paradoxically, though, a key article of the Puritans' faith insisted that people could not know for certain if they were "saved" because mere mortals could not comprehend or affect their predestination to heaven or hell. Thus pious Puritans daily confronted serious dilemmas: If the saved (or "elect") could not be identified with certainty, how could proper churches be constituted? If one was predestined for heaven or hell and could not alter one's fate, why should one

London in 1616, with London Bridge at center right. Overcrowding in the city led many observers to conclude that American colonization could remove "excess" population and provide new employment for poverty-stricken persons. The rapidly growing community of London merchants also sought to develop new sources of overseas profits.   (Trustees of the British Library)

attend church or do good works? Puritans dealt with the first conundrum by admitting that their judgments as to eligibility for church membership only approximated God's unknowable decisions. And they resolved the second by reasoning that God gave the elect the ability to accept salvation and to lead a good life. Therefore, even though one could not earn a place in heaven by piety and good works, such practices could indicate one's place in the ranks of the saved.

Elizabeth I's Stuart successors, her cousin James I (1603–1625) and his son Charles I (1625–1649), were less tolerant of Puritans than she. As Scots, they also had little respect for the traditions of representative government that had developed in England under the Tudors and their predecessors (see Table 2.2). The wealthy landowners who sat in Parliament had grown accustomed to having considerable influence on government policies, especially taxation. But James I, taking a position later endorsed by his son, publicly declared his adherence to the theory of the divine right of kings. The Stuarts insisted that a monarch's power came directly from God and that his subjects had a duty to obey him. A king's authority was absolute, they argued, just like the authority of a father over his children.

The First Stuart Monarchs

Both James I and Charles I believed that their authority included the power to enforce religious conformity among their subjects. Because Puritans were challenging many of the most important precepts of the English church, the monarchs authorized the removal of Puritan clergymen from their pulpits. In the 1620s and 1630s a number of English Puritans decided to move to America, where they hoped to put their religious beliefs into practice unmolested by the Stuarts or the church hierarchy. Some fled hurriedly to avoid arrest and imprisonment.

The Founding of Virginia

The initial impulse that would lead to England's first permanent colony in the Western Hemisphere came not from the Puritans but from a group of merchants and wealthy gentry. In 1606, envisioning the possibility of earning great profits by finding precious metals and opening new trade routes, the men established a joint-stock venture, the Virginia Company, to plant colonies in America.

Joint-stock companies had been developed in England during the sixteenth century as a mechanism for pooling the resources of many small investors. Stock sales funded these forerunners of modern corporations. Until the creation of the Virginia Company, they had been used primarily to finance trading voyages. For that purpose they worked well: no one risked too much money, and investors usually received quick returns. But joint-stock companies turned out to be a poor way to finance colonies because the early settlements required enormous amounts of capital and, with rare exceptions, failed to return much immediate profit. Colonies founded by joint-stock companies consequently suffered from a chronic lack of capital and from constant tension between stockholders and colonists, who claimed they were not being adequately supported by the investors.

Joint-Stock Companies

The Virginia Company was no exception. Chartered by James I in 1606, the company tried but failed to start a colony in Maine and barely succeeded in planting one in Virginia. In 1607 it dispatched to North America an expedition consisting exclusively of men and boys. In May, 104 Englishmen landed in a region the native inhabitants called Tsenacomoco. There they established the settlement called Jamestown on a swampy peninsula in a river they also named for their monarch. Ill-equipped for survival in the unfamiliar environment, the colonists were afflicted by dissension and disease. Moreover, through sheer bad luck they arrived in the midst of a severe drought (now known to be the worst in the region for nearly eight hundred years), which persisted until 1612. The lack of rainfall not only made it difficult to cultivate crops but also polluted their drinking water.

Jamestown

By January 1608, only thirty-eight of the original colonists remained alive. Many of the first immigrants were gentlemen unaccustomed to working with their hands and artisans with irrelevant skills like glassmak-

Table 2.2	**Tudor and Stuart Monarchs of England, 1509–1649**	
Monarch	**Reign**	**Relation to Predecessor**
Henry VIII	1509–1547	Son
Edward VI	1547–1553	Son
Mary I	1553–1558	Half-sister
Elizabeth I	1558–1603	Half-sister
James I	1603–1625	Cousin
Charles I	1625–1649	Son

ing. A few were soldiers who had fought against Spain in the Netherlands. Having come to Virginia expecting to make easy fortunes, many could not adjust to the conditions they encountered. They resisted hard labor, retaining elaborate English dress and casual work habits despite their desperate circumstances. Such attitudes, combined with the effects of chronic malnutrition and epidemic disease, took a terrible toll. Only when Captain John Smith, one of the colony's founders, imposed military discipline on the colonists in 1608 was Jamestown saved from collapse. But after Smith's departure the settlement experienced a severe "starving time" (the winter of 1609–1610), during which at least one colonist resorted to cannibalism. Although more settlers (including a few women and children) arrived in 1608 and 1609 and living conditions slowly improved, as late as 1624 only 1,300 of approximately 8,000 English immigrants to Virginia remained alive.

The survival of Jamestown may be attributed not to the English but rather to the Native Americans within whose territories they settled,

The Powhatan Confederacy

a group of six Algonquian tribes known as the Powhatan Confederacy (see Map 2.1). A shrewd and powerful leader, Powhatan was aggressively consolidating his authority over some twenty-five smaller bands when the Europeans arrived. Fortunately for the colonists, Powhatan at first viewed them as potential allies. He found the English colony a reliable source of useful items such as steel knives and guns, which gave him a technological advantage over his Indian neighbors. In return, Powhatan's people traded their excess corn and other foodstuffs to the starving settlers. The initially cordial relationship soon deteriorated, however. The English colonists kidnapped Powhatan's daughter, Pocahontas, holding her as a hostage in retaliation for Powhatan's seizure of several settlers. In captivity, she agreed in 1614 to marry a colonist, John Rolfe; she sailed with him to England, where she died in 1616.

The Jamestown colony and the coastal Indians had an uneasy relationship. English and Algonquian

Algonquian and English Cultural Differences

peoples had much in common: deep religious beliefs, a lifestyle oriented around agriculture, clear political and social hierarchies, and sharply defined gender roles. Yet the English and the Powhatans themselves focused on their cultural differences, not their similarities. English men regarded Indian men as lazy because they did not cultivate crops and spent much of their time hunting (a sport, not work, in English eyes). Indian men thought English men effeminate because they did "women's work" of cultivation. In the same vein, the English believed that Algonquian women were oppressed because they did heavy field labor.

Other differences between the two cultures caused serious misunderstandings. Although both societies were hierarchical, the nature of the hierarchies differed considerably. Among the East Coast Algonquians, people were not born to positions of leadership, nor were political power and social status necessarily inherited through the male line. Members of the English gentry inherited their position from their fathers, and English political and military leaders tended to rule autocratically. By contrast, the authority of Algonquian leaders rested on consensus. Accustomed to the European concept of powerful kings, the English sought such figures in native villages. Often (for example, when negotiating treaties) they willfully overestimated the ability of chiefs to make independent decisions for their people.

Furthermore, the Algonquians and the English had very different notions of property ownership. In most Algonquian villages, land was held communally by the entire group. It could not be bought or sold absolutely, although certain rights to use the land (for example, for hunting or fishing) could be transferred. English people, in contrast, were accustomed to individual farms and to buying and selling land. The English also refused to accept the validity of Indians' claims to traditional hunting territories, insisting that only land intensively cultivated could be regarded as owned or occupied. As one colonist put it, "salvadge peoples" who "rambled" over a region without farming it could claim no "title or propertye" in the land. Ownership of such "unclaimed" property, the English believed, lay with the English monarchy, in whose name John Cabot had laid claim to North America in 1497.

Above all, the English settlers believed unwaveringly in the superiority of their civilization. Although in the early years of colonization they often anticipated living peacefully alongside Native Americans, they always assumed that they would dictate the terms of such coexistence. Like Thomas Harriot at Roanoke, they expected Native Americans to adopt English customs and to convert to Christianity. They showed little respect for traditional Indian ways of life, especially when they believed their own interests were at stake. The Virginia colony's treatment of the Powhatan Confederacy in subsequent years clearly revealed that attitude.

How do historians know...

that the Jamestown settlers traded extensively with the neighboring Powhatan Indians?

The few surviving written descriptions of life in early Jamestown omit many details that would interest historians today. But excavations conducted each year since 1994 have located the site of the first permanent English settlement in North America (previously thought to have eroded long ago into the James River) and have unearthed artifacts that speak volumes about the settlers' lives in the first years of Virginia. The small scraps of copper and the Irish copper coins illustrated here, for example, were found within the remains of the original James Fort, constructed in 1607 and abandoned by 1624. The fragments show that Englishmen quickly learned that the Powhatans placed a great value on copper ornaments, which, before the English arrived, they could obtain only by trade with Indians living far to the west. So settler craftsmen fashioned items for Indian trade from coins that the English regarded as nearly worthless and perhaps from copper brought from Europe for the purpose. Undoubtedly the Jamestown residents gave such objects to the Powhatans in exchange for the food they desperately needed. Copper ornaments of English manufacture have been found in Indian burials at Pasbehegh, the Powhatan village nearest to Jamestown. (Photos: The Association for the Preservation of Virginia Antiquities)

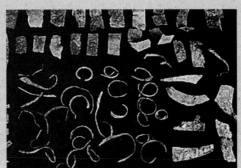

The Cultivation of Tobacco

The spread of tobacco cultivation upset the balance of power in early Virginia. In tobacco—the American crop previously introduced to Europe by the Spanish—the settlers and the Virginia Company found the salable commodity for which they had been searching. John Rolfe planted the first crop in 1611. Nine years later Virginians exported 40,000 pounds of cured leaves, and by the late 1620s shipments had jumped dramatically to 1.5 million pounds. The great tobacco boom had begun, fueled by high prices and substantial profits for planters. The price later fell almost as sharply as it had risen, fluctuating wildly from year to year in response to increasing supply and international competition. Nevertheless, tobacco made Virginia prosper, and the colony developed from a small outpost peopled exclusively by males into an agricultural settlement inhabited by both men and women.

Successful tobacco cultivation required abundant land, since the crop quickly drained soil of nutrients. Farmers soon learned that a field could produce only about three satisfactory crops before it had to lie fallow for several years to regain its fertility. Thus the once-small English settlements began to expand rapidly: eager applicants asked the Virginia Company for large land grants on both sides of the James River and its tributary streams. Lulled into a false sense of security by years of peace, Virginians established farms at some distance from one another along the river banks—a settlement pattern convenient for tobacco cultivation but dangerous for defense.

Virginia Company Policies

To attract more settlers to the colony, the Virginia Company in 1617 developed the "headright" system. Every new arrival paying his or her own way was promised a land grant of 50 acres; those who financed the passage of others received similar headrights for each person. To ordinary English farmers, many of whom owned little or no land, the headright system offered a powerful incentive to move to Virginia. To wealthy gentry, it promised even more: the possibility of establishing vast agricultural enterprises worked by large numbers of laborers. Two years later, the company introduced a second reform, authorizing the landowning men of the major Virginia settlements to elect representatives to an assembly called the House of Burgesses. Although England was a monarchy, English landholders had long been accustomed to electing members of Parliament and controlling their own local governments; therefore, they expected the same privilege in the nation's colonies.

Opechancanough, Powhatan's brother and successor, watched the English colonists steadily encroaching on the confederacy's lands and attempting to convert its members to

Indian Uprisings

Christianity. Recognizing the danger his brother had overlooked, the war leader launched coordinated attacks all along the James River on March 22, 1622. By the end of the day, 347 colonists (about one-quarter of the total) lay dead, and only a timely warning from two Christian converts saved Jamestown itself from destruction.

Virginia reeled from the blow but did not collapse. Reinforced by new shipments of men and arms from England, the settlers attacked Opechancanough's villages. For some years an uneasy peace prevailed, but then in April 1644 Opechancanough tried one last time to repel the invaders. He failed, losing his life in the war that ensued. In 1646, survivors of the Powhatan Confederacy accepted a treaty formally subordinating them to English authority. Although they continued to live in the region, their alliance crumbled and their efforts to resist the spread of European settlement ended.

The 1622 Powhatan uprising that failed to destroy the colony succeeded in killing its parent. The Virginia Company never made any profits from the enterprise, for all its

End of the Virginia Company

earnings were offset by the heavy cost of supporting the settlers and by internal corruption. In 1624 James I revoked the charter, transforming Virginia into a royal colony—a colony ruled by the king through appointed officials. James continued the headright policy the company had adopted. Because he distrusted legislative bodies, though, James at first abolished the assembly. But Virginians protested so vigorously that by 1629 the House of Burgesses was functioning once again. Only two decades after the first permanent English settlement was planted in North America, the colonists successfully insisted on governing themselves at the local level. Thus the political structure of England's American possessions came to differ from that of New Spain, New France, and New Netherland, all of which were ruled autocratically.

Life in the Chesapeake

By the 1630s, tobacco was firmly established as the staple crop and chief source of revenue in Virginia. It quickly became just as important in the second English colony planted on Chesapeake Bay: Maryland, given by Charles I to George Calvert, first Lord Baltimore, as a personal possession (proprietorship), which was settled in 1634. (Because Virginia and Maryland both border Chesapeake Bay—see Map 2.1—they are often referred to collectively as "the Chesapeake.") Members of the Calvert family intended the colony to serve as a haven for their fellow Roman Catholics, then being persecuted in England. Cecilius Calvert, second Lord Baltimore, became the first colonizer to offer freedom of religion to all Christian settlers; he understood that protecting the Protestant majority could also ensure Catholics' rights. (The policy was codified in Maryland's Act of Religious Toleration in 1649.)

In everything but religion the two Chesapeake colonies resembled each other. In Maryland as in Virginia, tobacco planters spread out along the river banks, establishing isolated farms instead of towns. The region's deep, wide rivers offered dependable water transportation in an age of few and inadequate roads. Each farm or group of farms had its own wharf, where oceangoing vessels could take on or discharge cargo. As a result, Virginia and Maryland had few towns, for their residents did not need commercial centers in order to buy and sell goods.

The planting, cultivation, and harvesting of tobacco had to be done by hand; such tasks were repetitious, time-consuming, and labor-

Need for Laborers

intensive. Clearing land for new fields, necessary every few years, was also a laborious job. Above all else, then, successful Chesapeake tobacco farms required laborers. But where and how could they be obtained? Nearby Indians, their numbers reduced by war and disease, could not supply the needed workers. Nor were enslaved Africans readily available: merchants could more easily and profitably sell those slaves to Caribbean sugar planters. In the first half of the seventeenth century, therefore, only a few people of African descent, some of them free or indentured laborers rather than slaves, arrived in the Chesapeake. By 1650 about three hundred blacks lived in Virginia—a tiny fraction of the population.

Chesapeake tobacco farmers thus looked primarily to England to supply their labor needs. Because of the headright system (which Maryland also adopted in

1640), a tobacco farmer anywhere in the Chesapeake could simultaneously obtain both land and labor by importing workers from England. Good management would make the process self-perpetuating: a farmer could use his profits to pay for the passage of more workers and thereby gain title to more land. Success could even bring movement into the ranks of the planter gentry that began to develop in the region.

Because men did the agricultural work in European societies, colonists assumed that field laborers should be men. Such male laborers, along with a few

Indentured Servant Immigrants

women, immigrated to America as indentured servants—that is, in return for their passage they contracted to work for farmers for periods ranging from four to seven years. Indentured servants accounted for 75 to 85 percent of the approximately 130,000 English immigrants to Virginia and Maryland during the seventeenth century. The rest tended to be young couples with one or two children.

Males between the ages of fifteen and twenty-four composed roughly three-quarters of the servants; only one immigrant in five or six was female. Most of these young men came from farming or laboring families, and many originated in regions of England experiencing severe social disruption. Some had already moved several times within England before relocating to America. Often they came from the middling ranks of society—what their contemporaries called the "common sort." Their youth indicated that most probably had not yet established themselves in their homeland.

For such people the Chesapeake appeared to offer good prospects. Servants who fulfilled the terms of their indentures earned "freedom dues" consisting of clothes, tools, livestock, casks of corn and tobacco, and sometimes even land. From a distance at least, America seemed to hold out chances for advancement unavailable in England. Yet immigrants' lives were difficult. Servants typically worked six days a week, ten to fourteen hours a day, in a climate much warmer than England's. Their masters could discipline or sell them, and they faced severe penalties for running away. Even so, the laws did offer them some protection. For example, their masters were supposed to supply them with sufficient food, clothing, and shelter, and they were not to be beaten excessively. Cruelly treated servants could turn to the courts for assistance, sometimes winning verdicts directing that they be sold to more humane masters or released from their indentures.

Servants and their owners alike had to contend with epidemic disease. Immigrants first had to survive the process the colonists called "seasoning"—a bout with disease (probably malaria) that usually occurred during their first Chesapeake summer. They then had to endure recurrences of malaria, along with dysentery, typhoid fever, and other diseases. As a result, approximately 40 percent of male servants did not survive long enough to become freedmen. Even young men of twenty-two who successfully weathered their seasoning could expect to live only another twenty years at best.

Conditions of Servitude

A surveyor's plat from Charles County, Maryland, late in the seventeenth century. The courthouse, the ordinary (inn), and the pillory and stocks are surrounded by old houses and a peach orchard, with roads and still uncleared land nearby. Such a landscape would have been familiar to any resident of the early Chesapeake.
(Maryland State Archives, Charles County Court records, No. 1 MDHR 8132)

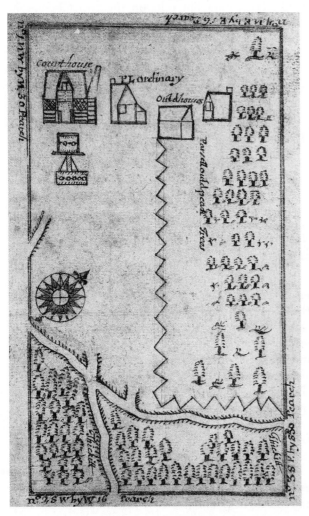

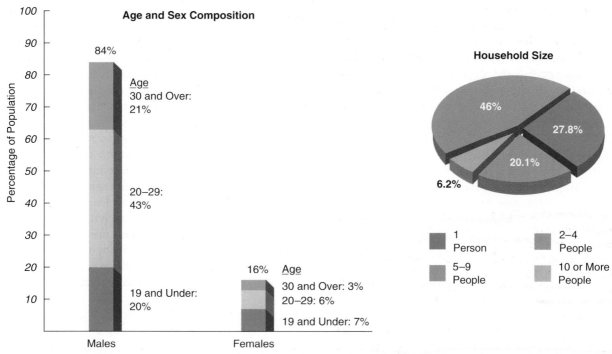

Figure 2.1   Population of Virginia, 1625   The only detailed census taken in the English mainland North American colonies during the seventeenth century was prepared in Virginia in 1625. It listed a total of 1,218 people, constituting 309 "households" and living in 278 dwellings—so some houses contained more than one family. The chart shows, on the left, the proportionate age and gender distribution of the 765 individuals for whom full information was recorded, and, on the right, the percentage variation in the sizes of the 309 households. The approximately 42 percent of the residents of the colony who were servants were concentrated in 30 percent of the households. Nearly 70 percent of the households had no servants at all. (Source of data: Robert V. Wells, *The Population of the British Colonies in America Before 1776: A Survey of Census Data* [Princeton: Princeton University Press, 1975], tables V-5 and V-6 and pp. 165–166.)

For those who survived the term of their indentures, however, the opportunities for advancement were real. Until the last decades of the seventeenth century, former servants were usually able to become independent farmers ("freeholders") and to live a modest but comfortable existence. Some even assumed positions of political prominence such as justice of the peace or militia officer. But in the 1670s tobacco prices entered a fifty-year period of stagnation and decline. Simultaneously, good land grew increasingly scarce and expensive. In 1681 Maryland dropped its legal requirement that servants receive land as part of their freedom dues, forcing large numbers of freed servants to live for years as wage laborers or tenant farmers. By 1700 the Chesapeake was no longer the land of opportunity it once had been.

Life in the early Chesapeake was hard for everyone, regardless of sex or status. Farmers (and sometimes their wives) toiled in the fields alongside

Standard of Living

servants, laboriously clearing land, then planting and harvesting tobacco and corn. Because hogs could forage for themselves in the forests and needed little tending, Chesapeake households subsisted mainly on pork and corn, a filling diet but not sufficiently nutritious. Families supplemented this monotonous fare by eating fish, shellfish, and wildfowl, in addition to vegetables such as lettuce and peas, which they grew in small gardens. The near impossibility of preserving food for safe winter consumption magnified the health problems caused by epidemic disease. Salting, drying, and smoking, the only methods the colonists knew, did not always prevent spoilage.

Few households had many material possessions other than farm implements, bedding, and basic cooking and eating utensils. Chairs, tables, candles, and knives and forks were luxury items. Most people rose and went to bed with the sun, sat on crude benches or storage chests, and held plates or bowls in their hands while eating meat and vegetable stews with spoons. The ramshackle houses commonly had just one or two rooms. Colonists devoted their income to improving their farms, buying livestock, and purchasing more laborers rather than to improving their standard of living. Instead of making items such as clothing and tools, tobacco-growing families imported necessary manufactured goods from England.

Chesapeake Families

The predominance of males, the incidence of servitude, and the high mortality rates combined to produce unusual patterns of family life. Female servants normally could not marry during their terms of indenture because masters did not want pregnancies to deprive them of workers. Many male ex-servants could not marry at all because of the scarcity of women; such men lived alone, in pairs, or as the third member of a household containing a married couple. In contrast, nearly every adult free woman in the Chesapeake married, and widows usually remarried within a few months of a husband's death. Yet because of high infant mortality and because almost all marriages were delayed by servitude or broken by death, Chesapeake women commonly reared only one to three healthy children, in contrast to English women, who normally had at least five.

Thus Chesapeake families were few, small, and short-lived. Youthful immigrants came to America as individuals free of familial control and tended to die while their children were still young. In one Virginia county, for example, more than three-quarters of the children had lost at least one parent by the time they either married or reached age twenty-one. For the most part, then, Chesapeake men (unlike their English fathers; see page 14) could not establish long-term control over their spouses or offspring. And the large number of orphaned children prompted a legal innovation: the establishment of orphans' courts to oversee the management of orphans' property and to ensure that such young people received the appropriate inheritance when they reached adulthood.

Chesapeake Politics

Because of the low rate of natural increase, throughout the seventeenth century immigrants composed a majority of the Chesapeake population, with important implications for regional political patterns. Most of the members of Virginia's House of Burgesses and Maryland's House of Delegates (established in 1635) were immigrants; they also dominated the governor's council,

which was simultaneously each colony's highest court, part of the legislature, and executive adviser to the governor. A cohesive, native-born ruling elite did not emerge until the early eighteenth century. Before that, the Chesapeake colonies' immigrant leaders engaged in bitter and prolonged struggles for power and personal economic advantage.

Representative institutions based on the consent of the governed usually function as a major source of political stability. In the seventeenth-century Chesapeake, most property-owning white males could vote, and such freeholders chose as their legislators the local elites who seemed to be the natural leaders of their respective areas. But because most such men were immigrants without strong ties to one another or to the colonies, the assemblies' existence did not create political stability. Unusual demographic patterns thus contributed to the region's contentious politics.

The Founding of New England

The economic motives that prompted English people to move to the Chesapeake colonies also drew men and women to New England (see Map 2.2). But because Puritans organized the New England colonies, and also because of environmental differences between the two regions, the northern settlements turned out very differently from those in the South. The northern climate was too cold and the soil too infertile to raise tobacco on a large scale or to raise sugar cane at all. Accordingly, diversified small farms dominated the landscape.

Contrasting Regional Religious Patterns

Except for the few Catholics who moved to Maryland, immigrants to the Chesapeake seem to have been little affected by religious motives. Yet religion motivated many, although certainly not all, of the people who colonized New England. Puritan congregations quickly became key institutions in colonial New England, whereas neither the Church of England nor Roman Catholicism had much impact on the settlers or the early development of the Chesapeake colonies. Catholic and Anglican bishops in England paid little attention to their coreligionists in America, and Chesapeake congregations languished in the absence of sufficient numbers of properly ordained clergymen. (For example, in 1665 an observer noted that only ten of the fifty Virginia parishes had resident ministers.) Not until the 1690s did the Church of England begin to take firmer root in Virginia; by then (see page 82) it had also replaced Catholicism as the established church in Maryland.

By contrast, religion was a constant presence in the lives of pious Puritans, who regularly reassessed the state of their souls. Many devoted themselves to self-examination and Bible study, and families prayed together each day under the guidance of the husband and father. Yet because even the most pious could never be certain that they were numbered among the elect, anxiety about their spiritual state troubled devout Puritans. That anxiety lent a special intensity to their religious beliefs and to their concern with proper behavior—their own and others'.

Some Puritans (called Congregationalists) wanted to reform the Church of England rather than abandon

Congregation-alists and Separatists

it. Other groups, known as Separatists, thought the Church of England too corrupt to be salvaged. Only by starting anew could the church be purified, they argued, and so they established their own religious bodies, with membership restricted to the saved, as nearly as they could be identified.

Separatists were the first to move to New England. In 1609 a Separatist congregation relocated to Leiden, in the Netherlands, where they found the freedom of worship denied them in Stuart England. But the Netherlands' tolerant atmosphere worried them: the nation that tolerated them also tolerated religions and behaviors that they abhorred. Hoping to isolate themselves and their children from the corrupting influence of worldly temptations, these people, who were to become known as Pilgrims, received permission from the Virginia Company to colonize the northern part of its territory.

In September 1620, more than one hundred people, only thirty of them Separatists, set sail from

Plymouth

England on the old and crowded *Mayflower.* Two months later they landed in America, but farther north than they had intended. Still, given the lateness of the season, they decided to stay where they were. Establishing their settlement on a fine harbor—the site of an Indian village wiped out by the epidemic of 1616–1618—the English people named it Plymouth.

Even before they landed, the Pilgrims had to surmount their first challenge—from the "strangers," or non-Puritans, who sailed with them to America. Because they landed outside the jurisdiction of the Virginia Company, some of the strangers questioned the

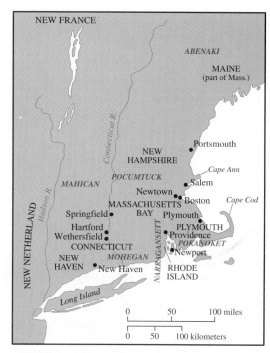

Map 2.2   New England Colonies, 1650   The most densely settled region of the mainland was New England, where English settlements and Indian villages existed side by side.

authority of the colony's leaders. In response, the Mayflower Compact, signed in November 1620 while everyone was still on board the ship, established a "Civil Body Politic" and a rudimentary legal authority for the colony. The settlers elected a governor and at first made all decisions for the colony at town meetings. Later, after more towns had been founded and the population increased, Plymouth, like Virginia and Maryland, created an assembly to which the landowning male settlers elected representatives.

A second challenge facing the Pilgrims was simple survival. Like the Jamestown settlers before them, they were poorly prepared to subsist in the new environment. Winter quickly descended, compounding their difficulties. Only half the *Mayflower*'s passengers were still alive by spring. But, again like the Virginians, the Pilgrims benefited from the political circumstances of nearby Indians.

The Pokanokets (a branch of the Wampanoags) controlled the area in which the Pilgrims settled.

Pokanokets

Their villages had suffered terrible losses in the recent epidemic, so to protect themselves from the powerful Narragansetts of the southern New England coast (who had been

Some scholars now believe that this 1638 painting by the Dutch artist Adam Willaerts depicts the Plymouth colony about fifteen years after its founding. The shape of the harbor, the wooden gate, and the houses straggling up the hill all coincide with contemporary accounts of the settlement. No one believes that Willaerts himself visited Plymouth, but people returning from the colony to Holland, where the Pilgrims had lived for years before emigrating, could well have described Plymouth to him. (© J. D. Bangs, Courtesy of Leiden American Pilgrim Museum, The Netherlands)

spared the ravages of the disease), the Pokanokets decided to ally themselves with the newcomers. In the spring of 1621, their leader, Massasoit, signed a treaty with the Pilgrims, and during the colony's first difficult years the Pokanokets supplied the English with essential foodstuffs. The settlers were also assisted by Squanto, a Pokanoket, who, like Malinche (see page 23), served as a conduit between the Native Americans and the Europeans. Captured by fishermen in the early 1610s and taken to Europe, Squanto learned to speak English. Upon returning to North America, he discovered that his village had been wiped out by the epidemic. Squanto became the Pilgrims' interpreter and a major source of information about the unfamiliar environment.

Before the 1620s ended, another group of Puritans—this time Congregationalists, not Separatists—launched the colonial enterprise that would come to dominate New England and would absorb Plymouth in 1691. Charles I, who became king in 1625, was more hostile to Puritans than his father had been. Under his leadership, the Church of England attempted to suppress Puritan

Massachusetts Bay Company

practices, driving clergymen from their pulpits and forcing congregations to hold clandestine meetings for worship. A group of Congregationalist merchants, concerned about their long-term prospects in England, sent out a body of colonists to Cape Ann (north of Cape Cod) in 1628. The following year the merchants obtained a royal charter, constituting themselves as the Massachusetts Bay Company.

The new joint-stock company quickly attracted the attention of Puritans of the "middling sort" who were becoming increasingly convinced that they no longer would be able to practice their religion freely in their homeland. They remained committed to the goal of reforming the Church of England but concluded that they should pursue that aim in America. In a dramatic move, the Congregationalist merchants boldly decided to transfer the Massachusetts Bay Company's headquarters to New England. The settlers would then be answerable to no one in the mother country and would be able to handle their affairs, secular and religious, as they pleased.

The most important recruit to the new venture was John Winthrop, a member of the lesser English gentry. In October 1629, the Massachusetts Bay Com-

Governor John Winthrop

pany elected Winthrop as its governor. (Until his death twenty years later, he served the colony continuously in one leadership post or another.) It fell to Winthrop to organize the initial segment of the great Puritan migration to America. In 1630 more than one thousand English men and women moved to Massachusetts—most of them to Boston, which soon became the largest town in English North America. By 1643 nearly twenty thousand compatriots had followed them.

On board the *Arbella*, en route to New England in 1630, John Winthrop preached a sermon, "A Model of Christian Charity," laying out his expectations for the new colony. Above all, he stressed the communal nature of the endeavor on which he and his fellow settlers had embarked. God, he explained, "hath so disposed of the condition of mankind as in all times some must be rich, some poor, some high and eminent in power and dignity, others mean and in subjection." But differences in status did not imply differences in worth. On the contrary: God had planned the world so that "every man might have need of other, and from hence they might be all knit more nearly together in the bond of brotherly affection." In America, Winthrop asserted, "we shall be as a city upon a hill, the eyes of all people are upon us." If the Puritans failed to carry out their "special commission" from God, "the Lord will surely break out in wrath against us."

Winthrop's was a transcendent vision. He foresaw in Puritan America a true commonwealth, a community in which each person put the good of the whole ahead of his or her private concerns. Although, as in seventeenth-century England, that society would be characterized by social inequality and clear hierarchies of status and power, Winthrop hoped that its members would live according to the precepts of Christian love. Of course, such an ideal was beyond human reach. Early New England had its share of bitter quarrels and unchristian behavior. What is remarkable is that the ideal persisted well into the third and fourth generations of the immigrants' descendants.

The Puritans expressed their communal ideal chiefly in the doctrine of the covenant. They believed

Ideal of the Covenant

God had made a covenant—that is, an agreement or contract—with them when they were chosen for the special mission to America. In turn they covenanted with one another, promising to work together toward their goals. The founders of churches and towns in the new land often drafted formal documents setting forth the principles on which such institutions would be based. The same was true of the colonial governments of New England. The Pilgrims' Mayflower Compact was a covenant; so too was the Fundamental Orders of Connecticut (1639), which laid down the basic law for the settlements established along the Connecticut River valley in 1636 and thereafter.

The leaders of Massachusetts Bay likewise transformed their original joint-stock company charter into the basis for a covenanted community based on mutual consent. Under strong and persistent pressure from landowning male settlers, they gradually changed the General Court—officially the company's small governing body—into a colonial legislature. They also granted the status of freeman, or voting member of the company, to all property-owning adult male church members. Like Virginia men who won the reestablishment of the House of Burgesses after the king had abolished it, the male residents of Massachusetts insisted that their reluctant leaders allow them a greater voice in their government. Less than two decades after the first large group of Puritans arrived in Massachusetts Bay, the colony had a functioning system of self-government composed of a governor and a two-house legislature. The General Court also established a judicial system modeled on England's, although the laws they adopted differed from those of their homeland (see page 55).

The colony's method of distributing land helped to further the communal ideal. Unlike Virginia and Maryland, where individual applicants acquired headrights

An English beaver felt hat, made by combining American beaver fur with wool and other fibers. Men and women in England and on the European continent wore such fashionable items, thus creating the insatiable demand for pelts that fueled the fur trade for many years. (The Pilgrim Society, Plymouth, Massachusetts)

New England Towns

and sited their farms separately, in Massachusetts groups of men—often from the same region of England—applied together to the General Court for grants of land on which to establish towns (novel governance units that did not exist in England). The men receiving such a grant determined how the land would be distributed. Understandably, the grantees copied the villages from which they had come. First they laid out lots for houses and a church. Then they gave each family parcels of land scattered around the town center: a pasture here, a woodlot there, an arable field elsewhere. They reserved the best and largest plots for the most distinguished among them (including the minister). People who had been low on the social scale in England received much smaller and less desirable allotments. Still, every man obtained land, thus sharply differentiating these villages from their English counterparts.

Thus New England settlements initially tended to be more compact than those of the Chesapeake. Town centers grew up quickly, developing in three distinctly different ways. Some, chiefly isolated agricultural settlements in the interior, tried to sustain Winthrop's vision of harmonious community life based on diversified family farms. A second group, the coastal towns like Boston and Salem, became bustling seaports, serving as focal points for trade and places of entry for thousands of new immigrants. The third category, commercialized agricultural towns, grew up in the Connecticut River valley, where easy water transportation made it possible for farmers to sell surplus goods readily. In Springfield, Massachusetts, for example, the merchant-entrepreneur William Pynchon and his son John began as fur traders and ended as large landowners with thousands of acres. Even in New England, then, the entrepreneurial spirit characteristic of the Chesapeake found some room for expression.

Internal Migration

When migrants began to move beyond the territorial limits of the Massachusetts Bay colony into Connecticut (1636), New Haven (1638), and New Hampshire (1638), the same pattern of land grants was maintained. (Only Maine, with coastal regions thinly populated by fishermen and their families, deviated from the standard practice.) The migration to the Connecticut valley ended the Puritans' relative freedom from clashes with nearby Indians. The first English people in the valley moved there from Massachusetts Bay under the direction of their minister, Thomas Hooker. Although their new settlements were remote from other English towns, the wide river promised ready access to the ocean. The site had just one problem: it fell within the territory controlled by the powerful Pequots.

Pequot War

The Pequots' dominance stemmed from their role as primary middlemen in the trade between New England Indians and the Dutch in New Netherland. The arrival of English settlers signaled the end of the Pequots' power over such regional trading networks, for previously subordinate bands could now trade directly with Europeans. Clashes between Pequots and English colonists began even before the establishment of settlements in the Connecticut valley, but their founding tipped the balance toward war. The Pequots tried without success to enlist other Indians in resisting English expansion. After two English traders were killed (not by Pequots), the English raided a Pequot village. In return, the Pequots attacked the new town of Wethersfield in April 1637, killing nine and capturing two of the colonists. To retaliate, a Massachusetts Bay expedition the following month attacked and burned the main Pequot town on the Mystic River. The Englishmen and their Narragansett allies slaughtered at least four hundred Pequots, mostly women and children, capturing and enslaving many of the survivors.

For the next thirty years, the New England Indians accommodated themselves to the spread of European

Among John Eliot's principal converts to Christianity was a young Native American named Daniel Takawampbartis. Ordained as a minister, he served at the head of the Indian congregation at Natick, Massachusetts, a "Praying Town," until his death in 1716. Members of his congregation made this desk for him in about 1677, incorporating elements of English design (brass pulls), Native American motifs (incised lines), and uniquely American hooved feet. The top, a hinged box, is intended to hold a Bible. (The Morse Institute, Natick, Massachusetts. Photo by Mark Sexton of the Peabody Essex Museum, Salem)

settlement. They traded with the newcomers and sometimes worked for them, but for the most part they resisted acculturation or incorporation into English society. Native Americans persisted in using traditional farming methods, which did not employ plows or fences, and women rather than men continued to be the chief cultivators. When Indian men learned "European" trades in order to survive, they chose those—like broom making, basket weaving, and shingle splitting—that most nearly accorded with their customary occupations and simultaneously ensured both independence and income. The one European practice they adopted was keeping livestock, for domesticated animals provided excellent sources of meat once earlier hunting territories had been turned into English farms and wild game had consequently disappeared.

Although the official seal of the Massachusetts Bay colony showed an Indian crying "Come over and help us," most colonists showed little interest in converting the Algonquians to Christianity. Only a few Massachusetts clerics, most notably John Eliot, seriously undertook missionary activities. Eliot insisted that converts reside in towns, farm the land in English fashion, assume English names, wear European-style clothing and shoes, cut their hair, and stop observing a wide range of their own customs. Since Eliot was demanding a total cultural transformation from his adherents—on the theory that Indians could not be properly Christianized unless they were also "civilized"—he understandably met with little success. At the peak of Eliot's efforts, only eleven hundred Native Americans (out of many thousands) lived in the fourteen "Praying Towns" he established, and just 10 percent of those town residents had been formally baptized.

John Eliot and the Praying Towns

The Jesuits' successful missions in New France contrasted sharply with the Puritans' failure to win many converts and the Franciscans' mixed results in New Mexico. Initially, Catholicism had several advantages over Puritanism (advantages more fully exploited by Jesuits than by Franciscans). The Catholic Church employed beautiful ceremonies, instructed converts that through good works they could help to earn their own salvation, and offered Indian women an inspiring role model—the Virgin Mary. In Montreal and Quebec but not in New Mexico, communities of nuns taught Indian women and children and ministered to their needs. Furthermore, the few French colonists on the St. Lawrence

Puritan, Franciscan, and Jesuit Missions Compared

Father Claude Chauchetière, a Jesuit in New France, sketched scenes of life in the colony's missions. His drawing of Indian women worshiping at a shrine of the Virgin Mary includes (at the rear) a view of one woman cutting her hair to conform more closely to European fashion. The other female converts show no evidence of having adopted European dress or hairstyles. (Archives Départmentales de la Gironde, France)

did not alienate potential converts by encroaching steadily on their lands (as did New Englanders) or by demanding labor tribute (as did New Mexicans). Perhaps most important, the Jesuits understood that Christian beliefs could be compatible with Native American culture. Unlike Puritans and Franciscans, Jesuits accepted converts who did not wholly adopt European styles of life.

What attracted Indians to these religious ideas? Conversion often alienated the new Christians (both Catholic and Puritan) from their relatives and traditions—a likely outcome that must have caused many potential converts to think twice about making such a commitment. But surely many hoped to use the Europeans' religion as a means of coping with the dramatic changes the intruders had wrought. The combination of disease, alcohol, new trading patterns, and loss of territory disrupted customary ways of life to an unprecedented extent. Shamans had little success in restoring traditional ways. Many Indians must have concluded that the Europeans' own ideas could provide the key to survival in the new circumstances.

John Winthrop's description of the great smallpox epidemic that swept through southern New England in the early 1630s reveals the relationship among smallpox, conversion to Christianity, and English land claims. "A great mortality among the Indians," he noted in his diary in 1633. "Divers of them, in their sickness, confessed that the Englishmen's God was a good God; and that if they recovered, they would serve him." But most did not recover: in January 1634 an English scout reported that smallpox had spread "as far as any Indian plantation was known to the west."

In 1664 an eight-year-old girl, Elizabeth Eggington, became the subject of the earliest known dated New England painting. Her mother died shortly after her birth, perhaps because of childbirth complications; the girl's rich clothing, elaborate jewelry, and feather fan not only reveal her family's wealth but also suggest that she was much loved by her father, a merchant and ship captain. Unfortunately, Elizabeth died about the time this portrait was painted; perhaps it—like some other colonial portraits of young children—was actually painted after her death to memorialize her.   (Wadsworth Atheneum, Hartford. Gift of Mrs. Walter H. Clark. Endowed by her daughter, Mrs. Thomas L. Archibald)

By July, Winthrop observed that most of the Indians within a 300-mile radius of Boston had died of the disease. Therefore, he declared with satisfaction, "the Lord hath cleared our title to what we possess."

Life in New England

New England's colonizers adopted lifestyles that differed considerably from those of both their Indian neighbors and their European counterparts in the Chesapeake. Algonquian bands usually moved four or five times each year to take full advantage of their environment. In spring, women planted the fields, but once crops were established, they did not need regular attention for several months. Villages then divided into small groups, women gathering wild foods and men hunting and fishing. The villagers returned to their fields for harvest, then separated again for fall hunting. Finally, the people wintered together in a sheltered spot before returning to the fields to start the cycle anew the following spring.

Unlike the mobile Algonquians, English people lived year-round in the same location. And unlike residents of the Chesapeake, New Englanders constructed sturdy dwellings intended to last. (Many still survive to this day.) They used the same fields again and again, believing it was less arduous to employ manure as fertilizer than to clear new fields every few years. Furthermore, they fenced their croplands to prevent them from being overrun by the cattle, sheep, and hogs that were their chief sources of meat. When New Englanders began to spread out over the countryside, the reason was less human crowding than animal crowding. All that livestock constantly needed more pasturage.

Because Puritans commonly moved to America in family groups, the age range in early New England was wide; and because many more women went to New England than to the tobacco colonies, the population could immediately begin to reproduce itself. Lacking such tropical diseases as malaria, New England was much healthier than the Chesapeake. Once Puritan settlements had survived the difficult first few years and established self-sufficiency in foodstuffs, New England proved to be even healthier than the mother country. Adult male migrants to the Chesapeake lost about ten years from their English life expectancy of fifty to fifty-five years; their Massachusetts counterparts gained five or more years.

New England Families

Consequently, while Chesapeake population patterns gave rise to families that were few in number, small in size, and transitory, the demographic characteristics of New England made families there numerous, large, and long-lived. In New England most men married; immigrant women married young (at age twenty, on the average); and marriages lasted longer and produced more children, who were more likely to live to maturity. If seventeenth-century Chesapeake women could expect to rear one to three healthy children, New England women could anticipate raising five to seven.

The nature of the population had other major implications for family life. New England in effect created grandparents, since in England people rarely lived long enough to know their children's children. And whereas early Chesapeake parents commonly died before their children married, New England parents exercised a good deal of control over their adult offspring. Young men could not marry without acreage to cultivate, and because of the communal land-grant system they had to depend on their fathers to give them that land. Daughters, too, needed a dowry of household goods supplied by their parents. Yet parents relied on their children's labor and often were reluctant to see them marry and start their own households. These needs at times led to considerable conflict between the generations. On the whole, though, children seem to have obeyed their parents' wishes, for they had few alternatives.

Another important difference lay in the influence of religion on New Englanders' lives. Puritans controlled the governments of Massachusetts Bay, Plymouth, Connecticut, and all the other early northern colonies. Congregationalism was the only officially recognized religion; except in Rhode Island, founded by dissenters from Massachusetts, members of other sects had no freedom of worship. Some non-Puritans voted in town meetings, but in Massachusetts Bay and New Haven, church membership was a prerequisite for voting in colony elections. All the early colonies taxed residents to build meetinghouses and pay ministers' salaries, but only in New England were provisions of criminal codes based on the Old Testament. Massachusetts's first bodies of law (1641 and 1648) incorporated regulations drawn from scriptures; New Haven, Plymouth, New Hampshire, and Connecticut later copied those codes. All colonists were required to attend religious services, whether or not they were church members, and people who expressed contempt for ministers or

Impact of Religion

their preaching could be punished with fines or whippings.

The Puritan colonies attempted to enforce strict codes of moral conduct. Colonists there were frequently tried for drunkenness, card playing, even idleness. Couples who had sex during their engagement—as revealed by the birth of a baby less than nine months after their wedding—were fined and publicly humiliated. (Maryland, by contrast, did not penalize premarital pregnancy, only bastardy.) More harshly treated were men—and a handful of women—who engaged in behaviors that today would be called homosexual. (The term did not then exist, nor were some people thought to be more likely than others to perform such acts.) Several men who had consenting same-sex relationships were hanged, as were other men suspected of bestiality (sex with animals). Executions for such offenses were far more common in New England than in the Chesapeake, even though men's behavior in the two regions was probably similar.

In New England, church and state were thus intertwined to a greater extent than they were in the Chesapeake. Puritans objected to secular interference in religious affairs but at the same time expected the church to influence the conduct of politics and the affairs of society. They also believed that the state was obliged to support and protect the one true church—theirs. As a result, although they came to America seeking freedom to worship as they pleased, they saw no contradiction in refusing to grant that freedom to others.

Roger Williams, a Separatist who immigrated to Massachusetts Bay in 1631, quickly ran afoul of that Puritan orthodoxy. He told his fellow settlers that the king of England had no right to grant them land already occupied by Indians, that church and state should be kept entirely separate, and that Puritans should not impose their religious beliefs on others. Because Puritan leaders placed a heavy emphasis on achieving consensus in both religion and politics, they could not long tolerate significant dissent. In October 1635, the Massachusetts General Court tried Williams for challenging the validity of the colony's charter and for maintaining that New England Congregationalists had not separated themselves, their churches, or their polity sufficiently from England's corrupt institutions and practices.

Convicted and banished, Williams journeyed in early 1636 to the head of Narragansett Bay, where he founded the town of Providence on land he obtained from the Narragansetts and Wampanoags. Because

Roger Williams

Williams believed that government should not interfere with religion in any way, Providence and other towns in what became Rhode Island adopted a policy of tolerating all religions, including Judaism. Along with Maryland (see page 45), the tiny colony founded by Williams thus presaged the religious freedom that eventually became one of the hallmarks of the United States.

A dissenter who presented a more sustained challenge to Bay colony leaders was Mistress Anne Marbury Hutchinson. (The title "Mistress" meant she had high status.) A skilled medical practitioner popular with the women of Boston, she greatly admired John Cotton, a minister who stressed the covenant of grace, or God's free gift of salvation to unworthy human beings. By contrast, most Massachusetts clerics emphasized the need for Puritans to engage in good works, study, and reflection in preparation for receiving God's grace. (In its most extreme form, such a doctrine could verge on the covenant of works, or the idea that people could earn their salvation.) After spreading her ideas for months in the context of childbed gatherings—when no men were present—Mistress Hutchinson began holding women's meetings in her home to discuss Cotton's sermons. She emphasized the covenant of grace more than did Cotton himself, and she even adopted the belief that the elect could be assured of salvation and communicate directly with God. Such ideas had an immense appeal for Puritans. Anne Hutchinson offered them certainty of salvation instead of a state of constant anxiety. Her approach also lessened the importance of the institutional church and its ministers.

Hutchinson's ideas posed a dangerous threat to Puritan orthodoxy. So in November 1637, officials charged her with having maligned the colony's ministers by accusing them of preaching the covenant of works. For two days she defended herself cleverly, matching scriptural references and wits with John Winthrop himself. But then Anne Hutchinson triumphantly and boldly declared that God had spoken to her directly, explaining that he would curse the Puritans' descendants for generations if they harmed her. That assertion assured her banishment, for what member of the court could acknowledge the legitimacy of such a revelation? After she had also been excommunicated from the church, she and her family, along with some faithful followers, were exiled to Rhode Island. Several years later, after she moved to New Netherland, she and most of her children were killed by Indians.

Anne Hutchinson

The authorities in Massachusetts Bay perceived Anne Hutchinson as doubly dangerous to the existing order: she threatened not only religious orthodoxy but also traditional gender roles. Puritans believed in the equality before God of all souls, including those of women, but they considered actual women (as distinct from their spiritual selves) inferior to men. Christians had long followed Saint Paul's dictum that women should keep silent in church and be submissive to their husbands. Mistress Hutchinson did neither. The magistrates' comments during her trial reveal that they were almost as outraged by her "masculine" behavior as by her religious beliefs. Winthrop charged her with having set wife against husband, since so many of her followers were women. A minister at her church trial told her bluntly: "You have stept out of your place, you have rather bine a Husband than a Wife and a preacher than a Hearer; and a Magistrate than a Subject."

The New England authorities' reaction to Anne Hutchinson reveals the depth of their adherence to European gender-role concepts. To them, an orderly society required the submission of wives to husbands as well as the obedience of subjects to rulers. English people intended to change many aspects of their lives by colonizing North America, but not the sexual division of labor or the assumption of male superiority.

Summary

By the middle of the seventeenth century, Europeans had unquestionably come to North America to stay, a fact that signaled major changes for the peoples of both hemispheres. Europeans had indelibly altered not only their own lives but also those of Native Americans. Europeans killed Indians with their weapons and diseases and had but limited success in converting them to European religions. Contacts with the Native Americans taught Europeans to eat new foods, speak new languages, and recognize—however reluctantly—the persistence of other cultural patterns. The prosperity and even survival of many of the European colonies depended heavily on the cultivation of American crops (maize and tobacco) and an Asian crop (sugar), thus attesting to the importance of post-Columbian ecological change.

European political rivalries, once confined to Europe, now spread around the globe, as England, Spain, Portugal, France, and the Netherlands vied for control of the peoples and resources of Asia, Africa, and the

Americas. In America, Spaniards reaped the benefits of their South and Central American gold and silver mines, while French people earned their primary profits from Indian trade (in Canada) and cultivating sugar cane (in the Caribbean). Sugar also enriched the Portuguese. The Dutch, by contrast, concentrated on commerce—trading in furs and sugar as well as carrying human cargoes of enslaved Africans to South America and the Caribbean.

Of these nations, only France and Spain went beyond the economic relationships they established with native peoples to attempt to Christianize them. In missions scattered in remote locations such as northern Florida, the St. Lawrence valley, and New Mexico, Catholic priests like Fray Alonso de Benavides worked with dedication to convert the Indians and to persuade them of the truth of Europeans' religious beliefs.

Although the English colonies, too, at first sought to rely on trade, they quickly took another form altogether when so many English people of the "middling sort" decided to migrate to North America. To a greater extent than their European counterparts, the English transferred the society and politics of their homeland to a new environment. Their sheer numbers, coupled with their need for vast quantities of land on which to grow their crops and raise their livestock, inevitably brought them into conflict with their Native American neighbors. New England and the Chesapeake differed in the sex ratio and age range of their immigrant populations, in the nature of their developing economies, in their settlement patterns, and in the impact of religious beliefs on their settlers' lives. Yet both were English in origin, and in the years to come both regions would be drawn into the increasingly fierce rivalries besetting the European powers. Those rivalries would continue to affect Americans of all races until after France and England in the mid-eighteenth century fought the greatest war yet known, and the Anglo-American colonies had won their independence.

LEGACY FOR A PEOPLE AND A NATION

The Foxwoods Casino and the Mashantucket Pequot Museum

In 1992 the Mashantucket Pequots opened the enormously successful Foxwoods Resort Casino on their small reservation in southeastern Connecticut. Just six years later, in August 1998, the Pequots proudly inaugurated a new museum (built with some of their

substantial profits) presenting their people's story, meticulously researched by historians and archaeologists. Both developments surprised many Americans, who associated Indians only with territories west of the Mississippi and did not realize that Native Americans still lived in New England. The existence of the Pequots was particularly startling, because histories had long recorded that the nation was destroyed in the Pequot War of 1637.

Survivors of the Mystic River massacre had regrouped in the Mashantucket swamps, building lives as farmers, laborers, and craftspeople. Some left the area, finding work on whaling vessels or eventually migrating to Wisconsin. But a few Pequots remained—the 1910 census, the source today for determining Pequot tribal membership, counted sixty-six residents of a reservation just 213 acres in size. By the 1970s, the residents had been reduced to two, and the state of Connecticut threatened to turn the reservation into a park. But an elder, Elizabeth George, persuaded several hundred people tracing descent from those listed in 1910 to return to live on the reservation. In 1983 the determined Pequots won formal federal recognition, and in turn that allowed them to build the profitable casino, a hotel, and several restaurants, and to begin purchasing more land.

Now the museum introduces the history of the Pequots and of eastern Algonquian peoples to hundreds of thousands of visitors each year. At its heart is a re-creation of a Pequot village as it would have looked shortly before Europeans first arrived on Connecticut's shores, complete with sounds and smells controlled by state-of-the-art computers. Exhibits detail the origins of the Pequot War, and a film narrates the tale of the massacre. Furthermore, excavations nearby continue to uncover new evidence about the overlooked history of these indomitable descendants of America's early residents.

The Pequots' success has helped to embolden other eastern Algonquian nations—for example, Wampanoags and Mashpees—to reassert publicly their long-suppressed Indian identities. The Pequot people's dedication to preserving their culture and reaffirming their history has created a remarkable legacy for the nation.

For Further Reading, see page A-2 of the Appendix. For Web resources, go to http://college.hmco.com.

Why why should I my Joyes be minding
Herein a World of Evils Finding thy Jarres
Then Farwell World: Farwell thy Wars
Thy Tales thy Toies thy Wiles thy Wants
Thy Joies thy Toies: I am not forye.
The Eternall Draines to him my heart
By Faith (which can my Force Subvert)
Shine me (after grace) with Glory.

The *Seaflower*, Captain Thomas Smith, master, lay at anchor in Boston harbor in early September 1676, awaiting official documents signed by Governor John Leverett of Massachusetts and his Plymouth counterpart, Josiah Winslow. Like other mariners of the period, Smith expected to sell the cargo in his hold in the West Indies. But that cargo differed from most: it comprised human beings, nearly two hundred "heathen Malefactors—men, women, and Children."

The certificates from the governors, dated September 12, explained "To all People" the origins of Captain Smith's human cargo: "Philip an heathen Sachem . . . with others his wicked complices and abettors have treacherously and perfidiously rebelled against" these colonies. "By due and legall procedure" the captives on board the *Seaflower* were "Sentenced & condemned to perpetuall Servitude" as punishment for their "inhumane and barbarous crueltys murder, outrages and vilainies." The Pokanoket leader King Philip (called Metacom at birth and later renamed "Philip" by New Englanders) had been killed a month earlier in the war that bore his name. His captured wife and young son subsequently languished for months in a Boston jail; her fate is unknown, but the boy seems to have been sold into slavery, along with many shiploads of Philip's followers.

Only one prominent New Englander objected on moral grounds to the policy of selling the vanquished Algonquians into West Indian slavery. The Reverend John Eliot (see page 53) reminded the authorities that the Bay colony's charter called for the conversion of Indians, "not theire exstirpation." The colonists had a solemn duty, he contended, to "inlarge the kingdom of Jesus Christ"; "to sell them away for slaves, is to hinder the inlargement of his kingdom." If the Indians deserved to die, then "godly governors" should ensure that they died "penitently," rather than depriving them

Captain Thomas Smith, a Boston mariner, painted this remarkable self-portrait in the late seventeenth century. It links his sailing career—illustrated in the background battle scene, which is thought to represent a combined Anglo-Dutch assault on a North African fort in 1670—with his pious Puritan faith. The skull under his hand serves to remind viewers of the brevity of life, which the poem underscores. "Why, why should I the World be minding?" the poet asks, looking forward to a future in which "The Eternall" would "Crowne me (after Grace) with Glory." (Worcester Art Museum, Worcester, Massachusetts, Museum purchase)

AMERICAN SOCIETIES TAKE SHAPE 1640–1720

of "all meanes of grace" by selling them as slaves. Not even Eliot, then, argued against enslavement itself, nor did he deny that the captured Algonquians deserved punishment. Rather, he believed that the chosen penalty would subvert God's plan for Massachusetts.

What the pious Captain Thomas Smith (whose self-portrait is reproduced on page 58) thought about his human cargo is unknown. The *Seaflower* arrived in Jamaica in November, and perhaps he disposed of some of the captives there. But the Reverend Eliot learned from a correspondent seven years later that at least a few New England Algonquians had ended up in Tangier (in the modern nation of Morocco) because so many countries had turned away the vessels carrying them.

The tale of Thomas Smith and the *Seaflower*'s human cargo illustrates not only the English colonists' willingness to enslave "heathen" peoples and their increasingly contentious relationship with Native Americans, but also the participation of the mainland colonies in a growing international network. North America, like England itself, was becoming embedded in a worldwide matrix of trade and warfare. The web woven by oceangoing vessels—once composed of only a few strands spun by Christopher Columbus, John Cabot, and their successors—now crisscrossed the globe, carrying European goods to America and Africa, West Indian sugar to New England and Europe, Africans to the Americas, and New England fish and wood products—and occasionally Indian slaves—to the Caribbean. Formerly tiny outposts, the North American colonies expanded their territorial claims and diversified their economies after the mid-seventeenth century.

Three developments shaped life in the mainland English colonies between 1640 and 1720: the introduction of a system of slavery, especially in the southern coastal regions; changes in the colonies' political and economic relationships with England; and escalating conflicts with Indians and other European colonies in North America.

The explosive growth of the slave trade significantly altered the Anglo-American economy. Carrying human cargoes paid off handsomely, as many mariners and ship owners learned; planters who could afford to buy slaves also reaped huge profits. At first primarily encompassing Indians and already enslaved Africans from the Caribbean, the trade soon came to focus almost exclusively on cargoes brought to the American mainland directly from Africa. The arrival of large numbers of West African peoples dramatically re-

shaped colonial society and fueled the international trading system.

The burgeoning North American economy, invigorated by the arrival of so many laborers, attracted new attention from colonial administrators. Especially after the Stuarts had been restored to the throne in 1660 (having lost it for a time as a result of the English Civil War), rulers and bureaucrats in London attempted to supervise the American settlements more effectively and to ensure that the mother country benefited from their economic growth. By the early eighteenth century, following a period of upheaval, a new stability characterized colonial political institutions.

Neither English colonists nor London administrators could ignore other peoples living on the North American continent. As the English settlements expanded, they came into violent conflict not only with powerful Indian nations but also with the Dutch, the Spanish, and especially the French. Moreover, all the European colonies confronted significant crises during the decade of the 1670s. By 1720, war—between Europeans and Indians, among Europeans, and among Indians allied with different colonial powers—had become an all-too-familiar feature of American life. No longer isolated from each other or from Europe, the people and products of the North American colonies had become integral to the world trading system and inextricably enmeshed in its conflicts. ■

The Restoration Colonies

In 1642 England erupted into civil war. Disputes over taxation, religion, and other issues led to armed conflict between supporters of the Stuart King Charles I and the Puritan-dominated Parliament. After four years of warfare, Parliament triumphed. Following the execution of Charles I in 1649, the parliamentary army's leader, Oliver Cromwell, assumed control of the government. Yet after Cromwell's death in 1658 Parliament decided to restore the monarchy if Charles I's son and heir would agree to restrictions on his authority. In 1660, Charles II ascended the throne (see Table 3.1), having promised to support the Church of England and to seek Parliament's consent for any new taxes. Thus the Stuart Restoration ended the tumultuous chapter in English history known as the Interregnum (Latin for "between reigns") or Commonwealth period.

The English Civil War, the Interregnum, and the reign of Charles II (1660–1685) had far-reaching sig-

IMPORTANT EVENTS

1642–46 English Civil War

1649 Charles I executed

1651 First Navigation Act passed to regulate colonial trade

1660 Stuarts restored to throne; Charles II becomes king

1663 Carolina chartered

1664 English conquer New Netherland; New York founded
New Jersey established

1670s Marquette, Jolliet, and La Salle explore the Great Lakes and Mississippi valley for France

1675–76 King Philip's War devastates New England

1676 Bacon's Rebellion disrupts Virginia government; Jamestown destroyed

1680–92 Pueblo revolt temporarily drives Spaniards from New Mexico

1681 Pennsylvania chartered

1685 James II becomes king

1686–89 Dominion of New England established, superseding all charters of colonies from Maine to New Jersey

1688–89 James II deposed in Glorious Revolution; William and Mary ascend throne

1689–97 King William's War fought on northern New England frontier

1692 Witchcraft crisis in Salem; nineteen executions result

1696 Board of Trade and Plantations established to coordinate English colonial administration

1701 Iroquois adopt neutrality policy toward France and England

1702–13 Queen Anne's War fought by French and English

1711–13 Tuscarora War (North Carolina) leads to capture or migration of most Tuscaroras

1715 Yamasee War nearly destroys South Carolina

1718 New Orleans founded in French Louisiana

Proprietorships nificance for the Anglo-American colonies. During the Civil War and the Commonwealth period, Puritans controlled the English government. Thus their migration to New England largely ceased, and some colonists packed up to return home. The subsequent reign of Charles II saw the founding of six of the thirteen colonies that eventually would form the American nation: New York, New Jersey, Pennsylvania (including Delaware), and North and South Carolina (see Map 3.1). All were proprietorships; in each of them, as in Maryland, one man or several men held title to the soil and controlled the government. Charles II gave such vast American holdings as rewards to men who had supported his family during the Civil War. Several of his favorites even shared in more than one grant. Collectively, these became known as the Restoration colonies because they were created by the restored Stuart monarchy.

Charles's younger brother James, the duke of York, quickly benefited from his brother's generosity. In 1664, acting as though the Dutch colony of New Netherland did not exist, Charles II gave James the re-

New York gion between the Connecticut and Delaware Rivers, including the Hudson valley and Long Island. James immediately organized an invasion fleet. In August James's warships anchored off Manhattan Island and demanded New Netherland's surrender. The colony complied without resistance. Although the Netherlands briefly retook the colony in a later war in 1672, the Dutch permanently ceded the province in 1674.

Table 3.1 Stuart Monarchs of England, 1660–1714

Monarch	Reign	Relation to Predecessor
Charles II	1660–1685	Son
James II	1685–1688	Brother
Mary	1688–1694	Daughter
William	1688–1702	Son-in-law
Anne	1702–1714	Sister, sister-in-law

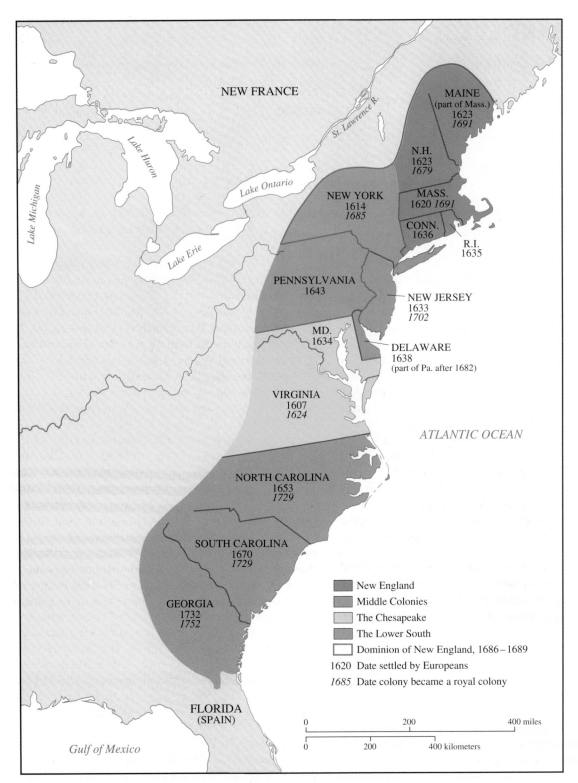

Map 3.1   The Anglo-American Colonies in the Early Eighteenth Century   By the early eighteenth century, the English colonies nominally dominated the Atlantic coastline of North America. But the colonies' formal boundary lines are deceiving because the western reaches of each colony were still largely unfamiliar to Europeans and because much of the land was still inhabited by Native Americans.

About 1650 a Dutch artist produced this copper engraving of New Amsterdam. Dominated by a prominent windmill, tall government buildings, and European-style row houses, the small community closely resembled towns in the Netherlands. Note the many contrasts to the view of Plymouth on page 50. (Museum of the City of New York. Gift of Dr. N. Sulzberber)

Thus James acquired a heterogeneous possession, which he renamed New York (see Table 3.2). In 1664 an appreciable minority of English people (mostly Puritan New Englanders who had moved to Long Island) already lived there, along with sizable numbers of Indians, Africans, Germans, French-speaking Walloons (from the southern part of modern Belgium), Scandinavians, and a smattering of other European peoples. The Dutch West India Company, the world's greatest slave-trading power at midcentury (see page 75), had actively imported slaves into the colony, intending some for resale in the Chesapeake. Many, though, remained in New Netherland as laborers; at the time of the English conquest, almost one-fifth of Manhattan's approximately fifteen hundred inhabitants were of African descent. Indeed, slaves then made up a higher proportion of New York's urban population than of the Chesapeake's rural people.

Recognizing the population's diversity, the duke of York's representatives moved cautiously in their efforts to establish English authority. The

The Duke's Laws

Duke's Laws, a legal code proclaimed in 1665, at first applied solely to the English settlements on Long Island, only later being extended to the rest of the colony. Dutch forms of local government were maintained, Dutch land titles confirmed, and Dutch residents allowed to maintain customary legal practices. Each town was permitted to decide which church (Dutch Reformed, Congregational, or Church of England) to support with its tax revenues. Much to the dismay of English residents of the colony, the Duke's Laws made no provision for a representative assembly. Like other Stuarts, James distrusted legislative bodies, and not until 1683 did he agree to the colonists' requests for an elected legislature. Before then, an auto-

cratic governor ruled New York, just as had been the practice under the Dutch.

The English takeover thus had little immediate effect on the colony. Its population grew slowly, barely reaching eighteen thousand by the time of the first English census in 1698. Until the second decade of the eighteenth century, New York City remained a commercial backwater within the orbit of Boston.

The English conquest brought so little change to New York primarily because the duke of York in 1664

Founding of New Jersey

regranted the land between the Hudson and Delaware Rivers—East and West Jersey—to his friends Sir George Carteret and John Lord Berkeley. That grant left the duke's own colony hemmed in between Connecticut to the east and the Jerseys to the west and south, depriving it of much fertile land and hindering its economic growth. He also failed to promote migration. Meanwhile, the Jersey proprietors acted rapidly to attract settlers, promising generous land grants, limited freedom of religion, and—without authorization from the Crown—a representative assembly. In response, large numbers of Puritan New Englanders migrated southward to the Jerseys, along with some Barbadians and Dutch New Yorkers. New Jersey grew quickly; in 1726, at the time of its first census as a united colony, it had 32,500 inhabitants, only 8,000 fewer than New York.

Within twenty years, Berkeley and Carteret sold their interests in the Jerseys to separate groups of investors. The purchasers of all of Carteret's share (West Jersey) and portions of Berkeley's (East Jersey) were members of the Society of Friends, seeking a refuge from persecution in England. The Society of Friends, also called Quakers, rejected earthly and religious

Table 3.2   The Founding of English Colonies in North America, 1664–1681

Colony	Founder(s)	Date	Basis of Economy
New York (formerly New Netherland)	James, duke of York	1664	Farming, fur trading
New Jersey	Sir George Carteret, John Lord Berkeley	1664	Farming
North Carolina	Carolina proprietors	1665	Tobacco, forest products
South Carolina	Carolina proprietors	1670	Rice, indigo
Pennsylvania	William Penn	1681	Farming

hierarchies and denied the need for intermediaries between individuals and God. They believed that anyone could be saved by the "inner light" and that all people were equal in God's sight. With no formally trained clergy, Quakers allowed anyone, male or female, to speak in meetings or become a "public Friend" and travel to spread God's word. The Quaker message of radical egalitarianism was not welcome in the hierarchical society of seventeenth-century England or, for that matter, in Puritan New England. For example, Mary Dyer—who had followed Anne Hutchinson into exile—became a Quaker, returned to Boston as a missionary, and was hanged in 1660 (along with several men) for preaching Quaker doctrines.

Pennsylvania: A Quaker Haven

The Quakers obtained their own colony in 1681, when Charles II granted the region between Maryland and New York to his close friend William Penn, a prominent member of the sect. Penn was then thirty-seven years old; he held the colony as a personal proprietorship, one that earned profits for his descendants until the American Revolution. Even so, Penn, like the Roman Catholic Calverts of Maryland before him, saw his province not merely as a source of revenue but also as a haven for persecuted coreligionists. Penn offered land to all comers on liberal terms, promised toleration of all religions (although only Christians were given the vote), guaranteed English liberties such as the right to bail and trial by jury, and pledged to establish a representative assembly. He also publicized the ready availability of land in Pennsylvania through promotional tracts printed in German, French, and Dutch and distributed widely throughout Europe.

Penn's activities and the Quakers' attraction to his lands gave rise to a migration whose magnitude equaled the Puritan exodus to New England in the 1630s. By mid-1683, more than three thousand people—among them Welsh, Irish, Dutch, and Germans—had already moved to Pennsylvania, and within five years the population reached twelve thousand. (By contrast, it took Virginia more than thirty years to achieve a comparable population.) Philadelphia, carefully sited on the easily navigable Delaware River and planned to be the major city in the province, drew merchants and artisans from throughout the English-speaking world. From mainland and Caribbean colonies alike came Quakers seeking religious freedom; they brought with them years of experience on American soil and well-established trading connections. Pennsylvania's plentiful and fertile lands soon enabled its residents to begin exporting surplus flour and other foodstuffs to the West Indies. Practically overnight Philadelphia acquired more than two thousand citizens and started to challenge Boston's commercial dominance.

William Penn's Indian Policy

A pacifist with egalitarian principles, Penn attempted to treat Native Americans fairly. He learned to speak the language of the Delawares (or Lenapes), from whom he purchased tracts of land to sell to European settlers. Penn also established strict regulations for trade and forbade the sale of alcohol to Indians. His policies attracted native peoples who moved to Pennsylvania near the end of the seventeenth century to escape repeated clashes with English colonists in Maryland, Virginia, and North Carolina. Most important were the Tuscaroras, whose experiences are described later in this chapter. Likewise, Shawnees and Miamis chose to move eastward from the Ohio valley. By a supreme irony, however, the same toleration that attracted Native Americans also brought non-Quaker Europeans who showed little respect for Indian claims to the soil.

William Penn, later the proprietor of Pennsylvania, as he looked during his youth in Ireland. In such pamphlets as the one shown here, Penn spread the word about his new colony to thousands of readers in England and its other colonial possessions. (Historical Society of Pennsylvania)

In effect, Penn's policy was so successful that it caused its own downfall. The Scots-Irish, Germans, and Swiss who settled in Pennsylvania in the first half of the eighteenth century clashed repeatedly over land with Indians who had also recently migrated to the colony.

The southernmost proprietary colony, granted by Charles II in 1663, encompassed a huge tract of land stretching from the southern boundary of Virginia to Spanish Florida. The area had great strategic importance: a successful English settlement there would prevent Spaniards from pushing farther north. The fertile semitropical land also held forth the promise of producing exotic and valuable commodities such as figs, olives, wines, and silk. The proprietors named their new province Carolina in honor of Charles, whose Latin name was Carolus. The "Fundamental Constitutions of Carolina," which they asked the political philosopher John Locke to draft for them, set forth an elaborate plan for a

Founding of Carolina

colony governed by a hierarchy of landholding aristocrats and characterized by a carefully structured distribution of political and economic power.

But Carolina failed to follow the course the proprietors laid out. Instead, it quickly developed two distinct population centers, which in 1729 split into separate colonies. Virginia planters settled the Albemarle region that became North Carolina. They established a society much like their own, with an economy based on cultivating tobacco and exporting such forest products as pitch, tar, and timber. Because North Carolina lacked a satisfactory harbor, its planters relied on Virginia's ports and merchants to conduct their trade, and the colonies remained tightly linked. The other population center, which eventually formed the core of South Carolina, developed at Charles Town, founded in 1670 near the juncture of the Ashley and Cooper Rivers. Many of its early residents migrated from Barbados, which was already overcrowded less than fifty years after English people first settled there.

South Carolina's first years were difficult. After learning that many tropical plants would not grow successfully on the mainland, Carolinians began to raise corn and herds of cattle, which they sold to Caribbean sugar planters hungry for foodstuffs. Like so many other colonists before them, they depended on trade with nearby Indians to supply the only commodity for which they found a ready market in Europe: deerskins, which were almost as valuable as beaver pelts. During the first decade of the eighteenth century, South Carolina exported an average of 54,000 skins annually, and exports later peaked at 160,000 a year.

1670–1680: A Decade of Crisis

 As the Restoration colonies were extending the range of English settlement on the North American landscape, existing English colonies and French and Spanish settlements in North America faced new crises caused primarily by their changing relationships with America's indigenous peoples. Between 1670 and 1680, New England, Virginia, New France, and New Mexico experienced bitter conflicts as their interests collided with those of America's original inhabitants. All the early colonies changed irrevocably as a result.

In the mid-1670s, Louis de Buade de Frontenac, the governor-general of Canada, decided to expand

New France and the Iroquois

New France's reach into the south and west, hoping to establish a trade route to Mexico and to gain direct control of the valuable fur trade on which the prosperity of the colony rested. Accordingly, he encouraged the explorations of Father Jacques Marquette, Louis Jolliet, and Robert Cavelier de La Salle in the Great Lakes and Mississippi valley regions. His goal, however, brought him into conflict with the powerful Iroquois Confederacy, comprising not one Indian nation but five—the Mohawks, Oneidas, Onondagas, Cayugas, and Senecas. (In 1722 the Tuscaroras became the sixth.)

Under the terms of a unique defensive alliance forged early in the sixteenth century, a representative council made decisions of war and peace for the entire Iroquois Confederacy, although each nation still retained some autonomy and could not be forced to comply with a council directive against its will. Before the arrival of Europeans, the Iroquois waged wars pri-

Trade between Europeans and Indians provided both societies with essential items. The Europeans manufactured tomahawks specifically for the Native American market. Likewise, the Indians of Long Island increased their production of wampum (made from clam shells) when English and Dutch colonists adopted the purple and white beads as a medium of exchange. Wampum served as a substitute for European coins, which were scarce in the remote colonial outposts. (Peabody Essex Museum/Peabody Museum Collections. Photos by Mark Sexton)

marily to acquire captives to replenish their population. Contact with foreign traders brought ravaging disease as early as 1633, intensifying the need for captives. Simultaneously, the Europeans' presence created an economic motive for warfare: the desire to dominate the fur trade and to gain unimpeded access to European goods. The war with the Hurons in the 1640s (see page 38) was but the first of a series of conflicts with other Indians known as the Beaver Wars, in which the Iroquois fought to achieve control of the lucrative peltry trade. Iroquois warriors did not themselves trap beaver; instead, they raided other villages in search of caches of pelts or attacked Indians from the interior as they carried furs to European outposts. Then the Iroquois traded that booty for European-made blankets, knives, guns, alcohol, and other desirable items.

In the mid-1670s, as Iroquois dominance grew, the French stepped in, for an Iroquois triumph would have destroyed France's plans to trade directly with western Indians. Over the next twenty years the French launched repeated attacks on Iroquois villages. The English offered little assistance other than weapons to their trading partners, even though in 1677 New Yorkers and the Iroquois established a formal alliance known as the Covenant Chain. Its people and resources depleted by constant warfare, the Confederacy in 1701 finally negotiated a neutrality treaty with France and other Indians. For the next half-century the Iroquois nations maintained their power through trade and skillful diplomacy rather than warfare.

The wars against the Iroquois initiated in the 1670s were crucial components of French Canada's plan to penetrate the heartland of North America. Unlike Spaniards, French adventurers did not attempt to subjugate the Indians they encountered. Nor, at first, did they even formally claim large territories for France. Still, when France decided to strengthen its presence near the Gulf of Mexico by founding New Orleans in 1718—to counter both westward thrusts of the English colonies and eastward moves of the Spanish—the Mississippi posts became the glue of empire. *Coureurs de bois* (literally, "forest runners") used the rivers and lakes of the American interior to travel regularly between Quebec and Louisiana, carrying French goods to outposts such as Michilimackinac (at the junction of Lakes Michigan and Huron), Cahokia and Kaskaskia (in present-day

French Expansion into the Mississippi Valley

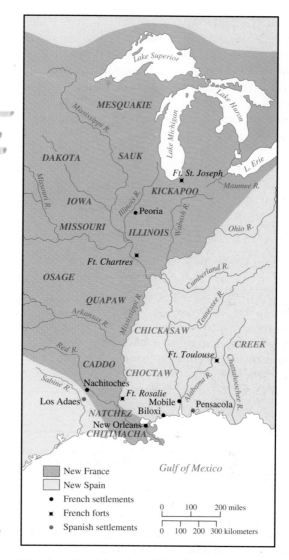

Map 3.2 Louisiana, c. 1720 By 1720 French forts and settlements dotted the Mississippi River and its tributaries in the interior of North America. Two isolated Spanish outposts were situated near the Gulf of Mexico. (Source: Adapted from *France in America,* by William J. Eccles. Copyright © 1972 by William J. Eccles. Reprinted by permission of HarperCollins Publishers, Inc.)

Illinois), and Fort Rosalie (Natchez), on the lower Mississippi River (see Map 3.2).

At most such sites lived a small military garrison and a priest, surrounded by powerful nations such as the Choctaws, Chickasaws, and Osages. Indians gained easy access to valuable European goods by tolerating the minimal European presence, and France's

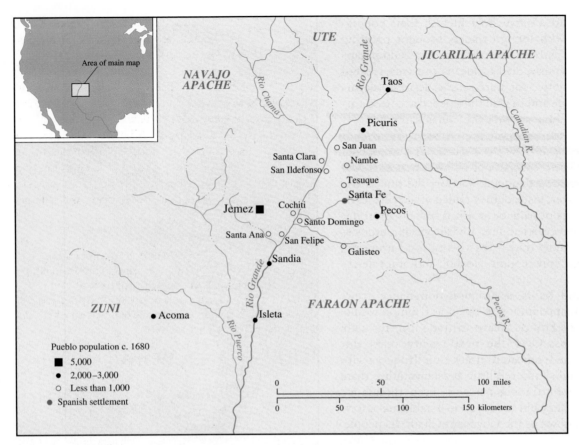

Map 3.3 New Mexico, c. 1680 In 1680, the lone Spanish settlement at Santa Fe was surrounded and vastly outnumbered by the many Pueblo villages nearby. (Source: Adapted from *Apache, Navaho, and Spaniard,* by Jack D. Forbes. Copyright © 1960 by the University of Oklahoma Press. Used by permission.)

primarily political and economic aims did not include systematic missionary work. The largest French settlements in the region, known collectively as *le pays de Illinois* ("the Illinois country"), never totaled much above three thousand in population. Located along the Mississippi just south of modern St. Louis and north of Fort Chartres, the settlements produced wheat for export to New Orleans. In all the French outposts, the shortage of European women led to interracial unions between French men and Indian women and to the creation of mixed-race people known as *metís.*

In New Mexico, too, events of the 1670s led to a crisis with long-term consequences. Over the years under Spanish domination, the Pueblo peoples had added Christianity to their religious beliefs while still retaining traditional rituals, engaging in syncretic practices as had

Popé and the Pueblo Revolt

Mesoamericans (see pages 24–25). But decade by decade Franciscans adopted increasingly brutal and violent tactics in order to erase all traces of the native religion. Priests and secular colonists who held *encomiendas* also placed heavy labor demands on the population. In 1680 the Pueblos revolted under the leadership of Popé, a respected shaman, successfully driving the Spaniards out of New Mexico (see Map 3.3). Although Spain managed to restore its authority in 1692, imperial officials had learned their lesson. Afterward, Spanish governors stressed cooperation with the Pueblos, no longer attempting to reduce them to bondage or to violate their cultural integrity. The Pueblo revolt of 1680 instigated the most successful and longest-sustained Indian resistance movement in colonial North America.

When the Spanish expanded their territorial claims to the east and north, they followed the same

Spain's North American Possessions

strategy they had adopted in New Mexico, establishing their presence through military outposts and Franciscan missions. The army's role was to maintain order among the subject Indians—to protect them from attack and ensure the availability of their labor—and to guard the boundaries of the New Spain from possible incursions, especially by the French. The friars concentrated on conversions and allowed religious syncretism. By the late eighteenth century, Spain claimed a vast territory that stretched from California (first colonized in 1769 to prevent Russian sea-otter trappers from taking over the region) through Texas (settled after 1700) to the Gulf Coast. Throughout that region, the Spanish presence consisted of a mixture of missions and forts dotting the countryside, sometimes at considerable distances from one another.

In the more densely settled English colonies, hostilities developed in the decade of the 1670s not over religion (as in New Mexico) or trade (as in New France) but rather over land. Put simply, the rapidly expanding Anglo-American population wanted more of it. In both New England and Virginia—though for different reasons—settlers began to encroach on territories that until then had remained in the hands of Native Americans.

In the north, the expansion of the population resulted not from continued immigration (for that largely ceased after the outbreak of the English Civil War in 1642) but rather from natural increase. The

Population Pressures in New England

original settlers' many children also produced many children, and subsequent generations followed suit. By the 1670s, New England's population had more than tripled to reach approximately seventy thousand. Such a rapid increase placed great pressure on available land. Colonial settlement spread far into the interior of Massachusetts and Connecticut, and many members of the third and fourth generations had to migrate—north to New Hampshire or Maine, south to New York or New Jersey, west beyond the Connecticut River—to find sufficient farmland for themselves and their children. Others abandoned agriculture and learned such skills as blacksmithing or carpentry to support themselves in the growing towns.

Colonial settlements eventually surrounded the ancestral lands of the Pokanokets (Wampanoags) on Narragansett Bay. The Pokanoket chief, King Philip, was the son of Massasoit, who had welcomed

King Philip's War

the Pilgrims in 1621. Troubled by the loss of Pokanoket lands and concerned about the impact of European culture and Christianity on his people, King Philip led his warriors in attacks on nearby communities in June 1675. Other Algonquian peoples, among them Nipmucks and Narragansetts, soon joined King Philip's forces. In the fall, the Indian nations jointly attacked settlements in the northern Connecticut River valley. In early 1676, they devastated well-established villages and even attacked Plymouth and Providence. Altogether, the alliance

In September 1671 a large number of Wampanoags renewed their long-standing alliance with the Plymouth colony by signing this document. Yet less than four years later the peace collapsed as King Philip launched devastating attacks on settlements in southern New England.   (Boston Athenaeum)

wholly or partially destroyed twenty-five of the ninety Puritan towns and attacked forty others, pushing the line of English settlement back toward the coast.

Still, the tide turned in the summer of 1676. The Indian coalition ran short of food and ammunition, and colonists began to use Christian Indians as guides and scouts. On June 12, the Mohawks—who as Iroquois were ancient enemies of the New England Algonquians—devastated a major Wampanoag encampment while most of the warriors were away attacking an English town on the Connecticut River. After King Philip's death that August, the alliance crumbled. As the chapter-opening vignette reveals, many surviving Pokanokets, Nipmucks, and Narragansetts were captured and sold into slavery, and still more died of starvation and disease. New Englanders had broken the power of the coastal tribes. Thereafter the Indians lived in small clusters, subordinated to the colonists and often working as servants or sailors. Only on the isolated island of Martha's Vineyard did some Wampanoags who had not participated in the war preserve their cultural identity intact.

But the settlers paid a terrible price for their victory in King Philip's War: an estimated one-tenth of the able-bodied adult male population was killed or wounded. Proportional to population, it was the most costly conflict in American history. New Englanders did not fully rebuild abandoned interior towns for another three decades, and not until the American Revolution did the region's per capita income again reach pre-1675 levels.

Not coincidentally, conflict with Indians wracked Virginia at precisely the same time. By the early 1670s,

Bacon's Rebellion

land-hungry Virginians eagerly eyed rich lands north of the York River reserved for Native Americans by early treaties. Using as a pretext the July 1675 killing of an English servant by some Doeg Indians, settlers attacked not only the Doegs but also the Susquehannocks, a powerful nation that had recently occupied the area. In retaliation, Susquehannock bands raided outlying farms in the winter of 1676. Governor William Berkeley, the leader of an entrenched coterie of large landowners, resisted starting a major war to further the aims of disgruntled men who overtly challenged his hold on power. Dissatisfied colonists, including former indentured servants unable to establish their own tobacco farms, rallied behind the leadership of a recent immigrant, the wealthy Nathaniel Bacon, who like other new ar-

rivals had found that all the desirable land in settled areas was already claimed by earlier residents.

Berkeley and Bacon soon clashed. After Bacon held members of the House of Burgesses hostage until they authorized him to attack the Indians, Berkeley declared Bacon and his men to be in rebellion. As the chaotic summer of 1676 wore on, Bacon alternately pursued Indians and battled the governor's supporters. In September Bacon marched on Jamestown itself, burning the capital to the ground. But when Bacon died of dysentery the following month, the rebellion began to collapse. Even so, the rebels had made their point, and a new treaty signed in 1677 opened much of the disputed territory to English settlement.

The war, a turning point in Virginia's relationship with nearby Indians, also marked a turning point in the colony's internal race relations. After Bacon's Rebellion, Virginia landowners began to purchase large numbers of imported African slaves for the first time. Historians disagree as to whether they did so in part because they feared dealing with successive waves of the discontented ex-servants who had followed Bacon's lead. But regardless of their motives, in the last two decades of the seventeenth century Anglo-Americans in the Chesapeake irrevocably altered the racial composition of their labor force.

The Introduction of African Slavery

In the 1670s and 1680s, the prosperity of the Chesapeake rested on tobacco, and successful tobacco cultivation depended, as it always had, on an ample labor supply. But fewer and fewer English men and women proved willing to indenture themselves for long terms of service in Maryland and Virginia. Population pressures had eased in England, and the founding of the Restoration colonies meant that people could choose other American destinations. Furthermore, fluctuating tobacco prices and the growing scarcity of land made the Chesapeake less appealing to potential immigrants. That posed a problem for wealthy Chesapeake tobacco growers, whose farms had by then developed into plantations—large enterprises encompassing a number of fields worked by many laborers. Where could they obtain the workers they needed? They found the answer in the Caribbean sugar islands, where since the 1640s Dutch, French, English, and Spanish planters had eagerly purchased African slaves.

European traders hoped to avoid purchasing sick slaves who would carry diseases on board their vessels, thereby causing high mortality rates among other bondspeople and destroying the profitability of the voyages. Some mistakenly believed that by tasting the slaves' sweat they could determine their captives' health. An artist sketched just such a scene in 1725. (*Traite général du commerce de l'Amérique,* by Chambon. Bibliothèque Municipale, Nantes, France)

Why African Slavery?

Slavery had been practiced in Europe (although not in England) for centuries. European Christians—both Catholics and Protestants—believed that enslaving heathen peoples, especially those of exotic origin, was justifiable in religious terms. Some argued, piously, that holding heathens in bondage would lead to their conversion. Others believed that any heathen taken prisoner in wartime could legitimately be enslaved. Consequently, when Portuguese mariners reached the sub-Saharan African coast and encountered non-Christian societies holding enslaved prisoners of war (see page 18), they did not hesitate to buy such slaves. After the 1440s, Portugal imported large numbers of these captives into the Iberian Peninsula and the Wine Islands; one historian has estimated that by 1500, enslaved Africans composed about one-tenth of the population of Lisbon and Seville, the chief cities of Portugal and Spain.

Iberians then exported African slavery to their American possessions, New Spain and Brazil. Because the Catholic Church prevented the formal enslavement of Indians in those domains (see pages 23–24) and free laborers saw no reason to work voluntarily in mines or on sugar plantations when they could earn better wages under easier conditions elsewhere, African bondspeople (who had no choice) became mainstays of the Caribbean and Brazilian economies. Sugar planters on English islands, who had the same problems of labor supply as did their French, Dutch, and Spanish counterparts, also purchased slaves.

Yet that slave system—well-established in the West Indies by the mid-1650s—did not immediately take root in the English mainland colonies, in large part because the colonies were then well-supplied with English laborers. Before the 1660s, the few residents of African descent on the mainland varied in

Atlantic Creoles in Societies with Slaves

status: some were free, some indentured, some enslaved. All came from a population that the historian Ira Berlin has termed Atlantic creoles. Often of mixed race, many came to the English colonies from elsewhere in the Americas. Already familiar with Europeans, the Atlantic creoles fitted easily into established niches in the many-faceted hierarchical social structures of the early colonies. Berlin has characterized all the early mainland colonies as "societies with slaves"— that is, societies in which some people were held in perpetual bondage but that did not rely wholly on slave labor. He usefully contrasts such communities with "slave societies," or societies in which slavery served as the fundamental basis of the economy.

The many ambiguities of status in societies with slaves are evident in early laws adopted by the Chesapeake assemblies. In several Virginia statutes the term *Christian* was used to mean "free person"; when at least one slave therefore claimed freedom as a consequence of conversion to Christianity, the House of Burgesses provided (in 1667) that "the blessed sacrament of baptism" would not liberate bondspeople from perpetual servitude. The two colonies did not agree on how slave status would be transmitted to the next generation: Virginia in 1662 declared that slavery followed "the condition of the mother," whereas Maryland two years later provided that children would be slaves "as their fathers were." And when in 1670 the House of Burgesses sought to define for the first time who was enslaveable and who was not, it declared that "all servants not being christians imported into this colony by shipping shalbe slaves for their lives," but similar servants that "shall come by land" would serve only for a term of years. The awkward phrases attempted to differentiate Africans from Indians; Virginians clearly saw both groups as distinguishable from English people, but expressed those distinctions in terms of religion and geography rather than race.

Yet just a few years later, Chesapeake legislators started to employ racial terminology. As increasing numbers of slaves arrived each year, first from the Caribbean and then directly from Africa, the majority of the enslaved population changed from acculturated creole to newly imported African. Virginia in 1682 altered its definition of who could be enslaved, declaring bluntly that "Negroes, Moors, Mollatoes or Indians" arriving "by sea or land" could all be held in bondage for life if their "parentage and native country

The Beginnings of Mainland Slave Societies

are not christian." Most of the English colonies, even those without many bondspeople, adopted detailed codes to govern slaves' behavior. By 1700 African slavery was firmly established as the basis of the economy in the Chesapeake and South Carolina as well as in the Caribbean. Under Berlin's definition, those colonies had become "slave societies."

English enslavers evidently had few moral qualms about these actions. Few at the time questioned the decision to hold Africans and their descendants—or Indians captured in wars, such as the New England Algonquians—in perpetual bondage. The convoluted and contradictory early attempts to define slave status and how it would pass to the next generation suggest, however, that seventeenth-century English colonists nevertheless initially lacked clear conceptual categories defining both "race" and "slave." They developed such categories and their meanings over time, through their experience with the institution of African (and Indian) slavery, which they originally adopted for economic reasons.

Between 1492 and 1770 more Africans than Europeans came to the Americas, the overwhelming majority of them as slaves. Most went to Brazil or the Caribbean: of at least 10 million enslaved people brought to the Americas during the existence of slavery, only about 120,000 by 1740, or 260,000 by 1775, were imported into the region that later became the United States. This massive trade in human beings is best understood within the context of the Atlantic trading system that developed during the middle years of the seventeenth century.

The Web of Empire and the Atlantic Slave Trade

 The elaborate Atlantic economic system is commonly called the triangular trade. In that context, the traffic in slaves from Africa to the Americas has become known as the middle passage because it constituted the middle leg of such a theoretical triangle. But both *triangular trade* and *middle passage* fail to convey the complexities of the commercial relationships that by the late seventeenth century linked the various elements of the Atlantic trading system in Europe, Africa, North and South America, and the Caribbean. People and products did not move across the ocean in easily diagrammed patterns. Instead, their movements created a complicated web of exchange that inextrica-

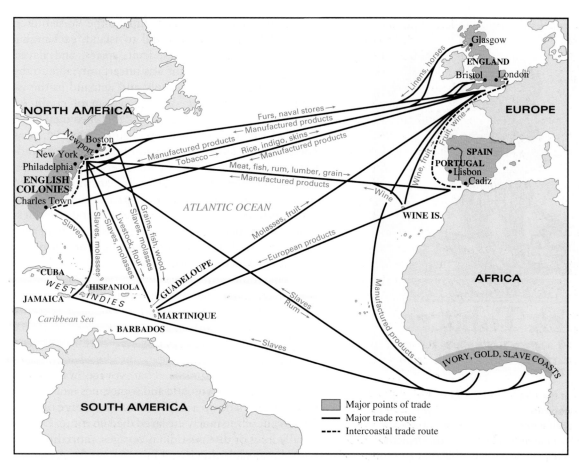

Map 3.4   Atlantic Trade Routes   By the late seventeenth century, an elaborate trade network linked the countries and colonies bordering the Atlantic Ocean. The most valuable commodities exchanged were enslaved people and the products of slave labor.

bly tied the peoples of the Atlantic world together (see Map 3.4).

The traffic in enslaved human beings served as the linchpin of the system. The expanding network of trade between Europe and its colonies was fueled by the sale and transport of slaves, the exchange of commodities produced by slave labor, and the need to feed and clothe so many bound laborers. Yet the various elements had different relationships within the system and with the wider web of exchange. Chesapeake tobacco and Caribbean and Brazilian sugar were in great demand in Europe, so planters shipped their products directly to their home countries. The profits paid for both the African laborers who grew their crops and European manufactured goods. The African coastal rulers who

Atlantic Trading System

ran the entrepots where European slavers acquired their human cargoes received their payment in European manufactures; they had little need for most American products. Europeans purchased slaves from Africa for resale in their colonies and acquired sugar and tobacco from America, in exchange dispatching their manufactures everywhere.

New England had the most complex relationship to the trading system. The region produced only one item England wanted: tall trees to serve as masts for sailing vessels. To buy English manufactures, New Englanders therefore needed profits earned elsewhere—the Wine Islands and such English islands as Barbados and St. Kitts. Those islands lacked precisely the items that New England could produce in abundance: cheap

New England and the Caribbean

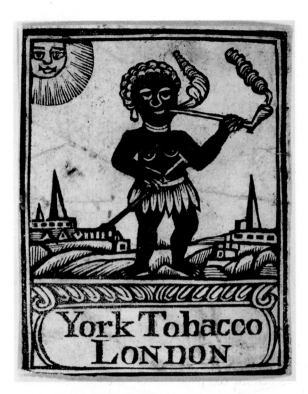

York Tobacco LONDON

By the middle of the eighteenth century, American tobacco had become closely associated with African slavery. An English woodcut advertising tobacco from the York River in Virginia accordingly depicted not a Chesapeake planter but rather an African, shown with a hoe in one hand and a pipe in the other. Usually, of course, slaves would not have smoked the high-quality tobacco produced for export, although they were allowed to cultivate small crops for their own use.   (Colonial Williamsburg Foundation)

food (primarily corn and salt fish) to feed the burgeoning slave population and wood for barrels to hold wine and molasses (the liquid form in which sugar was shipped). By the late 1640s, decades before the Chesapeake economy became dependent on *production* by slaves, New England's already rested on *consumption* by slaves and their owners. The sale of foodstuffs and wood products to Caribbean sugar planters provided New England farmers and merchants with a major source of income. After the founding of Pennsylvania, New York, and New Jersey, those colonies too participated in the lucrative West Indian trade.

Shopkeepers in the interior of New England and the middle colonies bartered with local farmers for grains, livestock, and barrel staves, then traded those items to merchants located in port towns. Such merchants then dispatched their ships to the West Indies, where they sailed from island to island, exchanging their cargoes for molasses, fruit, spices, and slaves. The system's sole constant was uncertainty, due to the weather, rapid shifts in supply and demand in the island markets, and the delicate system of credit on which the entire structure depended. Once they had a full load, the ships returned to Boston, Newport, New York, or Philadelphia to dispose of their cargoes, trading the items they did not use to other nearby colonies. Americans then distilled West Indian molasses into rum, a crucial aspect of the only part of the trade that could accurately be termed triangular. Rhode Islanders took rum to Africa and traded it for slaves, whom they carried to the West Indies to exchange for more molasses to produce still more rum.

The Human Tragedy of the Slave Trade

Tying the system together was the voyage that brought Africans (sold by coastal rulers, bought by European slavers) to the Americas, where they cultivated the profitable crops and—in the Caribbean—consumed foods produced in North America. That voyage was always traumatic and sometimes fatal for the people who made up a ship's cargo. An average of 10 to 20 percent of the newly enslaved died en route. On unusually long or disease-ridden voyages, mortality rates could be much higher. In addition, some slaves died either before the ships left Africa or shortly after their arrival in the Americas. Their European captors also died at high rates, chiefly through exposure to such diseases as yellow fever and malaria, which were endemic to Africa. Just 10 percent of the men sent to run the Royal African Company's forts in Lower Guinea lived to return home to England, and one in every four or five European sailors died on slaving voyages. Once again, the exchange of diseases caused unanticipated death and destruction.

Equiano's Story

Olaudah Equiano, just eleven years old in 1756 when African raiders kidnapped him from his Ibo village in what is now Nigeria, has left one of the most vivid accounts of such a voyage—as applicable to a century earlier as to his own time. Terrified by the light complexions, long hair, and strange language of the sailors, he feared that he "had gotten into a world of bad spirits and that they were going to kill me." Placed below decks, Equiano found that "with the loathsomeness of the stench and crying together, I became so sick and low that I was not able to eat, nor had I the least desire to taste anything."

The slavers flogged him to make him eat. Equiano thought about killing himself by jumping overboard but was too closely watched. At last some other Ibos told him that they were being taken to their captors' country to work. "I then was a little revived," Equiano remembered, "and thought if it were no worse than working, my situation was not so desperate."

After a long voyage during which many of the Africans died of disease brought on by the cramped, unsanitary conditions and poor food, the ship arrived at Barbados. Equiano and his shipmates suspected that "these ugly men" were cannibals, but experienced slaves came on board to assure them that they would not be eaten and that many Africans like themselves lived on the island. Equiano recalled that "sure enough soon after we landed there came to us Africans of all languages." Along with other less desirable slaves in the cargo, the youthful Equiano was carried to Virginia, where he was sold and put to work on an isolated part of a tobacco plantation. Resold to a visiting ship captain, he became a sailor, learned English, purchased his own freedom, and eventually published his autobiography.

The slave trade had political and economic consequences for the nations of West Africa. Coastal rulers served as middlemen, allowing the

West Africa and the Slave Trade

establishment of permanent slave-trading posts in their territories and supplying resident Europeans with slaves to fill ships that stopped regularly at the coastal forts. Such rulers controlled European traders' access to slaves and at the same time controlled inland peoples' access to desirable European goods such as cloth, alcohol, tobacco, firearms, and iron bars that could be made into useful tools. The centralizing tendencies of the slave trade helped to create such powerful eighteenth-century kingdoms as Dahomey and Asante (formed from the Akan States; see page 13). Traffic in slaves thus destroyed smaller polities and disrupted traditional economic patterns, as trade once sent north toward the Mediterranean was redirected to the coast, and as local manufactures declined in the face of European competition.

The trade in human beings did not uniformly depopulate Guinea, a fertile and densely inhabited region. Instead, the slave trade affected African societies unevenly. Because they primarily bartered prisoners of war with European slavers, coastal rulers' participation in the trade depended on their involvement in warfare. For example, the growing state of Benin actively sold wartime captives to the Portuguese in the late fifteenth century; did not do so at the height of its power in the sixteenth and seventeenth centuries; and renewed the sale of prisoners in the eighteenth century when its waning power led to conflict with neighboring states. Because American planters preferred to purchase male slaves, the trade did have an impact on the sex ratio of the remaining population. The relative shortage of men increased work demands on women, encouraged polygyny, and opened new avenues for advancement to women and their children.

This traffic in slaves chiefly benefited Europeans, despite its importance to some African kings. The European economy, previously oriented toward the Mediterranean and Asia,

European Rivalries and the Slave Trade

shifted its emphasis to the Atlantic Ocean. Whereas European merchants' profits had once come primarily from trade with North Africa, the eastern Mediterranean, and China, by the late seventeenth century commerce in slaves and the products of slave labor constituted the basis of the European economic system. The irony of Columbus's discoveries thus became complete: seeking the wealth of Asia, Columbus instead found the lands that—along with Africa—ultimately replaced Asia as the source of European prosperity.

European nations fought bitterly to control the slave trade. The Portuguese, who at first dominated the trade, were supplanted by the Dutch in the 1630s. The Dutch in turn lost out to the English, who controlled the trade through the Royal African Company, a joint-stock company chartered by Charles II in 1672. Holding a monopoly on all English trade with sub-Saharan Africa, the company built and maintained seventeen forts and trading posts, dispatched to West Africa hundreds of ships carrying English manufactured goods, and transported about 100,000 slaves to England's Caribbean colonies. It paid regular dividends averaging 10 percent yearly, and some of its agents made fortunes. Yet even before the company's monopoly expired in 1712, many individual English traders had illegally entered the market for slaves. By the early eighteenth century, such independent traders carried most of the Africans imported into the colonies, earning huge profits from successful voyages.

English officials seeking a new source of revenue after the disruptions of the Civil War decided to tap into the profits produced by the expanding Atlantic trading system. Chesapeake tobacco and West Indian sugar had obvious value, but other colonial products also had considerable potential. Additional tax revenues could put

The harbor of Christiansted, St. Croix, in the Danish West Indies. Although this view was painted over one hundred years after the events discussed in this chapter, the town had not changed much in the interim. Scenes like this would have been very familiar to seventeenth- and eighteenth-century colonial mariners, for such ports existed all over the Caribbean. Anchored merchant vessels await the hogsheads of molasses being prepared for shipment at the wharf.   (1996 MAPes MONDe Ltd.)

England back on a sound financial footing, and English merchants wanted to ensure that they—not their Dutch rivals—reaped the benefits of trading with English colonies. Parliament and the restored Stuart monarchs accordingly began to draft laws designed to confine the proceeds of the English imperial web of trade primarily to the mother country.

Like other European nations, England based its commercial policy on a series of assumptions about the operations of the world's economic system. Collectively, these assumptions are usually called mercantilism, although neither the term itself nor a unified mercantilist theory would be formulated until a century later. The theory viewed the economic world as a collection of national states, whose governments actively competed for shares of a finite amount of

Mercantilism

wealth. What one nation gained, another nation automatically lost. Each nation sought to become as economically self-sufficient as possible while maintaining a favorable balance of trade with other countries by exporting more than it imported. Colonies had an important role to play in such a scheme. They could supply the mother country with valuable raw materials to be consumed at home or sent abroad, and they could serve as a market for the mother country's manufactured goods.

Parliament applied mercantilist thinking to the American colonies in laws known as the Navigation Acts. The major acts—passed between 1651 and 1673—established three main principles. First, only English or colonial merchants and ships could engage in trade in the colonies.

Navigation Acts

Second, certain valuable American products could be sold only in the mother country or in other English colonies. At first, these "enumerated" goods included wool, sugar, tobacco, indigo, ginger, and dyes; later acts added rice, naval stores (masts, spars, pitch, tar, and turpentine), copper, and furs to the list. Third, all foreign goods destined for sale in the colonies had to be shipped by way of England, paying English import duties. Some years later, a new series of laws established a fourth principle: the colonies could not export items (such as wool clothing, hats, or iron) that competed with English products.

The Navigation Acts aimed at forcing American trade to center on England. The mother country would benefit from colonial imports and exports both. England had first claim on the most valuable colonial exports, and all foreign imports into the colonies had to pass through England first, enriching its customs revenues in the process. The laws adversely affected some colonies, like those in the West Indies and the Chesapeake, because planters there could not seek new markets for their staple crops. In others, the impact was minimal or even positive. Builders and owners of ships benefited from the monopoly on American trade given to English and colonial merchants; the laws stimulated the creation of a lucrative colonial shipbuilding industry, especially in New England. And the northern and middle colonies produced many unenumerated goods—for example, fish, flour, meat and livestock, and barrel staves. Such products could be traded directly to the French and Dutch Caribbean islands as long as they were carried in English or American ships.

The English authorities soon learned that writing mercantilist legislation was far easier than enforcing it. The many harbors of the American coast provided ready havens for smugglers, and colonial officials often looked the other way when illegally imported goods were offered for sale. In ports such as St. Eustatius in the Dutch West Indies, American merchants could easily dispose of enumerated goods and purchase foreign items on which duty had not been paid. Consequently, Parliament in 1696 enacted another Navigation Act. This law established in America a number of vice-admiralty courts, which operated without juries. In England such courts dealt only with cases involving piracy, vessels taken as wartime prizes, and the like. But since American juries had already demonstrated a tendency to favor local smugglers over customs officers (a colonial customs service was instituted in 1671), Parliament decided to remove Navigation Act cases from the regular colonial courts.

England took another major step in colonial administration in 1696 by creating the fifteen-member Board of Trade and Plantations, which thereafter served as the chief organ of government concerned with the American colonies. (Previously, no single body in London had that responsibility.) It gathered information, reviewed Crown appointments in America, scrutinized legislation passed by colonial assemblies, supervised trade policies, and advised successive ministries on colonial issues. Still, the Board of Trade did not have any direct powers of enforcement. It also shared jurisdiction over American affairs not only with the customs service and the navy but also with the secretary of state for the southern department, the member of the ministry responsible for the colonies. In short, although the Stuart monarchs' reforms considerably improved the quality of colonial administration, supervision of the American provinces remained decentralized and haphazard.

Board of Trade and Plantations

Enslavement in North America

The voyage Olaudah Equiano described was typical, for most slave ships followed the Northeast Trades to the Caribbean before heading north to the Chesapeake. So many Africans were imported into Virginia and Maryland so rapidly that as early as 1690 those colonies contained more slaves than English indentured servants, and by 1710 people of African descent composed one-fifth of the region's population. Even so, and despite sizable continuing imports, a decade later American-born slaves already outnumbered their African-born counterparts in the Chesapeake, and the native-born continued to grow thereafter as a proportion of the slave population.

Slaves brought from Africa tended to be assigned to outlying parts of the plantations (called quarters), at least until they learned some English and the routines of tobacco cultivation. Those from Upper Guinea might have grown the crop in Africa; one historian has speculated that slaves from that region, whence tobacco was exported by the 1680s, could have offered expert advice to Chesapeake planters, who at the time were still experimenting with curing and processing techniques. Such Africans—the vast majority of them men—lived in quarters composed of ten to fifteen workers housed

Enslavement in the Chesapeake

together in one or two buildings and supervised by an Anglo-American overseer. Each man was expected to cultivate about two acres of tobacco a year. Their lives must have been filled with toil and loneliness, for few spoke the same language and all were expected to work for their owners six days a week. On Sundays, planters allowed them a day off. Many used that time to cultivate their own gardens or to hunt or fish to supplement their meager diets. Only rarely could they form families because of the scarcity of women among newly imported Africans.

Such slaves usually cost about two and a half times as much as indentured servants, but they repaid the greater investment with a lifetime of service, assuming they survived—which large numbers, weakened by the voyage and sickened by exposure to new diseases, did not. Many planters could not afford to purchase such expensive workers. Thus the transition from indentured to enslaved labor increased the social and economic distance between richer and poorer planters. Those with enough money could acquire slaves, accumulate greater wealth, and establish large plantations worked by tens, if not hundreds, of bondspeople, whereas the less affluent could not even buy indentured servants, whose price rose because of scarcity. As time passed, Anglo-American society in the Chesapeake became more and more stratified— that is, the gap between rich and poor steadily widened. The introduction of large numbers of Africans into the Chesapeake thus had a significant impact on the shape of Anglo-American society, in addition to reshaping the population as a whole.

Impact of Slavery on the Anglo-American Chesapeake

Africans who had lived in the Caribbean came with their masters to South Carolina from Barbados in 1670, composing one-quarter to one-third of the early population. The Barbadian slaveowners quickly discovered that African-born slaves had a variety of skills well suited to the semitropical environment of South Carolina. African-style dugout canoes became the chief means of transportation in the colony, which was crossed by rivers. Fishing nets copied from African models proved more efficient than those of English origin. Baskets that enslaved laborers wove and gourds that they hollowed out came into general use as containers for food and drink. Africans' skill at killing crocodiles equipped them to handle alligators. And, finally, Africans adapted their traditional techniques of cattle

Enslavement in South Carolina

herding for use in America. Since meat and hides numbered among the colony's chief exports in its earliest years, Africans contributed significantly to South Carolina's prosperity.

Not until after 1700 did South Carolinians begin to import slaves directly from Africa. Nevertheless, by 1710 African-born slaves already outnumbered those born in the Americas, and they constituted a majority of the slave population in South Carolina until about midcentury. The similarity of the South Carolinian and West African environments, coupled with the large proportion of Africans in the population, ensured that more aspects of West African culture survived in that colony than elsewhere on the North American mainland. Only in South Carolina did enslaved parents continue to give their children African names; only there did a dialect develop that combined English words with African terms. (Known as Gullah, it has survived to the present day in isolated areas.) African skills remained useful, so techniques lost in other regions when the migrant generation died were instead passed down to the migrants' children. And in South Carolina African women became the primary petty traders, dominating the markets of Charles Town as they did those of Guinea.

The importation of large numbers of Africans coincided with the successful introduction of rice as a staple crop in South Carolina. English people knew little about the techniques of growing and processing rice, and they failed at their first attempts to raise the crop. But people from Africa's Rice Coast (see page 11) had spent their lives working with rice. Although the evidence is circumstantial, it seems likely that the Africans' expertise assisted their English masters in cultivating the crop profitably. Slaves on rice plantations, which were far larger than Chesapeake tobacco quarters, were each expected to cultivate three to four acres of rice a year. To cut expenses, planters also expected slaves to grow part of their own food. A universally adopted task system of predefined work assignments provided that after bondspeople had finished their set "tasks" for the day, they could then relax or work in their own garden plots or on other projects. Experienced slaves could often complete their tasks by early afternoon; after that, as on Sundays, their masters had no legitimate claim on their time.

Rice and Indigo

When South Carolina developed a second staple crop, its planters too used the task system and drew on slaves' specialized skills. Indigo was much prized in

How do historians know...

that enslaved Africans preserved important aspects of their culture in America? The vast majority of slaves could not read or write, so they did not leave the documentary evidence on which historians customarily rely to develop interpretations of cultural continuity among other peoples. Yet European observers commented on the activities and skills of Africans in their homelands and in the Americas, and the conjunctions are sometimes highly revealing. In 1726, for example, William Smith, an employee of the Royal African Company, drew the sketch below, showing an African musician playing a traditional marimba-like instrument called the *balafo*. Anglo-Americans reported seeing and hearing similar instruments both in the Caribbean islands and on the mainland. John Harrower, a schoolmaster who was an indentured servant in Virginia, recorded in his journal in March 1775 a visit to a tutor on another plantation. After dinner, he wrote, "I spent the afternoon with him in conversation & hearing him play the Fiddle. He also made a Niger come & play on an Instrument call'd a Barrafou." Harrower's description makes it clear that the instrument he heard closely resembled the one Smith had seen half a century earlier in Guinea: "The body of it is an oblong box with the mouth up & stands on four sticks put in bottom, & cross the [top] is laid 11 lo[o]se sticks upon [which] he beats." It is impossible to know who made the *balafo* Harrower heard, or whether the musician was African- or American-born. But the sketch and the description, taken together, show that African music came to North America along with the enslaved multitudes. (Photo: Joseph Regenstein Library, University of Chicago)

A Negro playing on the Ballafoe

Europe as a source of blue dye for cloth. In the early 1740s, Eliza Lucas, a young woman managing her father's plantations, began to experiment with indigo cultivation. Drawing on the knowledge of slaves and overseers from the West Indies, she developed the planting and processing techniques later adopted throughout the colony. Indigo grew on high ground, and rice was planted in low-lying swamps; rice and indigo also had different growing seasons. Thus the two crops complemented each other. South Carolina indigo never matched the quality of that from the Caribbean, but the indigo industry flourished because Parliament offered Carolinians a bounty on every pound they exported to Great Britain.

Indian Enslavement in North and South Carolina

Among the many people held in slavery in both the Carolinas were Indians, many of them Catholic converts from Spanish missions in northern Florida who had been captured by Englishmen or their Native American allies. A widespread traffic in Indian slaves developed in South Carolina, as some Indian nations (for example, the Creeks and the Tuscaroras) sold their captives to the colonists, who either retained them or exported them to other colonies. There are no reliable statistics on the extent of the trade in Indian slaves, but in 1708 they composed 14 percent of the South Carolina population.

Bitter conflicts between North Carolina settlers and indigenous peoples produced not only Indian slaves but also mass migrations. In 1711 the Tuscaroras, an Iroquoian people, attacked a Swiss-German settlement at New Bern that had expropriated their lands without payment. Because the Tuscaroras had been avid slavers, their Algonquian neighbors took the opportunity to settle old scores, joining with the English colonists to defeat their enemy in a bloody two-year war. In the end, more than a thousand Tuscaroras were themselves sold into slavery, and the remnants of the group drifted northward, where they joined the Iroquois Confederacy (see page 66).

The slave trade's abuses led as well to another Indian war in South Carolina. Colonial traders were well known for cheating Native Americans, physically abusing them, and selling friendly peoples into slavery when no enemy captives came readily to hand. In the spring and summer of 1715, the Yamasees, aided by Creeks and others, retaliated by attacking English settlements. Refugees by the hundreds streamed into Charles Town; the Creek-Yamasee offensive came close to driving the colonists from South Carolina. But reinforcements arrived from the north, the colonists hastily armed their slaves to help defend the territory, and Cherokees joined the English settlers to fight the Creeks, their ancient foes. In the end, the Creeks were forced to retreat to villages in the west and the Yamasees moved south into Florida, seeking refuge among the Spanish.

Yamasee War

Indian or African slavery was never of great importance in the economy of Spain's North American territories. (Required labor tribute from the Indian population supplied the Spaniards' needs.) But as slavery took deeper root in South Carolina, Florida officials in 1693 offered freedom to fugitives who would convert to Catholicism. Hundreds of South Carolina runaways took advantage of the offer; although not all won their liberty, others enlisted as free men in the Florida militia. Many settled in a town founded for them near St. Augustine, Gracia Real de Santa Teresa de Mose, which was led by a former slave and militia captain, Francisco Menéndez.

Slaves in Spanish North America

In early Louisiana, too, slaves—some Indians, some Atlantic creoles—at first composed only a tiny proportion of the residents. But a growing European population demanded that the French government supply them with slaves, and in 1719 officials finally acquiesced, dispatching more than six thousand Africans (most from Senegal) over the next decade. The residents failed to develop a successful crop (although they experimented with both tobacco and indigo), but they did succeed in angering the Natchez Indians, whose lands they had usurped. In 1729 the Natchez, assisted by newly arrived slaves, attacked northern reaches of the colony, killing more than 10 percent of its European people. The French struck back, slaughtering the Natchez and their enslaved allies, but throughout much of the century Louisiana remained a society with slaves rather than a slave society.

Slaves in French Louisiana

Atlantic creoles from the West Indies composed almost all the bondspeople in the northern mainland colonies; few vessels arrived in Boston, Newport, or Philadelphia directly from Africa. Yet the intricate involvement of northerners in the web of commerce surrounding the slave trade ensured that many people of African descent lived in America north of Virginia. Some bondspeople resided in urban areas, especially New York, which in 1700 had a larger black population than any other mainland city. Women tended to work as domestic servants, men as unskilled laborers, and one or two slaves were commonly found in the households of well-to-do families (including three-quarters of wealthy Philadelphians at the end of the seventeenth century). Yet even in the north most enslaved people worked in the countryside, the majority at agricultural tasks. Some men toiled in new rural enterprises such as ironworks, working with hired laborers and indentured servants at forges and foundries. Indeed, ironmasters owned some of the largest numbers of slaves in the north.

Enslavement in the North

Colonial Political Development, Imperial Reorganization, and the Witchcraft Crisis

The crises of the 1670s in Virginia and New England focused the attention of reform-minded English officials on the mainland colonies. In the early 1680s, London administrators confronted a bewildering array of colonial governments. Massachusetts Bay (including Maine) functioned under its original charter. Neighboring Connecticut (having absorbed New Haven) and Rhode Island were granted charters by Charles II in 1662 and 1663, respectively, but Plymouth remained autonomous. Virginia, a royal colony, was joined in that status by New Hampshire in 1679 and New York in 1685 when its proprietor ascended the throne as James II. All the other mainland settlements were proprietorships.

Still, the colonies shared characteristic political structures. A governor and a legislature ruled most. In

Colonial Political Structures

New England, property-holding men or the legislature elected the governors; in other regions, the king or the proprietor appointed such leaders. A council, either elected or appointed, advised the governor on matters of policy and sometimes served as the colony's highest court. The councils also served as upper houses of colonial legislatures. At first, councilors and elected representatives met jointly to debate and adopt laws affecting the colony. But as time passed, the fundamental differences between the two legislative groups' purposes and constituencies led them to separate (the first such division occurred in Massachusetts in 1644). Thus developed the two-house legislature still used in all but one of the states.

Meanwhile, local political institutions took shape. In New England, elected selectmen initially governed the towns, but by the end of the seventeenth century, town meetings—held at least annually and attended by most free adult male residents—handled matters of local concern. In the Chesapeake colonies and both of the Carolinas, appointed justices of the peace ran local governments. At first the same was true in Pennsylvania, but by the early eighteenth century elected county officials began to take over some government functions. And in New York, local elections were the rule even before the establishment of the colonial assembly in 1683.

By late in the seventeenth century, therefore, Anglo-American colonists everywhere had become

A Tradition of Autonomy Challenged

accustomed to exercising a considerable degree of local political autonomy. The tradition of consent was especially firmly established in New England. Massachusetts, Plymouth, Connecticut, and Rhode Island operated essentially as independent entities, subject neither to the direct authority of the king nor

to a proprietor. Everywhere in the English colonies, free adult men who owned more than a minimum amount of property (which varied from place to place) expected to have an influential voice in their governments—and especially in decisions concerning taxation.

After James II became king in 1685, such expectations clashed with those of the monarch. The new king and his successors sought to bring order to the apparently chaotic state of colonial administration by tightening the reins of government and by reducing the colonies' political autonomy. (Simultaneously, officials used the Navigation Acts to reduce the colonies' economic autonomy.) Administrators began to chip away at the privileges granted in colonial charters and to reclaim proprietorships for the Crown. Massachusetts (1691), New Jersey (1702), and the Carolinas (1729) all became royal colonies. The charters of Rhode Island, Connecticut, Maryland, and Pennsylvania were temporarily suspended but ultimately were restored to their original status.

The most drastic reordering of colonial administration targeted Puritan New England. Reports from

Dominion of New England

America convinced English officials that New England was a hotbed of smuggling. Moreover, Puritans refused to allow freedom of religion to non-Congregationalists and insisted on maintaining laws that ran counter to English practice. New England thus seemed an appropriate place to exert English authority with greater vigor. The charters of all the colonies from New Jersey to Maine were revoked, and a Dominion of New England established in 1686. (For the boundaries of the Dominion, see Map 3.1.) Sir Edmund Andros, the governor, had immense power: Parliament dissolved all the assemblies, and Andros needed only the consent of an appointed council to make laws and levy taxes.

New Englanders endured Andros's autocratic rule for more than two years. Then came the dramatic news that James II had been

Glorious Revolution in America

overthrown in a bloodless coup known as the Glorious Revolution and had been replaced on the throne by his daughter Mary and her husband, the Dutch prince of Orange. James II, like his father Charles I, had levied taxes without parliamentary approval. He also had announced his conversion to Roman Catholicism. When Parliament offered the throne to

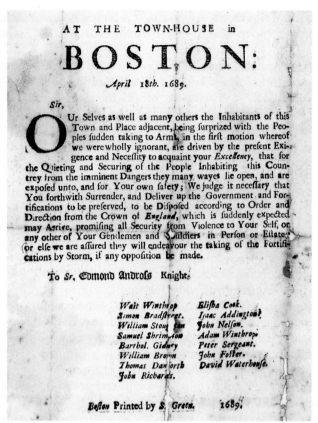

Sir Edmund Andros (1637–1714), the much-detested autocratic governor of the Dominion of New England, and a broadside issued at the height of the crisis caused by the Glorious Revolution, calling on Andros to surrender control of the government. The signers were the foremost leaders of the Massachusetts Bay colony, among them a son and grandson of John Winthrop. (Portrait: Massachusetts State Archives; Broadside: Massachusetts Historical Society)

the Protestants William and Mary, the Glorious Revolution affirmed the supremacy of both Parliament and Protestantism.

Seizing the opportunity to rid themselves of the hated Dominion, New Englanders jailed Andros and his associates, proclaimed their loyalty to William and Mary, and wrote to England for instructions about the form of government they should adopt. Most of Massachusetts Bay's political leaders hoped that the new monarchs would renew their original charter, revoked in 1684 prior to establishment of the Dominion. In other colonies, too, the Glorious Revolution emboldened people for revolt. In Maryland the Protestant Association overturned the government of the Catholic proprietor, and in New York a militia officer of German origin, Jacob Leisler, assumed control of the gov-

ernment. Like New Englanders, the Maryland and New York rebels allied themselves with the supporters of William and Mary. They saw themselves as carrying out the colonial phase of the English revolt against Stuart absolutism.

William and Mary, however, like James II, believed that England should exercise tighter control over its unruly American possessions. Consequently, only the Maryland rebellion received royal sanction, primarily because of its anti-Catholic thrust. In New York, Jacob Leisler was hanged for treason, and Massachusetts (including the formerly independent jurisdiction of Plymouth) became a royal colony with an appointed governor. The province retained its town meeting system of local government and continued to elect its council, but the new charter issued in 1691 (which arrived in Boston with the new governor in May 1692) eliminated the traditional religious test for voting and officeholding. A parish of the Church of England appeared in the heart of Boston. The "city upon a hill," as John Winthrop had envisioned it, was no more.

A war with the French and their Algonquian allies compounded New England's difficulties in a time of political upheaval and economic uncertainty. King Louis XIV of France allied himself with the deposed James II, and England declared war on France in 1689. In Europe, this conflict was known as the War of the League of Augsburg, but the colonists called it King William's War. Indian attacks wholly or partially destroyed a number of English settlements, including Schenectady (New York) and such Maine communities as Casco and Wells. Expeditions organized by the colonies against Montreal and Quebec in 1690 both failed miserably, and throughout the rest of the conflict New England found itself on the defensive. Even the Peace of Ryswick (1697), which formally ended the war in Europe, failed to bring much of a respite from warfare to the northern frontiers. For instance, Maine could not be fully resettled for several decades because of continuing unrest.

King William's War

Early in the conflict, New Englanders understandably feared a repetition of the devastation of King Philip's War. For eight months in 1692, witchcraft accusations spread like wildfire through the rural communities of northeastern Massachusetts—precisely the area most threatened by the Indian attacks in southern Maine and New Hampshire. Like their contemporaries elsewhere, seventeenth-century New Englanders believed in the existence of witches, whose evil powers came from the Devil. If people could not find other explanations for their troubles, they tended to suspect they were bewitched. Before 1689, about one hundred New Englanders, most of them middle-aged women, had been charged with practicing witchcraft, chiefly by neighbors who attributed misfortunes to the suspected witch. Only a few of the accused were convicted, and fewer still were executed. Such isolated incidents involving personal disputes bore little relationship to the witch fears that convulsed the region in 1692 while the war raged just to the north.

The 1692 Witchcraft Crisis

The crisis began in late February when several girls in Salem Village (an outlying precinct of the bustling port of Salem) accused some older female neighbors of having bewitched them. Soon other accusers chimed in, many of them female domestic servants who had been orphaned in the Indian attacks on Maine. (One, for example, lost her grandparents in King Philip's War and her parents in King William's War.) These traumatized young women, perhaps the most powerless people in a region apparently powerless to affect its fate, offered their fellow New Englanders a compelling explanation for the seemingly endless chain of troubles afflicting them: their province was under direct attack not only by the Indians but also by the Devil and his allied witches. Before the crisis ended, fourteen women and five men were hanged, one man was pressed to death with heavy stones, and more than one hundred fifty people were jailed, some for many months.

In October, the crisis ended rapidly, for three main reasons. First, the colony's ministers, led by the Reverend Increase Mather, formally expressed serious reservations about the validity of the evidence used to convict many of the accused. Second, the full implementation of the new royal charter ended the worst period of political uncertainty, eliminating one of the sources of stress and regularizing legal procedures. Third, opponents of the trials gained the ear of the new governor, publicly disparaging the "hysterical girls" who had begun the crisis and casting doubt on their credibility.

With the end of the witchcraft crisis and with colonial administration firmly in place, Massachusetts and the rest of the English colonies in America accommodated themselves to the new imperial order. Most colonists resented alien officials who arrived in America determined to implement the policies of king and Parliament, but they adjusted to their demands and to the trade restrictions imposed by the Navigation Acts. They fought another imperial war—the War of the Spanish Succession, or Queen Anne's War—from 1702 to 1713, without enduring the stresses of the first, despite the heavy economic burdens the conflict imposed. Colonists who allied themselves with royal government received patronage in the form of offices and land grants and composed "court parties" that supported English officials. Others, who were either less fortunate in their friends or more principled in defense of colonial autonomy, made up the opposition, or "country" interest. By the

Accommodation to Empire

end of the first quarter of the eighteenth century, most men in both groups had been born in America and were members of elite families whose wealth derived from staple-crop production in the South and commerce in the North.

The Reverend Cotton Mather of Boston, twenty-nine years old in 1692 at the time of the Salem witchcraft crisis, rushed this book—*The Wonders of the Invisible World*—into print shortly after the trials ended. He tried to explain to his fellow New Englanders the "Grievous Molestations by Daemons and Witchcrafts which have lately annoy'd the Countrey" by providing both brief trial narratives and examples of similar recent occurrences elsewhere, most notably in Mohra, Sweden.   (Massachusetts Historical Society)

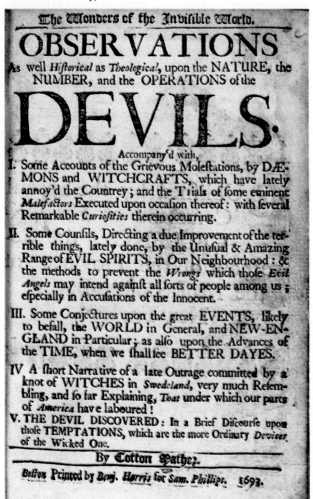

Summary

The eighty years from 1640 to 1720 established the basic economic and political patterns that were to structure subsequent changes in mainland colonial society. In 1640 just two isolated centers of English population, New England and the Chesapeake, existed along the seaboard, along with the tiny Dutch colony of New Netherland. In 1720 nearly the entire east coast of North America was in English hands, and Indian control east of the Appalachian Mountains had been broken by the outcomes of King Philip's War, Bacon's Rebellion, and Queen Anne's War. To the west of the mountains, though, Iroquois power still reigned supreme. What had been an immigrant population was now mostly American-born, except for the many African-born people in South Carolina; economies originally based on trade in fur and skins had become far more complex and more closely linked with the mother country; and a wide variety of political structures had been reshaped into a more uniform pattern. Yet at the same time the introduction of large-scale slavery into the Chesapeake and the Carolinas differentiated their societies from those of the colonies to the north. The production of tobacco, rice, and indigo for international markets distinguished the southern regional economies. They had become true slave societies, heavily reliant on a system of perpetual servitude, not societies with slaves, in which a few bondspeople mingled with larger numbers of indentured servants and laborers of other descriptions.

Even the economies of the northern colonies, though, rested on profits derived from the Atlantic trading system, the key element of which was traffic in enslaved humans, primarily Africans but also including Indians. New England sold corn, salt fish, and wood products to the West Indies, where slaves consumed the foodstuffs and planters shipped molasses in barrels made from staves crafted by northern farmers. Pennsylvania and New York too found in the Caribbean islands a ready market for their livestock, grains, and wheat flour. The rapid growth of enslavement drove all the English colonial economies in these years.

Meanwhile, from a small outpost in Santa Fe, New Mexico, and missions in Florida, the Spanish had expanded their influence throughout the Gulf Coast region and, by just after midcentury, as far north as California. The French had moved from a few settlements along the St. Lawrence to dominate the length of the Mississippi River and the entire Great Lakes region. Both groups of colonists lived near Indian nations and depended on the indigenous people's labor and goodwill. The French and Spanish could not fully control their Native American allies—and the French did not even try. The extensive Spanish and French presence to the south and west of the English settlements meant that future conflicts among the European powers in North America were nearly inevitable.

By 1720, the essential elements of the imperial administrative structure that would govern the English colonies until 1775 had been put firmly in place. The regional economic systems originating in the late seventeenth and early eighteenth centuries also continued to dominate North American life for another century—until after independence had been won. And Anglo-Americans had developed the commitment to autonomous local government that later would lead them into conflict with Parliament and the king.

LEGACY FOR A PEOPLE AND A NATION
"Witch Hunts"

Since the eighteenth century, the Salem witchcraft crisis has fascinated Americans, both scholars in many different fields and the general public. Movies, plays, television shows, and innumerable books and articles have examined the episode from a variety of perspectives. Some authors attribute the hysteria to food poisoning or disease (encephalitis); some accuse a "girl gang" of delinquents of making mischief because they were repressed by Puritan culture (or perhaps because they were simply bored with their lives); one historian even asserts that there really *were* practicing witches in Salem in 1692.

Yet everyone today agrees that what happened in northeastern Massachusetts in 1692 was a "witch hunt." Americans now regularly apply that term to a misguided search for scapegoats on whom to blame assorted troubles. In the early 1690s, those troubles stemmed from concerns about the future of the Bay colony—fears caused both by the absence of a fully implemented charter and by the ongoing King William's War being fought immediately to the north. Because seventeenth-century people believed that those who allied themselves with the Devil could thereby gain the power to harm individuals and animals, they singled out some of their unpopular neighbors as witches and jailed or hanged them.

During the last half-century, some Americans have likewise used the term "witch hunt" as a code phrase to describe searches for scapegoats of various sorts. In the early 1950s it was employed with respect to Senator Joseph McCarthy's campaign against reputed Communists in the State Department and the Army, and the House Un-American Activities Committee's attack on prominent stage and film professionals for Communist Party membership. In the early 1980s, prosecutions of daycare workers accused of child sexual abuse and engaging in satanic rituals were likewise termed "witch hunts" by their critics. Democrats charged that the 1999 impeachment of President Bill Clinton by the House of Representatives was yet another "witch hunt." Always the term is used pejoratively by opponents of the actions in question, for because of the episode commonly known simply as "Salem," the phrase "witch hunt" has become an American byword for unjustified and unfair legal proceedings that appear to result from communal hysteria. The accusations that so shook the people who lived in the tiny settlements of northeastern Massachusetts more than three hundred years ago have thus left an indelible legacy for the nation.

For Further Reading, see page A-3 of the Appendix. For Web resources, go to http://college.hmco.com.

aturina, a free black resident of New Orleans, awoke with a start at 3 A.M. on June 2 to the shouts of her neighbor, a slave woman named Louisa. "Maturina, someone has stolen your hens!" Louisa yelled. Leaping from her bed, Maturina ran to investigate, accompanied by her son and her brother Nicolas. They quickly located three of the hens, which had escaped from the robber's grasp, but could search no more until daylight.

Maturina knew where to look for missing chickens. At dawn, she and her relatives went to the city market on the levee (river bank), where they soon encountered a man carrying three fowls they recognized as hers. By threatening him with prosecution, they extracted the information that he had purchased the hens from a French grocer named La Rochelle. So the three confronted La Rochelle at his hut, where they found yet another of the birds. Under their questioning, the grocer reluctantly admitted that "it was a negro who had brought them to him to sell," informing Maturina and Nicolas that the culprit "must be on the levee, or in some of the huts."

Suspicious, Maturina searched La Rochelle's own hut, rousting out the thief, who was hiding within. He tried to escape, but Nicolas pursued and captured him. Brought before the authorities, the thief proved to be Juan, a runaway slave from the countryside. The official investigation revealed that several times in the previous month Juan had successfully sold other stolen poultry at the levee market, and he was convicted of theft.

That much of the action in the story of Maturina, Nicolas, and Juan took place on the Mississippi River levee is not surprising. In the mid-eighteenth century, the crude market centered there was as much a focal point of New Orleans as were its formal government buildings. (The theft occurred in 1782, when New Orleans was ruled by Spain [see page 120], but the same events could easily have happened under French governance, during the decades covered by this chapter.)

More than fifty years after Maturina found her missing chickens at the New Orleans market (see text above), Benjamin Henry Latrobe sketched these "Market Folks" buying and selling goods on the levee. Maturina would have recognized this scene, even though it occurred in 1819. African Americans, European Americans, and Native Americans all actively participated in market exchanges in both eras. (Maryland Historical Society, Baltimore)

4

A WORLD TRANSFORMED 1720–1770

Population Growth and Ethnic Diversity
Economic Growth and Development
Colonial Cultures
Colonial Families
Politics: Stability and Crisis in British America
A Crisis in Religion
LEGACY FOR A PEOPLE AND A NATION
Anti-Immigrant Sentiments

To the levee came Indian traders, French and German farmers, free and enslaved Africans—all intent on buying and selling. One contemporary observed in 1761 that the Germans' Saturday morning market on the levee supplied the city with "cabbages, salads, fruits, greens . . . as well as vast quantities of wildfowl, salt pork, and many excellent sorts of fish." About two thousand people, or one-fourth of the population of Louisiana, lived in New Orleans in 1763, and they regularly mingled at the levee market.

The lively markets in New Orleans and Anglo-American cities such as Boston, Charles Town, and Philadelphia illuminate several key themes of colonial development in the mid-eighteenth century: population growth, ethnic diversity, the increasing importance of colonial urban centers, the creation of an urban elite that purchased food and clothing from other colonists, rising levels of consumption for all social ranks, and the new significance of internal markets. In the French and English mainland colonies, exports continued to dominate the economy. Settlers along the Atlantic and Gulf of Mexico coasts were tied to an international commercial system that fluctuated wildly for reasons having little to do with the colonies but inescapable in their effects. Yet expanding local populations demanded greater quantities and types of goods, and Europe could not supply all those needs. Therefore, in English and French America, as well as in the northern portions of New Spain known as the Borderlands (where exports were never an important element of the economy), colonists came increasingly to depend on exploiting and consuming their own resources.

Ethnic diversity was especially pronounced in the small colonial cities, but even the countryside attracted settlers from many European nations. For example, an Englishman traveling in the vicinity of New Orleans in 1770 encountered not merely the French, Indian, and African residents one might expect, but also Germans, Acadians (see page 120), Irish, Scots, a native of the Spanish island of Minorca, a Slav, and several Anglo-Americans. The Spanish Borderlands and rural New England were the only exceptions; they attracted few new immigrants of any description, their population growth stemming almost entirely from natural increase. The middle and southern Anglo-American colonies attracted by far the largest number of newcomers. Their arrival not only swelled the population but also altered political balances and affected the religious climate by introducing new sects. Unwilling immigrants too (slaves and transported con-

victs) clustered primarily in the middle and southern colonies.

Intermarried networks of wealthy families developed in each of Europe's American possessions by the 1760s. These well-off, educated colonists participated in transatlantic intellectual life, such as the movement known as the Enlightenment, whereas many colonists of the "lesser sort" could neither read nor write. The elites lived in comfortable houses and enjoyed leisure-time activities. Most colonists, whether free or enslaved, struggled just to survive, working daily from dawn to dark. Such divisions were most pronounced in British America, the largest and most prosperous settlements on the continent. By the last half of the century, the social and economic distance among different ranks of Anglo-Americans had widened noticeably. As such stratification increased, so did conflicts—political, economic, and even religious—among people of diverse origins and social ranks.

In 1720 much of the North American continent still fell under Indian control. By 1770, in sharp contrast, settlements of Europeans and Africans ruled by Great Britain filled almost all of the region between the Appalachian Mountains and the Atlantic Ocean; and the British, thanks to their victory over France in the Seven Years War (see pages 118–120), dominated the extensive system of rivers and lakes running through the heart of the continent. Spanish missions extended in a great arc from present-day northern California to the Gulf Coast. Such geographical, economic, and social changes transformed the character of Europe's North American possessions. ■

Population Growth and Ethnic Diversity

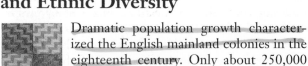

Dramatic population growth characterized the English mainland colonies in the eighteenth century. Only about 250,000 European and African Americans resided in the colonies in 1700. Thirty years later, that number had more than doubled, and by 1775 it had become 2.5 million. Such rapid expansion appears even more remarkable when it is compared with the modest changes that occurred in Louisiana, New Mexico, California, and Texas. By the last quarter of the eighteenth century, Texas contained only about 2,500 Spanish residents and California even fewer; the largest Spanish colony, New Mexico, included just 20,000 or so. The total European population of New France ex-

IMPORTANT EVENTS

1690 Locke's *Essay Concerning Human Understanding* published, a key example of Enlightenment thought

1720–40 Black population of Chesapeake begins to grow by natural increase, contributing to rise of large plantations

1732 Founding of Georgia

1739 Stono Rebellion (South Carolina) leads to increased white fears of slave revolts
George Whitefield arrives in America; Great Awakening broadens

1739–48 King George's War disrupts American economy

1741 New York City "conspiracy" reflects whites' continuing fears of slave revolts

1760s Baptist congregations take root in Virginia

1760–75 Peak of eighteenth-century European and African migration to English colonies

1765–66 Hudson River land riots pit tenants and squatters against large landlords

1767–69 Regulator movement (South Carolina) tries to establish order in backcountry

1771 North Carolina Regulators defeated by eastern militia at Battle of Alamance

panded from approximately 15,000 in 1700 to about 70,000 in the 1760s, but only along the St. Lawrence River between Quebec and Montreal and in New Orleans were there significant concentrations of French settlers.

Although migration accounted for a considerable share of the growth in English America, most of the gain resulted from natural increase. Once the difficult early decades of settlement had passed, the American population doubled approximately every twenty-five years. Such a rate of growth, unparalleled in human history until very recent times, had a variety of causes, chief among them women's youthful age at the onset of childbearing (early twenties for European Americans, late teens for African Americans). Since married women became pregnant every two or three years, women normally bore five to ten children. Because the colonies were relatively healthful places to live (especially north of Virginia), a large proportion of children who survived infancy reached maturity and began families of their own. As a result, about half of the American population was under sixteen years old in 1775. (By contrast, only about one-third of the American population was under sixteen in 1990.)

Africans (about 260,000) constituted the largest racial or ethnic group that came to the mainland English colonies during the eighteenth century. In the slaveholding societies of South America and the Caribbean, a surplus of males over females and appallingly high mortality rates meant that only a large, continuing

Newcomers from Africa and Europe

flow of enslaved Africans could maintain the captive work force at constant levels. South Carolina, where rice cultivation was difficult and unhealthy (chiefly because malaria-carrying mosquitoes bred in the rice swamps), and where planters preferred to purchase men, bore some resemblance to such colonies because it too required an inflow of Africans to sustain as well as expand its labor force. But in the Chesapeake the number of black residents grew especially rapidly because the new imports were added to an African American population that began to sustain itself through natural increase after 1740. Even in South Carolina, where imports continued, African-born slaves had become a minority by 1750.

The offspring of slaves were also slaves, whereas the children of servants were free. The consequences of this important difference between enslaved and indentured labor first became clear when the enslaved population began to grow primarily through natural increase. A planter who owned adult female slaves could watch the size of his labor force increase steadily—through the births of their children, by then declared to be slaves in all the colonies—without making additional major investments in workers. Not coincidentally, the first truly large Chesapeake plantations appeared in the 1740s. Some years later, the slaveholder Thomas Jefferson indicated that he fully understood the connections when he declared, "I consider a woman who brings a child every two years more profitable than the best man of the farm. What she produces is an addition to the capital, while his labors disappear in mere consumption."

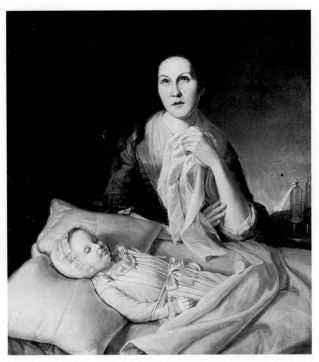

"Rachel Weeping," by Charles Willson Peale, conveys as few other colonial portraits can the affection of eighteenth-century parents for their children and the grief they felt when those children died (as was so often the case) at an early age. Peale movingly revealed his wife's sorrow at the death of their daughter; thus his painting helps to refute the interpretation—advanced by some historians—that high levels of infant mortality led colonists to avoid becoming too attached to their young children. (Philadelphia Museum of Art, the Barra Foundation)

In addition to the new group of Africans, about 585,000 Europeans moved to North America during the eighteenth century, most of them after 1730. Late in the seventeenth century, English officials decided to recruit foreign Protestant colonists in order to prevent further large-scale emigration from England itself, for, influenced by mercantilist thought, they had come to regard a large, industrious population at home as an asset rather than a liability. Thus they ordered the deportation to the colonies of "undesirables"—convicts and Jacobite rebels (supporters of the deposed Stuart monarchs)—but otherwise discouraged emigration. They offered foreign Protestants free lands and religious toleration, even financing the passage of some groups (for example, Germans sent to New York in the 1710s). After 1740 they relaxed citizenship (naturalization) requirements, insisting on only the payment of a small fee, seven years' colonial residence, evidence of adherence to Protestant beliefs, and an oath of allegiance to the king.

One of the largest groups of immigrants—nearly 150,000—came from Ireland or Scotland. About 66,000 Scots-Irish descendants of Presbyterian Scots who had settled in the north of Ireland during the seventeenth century joined some 35,000 people who came directly to America from Scotland (see Table 4.1). Another 43,000, both Protestants and Catholics, migrated from southern Ireland. Fleeing economic distress and (in Ireland) religious discrimination, they hoped to obtain their own land. Scots, Irish, and Scots-Irish immigrants usually landed in Philadelphia. They moved west and south, settling chiefly in Pennsylvania, Maryland, Virginia, and the Carolinas. Frequently unable to afford any acreage, they settled illegally on land belonging to Indians, land speculators, or colonial governments.

Scots-Irish, Germans, and Scots

Migrants from Germany numbered about 85,000. Most emigrated from the Rhineland between 1730 and 1755, also usually arriving in Philadelphia. They became known locally as Pennsylvania Dutch (a corruption of *Deutsch*, as the Germans called themselves); late in the century they and their descendants accounted for one-third of Pennsylvania's residents. But many other Germans moved west and then south along the eastern slopes of the Appalachian Mountains, eventually finding homes in western Maryland and Virginia. Others landed in Charles Town and settled in the southern interior. The Germans belonged to a wide variety of Protestant sects—primarily Lutheran, German Reformed, and Moravian—and therefore added to the already substantial religious diversity of Pennsylvania and New York.

The most concentrated period of immigration to the colonies fell between 1760 and 1775. Tough economic times in Germany and the British Isles led many to decide to seek a better life in America; simultaneously, the slave trade burgeoned. In those fifteen years alone more than 220,000 persons arrived—nearly 10 percent of the entire population of British North America in 1775. Late-arriving free immigrants had little choice but to remain in the cities or move to the edges of settlement; land elsewhere was fully occupied (see Map 4.1). In the peripheries they became the tenants of, or bought property from, land speculators who had purchased giant tracts in the (usually vain) hope of making a fortune.

Table 4.1   Who Moved to America from England and Scotland in the Early 1770s, and Why?

	English Emigrants	Scottish Emigrants	Free American Population
Destination			
13 British colonies	81.1%	92.7%	—
Canada	12.1	4.2	—
West Indies	6.8	3.1	—
Age Distribution			
Under 21	26.8	45.3	56.8%
21–25	37.1	19.9	9.7
26–44	33.3	29.5	20.4
45 and over	2.7	5.3	13.1
Sex Distribution			
Male	83.8	59.9	—
Female	16.2	40.1	—
Unknown	4.2	13.5	—
Traveling Alone or with Families			
In families	20.0	48.0	—
Alone	80.0	52.0	—
Known Occupation or Status			
Gentry	2.5	1.2	—
Merchandising	5.2	5.2	—
Agriculture	17.8	24.0	—
Artisanry	54.2	37.7	—
Laborer	20.3	31.9	—
Why They Left			
Positive reasons (e.g., desire to better one's position)	90.0	36.0	—
Negative reasons (e.g., poverty, unemployment)	10.0	64.0	—

Note: Between December 1773 and March 1776, the British government questioned individuals and families leaving ports in Scotland and England for the American colonies to learn who they were, where they were going, and why they were leaving. This table summarizes just a few of the findings of the official inquiries, which revealed a number of significant differences between the Scottish and English emigrants.

Source of data: Bernard Bailyn, *Voyagers to the West* (New York: Knopf, 1986), Tables 4.1, 5.2, 5.4, 5.7, 5.23, and 6.1.

Maintaining Ethnic Identities

Because of these migration patterns and the concentration of slaveholding in the South, half the colonial population south of New England had non-English origins by 1775. Whether the migrants assimilated readily into Anglo-American culture depended on patterns of settlement, the size of the group, and the strength of the migrants' ties to their common culture. For example, the Huguenots—French Protestants who fled religious persecution in their homeland after 1685—settled in tiny enclaves in American cities like Charles Town and New York. Unable to sustain either their language or their religious practices, they had almost

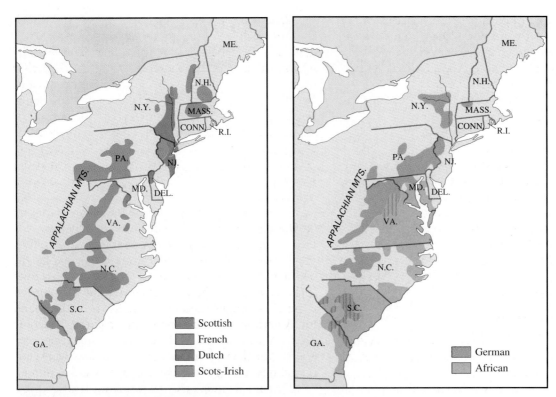

Map 4.1 Non-English Ethnic Groups in the British Colonies, c. 1775 Non-African immigrants arriving in the years after 1720 were pushed to the peripheries of settlement, as is shown by these maps. Scottish, Scots-Irish, French, and German newcomers had to move to the frontiers. The Dutch remained where they had originally settled in the seventeenth century. Africans were concentrated in coastal plantation regions.

wholly assimilated into the dominant culture within two generations. By contrast, the equally small group of colonial Jews maintained a distinct identity. Most were Sephardic, descended from Spanish and Portuguese Jews who had escaped persecution in those countries by migrating to the Netherlands and later to Dutch colonies in America. In a few cities—notably New York and Newport, Rhode Island—they established synagogues and worked actively to preserve their culture. For instance, when Phila Franks, the daughter of a prominent New York Jewish family, married a Christian in 1742, her devastated mother Abigail declared, "I am Determined I never will See nor Lett none of ye Family Goe near her." Few colonial children could defy such strong familial pressures.

Members of the larger groups of migrants (Germans, Irish, and Scots) found it easier to sustain Old World ways. Different ethnic groups each dominated certain localities. Near Frederick, Maryland, a visitor would have heard more German than English; in Anson and Cumberland Counties, North Carolina, the

same visitor might have thought she was in Scotland. Where migrants from different countries settled in the same region, ethnic antagonisms often surfaced. One German clergyman in Pennsylvania, for example, explained his efforts to prevent German youths from marrying people of different ethnic origins by asserting that the Scots-Irish were "lazy, dissipated and poor" and that "it is very seldom that German and English blood is happily united in wedlock."

Recognizing the benefits of keeping other racial and ethnic groups divided, the English elites on occasion deliberately fostered such antagonisms, and they frequently subverted the naturalization laws, thus depriving even long-resident immigrants of a voice in government. When the targets of their policies were European migrants, they hoped to maintain their political and economic power. When they targeted Indians and Africans, as in South Carolina, the stakes were considerably higher. In 1758 one official reported, "It has been allways the policy of this government to create an aversion in them [Indians] to Negroes."

South Carolinians of English origin, a minority of the population, wanted to prevent Indians and Africans from making common cause against them. To keep slaves from running away to join the Indians, Anglo-Americans hired Indians as slave catchers. To keep Indians from trusting Africans, slaves were employed as soldiers in Indian wars.

The elites probably would have preferred to ignore the English colonies' growing racial and ethnic diversity, but they could not do so for long and still maintain their power. When such men decided to lead a revolution in the 1770s, they recognized that they needed the support of non-English Americans. Quite deliberately, they began to speak of "the rights of man," rather than "English liberties," when they sought recruits for their cause.

Economic Growth and Development

The dramatic increase in the population of Anglo America served as one of the few sources of stability for the colonial economy, which was primarily driven by the vagaries of international markets. A comparison to French and Spanish America reveals significant differences. The population and economy of New Spain's Borderlands both stagnated. The isolated settlements produced few items for export (notably, hides and skins, most obtained through trade with Indians); residents were more likely to exchange goods illegally with their French and English neighbors than with the distant centers of Spanish Mexico or the Caribbean. French Canada exported large quantities of furs and fish, but monopolistic trade practices ensured that most of the profits ended up in the home country. The Louisiana colony required substantial government subsidies to survive, despite its active internal trade and some agricultural exports. Of France's American possessions, only the Caribbean islands flourished economically.

In British North America, by contrast, each year the rising population generated ever-greater demands for goods and services, which led to the development of small-scale colonial manufacturing and a complex network of internal trade. As the area of settlement expanded, roads, bridges, roads, mills, and stores were built to serve the new communities. A lively coastal trade developed; by the late 1760s, 54 percent of the vessels leaving Boston harbor were sailing to other

Overview of the Anglo-American Economy

mainland colonies rather than to foreign ports. Such ships not only collected goods for export and distributed imports but also sold items made in America. The colonies thus began to move away from their earlier pattern of near total dependence on Europe for manufactured goods. For the first time, the American population generated sufficient demand to encourage manufacturing enterprises. The largest indigenous industry was iron making; by 1775, 82 American furnaces and 175 forges produced more iron than did England itself. Almost all of that iron was for domestic consumption.

The major energizing, yet destabilizing, influence on the colonial economy nevertheless remained foreign trade. Colonial prosperity still depended heavily on overseas demand for American products like tobacco, rice, indigo, fish, and barrel staves. The sale of such items earned the colonists the credit they needed to purchase English and European imports. If demand for American exports slowed, the colonists' income dropped and so did their ability to buy imported goods. Merchants were particularly vulnerable to economic downswings, and bankruptcies were common.

Despite fluctuations, the economy slowly grew during the eighteenth century. That growth, which resulted in part from Americans' higher earnings from their exports, in turn produced better standards of living for all property-owning Americans. In the first two decades of the century, as the price of British manufactures fell in relation to Americans' incomes, households began to acquire amenities such as chairs and earthenware dishes. Diet also improved as trading networks brought access to more varied foodstuffs. After 1750, luxury items like silver plate could be found in the homes of the wealthy, and the "middling sort" started to purchase imported English ceramics and teapots. Even the poorest property owners had more and better household possessions. Thus the colonists became consumers, in the sense that for the first time they could make choices among a wide variety of products and also could afford to buy items not absolutely essential for survival and subsistence.

Growth of Consumption

Yet the benefits of economic growth were unevenly distributed: wealthy Americans improved their position relative to other colonists. The native-born elite families who dominated American political, economic, and social life by 1750 had begun the century with sufficient capital to take advantage of the changes caused by population growth. They were the urban merchants who exported raw materials and imported luxury goods, the large landowners who rented small farms to immigrant tenants, the slave traders who supplied equally wealthy planters with their bondspeople, and the owners of rum distilleries. The rise of this group of moneyed families helped to make the social and economic structure of mid-eighteenth-century America more stratified than before.

New arrivals did not have the opportunities for advancement that had greeted their predecessors.

Urban Poverty

Even so, there seems to have been relatively little severe poverty among free settlers in rural areas, where over 90 percent of the colonists lived. But in the cities, circumstances differed. Families of urban laborers lived on the edge of destitution. In Philadelphia, for instance, a male laborer's average annual earnings fell short of the amount needed to supply his family with the bare necessities. Even in a good year, his wife or children had to do wage work; in a bad year, the family could be reduced to beggary. By the 1760s

public urban poor-relief systems were overwhelmed with applicants for assistance, and some cities began to build workhouses or almshouses to shelter the growing number of poor people. Among them were recent immigrants, the elderly and infirm, and widows, especially those with small children.

Within this overall picture, it is important to distinguish among the various regions: New England, the middle colonies (Pennsylvania, New York, and New Jersey), the Chesapeake (including North Carolina), and the Lower South (South Carolina and Georgia). Each region of the colonies had its own economic rhythm derived from the nature of its export trade.

In New England, three elements combined to influence economic development: the nature of the landscape, New England's leadership in colonial shipping, and the impact of imperial wars. New England's poor soil did not produce surpluses other than livestock, so wood products constituted important salable commodities. Farms were worked primarily by family

Figure 4.1   Regional Trading Patterns: New England   New England's major exports—salt fish, livestock, and wood products—were sold primarily in the West Indies.   (Source: James F. Shepherd and Gary M. Walton, *Shipping, Maritime Trade, and the Economic Development of Colonial North America* [Cambridge: Cambridge University Press, 1972]. Copyright 1972. Used by permission of Cambridge University Press.)

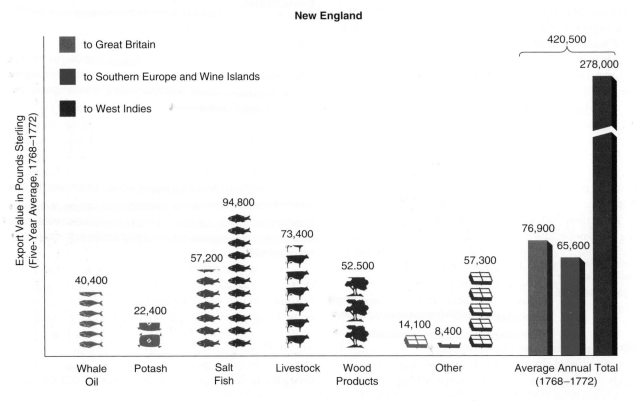

members; the region had relatively few hired laborers. It also had the lowest average wealth per freeholder in the colonies. But New England had many wealthy men: merchants and professionals whose income was drawn from trade with the West Indies in items such as salt fish, livestock, and molasses. (See Figure 4.1.)

Boston, by the 1730s a major shipbuilding center, soon felt the effects when warfare between European powers resumed in 1739. British vessels clashed with Spanish ships in the Caribbean, setting off a conflict that became known in America as King George's War. Nominally the war (called the War of the Austrian Succession in Europe) concerned who would sit on the Austrian throne, but European commercial rivalries in the Americas contributed greatly to its motivations. At first, the war had a positive impact on Boston's economy, for ships—and sailors—were in great demand to serve as privateers (privately owned vessels authorized

New England and King George's War

by the British to capture the enemy's commercial shipping). Wealthy merchants became even wealthier by profiting from contracts to supply military expeditions.

But New England suffered heavy losses of manpower in Caribbean battles and forays against Canada. In 1745 the most successful and expensive expedition captured the French fortress of Louisbourg (in modern Nova Scotia), which guarded the sea-lanes leading to New France. Afterward, though, Massachusetts had to levy heavy taxes on its residents to pay for the costly effort. For decades Boston's economy felt the continuing effects of King George's War. The city was left with unprecedented numbers of widows and children on its relief rolls. The boom in shipbuilding ended when the war did, and taxes remained high. As a final blow to the colony, Britain gave Louisbourg back to France in the Treaty of Aix-la-Chapelle (1748).

King George's War and its aftermath affected the middle colonies more positively because of the greater

Figure 4.2 Regional Trading Patterns: Middle Colonies The middle colonies' major trading partners were the West Indies, the Wine Islands, and southern Europe. Bread, flour, and grains were the region's most valuable exports. (Source: James F. Shepherd and Gary M. Walton, *Shipping, Maritime Trade, and the Economic Development of Colonial North America* [Cambridge: Cambridge University Press, 1972]. Copyright 1972. Used by permission of Cambridge University Press.)

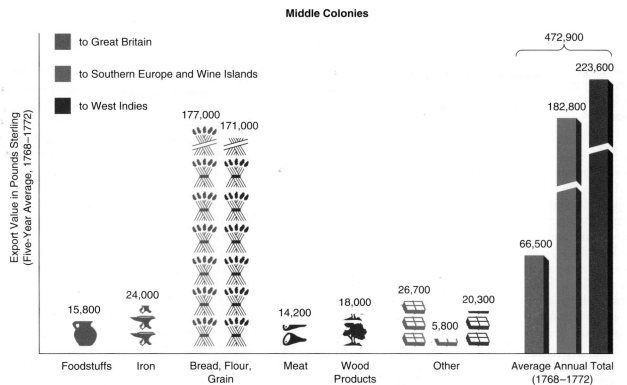

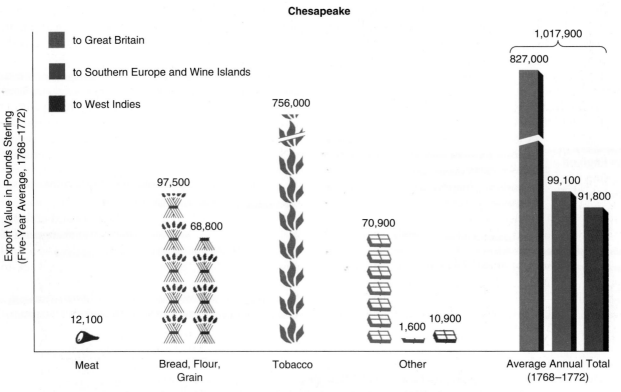

Figure 4.3   Regional Trading Patterns: The Chesapeake   Tobacco—legally exported only to Great Britain under the terms of the Navigation Acts—was the Chesapeake's dominant product. Grain made up an increasing proportion of the crops this region sold to other destinations.   (Source: James F. Shepherd and Gary M. Walton, *Shipping, Maritime Trade, and the Economic Development of Colonial North America* [Cambridge: Cambridge University Press, 1972]. Copyright 1972. Used by permission of Cambridge University Press.)

Prosperity of the Middle Colonies

fertility of the soil in New York and Pennsylvania, where commercial farming prevailed. An average Pennsylvania farm family consumed only 40 percent of what it produced, selling the rest. New York and New Jersey both had many tenant farmers, who rented acreage from large landowners and often paid their rental fees by sharing crops with their landlords. Prosperous landlords and farmers thus occupied an ideal position to profit from the wartime demand for grain and meat, especially in the West Indies (see Figure 4.2). After the war a series of poor grain harvests in Europe caused flour prices to rise rapidly. Philadelphia and New York, which could draw on large fertile grain- and livestock-producing areas, took the lead in the foodstuffs trade. Meanwhile, Boston, which had no such fertile hinterland, found its economy stagnating.

Increased European demand for grain had a significant impact on the Chesapeake as well. After 1745,

Change in the Chesapeake

when the price of grain began rising faster than that of tobacco, some Chesapeake planters began to convert tobacco fields to wheat and corn. By diversifying their crops, they could avoid dependency on one product for their income. Tobacco still ruled the region and remained the largest single export from the mainland colonies. (The value of tobacco exports was nearly double that of grain products, the next contender.) Yet the conversion to grain cultivation brought about the first significant change in Chesapeake settlement patterns by encouraging the development of port towns (like Baltimore) to house the merchants who marketed the new products. (See Figure 4.3.)

Like the Chesapeake, the Lower South depended on staple crops and an enslaved labor force, but it had a distinctive pattern of economic growth. In contrast to tobacco prices, which rose slowly through the middle decades of the century, rice prices climbed steeply,

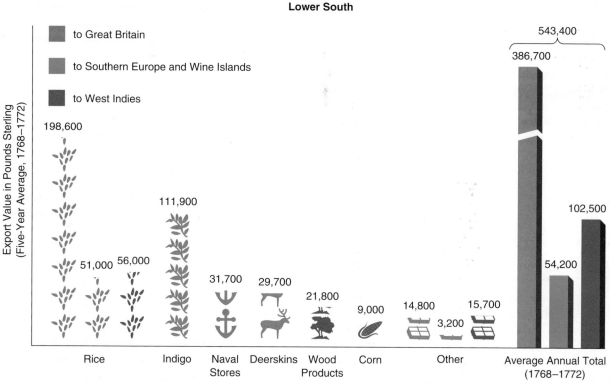

Figure 4.4   Regional Trading Patterns: The Lower South   Rice and indigo, sold primarily in the mother country, dominated the exports of the Lower South.   (Source: James F. Shepherd and Gary M. Walton, *Shipping, Maritime Trade, and the Economic Development of Colonial North America* [Cambridge: Cambridge University Press, 1972]. Copyright 1972. Used by permission of Cambridge University Press.)

Trade and the Lower South

doubling by the late 1730s, primarily because of heavy demand for rice in southern Europe (see Figure 4.4). After Parliament removed rice from the list of enumerated products (see page 77) in 1730, South Carolinians did what colonial tobacco planters could never do: trade directly with continental Europe. But dependence on European sales had its drawbacks, as rice growers discovered when the outbreak of King George's War in 1739 disrupted trade with the continent. Rice prices plummeted, and South Carolina entered a depression from which it did not emerge for a decade. Still, prosperity returned by the 1760s because of rapidly rising European demand for South Carolina's exports; indeed, the Lower South experienced more rapid economic growth in that period than did the other regions of the colonies. Partly as a result, it had the highest average wealth per freeholder in Anglo America by the time of the American Revolution.

Georgia

Closely linked to South Carolina geographically, demographically, and economically was the newest colony on the mainland, Georgia, chartered in 1732 as a haven for English debtors. Its founder James Oglethorpe envisioned Georgia as a garrison province peopled by sturdy farmers who would defend the southern flank of English settlement against Spanish Florida, and so its charter prohibited slavery. But Carolina rice planters successfully won the removal of the restriction in 1751. Thereafter, they essentially invaded Georgia, which—despite remaining politically independent and becoming a royal colony in 1752—developed into a rice-planting slave society resembling South Carolina.

King George's War at first helped New England and hurt the Lower South, but in the long run those effects were reversed. In the Chesapeake and the middle colonies, the war ushered in a long period of prosperity. These variations in economic experience point up a crucial fact about the English mainland colonies: they did not compose a unified whole. Although linked economically into regions, they had few political or social ties beyond or even within those regions. Despite the growing coastal trade, the individual colonies' economic fortunes depended not on their neighbors in America but rather on the shifting markets of Europe and the West Indies. Had it not been for an unprecedented crisis in the British imperial system (discussed in Chapter 5), it is hard to see how they could have been persuaded to join in a common endeavor. Even with that impetus, they found unity difficult to maintain.

Colonial Cultures

A seventeenth-century resident of England's American possessions miraculously transported to 1750 would have been surprised not only by the denser and more diverse population but also by the new extremes of wealth and poverty, primarily visible in the growing cities. Native-born colonial elites sought to distinguish themselves from ordinary folk in a variety of ways as they consolidated their hold on the local economy and political power.

One historian has termed these processes "the refinement of America." Those colonists who acquired wealth through trade, agriculture, or manufacturing spent their money ostentatiously, dressing at the height of fashion, traveling in horse-drawn carriages driven by uniformed servants, and entertaining one another at lavish parties. Most notably, they built large houses containing rooms specifically designed for such forms of socializing as dancing, cardplaying, or drinking tea. Sufficiently well-off to enjoy "leisure" time (a first for North America), they attended concerts and the theater, gambled at horse races, and played billiards and other games. They also cultivated polite manners, adopting stylized forms of address and paying attention to "proper" ways of behaving. Although the effects of accumulated wealth were most pronounced in Anglo America, elite families in New Mexico, Louisiana, and Quebec as well set themselves off from the "lesser sort." Together these wealthy families deliberately constructed a genteel culture quite different from that of the seventeenth-century colonies or of ordinary colonists in their own day.

Genteel Culture

Men from such families prided themselves not only on their possessions and on their positions in the

Education

colonial political, social, and economic hierarchy, but also on their level of education and their intellectual connections to Europe. Many had been tutored by private teachers hired by their families; some even attended college in Europe or America. (Harvard, the first colonial college, founded in 1636, was joined by William and Mary in 1693, Yale in 1701, and later by several others—for example, Princeton, established in 1747.) In the seventeenth century, only aspiring clergymen attended college, and their studies focused heavily on ancient languages and theology. But by the mid-eighteenth century, colleges broadened their curricula to include courses on mathematics, the natural sciences, law, and medicine. Accordingly, young men from elite or upwardly mobile families enrolled in college to study for careers other than the ministry. American women were mostly excluded from advanced education, with the exception of some who joined nunneries in Canada or Louisiana, and there could engage in sustained study within convent walls.

The intellectual current known as the Enlightenment deeply affected the learned clergymen who headed colonial colleges and their students. Around the middle of the seventeenth century, some European thinkers began to analyze nature in an effort to determine the laws that govern the universe. They employed experimentation and abstract reasoning to discover general principles behind phenomena such as the motions of planets and stars, the behavior of falling objects, and the characteristics of light and sound. Above all, Enlightenment philosophers emphasized acquiring knowledge through reason, taking particular delight in challenging previously unquestioned assumptions. John Locke's *Essay Concerning Human Understanding* (1690), for example, disputed the notion that human beings are born already imprinted with innate ideas. All knowledge, Locke asserted, derives from one's observations of the external world.

The Enlightenment

The Enlightenment had an enormous impact on educated, well-to-do people in Europe and America. It supplied them with a common vocabulary and a unified view of the world, one that insisted that the enlightened eighteenth century was better, and wiser, than all previous ages. It joined them in a common endeavor, the effort to make sense of God's orderly creation. Thus American naturalists like John and William Bartram supplied European scientists with information about New World plants and animals so

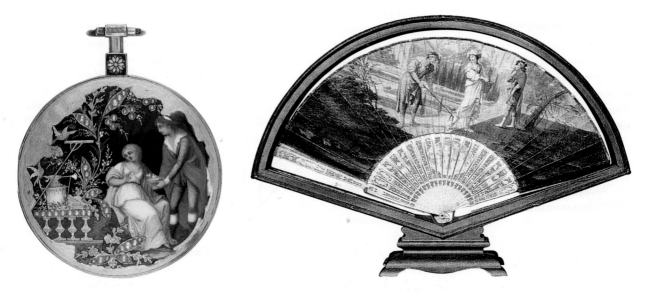

The profits earned by tobacco planters with large holdings of land and slaves enabled them to buy luxurious items unimaginable to earlier colonists. This handpainted ivory fan and elaborate gold and enamel watch belonged to female members of the Byrd family of Virginia in the mid-eighteenth century. (Virginia Historical Society)

that they could be included in newly formulated universal classification systems. So, too, Americans interested in astronomy took part in an international effort to learn about the solar system by studying a rare occurrence, the transit of Venus across the face of the sun in 1769. A prime example of America's participation in the Enlightenment was Benjamin Franklin, who retired from a successful printing business in 1748 when he was just forty-two, thereafter devoting himself to scientific experimentation and public service. His *Experiments and Observations on Electricity* (1751) established the terminology and basic theory of electricity still used today.

The Enlightenment had its greatest impact on the lives of ordinary Americans through advances in medicine—specifically, the treatment of smallpox. The Reverend Cotton Mather, a prominent Puritan cleric, read in a British publication about the benefits of inoculation (deliberately infecting a person with a mild case of a disease) as a protection against smallpox. When Boston in 1720–1721 suffered a major smallpox epidemic, Mather urged the adoption of inoculation despite fierce opposition from the city's leading physician. Mortality rates eventually supported Mather—of those inoculated, just 3 percent died; of others, 15 percent. Although inoculation was not widely accepted until midcentury, Enlightenment science had provided colonial Americans with a means of preventing the greatest killer disease of all.

Enlightenment rationalism affected politics as well as science. Locke's *Two Treatises of Government* (1691) and other works by French and Scottish philosophers challenged previous concepts of a divinely sanctioned, hierarchical political order originating in the power of fathers over families. Men created governments and so could alter them, Locke declared. A ruler who broke his contract with the people and failed to protect their rights could legitimately be ousted from power by peaceful— or even violent—means. Government should aim at the good of the people, Enlightenment theorists proclaimed. A proper political order could prevent the rise of tyrants; God's natural laws governed even the power of monarchs.

Contract Theory of Government

The world in which such ideas were discussed was that of the few, not the many. Most residents of North America did not know how to read or write. Even those with basic literacy skills—a small proportion in French or Spanish America, about half of the people in British America—knew only the rudiments. Books were scarce and expensive, and ordinary folk rarely had occasion to write a letter. No colony

Oral Cultures

required children to attend school; European American youngsters who learned to read usually did so in their own homes, taught by their parents or older siblings. A few months at a private "dame school" run by a literate local widow might complete their education by teaching them the basics of writing and simple arithmetic. Few Americans other than some Church of England missionaries in the South tried to teach enslaved children the rudiments. And only the most zealous Indian converts learned Europeans' literacy skills.

Thus the cultures of colonial North America were primarily oral, communal, and—at least through the first half of the eighteenth century—intensely local. In the absence of literacy, face-to-face conversation served as the major means of communication. Infor-

Religious Rituals

mation tended to travel slowly and within relatively confined regions. Different locales developed divergent cultural traditions, and racial and ethnic variations heightened those differences. Public rituals served as the chief means through which the colonists forged their cultural identities.

Attendance at church was perhaps the most important such ritual. In Congregational (Puritan) churches, church leaders assigned seating to reflect standing in the community. In early New England, men and women sat on opposite sides of a central aisle, arranged in ranks according to age, wealth, and church membership. By the mid-eighteenth century, wealthy

One of the very few institutions of higher learning open to females in eighteenth-century North America is clearly marked on this 1769 map from a Dutch atlas: the Ursuline convent in New Orleans. There young women studied religion and other subjects. As indicated in the label to the left, the convent is located at letter *k,* in the lower right corner of the map (which shows the area of the modern city known as the French Quarter).   (Private Collection)

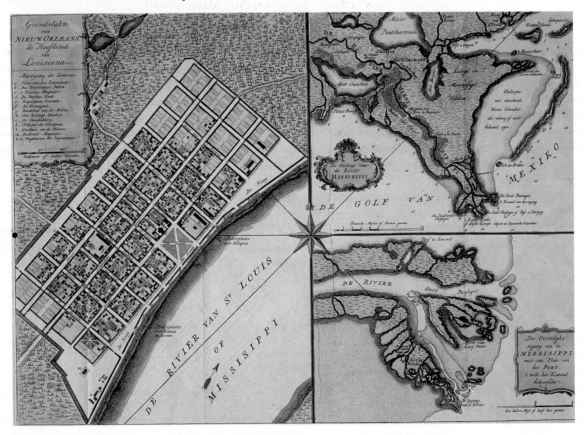

Convicted criminals were publicly punished and shamed in front of their friends, relatives, and neighbors. A man might be put in the stocks for offenses such as contempt of authority, drunken and disorderly conduct, or theft. The intent was not simply to deter him from future misbehavior but to let his fate serve as a warning to all who saw his humiliating posture. (Library of Congress)

men and their wives sat in privately owned pews; their children, servants, and the less fortunate still sat in sex-segregated fashion at the rear or sides of the church. In eighteenth-century Virginia, seating in Church of England parishes also conformed to the local status hierarchy. Planter families purchased their own pews, and in some parishes landed gentlemen customarily strode into church as a group just before the service, deliberately drawing attention to their exalted position. In Quebec city, formal processions of men into the parish church celebrated Catholic feast days; each participant's rank determined his placement in the procession. By contrast, Quaker meetinghouses in Pennsylvania and elsewhere used an egalitarian but sex-segregated seating system. The varying rituals surrounding people's entrance into and seating in colonial churches thus symbolized their place in society and the values of the local community.

Communal culture also centered on the civic sphere. In New England, colonial governments proclaimed official days of thanksgiving

Civic Rituals

(for good harvests, victories in war, and so forth) and days of fasting and prayer (when the colony was experiencing difficulties such as droughts or epidemics). Everyone was expected to participate in the public rituals held in churches on such occasions. Monthly militia musters (known as training days) also brought the community together, since all able-bodied men between the ages of sixteen and sixty participated in the militia.

In the Chesapeake, important cultural rituals occurred on court and election days. When the county court met, men came from miles around to file suits, appear as witnesses, serve as jurors, or observe the goings-on. Attendance at court functioned as a method of civic education; from watching the proceedings men learned what behavior their neighbors expected of them. Elections served the same purpose, for property-holding men voted in public. An election official, often flanked by the candidates for the office in question, would call each man forward to declare his preference. The voter would then be thanked politely by the gentleman for whom he had cast his oral ballot. Traditionally, the candidates afterward treated their supporters to rum at nearby taverns.

Everywhere in colonial North America, the public punishment of criminals served not just to humiliate the offender but also to remind the community of proper standards of behavior. Public hangings and whippings expressed the community's outrage about crimes and restored harmony to its ranks. Judges often assigned penalties that shamed miscreants in especially appropriate ways. In San Antonio, Texas, for example, one cattle thief was sentenced to be led through the town's streets "with the entrails hanging from his neck"; and when a New Mexico man assaulted his father-in-law, he was directed not merely to pay medical expenses but also to kneel before him and to beg his forgiveness publicly, in front of the entire community. New Englanders convicted of capital offenses but not hanged did not thereby escape public humiliation:

How do historians know...

that the residents of colonial North America began to purchase luxury items in the eighteenth century from wide-ranging international trade networks?

Probate inventories—written records of what people possessed at the time of their deaths—are a useful documentary source for scholars. But perhaps even more revealing are the results of archaeological excavations at the sites of colonial settlements. The shards shown here were found at one of the first French outposts in Louisiana—Old Mobile, established in 1702 on Mobile Bay, in what is now Alabama. The pots, of which only these small pieces remain (see the complete example), represent the final stage in a long trade route originating in China. The Chinese sold ceramics to traders in the Philippines, which Spain controlled, in exchange for Mexican silver. Spanish ships then carried the porcelain across the Pacific to Mexico, where it was purchased at annual fairs in Acapulco, carried by mule train across Mexico to Vera Cruz, then shipped to Caribbean and Gulf of Mexico ports and to Spain itself. The three hundred or so residents of Old Mobile bought such items

from the Spanish settlement at Pensacola in nearby Florida. A brief description in an inventory could not convey so much information nearly as vividly as do these small bits of pottery. (Photos: Chinese porcelain fragments: The Magazine Antiques; Chinese porcelain pot: The Metropolitan Museum of Art, Purchased by subscription, 1879)

frequently they were ordered to wear nooses around their necks for years as a constant reminder to themselves, their families, and their neighbors of their heinous violation of community norms.

The wide availability of consumer goods after the early years of the eighteenth century fostered new rituals centered on consumption, establishing novel links among the various residents of North America and creating what historians have termed "an empire of goods." The rituals began with the acquisition of desirable items. In the seventeenth century, settlers acquired necessities by bartering with neighbors or by ordering products from a home-country merchant. By the middle of the eighteenth century, specialized shops selling nonessentials had proliferated in cities such as New York, Philadel-

Rituals of Consumption

phia, and New Orleans. In 1770 Boston alone had more than five hundred stores, which offered consumers a vast selection of millinery, sewing supplies, tobacco, gloves, tableware, and the like. Even small and medium-size towns had one or two retail establishments. A colonist with money to spend would set aside time to "go shopping," a novel and pleasurable activity. The purchase of a desired object—for example, a ceramic bowl, a mirror, or a length of beautiful fabric—marked only the beginning of consumption rituals.

Consumers would then deploy their purchases in an appropriate manner: hanging the mirror prominently on a wall of the house, displaying the bowl on a table or sideboard, turning the fabric into a special piece of clothing. Individual colonists took pleasure in owning lovely objects, but they also could take pride in

This trade card (advertisement) issued by a Philadelphia tobacco dealer in 1770 shows a convivial group of wealthy men at a tavern. Both the leisurely activity depicted here and the advertisement itself were signs of the new rituals of consumption. Merchants began to advertise only when their customers could choose among different ways of spending money. (Library Company of Philadelphia)

displaying their acquisitions (and thus their wealth and good taste) publicly to kin and neighbors. A particularly rich man might even hire a portraitist to paint his family using the objects and wearing the clothing, thereby creating a pictorial record that also would be displayed for admiration.

Tea drinking played an especially important role in Anglo-American consumption rituals. From early in the eighteenth century, households with aspirations to genteel status sought to acquire the items necessary for the proper consumption of tea: not just pots and cups but also strainers, sugar tongs, bowls, and even special tables. Tea provided a focal point for socializing and, because of its cost, served as a crucial marker of status. A hot and mildly stimulating drink, it was seen as healthful as well. Thus poor households also consumed tea, although they could not afford the fancy equipment used by their better-off neighbors. Even some Mohawk Indians adopted the custom, much to the surprise of a traveler from Sweden, who observed them drinking tea in the late 1740s.

Importance of Tea

Other sorts of rituals allowed the disparate cultures of colonial North America to interact with one another. Particularly important rituals developed on what the historian Richard White has termed the "middle ground"—that is, the psychological and geographical space in which Indians and Europeans encountered each other. Most of those cultural encounters occurred in the context of trade or warfare.

Rituals on the "Middle Ground"

When Europeans sought to trade with Indians, they came into contact with an indigenous system of exchange that stressed gift giving rather than formalized buying and selling. Although French and English traders complained constantly about the need to present Indians with gifts prior to negotiating with them for furs and skins, successful bargaining required such a step. Over time, an appropriate ritual developed. A European trader arriving at a village would give gifts (cloth, rum, gunpowder, and other items) to Indian hunters. Eventually, those gifts would be reciprocated, and further exchanges would then take place. To the detriment of Indian societies, rum became a crucial component of these intercultural trading rituals. Traders soon concluded that drunken Indians would sell their furs more cheaply; and some Indians refused to hunt or trade unless they first received rum. Alcohol abuse hastened the deterioration of villages already devastated by disease and dislocation.

Intercultural rituals also developed to deal with murders. Indians and Europeans both believed that murders required a compensatory act, but the two groups had different notions of what that act should be. Europeans sought primarily to identify the murderer and to punish, perhaps even kill, the malefactor. To Indians, such "eye for an eye" revenge was just one of many possible responses to murder. Compensation could also be accomplished by capturing someone who could take the dead person's place or—most important for maintaining peace on the frontiers—by "covering the dead," or providing the family of the deceased with goods that compensated for the loss. Eventually, the French and the Algonquians in particular evolved an elaborate ritual for handling frontier murders—a ritual that encompassed elements of both societies' traditions: murders were investigated and murderers identified, but by mutual agreement deaths were usually "covered" by trade goods rather than by blood revenge.

Colonial Families

 Families (rather than individuals) constituted the basic units of colonial society. People living together as families, commonly under the direction of a marital pair, were everywhere the chief mechanisms for both production and consumption. Yet family forms and structures varied widely in the mainland colonies, and not all were headed by couples.

As Europeans consolidated their hold on the North American continent during the first three-quarters of the eighteenth century, Native Americans had to adapt to **Indian Families** novel circumstances. As Chapter 1 reveals, Spanish horses dramatically changed the lives of Plains Indians, and diseases ravaged even those groups that had little direct contact with Europeans. Bands reduced in numbers by disease and warfare recombined into new units; for example, the group later known as the Catawbas emerged in the 1730s in the western Carolinas from the fragmentary remains of several earlier Indian nations, including the

Yamasees. Likewise, Indian family forms were reshaped under pressure from European secular and religious authorities. Whereas many Indian societies had permitted easy divorce, English, French, and Spanish missionaries frowned on such practices; and those societies that had allowed polygynous marriages (including New England Algonquians) redefined such relationships, designating one wife as "legitimate" and others as "concubines."

Continued high mortality rates created Indian societies in which extended kin took on new importance, for when parents died, aunts, uncles, and other relatives—even occasionally nonkin—assumed child-rearing responsibilities. Furthermore, once Europeans established dominance in any region, Indians there could no longer pursue traditional modes of subsistence. That led to unusual family forms as well as to a variety of economic strategies. In New England, for instance, Algonquian husbands and wives often could not live together, for adults supported themselves by working separately for Anglo-Americans (perhaps wives as domestic servants, husbands as sailors). And in New Mexico, detribalized Navajos, Pueblos, and Apaches employed as servants by Spanish settlers clustered in the small towns of the Borderlands. Known collectively as *genizaros*, they lost contact with Indian cultures, instead living on the fringes of Hispanic society.

Wherever the population contained relatively few European women, sexual liaisons (both inside and outside marriage) occurred among European men and Indian women. The **Mixed-Race Families** resulting mixed-race population of *mestizos* and *métis* worked as a familial "middle ground" to ease other cultural interactions. In New France and the Anglo-American backcountry, such families frequently resided in Indian villages and were enmeshed in trading networks; often, children of these unions became prominent leaders of Native American societies. (For example, Peter Chartier, the son of a Shawnee mother and a French father, led a pro-French Shawnee band in western Pennsylvania in the 1740s.) By contrast, in the Spanish Borderlands the offspring of Europeans and *genizaros* were treated as degraded individuals. Largely denied the privilege of legal marriage, they bore generations of "illegitimate" children of various racial mixtures, giving rise in Hispanic society to a wide range of labels describing degrees of skin color with a precision unknown in English or French America.

Eighteenth-century Anglo-Americans used the word *family* to mean all the people who occupied one household (including any resident servants or slaves). Family life among the many European migrants to North America was far more stable than that among Indian and *mestizo* peoples. European men or their widows headed households considerably larger than American families today. In 1790 the average home in the United States housed 5.7 free people, and such sizable co-resident groups did not for the most part include extended kin like aunts, uncles, or grandparents. Family members—bound by ties of blood or servitude—worked together to produce goods for consumption or sale. The head of the household represented it to the outside world, managing the finances and holding legal authority over the rest of the family—his wife, his children, and his servants or slaves.

European American Families

In English, French, and Spanish America alike, the vast majority of European families supported themselves through agriculture by cultivating crops and raising livestock. The scale and nature of the work varied: the production of indigo in Louisiana or tobacco in the Chesapeake required different sorts of labor from subsistence farming in New England or cattle ranching in New Mexico and Texas. Still, just as in the European, African, and Native American societies discussed in Chapter 1, household tasks were allocated by sex. The master, his sons, and his male servants or slaves performed one set of chores; the mistress, her daughters, and her female servants or slaves, a different set.

The mistress took responsibility for what Anglo-Americans called "indoor affairs." She and her female helpers prepared food, cleaned the house, did laundry, and often made clothing. Preparing food alone involved planting and cultivating a garden, harvesting and preserving vegetables, salting and smoking meat, drying apples and pressing cider, milking cows and making butter and cheese, not to mention cooking and baking. The head of the household and his male helpers, responsible for "outdoor affairs," also had heavy workloads. They planted and cultivated the fields, built fences, chopped wood for the fireplace, harvested and marketed crops, cared for livestock, and butchered cattle and hogs to provide the household with meat. So extensive was the work involved in maintaining a farm household that a married couple

One of the few extant depictions of a mixed-race family in eighteenth-century North America, by the Mexican artist Miguel Cabrera, 1763. The Spanish father and Indian mother have produced a *mestiza* daughter. Families such as this would have been frequently seen in New Mexico as well.   (Private Collection)

could not do it alone. If they had no children to help them, they turned to servants or slaves.

Most African American families lived as components of European American households—often on plantations that masters perceived as one large family. More than 95 percent of colonial African Americans were held in perpetual bondage. Although many African Americans lived on farms with only one or two other slaves, others had the experience of living and working in a largely black setting. In South Carolina, a majority of the population was of African origin; in Georgia, about half; and in the Chesapeake, 40 percent. Portions of the Carolina low country were nearly 90 percent African American by 1790.

African American Families

The setting in which African Americans lived determined the shape of their family lives. In the North, the scarcity of other blacks often made it difficult for bondspeople to form stable family units. In the Chesapeake, men and women who regarded themselves as married (slaves could not legally wed) frequently lived on different quarters or even on different plantations. Children generally resided with their mothers, seeing their fathers only on Sundays. Simultaneously, the natural increase of the population created wide American-born kinship networks among Chesapeake slaves. On large Carolina and Georgia rice plantations, enslaved couples not only usually lived together with their children but also accumulated property through working for themselves after they had completed their daily "tasks" (see page 78). Some Georgia slaves sold their surplus produce at the market in Savannah, thereby earning money to buy nice clothing or such luxuries as tobacco or jewelry, but rarely enough to purchase themselves.

Running Away and Other Forms of Resistance

Because all the English colonies legally permitted slavery, bondspeople had few options other than Florida (see page 80) if they considered running away. Some recently arrived Africans stole boats to try to return home or ran off in groups to frontier regions to join the Indians or to establish independent communities. Among American-born slaves, family ties strongly affected such decisions. South Carolina planters soon learned, as one wrote, that slaves "love their families dearly and none runs away from the other," so many owners sought to keep families together for purely practical reasons. In the Chesapeake, where family members often lived separately, affectionate ties could by contrast cause slaves to run away, especially if a family member had been sold or moved to a distant quarter.

Although colonial slaves rarely rebelled collectively, they often resisted enslavement in other ways.

William L. Breton's watercolor of "The Old London Coffee House" in eighteenth-century Philadelphia shows a slave auction taking place on its porch. That such a scene could have occurred in front of such a prominent and popular meeting place serves as a reminder of the ubiquity of slavery in the colonies, north as well as south. (Historical Society of Pennsylvania)

Bondspeople uniformly rejected any attempts by their owners to commandeer their labor on Sundays without compensation. Slaves established strong family structures in which youngsters often carried relatives' names. Extended-kin groups protested excessive punishment of relatives and sought to live near each other. The links that developed among African American families who had lived on the same plantation for several generations served as insurance against the uncertainties of existence under slavery. If parents and children were separated by sale, other relatives could help with child rearing and similar tasks. Among African Americans, just as among Indians, the extended family thus served a more important function than it did among European Americans.

Most slave families managed to carve out a small measure of autonomy, especially in their working and spiritual lives and especially in the Lower South. Enslaved Muslims often clung to their Islamic faith, a pattern especially evident in Louisiana and South Carolina. Some African Americans preserved traditional beliefs and others converted to Christianity, finding comfort in the assurances of their new religion that all people would be free and equal in heaven. South Carolina and Georgia slaves jealously guarded their customary ability to control their own time after the completion of their "tasks." Even on Chesapeake tobacco plantations, slaves were allowed to plant their own gardens, hunt, or fish in order to supplement the minimal diet their masters supplied. Late in the century, some Chesapeake planters with a surplus of laborers began to hire out slaves to others, often allowing the workers to keep a small part of their earnings. Such accumulated property could buy desired goods or serve as a legacy for children.

Just as African and European Americans lived together on plantations, so too both groups were found side by side in cities. (Indeed, in

Life in the Cities

1760s Philadelphia one-fifth of the work force was enslaved, and by 1775 blacks composed nearly 15 percent of the population of New York City.) Yet such cities were nothing but large towns by today's standards. In 1750 the largest, Boston and Philadelphia, had just seventeen thousand and thirteen thousand inhabitants, respectively. Life in the cities differed considerably from that on northern farms, southern plantations, or southwestern ranches. City dwellers everywhere, not just those in New Orleans who went to the levee, purchased foodstuffs and wood at markets and cloth in shops instead of laboriously producing such items

themselves. Urban residents lived by the clock rather than the sun, and men's jobs frequently took them away from their households. City people also had much more contact with the world beyond their own homes than did their rural counterparts.

By the 1750s, most major cities had at least one weekly newspaper, and some had two or three. Anglo-American newspapers printed the latest "advices from London" (usually two to three months old) and news from other English colonies, as well as local reports. Newspapers were available at taverns, coffeehouses, and inns, so people who could not afford to buy them could catch up on the news. Even illiterates could do so, since literate customers often read the papers aloud. Contact with the outside world, however, had its drawbacks. Sailors sometimes brought exotic and deadly diseases into port. Boston, New York, Philadelphia, and New Orleans endured terrible epidemics of smallpox and yellow fever, which Europeans and Africans in the countryside largely escaped.

Politics: Stability and Crisis in British America

In the first decades of the eighteenth century, Anglo-American political life exhibited a new stability. Despite substantial migration from overseas, most residents of the mainland had been born in America. Men from genteel families dominated the political structures in each province, for voters (free male property holders) tended to defer to their well-educated "betters" on election days.

Throughout the Anglo-American colonies, political leaders sought to increase the powers of elected assemblies relative to the powers of the

Rise of the Assemblies

governors and other appointed officials. Assemblies began to claim privileges associated with the British House of Commons, such as the rights to initiate all tax legislation and to control the militia. The assemblies also developed effective ways of influencing British appointees, especially by threatening to withhold their salaries. In some colonies (Virginia and South Carolina, for example), elite members of the assemblies usually presented a united front to royal officials, but in others (such as New York), they fought among themselves long and bitterly. To win hotly contested elections, New York's genteel leaders began to appeal to "the people," competing openly for

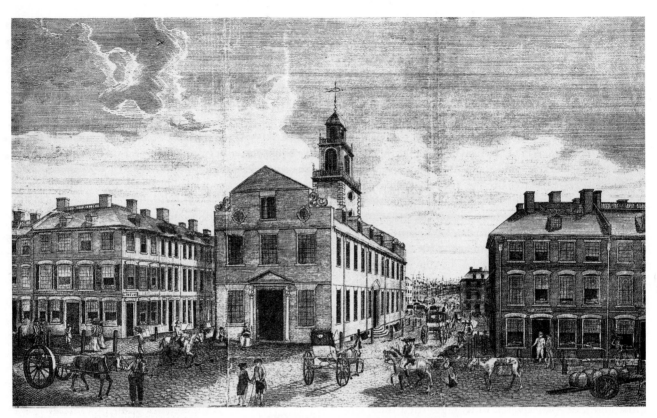

In 1713 the colony of Massachusetts constructed its impressive State House in Boston. Here met the assembly and the council. The solidity and imposing nature of the building must have symbolized for its users the increasing consolidation of power in the hands of the Massachusetts legislature.   (The Bostonian Society)

the votes of ordinary voters. Yet in 1733 that same New York government imprisoned a newspaper editor, John Peter Zenger, who had too vigorously criticized its actions. Defending Zenger against the charge of "seditious libel," his lawyer argued that the truth could not be defamatory, thus helping to establish a free-press principle now found in American law.

Eighteenth-century assemblies bore little resemblance to twentieth-century state legislatures. Much of their business would today be termed administrative; only on rare occasions did they formulate new policies or pass laws of real importance. Members of the assemblies also saw their roles differently than do modern legislators. Instead of believing that they should act positively to improve the lives of their constituents, eighteenth-century assemblymen saw themselves as acting defensively to prevent encroachments on the people's rights. In their minds, their primary function was, for example, stopping governors from imposing

oppressive taxes, rather than passing laws that would actively benefit their constituents.

By midcentury, politically aware colonists commonly linked their own governmental structures to Great Britain's balance of king, lords, and commons—a combination that had been thought to produce a stable polity since the days of ancient Greece and Rome. Drawing rough analogies, political leaders equated their governors with the monarch, their councils with the aristocracy, and their assemblies with the House of Commons. All three were believed essential to good government, but Americans did not regard them with the same degree of approval. They viewed governors and appointed councils as potential threats to colonial freedoms and customary ways of life, since such people primarily represented Britain. Colonists saw the assemblies, however, as the people's protectors. And in

Interpretations of the Assemblies

turn the assemblies regarded themselves as representatives of the people.

Again, though, such beliefs should not be equated with modern practice. The assemblies, firmly controlled by dominant families whose members were reelected year after year, rarely responded to the concerns of their poorer constituents. Although settlements continually expanded, assemblies failed to reapportion themselves to provide adequate representation for newer communities—a lack of action that led to serious grievances among frontier dwellers, especially those from non-English ethnic groups. The colonial ideal of the assembly as the defender of the people's liberties must therefore be distinguished from the colonial reality: the most dearly defended were the wealthy colonists, particularly the assembly members themselves.

At midcentury, the political structures that had stabilized in a period of relative calm confronted a series of crises. None affected all the mainland provinces, but no colony escaped wholly untouched. The crises of various descriptions—ethnic, racial, economic—exposed the internal tensions building in the pluralistic American society, foreshadowing the greater disorder of the revolutionary era. Most important, they demonstrated that the political accommodations arrived at in the aftermath of the Glorious Revolution were no longer adequate to govern Britain's American empire. Once again, changes appeared necessary, and imminent.

One of the first and greatest crises occurred in South Carolina. Early one morning in September 1739, about twenty South Carolina

Stono Rebellion

slaves, most from Angola, gathered near the Stono River south of Charles Town. Seizing guns and ammunition from a store, they killed the storekeepers and some nearby planter families. Then, joined by other local slaves, they headed toward Florida in hopes of finding refuge at Gracia Real de Santa Teresa de Mose. By midday, however, the alarm had been sounded among slaveowners in the district. That afternoon a troop of militia attacked the fugitives, who then numbered about a hundred, killing some and dispersing the rest. More than a week later, most of the remaining conspirators were captured. The colony quickly executed those not killed on the spot, but for over two years rumors about escaped renegades haunted the colony.

The Stono Rebellion shocked slaveholding South Carolinians as well as residents of other colonies.

New York Conspiracy

Throughout British America, laws governing the behavior of African Americans were stiffened. The most striking response came in New York City, which had suffered a slave revolt in 1712. There the news from the South, coupled with fears of Spain generated by the outbreak of King George's War, set off a reign of terror in the summer of 1741. Hysterical whites suspected a biracial gang of thieves and arsonists of conspiring to foment a slave uprising under the guidance of a supposed priest in the pay of Spain. By summer's end, thirty-one blacks and four whites had been executed for participating in the alleged plot. The Stono Rebellion and the New York conspiracy not only exposed and confirmed Anglo-Americans' deepest fears about the dangers of slaveholding but also revealed the assemblies' inability to prevent serious internal disorder. Events of the next two decades confirmed that pattern.

By midcentury most of the fertile land east of the Appalachians had been purchased or occupied. As a result, conflicts over land titles and

Land Riots in New Jersey and New York

conditions of landholding grew in number and frequency as colonists competed for control of land good for farming. In 1746, for example, some New Jersey farmers clashed violently with agents of the East Jersey proprietors. The proprietors claimed the farmers' land as theirs and demanded annual payments, called quit-rents, for the use of the property. Similar violence occurred in the 1760s in the region that later became Vermont. There, farmers holding land grants issued by New Hampshire battled with speculators claiming title to the area through grants from New York authorities.

The most serious land riots of the period took place along the Hudson River in 1765–1766. Late in the seventeenth century, the governor of New York had granted huge tracts in the lower Hudson valley to prominent colonial families. The proprietors in turn divided these estates into small farms, which they rented chiefly to poor Dutch and German migrants who regarded tenancy as a step on the road to independent freeholder status. By the 1750s some proprietors earned large sums annually from quit-rents and other fees.

After 1740, though, increasing migration from New England brought conflict to the great New York estates. The New Englanders did not want to become tenants. Many squatted on vacant portions of the manors, resisting all attempts at eviction. In the mid-

1760s the Philipse family sued New Englanders who had lived on Philipse land for two decades or more. New York courts upheld the Philipse claim, ordering squatters to make way for tenants with valid leases. Instead of complying, the farmers rebelled, terrorizing proprietors and loyal tenants, freeing their friends from jail, and on one occasion battling a county sheriff and his posse. The rebellion lasted nearly a year, ending only when British troops finally captured its leaders.

Violent conflicts of a different sort erupted just a few years later in the Carolinas. The Regulator

Regulators in the Carolinas

movements of the late 1760s (South Carolina) and early 1770s (North Carolina) pitted backcountry farmers against wealthy eastern planters who controlled the provincial governments. Frontier dwellers, most of Scots-Irish origin, protested their lack of an adequate voice in colonial political affairs. South Carolinians for months policed the countryside in vigilante bands, complaining of lax and biased law enforcement. North Carolinians, who primarily objected to heavy taxation, fought and lost a battle with eastern militiamen at Alamance in 1771. Regional, ethnic, and economic tensions thus combined to create these disturbances, which ultimately arose from frontier people's dissatisfaction with the Carolina governments.

A Crisis in Religion

The most widespread crisis was religious. From the mid-1730s through the 1760s, waves of religious revivalism—today known collectively as the First Great Awakening—swept over various parts of the colonies, primarily New England (1735–1745) and Virginia (1750s and 1760s). Orthodox Calvinists sought to combat Enlightenment rationalism, which denied innate human depravity. Simultaneously, the economic and political uncertainty accompanying King George's War made colonists receptive to the spiritual certainty offered by evangelical religion. In addition, many recent immigrants and residents of the backcountry had no prior religious affiliation, thus presenting evangelists with a potential source of converts.

The Great Awakening began in New England, where descendants of the Puritan founding generation still composed the membership of Congregational churches. Whether in full or "halfway" communion—

New England and the Great Awakening

the latter, a category established in 1662 to ensure that people who had not experienced saving faith would be subject to church discipline—such members were primarily female.

From the beginnings of the Awakening, though, both men and women responded with equal fervor. During 1734 and 1735, Reverend Jonathan Edwards, a noted preacher and theologian, noticed a remarkable reaction among the youthful members of his church in Northampton, Massachusetts, to a message based squarely on Calvinist principles. Individuals could attain salvation, Edwards contended, only through recognition of their own depraved natures and the need to surrender completely to God's will. Such surrender brought to Congregationalists of both sexes an intensely emotional release from sin and came to be seen as a single identifiable moment of conversion.

The effects of such conversions remained isolated until 1739, when George Whitefield, a Church of England clergyman already celebrated

George Whitefield

for leading revivals in England, arrived in America. For fifteen months he toured the British colonies, preaching to large audiences from Georgia to New England and concentrating his efforts in the major cities: Boston, New York, Philadelphia, Charles Town, and Savannah. A gripping orator, Whitefield in effect generated the Great Awakening. The historian Harry Stout has termed him "the first modern celebrity" because of his skillful self-promotion and clever manipulation of both his listeners and the newspapers. Everywhere he traveled, his fame preceded him. Thousands of free and enslaved folk turned out to listen—and to experience conversion. Whitefield's journey, the first such ever undertaken, created new interconnections among the previously distinct colonies.

Regular clerics initially welcomed Whitefield and the American-born itinerant evangelist preachers who sprang up to imitate him. Soon, however, many clergymen began to realize that although "revived" religion filled their churches, it ran counter to their own approach to doctrine and matters of faith. They disliked the emotional style of the revivalists, whose itinerancy also disrupted normal patterns of church attendance because it took churchgoers away from the services they usually attended. Particularly troublesome to the orthodox were the dozens of female exhorters who took to streets and pulpits, proclaiming their right (even duty) to expound God's word.

Opposition to the Awakening heightened rapidly, causing congregations to splinter. "Old Lights"—traditional clerics and their followers—engaged in bitter disputes with the "New Light" evangelicals. Already characterized by numerous sects, American Protestantism became further divided as the major denominations split into Old Light and New Light factions and as new evangelical sects—Methodists and Baptists—gained adherents. Paradoxically, the angry fights and the rapid rise in the number of distinct denominations eventually led to an American willingness to tolerate religious diversity. No single sect could make an unequivocal claim to orthodoxy, so they had to coexist if they were to exist at all.

Most significantly, the Awakening challenged traditional modes of thought, for the revivalists' message directly contested the colonial tradition of deference. Itinerant preachers, only a few of whom were ordained clergymen, claimed they understood the will of God better than did elite college-educated clerics. Moreover, they and their followers divided the world into two groups—the saved and the damned—without respect to gender, age, or status, the previously dominant social categories. The Awakening's emphasis on emotion rather than learning undermined the validity of received wisdom, and New Lights questioned not only religious but also social and political orthodoxy. For example, New Lights began to defend the rights of groups and individuals to dissent from a community consensus, thereby challenging one of the most fundamental tenets of colonial political life. Ordinary folk were especially attracted, and many elites repelled, by the egalitarian themes of the Awakening.

Impact of the Awakening

Nowhere was this trend more evident than in Virginia, where the Church of England, the established religion, was supported by tax moneys, and the plantation gentry and their ostentatious lifestyle dominated society. By the 1760s Baptists had gained a secure foothold in Virginia; inevitably, their beliefs and behavior clashed with the way most genteel families lived. They rejected as sinful the horseracing, gambling, and dancing that occupied much of the gentry's leisure time. They dressed plainly, in contrast to the gentry's fashionable opulence. They addressed one another as "brother" and

Virginia Baptists

Reverend George Whitefield, the charismatic evangelist who sparked the First Great Awakening in the mainland British colonies, attracted harsh critics as well as avid admirers. Here an English cartoonist satirizes him as a money-grubbing charlatan who hoodwinks his gullible followers into believing that he is a "Pious Churchman" motivated by "Holy Zeal." Whitefield's crossed eyes, obvious in this image as in others, played a prominent role in contemporary depictions of him.   (Trustees of the British Museum)

"sister" regardless of social status, and they elected the leaders of their congregations—more than ninety of them by 1776. Their monthly "great meetings," which attracted hundreds of people, introduced new public rituals that rivaled the weekly Anglican services.

Strikingly, almost all the Virginia Baptist congregations included both free and slave members. At the founding of the Dan River Baptist Church in 1760, for example, eleven of seventy-four members were African Americans; some congregations had African American majorities. Church rules applied equally to all members; interracial sexual relationships, divorce, and adultery were off limits to all. In addition, congregations forbade masters from breaking up slave couples through sale. Biracial committees investigated complaints about church members' misbehavior. Churches excommunicated slaves for stealing from their masters, but they also excommunicated masters for physically abusing their slaves. One such slaveowner so dismissed in 1772 experienced a true conversion. Penalized for "burning" one of his slaves, Charles Cook apologized to the congregation and became a preacher in a largely African American church. Other Baptists decided that owning slaves was "unrighteous" and freed their bondspeople; the immensely wealthy Robert Carter manumitted more than nine hundred slaves.

Summary

 The Great Awakening thus injected an egalitarian strain into Anglo-American life at midcentury. Although primarily a religious movement, the Awakening had important social and political consequences, calling into question habitual modes of behavior in the secular as well as the religious realm. In short, the Great Awakening helped to break Anglo-Americans' ties to their seventeenth-century origins. So, too, did the newcomers from Germany, Scotland, Ireland, and Africa, who brought their languages, customs, and religions to British North America. The European immigrants settled throughout the English colonies but were concentrated in the growing cities and in the backcountry. By contrast, enslaved migrants from Africa lived and worked primarily within 100 miles of the Atlantic coast. In many areas of the colonial South, 50 to 90 percent of the population was of African origin.

The economic life of all Europe's North American colonies proceeded simultaneously on two levels. On the farms, plantations, and ranches on which most colonists resided, the daily, weekly, monthly, and yearly rounds of chores for men, women, and children alike dominated people's lives while providing the goods consumed by households and sold in the markets. Simultaneously, the British, French, and Spanish colonies were enmeshed in an international network of trade that affected their local economic circumstances. The bitter wars fought by European nations during the eighteenth century inevitably involved the colonists by creating new opportunities for overseas sales or by disrupting their traditional markets. The volatile colonial economy fluctuated for reasons beyond Americans' control. Those fortunate few who—through skill, control of essential resources, or luck—reaped the profits of international trade made up the wealthy class of merchants and landowners who dominated colonial political and social life.

A century and a half after European peoples first settled in North America, the colonies mixed diverse European, American, and African traditions into a novel cultural blend that owed much to Europe but just as much, if not more, to North America itself. Europeans who interacted regularly with peoples of African and American origin—and with Europeans who came from nations other than their own—had to develop new methods of accommodating intercultural differences in addition to creating ties within their own potentially fragmenting communities. Yet at the same time the dominant colonists continued to identify themselves as French, Spanish, or British rather than as Americans. That did not change in Canada, Louisiana, or the Spanish Borderlands, but in the 1760s some Anglo-Americans began to realize that their interests did not necessarily coincide with those of Great Britain or its monarch. For the first time, they offered a direct challenge to British authority.

LEGACY FOR A PEOPLE AND A NATION
Anti-Immigrant Sentiments

In 1751 Benjamin Franklin tried to convince British authorities to halt immigration from Germany to the colonies. In *Observations Concerning the Increase of Mankind,* he contended that Britain's mainland possessions would be peopled by natural increase alone, so immigration was unnecessary. "Why should the Palatine [German] Boors be suffered to swarm into our Settlements, and by herding together establish their Language and Manners to the Exclusion of ours?" he asked. Pennsylvania would soon become "a Colony of *Aliens,*" who would "Germanize us instead of our Anglifying them"; and, he predicted, they "will never adopt our Language or Customs."

Such sentiments have a familiar ring, because policymakers and others today make similar comments about recent arrivals, primarily those from South and Central America and Asia. As the twenty-first century opens, the United States is grappling once again with immigration policy. State legislators, members of Congress, the courts, and public interest groups vie over such questions as how many immigrants to admit each year, what services and rights immigrants are entitled to, and how to deal with illegal aliens. Nativist groups argue for new controls on immigration, opposed by immigrants' rights organizations urging more lenient policies.

These current controversies have deep roots in American soil. More than two decades before Franklin published his essay, for example, Pennsylvania already levied heavy duties on all incoming aliens in hopes of preventing the immigration of "lewd, idle and ill-affected persons." And ever since the nation's founding, immigration policy has periodically caused vitriolic debates, as Americans argued over the admission of French and Haitian immigrants in the 1790s,

Irish immigrants in the 1840s and 1850s, Chinese and Japanese in the 1870s and 1880s, and eastern and southern Europeans around the turn of the century. Often, these debates ended with the passage of restrictive legislation—for example, Asian exclusion acts in the 1880s and laws setting immigration quotas for foreign countries in 1921 and 1924 (not removed until 1965).

Franklin's fears have thus been voiced repeatedly during the intervening 250 years. The first substantial wave of foreign immigration to the colonies and reactions to it have thereby left an enduring legacy to the American people.

For Further Reading, see page A-5 of the Appendix. For Web resources, go to http://college.hmco.com.

The two men must have found the occasion remarkable. The artist customarily painted portraits of the wealthy and high born, not of artisans, even well-connected, affluent ones. The subject himself was an artist—a maker of beautiful silver and gold objects, an engraver of cartoons and townscapes. The political sympathies of the painter, John Singleton Copley, lay primarily with Boston's conservatives, whereas the sitter, Paul Revere, was a noted leader of resistance to British policies. Yet sometime in 1768 Revere commissioned Copley to paint his portrait, and the result (opposite page) is one of the greatest works of American art.

Copley was thirty, Revere thirty-four. Each man had learned his trade from a parent. Revere's father Apollos, who had arrived in Boston as a teenage Huguenot refugee early in the century, was an accomplished gold- and silversmith; Paul served as his father's apprentice and took over the family business when Apollos died in 1754. Copley, whose Irish parents had immigrated to Boston in the 1730s, was taught to paint by his stepfather, Peter Pelham, an English artist. The two young tradesmen had undoubtedly known each other for years. In 1763 and thereafter, Copley hired Revere to make silver and gold frames for the miniature portraits that were among his earliest works.

But their finest collaboration was the painting reproduced here. Copley portrayed Revere surrounded by the tools of his trade and contemplating a teapot he was crafting. The silversmith wears a loose-fitting linen shirt and an open vest rather than the formal dress usually worn by colonial artists' subjects. Even so, Revere is not actually at work: his clothes are too clean, and the table is too polished to be a work surface. The silversmith's pose and apparel convey an impression of thoughtfulness, virtuous labor, and solidity. The teapot too carries a message, especially in the year 1768. Simultaneously a reflection of a craftsman's skills and a prominent emblem of the new "empire of goods" in British America, it resonated with symbolism because, as shall be seen later in this chapter, tea

John Singleton Copley's portrait of Paul Revere is generally regarded as one of his masterpieces. Copley captured Revere's character as a hard-working, respectable artisan—a man unafraid of displaying his humble origins to the world. (Museum of Fine Arts, Boston. Gift of Joseph W., William B., and Edward H. R. Revere)

5

SEVERING THE BONDS OF EMPIRE 1754–1774

boycotts were an important component of colonial resistance to Great Britain. Both artist and subject, indeed, were to be active participants (though in very different ways) in the 1773 event known to history as the Boston Tea Party.

In retrospect, John Adams identified the years between 1760 and 1775 as the era of the true American Revolution. The Revolution, Adams declared, ended before the fighting started, for it was "in the Minds of the people," involving not the actual winning of independence but a fundamental shift of allegiance from Britain to America. Today, not all historians would concur with Adams that the shift he identified constituted the Revolution. But none would deny the importance of the events of those crucial years, which divided the American population along political lines and set the colonies on the road to independence.

The story of the 1760s and early 1770s describes an ever-widening split between Great Britain and Anglo America and among their respective supporters in the colonies. In the long history of British settlement in the Western Hemisphere, considerable tension had occasionally marred the relationship between individual provinces and the mother country. Still, that tension had rarely persisted for long, nor had it been widespread, except during the crisis following the Glorious Revolution in 1689. The primary divisions affecting the colonies had been internal rather than external. In the 1750s, however, a series of events began to draw the colonists' attention from domestic matters to their relations with Great Britain. It all started with the Seven Years War.

Britain's overwhelming victory in that war, confirmed by treaty in 1763, forever altered the balance of power in North America. France was ousted from the continent and Spain from Florida, events with major consequences for both the indigenous peoples of the interior and the residents of the British colonies. Indians could no longer play off European powers against one another and so lost one of their major diplomatic tools. Anglo-Americans, for their part, no longer had to fear the French threat on their northern and western borders or the Spanish in the Southeast. The British colonies along the coast would never have dared to break with their mother country, some historians contend, if France had still controlled the Mississippi River and the Great Lakes.

The British victory in 1763, then, dramatically affected all the residents of North America. That victory also had a significant impact on Great Britain, one that soon involved the colonies. Britain's massive war-related debt needed to be paid, and so Parliament for the first time imposed revenue-raising taxes on the colonies in addition to the customs duties that had long regulated trade. That decision exposed differences in the political thinking of Americans and Britons—differences that until then had been obscured by a shared political vocabulary.

During the 1760s and early 1770s a broad coalition of the residents of Anglo America, men and women alike, resisted new tax levies and attempts by British officials to tighten controls over provincial governments. The colonies' elected leaders became ever more suspicious of Britain's motives as the years

Table 5.1 The Colonial Wars, 1689–1763

American Name	European Name	Dates	Participants	American Sites	Dispute
King William's War	War of the League of Augsburg	1689–97	England, Holland versus France, Spain	New England, New York, Canada	French power
Queen Anne's War	War of Spanish Succession	1702–13	England, Holland, Austria versus France, Spain	Florida, New England	Throne of Spain
King George's War	War of Austrian Succession	1739–48	England, Holland, Austria versus France, Spain, Prussia	West Indies, New England, Canada	Throne of Austria
French and Indian War	Seven Years War	1756–63	England versus France, Spain	Ohio country, Canada	Possession of Ohio country

IMPORTANT EVENTS

1754 Albany Congress meets to try to forge
colonial unity
Fighting breaks out with Washington's
defeat at Fort Necessity

1756 Britain declares war on France; Seven Years
War officially begins

1759 British forces take Quebec

1760 American phase of war ends with fall of
Montreal to British troops
George III becomes king

1763 Treaty of Paris ends Seven Years War
Pontiac's allies attack British forts in West
Proclamation of 1763 attempts to close land
west of Appalachians to English settlement

1764 Sugar Act lays new duties on molasses,
tightens customs regulations
Currency Act outlaws paper money issued
by the colonies

1765 Stamp Act requires stamps on all printed
materials in colonies
Sons of Liberty formed

1766 Stamp Act repealed
Declaratory Act insists that Parliament can
tax the colonies

1767 Townshend Acts lay duties on trade within
the empire, send new officials and judges
to America

1768–70 Resistance to Townshend duties takes
form of boycotts and public demonstrations but divides merchants and urban
artisans

1770 Lord North becomes prime minister
Townshend duties repealed, except for tea
tax
Boston Massacre kills five colonial rioters

1772 Boston Committee of Correspondence
formed

1773 Tea Act aids East India Company
Boston Tea Party protests the Tea Act

1774 Coercive Acts punish Boston and Massachusetts as a whole
Quebec Act reforms government of Quebec

passed. They laid aside old antagonisms to coordinate their responses to the new measures, and they slowly began to reorient their political thinking. As late as the summer of 1774, though, most were still seeking a solution within the framework of the empire; few harbored thoughts of independence. ■

Renewed Warfare Among Europeans and Indians

The English colonies along the Atlantic seaboard were surrounded by hostile, or potentially hostile, neighbors: Indians everywhere, the Spanish in Florida and along the coast of the Gulf of Mexico, the French along the great inland system of rivers and lakes that stretched from the St. Lawrence to the Mississippi. The Spanish outposts posed little direct threat, for Spain's days as a major power had passed. The French were another matter. Their long chain of forts and settlements dominated the North American interior, facilitating trading partnerships and alliances with the Indians. In none of the three wars fought between

1689 and 1748 was England able to shake France's hold on the American frontier. Under the Peace of Utrecht, which ended Queen Anne's War in 1713, the English won control of such peripheral northern areas as Newfoundland, Hudson's Bay, and Nova Scotia (Acadia). But Britain made no territorial gains in King George's War (see Table 5.1 and Map 5.2).

During both Queen Anne's War and King George's War, the Iroquois Confederacy maintained the policy of neutrality it first developed in 1701. While British and French forces fought for nominal control of the North American continent, the confederacy—which actually dominated a large portion of that continent—skillfully manipulated its favors with the Europeans, refusing to commit warriors fully to either side despite being showered with gifts by both. Instead, the Iroquois fought only their southern enemies, the Catawbas. Since France repeatedly urged them to attack the Catawbas, who were allied with Britain, the Iroquois achieved desirable goals. They appeased the French while simultaneously consolidating their control over the entire interior region north of Virginia. The cam-

Iroquois Neutrality

An eighteenth-century Iroquois warrior as depicted by a European artist. Such men of the Six Nations confederacy dominated the North American interior before the Seven Years War. Lines drawn on maps by colonizing powers and the incursions of traders made little impact on their power. (Library of Congress, Rare Book and Special Collections Division)

paign against a common enemy also enabled the confederacy to cement its alliance with its weaker tributaries, the Shawnees and Delawares, and to ensure the continued subordination of those groups.

But even careful Iroquois diplomats could not prevent the region inhabited by the Shawnees and Delawares (now western Pennsylvania and eastern Ohio) from providing the spark that set off a major war. That conflict spread from America to Europe (a significant reversal of previous patterns), proving decisive in the contest for North America. Trouble began in 1752 when Anglo-American fur traders ventured into the area known as the Ohio country (see Map 5.1). The French could not permit their rivals to gain a foothold in the region, for it contained the source of the Ohio River, which offered direct access by water to French posts on the Mississippi. A permanent British presence in the Ohio country could challenge France's

control of the western fur trade and even threaten its prominence in the Mississippi valley. Accordingly, in 1753 the French pushed southward from Lake Erie, building fortified outposts at strategic points.

In response to the French threat to their western frontiers, delegates from seven northern and middle colonies gathered in Albany, New York, in June 1754. With the backing of administrators in London, they sought two goals: to persuade the Iroquois to abandon their traditional neutrality and to coordinate the defenses of the colonies. They succeeded in neither. The Iroquois listened politely to the colonists' arguments but saw no reason to change a policy that had served them well for half a century. And although the Albany Congress delegates adopted a Plan of Union (which would have established an elected intercolonial legislature with the power to tax), their provincial governments uniformly rejected the plan—primarily because those governments feared a loss of autonomy.

Albany Congress

While the Albany Congress delegates deliberated, the war they sought to prepare for was already beginning. Governor Robert Dinwiddie of Virginia sent a small militia force westward to counter the French moves. Virginia claimed ownership of the Ohio country, and Dinwiddie hoped to prevent the French from establishing a permanent post there. But the Virginia militiamen arrived too late, for the French were already engaged in constructing Fort Duquesne at the strategic point—now Pittsburgh—where the Allegheny and Monongahela Rivers meet to form the Ohio. The inexperienced young officer who commanded the Virginians attacked a French detachment and then allowed himself to be trapped in his crudely built Fort Necessity at Great Meadows, Pennsylvania. After a day-long battle (on July 3, 1754), during which more than one-third of his men were killed or wounded, twenty-two-year-old George Washington surrendered. He and his men were allowed to return to Virginia.

Washington had blundered grievously, setting off a war that eventually would encompass nearly the entire world. He also ensured that the Ohio Indians, many of whom had moved west to escape Iroquois domination and to trade with the French, would support France in that conflict. The Indians took Washington's mistakes as an indication of Britain's weakness, and nothing that occurred in the next four years made them alter that judgment. In July 1755, a few miles south of Fort

Seven Years War

Map 5.1   European Settlements and Indians, 1754   By 1754, Europeans had expanded the limits of the English colonies to the eastern slopes of the Appalachian Mountains. Few independent Indian nations still existed in the East, but beyond the mountains they controlled the countryside. Only a few widely scattered English and French forts maintained the Europeans' presence there.

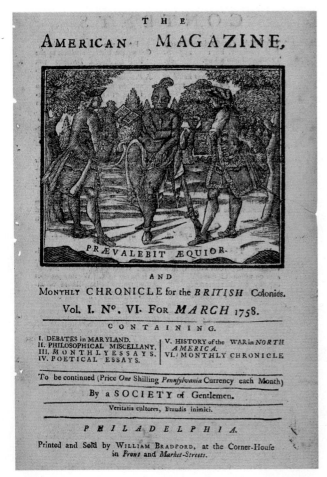

The frontispiece of *The American Magazine and Monthly Chronicle* for March 1758 reflected the struggle for the allegiance of Ohio valley Indians during the Seven Years War. The French representative on the left offers an undecided warrior a tomahawk and a flintlock, while the Englishman on the right presents him with bolts of cloth and a Bible. The Latin phrase at the base of the image translates as "grease takes precedence"; or, in other words, the better gift will win the contest for the Indians' assistance.   (Library of Congress)

Duquesne, a combined force of French and Indians ambushed British and colonial troops readying a renewed assault on the fort. In the devastating defeat, General Edward Braddock was killed and his surviving soldiers were demoralized. After news of the debacle reached London, Britain declared war on France in 1756, thus formally beginning the conflict known as the Seven Years War.

For three more years one disaster followed another. British officers tried without much success to coerce the colonies into supplying men and materiel to the army. The war went so badly that Britain began to fear that France would try to retake Newfoundland and Nova Scotia. Afraid that the approximately twelve thousand French residents of Nova Scotia would abandon the neutrality they had pledged, British commanders forced about half of them from their homeland—the first large-scale modern deportation. Ships crammed with Acadians sailed to each of the mainland colonies, where the dispirited exiles encountered hostility, discrimination, and disease. In Pennsylvania, for example, 450 Acadians were first imprisoned on shipboard, then ordered to live in widely scattered towns (which refused to accept them), then grudgingly allowed to remain in Philadelphia, where they eked out a meager living, in part by petty thievery. After 1763 the survivors dispersed to a variety of locations: some returned to Canada, others traveled to France or its West Indian islands, and many eventually settled in Louisiana, where they became known as Cajuns.

Led by William Pitt, the civilian official placed in charge of the war effort in 1757, Britain finally pursued a successful military strategy. Pitt agreed to reimburse the colonies for their wartime expenditures and placed troop recruitment wholly in local hands, thereby gaining wholehearted American support for the war. In July 1758, British forces recaptured the fortress at Louisbourg, winning control of the entrance to the St. Lawrence River and cutting the major French supply route. Then, in a stunning attack in September 1759, General James Wolfe's soldiers defeated the French on the Plains of Abraham and took Quebec. Sensing a British victory, the Iroquois abandoned their traditional neutrality, hoping to gain a postwar advantage by allying themselves with Britain. A year later the British captured Montreal, the last French stronghold on the continent, and the American phase of the war ended.

In the Treaty of Paris (1763), France ceded its major North American holdings to Britain. Spain, an ally of France toward the end of the war, gave Florida to the victors. France, meanwhile, ceded Louisiana west of the Mississippi to Spain, in partial compensation for its ally's losses elsewhere. The British thus gained control of the continent's fur trade. No longer would the English seacoast colonies have to worry about the threat to their existence posed by France's extensive North American territories (see Map 5.2).

Because most of the fighting occurred in the Northeast, the war had especially pronounced effects on New Englanders. As many as one-third of all Massachusetts men between the ages of sixteen and

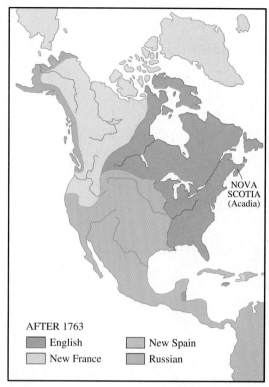

Map 5.2   European Claims in North America   The dramatic results of the British victory in the Seven Years (French and Indian) War are vividly demonstrated in these maps, which depict the abandonment of French claims to the mainland after the Treaty of Paris in 1763.

American Soldiers

twenty-nine served for a time in the provincial army. Wartime service left a lasting impression on these soldiers. For the first time, ordinary Americans came into extended contact with Britons—and they did not like what they saw. The provincials regarded the British troops (called "redcoats" because of the color of their uniforms) as haughty, profane Sabbath-breakers who arbitrarily imposed overly harsh punishments on anyone who broke the rules. Nearly sixty years later a veteran still vividly recalled an incident in 1762 when a British soldier inflicted hundreds of lashes on three men for "some trifling offense. . . . I felt at the time as though I could have taken summary vengeance on those who were the authors of it," he wrote in his memoirs.

The New England soldiers also learned that British troops did not share their adherence to principles of contract and consensus—the values that governed their lives at home. Colonial regiments mutinied or rebelled en masse if they believed they were being treated unfairly, as happened, for instance, when they were not allowed to leave when their enlistments expired. One private in these circumstances grumbled in his journal in 1759, "Although we be Englishmen born, we are debarred Englishmen's liberty. . . . [The British soldiers] are but little better than slaves to their officers. And when I get out of their [power] I shall take care how I get in again." Such men would later recall their personal experience of British "tyranny" when they decided to support the Revolution.

The overwhelming British triumph stimulated some Americans to think expansively. People like the Philadelphia printer Benjamin Franklin, who had long touted the colonies' wealth and potential, predicted a glorious new future for British North America—a future that included not just geographical expansion but also economic development and population growth. Such men were to lead the resistance to British measures in the years after 1763. They uniformly opposed

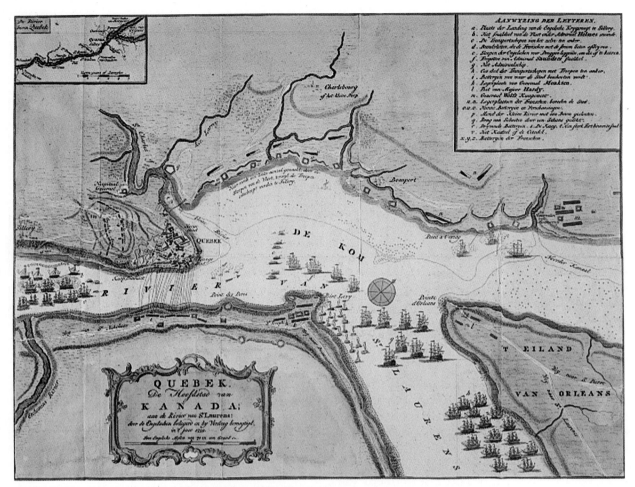

A 1769 Dutch atlas charted the successful British attack on Quebec ten years earlier. Ships of the British fleet fill the St. Lawrence River. Cannon on the southern shore bombard the fortified town (indicated by the lines across the river). And to the left of the city, on the Plains of Abraham, the string of small red blocks represents the British troops who had stealthily climbed the heights at night to confront Quebec's French defenders (the blue blocks). (Private Collection)

any laws that would retard America's growth and persistently supported steps to increase Americans' control over their own destiny.

1763: A Turning Point

 The great victory over France had an irreversible impact on North America, felt first by the indigenous peoples of the interior. With France excluded from the continent altogether and Spanish territory now confined to west of the Mississippi, the diplomatic strategy that had served the Indians well for so long was now obsolete. The consequences were immediate and devastating.

Even before the Treaty of Paris, southern Indians had to adjust to the new circumstances. After Britain gained the upper hand in the American war in 1758, Creeks and Cherokees lost their ability to force concessions by threatening to turn instead to France or Spain. In desperation, and in retaliation for British atrocities, Cherokees attacked the Carolina and Virginia frontiers in 1760. Though initially victorious, the Indians were defeated the following year by a force of British regulars and colonial militia. Late in 1761 the two sides concluded a treaty under which the Cherokees allowed the construction of British forts in their territories and opened a large tract of land to European settlement.

The fate of the Cherokees in the South portended events in the Ohio country. There, the Ottawas, Chippewas, and Potawatomis reacted angrily when Great Britain, no longer facing French competition, raised the price of trade goods and ended traditional gift-giving practices. Britain also allowed settlers to move into the Monongahela and Susquehanna valleys, onto Delaware and Iroquois lands. A shaman named Neolin (also known as the Delaware Prophet) urged Indians to oppose British incursion on their lands and European influence on their culture. Contending that native peoples were destroying themselves by becoming dependent on European goods and especially alcohol, Neolin advocated resistance, both peaceful and armed. If all Indians west of the mountains united to reject the invaders, Neolin declared, the Great Spirit would replenish the depleted deer herds and once again look kindly upon his people.

Neolin and Pontiac

Pontiac, the war chief of an Ottawa village near Detroit, became the leader of a movement based on Neolin's precepts. In the spring of 1763, Pontiac forged an unprecedented alliance among Hurons, Chippewas, Potawatomis, Delawares, Shawnees, and Mingoes (Pennsylvania Iroquois). Pontiac then laid siege to Fort Detroit while war parties attacked other British outposts in the Great Lakes region. Detroit withstood the siege, but by late June all the other forts west of Niagara and north of Fort Pitt (formerly the French Fort Duquesne) had fallen to the alliance. Indians then raided the Virginia and Pennsylvania frontiers at will throughout the summer, killing at least two thousand settlers. Still, they failed to take the strongholds of Niagara, Fort Pitt, or Detroit. In early August, colonial militiamen soundly defeated a combined force of Delawares, Shawnees, Hurons, and Mingoes at Bushy Run, Pennsylvania. Conflict ceased when Pontiac broke off the siege of Detroit in late October. A treaty ending the war was finally negotiated three years later.

The uprising showed Great Britain that the huge territory just acquired from France would not be easy to govern. Officials in London had no prior experience managing such a vast area, particularly one inhabited by such restive peoples—the remaining French settlers along the St. Lawrence and the many different Indian communities. In October, the ministry issued the Proclamation of 1763, which declared the headwaters of rivers flowing

Proclamation of 1763

Benjamin West, the first well-known American artist, engraved this picture of a prisoner exchange at the end of Pontiac's Uprising, with Colonel Henry Bouquet supervising the return of settlers abducted during the war. In the foreground, a child resists leaving the Indian parents he had grown to love. Many colonists were fascinated by the phenomenon West depicted—the reluctance of captives to abandon their adoptive Indian families. (Ohio Historical Society)

into the Atlantic from the Appalachian Mountains to be the temporary western boundary for colonial settlement (see Map 5.1). The proclamation was intended to prevent clashes by forbidding colonists to move onto Indian lands until tribes had given up their territory by treaty. But many Anglo-Americans had already established farms or purchased property west of the proclamation line; among them were wealthy speculators who hoped to control large tracts of fertile land. From the outset, then, the unenforceable policy was doomed to failure.

The hard-won victory in the Seven Years War had cost Britain millions of pounds and created an immense war debt. The problem of paying it bedeviled

George III

George III, who succeeded his grandfather, George II, on the British throne in 1760. The twenty-two-year-old king, a man of mediocre intellect and even more mediocre education, was unfortunately also an erratic judge of character. During the crucial years between 1763 and 1770, when the rift with the colonies grew ever wider and he faced a series of political crises in England, the king replaced ministries with bewildering rapidity. Although determined to assert the power of the monarchy, George III was immature and unsure of himself. He often substituted stubbornness for cleverness, and he regarded adherence to the status quo as the hallmark of patriotism.

The man he selected as prime minister in 1763, George Grenville, believed that the American colonies should be more tightly administered than in the past. Grenville confronted a financial crisis: England's burden of indebtedness had nearly doubled since 1754, from £73 million to £137 million. Annual expenditures before the war had amounted to no more than £8 million; now the yearly interest on the debt alone came to £5 million. Grenville's ministry had to find new sources of funds, and the British people themselves were already heavily taxed. Since the colonists had benefited greatly from the wartime expenditures, Grenville concluded that Anglo-Americans should be asked to pay a greater share of the cost of running the empire.

Grenville did not question Great Britain's right to levy taxes on the colonies. Like all his countrymen, he

Theories of Representation

believed that the government's legitimacy derived ultimately from the consent of the people, but he defined consent far more loosely than did the colonists. Americans had come to believe that they could be represented only by men who lived nearby and for whom they or their property-holding neighbors actually voted; otherwise, they could not count on legislators to represent their interests properly. Grenville and his English contemporaries, however, believed that Parliament—king, lords, and commons acting together—by definition represented all British subjects, wherever they resided (even overseas) and whether or not they could vote.

Parliament saw itself as collectively representing the entire nation; the particular constituency that chose a member of the House of Commons had no special claim on that member's vote, nor did he have to live near his constituents. According to this theory of government, called virtual representation, the colonists were seen as virtually, if not actually, represented in Parliament. Thus their consent to acts of Parliament could be presumed. In the colonies, by contrast, members of the lower houses of the assemblies were viewed as specifically representing the regions that had elected them. Before Grenville proposed to tax the colonists, the two notions coexisted because no major conflict arose to expose the central contradiction. But events of the 1760s revealed the incompatibility of the two definitions of representation.

The same events threw into sharp relief Americans' attitudes toward political power. The colonists

Real Whigs

had become accustomed to a central government that wielded only limited authority over them, affecting their daily lives very little. Consequently, they believed that a good government was one that largely left them alone, a view in keeping with the theories of a group of British writers known as the Real Whigs. Drawing on a tradition of dissenting thought that reached back to John Locke and even to the English Civil War, the Real Whigs stressed the dangers inherent in a powerful government, particularly one headed by a monarch. Some of them even favored republicanism, which proposed to eliminate monarchs altogether and rest political power more directly on the people. Real Whigs warned the people to guard constantly against government's attempts to encroach on their liberty and seize their property. Political power was always to be feared, wrote John Trenchard and Thomas Gordon in their essay series *Cato's Letters* (originally published in London in 1720–1723 and reprinted many times thereafter in the colonies). Rulers would try to corrupt and oppress the people. Only the perpetual vigilance of people and their elected representatives could preserve their precious yet fragile liberty, which was closely linked to their right to hold private property.

Britain's attempts to tighten the reins of government and to raise revenues from the colonies in the 1760s and early 1770s convinced many Americans that the Real Whigs' reasoning applied to their circumstances, especially because of the link between liberty and property rights. Excessive and unjust taxation, they believed, could destroy their freedoms. They began to interpret British measures in light of the Real Whigs' warnings and to see oppressive designs behind the actions of Grenville and his successors. Historians disagree over the extent to which those perceptions were correct, but by 1775 a large number of colonists believed they were. In the mid-1760s, however, colonial leaders did not immediately accuse Grenville of conspiring to oppress them. They at first merely questioned the wisdom of the laws he proposed.

Parliament passed the first such measures, the Sugar and Currency Acts, in 1764. The Sugar Act (also known as the Revenue Act) revised existing customs regulations, laid new duties on some foreign imports into the colonies, and aimed at stopping the widespread smuggling of molasses, one of the chief commodities in American trade. It also established a vice-admiralty court at Halifax, Nova Scotia. (Vice-admiralty courts considered cases arising under maritime law and operated without juries.) Although the Sugar Act appeared to resemble the Navigation Acts, which the colonies had long accepted as legitimate, it broke with tradition in being explicitly designed to raise revenue, not to channel American trade through Britain. The Currency Act effectively outlawed colonial issues of paper money. (British merchants had long complained that Americans were paying their debts in inflated local currencies.) Americans could accumulate little sterling, since they imported more than they exported; thus the act seemed to the colonists to deprive them of a useful medium of exchange.

Sugar and Currency Acts

The Sugar and Currency Acts were imposed on an economy already in the midst of depression. A business boom accompanied the Seven Years War, but the brief spell of prosperity ended abruptly in 1760 when the war shifted overseas. Urban merchants could not sell all their imported goods to colonial customers alone, and without the military's demand for foodstuffs, American farmers found fewer buyers for their products. The bottom dropped out of the European tobacco market, threatening the livelihood of Chesapeake planters. Sailors were thrown out of work, and artisans found few customers. In such circumstances, the prospect of increased import duties and inadequate supplies of currency aroused merchants' hostility.

Individual American essayists and incensed colonial governments protested the new policies. But, lacking any precedent for a united campaign against acts of Parliament, Americans in 1764 took only hesitant and uncoordinated steps. Eight colonial legislatures sent separate petitions to Parliament requesting the Sugar Act's repeal. They argued that its commercial restrictions would hurt Britain as well as the colonies and that they had not consented to its passage. The protests had no effect. The law remained in force, and Grenville proceeded with another revenue plan.

The Stamp Act Crisis

The Stamp Act (1765), Grenville's most important proposal, was modeled on a law that had been in effect in Great Britain for almost a century. It touched nearly every colonist by requiring tax stamps on most printed materials, but it placed the heaviest burden on merchants and other members of the colonial elite, who used printed matter more frequently than did ordinary folk. Anyone who purchased a newspaper or pamphlet, made a will, transferred land, bought dice or playing cards, applied for a liquor license, accepted a government appointment, or borrowed money would have to pay the tax. Never before had a revenue measure of such scope been proposed for the colonies. The act also required that tax stamps be paid for with sterling, which was scarce, and that violators be tried in vice-admiralty courts. Americans feared the loss of their right to trial by a jury of their peers. Finally, such a law would break decisively with the colonial tradition of self-imposed taxation.

The most important colonial pamphlet protesting the Sugar Act and the proposed Stamp Act was *The Rights of the British Colonies Asserted and Proved*, by James Otis, Jr., a brilliant young Massachusetts attorney. Otis starkly exposed the ideological dilemma that confounded the colonists for the next decade. How could they justify their opposition to certain acts of Parliament without questioning Parliament's authority over them? On the one hand, Otis asserted, Americans were "entitled to all the natural, essential, inherent, and inseparable rights" of Britons, including the right not to be taxed without their consent. "No man or body of men, not excepting the parliament . . . can take [those rights] away," he declared. On the other hand, Otis was forced to admit, under the British system established after the Glorious Revolution, "the power of parliament is uncontrollable but by themselves, and we must obey. . . . Let the parliament lay what burthens they please on us, we must, it is our duty to submit and patiently bear them, till they will be pleased to relieve us."

James Otis's Rights of the British Colonies

Otis's first contention, drawing on colonial notions of representation, implied that Parliament could not constitutionally tax the colonies because Americans were not represented in its ranks. Yet his second point both acknowledged political reality and accepted the prevailing theory of British government: that Parliament was the sole, supreme authority in the empire. Even unconstitutional laws enacted by Parliament had to be obeyed until Parliament decided to repeal them. According to orthodox British political theory, there could be no middle ground between absolute submission to Parliament and a frontal challenge to its authority. Otis tried to find such a middle ground by proposing colonial representation in Parliament, but his idea was never taken seriously on either side of the Atlantic. The British believed that colonists were already virtually represented in Parliament, and Anglo-Americans quickly realized that a handful of colonial delegates to London would simply be outvoted.

Otis published his pamphlet before the Stamp Act was passed. When Americans first learned of the act's adoption in the spring of 1765, they reacted indecisively. Few colonists—even appointed government officials—publicly favored the law. But colonial petitions had already failed to prevent its adoption, and further lobbying appeared futile. Perhaps Otis was correct: the only course open to Americans was to pay the stamp tax, reluctantly but loyally. Acting on that assumption, colonial agents in London sought the appointment of their American friends as stamp distributors so that the law would at least be enforced equitably.

Not all the colonists resigned themselves to paying the new tax. A twenty-nine-year-old lawyer serving his first term in the Virginia House of Burgesses was appalled by his fellow legislators' unwillingness to oppose the Stamp Act. Patrick Henry later recalled that he was "young, inexperienced, unacquainted with the forms of the house and the members that composed it"—but he decided to act. "Alone, unadvised, and unassisted, on a blank leaf of an old law book," he wrote the Virginia Stamp Act Resolves.

Patrick Henry and the Virginia Stamp Act Resolves

Little in Henry's earlier life foreshadowed his success in the political arena he entered so dramatically. The son of a prosperous Scottish immigrant to western Virginia, Henry had little formal education. After marrying at eighteen, he failed at both farming and storekeeping before turning to the law as a means of supporting his wife and their six children. Henry lacked legal training, but his oratorical skills made him an effective advocate, first for his clients and later for his political beliefs. A prominent Virginia lawyer observed, "He is by far the most powerful speaker I ever heard. Every word he says not only engages, but commands the attention; and your passions are no longer your own when he addresses them."

Patrick Henry introduced his seven proposals near the end of the legislative session, when many burgesses had already departed for home. Henry's fiery speech led the Speaker of the House to accuse him of treason. (Henry denied the charge, contrary to the nineteenth-century myth that he exclaimed, "If this be treason, make the most of it!") The few burgesses remaining in Williamsburg adopted five of Henry's resolutions by a bare majority. Although they repealed the most radical

In 1765 a clerk in the offices of British tax officials prepared this register to contain examples of the tax stamps intended for use in the American colonies. But because the law was never enforced and soon repealed, the register is largely empty, and the other volumes the clerk anticipated were never readied at all.   (The British Library Philatelic Section, Inland Revenue Archives)

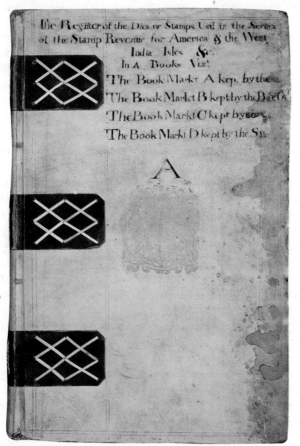

of the five the next day, their action had far-reaching effects. Some colonial newspapers printed Henry's seven original resolutions as if they had been uniformly passed by the House, even though one was rescinded and two others were never debated or voted on at all.

The four propositions adopted by the burgesses repeated Otis's arguments, asserting that the colonists had never forfeited the rights of British subjects, among which was consent to taxation. The other three resolutions went much further. The one that was repealed claimed for the burgesses "the only exclusive right" to tax Virginians, and the final two (those never considered) asserted that residents of Virginia need not obey tax laws passed by other legislative bodies (namely Parliament), terming any opponent of that opinion "an Enemy to this his Majesty's Colony."

The burgesses' decision to accept only the first four of Henry's resolutions anticipated the position most Americans would adopt throughout the following decade.

Continuing Loyalty to Britain

Though willing to contend for their rights, the colonists did not seek independence. They rather wanted some measure of self-government. Accordingly, they backed away from the assertions that they owed Parliament no obedience and that only their own assemblies could tax them. Indeed, declared the Maryland lawyer Daniel Dulany, whose *Considerations on the Propriety of Imposing Taxes on the British Colonies* was the most widely read pamphlet of 1765, "The colonies are dependent upon Great Britain, and the supreme authority vested in the king, lords, and commons, may justly be exercised to secure, or preserve their dependence." But, warned Dulany, a superior did not have the right "to seize the property of his inferior when he pleases"; there was a crucial distinction between a condition of "dependence and inferiority" and one of "absolute vassalage and slavery."

Over the next ten years, America's political leaders searched for a formula that would enable them to control their internal affairs, especially taxation, but remain under British rule. The chief difficulty lay in British officials' inability to compromise on the issue of parliamentary power. The notion that Parliament could exercise absolute authority over all colonial possessions inhered in the British theory of government. Even the harshest British critics of the ministries of the 1760s and 1770s questioned only the wisdom of specific policies, not the principles on which they rested. In effect, the Americans wanted British leaders

In 1795 the artist Lawrence Sully painted the only known life portrait of Patrick Henry. The old man's fierce gaze reflects the same intensity that marked his actions thirty years earlier, when he introduced the Virginia Stamp Act Resolves in the House of Burgesses.   (Mead Art Museum, Amherst College. Bequest of Herbert L. Pratt, Class of 1985)

to revise their fundamental understanding of the workings of their government. But that was simply too much to expect.

The ultimate effectiveness of Americans' opposition to the Stamp Act rested on more than ideological arguments over parliamentary power. The decisive and inventive actions of some colonists during the late summer and fall of 1765 gave the resistance its primary force.

In August the Loyal Nine, a Boston social club of printers, distillers, and other artisans, organized a demonstration against the Stamp Act. Hoping to show that people of all ranks opposed the act, they approached the leaders of the city's rival laborers' associations, based in Boston's North End and South End neighborhoods. The two gangs, composed of unskilled workers and poor tradesmen, often battled each other, but the Loyal Nine convinced them to lay aside their differences to participate in th[e]

Loyal Nine

demonstration. All colonists, not just affluent ones, would have to pay the stamp taxes.

Early on August 14, the demonstrators hung an effigy of Andrew Oliver, the province's stamp distributor, from a tree on Boston Common. That night a large crowd led by a group of about fifty well-dressed tradesmen paraded the effigy around the city. The crowd tore down a small building they thought was intended as the stamp office, making a bonfire near Oliver's house with wood from the structure. Beheading the effigy, they added it to the flames. Demonstrators broke most of Oliver's windows and threw stones at officials who tried to disperse them. In the midst of the melée, the North End and South End leaders drank a toast to their successful union. The Loyal Nine achieved success when Oliver publicly promised not to fulfill the duties of his office. One Bostonian jubilantly wrote to a relative, "I believe people never was more Universally pleased not so much one could I hear say he was sorry, but a smile sat on almost every ones countinance."

But another crowd action twelve days later, aimed this time at Oliver's brother-in-law, Lieutenant Governor Thomas Hutchinson, drew no praise from Boston's respectable citizens. On the night of August 26, a mob reportedly led by the South End leader Ebenezer MacIntosh attacked the homes of several customs officers. The crowd then completely destroyed Hutchinson's elaborately furnished townhouse in one of Boston's most fashionable districts. The lieutenant governor reported that by the next morning "one of the best finished houses in the Province had nothing remaining but the bare walls and floors." His trees and garden were ruined, his valuable library was lost, and the mob "emptied the house of every thing whatsoever except a part of the kitchen furniture." But Hutchinson took some comfort in the fact that "the encouragers of the first mob never intended matters should go this length and the people in general express the utmost detestation of this unparalleled outrage." (A portrait of Hutchinson is on page 137.)

The differences between the two Boston mobs of August 1765 exposed divisions that would continue to characterize subsequent colonial protests. Few residents of the colonies sided with Great Britain during the 1760s, but various colonial groups had divergent goals. The skilled craftsmen who composed the Loyal Nine, and merchants, lawyers, and other members of the educated elite preferred orderly demonstrations con-

Americans' Divergent Interests

fined to political issues. For the city's laborers, by contrast, economic grievances may have been paramount. Certainly, their "hellish Fury" as they wrecked Hutchinson's house suggests a resentment against his ostentatious display of wealth.

Colonists, like Britons, had a long tradition of crowd action in which disfranchised people took to the streets to redress deeply felt local grievances. But the Stamp Act controversy drew ordinary urban folk into the vortex of transatlantic politics for the first time. Matters that previously had been of concern only to the gentry or to members of colonial legislatures were now discussed on every street corner. Benjamin Franklin's daughter observed as much when she informed her father, then serving as a colonial agent in London, that "nothing else is talked of, the Dutch [Germans] talk of the stompt act the Negroes of the tamp, in short every body has something to say."

The entry of unskilled workers, slaves, and women into the realm of imperial politics both threatened and aided the elite men who wanted to mount effective opposition to British measures. On the one hand, crowd action could have a stunning impact. Anti–Stamp Act demonstrations occurred in cities and towns stretching from Halifax in the north to the Caribbean island of Antigua in the south (see Map 5.3). They were so successful that by November 1, when the law was scheduled to take effect, not one stamp distributor was willing to carry out his official duties. Thus the act could not be enforced. But on the other hand, wealthy men recognized that mobs composed of the formerly powerless—whose goals were not always identical to theirs (as the Boston experience showed)—could endanger their own dominance of the society. What would happen, they wondered, if the "hellish Fury" of the crowd turned against them?

They therefore attempted to channel resistance into acceptable forms by creating an intercolonial association, the Sons of Liberty. New Yorkers organized the first such group in early November, and branches spread rapidly through the coastal cities. Composed of merchants, lawyers, and prosperous tradesmen like Paul Revere, the Sons of Liberty by early 1766 linked protest leaders from Charleston, South Carolina, to Portsmouth, New Hampshire.

Sons of Liberty

The Sons of Liberty could influence events but not control them. In Charleston in October 1765, an informally organized crowd shouting "Liberty Liberty and stamp'd paper" forced the resignation of the South

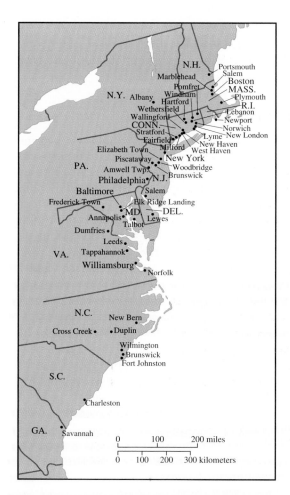

Map 5.3   Sites of Major Demonstrations Against the Stamp Act   Every place named on these maps was the site of a demonstration against the Stamp Act of 1765; British colonies outside the eventual United States joined in the nearly universal opposition to the hated measure. (Source: From Lester J. Cappon et al., eds., *Atlas of Early American History: The Revolutionary Era, 1760–1790.* Copyright © 1976 by Princeton University Press. Reprinted by permission of Princeton University Press.)

Carolina stamp distributor. The victory celebration a few days later—the largest demonstration the city had ever known—featured a British flag with the word "Liberty" emblazoned on it. But the new Charleston chapter of the Sons of Liberty was horrified when in January 1766 local slaves paraded through the streets similarly crying "Liberty!" Freedom from slavery was not the sort of liberty elite slaveowners had in mind.

In Philadelphia, too, resistance leaders were dismayed when an angry mob threatened to attack Benjamin Franklin's house. The city's laborers believed Franklin to be partly responsible for the Stamp Act, since he had obtained the post of stamp distributor for a close friend. But Philadelphia's artisans—the backbone of the opposition movement there and elsewhere—were fiercely loyal to Franklin, one of their own who had made good. They gathered to protect his home and family from the crowd. The house was saved, but the resulting split between the better-off tradesmen and the common laborers prevented the establishment of a successful workingmen's alliance like that of Boston.

During the fall and winter of 1765–1766, opposition to the Stamp Act proceeded on three separate fronts. Colonial legislatures petitioned Parliament to repeal the hated law, and courts closed because they could not obtain the stamps now required for all legal documents. In October nine colonies sent delegates to a general congress, the first since the 1754 Albany Congress. The Stamp Act Congress met in New York to draft a unified but conservative statement of protest that stressed the law's adverse economic effects rather than its perceived violations of Americans' rights. At the same time, the Sons of Liberty held mass meetings, attempting to rally public support for the resistance movement. Finally, American merchants organized nonimportation associations to pressure British exporters. By the 1760s, one-quarter of all British exports went to the colonies, and American merchants reasoned that London merchants whose sales suffered severely would lobby for repeal. Since times were bad and American merchants were finding few customers for imported goods anyway, a general moratorium on future purchases would also help to reduce their bloated inventories.

In March 1766, Parliament repealed the Stamp Act. The nonimportation agreements had had the anticipated effect, creating allies for the colonies among wealthy London merchants. But boycotts, formal protests, and crowd actions were less important in winning repeal than was the appointment of a new prime minister, chosen by George III for reasons unrelated to colonial politics. Lord Rockingham, who replaced Grenville in the summer of 1765, had opposed the Stamp Act, not because he believed Parliament lacked power to tax the colonies but because he thought the law unwise and divisive. Thus although Rockingham proposed repeal, he linked it to passage of a Declaratory Act, which asserted Parliament's authority to tax and legislate for Britain's American possessions "in all cases whatsoever."

Repeal of the Stamp Act

News of the repeal arrived in Newport, Rhode Island, in May, and the Sons of Liberty quickly dispatched messengers to carry the welcome tidings throughout the colonies. They organized celebrations commemorating the glorious event, all of which stressed the Americans' unwavering loyalty to Great Britain. Their goal achieved, the Sons of Liberty dissolved. Few colonists saw the ominous implications of the Declaratory Act.

Resistance to the Townshend Acts

The colonists had accomplished their immediate aim, but the long-term prospects were unclear. In the summer of 1766, another change in the ministry in London revealed how fragile their victory had been. The new prime minister, William Pitt, had fostered cooperation between the colonies and Great Britain during the Seven Years War (see page 118). Now, however, Pitt was ill much of the time, and another minister, Charles Townshend, became the dominant force in the ministry. An ally of Grenville and a supporter of colonial taxation, Townshend decided to renew the attempt to obtain additional funds from Britain's American possessions (see Table 5.2.).

The duties Townshend proposed in 1767 were to be levied on trade goods like paper, glass, and tea, and thus seemed to be nothing more than extensions of the existing Navigation Acts. But the Townshend duties differed from previous customs levies in two ways. First, they applied to items imported into the colonies from Britain, not from foreign countries. Thus they violated mercantilist theory (see page 76). Second, they were designed to raise money to pay the salaries of some royal officials in the colonies. That posed a direct challenge to the colonial assemblies, which derived considerable power from threatening to withhold officials' salaries. In addition, Townshend's scheme provided for the creation of an American Board of Customs Commissioners and of vice-admiralty courts at Boston, Philadelphia, and Charleston. Both moves angered merchants, whose profits would be threatened by more vigorous enforcement of the Navigation Acts.

In 1765, months had passed before the colonists began to protest the Stamp Act. The passage of the Townshend Acts, however, drew a quick response. One series of essays in particular, *Letters from a Farmer in Pennsylvania* by the prominent lawyer John Dickinson, expressed a broad consensus. Eventually all but four colonial newspapers printed Dickinson's essays; in pamphlet form they went through seven American editions. Dickinson con-

John Dickinson's Farmer's Letters

Table 5.2	British Ministries and Their American Policies
Head of Ministry	**Major Acts**
George Grenville	Sugar Act (1764)
	Currency Act (1764)
	Stamp Act (1765)
Lord Rockingham	Stamp Act repealed (1766)
	Declaratory Act (1766)
William Pitt/ Charles Townshend	Townshend Acts (1767)
Lord North	Townshend duties (except for the tea tax) repealed (1770)
	Coercive Acts (1774)
	Quebec Act (1774)

tended that Parliament could regulate colonial trade but could not exercise that power to raise revenue. By drawing a distinction between trade regulation and unacceptable commercial taxation, Dickinson avoided the sticky issue of consent and how it affected colonial subordination to Parliament. But his argument created a different, and equally knotty, problem. In effect it obligated the colonies to assess Parliament's motives in passing any law pertaining to trade before deciding whether to obey it. That was in the long run an unworkable position.

The Massachusetts assembly responded to the Townshend Acts by drafting a letter to circulate among the other colonial legislatures, calling

Massachusetts Assembly Dissolved

for unity and suggesting a joint petition of protest. Not the letter itself but the ministry's reaction to it united the colonies. When Lord Hillsborough, recently named to the new post of secretary of state for America, learned of the circular letter, he ordered Governor Francis Bernard of Massachusetts to insist that the assembly recall it. He also directed other governors to prevent their assemblies from discussing the letter. Hillsborough's order gave

colonial assemblies the incentive they needed to join forces to oppose this new threat to their prerogatives. In late 1768 the Massachusetts legislature met, debated, and resoundingly rejected recall by a vote of 92 to 17. Bernard immediately dissolved the assembly, and other governors followed suit when their legislatures debated the circular letter.

The number of votes cast against recalling the circular letter—92—assumed ritual significance for the supporters of resistance. The figure

Rituals of Resistance

45 already had symbolic meaning because John Wilkes, a radical Londoner sympathetic to the American cause, had been jailed for libel in Britain for publishing an essay entitled *The North Briton*, No. 45. In Boston, Paul Revere made a punchbowl weighing 45 ounces that held 45 gills (half-cups) and was engraved with the names of the 92 legislators; James Otis, John Adams, and others publicly drank 45 toasts from it (see the photo below). In Charleston the city's tradesmen decorated a tree with 45 lights and set off 45 rockets. Carrying 45 candles, they adjourned to a tavern, where 45 tables were set with 45 bowls of wine, 45 bowls of punch, and 92 glasses.

Paul Revere crafted a punchbowl to commemorate the 92 members of the Massachusetts Assembly who in 1768 voted against rescinding the circular letter. The bowl was also linked symbolically to John Wilkes by its size and weight, and through its use in rituals incorporating the number 45.   (Courtesy, Museum of Fine Arts, Boston. Gift by Subscription and Francis Bartlett Fund. Reproduced with permission. © 1999 Museum of Fine Arts, Boston. All rights reserved.)

Such public rituals served important educational functions. Just as the pamphlets by Otis, Dulany, Dickinson, and others acquainted literate colonists with the issues raised by British actions, so public rituals taught illiterate Americans about the reasons for resistance and familiarized them with the terms of the argument. When Boston's revived Sons of Liberty invited hundreds of city residents to dine with them each August 14 to commemorate the first Stamp Act uprising, and the Charleston Sons of Liberty held their meetings in public, crowds gathered to watch and listen. Likewise, the public singing of songs supporting the American cause helped to spread the word. The participants in such events openly expressed their commitment to the cause of resistance and encouraged others to join them.

During the campaign against the Townshend duties, the Sons of Liberty and other American leaders made a deliberate effort to involve ordinary folk in the resistance movement. Most important, they urged colonists of all ranks and both sexes to sign agreements not to purchase or consume British products. The new consumerism that previously had linked colonists economically now linked them politically as well, supplying them with a ready method of displaying their allegiance. As "A Tradesman" wrote in a Philadelphia paper in 1770, it was essential "for the Good of the Whole, to strengthen the Hands of the Patriotic Majority, by agreeing not to purchase British Goods."

As the primary purchasers of textiles and household goods, women played a central role in the non-consumption movement. In Boston

Daughters of Liberty

more than three hundred matrons publicly promised not to buy or drink tea, "Sickness excepted." The women of Wilmington, North Carolina, burned their tea after walking through town in a solemn procession. Women throughout the colonies exchanged recipes for tea substitutes or drank coffee instead. The best known of the protests, the so-called Edenton Ladies Tea Party, actually had little to do with tea. It was a meeting of prominent North Carolina women who pledged formally to work for the public good and to support resistance to British measures.

Women also encouraged home manufacturing. In many towns, young women calling themselves Daughters of Liberty met to spin in public in an effort to persuade other women to make homespun, thereby ending the colonies' dependence on British cloth. These symbolic displays of patriotism—publicized by newspapers and broadsides—served the same purpose as the male rituals involving the numbers 45 and 92. When young ladies from well-to-do families sat publicly at spinning wheels all day, eating only American food and drinking local herbal tea, and later listening to patriotic sermons, they were serving as political instructors. Many women took great satisfaction in their newfound role. When a New England satirist hinted that women discussed only "such triffling subjects as Dress, Scandal and Detraction" during their spinning bees, three Boston women replied angrily: "Inferior in abusive sarcasm, in personal invective, in low wit, we glory to be, but inferior in veracity, sincerity, love of virtue, of liberty and of our country, we would not willingly be to any."

But the colonists were by no means united in support of nonimportation and nonconsumption. If the Stamp Act protests had occasionally

Divided Opinion over Boycotts

(as in Boston and Philadelphia) revealed a division between artisans and merchants on the one side and common laborers on the other, resistance to the Townshend Acts exposed new splits in American ranks. The most significant—which arose from a change in economic circumstances—divided urban artisans and merchants, allies in 1765 and 1766.

The Stamp Act boycotts had helped to revive a depressed economy by creating a demand for local products and reducing merchants' inventories. But in 1768 and 1769, merchants were enjoying boom times and had no financial incentive to support a boycott. As a result, merchants signed the agreements only reluctantly, sometimes violating them secretly. In contrast, artisans supported nonimportation enthusiastically, recognizing that the absence of British goods would create a ready market for their own manufactures. Thus tradesmen formed the core of the crowds that coerced both importers and their customers by picketing stores, publicizing offenders' names, and sometimes destroying property.

Such tactics were effective: colonial imports from England dropped dramatically in 1769, especially in New York, New England, and Pennsylvania. But they also aroused heated opposition, creating a second major division among the colonists. Some Americans who supported resistance to British measures began to question the use of violence to force others to join the boycott. In addition, wealthier and more conservative colonists were frightened by the threat to private property inherent in the campaign. Political activism by ordinary colonists challenged the ruling elite's domination, just as its members had feared in 1765.

Disclosures that leading merchants had violated the nonimportation agreement caused dissension in the ranks of the boycotters, so Americans were relieved when news arrived in April 1770 that the Townshend duties had been repealed, with the exception of the tea tax. A new prime minister, Lord North, persuaded Parliament that duties on trade within the empire were ill-advised. Although some colonial leaders argued that nonimportation should continue until the tea tax was repealed, merchants quickly resumed importing. The rest of the Townshend Acts remained in force, but repealing the duties made the other provisions (establishing vice-admiralty courts and the American Board of Customs Commissioners, and promising to pay officials' salaries from customs revenues at some time in the future) appear less objectionable.

Repeal of the Townshend Duties

Confrontations in Boston

At first the new ministry in London did nothing to antagonize the colonists. Yet on the very day Lord North proposed repeal of the Townshend duties, a confrontation between civilians and soldiers in Boston led to the death of five Americans. The origins of the event that patriots called the Boston Massacre lay in repeated clashes between customs officers and the people of Massachusetts. The decision to base the American Board of Customs Commissioners in Boston was the source of the problem.

Mobs targeted the customs commissioners from the day they arrived in November 1767. In June 1768 their seizure of the patriot leader John Hancock's sloop *Liberty* on suspicion of smuggling caused a riot in which prominent customs officers' property was destroyed. The riot in turn helped to convince the ministry in London that troops were needed to maintain order in the unruly port. The assignment of two regiments of regulars to their city confirmed Bostonians' worst fears; the redcoats constantly reminded city dwellers of the oppressive potential of British power. Guards on Boston Neck, the entrance to the city, checked all travelers and their goods. Redcoat patrols

A 1769 Boston broadside commended the spinners, "Rich and Poor," who had "Compassion for their Country" and promoted "Frugality" during the Townshend Act crisis. The poet put into verse precisely the message the spinners intended to convey.   (Massachusetts Historical Society)

roamed the city day and night, questioning and sometimes harassing passersby. Military parades were held on Boston Common, accompanied by martial music and often the public whipping of deserters and other violators of army rules. Parents began to fear for the safety of their daughters, who were subjected to soldiers' coarse sexual insults. But the greatest potential for violence lay in the uneasy relationship between the soldiers and Boston laborers. Many redcoats sought employment in their off-duty hours, competing for unskilled jobs with the city's ordinary workingmen. Members of the two groups brawled repeatedly in taverns and on the streets.

Early on the evening of March 5, 1770, a crowd of laborers began throwing hard-packed snowballs at soldiers guarding the Customs House.

Boston Massacre

Goaded beyond endurance, the sentries acted against express orders to the contrary and fired on the crowd, killing four and wounding eight, one of whom died a few days later. Resistance leaders idealized the dead rioters as martyrs for the cause of liberty, holding a solemn funeral and later commemorating March 5 annually with patriotic orations. Paul Revere's engraving of the massacre (based on a drawing by John Singleton Copley's half-brother Henry Pelham and reproduced on page 135) was part of the propaganda campaign.

Leading patriots wanted to ensure that the soldiers did not become martyrs as well. Despite the political benefits the patriots derived from the massacre, they probably did not approve the crowd action that provoked it. Ever since the destruction of Hutchinson's house in August 1765, men allied with the Sons of Liberty had supported orderly demonstrations and expressed distaste for uncontrolled riots, of which the Boston Massacre was a prime example. Thus when the soldiers were tried for the killings in November, John Adams and Josiah Quincy, Jr., both unwavering patriots, acted as their defense attorneys. All but two of the accused men were acquitted, and those convicted were released after being branded on the thumb. Undoubtedly the favorable outcome of the trials prevented London officials from taking further steps against the city.

For more than two years after the Boston Massacre and the repeal of the Townshend duties, a superficial calm descended on the colonies.

A British Plot?

The most outspoken colonial newspapers, such as the *Boston Gazette*, the *Pennsylvania Journal*, and the *South Carolina Gazette*, published essays drawing on Real Whig ideology and accusing Great Britain of deliberately scheming to oppress the colonies. After the Stamp Act's repeal, the patriots had praised Parliament; following repeal of the Townshend duties, they warned of impending tyranny. What had seemed to be an isolated mistake, a single ill-chosen stamp tax, now appeared to be part of a plot against American liberties. Essayists pointed to Parliament's persecution of the British radical John Wilkes, the stationing of troops in Boston, and the growing number of vice-admiralty courts as evidence of plans to enslave the colonists. Indeed, patriot writers played repeatedly on the word *enslavement*. Most white colonists had direct knowledge of slavery (either as slaveholders themselves or as neighbors of slaveowners), and the threat of enslavement by Britain must have hit them with peculiar force.

Still, no one yet advocated complete independence from the mother country. Although the patriots were becoming increasingly convinced that they should seek freedom from parliamentary authority, they continued to acknowledge their British identity and their allegiance to George III. They began, therefore, to envision a system that would enable them to be ruled by their own elected legislatures while remaining loyal to the king. But any such scheme violated Britons' conception of the nature of their government, which posited that Parliament wielded sole undivided sovereignty over the empire. Furthermore, in the British mind, Parliament encompassed the king as well as lords and commons, so separating the monarch from the legislature was impossible.

Then, in the fall of 1772, the North ministry began to implement the Townshend Act that provided for governors and judges to be paid from customs revenues. In early November, voters at a Boston town meeting established a Committee of Correspondence to publicize the decision by exchanging letters with other Massachusetts towns. Heading the committee was the man who had proposed its formation, Samuel Adams.

Fifty-one in 1772, Samuel Adams was thirteen years older than his distant cousin John and by a decade the senior of most other leaders of American resistance. He had

Samuel Adams

been a Boston tax collector, a member and clerk of the Massachusetts assembly, an ally of the Loyal Nine, and a member of the Sons of Liberty. His primary forum was the Boston town meeting. Unswerving in his devotion to the American cause, Adams drew a sharp contrast between a corrupt, vice-ridden Britain and the colonies, peopled by simple, liberty-loving folk. An experienced political organizer, Adams continually stressed the necessity of prudent collective action. His Committee of Correspondence thus undertook the task of creating an informed consensus among all the residents of Massachusetts.

How do historians know...

that ordinary people became familiar with the ideas propounded by the leaders of the American Revolution?

This is a difficult question to answer because most of the evidence about the patriots' ideology comes from pamphlets and newspapers aimed at the well-educated. People who could read at only a basic level might not have been able to understand the sophisticated criticisms of British policies advanced in such writings. But because an engraver made his point visually rather than verbally, anyone, even illiterate folk, could interpret an image such as Paul Re-

vere's masterful portrayal of the Boston Massacre. The label "Butcher's Hall" on the Customs House merely reinforces the patriot view of the incident on March 5, 1770. The British soldiers are shown firing on an unresisting crowd, not the aggressive, angry mob described at the soldiers' trial. Even worse, a gun with smoke drifting up from its barrel emerges from a window above the redcoats, suggesting the complicity of civilian officials in what the patriots interpreted as an outrageous act. (Photo: Courtesy of the John Carter Brown Library, Brown University)

Such committees, which were eventually established throughout the colonies, represented the next logical step in the organization of American resistance. Until 1772, the protest movement was largely confined to the seacoast and primarily to major cities and towns (see Map 5.3).

Boston Committee of Correspondence

Adams realized that the time had come to widen the movement's geographic scope, to attempt to involve the residents of the interior in the struggle. Accordingly, the Boston town meeting directed the Committee of Correspondence "to state the Rights of the Colonists and of this Province in particular," to list "the Infringements and Violations thereof that have been, or from time to time may be made," and to send copies to the other towns in the province. In return, Boston requested "a free communication of their Sentiments on this Subject."

The statement of colonial rights prepared by the Bostonians declared that Americans had absolute rights to life, liberty, and property. The idea that "a British house of commons, should have a right, at pleasure, to give and grant the property of the colonists" was "irreconcileable" with "the first principles of natural law and Justice . . . and of the British Constitution in particular." The list of grievances complained of taxation without representation, the presence of unnecessary troops and customs officers on American soil, the use of imperial revenues to pay colonial officials, the expanded jurisdiction of vice-admiralty courts, and even the nature of the instructions given to American governors by their superiors in London.

The entire document, which was printed as a pamphlet for distribution to the towns, exhibited none of the hesitation that had characterized colonial claims against Parliament in the 1760s. No longer were patriots—at least in Boston—preoccupied with defining the precise limits of parliamentary authority. No longer did they mention the necessity of obedience to Parliament. They were committed to a course that placed American rights first, loyalty to Great Britain a distant second.

The response of the Massachusetts towns to the committee's pamphlet must have caused Samuel Adams to rejoice. Some towns disagreed with Boston's assessment of the state of affairs, but most aligned themselves with the city. From Braintree came the assertion that "all civil officers are or ought to be Servants to the people and dependent upon them for their official Support, and every instance to the Contrary from the Governor downwards tends to crush and destroy civil liberty." The town of Holden declared that "the People of New England have never given the People of Britain any Right of Jurisdiction over us." The citizens of Petersham commented that resistance to tyranny was "the first and highest social Duty of this people." And Pownallborough warned, "Allegiance is a relative Term and like Kingdoms and commonwealths is local and has its bounds." Beliefs like these made the next crisis in Anglo-American affairs the final one.

Tea and Turmoil

The tea tax was the only Townshend duty still in effect by 1773. In the years after 1770, some Americans continued to boycott English tea, while others resumed drinking it either openly or in secret. As was explained in Chapter 4, tea figured prominently in both the colonists' diet and their social lives, so observing the boycott required them not only to forgo a favorite beverage but also to alter habitual forms of socializing. Tea thus retained an explosively symbolic character even though the boycott began to fall apart after 1770.

In May 1773, Parliament passed an act designed to save the East India Company from bankruptcy.

Tea Act

The company, which held a monopoly on British trade with the East Indies, was critically important to the British economy (and to the financial well-being of many prominent British politicians who had invested in its stock). According to the Tea Act, legal tea would henceforth be sold in America only by the East India Company's designated agents, which would enable the company to avoid middlemen in both England and the colonies and to price its tea competitively with that offered by smugglers. The net result would be cheaper tea for American consumers. Resistance leaders, however, interpreted the new measure as a pernicious device to make them admit Parliament's right to tax them, for the less-expensive tea would still be taxed under the Townshend law. Others saw the Tea Act as the first step in the establishment of an East India Company monopoly of all colonial trade. Residents of the four cities designated to receive the first shipments of tea accordingly prepared to respond to what they perceived as a new threat to their freedom.

In New York City, the tea ships failed to arrive on schedule. In Philadelphia, the governor of Pennsylvania persuaded the captain to turn around and sail back to Britain. In Charleston, the tea was unloaded and stored; some was destroyed, the rest sold in 1776 by the new state government. The only confrontation occurred in Boston, where both sides—the town meeting, joined by participants from nearby towns, and Governor Thomas Hutchinson, two of whose sons were tea agents—rejected compromise.

The first of three tea ships, the *Dartmouth*, entered Boston harbor on November 28. The customs

The Boston Tea Party

laws required cargo to be landed and the appropriate duty paid by its owners within twenty days of a ship's arrival; otherwise, the cargo had to be seized by customs officers and sold at auction. After a series of mass meetings, Bostonians voted to post guards on the wharf to prevent the tea from being unloaded. Hutchinson refused to permit the vessels to leave the harbor. John Singleton Copley, whose father-in-law was a tea agent, tried to mediate the dispute.

On December 16, one day before the cargo would have been confiscated, more than five thousand people (nearly a third of the city's population) crowded into Old South Church. The meeting, chaired by Samuel Adams, made a final attempt to persuade Hutchinson to send the tea back to England. But the governor remained adamant. In the early evening Adams reportedly announced "that he could think of nothing further to be done—that they had now done all they could for the Salvation of their Country." Cries then rang out from the back of the crowd: "Boston harbor a tea-pot tonight! The Mohawks are come!" Small groups pushed their way out of the meeting. Within a few minutes, about sixty men crudely disguised as Indians assembled at the wharf, boarded the three ships, and dumped the cargo into the harbor. By 9 P.M. their work was done: 342 chests of tea worth approximately £10,000 floated in splinters on the water.

Among the "Indians" were many representatives of Boston's artisans, including the silversmith Paul Revere. Five masons, eleven carpenters and builders, three leatherworkers, a blacksmith, two barbers, a coachmaker, a shoemaker, and twelve apprentices have been identified as participants. That their ranks also included four farmers from outside Boston, ten merchants, two doctors, a teacher, and a bookseller illustrated the widespread support for the resistance

Thomas Hutchinson, the governor of Massachusetts, helped to incite the Boston Tea Party by refusing to allow the tea ships to leave the harbor. This portrait conveys the governor's haughty demeanor. (Massachusetts Historical Society)

movement. The next day John Adams exulted in his diary that the Tea Party was "so bold, so daring, so firm, intrepid and inflexible" that "I cant but consider it as an Epocha in history."

The North administration reacted with considerably less enthusiasm when it learned of the Tea Party.

Coercive and Quebec Acts

In March 1774, Parliament adopted the first of four laws that became known as the Coercive, or Intolerable, Acts. It ordered the port of Boston closed until the tea was paid for, prohibiting all but coastal trade in food and firewood. Later in the spring, Parliament passed three other punitive measures. The Massachusetts Government Act altered the province's charter, substituting an appointed council for the elected one, increasing the governor's powers, and forbidding most town meetings. The Justice Act provided that a person accused of committing murder in the course of suppressing a riot or enforcing the laws could be tried outside the colony where the incident had occurred. Finally, the Quartering Act allowed military officers to commandeer privately owned buildings to house their troops. Thus the Coercive Acts punished not only Boston but also Massachusetts as a whole, alerting other colonies to the possibility that their residents, too, could be subject to retaliation if they opposed British authority.

After passing the last of the Coercive Acts, Parliament turned its attention to much-needed reforms in the government of Quebec. The Quebec Act thereby became linked with the Coercive Acts in the minds of the patriots. Intended to ease strains that had arisen since the British conquest of the formerly French colony, the Quebec Act granted greater religious freedom to Catholics—alarming Protestant colonists, who equated Roman Catholicism with religious and political despotism. It also reinstated French civil law, which had been replaced by British procedures in 1763, and it established an appointed council (rather than an elected legislature) as the governing body of the colony. Finally, in an attempt to provide northern Indians with some protection against Anglo-American settlement, the act annexed to Quebec the area east of the Mississippi River and north of the Ohio River. That region, parts of which were claimed by individual seacoast colonies, was thus removed from their jurisdiction.

Members of Parliament who voted for the punitive legislation believed that the acts would be obeyed and that at long last they had solved the problem posed by the troublesome Americans. But the patriots showed little inclination to bow to the wishes of Parliament. In their eyes, the Coercive Acts and the Quebec Act proved what they had feared since 1768: that Great Britain had embarked on a deliberate plan to oppress them. If the port of Boston could be closed, why not the ports of Philadelphia or New York? If the royal charter of Massachusetts could be changed, why not the charter of South Carolina? If certain people could be transferred to distant colonies for trial, why not any violator of any law? If troops could be forcibly quartered in private houses, did not that action pave the way for the occupation of all of America? If the Roman Catholic Church could receive favored status in Quebec, why not everywhere? It seemed as though the full dimensions of the plot against American rights and liberties had at last been revealed.

Implications of the Coercive Acts

The Boston Committee of Correspondence urged all the colonies to join in an immediate boycott of British goods. But the other provinces hesitated to take such a drastic step. Rhode Island, Virginia, and Pennsylvania each suggested that another intercolonial congress be convened to consider an appropriate response, and in mid-June 1774 Massachusetts acquiesced. Few people wanted to take hasty action; even the most ardent patriots remained loyal to Britain and hoped for reconciliation with its leaders. Despite their objections to British policy, they continued to see themselves as part of the empire. Americans were approaching the brink of confrontation, but they had not committed themselves to an irrevocable break. So the colonies agreed to send delegates to Philadelphia in September to attend a Continental Congress.

Summary

 Just twenty years earlier, at the outbreak of the Seven Years War in the wilderness of western Pennsylvania, no one could have predicted that the future would bring such swift and dramatic change to Britain's mainland colonies. Yet that conflict—which simultaneously removed France from North America and created a huge war debt Britain had to find ways to pay—set in motion the process leading to the convening of the First Continental Congress.

In the years after the war ended in 1763, momentous changes occurred in the ways colonists thought about themselves and their allegiances. The number of colonists who defined themselves as political actors increased substantially. Once linked unquestioningly to Great Britain, they began to develop a sense of their own identity as Americans, including a recognition of the cultural and social gulf that separated them from Britons. They started to realize that their concept of the political process differed from that held by people in the mother country. They also came to understand that their economic interests did not necessarily coincide with those of Great Britain. Colonial political leaders reached such conclusions only after a long train of events, some of them violent, altered their understanding of their relationship with the mother country. Parliamentary acts such as the Stamp Act and the Townshend Acts elicited colonial responses—both ideological and practical—that produced further responses from Britain. Tensions escalated until they climaxed in the Tea Party. From that point on, there was to be no turning back.

In the late summer of 1774, the Americans were committed to resistance but not to independence. Even so, they had started to sever the bonds of empire. During the next decade, they would forge the bonds of a new American nationality to replace those rejected Anglo-American ties.

LEGACY FOR A PEOPLE AND A NATION
The Census and Reapportionment

When in the prerevolutionary years American colonists argued that "they were not represented in" Parliament, they developed a definition of *representation* very different from the understanding traditionally accepted in Great Britain. There, numbers did not matter: the entire British population was seen as being "virtually" represented in Parliament, regardless of how many men had the vote or how many electors lived in each district. In eighteenth-century Britain, some districts had few or no voters, some had many, and some heavily populated areas could vote for no one, because Parliament had not been reapportioned for centuries.

Americans, by contrast, placed great emphasis on the importance of being represented in government by someone for whom they—or at least their better-off male neighbors—had actually voted. And that carried with it the related desire for election districts that were regularly reapportioned in accordance with the movements and increase of the population; otherwise the goal of actual representation could not be ensured. Article 1, Section 2, of the U.S. Constitution thus provides for an "actual enumeration" of the nation's residents every ten years so that "representatives and direct taxes shall be apportioned among the several States . . . according to their respective numbers." Only once, in the 1790s, did Congress levy direct taxes, so the chief effect of this clause has been its requirement for a decennial census. Each decade, from 1790 to 2000, the government has tried to count the nation's residents accurately—although, according to historians and demographers, it has often failed to achieve that goal. Even Thomas Jefferson, who as secretary of state oversaw the first census in 1790, recognized that it undercounted the population and should be adjusted upward.

The planning for the year 2000 census led to heated debates in Congress and to a Supreme Court decision outlining appropriate techniques for conducting the mandated "actual enumeration" of the American population. In other years as well (especially 1920, near the close of an era of dramatic demographic change), planning and conducting the census proved extremely contentious. The origin of such contests lies in Americans' prerevolutionary experience, for the clause the Founding Fathers incorporated into the Constitution stemmed from ideological battles of the 1760s.

Thus every ten years the nation must still wrestle with an enduring legacy of the colonial period: the need to enumerate the American people and to alter the boundaries of electoral districts according to the results.

For Further Reading, see page A-6 of the Appendix. For Web resources, go to http://college.hmco.com.

The Shawnee chief Blackfish named his new captive Sheltowee, or Big Turtle, and adopted him as his son. Blackfish's warriors had easily caught the lone hunter, who was returning with a slaughtered buffalo to an encampment of men making salt at the briny spring known as Blue Licks. The captive then persuaded his fellow frontiersmen to surrender to the Shawnees (who were allied to the British) without a fight. It was February 1778. The hunter was Daniel Boone, who less than three years earlier had moved his family from North Carolina to the western region of Virginia known as Kentucke. Both his contemporaries and some historians have wondered about Boone's allegiance during the American Revolution, for he moved to the frontier just as the war began. His encounter with the Shawnees in 1778, which can be interpreted in several ways, highlights many of the ambiguities of revolutionary-era loyalties.

The Shawnees were seeking captives to cover the death (see page 104) of their chief Cornstalk, who had been killed several months earlier while a prisoner of American militiamen in the Ohio country. Of the twenty-six men taken at the spring, about half were adopted into Shawnee families; the others—less willing to conform to Indian ways—were dispatched as prisoners to the British fort at Detroit. Boone, who assured Blackfish that in the spring he would negotiate the surrender of the women and children remaining at his home settlement of Boonesborough, watched and waited, outwardly content with his new life. In June 1778 he escaped, hurrying home to warn the Kentuckians of impending attack.

When Blackfish's Shawnees and their British allies appeared outside the Boonesborough stockade in mid-September, Boone proved amenable to negotiations. Although the settlers adamantly refused to move back across the mountains, fragmentary evidence suggests that they agreed to swear allegiance to the British in order to avert a bloody battle. But the discussions dissolved into a melee and the Indians then futilely

A REVOLUTION, INDEED 1774–1783

A statue of George III standing in the Bowling Green in New York City was one of the first casualties of the American Revolution, as colonists marked the adoption of the Declaration of Independence by pulling it down. Much of the metal was melted to make bullets, but in the twentieth century the head—largely intact—was unearthed in Connecticut. (Lafayette College Art Collection, Easton, Pennsylvania)

besieged the fort for a week before withdrawing. With that threat gone, Boone was charged with treason and court-martialed by Kentucky militia. Although he was cleared, questions about the incident at Blue Licks and its aftermath haunted him for the rest of his life.

Where did Daniel Boone's loyalties lie? To the British? to the Americans? to other Kentuckians? His actions could be viewed in all three lights. Had he betrayed the settlers to Shawnees and sought to establish British authority in Kentucky? Had he—as he later claimed—twice deceived the Shawnees? Or had he rather made the survival of the fragile settlements his highest priority? Kentucky was a borderland—a region where British, Indians, and various groups of American settlers all vied for control. Boone and other residents of the Appalachian backcountry did not always face clear-cut choices as they struggled to establish themselves securely under such precarious circumstances.

Daniel Boone was not the only American of uncertain or shifting allegiance in the 1770s. As a civil war that affected much of North America east of the Mississippi River, the American Revolution uprooted thousands of families, disrupted the economy, reshaped society by forcing many colonists into permanent exile, led Americans to develop new conceptions of politics, and created a nation from thirteen separate colonies. Much more than a series of clashes between the British and patriot armies, it marked a significant turning point in Americans' collective history.

The struggle for independence required revolutionary leaders to accomplish three separate but closely related tasks. The first was political and ideological: transforming a consensus favoring loyal resistance into a coalition supporting independence. Pursuing a variety of measures (ranging from persuasion to coercion) to enlist all European Americans in the patriot cause, the colonies' elected leaders also tried to ensure the neutrality of Indians and slaves in the impending conflict.

The second task involved foreign relations. To win independence, patriot leaders knew they needed international recognition and aid, particularly from France. Thus they dispatched to Paris the most experienced American diplomat, Benjamin Franklin, who had served for years as a colonial agent in London. Franklin skillfully negotiated the Franco-American alliance of 1778, which was to prove crucial to winning independence.

Only the third task directly involved the British. George Washington, commander-in-chief of the American army, soon recognized that his primary goal should be not to win battles but to avoid losing them decisively. The outcome of any one battle was less important than ensuring that his army survived to fight another day. Consequently, the story of the Revolutionary War reveals British action and American reaction, British attacks and American defenses and withdrawals. The American war effort was aided by the failure of British military planners to analyze accurately the problem confronting them. Until it was too late, they treated the war against the colonists as they treated wars against other Europeans: they concentrated on winning battles and did not consider the difficulties of achieving their main goal, retaining the colonies' allegiance. In the end, the Americans' triumph owed more to their own endurance and to Britain's mistakes than to their military prowess. ■

Government by Congress and Committee

 When the fifty-five delegates to the First Continental Congress convened in Philadelphia in September 1774, they knew that any measures they adopted were likely to enjoy support among many of their fellow countrymen and countrywomen. That summer, open meetings held throughout the colonies had endorsed the idea of another nonimportation pact. Participants in such meetings promised (in the words of the freeholders of Johnston County, North Carolina) to "strictly adhere to, and abide by, such Regulations and Restrictions as the Members of the said General Congress shall agree to and judge most convenient." Committees of correspondence publicized these meetings so effectively that Americans everywhere knew about them. Most of the congressional delegates were selected by extralegal provincial conventions whose members were chosen at local gatherings, since governors had forbidden regular assemblies to conduct formal elections. Thus the very act of designating delegates to attend the Congress involved Americans in open defiance of British authority.

The colonies' leading political figures—most of them lawyers, merchants, and planters representing every colony but Georgia—attended the Philadelphia Congress. The Massachusetts delegation included both Samuel Adams, the experienced organizer of Boston resistance, and

First Continental Congress

IMPORTANT EVENTS

1774 First Continental Congress meets in Philadelphia, adopts Declaration of Rights and Grievances
Continental Association implements economic boycott of Britain; committees of observation established to oversee boycott

1774–75 Provincial conventions replace collapsing colonial governments

1775 Battles of Lexington and Concord; first shots of war fired
Second Continental Congress begins
Dunmore's proclamation offers freedom to patriots' slaves who join British forces

1776 Paine publishes *Common Sense*, advocating independence

British evacuate Boston
Declaration of Independence adopted
New York City falls to British

1777 British take Philadelphia Burgoyne surrenders at Saratoga

1778 French alliance brings vital assistance to the United States British evacuate Philadelphia

1779 Sullivan expedition destroys Iroquois villages

1780 British take Charleston

1781 Cornwallis surrenders at Yorktown

1782 Peace negotiations begin

1783 Treaty of Paris signed, granting independence to the United States

his younger cousin John, an ambitious lawyer. Among others, New York sent John Jay, a talented young attorney. From Pennsylvania came the conservative Joseph Galloway and his long-time rival, John Dickinson. Virginia elected Richard Henry Lee and Patrick Henry, both noted for their patriotic zeal, as well as George Washington. Most of these men had never met, but in the weeks, months, and years that followed they became the chief architects of the new nation.

The congressmen faced three tasks when they convened at Carpenters Hall on September 5, 1774. The first two were explicit: defining American grievances and developing a plan for resistance. The third—articulating their constitutional relationship with Great Britain—was less clear-cut and proved troublesome. The most radical congressmen, like Lee of Virginia, argued that colonists owed allegiance only to George III and that Parliament was nothing more than a local legislature for Great Britain with no authority over the colonies. The conservatives—Joseph Galloway and his allies—proposed a formal plan of union that would have required Parliament and a new American legislature to consent jointly to all laws pertaining to the colonies. After heated debate, delegates narrowly rejected Galloway's proposal, but they were not prepared to embrace the radicals' position either.

Finally, they accepted a compromise position worked out by John Adams. The crucial clause that Adams drafted in the Congress's Declaration of Rights and Grievances read in part: "From the necessity of the case, and a regard to the mutual interest of both countries, we cheerfully consent to the operation of such acts of the British parliament, as are bona fide, restrained to the regulation of our external commerce." Notice the key phrases. "From the necessity of the case" declared that Americans would obey Parliament only because they thought that doing so was in the best interest of both countries. "Bona fide, restrained to the regulation of our external commerce" made it clear to Lord North that they would continue to resist taxes in disguise, like the Townshend duties. Most striking of all was that such language—which only a few years before would have been regarded as irredeemably extreme—could be presented and accepted as a compromise in the fall of 1774. The Americans had come a long way since their first hesitant protests against the Sugar Act ten years earlier.

With the constitutional issue resolved, the delegates readily agreed on the laws they wanted repealed (notably the Coercive Acts) and decided to implement an economic boycott while petitioning the king for

Declaration of Rights and Grievances

In 1775 a British cartoonist demonstrated his contempt for the pronouncements of the Continental Congress by setting his satire in a privy, or "necessary house," and showing a politician who has used a torn congressional resolution as toilet paper. The person at right is poring over a political pamphlet while portraits of John Wilkes and a man who has been tarred and feathered decorate the walls.   (Library of Congress)

relief. They adopted the Continental Association, which called for nonimportation of British goods (effective December 1, 1774), nonconsumption of British products (effective March 1, 1775), and nonexportation of American goods to Britain and the British West Indies (effective September 10, 1775, so that southern planters could market their 1774 tobacco crop, which had to be dried and cured before sale).

To enforce the Continental Association, Congress recommended the election of committees of observation and inspection in every American locality. By specifying that committee members be chosen by all persons qualified to vote for members of the lower house of the colonial legislatures, Congress guaranteed the committees a broad popular base. In some places the committeemen were former local officeholders; in other towns they were men who had never before held office. Everywhere, these committeemen—perhaps seven to eight thousand of them in the colonies as a whole—became the local leaders of American resistance.

Committees of Observation

Such committees were officially charged only with overseeing implementation of the boycott, but over the next six months they became de facto governments. They examined merchants' records and published the names of those who continued to import British goods. They also promoted home manufactures, encouraging Americans to adopt simple modes of dress and behavior to symbolize their commitment to liberty and virtuous conduct. Since expensive leisure-time activities were believed to reflect vice and corruption, Congress urged Americans to forgo dancing, gambling, horseracing, cockfighting, and other forms of "extravagance and dissipation." Some committees extracted apologies from people caught gambling, partying, or racing, prohibited the slaughter of lambs (so that sheep could grow up to produce wool), and offered prizes for the best locally made cloth.

Thus the committees gradually extended their authority over many aspects of American life. They attempted to identify opponents of American resistance, developing elaborate spy networks, circulating copies of the Continental Association for signatures, and investigating reports of dissident remarks and activities. Suspected dissenters were first urged to support the colonial cause; if they failed to do so, the committees had them watched, restricted their movements, or tried to force them to leave the area. People engaging in casual political exchanges with friends one day could find themselves charged with "treasonable conversation" the next. One Massachusetts man, for example, was called before his local committee for maligning the Congress as "a Pack or Parcell of Fools" that was "as tyrannical as Lord North and ought to be opposed & resisted." When he refused to recant, the committee put him under surveillance.

Those who dissented more openly received harsher treatment, as the experiences of the Reverend John Agnew of Virginia demonstrate. Agnew, an Anglican, insisted on warning his congregation of "the danger and sin of rebellion." He rejected the committee's summons and was thereafter ostracized by its order. Millers would not grind his corn, and doctors would not treat his sick wife and children. The committee tried to intimidate him by sending armed men to his church to beat drums and drill during services. When that failed, patriots nailed shut the church's doors and windows. Finally Agnew and his oldest son fled, but the persecution of his wife and younger children continued. She was, she later recalled, "daily insulted and robbed . . . [and] searched under various pretense."

While the committees of observation were expanding their power during the winter and early spring of 1775, the regular colonial

Provincial Conventions

governments were collapsing. Only a few legislatures continued to meet without encountering patriot challenges to their authority. In most colonies, popularly elected provincial conventions took over the task of running the government, sometimes entirely replacing the legislatures and at other times holding concurrent sessions. In late 1774 and early 1775, these conventions approved the Continental Association, elected delegates to the Second Continental Congress (scheduled for May), organized militia units, and gathered arms and ammunition. Unable to stem the tide of resistance, the British-appointed governors and councils watched helplessly as their authority crumbled.

The frustrating experience of Governor Josiah Martin of North Carolina is a case in point. After a provincial convention was called to meet at New Bern on April 4, 1775—the same day the legislature was to convene—Martin asked all citizens to "renounce disclaim and discourage all such meetings cabals and illegal proceedings . . . which can only tend to introduce disorder and anarchy." When the convention met at New Bern, its membership proved to be virtually identical to that of the colonial legislature. The delegates proceeded to act alternately in both capacities and even passed some joint resolves. Continuing the farce, the exasperated Martin delivered a speech to the assembly denouncing the convention. Three days later, Martin wrote to officials in London, admitting that his government was "absolutely prostrate, impotent, and that nothing but the shadow of it is left."

Royal officials in other colonies suffered similar humiliations. Courts were prevented from holding sessions; taxes were paid to the conventions' agents rather than to provincial tax collectors; sheriffs' powers were challenged; and militiamen would muster only when committees ordered. In short, during the six months preceding the battles at Lexington and Concord, independence was being won at the local level, but without formal acknowledgment and for the most part without bloodshed. Not many Americans fully realized what was happening. The vast majority still proclaimed their loyalty to Great Britain, denying that they sought to leave the empire. Among the few who clearly recognized the trend toward independence were those who opposed it.

Choosing Sides: Loyalists, African Americans, and Indians

The first protests against British measures in the mid-1760s won the support of most colonists. Only in the late 1760s and early 1770s did a significant number of Americans begin to question both the aims and the tactics of the resistance movement. By 1774 and 1775 such people found themselves in a difficult position. Like their more radical counterparts, most of them objected to parliamentary policies, favoring some kind of constitutional reform. Joseph Galloway, for instance, was a conservative by American standards, but his plan for restructuring the empire was too novel for Britain to accept. Nevertheless, if forced to a choice, colonists like Galloway sympathized with Great Britain rather than with an independent America. The events of the crucial year between the passage of the Coercive Acts and the outbreak of fighting in Massachusetts crystallized their thinking. Their objections to violent protest, their desire to uphold legally constituted government, and their fears of anarchy combined to make them especially sensitive to the dangers of resistance.

Some conservatives thus began to publish essays and pamphlets critical of the Congress and its allied

Loyalists

committees. In New York City a group of Anglican clergymen publicly supported maintaining a cordial connection between Britain and America. In Pennsylvania, Joseph Galloway published *A Candid Examination of the Mutual Claims of Great Britain and the Colonies*, attacking the Continental Congress for rejecting his plan of union. In Massachusetts the young attorney Daniel Leonard, writing under the pseudonym Massachusettensis, engaged in a prolonged newspaper debate with Novanglus (John Adams). Leonard and others realized that what had begun as a dispute over the nature of American subordination to Parliament was now raising the question of whether the colonies would remain linked to Great Britain at all. "Rouse up at last from your slumber!" the Reverend Thomas Bradbury Chandler of New Jersey penned passionately. "There is a set of people among us . . . who have formed a scheme for establishing an independent government or empire in America."

John Singleton Copley married into a loyalist family. His father-in-law, Richard Clarke, was one of the Boston tea agents in 1773. Copley was in Italy studying art when the war began but joined his exiled wife and father-in-law in London in 1776. His sentimental portrait of the family (with himself in the background) commemorated their reunion. The only person in the painting who ever returned to America was his daughter Elizabeth *(center),* who grew up to marry a Bostonian. (Andrew W. Mellon Fund, © 1996 Board of Trustees, National Gallery of Art, Washington, D.C.)

Some colonists did heed the conservative pamphleteers' warnings. About one-fifth of the European American population remained loyal to Great Britain, firmly rejecting independence. Most loyalists had one thing in common: they had long opposed the men who became patriot leaders, though for varying reasons. British-appointed government officials; Anglican clergy everywhere and lay Anglicans in the North, where their denomination was in the minority; tenant farmers, particularly those whose landlords sided with the patriots; members of persecuted religious sects; many of the backcountry southerners who had rebelled against eastern rule in the late 1760s and early 1770s; and non-English ethnic minorities, especially Scots: all these groups feared the power wielded by those who controlled the colonial assemblies and who had shown little concern for their welfare in the past. Joined by merchants whose trade depended on imperial connections and by former officers and enlisted men from the British army who had settled in America after 1763, they formed a loyalist core that remained true to a self-conception that revolutionaries proved willing to abandon.

During the war, loyalists congregated in cities held by the British army. When those posts were evacuated at war's end, loyalists scattered to different parts of the British Empire—Britain, the West Indies, and especially Canada. In the provinces of Nova Scotia, New Brunswick, and Ontario they re-created their lives as colonists, laying the foundations of British Canada. All told, perhaps as many as 100,000 Americans preferred to leave their homeland rather than live in a nation independent of British rule.

Active revolutionaries, who accounted for about two-fifths of the population, came chiefly from the

Patriots and Neutrals

groups that had dominated colonial society, either numerically or politically. Among them were yeoman farmers, members of dominant Protestant sects (both Old and New Lights), Chesapeake gentry, merchants dealing mainly in American commodities, city artisans, elected officeholders, and people of English descent. Wives usually but not always adopted their husbands' political beliefs. Although all these patriots supported the Revolution, they pursued divergent goals within the broader coalition, as they had in the 1760s. Some sought limited political reform, others extensive political change, and still others social and economic reforms. (The ways in which their concerns interacted are discussed in Chapter 7.)

Between the patriots and the loyalists, there remained in the middle perhaps two-fifths of the European American population. Some of those who tried to avoid taking sides were sincere pacifists, such as Quakers. Others opportunistically shifted their allegiance to whatever side happened to be winning at the time. Still others simply wanted to be left alone; they cared little about politics and usually obeyed whoever was in power. Such colonists also resisted British and Americans alike when the demands on them seemed too heavy—when taxes became too high, for example, or when calls for militia service came too often. Their attitude might best be summed up in the phrase "a plague on both your houses." Such people made up an especially large proportion of the population in the southern backcountry (including Boone's Kentucky), where Scots-Irish settlers had little love for either the patriot gentry or the English authorities.

To patriots, apathy or neutrality was a crime as heinous as loyalism: those who were not for them were

Barzillai Lew, a free African American born in Groton, Massachusetts, in 1743, served in the Seven Years War before enlisting with patriot troops in the American Revolution. An accomplished fifer, Lew fought at the Battle of Bunker Hill. Like other freemen in the north, he cast his lot with the revolutionaries, in contrast to southern bondspeople, who tended to favor the British.   (Courtesy of Mae Theresa Bonitto)

surely against them. By the winter of 1775–1776, the Second Continental Congress was recommending that all "disaffected" persons be disarmed and arrested. State legislatures passed laws prescribing severe penalties for suspected loyalists or neutrals. Many began to require all voters (or, in some cases, all free adult men) to take oaths of allegiance; the penalty for refusal was usually banishment or extra taxes. After 1777 many states confiscated the property of banished persons, using the proceeds for the war effort.

The patriots' policies helped to ensure that their scattered and persecuted opponents could not band together to threaten the revolutionary cause. But loyalists and neutrals were not the patriots' only worry, for they also feared that Indians and slaves might join the forces arrayed against them. Early in the war, free blacks from New England enthusiastically enlisted in local patriot militias, but the revolutionaries could not assume that *enslaved* African Americans would also support the struggle for independence.

Bondspeople faced a dilemma at the beginning of the Revolution: how could they best pursue their goal of escaping slavery? Should they

The Slaves' Dilemma

fight with or against their masters? African Americans made different decisions, but to most slaves, supporting the British appeared more promising. Thus news of slave conspiracies surfaced in different parts of the colonies in late 1774 and early 1775. All shared a common element: a plan to assist the British army in return for freedom. One group of slaves futilely petitioned General Thomas Gage, the commander-in-chief of British forces in Boston, promising to fight for the redcoats if he would liberate them. The most serious incident occurred in 1775 in Charleston, where Thomas Jeremiah, a free black harbor pilot, was brutally executed after being convicted of attempting to foment a slave revolt.

Although the Caribbean islands too had protested British taxation in the 1760s (see Map 5.3 on page 129), sugar planters in the British West Indies were more cautious in opposing parliamentary policies than were residents of the mainland. On most of the Caribbean islands, slaves outnumbered their masters by six or seven to one. With the ever-present threat of slave revolt or foreign attack hanging over their heads, planters could not afford to risk opposing Britain, their chief protector. The Jamaica assembly agreed with the mainland colonial legislatures that citizens should not be bound by laws to which they had not consented. Nevertheless, its members assured the king in 1774 that "it cannot be supposed, that we now intend, or ever could have intended Resistance to Great Britain." They cited as reasons Jamaica's "weak and feeble" condition, "its very small number of white inhabitants, and . . . the incumbrance of more than Two hundred thousand Slaves."

Slavery affected politics on the mainland as well. In New England, with few resident slaves, revolutionary fervor reached a peak. In Virginia

Slavery and Revolutionary Fervor

and Maryland, where free people constituted a safe majority, the potential for slave revolts raised occasional but not disabling fears. By contrast, South Carolina and Georgia, where slaves composed more than half of the population, were no-

ticeably less enthusiastic about resistance. Georgia sent no delegates to the First Continental Congress and reminded its representatives at the second one to consider its circumstances, "with our blacks and tories [loyalists] within us," when voting on the question of independence.

The slaveowners' worst fears were realized in November 1775, when Lord Dunmore, the governor of Virginia, offered to free any slaves and indentured servants who would leave their patriot masters to join the British forces. Dunmore hoped to use African Americans in his fight against the revolutionaries and to disrupt the economy by depriving planters of their labor force. But at most only two thousand African Americans rallied to the British standard, and many of them perished in a smallpox epidemic. Even so, Dunmore's proclamation led Congress in January 1776 to modify an earlier policy that had prohibited the enlistment of African Americans in the regular American army.

Although slaves did not pose a serious threat to the revolutionary cause in its early years, the patriots turned rumors of slave uprisings to their own advantage. In South Carolina resistance leaders argued that unity under the Continental Association would protect masters from their slaves at a time when royal government was unable to muster adequate defense forces. Undoubtedly many wavering Carolinians were drawn into the revolutionary camp by fear that an overt division among the colony's free people would encourage rebellion among the bondspeople.

Similarly, the threat of Indian attacks helped persuade some reluctant westerners to support the struggle against Great Britain. In the years since the Proclamation of 1763, British officials had won the Indians' trust by attempting to protect them from land-hungry European Americans. The British-appointed superintendents of Indian affairs, John Stuart in the South and Sir William Johnson in the North, lived among and understood the Indians. In 1768 Stuart and Johnson negotiated separate agreements modifying the proclamation line and trying to draw realistic, defensible boundaries between tribal holdings and European American settlements. The treaties supposedly established permanent western borders for the colonies. But just a few years later, in 1770 and 1773, the British pushed the southern boundary even farther west to accommodate the demands of settlers in western Georgia and Kentucky.

By 1775 many Indian groups were provoked beyond endurance by such aggressive pressure on their lands. Bitterness, misunderstanding, and occasional

Indians' Grievances

bloody encounters characterized relationships on the frontier. Such grievances and the tribes' confidence in Stuart and Johnson predisposed most Indians toward an alliance with Great Britain. Even so, the latter hesitated to make full and immediate use of these potential allies. The superintendents knew that neither the Indians' style of fighting nor their war aims would necessarily be compatible with those of the British. Accordingly, Stuart and Guy Johnson (who became northern superintendent following his uncle's death) at first sought from native peoples only a promise of neutrality. The superintendents even helped to avert a general Indian uprising in the summer of 1774 by preventing the Shawnees from recruiting allies for attacks on Kentucky villages. Lord Dunmore's War, between the Shawnees and the Virginia militia, ended with Kentucky being opened to European American settlers such as Daniel Boone and his associates, but with hunting and fishing rights still reserved to the Shawnees.

Recognizing that their standing with native peoples was poor, the patriots also sought the Indians' neutrality. In 1775 the Second Continental Congress sent a general message to Indian communities describing the war as "a family quarrel between us and Old England" and requesting that they "not join on either side" since "you Indians are not concerned in it." A group of Cherokees led by Chief Dragging Canoe nevertheless decided that the "family quarrel" would allow them to settle some old scores. They attacked settlements along the western borders of the Carolinas and Virginia in the summer of 1776. But a militia campaign destroyed many of their towns, along with crops and large quantities of supplies. Dragging Canoe and his diehard followers fled to the west, establishing new outposts; the rest of the Cherokees agreed to a treaty that ceded still more of their land.

Bands of Shawnees and Cherokees continued to attack frontier settlements in Kentucky and elsewhere throughout the war, but dissent in their own ranks crippled their efforts.

Indians During the Revolution

The British victory over France in 1763 had destroyed the Indian nations' most effective means of maintaining their independence: their ability to play European powers off against one another. Successful strategies were difficult to envision under these new circumstances, and Indian leaders could no longer concur on a unified course of action. Communities split asunder as older and younger men, or civil and

In 1776 the American artist Benjamin West—based in London after the mid-1760s—painted Colonel Guy Johnson, the superintendent of Indian affairs for the northern district, while he was in London for consultations with British officials. In the background is the Iroquois chief Karonghyontye, also known as Captain David Hill. (Andrew W. Mellon Collection, © 1996 Board of Trustees, National Gallery of Art, Washington, D.C.)

war leaders, disagreed vehemently over what policy to adopt. Only a few communities (among them the Stockbridge Indians of New England and the Oneidas in New York) unwaveringly supported the American revolt; most other native villages either tried to remain neutral or at least partly aligned themselves with the British. Warfare between settlers and Indian bands allied with the British persisted on the frontier long after fighting between the main armies had ceased, and even after the signing of the peace treaty.

Although patriots could never completely ignore the threats posed by loyalists, neutrals, slaves, and Indians, only rarely did fear of these groups seriously hamper the revolutionary movement. Occasionally frontier militiamen refused to turn out for duty on the seacoast because they feared Indians would attack in their absence. Sometimes southern troops refused to serve in the North because they (and their political leaders) were unwilling to leave their regions unprotected against a slave insurrection. But the practical impossibility of a large-scale slave revolt, coupled with dissension in Indian communities and the patriots' successful campaign to disarm and neutralize loyalists, ensured that the revolutionaries would by and large remain firmly in control of the countryside as they fought for independence.

War and Independence

 On January 27, 1775, Lord Dartmouth, secretary of state for America, addressed a fateful letter to General Thomas Gage in Boston. Expressing his belief that American resistance was nothing more than the response of a "rude rabble without plan," Dartmouth urged Gage to take a decisive step. Opposition could not be "very formidable," Dartmouth wrote, and even if it were, "it will surely be better that the Conflict should be brought on, upon such ground, than in a riper state of Rebellion."

Battles of Lexington and Concord

Dartmouth's letter did not reach Gage until April 14. He responded by sending an expedition to confiscate provincial military supplies stockpiled at Concord. Bostonians dispatched two messengers, William Dawes and Paul Revere (later joined by Dr. Samuel Prescott), to rouse the countryside. So when the British vanguard of several hundred men approached Lexington at dawn on April 19, they found a ragtag group of seventy militiamen—about half of the adult male population of the town—drawn up before them on the common. The Americans' commander ordered his men to withdraw, realizing they could not halt the redcoats' advance. But as they began to disperse, a shot rang out; the British soldiers then fired several volleys. When they stopped, eight Americans lay dead and another ten had been wounded. The British moved on to Concord, 5 miles away.

There the contingents of militia were larger, Concord residents having been joined by groups of men from nearby towns. An exchange of gunfire at the North Bridge spilled the first British blood of the Revolution: three men were killed and nine wounded.

Thousands of militiamen then fired from houses and from behind trees and bushes at the British forces as they retreated to Boston. By the end of the day, the redcoats had suffered 272 casualties, including 70 deaths. Only the arrival of reinforcements and the American militia's lack of coordination prevented much heavier British losses. The patriots suffered just 93 casualties.

First Year of War

By the evening of April 20, perhaps as many as twenty thousand American militiamen had gathered around Boston, summoned by local committees that spread the alarm across the countryside. Many did not stay long since they were needed at home for spring planting, but those who remained dug in along siege lines encircling the city. For nearly a year the two armies sat and stared at each other across those lines. The redcoats attacked their besiegers only once, on June 17, when they drove the Americans from trenches atop Breed's Hill in Charlestown. In that misnamed Battle of Bunker Hill, the British incurred their greatest losses of the entire war: over 800 wounded and 228 killed. The Americans, though forced to abandon their position, lost less than half that number.

During the same eleven-month period, patriots captured Fort Ticonderoga, a British fort on Lake Champlain, acquiring much-needed cannon. Trying to bring Canada into the war on the American side, they also mounted an uncoordinated northern campaign that ended in disaster at Quebec in early 1776. But the chief significance of the war's first year lay in the long lull in fighting between the main armies at Boston. The delay gave both sides a chance to regroup, organize, and plan their strategies.

British Strategy

Lord North and his new American secretary, Lord George Germain, made three central assumptions about the war they faced. First, they concluded that patriot forces could not withstand the assaults of trained British regulars. They and their generals were convinced that the 1776 campaign would be the first and last of the war. Accordingly, they dispatched to America the largest force Great Britain had ever assembled anywhere: 370 transport ships carrying 32,000 troops and tons of supplies, accompanied by 73 naval vessels and 13,000 sailors. Such an extraordinary effort, they thought, would ensure a quick victory. Among the troops were thousands of German mercenaries (many from the German state of Hesse); eighteenth-century armies were often composed of

In 1775 an unknown artist painted the redcoats entering Concord. The fighting at North Bridge, which occurred just a few hours after this triumphal entry, signaled the start of open warfare between Britain and the colonies.   (Photography Courtesy of Concord Museum, Concord, Mass.)

such professional soldiers who hired out to the highest bidder.

Second, British officials and army officers treated this war as comparable to wars they had fought successfully in Europe. They adopted a conventional strategy of capturing major American cities and defeating the rebel army decisively without suffering serious casualties themselves. Third, they assumed that a clear-cut military victory would automatically bring about their goal of retaining the colonies' allegiance.

All these assumptions proved false. North and Germain, like Lord Dartmouth before them, vastly underestimated Americans' commitment to armed resistance. Battlefield defeats did not lead patriots to abandon their political aims and sue for peace. The ministers in London also failed to recognize the significance of the American population's dispersal over an area 1,500 miles long and more than 100 miles wide. Although Great Britain would control each of the most important American ports at one time or another during the war, less than 5 percent of the population lived in those cities. Furthermore, the coast offered so many excellent harbors that essential commerce was easily rerouted. In other words, the loss of cities did little to damage the American cause, while redcoat generals repeatedly squandered their resources to capture such ports.

Most of all, British officials did not at first understand that military triumph would not necessarily lead to political victory. Securing the colonies permanently

The plight of the redcoat soldiers besieged in Boston during the fall and winter of 1775–1776 attracted the sympathies of a British cartoonist. For "Six-Pence a Day," he noted, soldiers were exposed to "Yankees, Fire and Water, Sword and Famine," while their wives and children begged for assistance at home. The artist hoped to persuade men not to enlist in the British army.   (Courtesy of the British Museum, Department of Prints and Drawings, Satires)

would require hundreds of thousands of Americans to return to their original allegiance. The conquest of America was thus a far more complicated task than the defeat of France twelve years earlier. Great Britain needed not only to overpower the patriots but also to convert them. After 1778 the ministry adopted a strategy designed to achieve that goal through the expanded use of loyalist forces and the restoration of civilian authority in occupied areas. But the new policy came too late. Britain's leaders never fully realized that they were fighting not a conventional European war but rather an entirely new kind of conflict: the first modern war of national liberation.

Great Britain at least had a bureaucracy ready to supervise the war effort. The Americans had only the Second Continental Congress, originally planned as a brief gathering to consider the ministry's response to the Continental Association. Instead, the delegates who convened in Philadelphia on May 10, 1775, had to assume the man-

Second Continental Congress

tle of intercolonial government. "Such a vast Multitude of objects, civil, political, commercial and military, press and crowd upon us so fast, that we know not what to do first," John Adams wrote a close friend early in the session. Yet as the summer passed, Congress slowly organized the colonies for war. It authorized the printing of money with which to purchase necessary goods, established a committee to supervise relations with foreign countries, and took steps to strengthen the militia. Most important, it created the Continental Army and appointed its generals.

Until Congress met, the Massachusetts provincial congress had taken responsibility for organizing the militiamen encamped at Boston. But that army, composed of men from all over New England, constituted a heavy drain on limited local resources. Consequently, Massachusetts asked the Continental Congress to assume the task of directing the army. As a first step, Congress had to choose a commander-in-chief, and many delegates recognized the importance of naming someone who was not a New Englander. John

Adams later recalled that in mid-June he proposed the appointment of a Virginian "whose Skill and Experience as an Officer, whose independent fortune, great Talents and excellent universal Character, would command the Approbation of all America": George Washington. The Congress unanimously concurred.

Washington was no fiery radical, nor was he a reflective political thinker. He had not played a prominent role in the prerevolutionary agitation, but his devotion to the American cause was unquestioned. He was dignified, conservative, and respectable—a man of unimpeachable integrity. The younger son of a Virginia planter, Washington did not expect to inherit substantial property, planning to make his living as a surveyor. But the early death of his older brother and his marriage to the wealthy widow Martha Custis made George Washington one of the largest slaveholders in Virginia. Though unmistakably an aristocrat, he was unswervingly committed to representative government and—thanks to his service in the Seven Years War (see page 118)—he had considerable military experience. He had other desirable traits as well. His stamina was remarkable; in more than eight years of war, Washington never had a serious illness and took only one brief leave of absence. Moreover, he both looked and acted like a leader. More than six feet tall in an era when most men were five inches shorter, he displayed a stately and commanding presence. Other patriots praised his judgment, steadiness, and discretion, and even a loyalist admitted that Washington could "atone for many demerits by the extraordinary coolness and caution which distinguish his character."

George Washington: A Portrait of Leadership

Washington needed all the coolness and caution he could muster when he took command of the army outside Boston in July 1775. It took him months to impose hierarchy and discipline on the unruly troops and to bring order to the supply system. But by March 1776, when the arrival of cannon from Ticonderoga finally enabled him to put direct pressure on the redcoats in the city, the army was prepared to act. As it happened, an assault on Boston proved unnecessary. Sir William Howe, who had replaced Gage, had for some time been considering an evacuation; he wanted to transfer his troops to New York City. The patriots' new cannon decided the matter. On March 17, the British and more than a thousand of their loyalist allies abandoned Boston forever.

British Evacuation of Boston

That spring of 1776, as the British fleet left Boston for the temporary haven of Halifax, Nova Scotia, the colonies were moving inexorably toward the act the Massachusetts loyalists on board the British ships feared most: a declaration of independence. Even months after fighting began, American leaders still denied seeking a break with Great Britain. But in January 1776 there appeared a pamphlet by a man who advocated such a step.

Thomas Paine's *Common Sense* exploded on the American scene like a bombshell. Within three months of publication, it sold 120,000 copies. The author, a radical English printer who had lived in America only since 1774, called stridently for independence. Paine also challenged many

Thomas Paine's *Common Sense*

That America's patriot leaders read Thomas Paine's inflammatory *Common Sense* soon after it was published in early 1776 is indicated by this first edition, owned by George Washington himself. (Boston Athenaeum)

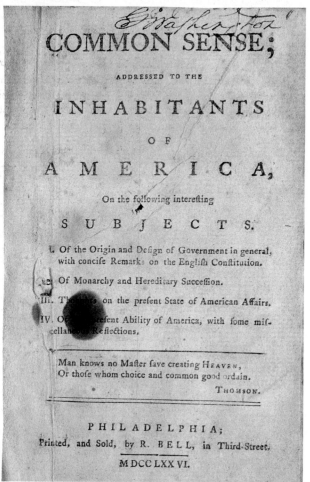

COMMON SENSE;

ADDRESSED TO THE

INHABITANTS

OF

AMERICA,

On the following interesting

SUBJECTS.

I. Of the Origin and Design of Government in general, with concise Remarks on the English Constitution.

II. Of Monarchy and Hereditary Succession.

III. Thoughts on the present State of American Affairs.

IV. Of the present Ability of America, with some miscellaneous Reflections.

Man knows no Master save creating HEAVEN,
Or those whom choice and common good ordain.
THOMSON.

PHILADELPHIA;

Printed, and Sold, by R. BELL, in Third-Street.

MDCCLXXVI.

common American assumptions about government and the colonies' relationship to Britain. Rejecting the notion that a balance of monarchy, aristocracy, and democracy was necessary to preserve freedom, he advocated the establishment of a republic, a government by the people with no king or nobility. Instead of acknowledging the benefits of links to the mother country, Paine insisted that Britain had exploited the colonies unmercifully. And for the frequently heard assertion that an independent America would be weak and divided, he substituted an unlimited confidence in America's strength once freed from European control.

He expressed these striking sentiments in equally striking prose. Scorning the rational style of most other pamphleteers, Paine adopted an enraged tone, describing the king as a "royal brute," a "wretch" who only pretended concern for the colonists' welfare. His pamphlet reflected the oral culture of ordinary folk. Couched in everyday language, it relied heavily on the Bible—the only book familiar to most Americans—as a primary source of authority. No wonder the pamphlet had a wider distribution than any other political publication of its day.

There is no way of knowing how many people were converted to the cause of independence by reading *Common Sense*. But by late spring in 1776 independence had become inevitable. On May 10, the Second Continental Congress formally recommended that individual colonies "adopt such governments as shall, in the opinion of the representatives of the people, best conduce to the happiness and safety of their constituents in particular, and America in general." From that source stemmed the first state constitutions. Perceiving the trend of events, the few loyalists still connected with Congress severed their ties to that body.

Then on June 7 came confirmation of the movement toward independence. Richard Henry Lee of Virginia, seconded by John Adams of Massachusetts, introduced the crucial resolution: "that these United Colonies are, and of right ought to be, free and independent States, that they are absolved of all allegiance to the British Crown, and that all political connection between them and the State of Great Britain is, and ought to be, totally dissolved." Congress debated but did not immediately adopt Lee's resolution. Instead, it postponed a vote until early July, to allow time for consultation and public reaction. In the meantime, a five-man committee—including Thomas Jefferson, John Adams, and Benjamin Franklin—was directed to draft a declaration of independence.

The committee assigned primary responsibility for writing the declaration to Jefferson, who was well known for his apt and eloquent style. Years later John Adams recalled that Jefferson had modestly protested his selection, suggesting that Adams prepare the initial draft. The Massachusetts revolutionary recorded his frank response: "You can write ten times better than I can."

The thirty-four-year-old Thomas Jefferson, a Virginia lawyer, had been educated at the College of William and Mary and in the law offices of a prominent attorney. A member of the House of Burgesses, he had read widely in history and political theory. That broad knowledge was evident not only in the declaration but also in his draft of the Virginia state constitution, completed just a few days before his appointment to the committee. Jefferson, an intensely private man, loved his home and family deeply. This early stage of his political career was marked by his beloved wife Martha's repeated difficulties in childbearing. While he wrote and debated in Philadelphia, she suffered a miscarriage at their home, Monticello. Not until after her death in 1782, from complications following the birth of their sixth (but only third surviving) child in ten years of marriage, did Jefferson fully commit himself to public service.

Thomas Jefferson and the Declaration of Independence

The draft of the declaration was laid before Congress on June 28, 1776. The delegates officially voted for independence four days later, then debated the wording of the declaration for two more days, adopting it with some changes on July 4. Since Americans had long ago ceased to see themselves as legitimate subjects of Parliament, the Declaration of Independence concentrated on George III (see the appendix). That focus also provided an identifiable villain. The document accused the king of attempting to destroy representative government in the colonies and of oppressing Americans through the unjustified use of excessive force.

The declaration's chief long-term importance, however, did not lie in its lengthy catalogue of grievances against George III (including, in a section deleted by Congress, Jefferson's charge that the British monarchy had introduced slavery into America). It lay instead in the ringing statements of principle that have served ever since as the ideal to which Americans aspire: "We hold these truths to be self-evident: That all men are created equal; that they are endowed by their

Creator with certain unalienable rights; that among these are life, liberty and the pursuit of happiness; that, to secure these rights, governments are instituted among men, deriving their just powers from the consent of the governed; that whenever any form of government becomes destructive of these ends, it is the right of the people to alter or to abolish it, and to institute new government." These phrases have echoed down through American history like no others.

The delegates in Philadelphia who voted to accept the Declaration of Independence did not have the advantage of our two centuries of hindsight. When they adopted the declaration, they risked their necks: they were committing treason. Therefore, when they concluded the declaration with the assertion that they "mutually pledge[d] to each other our lives, our fortunes, and our sacred honor," they spoke no less than the truth. The real struggle still lay before them, and not many of them had Thomas Paine's boundless confidence in success.

The Long Struggle in the North

In late June 1776, the first ships carrying Sir William Howe's troops from Halifax appeared off the coast of New York (see Map 6.1). On July 2, the day Congress voted for independence, redcoats landed on Staten Island. Washington marched his army of seventeen thousand south from Boston to defend Manhattan. Because Howe waited until more troops arrived from England before attacking, the American army was able to prepare to defend the city.

But Washington and his men, still inexperienced in fighting and maneuvering, made major mistakes,

Loss of New York

losing battles at Brooklyn Heights and on Manhattan Island. The city fell to the British, who captured nearly three thousand American soldiers. Those men spent most of the rest of the war imprisoned on British vessels anchored in New York harbor, where many died of disease.

During the autumn months, Washington retreated across New Jersey, with Howe in leisurely pursuit. The British took control of most of the state, and hundreds of New Jerseyites and Pennsylvanians (among them Joseph Galloway) accepted pardons for their "treasonous" activities. Occupying troops met little opposition, and the revolutionary cause appeared to be in disarray. "These are the times that try men's souls," wrote Thomas Paine in his pamphlet *The Cri-*

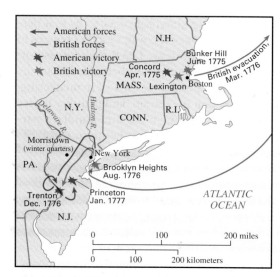

Map 6.1   The War in the North, 1775–1777
The early phase of the Revolutionary War was dominated by British troop movements in the Boston area, the redcoats' evacuation to Nova Scotia in the spring of 1776, and the subsequent British invasion of New York and New Jersey.

sis. "The summer soldier and the sunshine patriot will, in this crisis, shrink from the service of his country; . . . yet we have this consolation with us, that the harder the conflict, the more glorious the triumph."

The British let their advantage slip away as redcoats stationed in New Jersey went on a rampage of

Battles in New Jersey

rape and plunder. Because the invading troops failed to distinguish between loyalists and patriots, families on both sides suffered losses of livestock, crops, and firewood. Redcoats looted and burned houses and desecrated churches and public buildings. The murder and rape of innocent civilians alienated potentially loyal New Jerseyites whose allegiance the British could ill afford to lose. It also spurred Washington's determination to strike back. Moving quickly, he attacked a Hessian encampment at Trenton early in the morning of December 26, while the redcoats were still reeling from their Christmas celebration. The patriots captured more than nine hundred Hessians and killed another thirty; only three Americans were wounded. A few days later, Washington attacked again at Princeton. Having gained command of the field and buoyed American spirits with the two swift victories, Washington set up winter quarters at Morristown, New Jersey.

The 1776 campaign established patterns that persisted throughout much of the war, despite changes in British leadership and strategy. The British forces usually outnumbered and were often better led than the Americans. But their ponderous style of maneuvering, lack of familiarity with the terrain, and inability to live off the land without antagonizing the populace partially offset those advantages. Furthermore, although Washington always seemed to lack regular troops—the Continental Army never numbered more than 18,500 men—he could usually count on the militia to join him at crucial times. American militiamen preferred not to enlist for long terms of service or to fight far from home; but when their homes were threatened, they rallied to the cause. Washington and his officers complained about the militiamen's habit of disappearing during planting or harvesting. But time and again their presence, however brief, enabled the Americans to launch an attack or counter a strategic British thrust.

As the war dragged on, the Continental Army and the militia took on decidedly different characters.

The American Army

State governments, responsible for filling military quotas, discovered that most men willing to enlist for long periods in the regular army were young, single, and footloose. Farmers with families tended to prefer short-term militia duty. As the supply of men willing to join the Continentals dwindled, recruiters in northern states turned increasingly to African Americans, both slave and free. Approximately five thousand blacks eventually served in the army, most of them winning their freedom as a result. They commonly served in racially integrated units but were assigned tasks that others shunned, such as cooking, foraging for food, and driving wagons. Also attached to the American forces were a number of women, the wives and widows of poor soldiers. Such camp followers worked as cooks, nurses, and launderers in return for rations and low wages.

At the Battle of Princeton in early 1777, American forces under George Washington cemented the victory they had won a few days earlier at Trenton. This view was painted in 1787 by James Peale, who fought in the battle.   (Princeton University Library)

The presence of women, as well as militiamen who floated in and out of the American camp at irregular intervals, made for an unwieldy army that officers found difficult to manage. Yet the army's shapelessness also reflected its greatest strength: an almost unlimited reservoir of manpower and womanpower.

The officers of the Continental Army—those who enlisted for long periods or for the war's duration—developed an intense sense of pride and commitment to the revolutionary cause. The hardships they endured, the battles they fought, the difficulties they overcame all helped to forge an *esprit de corps* that outlasted the war. The realities of warfare were often dirty, messy, and corrupt, but the officers drew strength from a developing image of themselves as professionals who sacrificed personal gain for the good of the entire nation. When Benedict Arnold—an officer who fought heroically for the patriot cause early in the war—violated that virtuous self-image by defecting to the British, they made his name a metaphor for villainy. "How black, how despised, loved by none, and hated by all," wrote one patriot.

The flashy "Gentleman Johnny" Burgoyne, a playboy general as much at home at London's gaming tables as on the battlefield, planned the major British effort in 1777. A subordinate of Howe, Burgoyne spent the winter in London, where he gained the ear of Lord George Germain. Burgoyne convinced Germain that he could lead an invading force of redcoats and Indians down the Hudson River from Canada, cutting off New England from the rest of the states. He proposed to rendezvous near Albany with a similar force that would move east along the Mohawk River valley. The combined forces would then presumably link up with Sir William Howe's troops in New York City.

Planning the 1777 Campaign

That Burgoyne's scheme would give "Gentleman Johnny" all the glory and relegate Howe to a supporting role did not escape Sir William's notice. While Burgoyne plotted in London, Howe prepared his own plans in New York. Joseph Galloway and other Pennsylvania loyalists persuaded Howe that Philadelphia could be taken easily and that many loyal residents would welcome his troops. Just as Burgoyne omitted Howe from his plans, so too Howe omitted Burgoyne, and officials in London failed to order them to coordinate their campaigns. The two major British armies in America would operate independently in 1777; the result would be a disaster (see Map 6.2).

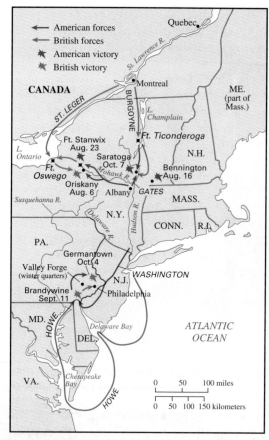

Map 6.2   Campaign of 1777   The crucial campaign of 1777 was fought on two fronts: along the upper Hudson and Mohawk River valleys, and in the vicinity of Philadelphia. The rebels won in the north; the British triumphed—at least nominally—in the south. The capture of Philadelphia, however, did the redcoats little good, and they abandoned the city the following year.

Howe captured Philadelphia, but he did so in inexplicable fashion, delaying for months before beginning the campaign, then taking six weeks to transport his troops by sea instead of marching them overland. That maneuver cost him at least a month, debilitated his men, and depleted his supplies. Incredibly, at the end of the lengthy voyage, he ended up only 40 miles closer to Philadelphia than when he started. By the time Howe advanced on Philadelphia, Washington had had time to prepare its defenses. Twice, at Brandywine Creek and again at Germantown, the two armies clashed near the patriot capital. Although the British won both en-

Howe Takes Philadelphia

This kettledrum belonged to the band of the Royal Norfolk Regiment, a British infantry unit that surrendered to the Americans at Saratoga. The drum was sent to West Point, where it has remained ever since, a symbol of the new nation's first great victory of the Revolution.   (The West Point Museum Collection, U.S. Military Academy, West Point, N.Y. Photo by Paul Warchal)

gagements, the Americans handled themselves well. The redcoats took Philadelphia in late September, but to little effect. The campaign season was nearly over; the revolutionary army had gained confidence in itself and its leaders; few welcoming loyalists had materialized; and, far to the north, Burgoyne was going down to defeat.

Burgoyne's Campaign in New York

Burgoyne and his men set out from Montreal in mid-June 1777, floating down Lake Champlain into New York in canoes and flat-bottom boats. They easily captured Fort Ticonderoga from its outnumbered and outgunned patriot defenders. Trouble began, however, when Burgoyne started an overland march. His clumsy artillery carriages and baggage wagons foundered in the heavy forests and ravines. Patriot militia felled giant trees across his path to slow his progress. Consequently, Burgoyne's troops took twenty-four days to travel 23 miles. In August the campaign suffered two sharp blows—first, when the redcoats and Indians marching east along the Mohawk River turned back after a battle at Oriskany, New York; second, when in a clash near Bennington, Vermont, American militiamen nearly wiped out eight hundred of Burgoyne's German mercenaries. Yet the general continued to dawdle, giving the Americans more than enough time to prepare for his coming. After several skirmishes with an American army commanded by General Horatio Gates, Burgoyne was surrounded near Saratoga, New York. On October 17, 1777, he surrendered his entire force of more than six thousand men.

Split of the Iroquois Confederacy

The August 1777 battle at Oriskany divided the Iroquois Confederacy (see pages 66–67). In 1776 the Six Nations formally pledged to remain neutral in the Anglo-American struggle. But two influential Mohawk leaders worked tirelessly to persuade their fellow Iroquois to join the British. Both Mary Brant, a powerful tribal matron and the widow of the Indian superintendent Sir William Johnson, and her younger brother Joseph, a renowned warrior, strongly believed that the

Six Nations should ally themselves with the British in order to prevent American encroachment on their lands. The Brants won over to the British the Senecas, Cayugas, and Mohawks, all of whom contributed warriors to the 1777 expedition. But the Oneidas—who had been converted to Christianity by Protestant missionaries—preferred the American side and brought the Tuscaroras with them. The Onondagas split into three factions, one on each side and one supporting neutrality. At Oriskany, some Oneidas and Tuscaroras joined patriot militiamen in fighting their Iroquois brethren, shattering a league of friendship that had survived for over three hundred years.

The collapse of Iroquois unity and the confederacy's abandonment of neutrality had significant consequences. In 1778 Iroquois warriors allied with the British raided frontier villages in Pennsylvania and New York. To retaliate, the Americans the following summer dispatched an expedition under General John Sullivan to burn Iroquois crops, orchards, and settlements. The resulting devastation forced many bands to leave their ancestral homeland to seek food and shelter north of the Great Lakes during the winter of 1779–1780. A large number of Iroquois people never returned to New York but settled permanently in British Canada.

Burgoyne's surrender at Saratoga brought joy to patriots, discouragement to loyalists and Britons. In exile in London, Thomas Hutchinson wrote of "universal dejection" among loyalists there. "Everybody in a gloom," he commented; "most of us expect to lay our bones here." The disaster prompted Lord North to authorize a peace commission to offer the Americans what they had requested in the Declaration of Rights and Grievances in 1774—in effect, a return to the imperial system of 1763. That proposal came far too late: the patriots rejected the overture, and the peace commission sailed back to England empty-handed in mid-1778.

Most important, the American victory at Saratoga drew France formally into the conflict. Ever since 1763, the French had sought to avenge their defeat in the Seven Years War, and the American Revolution gave them that opportunity. Even before Benjamin Franklin arrived in Paris in late 1776, France covertly supplied the revolutionaries with military necessities. Indeed, 90 percent of the gunpowder used by the Americans during the war's first two years came from France.

Benjamin Franklin worked tirelessly to strengthen ties between the two nations. He deliberately assumed

Joseph Brant, the Iroquois leader who helped to persuade the Mohawks, Senecas, and Cayugas to support the British in the latter stages of the Revolution, as painted by Charles Willson Peale in 1797. (Independence National Historic Park Collection)

Franco-American Alliance of 1778

a plain style of dress that made him stand out amid the luxury of the court of King Louis XVI. Presenting himself as a representative of American simplicity, Franklin played on the French image of Americans as virtuous yeomen. His efforts culminated in 1778 when the countries signed two treaties. In the Treaty of Amity and Commerce, France recognized American independence, establishing trade ties with the new nation. In the Treaty of Alliance, France and the United States promised—assuming that France would go to war with Britain, which it soon did—that neither would negotiate peace with the enemy without consulting the other. France also formally abandoned any claim to Canada and to North American territory east of the Mississippi River. In the years that followed, the most visible symbol of Franco-American cooperation was the Marquis de Lafayette, a young nobleman who volunteered for service with George Washington in 1777 and fought with American forces until the conflict ended.

The French alliance had two major benefits for the patriot cause. First, France began to aid the Americans

A British cartoon published in 1780. Even after Spain and the Netherlands had joined
France in supporting the Americans' quest for independence, this artist had confidence in
Britain's ability to outweigh the alliance in "The Ballance of Power."   (Print Collection,
Miriam and Ira D. Wallach Division of Art, Prints and Photographs. The New York Public
Library, Astor, Lenox, and Tilden Foundations)

openly, sending troops and naval vessels in addition to
arms, ammunition, clothing, and blankets. Second,
Great Britain could no longer focus solely on the
American mainland, for it had to fight France in the
Caribbean and elsewhere. Spain's entry into the war in
1779 as an ally of France (but not of the United States)
further magnified Britain's problems, for the Revolution then became a global war. The French aided the
Americans throughout the conflict, but in its last years
the assistance was particularly vital.

The Long Struggle in the South

In the aftermath of the Saratoga disaster,
Lord George Germain and British military officials reassessed their strategy. Maneuvering in the North had done them
little good; perhaps shifting the field of battle south-

ward would bring success. Many loyalist exiles in London encouraged this line of thinking. They argued
that loyal southerners would welcome the redcoat
army as liberators and that the region could serve as a
base for attacking the North, once it had been pacified
and returned to friendly civilian control.

Sir Henry Clinton, who replaced Howe, therefore
oversaw the regrouping of British forces in America.

**British Victories
in South
Carolina**

He ordered the evacuation of Philadelphia in June 1778 and then dispatched a small expedition to
Georgia at the end of the year. When
Savannah and then Augusta fell easily
into British hands, Clinton became
convinced that a southern strategy would succeed. In
late 1779 he sailed down the coast from New York to
besiege Charleston, the most important city in the
South (see Map 6.3). The Americans held out for

months, but on May 12, 1780, General Benjamin Lincoln surrendered the entire southern army—5,500 men—to the invaders. In the following weeks, the redcoats spread through South Carolina, establishing garrisons at key points in the interior. Hundreds of South Carolinians renounced allegiance to the United States, proclaiming their renewed loyalty to the Crown. Clinton organized loyalist regiments, and the process of pacification began.

Yet the triumph was less complete than it appeared. The success of the southern campaign depended on control of the seas, for the British armies were so widely dispersed and travel by land was so difficult that only through British naval vessels could the armies coordinate their efforts. For the moment, the Royal Navy safely dominated the American coastline, but French naval power posed a threat to the entire southern enterprise. Moreover, the redcoats never managed to establish full control of the areas they seized. Patriot bands operated freely throughout the state, and loyalists could not be guaranteed protection against their enemies. Last but not least, the fall of Charleston failed to dishearten the patriots; instead, it spurred them to greater exertions. As one Marylander declared confidently, "The Fate of America is not to be decided by the Loss of a Town or Two." Patriot women in four states formed the Ladies Association, which collected money to purchase shirts for needy soldiers. Recruiting efforts were stepped up.

Nevertheless, the war in South Carolina went badly for the patriots throughout most of 1780. At Camden in August, forces under Lord Cornwallis, the new British commander in the South, crushingly defeated a reorganized southern army led by Horatio Gates. Hundreds, even thousands, of enslaved African Americans joined the redcoats, seeking freedom on the basis of Lord Dunmore's 1775 proclamation. Running away from their patriot masters individually and as families, they seriously disrupted planting and harvesting in the Carolinas in 1780 and 1781. More than fifty-five thousand slaves were lost to their owners as a result of the war. Not all of them joined the British or won their freedom if they did, but their flight had exactly the effect Dunmore sought. Many served the British well as scouts, guides, and laborers.

After the Camden defeat, Washington (who had to remain in the North to contain the British army occupying New York) appointed General Nathanael Greene to command the southern campaign. Appalled by the conditions in South Carolina, Greene told a friend that "the word difficulty when applied to the

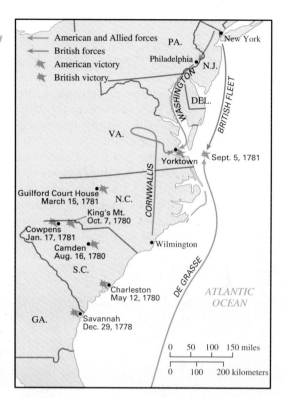

Map 6.3   The War in the South   The southern war—after the British invasion of Georgia in late 1778—was characterized by a series of British thrusts into the interior, leading to battles with American defenders in both North and South Carolina. Finally, after promising beginnings, Cornwallis's foray into Virginia ended with disaster at Yorktown in October 1781.

Greene and the Southern Campaign

state of things here . . . is almost without meaning, it falls so far short" of reality. His troops needed clothing, blankets, and food, but "a great part of this country is already laid waste and in the utmost danger of becoming a desert." Incessant guerrilla warfare had, he commented, "so corrupted the principles of the people that they think of nothing but plundering one another."

In such dire circumstances, Greene had to move cautiously. Adopting a conciliatory policy toward loyalists and neutrals, he persuaded the governor of South Carolina to pardon those who had fought for the British if they would now join the patriot militia. He also ordered his troops to treat captives fairly and not to loot loyalist property. Recognizing that the patriots needed to convince a war-weary populace that they could bring stability to the region, he helped the

How do historians know...

that many Americans were intensely patriotic during the Revolution and in the early years of the republic?

Evidence of a wave of nationalistic pride is supplied by the many items incorporating patriotic motifs that soon decorated the homes of American citizens. The artisans of the new nation quickly recognized that "patriotism sold," so they created a wide variety of objects to satisfy Americans' demand for furniture, wallpaper, curtains, and pottery goods displaying such themes. Only middling and well-to-do Americans could afford to buy such items, but a less-well-off American woman could produce some of these goods for herself. We do not know who made this eagle hooked rug, but a poor woman with just a few moments to spare each day could well have labored for months to display her allegiance to the newly independent United States in this fashion. (Photo: New York State Historical Association, Cooperstown)

shattered provincial congresses of Georgia and South Carolina to reestablish civilian authority in the interior—a goal the British were never able to accomplish. Since he had so few regulars (only sixteen hundred when he took command), Greene had to rely on western volunteers and could not afford to have frontier militia companies occupied in defending their homes from Indian attack. He accordingly pursued diplomacy aimed at keeping the Indians out of the war. Although royal officials cooperating with the redcoat invaders initially won some Indian allies, Greene's careful maneuvers eventually proved successful. By war's end, only the Creeks remained allied with Great Britain.

Even before Greene took command of the southern army in December 1780, the tide had begun to turn. In October, at King's Mountain, a force from the settlements west of the Appalachians defeated a large party of redcoats and loyalists. Then in January 1781 Greene's trusted aide Daniel Morgan brilliantly routed the crack British regiment Tarleton's Legion at Cowpens. Greene himself confronted the main body of British troops under Lord Cornwallis at Guilford Court House, North Carolina, in March. Although

Cornwallis controlled the field at the end of the day, most of his army had been destroyed. He had to retreat to Wilmington, on the coast, to receive supplies and fresh troops from New York by sea. Meanwhile, Greene returned to South Carolina, where, in a series of swift strikes, he forced the redcoats to abandon their interior posts and retire to Charleston.

Yorktown and the Treaty of Paris

 Lord Cornwallis headed north into Virginia, where he joined forces with a detachment of redcoats commanded by the American traitor Benedict Arnold. Instead of acting decisively with his new army of 7,200 men, Cornwallis withdrew to the peninsula between the York and James Rivers, where he fortified Yorktown and awaited more supplies and reinforcements. Seizing the opportunity, Washington quickly moved more than 7,000 troops south from New York City. When a French fleet under the Comte de Grasse arrived from the Caribbean in time to defeat the Royal Navy vessels sent to relieve Cornwallis, the British general was trapped (see Map 6.3). On October 19, 1781, Cornwallis surrendered to the combined American and French forces.

When news of the surrender reached London, Lord North's ministry fell. Parliament voted to cease offensive operations in America, authorizing peace negotiations. Washington returned with the main army to the environs of New York, where his underpaid—and, they thought, underappreciated—officers grew restive. In March 1783 they threatened to mutiny unless Congress guaranteed them adequate compensation for their services. Washington, warned in advance of the so-called Newburgh Conspiracy, met the challenge brilliantly. Summoning his officers, he defused the crisis with a well-reasoned but emotional speech drawing on their patriotism. How could they, he asked, "open the flood Gates of Civil discord, and deluge our rising Empire in Blood"? When at one point he fumbled for glasses, remarking in passing that "I have grown gray in your service and now find myself growing blind," eyewitnesses reported that many of the rebellious officers began to cry. At the end of the year, he stood before Congress and formally resigned his commission as commander-in-chief. Through such actions at the end of the conflict, Washington established an enduring precedent: civilian control of the American military.

The war had been won, but at terrible cost. More than twenty-five thousand American men died in the war, only about one-quarter of them from wounds suffered in battle. The rest were declared missing in action or died of disease or as prisoners of war. In the South, years of guerrilla warfare and the loss of thousands of runaway slaves shattered the economy. Indebtedness soared, and local governments were crippled for lack of funds, since few people could afford to pay their taxes. In the 1780s in Charles County, Maryland, for example, men commonly refused to serve in elective or appointive office because their personal estates would become liable for any taxes or fines they were unable to collect. Many of the county's formerly wealthy planters descended into insolvency, and in the 1790s a traveler observed that "the country . . . wears a most dreary aspect," remarking on the "old dilapidated mansions" that had once housed well-to-do slaveowners.

The Cost of Victory

Yet Charles County residents and Americans in general "all rejoiced" when they learned of the signing of the preliminary peace treaty at Paris in November 1782. The American diplomats—Benjamin Franklin, John Jay, and John Adams—ignored their instructions from Congress to be guided by France and instead negotiated directly with Great Britain. Their instincts were sound: the French government was more an enemy to Britain than a friend to the United States. In fact, French ministers worked secretly behind the scenes to try to prevent the establishment of a strong and unified government in America. Spain's desire to lay claim to the region between the Appalachian Mountains and the Mississippi River further complicated the negotiations. But the American delegates proved adept at power politics, achieving their main goal: independence as a united nation. Weary of war, the new British ministry, headed by Lord Shelburne (formerly an outspoken critic of Lord North's American policies), made numerous concessions—so many, in fact, that Parliament ousted the ministry shortly after peace terms were approved.

Treaty of Paris

The treaty, signed formally on September 3, 1783, granted the Americans unconditional independence. Generous boundaries delineated the new nation: to the north, approximately the present-day boundary with Canada; to the south, the 31st parallel (about the modern northern border of Florida); to the west, the Mississippi River. Florida, which Britain had acquired

Measles, typhus, diphtheria, dysentery, and other diseases ravaged military encampments, so medicine chests like the one shown here were essential equipment for the army. Doctors used crude remedies that often did more harm than good, for little was known about the causes of such afflictions. Smallpox was one of the few epidemics that eighteenth-century doctors could combat: inoculation was known to be an effective preventive measure as early as the 1720s.   (The West Point Museum Collection, U.S. Military Academy, West Point, N.Y. Photo by Josh Nefsky)

in 1763, reverted to Spain. The Americans also gained unlimited fishing rights off Newfoundland. In ceding so much land to the United States, Great Britain ignored the territorial rights of its Indian allies, sacrificing their interests to the demands of European politics. British diplomats also poorly served loyalists and British merchants. The treaty's ambiguously worded clauses pertaining to the payment of prewar debts and the postwar treatment of loyalists caused trouble for years to come, proving impossible to enforce.

Summary

The long war finally over, the victorious Americans could look back on their achievement with satisfaction and awe. Having unified the disparate mainland colonies, they had claimed their place in the family of nations and forged a successful alliance with France. With an inexperienced ragtag army, they had taken on the greatest military power in the world—and eight years later they had won. They accomplished their goal more through persistence and commitment than through brilliance on the battlefield. Actual victories were few, but their army always survived defeats and standoffs to fight again. Ultimately, the Americans simply wore their enemy down.

In winning the war, the Americans reshaped the physical and mental landscapes in which they lived. They abandoned the British identity once so important to them, excluding from their new nation all those unwilling to make a break with the mother country. In the Continental Army in particular they began the process of creating loyalty to an entity that had no prior existence—a nation they named "the United States of America." They also established a claim to most of the territory east of the Mississippi River and south of the Great Lakes, thereby greatly expanding the land potentially open to their settlements.

In achieving independence, Americans surmounted formidable challenges. But in the future they faced perhaps even greater ones: establishing stable republican governments at the state and national levels to replace the monarchy they had rejected, and ensuring their government's continued existence in a world of bitter rivalries among the major powers—Britain, France, and Spain. Those European rivalries worked to the Americans' advantage during the war, but in the decades to come they would pose significant threats to the survival of the new nation.

LEGACY FOR A PEOPLE AND A NATION
The Black Patriots' Memorial

The Black Patriots Foundation has been actively soliciting private funds to build a memorial to the approximately five thousand African Americans who fought in the revolutionary army. The National Capital Planning Commission has approved a site on the mall in Washington, D.C., and a commemorative silver dollar, authorized by Act of Congress, is being sold to raise money. A sculptor has been selected, a design chosen. The black soldiers of the Revolution "provided critical service to the founding of America," declared a foundation supporter at a Memorial Day, 1996, ceremony. Their "gallant efforts . . . have been tragically overlooked by history. It's time—past time—that we right this historical wrong by honoring their noble service with a fitting memorial."

Although historians of the American Revolution appreciate the impulse behind the campaign, many find the project ironic. A prime example of what scholars have termed "contribution history"—that is, the notion that a people's history is important primarily insofar as it has contributed to the history of the nation—the Black Patriots' Memorial would enshrine in bronze the story of only approximately 10 percent of the African Americans who fought in the Revolutionary War. The other 90 percent aligned themselves with the British.

And with good reason. Enslaved African Americans understandably sought their own personal freedom during the Revolution. The British held out that prospect to *any* slave of a rebel—man, woman, or child—who joined them during the conflict. Only a few African American men received similar promises from individual patriots or from the states. Black loy-

alists, who at the end of the war emigrated to the Bahamas, England, or Nova Scotia, and some of whom later founded Sierra Leone on the African continent, represented the vast majority of black participants in the Revolution.

The Black Patriots' Memorial thus ignores the experience of most revolutionary-era African Americans. Moreover, its exclusive focus on patriots obscures the fact that—judging by the number of slaves who seized freedom by joining the British forces—the Revolution was by far the most successful slave revolt in American history. Through their devotion to personal liberty and their open challenge to enslavement, the black people who chose loyalism have left at least as great a legacy to the nation today as did the much smaller number of black patriots who contributed more formally to the nation's founding.

For Further Reading, see page A-7 of the Appendix. For Web resources, go to http://college.hmco.com.

On December 26, 1787, a group of Federalists—supporters of the proposed Constitution—gathered in Carlisle, a town on the Pennsylvania frontier. The men planned to fire a cannon to celebrate their state convention's ratification vote two weeks earlier, but a large crowd of Antifederalists prevented them from doing so. First the Antis stood in front of the cannon, refusing to budge even though the Federalists threatened to fire the gun anyway. Then, moving from passive to active resistance, they attacked the Federalists, who eventually fled the scene as the angry Antis publicly burned a copy of the Constitution.

The next day, the Federalists returned in force to fire their cannon and to read the convention's ratification proclamation. Choosing not to create another violent confrontation, Antifederalists instead paraded around the town effigies of two supporters of the Constitution, then burned them. When Federalist officials later arrested several Antifederalists on riot charges, the Antifederalist-dominated militia mustered to break the men out of jail. Only a flaw in the warrant—which freed the arrestees legally—prevented another bloody brawl.

For several weeks thereafter, the participants in these events argued back and forth in the Carlisle newspaper about the meaning of the demonstrations and counterdemonstrations. Pro-Federalist authors proclaimed that the respectable initial celebrants acted with "good order and coolness"; their Antifederalist opponents, by contrast, were "obscure" men, nothing but "a few worthless ragamuffins." In response, "One of the People" pronounced the Federalists "an unhallowed riotous mob." Although the Constitution's supporters had declared themselves to be "friends of government," he wrote, in fact they were not: through their support of a form of government that aimed to suppress the people's liberties, they had revealed their true identity as secret aristocrats.

William Smith, painted with his grandson in 1788 by Charles Willson Peale, presented the public image appropriate to a dignified citizen of the new republic. Peale and other artists of the time tried to promote republican values visually in their work. Here, the images of the well-tended farm, a mill, books, and a cherished child combine to symbolize virtuous labor, rational thought, and a concern for the "rising generation." (Virginia Museum of Fine Arts)

7

FORGING A NATIONAL REPUBLIC 1776–1789

The Carlisle riots presaged violent disputes over the new Constitution in Albany (New York), Providence (Rhode Island), and other cities. In late 1787, Carlisle witnessed one incident in an ongoing struggle that began in 1775 and continued until the end of the century. In that contest, Americans argued continually—in print and in person—over how to implement republican principles and who represented the people's will. Easterners debated with westerners; in both regions, elites contended with ordinary folk. Public celebrations, like those in the small Pennsylvania town, played an important part in the struggle. After all, in a world in which only relatively few property-holding men had the right to vote, other people—and even voters themselves—expressed their political opinions in the streets rather than at the ballot box.

Republicanism—the idea that governments should be based wholly on the consent of the people—originated with political theorists in ancient Greece and Rome. Republics, theorists declared, were desirable yet fragile forms of government. Unless their citizens were especially virtuous—that is, sober, moral, and industrious—and largely in agreement on key issues, republics were doomed to failure. When Americans left the British Empire, they abandoned the idea that the best system of government balanced monarchy, aristocracy, and democracy—or, to put it another way, that a stable polity required participation by a king, the nobility, and the people. They substituted a belief in the superiority of republicanism, in which the people, not Parliament, were sovereign. During and after the war, Americans had to deal with the potentially unwelcome consequences of that decision, such as those evident in the Carlisle demonstrations. How could they best ensure political stability? How could they foster consensus among the populace? How could they create and sustain a virtuous republic?

America's political and intellectual leaders worked hard to inculcate virtue in their fellow countrymen and countrywomen. After 1776, American literature, theater, art, architecture, and education all pursued explicitly moral goals. The education of women was considered particularly important, for as the mothers of the republic's children, they were primarily responsible for ensuring the nation's future. On such matters Americans could agree, but they disagreed on many other critical issues. Almost all white men assumed that women, Indians, and African Americans should have no formal role in politics, but they found it diffi-

cult to reach a consensus on how many of their own number should be included, how often elections should be held, or how their new governments should be structured.

Republican citizens had to make many other decisions as well. Should a republic's diplomacy differ from that of other nations? (For example, should the United States work to advance the cause of republicanism elsewhere?) And then there were Thomas Jefferson's words in the Declaration of Independence: "all men are created equal." Given that bold statement of principle, how could white republicans justify holding African Americans in perpetual bondage? Some answered that question by freeing their slaves or by voting for state laws that abolished slavery. Others responded by denying that blacks were "men" in the same sense as whites.

The most important task facing Americans in these years was the construction of a genuinely national government. Before 1765 the British mainland colonies had rarely cooperated on common endeavors. Many circumstances separated them: their diverse economies, varying religious traditions and ethnic compositions, competing land claims (especially in the West), and different political systems. But fighting the Revolutionary War brought them together and created a new nationalistic spirit, especially among those who served in the Continental Army or the diplomatic corps. Wartime experiences broke down at least some of the boundaries that previously had divided Americans, replacing loyalties to state and region with loyalties to the nation.

Still, forging a national republic (as opposed to a set of loosely connected state republics) was neither easy nor simple. America's first such government, under the Articles of Confederation, proved too weak and decentralized. But some of the nation's political leaders learned from their experiences and tried another approach when they drafted the Constitution in 1787. Some historians have argued that the Articles of Confederation and the Constitution reflect opposing political philosophies, the Constitution representing an "aristocratic" counterrevolution against the "democratic" Articles. The two documents are more accurately viewed as successive attempts to solve the same problems—for instance, the relationship of states and nation and the extent to which authority should be centralized. Both applied theories of republicanism to practical problems of governance; neither was entirely successful in resolving those difficulties. ■

IMPORTANT EVENTS

1776 Second Continental Congress directs states to draft constitutions

1777 Articles of Confederation sent to states for ratification
Vermont becomes first state to abolish slavery

1781 Articles of Confederation ratified

1786 Annapolis Convention meets, discusses reforming government

1786–87 Shays's Rebellion in western Massachusetts raises questions about future of the republic

1787 Northwest Ordinance organizes territory north of Ohio River and east of Mississippi River
Constitutional Convention drafts new form of government

1788 Hamilton, Jay, and Madison write *The Federalist* to urge ratification of the Constitution by New York
Constitution ratified

1794 Wayne defeats Miami Confederacy at Fallen Timbers

1795 Treaty of Greenville opens Ohio to white settlement

1800 Weems publishes his *Life of Washington*

Creating a Virtuous Republic

When the colonies declared their independence from Great Britain, John Dickinson recalled many years later, "there was no question concerning forms of Government, no enquiry whether a Republic or a limited Monarchy was best. . . . We knew that the people of this country must unite themselves under some form of Government and that this could be no other than the republican form"—in short, self-government by the people. But how should that goal be implemented?

Three different definitions of *republicanism* emerged in the new United States. Ancient history and political theory informed the first,

Varieties of Republicanism

held chiefly by members of the educated elite (such as the Adamses of Massachusetts). The histories of popular governments in Greece and Rome suggested that republics could succeed only if they were small in size and homogeneous in population. Unless a republic's citizens were willing to sacrifice their own private interests for the good of the whole, the government would collapse. A truly virtuous man, classical republican theory insisted, had to forgo personal profit and work solely for the best interests of the nation. In return for sacrifices, though, a republic offered its citizens equality of opportunity.

Under such a government, rank would be based on merit rather than on inherited wealth and status. Society would be governed by members of a "natural aristocracy," men whose talent had elevated them from what might have been humble beginnings to positions of power and privilege. Rank would not be abolished but instead would be founded on merit.

A second definition, advanced by other members of the elite but also by some skilled craftsmen, drew more on economic theory than on political thought. Instead of perceiving the nation as an organic whole composed of people nobly sacrificing for the common good, this version of republicanism followed the Scottish theorist Adam Smith in emphasizing individuals' pursuit of rational self-interest. The huge profits some men reaped from patriotism by selling supplies to the army underscored such an approach. The nation could only benefit from aggressive economic expansion, argued men such as Alexander Hamilton. When republican men sought to improve their own economic and social circumstances, the entire nation would benefit. Republican virtue would be achieved through the pursuit of private interests, rather than through subordination to some communal ideal. Such thinking decisively abandoned the old notion of the Puritan covenant, which the first definition perpetuated in its emphasis on consensus though not in its stress on an aristocracy of talent rather than birth (see page 51).

When the great French sculptor Jean-Antoine Houdon prepared this bust of George Washington in 1785, he chose to show the revolutionary leader in classical garb rather than in contemporary clothing. Such images linked the aspirations of the new nation to the ancient republics American thinkers revered.   (Collection of Dr. Gary Milan)

The third notion of republicanism was less influential but more egalitarian than the other two, which both contained considerable potential for inequality. Many of its illiterate or barely literate proponents could write little to promote their beliefs. Men who advanced the third version of republicanism, the most prominent of whom was Thomas Paine, called for widening men's participation in the political process. They also wanted government to respond directly to the needs of ordinary folk, rejecting any notion that the "lesser sort" should automatically defer to their "betters." They were, indeed, democrats in more or less the modern sense. For them, republican virtue was embodied in the untutored wisdom of the people as a whole, rather than in the special insights of a natural aristocracy or the pronouncements of wealthy individuals.

Despite the differences, the three strands of republicanism shared many of the same assumptions.

For example, all three contrasted the industrious virtue of America to the corruption of Britain and Europe. In the first version, that virtue manifested itself in frugality and self-sacrifice; in the second, it would prevent self-interest from becoming vice; in the third, it was the justification for including even propertyless free men in the ranks of voters. "Virtue, Virtue alone . . . is the basis of a republic," asserted Dr. Benjamin Rush of Philadelphia, an ardent patriot, in 1778. His fellow Americans concurred, even if they defined virtue differently. Most agreed that a virtuous country would be composed of hard-working citizens who would dress simply and live plainly, elect wise leaders to public office, and forgo the conspicuous consumption of luxury goods.

As citizens of the United States set out to construct their republic, they believed they were embarking on an unprecedented enterprise.

Virtue and the Arts

With great pride in their new nation, they expected to replace the vices of monarchical Europe—immorality, selfishness, and lack of public spirit—with the sober virtues of republican America. They wanted to embody republican principles not only in their governments but also in their society and culture. They looked to painting, literature, drama, and architecture to convey messages of nationalism and virtue to the public, focusing on such themes until after the turn of the century.

Americans faced a crucial contradiction at the very outset of their efforts. To some republicans, the fine arts themselves were manifestations of vice. Their existence in a virtuous society, many contended, signaled the arrival of luxury and corruption. What need did a frugal yeoman have for a painting—or, worse yet, a novel? Why should anyone spend hard-earned wages to see a play in a lavishly decorated theater? The first American artists, playwrights, and authors thus confronted an impossible dilemma. They wanted to produce works embodying virtue, but those very works, regardless of their content, were viewed by many as corrupting.

Still, they tried. William Hill Brown's *The Power of Sympathy* (1789), the first novel written in the United States, was a lurid tale of seduction intended as a warning to young women, who made up a large proportion of America's fiction readers. In Royall Tyler's *The Contrast* (1787), the first successful American play, the virtuous conduct of Colonel Manly was contrasted (hence the title) with the reprehensible behavior of the fop Billy Dimple. The most popular book of the era,

Mason Locke Weems's *Life of Washington*, published in 1800 shortly after George Washington's death, was intended by its author to "hold up his great Virtues . . . to the imitation of Our Youth." Weems could hardly be accused of subtlety. The famous tale he invented—six-year-old George bravely admitting cutting down his father's favorite cherry tree—ended with George's father exclaiming, "Run to my arms, you dearest boy. . . . Such an act of heroism in my son, is worth more than a thousand trees, though blossomed with silver, and their fruit of purest gold."

Painting and architecture, too, were expected to embody high moral standards. Two of the most prominent artists of the period, Gilbert Stuart and Charles Willson Peale, painted innumerable portraits of upstanding republican citizens. John Trumbull's vast canvases depicted milestones of American history such as the Battle of Bunker Hill, Burgoyne's surrender at Saratoga, and Cornwallis's capitulation at Yorktown. Such portraits and historical scenes were intended to instill patriotic sentiments in their viewers. Architects likewise hoped to convey in their buildings a sense of the young republic's ideals. When the Virginia government asked Thomas Jefferson, then minister to France, for advice on the design of the state capitol in Richmond, Jefferson unhesitatingly recommended copying a Roman building, the Maison Carrée at Nîmes. "It is very simple," he explained, "but it is noble beyond expression." Jefferson set forth ideals that would guide American architecture for a generation to come: simplicity of line, harmonious proportions, a feeling of grandeur.

Despite the artists' efforts (or, some would have said, because of them), some Americans began to detect signs of luxury and corruption by the mid-1780s. The resumption of European trade after the war brought a return to fashionable clothing for both men and women and abandonment of the simpler homespun garments patriots had once worn with pride. Elite families again attended balls and concerts. Parties no longer seemed complete without gambling and cardplaying. Social clubs for young people multiplied; Samuel Adams worried in print about the opportunities for corruption lurking behind plans for tea drinking and genteel conversation among Boston youths. Especially alarming to fervent republicans was the establishment in 1783 of the Society of the Cincinnati, a hereditary association for Revolutionary War officers and their descendants. Although the organizers hoped to advance the notion of the citizen-soldier, opponents feared that the group would become the nucleus of a native-born aristocracy. All these developments directly challenged the United States's self-image as a virtuous republic.

Americans' deep-seated concern for the future of the infant republic focused their attention on their children, the "rising generation."

Educational Reform

Education had previously been seen as a private means to personal advancement, a concern only for individual families. Now, though, schooling would serve a public purpose. If young people were to resist the temptations of vice and become useful citizens prepared for self-government, they would need a better education. In fact, the very survival of the nation depended on it. The 1780s and 1790s thus witnessed two major changes in educational practice.

First, in contrast to the colonies, where nearly all education had been privately financed, some northern states began to use tax money to support public elementary schools. In 1789 Massachusetts became one of the first states to require towns to offer their citizens free public elementary education. Second, schooling for girls was improved. Americans' recognition of the importance of the rising generation led to the realization that mothers would have to be properly educated if they were to instruct their children adequately. Therefore, Massachusetts insisted in its 1789 law that town elementary schools be open to girls as well as boys. Throughout the United States, private academies were founded to give teenage girls from well-to-do families an opportunity for advanced schooling. No one yet proposed opening colleges to women, but a few fortunate girls could study history, geography, rhetoric, and mathematics. The academies also trained female students in fancy needlework—the only artistic endeavor considered appropriate for genteel women.

The chief theorist of women's education in the early republic was Judith Sargent Murray of Gloucester, Massachusetts. In a series of essays published in the 1780s and 1790s, Murray argued that women and men had equal intellectual capacities, although women's inadequate education might make them seem less intelligent. "We can only reason from what we know," she declared, "and if an opportunity of acquiring knowledge hath been denied us, the inferiority of our sex cannot fairly be deduced from thence." Therefore, concluded Murray, boys and girls should be offered equivalent scholastic training.

Judith Sargent Murray and Women's Education

She further contended that girls should be taught to support themselves by their own efforts: "Independence should be placed within their grasp."

Murray's direct challenge to the traditional colonial belief that, as one man put it, girls "knew quite enough if they could make a shirt and a pudding" was part of a general rethinking of women's position that occurred as a result of the Revolution. Male patriots who enlisted in the army or served in Congress were away from home for long periods of time. In their absence their wives, who previously had handled only the "indoor affairs" of the household, shouldered the responsibility for "outdoor affairs" as well. As the wife of a Connecticut militiaman later recalled, her husband "was out more or less during the remainder of the war [after 1777], so much so as to be unable to do anything on our farm. What was done, was done by myself."

The American artist Benjamin Blythe painted this portrait of Abigail Smith Adams in 1766, shortly after her marriage. Less than a decade later she would join her husband John in eager support of the revolutionary cause. At the same time, however, she forthrightly challenged him to "remember the ladies" in the nation's "new code of laws."   (Massachusetts Historical Society)

Similarly, John and Abigail Adams took great pride in Abigail's developing skills as a "farmeress." Like her female contemporaries, Abigail Adams stopped calling the farm "yours" in letters to her husband and began referring to it as "ours"—a revealing change of pronoun. Both men and women realized that female patriots had made vital and important contributions to winning the war through their work at home and that their notions of proper gender roles had to be rethought. Americans began to develop new ideas about the role women should play in a republican society.

The best-known expression of those new ideas appears in a letter Abigail Adams addressed to her husband in March 1776. "In the new Code of Laws which I suppose it will be necessary for you to make I desire you would Remember the Ladies," she wrote. "Remember all Men would be tyrants if they could. . . . If perticuliar care and attention is not paid to the Laidies [*sic*] we are determined to foment a Rebelion, and will not hold ourselves bound by any Laws in which we have no voice, or Representation." With these words, Abigail Adams took a step that was soon to be duplicated by other disfranchised Americans. She deliberately applied the ideology developed to combat parliamentary supremacy to purposes revolutionary leaders had never intended. Since men were "Naturally Tyrannical," she argued, the United States should reform colonial marriage laws, which made wives subordinate to their husbands.

Abigail Adams: "Remember the Ladies"

Abigail Adams did not ask that women be allowed to vote, but others claimed that right. The men who drafted the New Jersey state constitution in 1776 defined voters carelessly as "all free inhabitants" who met certain property qualifications. They thereby unintentionally gave the vote to property-holding white spinsters and widows, as well as to free black landowners. Qualified women and African Americans regularly voted in New Jersey's local and congressional elections until 1807, when they were disfranchised by the state legislature, which falsely alleged that they had engaged in widespread vote fraud. Yet the fact that women voted at all was evidence of their altered perception of their place in the political life of the country.

Such dramatic episodes were unusual. After the war, European Americans still viewed women in traditional terms, continuing to believe that women's primary function was to be good wives, mothers, and mistresses of households. They perceived significant

Women's Role in the Republic

differences between male and female characters. That distinction eventually enabled Americans to resolve the conflict between the two most influential strands of republican thought and led to new roles for some women. Because wives could not own property or participate directly in economic life, women in general came to be seen as the embodiment of self-sacrificing, disinterested republicanism. Through new female-run charitable associations founded after the war, better-off women assumed public responsibilities, in particular through caring for poor widows and orphaned children. Thus men were freed from the naggings of conscience as they pursued their economic self-interest (that other republican virtue), secure in the knowledge that their wives and daughters were fulfilling the family's obligation to the common good. The ideal republican man, therefore, was an individualist, seeking advancement for himself and his family. The ideal republican woman, by contrast, always put the well-being of others ahead of her own.

Together European American men and women established the context for the creation of a virtuous republic. But nearly 20 percent of the American population was of African descent. How did approximately 700,000 African Americans fit into the developing national plan?

The First Emancipation and the Growth of Racism

Revolutionary ideology exposed one of the primary contradictions in American society. Both European and African Americans saw the irony in slaveholders' claims that they sought to prevent Britain from "enslaving" them. Many revolutionary leaders voiced the theme. In 1773 Dr. Benjamin Rush called slavery "a vice which degrades human nature," warning ominously that "the plant of liberty is of so tender a nature that it cannot thrive long in the neighborhood of slavery." Common folk also saw the contradiction. When Josiah Atkins, a Connecticut soldier marching south, saw Washington's plantation, he observed in his journal: "Alas! That persons who pretend to stand for the rights of mankind for the liberties of society, can delight in oppression, & that even of the worst kind!"

African Americans did not need revolutionary ideology to tell them that slavery was wrong, but they quickly took advantage of that ideology. In 1779 a group of slaves from Portsmouth, New Hampshire, asked the state legislature "from what authority [our masters] assume to dispose of our lives, freedom and property," pleading "that the name of slave may not more be heard in a land gloriously contending for the sweets of freedom." The same year several bondspeople in Fairfield, Connecticut, petitioned the legislature for their freedom, characterizing slavery as a "dreadful Evil" and "flagrant Injustice." How could men who were "nobly contending in the Cause of Liberty," they asked, continue "this detestable Practice"?

Both legislatures responded negatively, but the postwar years witnessed the gradual abolition of slavery in the North, a process that has become known as "the first emancipation." Vermont abolished slavery in its 1777 constitution. Massachusetts courts decided in the 1780s that a clause in the state constitution prohibited slavery. Most of the other northern and middle states adopted gradual emancipation laws between 1780 (Pennsylvania) and 1804 (New Jersey). Although New Hampshire did not formally abolish slavery, only eight slaves were reported on the 1800 census, and none remained a decade later. No southern state adopted similar general emancipation laws, but the legislatures of Virginia (1782), Delaware (1787), and Maryland (1790 and 1796) altered laws that earlier had restricted slaveowners' ability to free their bondspeople. South Carolina and Georgia never considered adopting such acts, and North Carolina insisted that all manumissions (emancipations of individual slaves) be approved by county courts.

Emancipation and Manumission

Revolutionary ideology thus had limited impact on the well-entrenched economic interests of large slaveholders. Only in the North, where slaves were less common and where less money was invested in human capital, could state legislatures vote to abolish slavery. Even there, legislators' concern for property rights—the Revolution, after all, was fought for property as well as life and liberty—led them to favor gradual emancipation over immediate abolition. Most states provided only for the freeing of children born after passage of the law, not for the emancipation of adults. And even those children were to remain slaves until reaching adulthood. Still, by 1840 only one northern state—New Jersey—permitted holding African Americans in bondage.

Despite the slow progress of abolition, the number of free people of African descent in the United States grew dramatically in the first years after the

Robert Carter was one of the largest slaveholders in Virginia. After the state altered its manumission laws and he had become a Baptist, he decided to free all of his bondspeople. He worked out a plan of gradual emancipation, freeing some slaves each year for several years. Hannah, one of his weavers, wrote to him in April 1792, requesting that she be allowed to buy her loom when she was emancipated the following January. This is one of only a handful of documents known to be written by literate slave women during the eighteenth century. (Chicago Historical Society, Robert Carter Papers)

Growth of Free Black Population

Revolution. Before the war they had been few in number; in 1755, for example, only 4 percent of African Americans in Maryland were free. Most slaves emancipated before the war were mulattos, born of unions between bondswomen and their masters, who then manumitted the children. But wartime disruptions radically augmented the freed population. Slaves who had escaped from plantations during the war, others who had served in the American army, and still others who had been emancipated by their owners or by state laws were now free. By 1790 nearly 60,000 free people of color lived in the United States; ten years later they numbered more than 108,000, nearly 11 percent of the total African American population.

The Chesapeake, where manumissions were speeded by economic changes such as declining soil fertility and the shift from tobacco to grain production, felt the effects of the postwar trend most sharply. Since grain cultivation was less labor-intensive than tobacco growing, planters began to complain about "excess" slaves. They occasionally solved that problem by freeing some of their less productive or more favored bondspeople. The free black population of Virginia more than doubled between 1790 and 1810, and by the latter year nearly one-quarter of Maryland's African American population was no longer in legal bondage.

Migration to Northern Cities

In the 1780s and thereafter, freed people from rural areas often made their way to northern port cities. Boston and Philadelphia, where slavery was abolished sooner than in New York City, were popular destinations. Women outnumbered men among the migrants by a margin of three to two, for they had better employment opportunities in the cities, especially in domestic service. Some freedmen also worked in domestic service, but larger numbers were employed as unskilled laborers and sailors. A few of the women and a sizable proportion of men (nearly one-third of those in Philadelphia in 1795) were skilled workers or retailers. These people chose new names for themselves, exchanging the surnames of former masters for names like Newman or Brown, and as soon as possible they established independent two-parent nuclear families instead of continuing to live in their employers' households. They also began to occupy distinct neighborhoods, probably as a result of discrimination.

Emancipation did not bring equality. Even whites who recognized African Americans' right to freedom were unwilling to accept them as equals. Laws discriminated against freed people as they had against slaves. South Carolina, for example, did not permit free blacks to testify against whites in court. Public schools often refused to educate their children. Freedmen found it difficult to purchase property and find good jobs. And though in many areas African Americans were accepted as members—even ministers—of evangelical churches, they were rarely allowed an equal voice in church affairs.

Gradually, freed people developed their own institutions, often based in their own neighborhoods. In Charleston mulattos formed the Brown Fellowship Society, which provided insurance coverage for its members, financed a school, and helped to support or-

Freed People's Churches and Associations

phans. In 1794 former slaves in Philadelphia and Baltimore founded societies that eventually became the African Methodist Episcopal (AME) denomination. AME churches later sponsored schools in a number of cities and, along with African Baptist, African Episcopal, and African Presbyterian churches, became cultural centers of the free black community. Freed people quickly learned that, to survive and prosper, they had to rely on their own collective efforts rather than on the benevolence or goodwill of their white compatriots.

Their endeavors were all the more important because the postrevolutionary years witnessed the development of a formal racist theory in the United States. European Americans had long regarded their slaves as inferior, but the most influential writers attributed that inferiority to environmental factors. They argued that African slaves' seemingly debased character derived from their enslavement, rather than enslavement being the consequence of inherited inferiority. In the Revolution's aftermath, though, slaveowners needed to defend holding other human beings in bondage against the notion that "all men are created equal." Consequently, they began to argue that people of African descent were less than fully human and that the principles of republican equality applied only to European Americans. In other words, to avoid having to confront the contradiction between their practice and the egalitarian implications of revolutionary theory, they redefined the theory so that it would not apply to African Americans.

Development of Racist Theory

Simultaneously, the very notion of "race" appeared in coherent form, applied to groups defined by skin color as "whites" and "blacks." The rise of egalitarian thinking among European Americans both downplayed status distinctions within their own group and differentiated all "whites" from people of color—Indians and African Americans. (That differentiation soon manifested itself in new miscegenation laws adopted in both northern and southern states to forbid intermarriage among whites and blacks or Indians.) Meanwhile, a generation or two of experience as slaves on American soil forged the identity "African" or "black" from the various ethnic and national affiliations of people who had survived the transatlantic crossing. Strikingly, among the first to term themselves "Africans" were Olaudah Equiano (see pages 74–75) and his fellow oceanic sailors—men whose wide-ranging contacts with Europeans caused them to construct a unified (and separate) identity for themselves. Thus in the revolutionary era "whiteness" and "blackness"—along with the superiority of the former, the inferiority of the latter—developed as contrasting terms in tandem with each other.

Such racism had several intertwined elements. First came the assertion that, as Thomas Jefferson insisted in 1781, blacks were "inferior to the whites in the endowments both of body and mind." There followed the belief that blacks were congenitally lazy, dishonest, and uncivilized (or uncivilizable). Third, and of crucial importance, was the notion that all blacks were sexually promiscuous and that African American men lusted after European American women. The specter of interracial sexual intercourse involving black men and white women haunted early American racist thought. Significantly, the more common reverse circumstance—the sexual exploitation of enslaved women by their masters—aroused little comment or concern.

African Americans did not allow these developing racist notions to go unchallenged. Benjamin Banneker, a free black surveyor, astronomer, and mathematical genius, directly disputed Thomas Jefferson's belief in Africans' intellectual inferiority. In 1791 Banneker sent Jefferson a copy of his latest almanac (which included his astronomical calculations) as an example of blacks' mental powers. Jefferson's response admitted Banneker's capability but indicated that he regarded Banneker as exceptional; Jefferson insisted that he needed more evidence before he would change his mind.

At its birth, then, the republic was defined by its leaders as an exclusively white male enterprise. Indeed, some historians have argued that the subjugation of blacks and women was a necessary precondition for theoretical equality among white men. They have pointed out that identifying a common racial antagonist helped to create white solidarity and to lessen the threat to gentry power posed by the enfranchisement of poorer white men. Moreover, excluding women from the political realm preserved all power for men, specifically those of the "better sort." Some scholars have pointed out that it was less dangerous to allow white men with little property to participate formally in politics than to open the possibility that they might join with former slaves to question the rule of elites. That was perhaps one reason why after the Revolution the division of American

A Republic for White Men Only

How do historians know...

that the 1780s and 1790s marked a crucial turning point in the history of slavery and racism in the United States?

Emancipation, manumission, and miscegenation laws adopted by state legislatures, coupled with debates in pamphlets and newspapers, indicate a shift in Americans' thinking. A painting such as the one reproduced here, *Liberty Displaying the Arts and Sciences*, offers a unique visual perspective on the same developments. In 1792 the Library Company of Philadelphia, a private lending library founded in the mid-eighteenth century, commissioned the artist Samuel Jennings to produce a depiction of slavery and abolitionism showing the "figure of Liberty (with her Cap and proper Insignia) displaying the arts." The results reportedly pleased the library's directors. The painting, probably the first to celebrate emancipation, shows the blonde goddess presenting books (symbolizing knowledge and freedom) to several suppliant and grateful blacks, while in the background former slaves dance joyfully around a liberty pole. Although the theme is abolition and the African Americans in the foreground have realistic features, the portrayal of blacks in passive roles and diminutive sizes portended future stereotypes. Thus the picture linked emancipation and the growth of racism. (Photo: The Library Company of Philadelphia)

society between slave and free was transformed into a division between blacks—some of whom were free—and whites. The white male wielders of power ensured their continued dominance in part by substituting race for enslavement as the primary determinant of African Americans' status.

Designing Republican Governments

In May 1776, even before adoption of the Declaration of Independence, the Second Continental Congress directed states to devise new republican governments to replace the provincial congresses and committees that had met since 1774. Thus American men initially concentrated on drafting state constitutions and devoted little attention to their national government—an oversight they later had to remedy.

At the state level, they immediately faced the problem of defining a "constitution." Americans

Drafting of State Constitutions

wanted to create tangible documents specifying the fundamental structures of government, but at first legislators could not decide how best to accomplish that goal. States eventually concluded that their constitutions should not be drafted by regular legislative bodies. Following the lead established by Vermont in 1777 and Massachusetts in 1780, they began to elect conventions for the sole purpose of drafting constitutions. Thus states sought direct authorization from the people—the theoretical sovereigns in a republic—before establishing new governments. After preparing new constitutions, delegates submitted them to voters for ratification.

The framers of state constitutions concerned themselves primarily with outlining the distribution of and limitations on government power—both crucial to the survival of republics. If authority was improperly distributed among the branches of government, or not confined within reasonable limits, the states might become tyrannical, as Britain had. Americans' experience with British rule permeated every provision of their new constitutions. States experimented with different solutions to the problems the framers perceived, and the early constitutions varied considerably in specifics while remaining broadly comparable in outline.

Under their colonial charters, Americans had learned to fear the power of the governor—usually, the appointed agent of the king or proprietor—and to see the legislature as their defender. Accordingly, the first state constitutions typically provided for the governor to be elected annually (commonly by the legislature), limited the number of terms he could serve, and gave him little independent authority. Simultaneously, the constitutions expanded the legislature's powers. Every state except Pennsylvania and Vermont retained a two-house structure, with members of the upper house having longer terms and being required to meet higher property-holding standards than members of the lower house. But they also redrew electoral districts to reflect population patterns more accurately, and they increased the number of members in both houses. Finally, most states lowered property qualifications for voting. As a result the legislatures came to include some members who before the war would not have been eligible to vote. Thus the revolutionary era witnessed the first deliberate attempt to broaden the base of American government, a process that has continued into our own day.

But the state constitutions' authors knew that governments designed to be responsive to the people would not necessarily provide sufficient protection if tyrants were elected to office. They consequently included explicit limitations on government authority in the documents they composed, attempting to protect what they regarded as the inalienable rights of individual citizens. Seven of the constitutions contained formal bills of rights, and the others had similar clauses. Most guaranteed citizens freedom of the press and of religion, the right to a fair trial, the right of consent to taxation, and protection against general search warrants. An independent judiciary was charged with upholding such rights.

Limits on State Governments

In sum, the constitution makers put far greater emphasis on preventing state governments from becoming tyrannical than on making them effective wielders of political authority. Their approach to shaping governments was understandable, given the American experience with Great Britain. But establishing such weak political units, especially in wartime, practically ensured that the constitutions soon would need revision. Soon some states began to rewrite constitutions they had drafted in 1776 and 1777.

Invariably, the revised versions increased the powers of the governor and reduced the scope of the legislature's authority. In the mid-1780s, some American

Rewriting the State Constitutions

political leaders started to develop a theory of checks and balances as the primary means of controlling government power. (In the mid-1770s, constitutions prescribed powerful legislatures to ensure good government, but warime experiences led many to conclude that such arrangements often failed.) Americans sought to balance the powers of the legislative, executive, and judicial branches against one another. The national constitution they drafted in 1787 also embodied that principle.

Yet the constitutional theories that Americans applied at the state level did not at first influence their conception of national government. Since American officials initially focused on organizing the military struggle against Britain, the powers and structure of the Continental Congress evolved by default early in the war. Not until late 1777 did Congress send the Articles of Confederation to the states for ratification, and those Articles simply wrote into law the unplanned arrangements of the Continental Congress.

Articles of Confederation

The chief organ of national government was a unicameral (one-house) legislature in which each state had one vote. Its powers included conducting foreign relations, mediating disputes between states, controlling maritime affairs, regulating Indian trade, and valuing state and national coinage. The Articles did not give the national government the ability to raise revenue effectively or to enforce a uniform commercial policy. The United States of America was described as "a firm league of friendship" in which each state "retains its sovereignty, freedom and independence, and every Power, Jurisdiction and right, which is not by this confederation expressly delegated to the United States, in Congress assembled." (See the appendix for the text of the Articles.)

The Articles required unanimous consent of state legislatures for ratification or amendment, and a clause concerning western lands proved troublesome. The draft accepted by Congress allowed states to retain all land claims derived from their original charters. But states with definite western boundaries in their charters (such as Maryland and New Jersey) wanted other states to cede to the national government their landholdings west of the Appalachian Mountains. Otherwise, they feared, states with large claims could expand and overpower their smaller neighbors. Maryland refused to accept the Articles until 1781, when Virginia finally promised to surrender its western holdings to

national jurisdiction (see Map 7.1). Other states followed suit, establishing the principle that unorganized lands would be held by the nation as a whole.

The capacity of a single state to delay ratification for three years portended the fate of American government under the Articles of Confederation. The unicameral legislature, whether it was called the Second Continental Congress (until 1781) or the Confederation Congress (thereafter), was too inefficient and unwieldy to govern effectively. The Articles' authors had not given adequate thought to the distribution of power within the national government or to the relationship between the Confederation and the states. The Congress they created was simultaneously a legislative body and a collective executive (there was no judiciary), but it had no independent income and no authority to compel the states to accept its rulings. Under the Articles, national government lurched from crisis to crisis.

Trials of the Confederation

Finance posed the most persistent problem faced by both state and national governments. Because legislators at all levels levied taxes only reluctantly, both Congress and the states at first tried to finance the war simply by printing currency. Even though the money was backed by nothing but good faith, it circulated freely and without excessive depreciation during 1775 and most of 1776. Demand for military supplies and civilian goods was high, stimulating trade (especially with France) and local production. Indeed, the amount of money issued in those years was probably no more than what a healthy economy required as a medium of exchange.

But in late 1776, as the American army suffered reverses in New York and New Jersey, prices began to rise and inflation set in. The cur-

Inflation and Taxation

rency's value rested on Americans' faith in their government, a faith that was sorely tested in the years that followed, especially during the dark days of early British triumphs in the South (1779 and 1780). State governments fought inflation by controlling wages and prices and requiring acceptance of paper currency on an equal footing with hard money. States also borrowed funds, established lotteries, and even levied taxes. Their efforts were futile. So too was Congress's attempt to stop printing currency altogether and to rely solely on money contributed by the

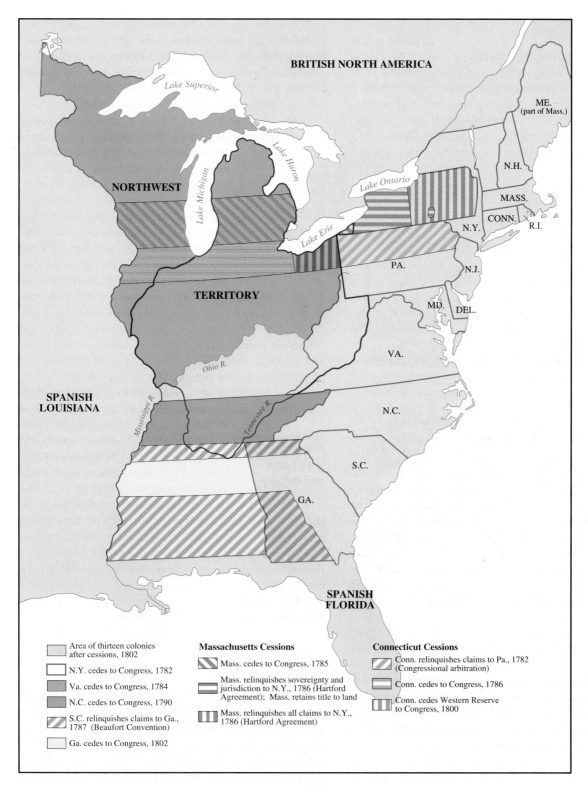

BRITISH NORTH AMERICA

Lake Superior

NORTHWEST

Lake Michigan

Lake Huron

Lake Erie

Lake Ontario

ME.
(part of Mass.)

N.H.

MASS.

CONN.

R.I.

N.Y.

PA.

N.J.

TERRITORY

MD.

DEL.

Ohio R.

VA.

SPANISH
LOUISIANA

Mississippi R.

Tennessee R.

N.C.

S.C.

GA.

SPANISH
FLORIDA

Area of thirteen colonies
after cessions, 1802

N.Y. cedes to Congress, 1782

Va. cedes to Congress, 1784

N.C. cedes to Congress, 1790

S.C. relinquishes claims to Ga.,
1787 (Beaufort Convention)

Ga. cedes to Congress, 1802

Massachusetts Cessions

Mass. cedes to Congress, 1785

Mass. relinquishes sovereignty and
jurisdiction to N.Y., 1786 (Hartford
Agreement); Mass. retains title to land

Mass. relinquishes all claims to N.Y.,
1786 (Hartford Agreement)

Connecticut Cessions

Conn. relinquishes claims to Pa., 1782
(Congressional arbitration)

Conn. cedes to Congress, 1786

Conn. cedes Western Reserve
to Congress, 1800

Map 7.1   Western Land Claims and Cessions, 1782–1802   After the United States achieved independence, states competed with each other for control of valuable lands to which they had possible claims under their original charters. That competition led to a series of compromises among the states or between individual states and the new nation, which are indicated on this map.

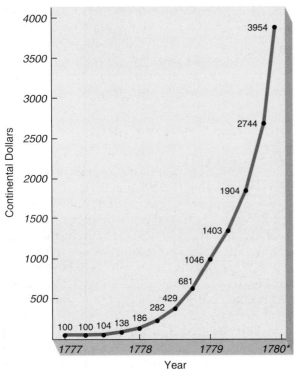

* Currency abandoned in April 1780

Figure 7.1 Depreciation of Continental Currency, 1777–1780 The depreciation of Continental currency accelerated in 1778, as is shown in this graph measuring its value against one hundred silver dollars. Thereafter, its value dropped almost daily. (Source: Data from John J. McCusker, "How Much Is That in Real Money? A Historical Price Index for Use as a Deflator of Money Values in the Economy of the United States," *Proceedings of the American Antiquarian Society,* Vol. 101, Pt. 2 [1991], Table C-1.)

states. By early 1780 it took forty paper dollars to purchase one silver dollar. Soon, Continental currency was worthless (see Figure 7.1).

In 1781, faced with total collapse of the monetary system, the congressmen undertook ambitious reforms. After establishing a department of finance under the wealthy Philadelphia merchant Robert Morris, they asked the states to amend the Articles of Confederation to allow Congress to levy a duty of 5 percent on imported goods. Morris put national finances on a solid footing, but the customs duty was never adopted. First Rhode Island and then New York refused to agree to the tax. The states' resistance reflected fear of a too-powerful central government. As one worried citizen wrote in 1783, "If permanent Funds are given

to Congress, the aristocratical Influence, which predominates in more than a major part of the United States, will fully establish an arbitrary Government." But states too needed revenue, and found it just as hard to come by. When they enacted new, heavy taxes after the war, farmers resisted their authority.

Because the Articles denied Congress the power to establish a national commercial policy, the realm of foreign trade also exposed the new government's weaknesses. Immediately after the war, Britain, France, and Spain restricted American trade with their colonies. Americans, who had hoped independence would bring about trade with all nations, were outraged but could do little to change matters. Members of Congress watched helplessly as British manufactured goods flooded the United States while American produce could no longer be sold in the British West Indies, once its prime market. Although Americans reopened commerce with other European countries and started a profitable trade with China in 1784, neither substituted for access to closer and larger markets.

Inability to Regulate Commerce

Congress furthermore had difficulty dealing with the Spanish presence on the nation's southern and western borders. Determined to prevent the republic's expansion, Spain in 1784 closed the Mississippi River to American navigation, thereby depriving the growing settlements west of the Appalachians of their access to the Gulf of Mexico. Congress, through its department of foreign affairs, opened negotiations with Spain in 1785, but even John Jay, one of the nation's most experienced diplomats, could not win the necessary concessions. The talks collapsed the following year after Congress divided sharply: southerners and westerners insisted on navigation rights on the Mississippi; northerners were willing to abandon that claim in order to win commercial concessions in the West Indies. The impasse raised doubts about the possibility of any national consensus on foreign affairs.

Relations with Spain and Britain

Provisions of the 1783 Treaty of Paris too caused serious problems. Article Four, which promised the repayment of prewar debts (most of them owed by Americans to British merchants), and Article Five, which recommended that states allow loyalists to recover their confiscated property, aroused considerable opposition. States passed laws denying British subjects the right to sue for recovery of debts or property in American courts, and town meetings decried the loyal-

treaty, however unpopular, was a crucial test of the republic's credibility in foreign affairs. "Will foreign nations be willing to undertake anything with us or for us," asked Alexander Hamilton, "when they find that the nature of our governments will allow no dependence to be placed on our engagements?"

Order and Disorder in the West

Because of their citizens' resistance to taxation, the early state governments found it hard to raise sufficient revenues. Some, like Massachusetts, turned to state-run lotteries to make up the shortfall. Here a New Englander proudly poses with a lottery ticket, demonstrating his support for the state. (Milwaukee Art Museum Purchase, Layton Art Collection)

Congressmen also confronted knotty problems when they considered the status of land beyond the Appalachians. Although British and American diplomats did not discuss tribal claims, the United States assumed that the Treaty of Paris cleared its title to all land east of the Mississippi except the area still held by Spain. Still, recognizing that land cessions should be obtained from the most powerful tribes, Congress initiated negotiations with both northern and southern Indians (see Map 7.2).

At Fort Stanwix, New York, in 1784, American diplomats negotiated a treaty with chiefs who said they represented the Iroquois; and at Hopewell, South Carolina, in late 1785 and early 1786, they did the same with emissaries from the Choctaw, Chickasaw, and Cherokee nations. In 1786 the Iroquois formally repudiated the Fort Stanwix treaty, denying that the men who attended the negotiations had been authorized to speak for the Six Nations. The confederacy threatened new attacks on frontier settlements, but everyone knew the threat was empty; the flawed treaty stood by default. At intervals until the end of the decade New York State purchased large tracts of land from individual Iroquois nations. By 1790 the once-dominant confederacy was confined to a few scattered reservations. In the South as well the United States took the treaties as confirmation of its sovereignty, authorizing settlers to move onto the territories in question. European Americans poured over the southern Appalachians, provoking the Creeks—who had not agreed to the Hopewell treaties—to defend their territory by declaring war. Only in 1790 did they come to terms with the United States.

Relations with the Indians

ists' return. As residents of Norwalk, Connecticut, put it, few Americans wanted to permit the "Tory Villains" to return "while filial Tears are fresh upon our Cheeks and our Murdered Brethren scarcely cold in their Graves." State governments also had reason to oppose enforcement of the treaty. Sales of loyalists' land, houses, and other possessions had helped finance the war. Since most of the purchasers were prominent patriots, states had no desire to raise questions about the legitimacy of their property titles.

The refusal of state and local governments to comply with Articles Four and Five gave Britain an excuse to maintain military posts on the Great Lakes long after its troops were supposed to have withdrawn. Furthermore, Congress's inability to convince states to implement the treaty disclosed its lack of power, even in an area—foreign affairs—in which it had authority under the Articles of Confederation. Concerned nationalists argued publicly that enforcement of the

Western nations such as the Shawnees, Chippewas, Ottawas, and Potawatomis previously had allowed the Iroquois to speak for them. After the collapse of Iroquois power, they formed their own confederacy and demanded direct negotiations with the United States. They intended to present a united

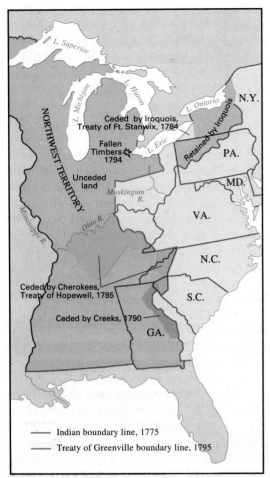

Map 7.2 Cession of Tribal Lands to the United States, 1775–1790 The land claims of the United States meant little as long as Indian nations still controlled vast territories within the new country's formal boundaries. A series of treaties in the 1780s and 1790s opened some lands to white settlement. (Source: From Lester J. Cappon et al., eds., *Atlas of Early American History: The Revolutionary Era, 1760–1790.* Copyright © 1976 by Princeton University Press. Reprinted by permission of Princeton University Press.)

front so as to avoid the piecemeal surrender of land by individual bands and villages. But they faced a difficult task. In the postwar world, Indian nations could no longer pursue the diplomatic strategy that had worked so well for so long: playing off European and American powers against one another. France was gone; Spanish territory lay far to the west and south; and British power was confined to Canada, north of the Great Lakes. Only the United States remained.

At first the national government ignored the western confederacy. Shortly after state land cessions were completed, Congress began to organize the Northwest Territory, bounded by the Mississippi River, the Great Lakes, and the Ohio River (see Map 7.1). Ordinances passed in 1784, 1785, and 1787 outlined the process through which the land could be sold to settlers and formal governments could be organized.

Ordinances of 1784 and 1785

To ensure orderly development, Congress in 1785 directed that the land be surveyed into townships 6 miles square, each divided into thirty-six sections of 640 acres (1 square mile). Revenue from the sale of the sixteenth section of each township was to be reserved for the support of public schools—the first instance of federal aid to education in American history. One dollar was the minimum price per acre; the minimum sale was one section. Thus Congress showed little concern for the small farmer: the resulting minimum outlay, $640, lay beyond the reach of ordinary Americans, except those veterans who received part of their army pay in land warrants. Proceeds from western land sales constituted the first independent revenues available to the national government.

The most important of the three land policies—the Northwest Ordinance of 1787—contained a bill of rights guaranteeing settlers freedom of religion and the right to a jury trial, forbidding cruel and unusual punishments, and nominally prohibiting slavery. Eventually, that prohibition became an important symbol for antislavery northerners, but at the time it had little effect. Some residents of the territory already held slaves, and Congress did not intend to deprive them of their property. Moreover, the ordinance also contained a provision allowing slaveowners to "lawfully reclaim" runaway bondspeople who took refuge in the territory—the first national fugitive slave law. The ordinance prevented slavery from taking deep root by discouraging slaveholders from moving into the territory with their human chattel, but not until 1848 was enslavement abolished throughout the region, now known as the Old Northwest.

Northwest Ordinance

The ordinance of 1787 also specified the process by which residents of the territory could organize state governments and seek admission to the Union "on an equal footing with the original States." Early in the nation's history, therefore, Congress laid down a policy of admitting new states on the same basis as the old

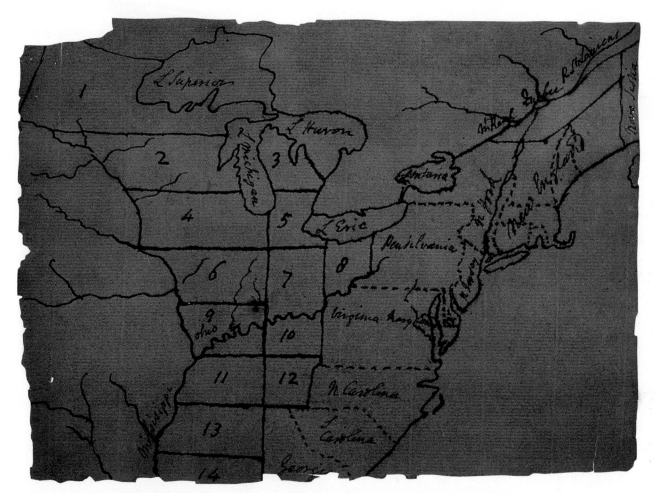

In 1784 Thomas Jefferson proposed a scheme for organizing the new nation's western lands. His plan would have divided the region on a grid pattern, yielding fourteen new states (with names such as "Metropotamia" and "Pelisipia") composed of 10-mile-square "hundreds." After a year of debate, Jefferson's plan was replaced by the one adopted in the Land Ordinance of 1785, which is described in the text.   (Clements Library, University of Michigan)

and assuring residents of the territories the same rights held by citizens of the original states. Having suffered under the rule of a colonial power, congressmen understood the importance of preparing the new nation's first "colony" for eventual self-government. Nineteenth- and twentieth-century Americans were to be less generous in their attitudes toward residents of later territories, many of whom were non-European or non-Protestant. But the nation never fully lost sight of the egalitarian principles of the Northwest Ordinance.

In a sense, though, in 1787 the ordinance was purely theoretical. The Miamis, Shawnees, and Delawares refused to acknowledge American sovereignty. They opposed settlement violently, attacking unwary pioneers who ventured too far north of the Ohio River. In 1788 the Ohio Company, to which Congress had sold a large tract of land at reduced rates, established the town of Marietta at the juncture of the Ohio and Muskingum Rivers. But Indians prevented the company from extending settlement very far into the interior. After General Arthur St. Clair, the Northwest Territory's first governor, failed to negotiate a meaningful treaty with the Indians in early 1789, the United States could not avoid clashing with the western confederacy, composed of eight nations and led by the Miamis.

Little Turtle, the able war chief of the Miami Confederacy, defeated first General Josiah Harmar (1790) and then St. Clair himself (1791) in major battles near the present border between Indiana and

In the summer of 1795, the United States and the Miami Confederacy signed the Treaty of Greenville, bringing an end to open conflict after several years of warfare. All the participants smoked the calumet (peace pipe) pictured here, symbolizing their acceptance of the treaty. Because there were so many signatories, the ceremony took a long time.   (Pipe: Ohio Historical Society; Treaty: National Archives)

War in the Old Northwest

Ohio. More than six hundred of St. Clair's men died, and scores more were wounded, in the United States' worst defeat in the entire history of the American frontier. In 1793 the Miami Confederacy declared that peace could be achieved only if the United States recognized the Ohio River as its northwestern boundary. But the national government refused to relinquish its claims in the region. A new army under the command of General Anthony Wayne, a Revolutionary War hero, attacked and defeated the confederacy in August 1794 at the Battle of Fallen Timbers (near present-day

Toledo, Ohio; see Map 7.2). Peace negotiations began after the victory.

By the summer of 1795, Wayne reached agreement with the Miami Confederacy. The Treaty of Greenville gave each side a portion of what it wanted. The United States gained the right to settle much of what was to become Ohio, the indigenous peoples retaining only the northwest corner of the region. Indians, though, received the acknowledgment they had long sought: American recognition of their rights to the soil. At Greenville, the United States formally accepted the principle of Indian sovereignty, by virtue of residence, over all lands the native peoples had not ceded. Never again would the United States government claim that it had acquired Indian territory solely through negotiation with a European or North American country.

The problems the United States encountered in ensuring safe settlement of the Northwest Territory revealed the basic weakness of the Confederation government. Not until after the Articles of Confederation were replaced with a new constitution could the United States muster sufficient force to implement the Northwest Ordinance. Thus, although the ordinance is often viewed as one of the few lasting accomplishments of the Confederation Congress, it must be seen within a context of political impotence.

From Crisis to the Constitution

Americans involved in finance, overseas trade, and foreign affairs became acutely aware of the inadequacies of the Articles of Confederation. In those areas the Articles had obvious deficiencies: Congress could not levy taxes, nor could it impose its will on the states to establish a uniform commercial policy or to ensure the enforcement of treaties. Partly as a result, the American economy slid into a depression less than a year after war's end. Exporters of staple crops (especially tobacco and rice) and importers of manufactured goods suffered from the postwar restrictions European powers imposed on American commerce. Although recovery began by 1786, the war's effects proved impossible to erase, particularly in the Lower South. Some estimates suggest that between 1775 and 1790 America's per capita gross national product declined by nearly 50 percent.

The war, indeed, wrought permanent change in the American economy. The near total cessation of foreign commerce in nonmilitary items during the war stimulated domestic manufacturing. Consequently, despite the influx of European goods after 1783, the postwar period witnessed the stirrings of American industrial development. For example, the first American textile mill began production in Pawtucket, Rhode Island, in 1793. Because of continuing population growth, the domestic market assumed greater relative importance in the overall economy. Moreover, foreign trade patterns shifted from Europe and toward the West Indies, continuing a trend that had begun before the war. Foodstuffs shipped to the French and Dutch

Economic Change

Caribbean islands became America's largest single export, replacing tobacco (and thus accelerating the Chesapeake's conversion from tobacco to grain production). South Carolina resumed importing slaves on a large scale, as planters sought to replace workers lost to wartime disruptions. Yet without British subsidies American indigo could not compete with that produced in the Caribbean, and even rice planters struggled to find new markets.

Recognizing the Confederation Congress's inability to deal with commercial matters, representatives of Virginia and Maryland met at Mt. Vernon (George Washington's plantation) in March 1785 to negotiate an agreement about trade on the Potomac River, which divided the two states for much of its length. The successful meeting led to an invitation to other states to discuss trade policy generally at a convention in Annapolis, Maryland. Although nine states named representatives to the meeting in September 1786, only five delegations attended. Those present realized that so few people could not have any significant impact on the political system. They issued a call for another convention, to be held in Philadelphia nine months later, "to devise such further provisions as shall . . . appear necessary to render the constitution of the federal government adequate to the exigencies of the Union."

Annapolis Convention

The other states did not respond immediately. But then an armed rebellion in Massachusetts did what a polite invitation to convene could not: convince doubters that reform was needed. Farmers from the western part of the state, many of them veterans, violently opposed high taxes (levied by the eastern-dominated legislature to pay off war debts) and an allied policy of foreclosing on the lands of tax defaulters. Daniel Shays, a former officer in the Continental Army, assumed the nominal leadership of the disgruntled western farmers. On January 25, 1787, he led about 1,500 men in an assault on the federal armory at Springfield, attempting to capture the military stores housed there. The militiamen mustered to defend the armory fired on their former comrades in arms, who then withdrew after suffering twenty-four casualties. The westerners did not confine to the battlefield their challenge to the legitimacy of a government controlled by eastern merchants. Terming Massachusetts "tyrannical," they insisted that "whenever any encroachments are made either upon the liberties or properties of the people, if redress

Shays's Rebellion

cannot be had without, it is virtue in them to disturb government." They thereby explicitly linked their rebellion to the earlier independence struggle.

Such explosive assertions convinced many political leaders that the nation's problems extended far beyond trade policy. To some, the rebellion confirmed the need for a much stronger federal government. After most of the states had already appointed delegates, the Confederation Congress belatedly endorsed the convention, "for the sole and express purpose of revising the Articles of Confederation." In mid-May 1787, fifty-five men, representing all the states but Rhode Island, assembled in Philadelphia to begin their deliberations.

Constitutional Convention in Philadelphia

The vast majority of delegates to the Constitutional Convention were men of property and substance. They all favored reform; otherwise, they would not have come to Philadelphia. Most wanted to invigorate the national government and to give it new authority over taxation and foreign commerce. Many had been members of state legislatures, and some had helped to draft state constitutions. All were influenced in their Philadelphia deliberations by their understanding of the success or failure of those constitutions' provisions. Their ranks included merchants, planters, physicians, generals, governors, and especially lawyers—twenty-three had studied the law. Most had been born in America, and many came from families that had arrived in the seventeenth century. In an era when only a tiny proportion of the population had any advanced education, more than half of the delegates had attended college. A few had been educated in Britain, but most had graduated from American institutions: Princeton, with ten, counted the most alumni participants. The youngest delegate was twenty-six, the oldest—Benjamin Franklin—eighty-one. Like George Washington, whom they elected their presiding officer, most were in their vigorous middle years. A dozen men did the bulk of the convention's work. Of these, James Madison of Virginia was by far the most important; he deserves the title "Father of the Constitution."

James Madison: Father of the Constitution

The frail, shy James Madison was thirty-six years old in 1787. A Princeton graduate raised in western Virginia, he served on the local Committee of Safety and was elected successively to the provincial convention, the state's lower and upper houses, and the Continental Congress (1780–1783). Although Madison returned to Virginia to serve in the state legislature in 1784, he remained in touch with national politics, partly through his continuing correspondence with his close friend Thomas Jefferson. A promoter of the Annapolis Convention, he strongly supported its call for further reform.

Madison stood out among the delegates for his systematic preparation for the Philadelphia meeting. Through Jefferson in Paris he bought more than two hundred books on history and government, carefully analyzing their accounts of past confederacies and republics. A month before the Constitutional Convention began, he summed up the results of his research in a lengthy paper entitled "Vices of the Political System of the United States." After listing the flaws he perceived in the current structure of the government (among them "encroachments by the states on the federal authority" and lack of unity "in matters where common interest requires it"), Madison revealed the conclusion that would guide his actions over the next few months. What the government most needed, he declared, was "such a modification of the sovereignty as will render it sufficiently neutral between the different interests and factions, to controul one part of the society from invading the rights of another, and at the

James Madison (1751–1836), the youthful scholar and skilled politician who earned the title "Father of the Constitution." (Library of Congress)

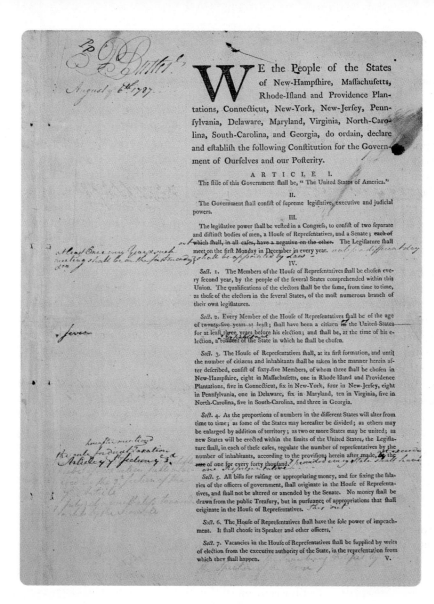

In August 1787 a first draft of the Constitution was secretly printed in Philadelphia for the use of convention members. Wide margins left room for additions and amendments, such as those made on this copy by the South Carolina delegate Pierce Butler. Note that in this early version the preamble does not yet read "We the people of the United States," but instead begins by listing the individual states. (The Gilder Lehrman Collection, on deposit at the Pierpont Morgan Library/Art Resource, N.Y.)

same time sufficiently controuled itself, from setting up an interest adverse to that of the whole Society."

Thus Madison set forth the principle of checks and balances. The government, he believed, had to be constructed in such a way that it could not become tyrannical or fall wholly under the influence of a particular faction. He regarded the large size of a potential national republic as an advantage in that respect. Rejecting the common assertion that republics had to be small to survive, Madison argued that a large, diverse republic should be preferred. Because the nation would include many different factions, no one of them would be able to control the government. Political stability would result from compromises among the contending parties.

The so-called Virginia Plan, introduced on May 29 by Edmund Randolph, embodied Madison's con-

Virginia and New Jersey Plans

ception of national government. The plan provided for a two-house legislature, the lower house elected directly by the people and the upper house selected by the lower; representation in both houses proportional to property or population; an executive elected by Congress; a national judiciary; and congressional veto over state laws. The Virginia Plan gave Congress the broad power to legislate "in all cases to which the separate states are incompetent." Had it been adopted intact, it would have created a government in which national authority reigned unchallenged and state power was greatly diminished. Proportional representation in both houses (however reckoned) would also have given large states a dominant voice in the national government.

The convention included many delegates who recognized the need for change but believed the Virginia Plan went too far in the direction of national consolidation. After two weeks of debate on Randolph's proposal, disaffected delegates—particularly those from small states—united under the leadership of William Paterson of New Jersey. On June 15 Paterson presented an alternative scheme, the New Jersey Plan, calling for strengthening the Articles rather than completely overhauling the government. Paterson proposed retaining a unicameral congress in which each state had an equal vote, but giving Congress new powers of taxation and trade regulation. Paterson earlier had made his position clear in debate. Asserting that the Articles were "the proper basis of all the proceedings of the convention," he contended that the delegates' proper task was "to mark the orbits of the states with due precision and provide for the use of coercion" by the national government. Although the convention initially rejected Paterson's position, he and his allies won a number of victories in the months that followed.

The delegates began their work by discussing the structure and functions of Congress. They readily agreed that the new national government should have a two-house (bicameral) legislature. In addition, they concurred, in accordance with Americans' long-standing opposition to virtual representation (see page 124), that "the people" (however that term was defined) should be directly represented in at least one house of Congress. But they discovered that they differed widely in their answers to three key questions: Should representation in *both* houses of Congress be proportional to population? How was representation in either or both houses to be apportioned among the states? And, finally, how were the members of the two houses to be elected?

The Debates: Houses of Congress

The last issue proved the easiest to resolve. To quote John Dickinson, the delegates thought it "essential" that members of the lower branch of Congress be elected directly by the people and "expedient" that members of the upper house be chosen by state legislatures. Since legislatures had selected delegates to the Confederation Congress, they would expect a similar privilege in the new government. If the convention had not agreed to allow state legislatures to elect senators, the Constitution would have run into significant opposition among state political leaders. The plan also had the virtue of placing the election of one house of Congress one step removed from the "lesser sort," whose judgment the elites at the convention did not wholly trust.

The possibility of representation proportional to population in the Senate caused considerably greater disagreement. The delegates accepted without much debate the principle of proportional representation in the House of Representatives. But small states, through their spokesman Luther Martin of Maryland, argued for equal representation in the Senate. Such a scheme, they rightly supposed, would give them relatively more power at the national level. Large states, on the other hand, supported a proportional plan, for they would then be allotted more votes in the upper house. For weeks the convention deadlocked, neither side able to obtain a majority. A committee appointed to work out a compromise recommended equal representation in the Senate, coupled with a proviso that all appropriation bills originate in the lower house. But not until the convention accepted a suggestion that a state's two senators vote as individuals rather than as a unit was a breakdown averted.

The remaining critical question divided the nation along sectional lines rather than by size of state: how was representation in the lower house to be apportioned among states? Delegates from states with large numbers of slaves wanted African and European inhabitants to be counted equally; delegates from states with few slaves wanted only free people to be counted. Slavery thus became inextricably linked to the foundation of the new government. Delegates resolved the dispute by using a formula developed by the Confederation Congress in 1783 to allocate financial assessments among states: three-fifths of slaves would be included in population totals. (The formula reflected delegates' judgment that slaves were less efficient producers of wealth than free people, not that they were 60 percent human and 40 percent property.) The three-fifths compromise on representation won unanimous approval. Only two delegates, Gouverneur Morris of New York and George Mason of Virginia, later spoke out against the institution of slavery.

The Debates: Slavery and Representation

Although the words *slave* and *slavery* do not appear in the Constitution (the framers used euphemisms such as "other persons"), the document contained both direct and indirect protections for slavery. The three-fifths clause, for example, assured white southern male voters not

Constitutional Protections for Slavery

only congressional representation out of proportion to their numbers but also a disproportionate influence on the selection of the president, since the number of each state's electoral votes was determined by the size of its congressional delegation. The Constitution prohibited Congress from outlawing the slave trade for at least twenty years, and the fugitive slave clause required all states to return runaways to their masters. By guaranteeing that the national government would aid any states threatened with "domestic violence," the Constitution promised aid in putting down future slave revolts, as well as incidents like Shays's Rebellion.

Once delegates agreed on the knotty, conjoined problems of slavery and representation, they readily achieved consensus on the other issues confronting them. All agreed that the national government needed the authority to tax and to regulate commerce. But instead of giving Congress the nearly unlimited scope proposed in the Virginia Plan, delegates enumerated congressional powers and then provided for flexibility by granting it all authority "necessary and proper" to carry out those powers. Discarding the congressional veto contained in the Virginia Plan, the convention implied but did not explicitly authorize a national judicial veto of state laws. The Constitution plus national laws and treaties would constitute "the supreme law of the land; and the judges in every state shall be bound thereby," Article VI declared ambiguously. As another means of circumscribing state powers, delegates drafted a long list of actions forbidden to states.

The convention placed primary responsibility for conducting foreign affairs in the hands of the president, who was also designated commander-in-chief of the armed forces.

The Presidency

That decision raised the question, left unspecified in the Constitution's text, of whether the president (or Congress, for that matter) acquired special powers in times of war. With the consent of the Senate, the president could appoint judges and other federal officers. To select the president, delegates established an elaborate mechanism, the electoral college, whose members would be chosen in each state by legislatures or qualified voters. This system, they hoped, would ensure that the executive would be independent of the national legislature—and of the people. They also agreed that the chief executive should serve a four-year term but be eligible for reelection.

The final document still showed signs of its origins in the Virginia Plan, but compromises created a system of government less powerful at the national

Separation of Powers

level than Madison and Randolph had envisioned. The key to the Constitution was the distribution of political authority—that is, separation of powers among executive, legislative, and judicial branches of the national government, and division of powers between states and nation. Two-thirds of Congress and three-fourths of the states, for example, had to concur on amendments. The branches balanced one another, their powers deliberately entwined to prevent each from acting independently. The president could veto congressional legislation, but that veto could be overridden by two-thirds majorities in both houses, and his treaties and major appointments required the Senate's consent. Congress could impeach the president and federal judges, but courts appeared to have the final say on interpreting the Constitution. These checks and balances would make it difficult for the government to become tyrannical. At the same time, though, the elaborate system would sometimes prevent the government from acting quickly and decisively. Furthermore, the Constitution drew such a vague line between state and national powers that the United States fought a civil war in the next century over that very issue.

The convention held its last session on September 17, 1787. Of the forty-two delegates present (others had returned home weeks earlier), only three refused to sign the Constitution, two of them in part because of the lack of a bill of rights. Benjamin Franklin had written a speech calling for unity; because his weak voice could not be heard, another delegate read it for him. "I confess that there are several parts of this constitution which I do not at present approve," Franklin admitted. Yet he urged its acceptance "because I expect no better, and because I am not sure, that it is not the best." Only then was the Constitution made public. The convention's proceedings had been entirely secret—and remained so until the delegates' private notes were published in the nineteenth century. (See the Appendix for the full text of the Constitution.)

Opposition and Ratification

 Later the same month, the Confederation Congress submitted the Constitution to the states but did not formally recommend approval. The ratification clause provided for the new system to take effect once it was approved by special conventions in at least nine states, with delegates being elected by qualified voters. Thus the national Constitution, unlike the Articles of Confederation, would rest directly on popular authority (and the presumably hostile state legislatures would be circumvented).

As states began to elect delegates to the special conventions, discussion of the proposed government grew more heated. Newspaper essays and pamphlets vigorously defended or attacked the Philadephia convention's decisions. The extent of the debate was unprecedented. Every newspaper in the country printed the full text of the Constitution, and most supported its adoption. It quickly became apparent, though, that disputes within the Constitutional Convention had been mild compared to divisions of opinion within the populace as a whole. Although most citizens concurred that the national government should have more power over taxation and foreign commerce, some believed that the proposed government held the potential for tyranny. As happened in Carlisle, Pennsylvania, the vigorous debate between the two sides frequently spilled out into the streets.

Those supporting the proposed Constitution called themselves Federalists. They built on the

Federalists

notions of classical republicanism, holding forth a vision of a virtuous, self-sacrificing republic vigorously led by a manly aristocracy of talent. Claiming that the nation did not need to fear centralized authority when good men drawn from the elite were in charge, they argued that the carefully structured government would preclude the possibility of tyranny. A republic could be large, they declared, if the government's design prevented any one group from controlling it. The separation of powers among legislative, executive, and judicial branches, and the division of powers between states and nation, would accomplish that goal. Thus people did not need to be protected from the powers of the new government in a formal way. Instead, their liberties would be guarded by "distinguished worthies"—men of the "better sort" whose only goal (said George Washington) was "to merit the approbation of good and virtuous men."

The Federalists termed those who opposed the Constitution Antifederalists, thus tagging them with

Antifederalists

negative nomenclature. Antifederalists, while recognizing the need for a national source of revenue, feared a too-powerful central government. They saw the states as the chief protectors of individual rights; consequently, weakening the states could bring the onset of arbitrary power. Antifederalist arguments against the Constitution often consisted of lists of potential abuses of government authority.

Heirs of the Real Whig ideology of the late 1760s and early 1770s, Antifederalists stressed the need for constant popular vigilance to avert oppression. Indeed, some of the Antifederalists had originally promulgated those ideas—Samuel Adams, Patrick Henry, and Richard Henry Lee led the opposition to the Constitution. Such older Americans, whose political opinions had been shaped prior to the centralizing, nationalistic Revolution, peopled the Antifederalist ranks. Joining them were small farmers preoccupied with guarding their property against excessive taxation, and ambitious, upwardly mobile men who would benefit from an economic and political system less tightly controlled than that the Constitution envisioned. Federalists denigrated such men as disorderly, licentious, and even "unmanly" and "boyish" because they would not follow the elites' lead in supporting the Constitution.

As public debate continued, Antifederalists focused on the Constitution's lack of a bill of rights.

Importance of a Bill of Rights

Even if the new system weakened the states, Antis believed, people could still be protected from tyranny by specific guarantees of rights. The Constitution did contain some prohibitions on congressional power. For example, the writ of habeas corpus, which prevented arbitrary imprisonment, could not be suspended except in dire emergencies. But Antifederalists found such constitutional provisions to be few and inadequate. Nor were they reassured by Federalist assertions that the new government could not violate people's rights because it had only limited powers. Antis wanted the national governing document to incorporate a bill of rights, as had most state constitutions.

Letters of a Federal Farmer, perhaps the most widely read Antifederalist pamphlet, listed the rights that should be protected: freedom of the press and religion, trial by jury, and guarantees against unreasonable searches. From Paris, Thomas Jefferson added his voice to the chorus. Replying to Madison's letter conveying a copy of the Constitution, Jefferson declared, "I like much the general idea" but not "the omission of a bill of rights. . . . A bill of rights is what the people are entitled to against every government on earth, general or particular, and what no just government should refuse, or rest on inference."

As state conventions considered ratification, the lack of a bill of rights loomed ever larger as a flaw in

Ratification of the Constitution

the proposed government. Four of the first five states to ratify did so unanimously, but serious disagreements then surfaced. Massachusetts, in which Antifederalist forces had been bolstered by a backlash against the state government's heavy-handed treatment of the Shays rebels, ratified by a majority of only 19 votes out of 355 cast. In June 1788, when New Hampshire ratified, the requirement of nine states was satisfied. But New York and Virginia had not yet voted, and everyone realized the new Constitution could not succeed unless those key states accepted it.

Despite a valiant effort by the Antifederalist Patrick Henry, pro-Constitution forces won by 10 votes in the Virginia convention. In New York, James Madison, John Jay, and Alexander Hamilton campaigned for ratification by publishing *The Federalist*, a political tract that explained the theory behind the Constitution and masterfully answered its critics. Their reasoned arguments, coupled with Federalists' promise to add a bill of rights to the Constitution, helped win the battle. On July 26, 1788, New York ratified the Constitution by the slim margin of 3 votes. Although the last states—North Carolina and Rhode Island—did not join the Union until November 1789 and May 1790, respectively, the new government was a reality.

Americans in many cities celebrated ratification (somewhat prematurely) with a series of parades on

Celebrating Ratification

July 4, 1788. The carefully planned processions dramatized the history and symbolized the unity of the new nation, seeking to counteract memories of the dissent that had so recently engulfed such cities as Carlisle, Pennsylvania (see page 167). Like pre-Revolution protest meetings, the parades served as political lessons for literate and illiterate Americans alike. The processions aimed to educate men and women about the significance of the new Constitution and to instruct them about political leaders' hopes for industry and frugality on the part of a virtuous American public.

Symbols expressing those goals filled the Philadelphia parade, planned by the artist Charles Willson Peale. About five thousand people participated in the procession, which featured floats portraying such themes as "The Grand Federal Edifice" and stretched for a mile and a half. Marchers representing the first pioneers and Revolutionary War troops paraded with groups of farmers and artisans dramatizing their work.

The Federal Almanack for 1789 trumpeted the virtues of the new Constitution. Not all Americans were so certain that the national government, here symbolized as an edifice supported by thirteen pillars, was as "solid, strong as time" as the printer proclaimed.   (American Antiquarian Society)

More than forty groups of tradesmen, including barbers, hatters, printers, cloth manufacturers, and clockmakers, sponsored floats. Lawyers, doctors, clergymen of all denominations, and congressmen followed the artisans. A final group of marchers symbolized the nation's future: students from the University of Pennsylvania and other city schools bore a flag labeled "The Rising Generation."

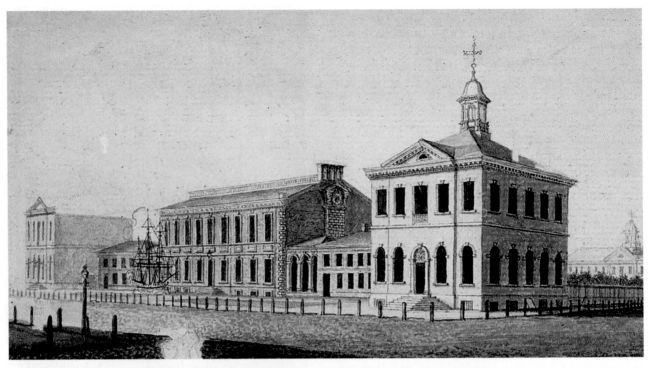

The Philadelphia State House (the building now known as Independence Hall, but without its familiar tower), on the left; and, to its right, Congress Hall, where Congress met when Philadelphia served as the U.S. capital. Portrayed in front of the state house in this 1792 watercolor is the 33-foot-long vessel *Union,* an elaborately constructed ship carried through the city streets in the grand ratification parade of July 4, 1788.   (Philadelphia Museum of Art, Lent by the Dietrich American Foundation)

Summary

During the 1770s and 1780s the nation took shape as a political union. It began to develop an economy independent of the British Empire and attempted to chart its own course in the world in order to protect the national interest, defend the country's borders, and promote beneficial trade. Some Americans prescribed rules for the cultural and intellectual life they thought appropriate for a republic, outlining artistic and educational goals for a properly virtuous people. An integral part of the formation of the Union was the systematic formulation of American racist thought. Emphasizing race (rather than status as slave or free) as a determinant of African Americans' standing in the nation, and defining women as nonpolitical, allowed men who now termed themselves "white" to define *republicanism* to exclude all people but themselves and to ensure that they would dominate the country for the foreseeable future.

The experience of fighting a war and of struggling for survival as an independent nation altered the political context of American life in the 1780s. At the outset of the war, most Americans believed that "that government which governs best governs least," but by the late 1780s many had changed their minds. They were the drafters and supporters of the Constitution, who concluded from the republic's vicissitudes under the Articles of Confederation that the United States needed a more powerful central government. They contended during ratification debates that their proposed solution to the nation's problems was just as "republican" in conception (if not more so) as the Articles.

Both sides concurred in a general adherence to republican principles, but they emphasized different views of republicanism. Federalists advanced a position based on the principles of classical republicanism. Antifederalists, fearing that elected leaders would not subordinate personal gain to the good of the whole, wanted a weak central government, formal protection of individual rights, and a loosely regulated economy.

The Federalists won their point when the Constitution was adopted, however narrowly. The process of consolidating the states into a national whole was thereby formalized. The 1790s, the first decade of government under the Constitution, would witness hesitant steps toward the creation of a true nation, the United States of America.

LEGACY FOR A PEOPLE AND A NATION
Women's Education

In the early years of the twenty-first century, women comprise a slim majority of the students enrolled in U.S. colleges and universities. Because women were denied all access to collegiate education in this country until the middle of the nineteenth century, that is a remarkable development. Its roots lie deep, in the republican ideology of the 1770s and 1780s.

Once the United States had established republican forms of government at both state and national levels, its citizens began to worry about sustaining those governments—thought to be fragile and easily disrupted—for the decades and centuries to come. The future, everyone knew, lay in the hands of the nation's children, especially its sons. And theorists concluded that those sons could successfully perpetuate the republic only if they learned the lessons of patriotism from their mothers. Male and female reformers therefore began to argue that women in the United States should be better educated than those who lived under other forms of government. If American women were ignorant of the nation's history or principles of government, or if they did not know enough basic reading or arithmetic to assist their husbands in running farms or businesses, the republic was doomed to collapse in just a generation or two.

Some of those reformers accordingly founded private academies (roughly equivalent to modern high schools) to teach young women from leading families such subjects as history, geography, mathematics, and languages. Some of the women who attended those academies later started educational establishments of their own—including Mary Lyon, who in 1837 founded Mt. Holyoke College in western Massachusetts, the first institution of higher education for women in the United States. A few years later, some colleges for men (such as Oberlin, in Ohio) and state universities (for example, Michigan) admitted women as students, and a number of women's colleges were established. Not until the second half of the twentieth century, however, did American women gain truly equal access to higher education. In the 1970s such Ivy League universities as Yale and Princeton finally opened their doors to women students, and others (such as Cornell) that had sharply restricted women's enrollment through admissions quotas removed all constraints.

Along with the existence of the nation itself, increased educational opportunity for women is therefore one of the most important legacies of the revolutionary era for the American people.

For Further Reading, see page A-9 of the Appendix. For Web resources, go to http://college.hmco.com.

The twenty-eight-year-old guest on the Georgia plantation, a recent graduate of Yale College, had already proved himself to be good with his hands. His hostess, Catherine Greene (the widow of the Revolutionary War general Nathanael Greene), had complained that her embroidery frame was poorly designed—and so he quickly constructed a replacement. Thus when some neighboring planters discussed in Mrs. Greene's presence the seemingly insurmountable problem of extracting seeds from cotton fibers, she told them, "apply to my young friend, Mr. Whitney, he can make any thing."

Catherine Greene's "young friend," Eli Whitney, attacked the planters' challenge with the same ingenuity that had led him, while still a teenager, to develop methods for manufacturing nails on a large scale. Within ten days, he later recalled, he produced a small working model of the machine that would become known as the cotton gin. Whitney's device changed the lives of millions of people, for good and ill.

In the years after the Revolution, the United States sought another staple crop to augment such exports as tobacco and salt fish. When new spinning and weaving machines caused a boom in the British textile manufacturing industry in the 1780s, cotton seemed a possibility. But the only kind of cotton that could be grown widely in the United States had fibers that twisted tightly around its seeds. Removing the seeds by hand was costly, labor-intensive, and agonizingly slow. Before Whitney invented his cotton gin in 1793, few Americans planted much cotton because of such processing difficulties.

Whitney attached wire teeth to two adjacent rollers turned by a hand crank. The teeth tore the seeds from fibers fed between the rollers; the seeds then dropped through a screen into a receptacle. To prevent fibers from clogging the machine, Whitney also rigged a set of brushes that turned in the opposite direction, continually cleaning the rollers. This gin, its inventor proudly noted, processed cotton fifty times faster than hand workers could. The Georgia planters

Eli Whitney, the inventor of the cotton gin, in a portrait by his fellow Yale graduate Samuel F. B. Morse. Although the gin did not earn him the fortune Whitney had anticipated, it did eventually bring him great fame. (Yale University Art Gallery, Gift of George Hoadley, B.A., 1801)

8

THE EARLY REPUBLIC: CONFLICTS AT HOME AND ABROAD 1789–1800

who saw the machine quickly recognized its potential. Someone stole the model even before Whitney could request a patent on it, and thereafter he spent years in court defending his right to his invention. He did not fully establish his legal claims until shortly before the patent expired.

Whitney therefore did not profit greatly from the cotton gin, but many others did. Cotton exports became one of the mainstays of the American economy in the nineteenth century. The surge in cotton cultivation revived the institution of slavery, which in the immediate postrevolutionary period had appeared to be losing its reason for being, as Chesapeake tobacco planters switched to less labor-intensive grains, indigo cultivation collapsed, and new markets for rice had to be established. Southern planter families and New England capitalists gained a great deal by his invention, but enslaved people thus lost much more.

In the 1790s, before the full impact of Whitney's invention, the American economy still rested in large part on traditional exports. Americans found their vital commerce disrupted once more—with consequent fluctuations in their income and profits—when in 1793 England and France again went to war. The fight over ratifying the Constitution turned out to presage an even wider division over the major political, economic, and diplomatic questions confronting the young republic: the extent to which authority (especially fiscal authority) should be centralized in the national government; the relationship of national power and states' rights; the formulation of foreign policy in an era of continual warfare in Europe; and the limits of dissent. Americans did not anticipate the acrimonious disagreements that rocked the 1790s. Believing that the Constitution would resolve the problems that had arisen under the Confederation, they mistakenly expected the new government to rule largely by consensus. And no one predicted the difficulties that would develop as the United States attempted to deal with Indian nations now wholly encompassed within its borders.

Most important of all, perhaps, they could not understand or fully accept the division of America's political leaders into two factions—not yet political parties—known as Federalists and Democratic-Republicans, believing that only monarchies should experience such factional disputes. In republics, they believed, the rise of factions signified decay and corruption. As the decade closed with the first fully partisan presidential election, Americans still had not come to terms with the implications of partisan politics. ■

Building a Workable Government

 The nationalistic spirit expressed in the processions celebrating ratification of the Constitution carried over to the first session of Congress. Only a few Antifederalists ran for office in the congressional elections held late in 1788, and even fewer were elected. Thus the First Congress consisted chiefly of men who supported a strong national government. The drafters of the Constitution had deliberately left many key issues undecided, so the nationalists' domination of Congress meant that their views on those points quickly prevailed.

Congress faced four immediate tasks when it convened in April 1789: raising revenue to support the new government, responding to states' calls for a bill of rights, setting up executive departments, and organizing the federal judiciary. The last task was especially important. The Constitution established a Supreme Court but left it to Congress to decide whether to have other federal courts as well.

James Madison, who had been elected to the House of Representatives, soon became as influential in Congress as he had been at the Constitutional Convention. A few months into the first session, he persuaded Congress to adopt the Revenue Act of 1789, imposing a 5 percent tariff on certain imports. Thus the First Congress quickly achieved what the Confederation Congress never had: an effective national tax law. The new government would have problems in its first years, but lack of revenue was not one of them.

Madison and the First Congress

Madison also took the lead with respect to constitutional amendments. At the convention and thereafter, he had consistently opposed additional limitations on the national government. He believed it unnecessary to guarantee people's rights explicitly when the government was one of limited powers. But Madison recognized that Congress should respond to public opinion as expressed in state ratifying conventions. Accordingly, he placed nineteen proposed amendments before the House. The states soon ratified ten, which officially became part of the Constitution on December 15, 1791 (see the appendix for the Constitution and all amendments, including the twenty-seventh, which was one of Madison's nineteen). Their adoption defused Antifederalist opposition and rallied support for the new government.

IMPORTANT EVENTS

1789 Washington inaugurated as first president
Judiciary Act of 1789 organizes federal
court system
French Revolution begins

1790 Hamilton's *Report on Public Credit* proposes
assumption of state debts

1791 First ten amendments (Bill of Rights)
ratified
First national bank chartered

1793 France declares war on Britain, Spain, and
the Netherlands
Washington's neutrality proclamation keeps
the United States out of war
Democratic-Republican societies founded,
the first grassroots political organizations

1794 Whiskey Rebellion in western Pennsylvania
protests taxation

1795 Jay Treaty with England
Pinckney's Treaty with Spain

1796 First contested presidential election: Adams
elected president, Jefferson vice president

1798 XYZ affair arouses American opinion
against France
Sedition Act penalizes dissent
Virginia and Kentucky resolutions protest
suppression of dissent

1798–99 Quasi-War with France

1800 Franco-American Convention ends Quasi-
War
Jefferson elected president, Burr vice
president
Gabriel's Rebellion threatens Virginia
slaveowners

The First Amendment specifically prohibited Congress from passing any law restricting the right to freedom of religion, speech, press, peaceable assembly, or petition. The

Bill of Rights

next two amendments arose directly from the former colonists' fear of standing armies as a threat to freedom. The Second Amendment guaranteed the right "to keep and bear arms" because of the need for a "well-regulated Militia." Thus the constitutional right to bear arms was based on the expectation that most able-bodied men would serve the nation as citizen-soldiers, and there would be little need for a standing army. The Third Amendment limited the conditions under which troops could be quartered in private homes. The next five pertained to judicial procedures. The Fourth Amendment prohibited "unreasonable searches and seizures"; the Fifth and Sixth established the rights of accused persons; the Seventh specified the conditions for jury trials in civil (as opposed to criminal) cases; and the Eighth forbade "cruel and unusual punishments." The Ninth and Tenth Amendments reserved to the people and the states other unspecified rights and powers. In short, the amendments' authors made clear that, in listing some rights, they did not mean to preclude the exercise of others.

While debating proposed amendments, Congress also considered the organization of the executive branch. It readily agreed to continue the three administrative departments established under the Articles of Confederation: War, Foreign Affairs (renamed State), and Treasury. Congress instituted two lesser posts: the attorney general—the nation's official lawyer—and the postmaster general. Controversy arose over whether the president alone could dismiss officials whom he originally had appointed with the Senate's consent. After some debate, the House and Senate agreed that he had such authority. Thus was established the important principle that the heads of executive departments are accountable solely to the president.

Aside from constitutional amendments, the most far-reaching piece of legislation enacted by the First

**Federal
Judiciary**

Congress was the Judiciary Act of 1789, which defined the jurisdiction of the federal judiciary and established a six-member Supreme Court, thirteen district courts, and three circuit courts of appeal. Its most important provision, Section 25, allowed appeals from state courts to federal courts when cases raised certain types of constitutional issues. Section 25 thus implemented Article VI of the Constitution, which stated that federal laws and treaties were to be considered "the supreme Law of the Land." For Article VI to be enforced uniformly, the national judiciary had to be able to overturn state court decisions in cases involving the Constitution, federal laws, or treaties. Yet nowhere did the Constitution explicitly permit such action by federal courts.

The Judiciary Act of 1789 presumed that the wording of Article VI implied the right of appeal from state to federal courts. In the nineteenth century, however, judges and legislators committed to states' rights challenged that interpretation.

During its first decade, the Supreme Court handled few cases of any importance, and several members resigned. (John Jay, the first chief justice, served only six years.) But in a significant 1796 decision, *Ware v.*

When George Washington toured the nation during his first term in office, he was greeted by local leaders in elaborately orchestrated rituals. The organizers of the ceremony at Providence, Rhode Island, on August 17, 1790, issued this broadside to inform participants of their plans for a formal procession. While some Americans gloried in such displays of pomp, others feared they presaged the return of monarchy.   (The Huntington Library & Art Collections, San Marino, California)

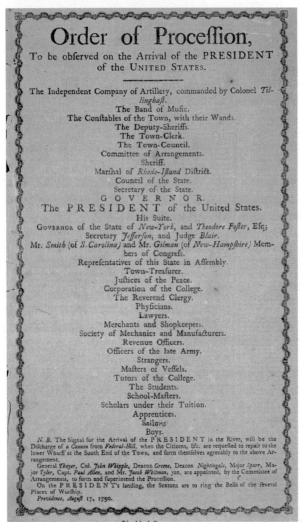

Hylton, the Court for the first time declared a state law unconstitutional. That same year it also reviewed the constitutionality of an act of Congress, upholding its validity in the case of *Hylton v. U.S.* The most important case of the decade, *Chisholm v. Georgia* (1793), established that states could be sued in federal courts by citizens of other states. This decision, unpopular with state governments, was overruled five years later by the Eleventh Amendment to the Constitution.

Domestic Policy Under Washington and Hamilton

George Washington did not seek the presidency. In 1783 he returned to Mount Vernon eager for the peaceful life of a Virginia planter. But his fellow countrymen never regarded Washington as just another private citizen. Unanimously elected to preside at the Constitutional Convention, he did not participate in debates but consistently voted for a strong national government. After the adoption of the new governmental structure, Americans concurred that only George Washington had sufficient stature to serve as the republic's first president, an office designed largely with him in mind. The unanimous vote of the electoral college merely formalized that consensus.

Reluctant to return to public life, George Washington nevertheless knew he could not ignore his country's call. Awaiting the summons to New York City, the nation's capital, he wrote to an old friend, "My movements to the chair of Government will be accompanied by feelings not unlike those of a culprit who is going to the place of his execution. . . . I am sensible, that I am embarking the voice of my Countrymen and a good name of my own, on this voyage, but what returns will be made for them, Heaven alone can foretell."

Washington acted cautiously during his first months in office, knowing that whatever he did would set precedents for the future. When the title by which he should be addressed aroused controversy (Vice President John Adams favored "His Highness, the President of the United States of America, and Protector of their Liberties"), Washington said nothing. The accepted title soon became a plain "Mr. President." By using the heads of the executive departments collectively as his chief advisers, he created the cabinet. As the Constitution required, he sent Congress an annual State of the

Washington's First Steps

Alexander Hamilton, by James Sharpless, about 1796. This profile of Hamilton, painted near the end of Washington's presidency, shows the secretary of the treasury as he looked during the years of his first heated partisan battles with Thomas Jefferson and James Madison (see page 203). (National Portrait Gallery, Smithsonian Institution/Art Resource, N.Y.)

John Trumbull, known primarily for his larger-than-life portraits of patriot leaders, painted this miniature (c. 1792–1794) of George Washington, who posed for it during his presidency. (Division of Political History, Smithsonian Institution, Washington, D.C.)

Union message. Washington also concluded that he should exercise his veto power over congressional legislation very sparingly—only, indeed, if he became convinced a bill was unconstitutional.

Early in his term, Washington undertook elaborately organized journeys to all the states. At each stop, he was ritually welcomed by uniformed militia units, young women strewing flowers in his path, local leaders, groups of Revolutionary War veterans, and respectable citizens who presented him with formal addresses reaffirming their loyalty to the United States. The president thus personally came to embody national unity, simultaneously drawing ordinary folk into the sphere of national politics.

Washington's first major task as president was to choose the heads of the executive departments. For the War Department he selected an old comrade-in-arms, Henry Knox of Massachusetts, who had been his reliable general of artillery during much of the Revolution. His choice for the State Department was his fellow Virginian Thomas Jefferson, who had just re-

turned to the United States from his post as minister to France. And for the crucial position of secretary of the treasury, the president chose the brilliant, intensely ambitious Alexander Hamilton.

The illegitimate son of a Scottish aristocrat and a woman whose husband had divorced her for adultery and desertion, Hamilton was born in the British West Indies in 1757. His early years were spent in poverty; after his mother's death when he was eleven, he worked as a clerk for a mercantile firm. In 1773 Hamilton enrolled in King's College (later Columbia University) in New York City. Only eighteen months later, in late 1774, the precocious seventeen-year-old contributed a pamphlet to the prerevolutionary publication wars. Devoted to the patriot cause, Hamilton volunteered for service in the American army, where he came to Washington's attention. In 1777 Washington appointed the young man as one of his aides, and the two developed great mutual affection.

Alexander Hamilton

The general's patronage helped the poor youth of dubious background to marry well. At twenty-three he took as his wife Elizabeth Schuyler, daughter of a wealthy New York family. After the war, Hamilton practiced law in New York City and served as a delegate first to the Annapolis Convention and then to the Constitutional Convention. Although he exerted little influence at either gathering, his contributions to *The Federalist* in 1788 revealed him as one of the chief political thinkers in the republic.

In his dual role as secretary of the treasury and one of Washington's major advisers, Hamilton exhibited two traits that distinguished him from most of his contemporaries. First, he displayed an undivided loyalty to the nation as a whole. As a West Indian who had lived on the mainland only briefly before the war, Hamilton had no ties to a particular state. He showed little sympathy for, or understanding of, demands for local autonomy. Thus the aim of his fiscal policies was always to consolidate power at the national level. Further, he never feared the exercise of centralized executive authority, as did older counterparts who had clashed repeatedly with colonial governors, nor was he afraid of maintaining close political and economic ties with Britain.

Second, Hamilton regarded his fellow human beings with unvarnished cynicism. Perhaps because of his difficult early life and his own overriding ambition, Hamilton believed people to be motivated primarily by self-interest—particularly economic self-interest. He placed no reliance on people's capacity for virtuous and self-sacrificing behavior. This outlook set him apart from those Americans who foresaw a rosy future in which public-spirited citizens would pursue the common good rather than their own private advantage. Although other Americans (for example, Madison) also stressed the role of private interests in a republic, Hamilton went beyond them in his emphasis on self-interest as the major motivator of human behavior. And his beliefs significantly influenced the way in which he tackled the monumental task before him: straightening out the new nation's tangled finances.

In 1789, Congress ordered the new secretary of the treasury to assess the public debt and to submit recommendations for supporting the government's credit. Hamilton found that the country's remaining war debts fell into three categories: those owed by the nation to foreign governments and investors, mostly to France (about $11 million); those owed by the national government to

National and State Debts

merchants, former soldiers, holders of revolutionary bonds, and the like (about $27 million); and, finally, similar debts owed by state governments (roughly $25 million). With respect to the national debt, few disagreed: Americans recognized that if their new government was to succeed, it would have to repay at full face value those financial obligations incurred by the nation while winning independence.

The state debts were another matter. Some states—notably Virginia, Maryland, North Carolina, and Georgia—already had paid off most of their war debts by levying taxes and handing out land grants in lieu of monetary payments. They would oppose the national government's assumption of responsibility for other states' debts because their citizens would be taxed to pay such obligations. Massachusetts, Connecticut, and South Carolina, by contrast, still had sizable unpaid debts and would welcome a system of national assumption. The possible assumption of state debts also had political implications. Consolidating the debt in the hands of the national government would help to concentrate economic and political power at the national level. A contrary policy would reserve greater independence of action for the states.

Hamilton's first *Report on Public Credit*, sent to Congress in January 1790, stimulated lively debate. The treasury secretary proposed that Congress assume outstanding state debts, combine them with national obligations, and issue new securities covering both principal and accumulated unpaid interest. Hamilton thereby hoped to ensure that holders of the public debt—many of them wealthy merchants and speculators—had a significant financial stake in the new government's survival. The opposition coalesced around James Madison, who was against the assumption of state debts for two reasons. Not only had his state already paid off most of its obligations, but he also wanted to avoid rewarding wealthy speculators who had purchased state and national debt certificates at a small fraction of their face value from needy veterans and farmers.

Hamilton's Financial Plan

Prompted in part by Madison, the House initially rejected the assumption of state debts. The Senate, however, adopted Hamilton's plan largely intact. A series of compromises followed, in which the assumption bill became linked to the other major controversial issue of that congressional session: the location of the permanent national capital. The legend that Hamilton and Madison agreed over Jefferson's dinner table to exchange assumption of state debts for a southern site is not supported by the surviving evidence, but a political deal was undoubtedly struck. The Potomac River was designated as the site for the capital, and the first part of Hamilton's financial program became law in August 1790.

Four months later Hamilton submitted to Congress a second report on public credit, recommending the chartering of a national bank. This proposal too aroused much opposition, though primarily after Congress had already passed the bill to establish the bank.

Hamilton modeled his bank on the Bank of England. The Bank of the United States was to be capitalized at $10 million, of which only $2 million would come from public funds. Private investors would supply the rest. The bank's charter would run for twenty years, and the government would name one-fifth of the directors. The bank's notes would circulate as the nation's currency. The bank would also act as collecting and disbursing agent for the Treasury and would lend money to the government. Most political leaders

**First Bank
of the United
States**

recognized that such an institution would be beneficial, especially because it would solve the problem of America's perpetual shortage of an acceptable medium of exchange. But another issue loomed large: did the Constitution give Congress the power to establish such a bank?

James Madison answered that question with a resounding *no*. He pointed out that Constitutional Convention delegates had specifically rejected a clause authorizing Congress to issue corporate charters. Consequently, he argued, that power could not be inferred from other parts of the Constitution. Madison's contention disturbed President Washington, who decided to request other opinions before signing the bill into law. Edmund Randolph, the attorney general, and Thomas Jefferson, the secretary of state, agreed with Madison that the bank was unconstitutional. Jefferson referred to Article I, Section 8, of the Constitution, which gave Congress the power "to make all Laws which shall be necessary and

**Strict and Broad
Constructions
of the
Constitution**

Although Congress did not react positively to the arguments in Hamilton's *Report on Manufactures,* the owners of America's burgeoning industries recognized the importance of the policy Hamilton advocated. Ebenezer Clough, a Boston maker of wallpaper, incorporated into his letterhead the exhortation "Americans, Encourage the Manufactories of your Country, if you wish for its prosperity." (American Antiquarian Society)

proper for carrying into Execution the foregoing Powers." The key word, Jefferson argued, was *necessary:* Congress could do what was needed but without specific constitutional authorization could not do what was merely desirable. Thus Jefferson formulated the strict-constructionist interpretation of the Constitution.

Washington asked Hamilton to reply to the negative assessments of his proposal. Hamilton's *Defense of the Constitutionality of the Bank*, presented to the president in February 1791, brilliantly expounded a broad-constructionist view of the Constitution. Hamilton argued forcefully that Congress could choose any means not specifically prohibited by the Constitution to achieve a constitutional end. He reasoned thus: if the end was constitutional and the means was not *un*constitutional, then the means was constitutional.

Washington concurred, and the bill became law. The bank proved successful, as did the scheme for funding the national debt and assuming the states' debts. The new nation's securities became desirable investments for its own citizens and for wealthy foreigners, especially those in the Netherlands, who rushed to purchase American debt certificates. The influx of new capital, coupled with the high prices American produce now commanded in European markets, eased farmers' debt burdens and contributed to a new prosperity. But two other aspects of Alexander Hamilton's wide-ranging financial scheme did not fare so well.

In December 1791, Hamilton presented to Congress his *Report on Manufactures*, the third and last of his prescriptions for the American economy. In it he outlined an ambitious plan for encouraging and protecting the United States's infant industries, such as shoemaking and textile manufacturing. Hamilton argued that the nation could never be truly independent as long as it relied heavily on Europe for manufactured goods. He thus urged Congress to promote the immigration of technicians and laborers and to support industrial development through a limited use of protective tariffs. Many of Hamilton's ideas were implemented in later decades, especially after the United States greatly increased its cultivation of cotton and could therefore amply supply its textile mills, but few congressmen in 1791 could see much merit in his proposals. They firmly believed that America's future lay in agriculture and the carrying trade and that the mainstay of the republic was the virtuous small farmer. Therefore, Congress rejected the report.

Hamilton's Report on Manufactures

That same year Congress accepted another feature of Hamilton's financial program, levying a tax on whiskey produced within the United States. Although proceeds from the Revenue Act of 1789 covered the interest on the national debt, the decision to fund state debts meant that the national government required additional income. A tax on whiskey affected relatively few farmers—those west of the mountains who sold their grain in the form of distilled spirits as a means of avoiding the high cost of transportation—and might also reduce the consumption of whiskey. (Eighteenth-century Americans, notorious for their heavy drinking, consumed about twice as much alcohol per capita as today's rate.) Moreover, Hamilton knew that those western farmers were Jefferson's supporters, and he saw the benefits of taxing them rather than the merchants who supported his own policies.

News of the tax set off protests in frontier areas of Pennsylvania, where residents were already dissatisfied with the army's as yet unsuccessful attempts to defeat the Miami Confederacy (see pages 184–185). To their minds, the same government that protected them inadequately was now proposing to tax them disproportionately. Unrest continued for two years on the frontiers of Pennsylvania, Maryland, and Virginia. Large groups of men drafted petitions protesting the tax, deliberately imitated crowd actions of the 1760s, and occasionally harassed tax collectors.

Whiskey Rebellion

President Washington responded with restraint until violence erupted in July 1794, when western Pennsylvania farmers resisted a federal marshal and a tax collector trying to enforce the law. Three rioters were killed and several militiamen wounded. About seven thousand rebels convened on August 1 to plot the destruction of Pittsburgh but decided not to face the heavy guns of the fort guarding the town. Washington then took decisive action to prevent a crisis reminiscent of Shays's Rebellion. On August 7, he called on the insurgents to disperse and summoned nearly thirteen thousand militia from Pennsylvania and neighboring states. By the time federal forces marched westward in October and November (led at times by Washington himself), the disturbances had ceased. The troops met no resistance and arrested only twenty suspects. Two, neither of them prominent leaders of the rioters, were convicted of treason, but—continuing his policy of restraint—Washington pardoned both. The leaderless and unorganized rebellion ended with little bloodshed.

The chief importance of the Whiskey Rebellion lay not in military victory over the rebels—for there was none—but in the forceful message it conveyed to the American people. The national government, Washington had demonstrated, would not allow violent resistance to its laws. In the republic, change would be effected peacefully, by legal means. People dissatisfied with the law should try to amend or repeal it, not take extralegal action as they had during the colonial era.

The French Revolution and the Development of Partisan Politics

 By 1794, some Americans were already beginning to seek change systematically through electoral politics, even though traditional political theory regarded organized opposition—especially in a republic—as illegitimate. In a monarchy, formal opposition groups were to be expected. In a government of the people, by contrast, serious and sustained disagreement was taken as a sign of corruption and subversion. Such negative judgments, while widely held, still did not halt the growth of partisan sentiment.

Thomas Jefferson and James Madison became convinced as early as 1792 that Hamilton's policies of

Democratic-Republicans and Federalists

favoring wealthy commercial interests at the expense of agriculture aimed at imposing a corrupt, aristocratic government on the United States. Characterizing themselves as the true heirs of the Revolution, they charged that Hamilton was plotting to subvert republican principles. To dramatize their point, Jefferson, Madison, and their followers in Congress began calling themselves Democratic-Republicans. Hamilton in turn accused Jefferson and Madison of the same crime: attempting to destroy the republic. Hamilton and his supporters began calling themselves Federalists, to legitimize their claims and link themselves with the Constitution. Each group accused the other of being an illicit faction working to sabotage the republican principles of the Revolution. (In the traditional sense of the term, a faction was by definition dangerous and opposed to the public good.)

At first, President Washington tried to remain aloof from the political dispute that divided Hamilton and Jefferson, his chief advisers. Yet the growing controversy helped persuade him to seek a second term of office in 1792 in hopes of promoting political unity.

A Federalist political cartoon from the 1790s shows "Mad Tom" Paine "in a rage," trying to destroy the federal government as carefully constructed (in classical style) by President Washington and Vice President Adams. That Paine is being aided by the Devil underscores the hostility to partisanship common in the era.   (The Huntington Library & Art Collections, San Marino, California)

But in 1793 and thereafter, developments in foreign affairs magnified the disagreements, for France—America's wartime ally—and Great Britain—America's most important trading partner—resumed the periodic hostilities that had originated a century earlier (see page 83).

In 1789 Americans welcomed the news of the French Revolution. The French people's success in

The French Revolution

limiting, and then overthrowing, an oppressive monarchy seemed to vindicate the United States's own revolution. Americans saw themselves as the vanguard of an inevitable historical trend that would reshape the world in a republican mold. But by the early 1790s the reports from France were disquieting. Outbreaks of violence continued and ministries succeeded each other with bewildering rapidity. Executions mounted; the king himself was beheaded in early 1793. Although many Americans, including Jefferson and Madison, retained a sympathetic view of the revolution, others began to cite France as a prime example of the perversion of republicanism. As might be expected, Alexander Hamilton spoke for the latter group.

When France declared war on Britain, Spain, and Holland in 1793, the Americans faced a dilemma. The 1778 Treaty of Alliance with France bound them to that nation "forever," and a mutual commitment to republicanism created ideological bonds. Yet the United States was connected to Great Britain as well. In addition to their shared history and language, America and Britain had again become important economic partners. Americans still purchased most of their manufactured goods from Great Britain. Indeed, since the financial system of the United States depended heavily on import tariffs as a source of revenue, the nation's economic health in effect required uninterrupted trade with the former mother country.

The political and diplomatic climate grew even more complicated in April 1793, when Citizen Edmond Genêt, a representative of the French government, landed in Charleston, South Carolina. As Genêt made his way north to New York City, he recruited Americans for expeditions against British and Spanish colonies in the Western Hemisphere, freely distributing privateering commissions. Genêt's arrival raised troubling questions for President Washington. Should he receive Genêt, thus officially recognizing the French revolutionary government? Should he acknowledge an obligation to aid France under the terms of the 1778 Treaty of Alliance? Or should he proclaim American neutrality?

Citizen Genêt

For once, Hamilton and Jefferson saw eye to eye. Both told Washington that the United States could not afford to ally itself with either side. Washington agreed. He received Genêt but also issued a proclamation informing the world that the United States would adopt "a conduct friendly and impartial toward the belligerent powers." In deference to Jefferson's continued support for France, though, the word *neutrality* did not appear in the declaration.

Genêt himself was removed from politics when his faction fell from power in Paris; he subsequently sought political asylum in the United States. But his disappearance from the diplomatic scene did not diminish the impact of the French Revolution in America. The domestic divisions Genêt helped to widen were perpetuated by clubs called Democratic-Republican societies, formed by Americans sympathetic to the French Revolution and worried about the policies of the Washington administration. Such societies reflected a growing grassroots concern about the same developments that troubled Jefferson and Madison.

Citizen Edmond Genêt's visit caused the first major diplomatic crisis in the new nation. His attempts to enlist Americans in support of the French Revolution raised troubling questions about the international role of the United States.   (Collection of the Albany Institute of History and Art. Bequest of George Genêt)

More than forty Democratic-Republican societies organized between 1793 and 1800. Their members saw themselves as heirs of the Sons of Liberty, seeking the same goal as their predecessors: protection of people's liberties against encroachments by corrupt and self-serving rulers. To that end, they publicly protested government fiscal and foreign policy and repeatedly proclaimed their belief in "the equal rights of man," particularly the rights to free speech, free press, and assembly. Like the Sons of Liberty, the Demo-

Democratic-Republican Societies

cratic-Republican societies chiefly comprised artisans and craftsmen, although professionals, farmers, and merchants also joined.

The rapid growth of such groups, outspoken in their criticism of the Washington administration for its failure to come to the aid of France and for its domestic economic policies, deeply disturbed Hamilton and eventually Washington himself. Some newspapers charged that the societies were subversive agents of a foreign power. Their "real design," one asserted, was "to involve the country in war, to assume the reins of government and tyrannize over the people." The counterattack climaxed in the fall of 1794, when Washington accused the societies of having fomented the Whiskey Rebellion.

In retrospect, Washington and Hamilton's reaction to the Democratic-Republican societies seems disproportionately hostile. But it must be recalled that factional disputes were believed to endanger the survival of republics. As the first organized political dissenters in the United States, the Democratic-Republican societies alarmed elected officials, who had not yet accepted the idea that one component of a free government was an organized loyal opposition.

Partisan Politics and Relations with Great Britain

In 1794 George Washington dispatched Chief Justice John Jay to London to negotiate four unresolved questions in Anglo-American relations. The first point at issue was recent British seizures of American merchant ships trading in the French West Indies. The United States wanted to establish the principle of freedom of the seas and to assert its right, as a neutral nation, to trade freely with both combatants. Second, in violation of the 1783 peace treaty, Great Britain had not yet evacuated its posts in the American Northwest. Settlers there believed that the British were responsible for the renewed warfare in the region (see pages 182–185), and they wanted that threat removed. The Americans also hoped for a commercial treaty and sought compensation for the slaves who left with the British army at the end of the war.

The negotiations in London proved difficult, since Jay had little to offer in exchange for the concessions he sought. Britain did agree to evacuate the western forts and ease restrictions on American trade to England and the West Indies. (Some

Jay Treaty

limitations were retained, however, violating the Americans' stated commitment to open commerce.) The treaty established two arbitration commissions— one to deal with prewar debts Americans owed to British creditors and the other to hear claims for captured American merchant ships—but Britain adamantly refused slaveowners compensation for their lost bondspeople. Under the circumstances, Jay did remarkably well: the treaty averted war with England at a time when the United States, which lacked an effective navy, could not have won such a conflict. Nevertheless, most Americans, including the president, expressed dissatisfaction with at least some parts of the treaty.

The Senate debated the Jay Treaty in secret, so members of the public did not learn its provisions until after Senate ratification (by a vote of 20 to 10) in June 1795. The Democratic-Republican societies led protests against the treaty. Especially vehement opposition arose in the South, as planters criticized the failure to obtain compensation for runaway slaves and objected to the commission on prewar debts, which might make them pay off sizable obligations to British merchants dating back to the 1760s. Once President Washington had signed the treaty, though, there seemed little the Democratic-Republicans could do to prevent it from taking effect. Just one opportunity remained: Congress had to appropriate funds to carry out the treaty provisions and, according to the Constitution, appropriation bills had to originate in the House of Representatives.

When the House debated the issue in March 1796, members opposing the treaty tried to prevent approval of the appropriations. To that end, they asked Washington to submit to the House all documents pertinent to the negotiations. In successfully resisting the House's request, Washington established the doctrine of executive privilege—the power of the president to withhold information from Congress if he believes circumstances warrant doing so.

The treaty's opponents initially appeared to be in the majority, but pressure for appropriating the necessary funds built as time passed. Frontier residents eagerly sought Britain's evacuation of its remaining outposts, for they feared a new outbreak of Indian war despite the signing of the Treaty of Greenville. Merchants wanted to reap benefits from expanded trade. Furthermore, Thomas Pinckney of South Carolina had negotiated a treaty with Spain giving the United States navigation privileges on the Mississippi River, which would be an economic boost to the West and

South. The popularity of Pinckney's Treaty (the Senate ratified it unanimously) helped to overcome opposition to the Jay Treaty. For all these reasons, the House appropriated the money by the narrow margin of 51 to 48.

Analysis of the vote reveals both the regional nature of the division and the growing cohesion of the Democratic-Republican and Federalist factions in Congress. Voting for the appropriations were 44 Federalists and 7 Democratic-Republicans; voting against were 45 Democratic-Republicans and 3 Federalists. The final tally also divided by region. Southerners (including three Virginia Federalists) cast the vast majority of votes against the bill. Its supporters hailed from New England and the middle states, with the exception of two South Carolina Federalists. The seven Democratic-Republicans who voted for the appropriations came from commercial areas in New York, Pennsylvania, and Maryland.

Partisan Divisions in Congress

The small number of defectors on both sides reveals a new force at work in American politics: partisanship. Voting statistics from the first four Congresses show the ever-increasing tendency of members of the House of Representatives to vote as cohesive groups, rather than as individuals. If factional loyalty is defined as voting together at least two-thirds of the time on national issues, the percentage of nonaligned congressmen dropped from 42 percent in 1790 to just 7 percent in 1796. Significantly, this trend toward party cohesion occurred even though Congress experienced heavy turnover. Most congressmen served only one or two terms in office, and fewer than 10 percent were reelected more than three times. During the 1790s the majority slowly shifted from Federalist to Democratic-Republican. Federalists controlled the first three Congresses, through the spring of 1795. Democratic-Republicans gained ascendancy in the Fourth Congress. Federalists returned to power with slight majorities in the Fifth and Sixth Congresses, but the Democratic-Republicans took over—more or less for good—in the Seventh Congress in 1801.

Bases of Partisanship

To describe these shifts is easier than to explain them. The terms used by Jefferson and Madison (aristocrats versus the people) or by Hamilton and Washington (true patriots versus subversive rabble) do not adequately explain the growing divisions. Simple economic differences between agrarian and commercial interests do not provide the answer either, since more than 90

percent of Americans still lived in rural areas. Moreover, Jefferson's vision of a prosperous agrarian America rested on commercial farming, not rural self-sufficiency. Nor did the divisions in the 1790s simply repeat the Federalist-Antifederalist debate of 1787–1788. Even though most Antifederalists became Democratic-Republicans, the party's leaders, Madison and Jefferson, had supported the Constitution.

Yet certain distinctions can be made. Democratic-Republicans, especially prominent in the southern and middle states, tended to be self-assured, confident, and optimistic about both politics and the economy. Southern planters, firmly in control of their region and of a class of enslaved laborers, did not fear instability, at least among the European American population. They foresaw a prosperous future based partly on continued westward expansion, a movement they expected to dominate. Democratic-Republicans employed democratic rhetoric to win the allegiance of small farmers south of New England. Members of non-English ethnic groups—especially Irish, Scots, and Germans—found Democratic-Republicans' words attractive. Artisans also joined the coalition; they saw themselves as the urban equivalent of small farmers and valued their independence from domineering bosses. Democratic-Republicans of all descriptions emphasized developing America's own resources, worrying less than Federalists did about the nation's place in the world. Democratic-Republicans also remained sympathetic to France in international affairs.

By contrast, Federalists, concentrated in New England, came mostly from English stock. Insecure and uncertain of the future, they drew considerable support from commercial interests. They stressed the need for order, authority, and regularity in the political world. Federalists had no grassroots political organization and put little emphasis on involving ordinary people in government. Wealthy New England merchants aligned themselves with the Federalists, but so too did the region's farmers who, prevented from expanding agricultural production because of New England's poor soil, gravitated toward the more conservative party. Federalists, like Democratic-Republicans, assumed that southern and middle-state interests would dominate the land west of the mountains, so they had little incentive to work actively to develop that potentially rich territory. In Federalist eyes, potential enemies—both internal and external—perpetually threatened the nation, which required a continuing alliance with Great Britain for its own protection. Their vision of international affairs may have been more accurate than that of the Democratic-

Republicans, given the warfare in Europe, but it was also narrow and unattractive. Since the Federalist view held out little hope of a better future to the voters of any region, the Democratic-Republicans unsurprisingly prevailed in the end.

The presence of the two organized groups—not yet parties in the modern sense but active contenders for office nonetheless—made the presidential election of 1796 the first serious contest for the position. Wearied by the criticism to which he had been subjected,

Washington's Farewell Address

George Washington decided to retire from office. (Presidents had not yet been limited to two terms, as they have been since the adoption of the Twenty-second Amendment in 1951.) In September Washington published his Farewell Address, most of which had been written by Hamilton. In it Washington outlined two principles that guided American foreign policy at least until the late 1940s: to maintain commercial but not political

How do historians know...

that in all probability starting in the 1790s Thomas Jefferson fathered the children born to his slave Sally Hemings?

Tales that Jefferson fathered Hemings's children surfaced early in his presidency. For many years historians rejected those stories as scurrilous rumors spread by Jefferson's enemies, accepting the Jefferson family's explanation that Sally Hemings's children (who resembled the third president) had been fathered by one of his sister's sons, Peter or Samuel Carr. Most scholars and Jefferson family members argued that the acknowledged special treatment accorded the entire Hemings clan at Monticello stemmed from the fact that Sally and her siblings were the acknowledged offspring of Jefferson's father-in-law by his mulatto slave mistress, Betty Hemings (and thus that Sally was Jefferson's dead wife's half-sister). In 1974, however, the historian Fawn Brodie's assertion in her *Thomas Jefferson: An Intimate History* that Jefferson had fathered the younger Hemingses reignited the controversy. Recent advances in DNA testing permitted a scientific analysis of the alternative theories, at least with respect to the parentage of Sally's youngest son, Eston Hemings. It is now

known that men pass Y chromosomes on to their male children largely intact. Because no sons were born to the marriage of Martha Randolph and Thomas Jefferson, male-line descendants of Jefferson's paternal uncle were tested, along with similar descendants of the Carr brothers and Eston Hemings. British scientists, working blindly—that is, without knowing the origins of the blood samples they were studying—demonstrated to their own satisfaction that Jefferson had indeed fathered Eston Hemings, and by implication Sally Hemings's earlier children as well. The DNA samples of the Hemings and Jefferson descendants match almost perfectly (as illustrated here), whereas those of the Carrs differ significantly from both of the others. (Photo: *Nature*, vol. 396)

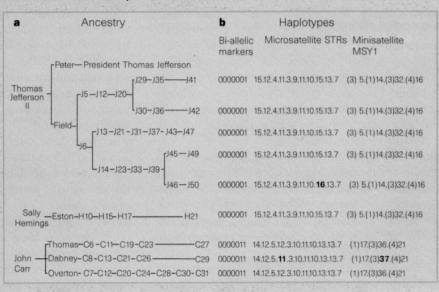

ties to other nations and to enter no permanent alliances. He also drew sharp distinctions between the United States and Europe, stressing America's uniqueness—its exceptionalism—and the need for unilateralism (independent action in foreign affairs).

Washington also lamented the existence of factional divisions among his countrymen. Historians have often interpreted his call for an end to partisan strife as the statement of a man who could see beyond political affiliations to the good of the whole. But in the context of the impending presidential election, the Farewell Address appears rather as an attack on the legitimacy of the Democratic-Republican opposition. Washington advocated unity behind the Federalist banner, which he viewed as the only proper political stance. The Federalists (like the Democratic-Republicans) continued to see themselves as the sole guardians of the truth and the only true heirs of the Revolution. Both sides perceived their opponents as misguided, unpatriotic troublemakers who sought to undermine revolutionary ideals.

Election of 1796

To succeed Washington, the Federalists in Congress put forward Vice President John Adams, with the diplomat Thomas Pinckney as his running mate. Congressional Democratic-Republicans met and chose Thomas Jefferson as their presidential candidate; the lawyer, Revolutionary War veteran, and active Democratic-Republican politician Aaron Burr of New York agreed to run for vice president.

That the election was contested does not mean that the people decided its outcome. Voters could cast their ballots only for electors, not for the candidates themselves, and not all electors publicly declared their preferences. State legislatures, not a popular vote, selected more than 40 percent of the members of the electoral college; some electors had been picked even before Federalists and Democratic-Republicans named their presidential candidates. Moreover, the method of voting in the electoral college did not take into account the possibility of party slates. The Constitution's drafters had not foreseen the development of competing national political organizations, so the Constitution provided no way to express support for one person for president and another for vice president. The electors simply voted for two people. The man with the highest total became president; the second highest, vice president.

This procedure proved to be the Federalists' undoing. Adams won the presidency with 71 votes, but a number of Federalist electors (especially those from New England) failed to cast ballots for Pinckney. Thomas Jefferson won 68 votes, 9 more than Pinckney, to become vice president. The incoming administration was thus politically divided. During the next four years the new president and vice president, once allies and close friends, became bitter enemies.

John Adams and Political Dissent

John Adams took over the presidency peculiarly blind to the partisan developments of the previous four years. As president he never abandoned an outdated notion discarded by George Washington as early as 1794: that the president should be above politics, an independent and dignified figure who did not seek petty factional advantage. Thus Adams kept Washington's cabinet intact, despite its key members' allegiance to his chief rival, Alexander Hamilton. Adams often adopted a passive posture, letting others (usually Hamilton) take the lead when the president should have acted decisively. As a result, his administration gained a reputation for inconsistency. When Adams's term ended, the Federalists were severely divided, and the Democratic-Republicans had won the presidency. But Adams's detachment from Hamilton's maneuverings did enable him to weather the greatest international crisis the republic had yet faced: the Quasi-War with France.

The Jay Treaty improved America's relationship with Great Britain, but it provoked French retaliation. Angry that the United States had reached agreement with its enemy, the French government ordered its ships to seize American vessels carrying British goods. In response, Congress increased military spending, authorizing the building of ships and the stockpiling of weapons and ammunition. President Adams also sent three commissioners to Paris to negotiate a settlement. For months, the American commissioners sought talks with Talleyrand, the French foreign minister, but Talleyrand's agents demanded a bribe of $250,000 before negotiations could begin. The Americans retorted, "No, no; not a sixpence," and reported the incident in dispatches that the president received in early March 1798. Adams informed Congress of the impasse and recommended further increases in defense appropriations.

Convinced that Adams had deliberately sabotaged the negotiations, congressional Democratic-Republicans insisted that the dispatches be turned over

This cartoon drawn during the XYZ affair depicts the United States as a maiden being victimized by the five leaders of the French government's directorate. In the background, John Bull (England) watches from on high, while other European nations discuss the situation.   (The Lilly Library, Indiana University, Bloomington, Indiana)

XYZ Affair

to Congress. Adams complied, aware that releasing the reports would work to his advantage. He withheld only the names of the French agents, referring to them as X, Y, and Z. The revelation that the Americans had been treated with contempt stimulated a wave of anti-French sentiment in the United States. A journalist's version of the commissioners' reply, "Millions for defense, but not a cent for tribute," became the national slogan. Cries for war filled the air. Congress formally abrogated the Treaty of Alliance and authorized American ships to seize French vessels.

Thus began an undeclared war with France. Warships of the U.S. Navy and French privateers seeking to capture American merchant vessels fought the Quasi-War in Caribbean waters. Although Americans initially suffered heavy losses of merchant shipping, by early 1799 the U.S. Navy had established its superiority in the West

Quasi-War with France

Indies. Its ships captured eight French privateers and naval vessels, easing the threat to America's vital Caribbean trade.

The Democratic-Republicans, who opposed war and continued to sympathize with France, could do little to stem the tide of anti-French feelings. Since Agent Y had boasted of the existence of a "French party in America," Federalists flatly accused Democratic-Republicans of traitorous designs. A New York newspaper declared that anyone who remained "lukewarm" after reading the XYZ dispatches was a "criminal—and the man who does not warmly reprobate the conduct of the French must have a soul black enough to be fit for treason Strategems and spoils." John Adams wavered between calling the Democratic-Republicans traitors and acknowledging their right to oppose administration measures. His wife was less tolerant. "Those whom the French boast of as their Partizans," Abigail Adams declared, should be "adjudged traitors to their country." If Jefferson had been president, she added, "we should all have been sold to the French."

Federalists saw this climate of opinion as an opportunity to deal a death blow to their Democratic-Republican opponents. Now that the country seemed to see the truth of

Alien and Sedition Acts

what they had been saying ever since the Whiskey Rebellion in 1794—that Democratic-Republicans were subversive foreign agents—Federalists sought to codify that belief into law. In 1798 the Federalist-controlled Congress adopted a set of four laws known as the Alien and Sedition Acts, intended to suppress dissent and to prevent further growth of the Democratic-Republican faction.

Three of the acts targeted recently arrived immigrants, whom Federalists accurately suspected of being Democratic-Republican in their sympathies. The Naturalization Act lengthened the residency period required for citizenship and ordered all resident aliens to register with the federal government. The two Alien Acts provided for the detention of enemy aliens in time of war and gave the president authority to deport any alien he deemed dangerous to the nation's security. Neither act was implemented during the Adams administration, however.

The fourth statute, the Sedition Act, sought to control both citizens and aliens. It outlawed conspiracies to prevent the enforcement of federal laws, setting the maximum punishment for such offenses at five years in prison and a $5,000 fine. The act also tried to control speech. Writing, printing, or uttering "false, scandalous and malicious" statements against the government or the president "with intent to defame . . . or to bring them or either of them, into contempt or disrepute" became a crime punishable by as much as two years' imprisonment and a fine of $2,000. Today any such law punishing speech alone would be considered unconstitutional. But in the eighteenth century, when organized political opposition was by definition suspect, many Americans supported the Sedition Act's restrictions on free speech.

The Sedition Act led to fifteen indictments and ten convictions. Outspoken Democratic-Republican newspaper editors who failed to mute their criticism of the administration composed most of the accused. But the first victim—whose story may serve as an example of the rest—was a hot-tempered Democratic-Republican congressman from Vermont, Matthew Lyon. The Irish-born Lyon, a former indentured servant who had purchased his freedom and fought in the Revolution, was indicted for declaring in print that John Adams had displayed "a continual grasp for

power" and "an unbounded thirst for ridiculous pomp, foolish adulation, and selfish avarice." Though convicted, fined $1,000, and sent to prison for four months, Lyon did not lapse into silence. He conducted his reelection campaign from jail, winning an overwhelming majority. Leading Democratic-Republicans from around the country contributed to pay his fine.

Faced with prosecutions of their supporters, Jefferson and Madison sought an effective means of combating the acts. Petitioning the

Virginia and Kentucky Resolutions

Federalist-controlled Congress to repeal the laws would clearly fail. Furthermore, Federalist judges refused to allow accused individuals to question the Sedition Act's constitutionality. Accordingly, the Democratic-Republican leaders turned to the only other forum available for protest: state legislatures. Carefully concealing their own role—it would not have been desirable for the vice president to be indicted for sedition—Jefferson and Madison each drafted a set of resolutions. Introduced into the Kentucky and Virginia legislatures, respectively, in the fall of 1798, the resolutions differed somewhat but had the same import. Since a compact among the states created the Constitution, they contended, people speaking through their states had a legitimate right to judge the constitutionality of actions taken by the federal government. Both sets of resolutions pronounced the Alien and Sedition Acts unconstitutional, asking other states to join in a concerted protest against them.

Although no other state endorsed them, the Virginia and Kentucky resolutions nevertheless had considerable influence. First, they constituted superb political propaganda, rallying Democratic-Republican opinion throughout the country. They placed the opposition party squarely in the revolutionary tradition of resistance to tyrannical authority. Second, the theory of union they proposed inspired southern states' rights advocates in the 1830s and thereafter. Jefferson and Madison had identified a key constitutional issue: how far could states go in opposing the national government? How could a conflict between the two be resolved? These questions would not be definitively answered until the Civil War.

Just as the Sedition Act was being implemented and northern state legislatures were rejecting the Virginia and Kentucky resolutions, Fed-

Convention of 1800

eralists split over the course of action the United States should take toward France. Hamilton and his supporters called for a declaration legitimizing the undeclared naval war. But Adams received a number of private signals that the French government regretted its treatment of the American commissioners. Acting on such assurances, he dispatched the envoy William Vans Murray to Paris. The United States sought two goals: compensation for ships the French had seized since 1793 and abrogation of the treaty of 1778. The Convention of 1800, which ended the Quasi-War, provided for the latter but not the former. Still, it freed the United States from its only permanent alliance, thus allowing it to follow the independent diplomatic course George Washington had urged in his Farewell Address.

The results of the negotiations did not become known in the United States until after the presidential election of 1800. Even so, since Hamilton and many of his followers wanted to widen the Quasi-War, Adams's decision to seek a peaceful settlement probably cost him reelection because of the divisions it caused in Federalist ranks.

The Democratic-Republicans entered the 1800 presidential race firmly united behind Thomas Jefferson and Aaron Burr, their candidates

Election of 1800

from four years earlier. Although they won the election, their lack of foresight almost cost them dearly. The system of voting in the electoral college, which Federalists understood better than Democratic-Republicans, nearly derailed the Democratic-Republicans' plans. The Federalists arranged in advance for one of their electors to fail to vote for Charles Cotesworth Pinckney, their vice-presidential candidate. John Adams thus received the higher number of Federalist votes (65 to Pinckney's 64). Democratic-Republicans failed to make the same distinction between their candidates, and all 73 of their electors cast ballots for both Jefferson and Burr (see Map 8.1). Because neither man had a plurality, the Constitution required that the contest be decided in the House of Representatives, with each state's congressmen voting as a unit. Since the new House, dominated by Democratic-Republicans, would not take office for some months, Federalist congressmen decided the election. It took them thirty-five ballots to decide that Jefferson would be a lesser evil than Burr, who revealed his ambition (and alienated Jefferson) by promoting his own candidacy for president. In response to the tangle, the Twelfth Amendment to the Constitution (1804) changed the method of voting in the electoral college to allow for a party ticket.

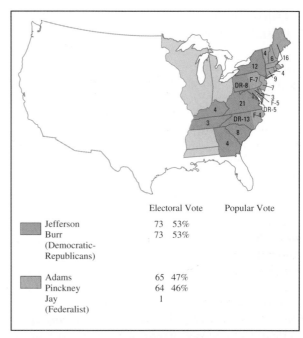

	Electoral Vote	Popular Vote
Jefferson	73	53%
Burr (Democratic-Republicans)	73	53%
Adams	65	47%
Pinckney	64	46%
Jay (Federalist)	1	

Map 8.1 Presidential Election, 1800 The Democratic-Republicans, with their candidates Thomas Jefferson and Aaron Burr, won the electoral votes of the southern states, while the Federalists, the party of John Adams and Charles Cotesworth Pinckney, received votes primarily in New England. The parties split the votes of the middle states, but the Democratic-Republicans dominated the electoral-vote count there and won the election.

Race Relations at the End of the Century

 As the nation anticipated the inauguration of a new president, it had added three states (Vermont, Kentucky, and Tennessee) to the original thirteen and more than 1 million people to the nearly 4 million counted by the 1790 census. Nine-tenths of the approximately 1 million resident African Americans—most still enslaved—lived in the Chesapeake or the Lower South. After the signing of the Treaty of Greenville in 1795 (see pages 184–185), all the Indian nations residing in U.S. territory east of the Mississippi River had made peace with the republic. Even though many Indian peoples still lived independently of federal authority, they came increasingly within the orbit of U.S. influence.

The new nation's policymakers, all of European American descent, could not ignore such large proportions of the population. How should the republic deal with eastern Indians, who no longer posed a military threat to the country? Did the growing population of bondspeople (augmented by more than ninety thousand imports directly from Africa before Congress ended the slave trade in 1808) present new hazards? The second question took on added significance after 1793, when in the French colony of Saint Domingue (Haiti), mulattos and blacks under the leadership of Toussaint L'Ouverture overthrew European rule in a bloody revolt characterized by numerous atrocities on both sides.

In 1789 Henry Knox, Washington's secretary of war, proposed that the new national government assume the task of "civilizing" America's indigenous population. "Instead of exterminating a part of the human race," he contended, the government

"Civilizing" the Indians

should "impart our knowledge of cultivation and the arts to the aboriginals of the country." The first step in such a project, Knox suggested, should be to introduce to Indian peoples "a love for exclusive property"; to that end, he proposed that the government give livestock to individual Indians. Four years later, the Indian Trade and Intercourse Act of 1793 codified Knox's plan, promising that the federal government would supply Indians with animals and agricultural implements and would also provide appropriate instructors.

The well-intentioned plan reflected federal officials' blindness to the realities of native peoples' lives. Not only did it incorrectly posit that the Indians' traditional commitment to communal notions of landowning (see page 43) could easily be overcome, it also ignored the centuries-long agricultural experience

In 1805, an unidentified artist painted Benjamin Hawkins, a trader and U.S. agent to the Indians of the Southeast, at the Creek agency near Macon, Georgia. Hawkins introduced European-style agriculture to the Creeks, who are shown here with vegetables from their fields. Throughout the eastern United States, Indian nations had to make similar adaptations of their traditional lifestyles in order to maintain their group identity.   (Collection of the Greenville County Art Museum, South Carolina)

of eastern Indian peoples. The policymakers focused only on Indian *men:* since they hunted, male Indians were "savages" who had to be "civilized" by being taught to farm. That in these societies *women* traditionally did the farming was irrelevant because in the eyes of the officials, Indian women—like those of European descent—should properly confine themselves to child rearing, household chores, and home manufacturing.

Indian nations at first responded cautiously to the "civilizing" plan. The Iroquois Confederacy had been devastated by the war; its people in the 1790s lived in what one historian has called "slums in the wilderness." Restricted to small reservations increasingly surrounded by Anglo-American farmlands, men could no longer hunt and often spent their days in idle carousing. Quaker missionaries started a demonstration farm among the Senecas, intending to teach men to plow, but they quickly learned that women showed greater interest in their message. The same was true among the Cherokees of Georgia, where Indian agents found that women eagerly sought to learn both new farming methods and textile manufacturing skills. As their southern hunting territories were reduced, Cherokee men did begin to raise cattle and hogs, but they startled the reformers by treating livestock like wild game, allowing the animals to run free in the woods and simply shooting them when needed, in the same way they had once killed deer. Men also started to plow the fields, although Cherokee women continued to bear primary responsibility for cultivation and harvest.

Iroquois and Cherokees

Iroquois men became more receptive to the Quakers' lessons after the spring of 1799, when a Seneca named Handsome Lake experienced a remarkable series of visions. Like other prophets stretching back to Neolin (see page 123), Handsome Lake preached that Indian peoples should renounce alcohol, gambling, and other destructive European customs. Even though he directed his followers to reorient men's and women's work assignments as the Quakers advocated, Handsome Lake aimed above all to preserve Iroquois culture by doing so. He recognized that, since men could no longer obtain meat through hunting, only by adopting a sexual division of labor that had originated in Europe could the Iroquois retain an autonomous existence.

African Americans had long been forced to conform to European American notions of proper gender roles and, unlike Indians, they had embraced Christianity as well during the Great Awakening (see page

African Americans and Ideas of Freedom

110). Yet, just as Cherokees and Iroquois adapted the reformers' plans to their own purposes, so too enslaved blacks found new meanings in the dominant society's ideas. Like their white compatriots, African Americans (both slave and free) became familiar with concepts of liberty and equality during the Revolution. They also witnessed the benefits of fighting collectively for freedom, rather than resisting individually or running away—a message reinforced by the dramatic news of the successful slave revolt in St. Domingue in 1793. And, as white evangelicals by the end of the century began to back away from the earlier racial egalitarianism of their movement, African Americans increasingly formed their own separate Baptist and Methodist congregations in the Chesapeake, as they did in Philadelphia and other urban centers (see pages 174–175).

Such congregations near Richmond became the seedbeds of revolt. Gabriel, an enslaved blacksmith who argued that African Americans should fight for their freedom, carefully planned a large-scale revolt. Often accompanied by his brother Martin, a preacher, he visited Sunday church services, where blacks gathered outside of the watchful eyes of their owners. Gabriel first recruited to his cause other skilled African Americans who like himself lived in semifreedom under minimal supervision. Next he enlisted rural slaves (see Map 8.2). The conspirators planned to attack Richmond on the night of August 30, 1800, set fire to the city, seize the state capitol, and capture the governor, James Monroe. At that point, Gabriel believed, other slaves and sympathetic poor whites would join in.

Gabriel's Rebellion

The plan showed considerable political sophistication, but heavy rain forced a postponement. Several planters then learned of the plan from slave informers and spread the alarm. Gabriel avoided arrest for some weeks, but militia troops quickly apprehended and interrogated most of the other leaders of the rebellion. Twenty-six conspirators, including Gabriel himself, were hanged. Ironically, only those slaves who betrayed their fellows won their freedom as a consequence of the conspiracy.

That disastrous outcome did not end the unrest among Virginia's slaves. In 1802 a waterman named Sancho—a peripheral participant in Gabriel's plot—revived the plans for a revolt. This time word spread along Virginia and North Carolina rivers, carried by slaves who, like Sancho, worked on the boats that plied

Richmond, Virginia, at the time of Gabriel's Rebellion. This was the city as Gabriel knew it. The state capitol, the rebels' intended target, dominates the city's skyline as it dominated Gabriel's thinking. (Virginia Historical Society)

the two states' interconnected waterways. The incomplete plans disintegrated when the plots were revealed prematurely. Again, trials and executions followed, and twenty-five more African Americans lost their lives on the gallows.

At his trial two years earlier, one of Gabriel's followers had made explicit the links that so frightened Chesapeake slaveholders. He told his judges that, like George Washington, "I have adventured my life in endeavouring to obtain the liberty of my countrymen, and am a willing sacrifice in their cause." Southern state legislatures responded to such claims by increasing the severity of the laws regulating slavery. Before long, all talk of emancipation (gradual or otherwise) ceased, and slavery became even more firmly entrenched as an economic institution and way of life, especially as cotton cultivation spread rapidly in the wake of Whitney's invention of the cotton gin.

Summary

 As the nineteenth century began, inhabitants of the United States faced changed lives in the new republic. Indian peoples east of the Mississippi River found that they had to give up some parts of their traditional culture to preserve others. Some African Americans struggled unsuccessfully to free themselves from the inhuman bonds of slavery, then subsequently confronted more constraints than ever because of increasingly restrictive laws.

European Americans too adjusted to changed circumstances. The first eleven years of government under the Constitution established many enduring precedents for congressional, presidential, and judicial action—among them the establishment of the cabinet, the interpretations of key clauses of the Constitution, and the stirrings of judicial review of state and federal legislation. Building on successful negotiations with Spain (Pinckney's Treaty), Britain (the Jay Treaty), and France (the Convention of 1800), the United States developed its diplomatic independence, striving to avoid entanglement with European powers. Yet especially after 1793 internal political consensus proved elusive. The 1790s spawned vigorous debates over foreign and domestic policy and saw the beginnings of a system of organized political factionalism, if not yet formal parties. The Whiskey Rebellion, instigated by westerners outraged at tax policies formulated by eastern elites, showed that regional conflicts continued even under the new government. And the waging of an undeclared war proved extremely contentious, splitting one faction and energizing another.

At the end of the 1790s, after more than a decade of struggle, the Jeffersonian view of the future of republicanism prevailed over Alexander Hamilton's vision of a powerful centralized economy and a strong national government. As a result, in the years to come

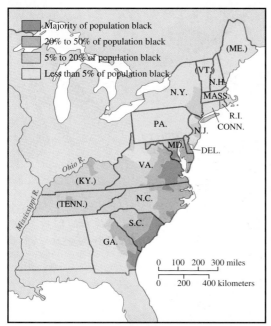

Map 8.2   African American Population, 1790: Proportion of Total Population   The first census clearly indicated that the African American population was heavily concentrated in just a few areas of the United States, most notably in coastal regions of South Carolina, Georgia, and Virginia. Although there were growing numbers of blacks in the backcountry—presumably taken there by migrating slaveowners—most parts of the North and East, with the exception of the immediate vicinity of New York City, had few African American residents.   (Source: From Lester J. Cappon et al., eds., *Atlas of Early American History: The Revolutionary Era, 1760–1790.* Copyright © 1976 by Princeton University Press. Reprinted by permission of Princeton University Press.)

the country would be characterized by a decentralized economy, minimal government (especially at the national level), and maximum freedom of action and mobility for individual white men. Jeffersonian Democratic-Republicans, like other white men before them, failed to extend to white women, Indian peoples, and African Americans the freedom and individuality they recognized as essential for themselves.

LEGACY FOR A PEOPLE AND A NATION
Dissent During Wartime

The Quasi-War with France in 1798 and 1799, the nation's first overseas conflict, brought the first attempt to suppress dissent. By criminalizing dissenting speech, the Sedition Act of 1798 tried to quiet the Democratic-Republicans' criticism of the war in general and President John Adams in particular. Fifteen men (including a member of Congress) were fined and jailed after being convicted under the statute's provisions.

Although Americans might assume that their right to free speech under the First Amendment, more fully accepted now than it was two hundred years ago, would today protect dissenters in the event of another war, the history of the nation suggests otherwise. Each major conflict fought under the Constitution—the Civil War, World War I, World War II, and Vietnam—has stimulated efforts by both government and individual citizens to suppress dissenting voices. For example, during the Civil War, the Union jailed civilian Confederate sympathizers, holding them under martial law for long periods. During the First World War, a later Sedition Act allowed the government to deport immigrant aliens who too vocally criticized the war effort, among them several outspoken Socialists and anarchists. Moreover, citizens who objected to government policies were subjected to a variety of formal and informal sanctions by their neighbors. World War II brought the silencing of isolationists' voices, as those who had opposed American entry into the war were denied public outlets for their ideas. The consequences of antiwar protests in the Vietnam era still affect the nation today, as the American people remain divided over whether the proper course of action in the 1960s was dissent from, or acquiescence in, government policy. And during the Gulf War in the early 1990s, military officials restricted reporters' access to the battlefront to forestall potential criticism.

Freedom of speech is never easy to maintain, and wartime conditions make it much more difficult. When the nation comes under attack from a foreign power, many patriotic Americans argue that the time for dissent has ceased and that all citizens should support the government. Others contend that, if freedom in the nation is to mean anything, people must have the right to speak their minds freely at all times. Tracing the history of wartime dissent in the United States suggests that this legacy will remain extremely contentious.

For Further Reading, see page A-10 of the Appendix. For Web resources, go to http://www.college.hmco.com.

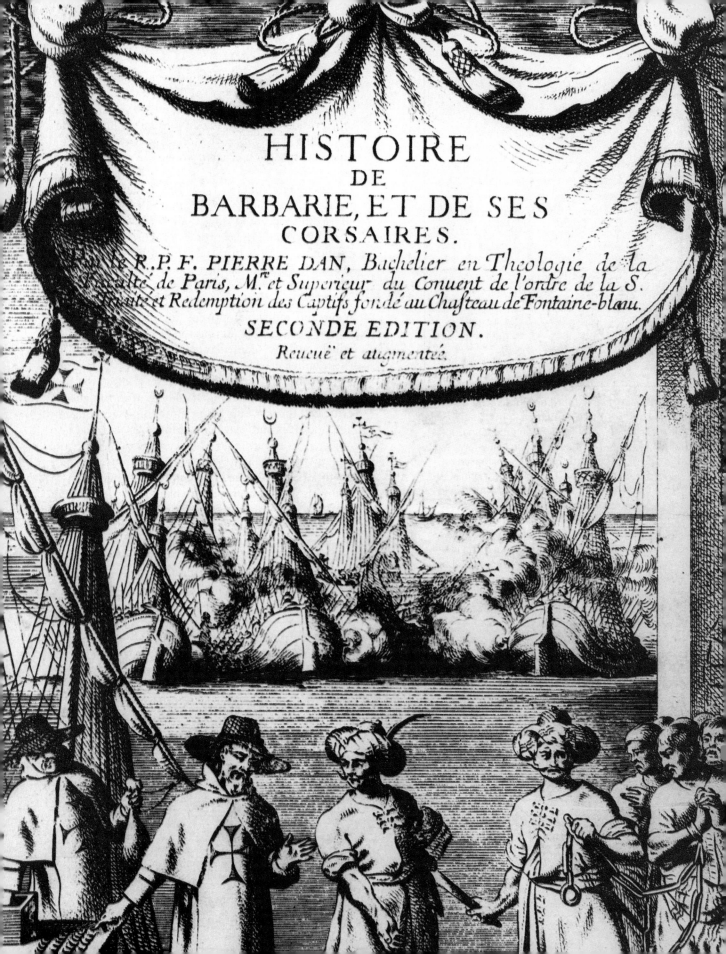

HISTOIRE
DE
BARBARIE, ET DE SES
CORSAIRES.

Par R. P. F. PIERRE DAN, Bachelier en Theologie de la Faculté de Paris, M.re et Superieur du Conuent de l'ordre de la S. Trinité et Redemption des Captifs fondé au Chasteau de Fontaine-bleau.

SECONDE EDITION.
Reueuë et augmentée.

John Foss, captured by "pirates" off the Barbary Coast of North Africa in the 1790s, wrote of the "hellish tortures and punishments" inflicted "on the unfortunate Christians." Marched through Algiers, the party of nine ragged sailors heard shouts from the Islamic crowds praising the victories over "Christian dogs," and in prison they learned of ten other American vessels recently captured. In Algiers they became white slaves under African masters. Eventually the United States ransomed the captives, and four of the nine made it back to America; the others died of plague.

In the early nineteenth century, the Barbary captivity stories had the drama of modern gothic novels. "Pirates" took American men and women hostage from ships, held them in confinement, stripped and beat them as Christians, and humiliated them as Americans. In telling of white slaves with black masters, the tales turned American assumptions of the natural order on their heads. Firsthand descriptions of Africa projected negative images of a despotic, depraved people, so very different from Americans. In the end, the Americans—at least those who survived to tell their stories—prevailed, and so the stories became epic affirmations of Western culture over "barbarians."

Americans loved to read these harrowing stories. John Foss's account of his captivity was reprinted twice in 1798. The fictional account of a woman held a slave in Algiers from 1800 to 1806, *History of the Captivity and Sufferings of Mrs. Maria Martin*, titillated Americans and went through twelve editions in eleven years following its 1807 printing. Chained in prison, Martin described how "the enormous iron round my neck pained me," and how "her mind sunk under this accumulation of miserable sufferings." Finally, she wrote, "my liberty had been purchased by my country," and she heard the door of the dungeon slam shut for the last time. As a Christian, in chains and afterward, she felt morally superior to her captors.

In reality the "pirates"—from what Europeans called the Barbary states and Africans the Maghreb— had challenged the United States in a most fundamental way: was this new nation an independent, sovereign

Christian monks purchase the freedom of Barbary Coast captives, held in chains, from their Muslim captors.   (James Ford Bell Library, University of Minnesota)

"A Wise and Frugal Government": The Democratic-Republicans in Power 1801–1815

217

state that could protect its citizens and commerce abroad?

The issue was money. In 1801 the *bashaw* of Tripoli, angry over the United States's refusal to pay tribute for safe passage of its ships, sailors, and passengers through the Mediterranean, declared war on the United States. President Thomas Jefferson responded by sending a naval squadron to protect American ships in the area. The only other alternative was to abandon the Mediterranean Sea, which would have severely damaged American trade. After two years of stalemate, Jefferson ordered a blockade of Tripoli, but the American frigate *Philadelphia* ran aground in its harbor and three hundred American officers and sailors were taken captive. Jefferson refused to ransom them. With the blockade still in place, seven marines and four hundred soldiers of fortune marched overland from Egypt to seize the port of Derne, on the shores of Tripoli. Finally, by treaty with Tripoli in 1805, the United States paid $60,000 to free the *Philadelphia* prisoners, and the war was over. But the United States continued to pay tribute to the other three Barbary states until 1815. Was the United States an independent sovereign nation? The question rankled, especially as Great Britain seemed to think not, and continued to treat the new nation as a colony.

American independence and stability passed a political test at home as well when presidential succession took place in 1801 by ballot rather than by arms, which some feared. Despite the bitterness of the campaign and the ensuing political intrigue, Thomas Jefferson replaced John Adams as president. The Constitution withstood the test, but the transfer of power to the Democratic-Republicans from the Federalists intensified political conflict. In the tradition of the Revolution, Democratic-Republican presidents soon sought to restrain the national government, believing that limited government would foster republican virtue. The Federalists, in contrast, advocated a strong national government with centralized authority to promote economic development. As both factions competed for popular support, they laid the basis for the evolution of party politics. Factionalism did not spring only from politics, however. Americans also divided along other lines: by class, race, ethnicity, gender, religion, and region.

Events abroad and in the West both encouraged and threatened Americans. Seizing one opportunity, the United States purchased the Louisiana Territory, adding a vast territory from which new states would soon be carved. But even as American interests turned westward, events in Europe and on the high seas of the Atlantic wrenched an about-face. Caught between the warring British and French, the United States found its ships seized, its foreign commerce interrupted, and its sailors impressed (forcibly drafted), all in violation of its rights as a neutral and independent nation. In what some have called the second war for independence, the United States fought Great Britain to a standoff, while on another front routing Indian resistance and shattering Native American unity. A peace treaty restored the prewar status quo, but the war and the treaty reaffirmed U.S. sovereignty and strengthened American's determination to steer clear of further European conflicts. The war also stimulated industry and nationalism. In 1815 a secure, independent, and self-confident nation looked to the future with optimism. ∎

The Jefferson Presidency and Marshall Court

 In later years Thomas Jefferson would always refer to his taking office as the "Revolution of 1800." He viewed his victory that year as a revolution that restored government to its limited role, restrained and frugal. He stressed the republican virtues of independence, self-reliance, and equality, and in contrast to the formality of the Federalist presidents, he and his fellow Democratic-Republicans preferred simplicity. They wore ordinary clothes instead of the aristocratic wigs and breeches (knee-length trousers) that George Washington and John Adams had favored. Jefferson believed that the austerity of the revolutionary period should be the model for personal conduct.

The election campaign of 1800 had been bitter, and writing to English scientist Joseph Priestly in 1801, Jefferson described his victory as defeating "the Barbarians." The Federalists, Jefferson wrote, had looked "backwards not forwards." But now, a new age had dawned: "The great extent of our republic is new. Its sparse habitation is new. The mighty wave of public opinion which has rolled over is new."

Yet in public, Jefferson sought unity by reaching out to his opponents, to heal the wounds of the campaign and to bridge policy differences. Unity and nation building were the order of the day and the theme of his inaugural address. Standing in the Senate chamber, the only part of the Capitol that had been completed, he

Jefferson's Inaugural

IMPORTANT EVENTS

1801 Marshall becomes chief justice of the United States

Jefferson inaugurated as first Republican president

1801–05 United States defeats Barbary pirates in Tripoli War

1803 *Marbury v. Madison* establishes judicial review

United States purchases Louisiana Territory from France

1804 Burr kills Hamilton in a duel

Jefferson reelected

1804–06 Lewis and Clark explore Louisiana Territory

1805 Prophet emerges as Shawnee leader

1807 *Chesapeake* affair almost leads to war with Great Britain

Embargo Act halts foreign trade

1808 Congress bans importation of slaves to the United States

Madison elected president

1808–13 Prophet and Tecumseh organize Native American tribal resistance

1808–15 Embargoes and war stimulate domestic manufacturing

1812–15 United States and Great Britain fight the War of 1812

1813 Death of Tecumseh ends effective pan-Indian resistance

New England capitalists form Boston Manufacturing Company

1814 Jackson's defeat of Creeks at Battle of Horseshoe Bend begins Indian removal from the South

Treaty of Ghent ends the War of 1812

1814–15 Hartford Convention undermines Federalists

1815 Battle of New Orleans makes Jackson a national hero

1816 James Monroe elected president

declared: "We are all republicans, we are all federalists." He thus appealed to the electorate not as party members but as citizens who shared common beliefs in republicanism and federalism. Nearly a thousand people strained to hear him lay out his vision of a restored republicanism: "A wise and frugal government, which shall restrain men from injuring one another, which shall leave them free to regulate their pursuits of industry and improvement, and shall not take from the mouth of labor the bread it has earned. This is the sum of good government," he concluded.

Still, Federalists and Democratic-Republicans continued to distrust each other. John Adams did not attend the inaugural; he had left Washington before dawn to avoid the Democratic-Republican takeover. He and Jefferson had once been close friends but now disliked each other intensely. Both were thin-skinned, quick to take offense and quick to give it.

To implement the restoration of republican values, Jefferson aggressively extended the Democratic-Republicans' grasp on the national government. Virtually all of the six hundred or so officials appointed during the administrations of Washington and Adams

Democratic-Republican Ascendancy

had been loyal Federalists; only six were known Democratic-Republicans. To bring into his administration men who shared his vision of an agrarian republic and individual liberty, Jefferson refused to recognize appointments that Adams had made in the last days of his presidency and dismissed Federalist customs collectors from New England ports. He awarded vacant treasury and judicial offices to Democratic-Republicans. By July 1803, Federalists held only 130 of 316 presidentially controlled offices. They accused Jefferson of "hunting the Federalists like wild beasts" and abandoning the olive leaf extended in his inaugural address.

The Democratic-Republican Congress, swept into office in the election of 1800, proceeded to affirm its belief in limited government. Albert Gallatin, secretary of the treasury, and John Randolph of Virginia, Jefferson's ally in the House of Representatives, translated ideology into policy, putting the federal government on a diet. Congress repealed all internal taxes, including the whiskey tax. Gallatin cut the army budget in half and reduced the 1802 navy budget by two-

This portrait of President Thomas Jefferson was painted by Rembrandt Peale in 1805. Charles Willson Peale (Rembrandt's father) and his five sons helped establish the reputation of American art in the new nation. Rembrandt Peale achieved fame for his presidential portraits; here he has captured Jefferson in a noble pose without the usual symbols of office or power, befitting the Republican age. (© Collection of The New-York Historical Society)

had done in suppressing Democratic-Republican editors) and pardoned those who had been convicted under their provisions. Congress let expire the Sedition Act in 1801 and the Alien Act in 1802. Congress also repealed the Naturalization Act of 1798, which had required fourteen years of residency for citizenship. The 1802 act that replaced it, while stipulating the registration of aliens, required of would-be citizens only five years of residency, loyalty to the Constitution, and the forsaking of foreign allegiance and titles. The new act would remain the basis of naturalized American citizenship into the twentieth century.

The Democratic-Republicans turned next to the judiciary, the last stronghold of Federalist power. To

War on the Judiciary

many Democratic-Republicans, the judiciary represented a centralizing force, one undemocratic by virtue of rule by unelected judges appointed for life. Especially galling to Jefferson, John Marshall had become chief justice of the United States, appointed after Adams's defeat. During the 1790s not a single Democratic-Republican had occupied the federal bench; thus the judiciary became a battlefield following the revolution of 1800.

The first skirmish erupted over repeal of the Judiciary Act of 1801, which had been passed in the final days of the Adams administration. The act, designed to maintain Federalist control over the courts, created fifteen new judgeships, which Adams filled by signing "midnight" appointments until his term was just hours away from expiring. The act also reduced by attrition the number of justices on the Supreme Court from six to five. Since that reduction would have denied Jefferson a Supreme Court appointment until two vacancies occurred, the new Democratic-Republican–dominated Congress repealed the 1801 act.

Partisan Democratic-Republicans created another front in the war for control of the judiciary by targeting opposition judges for removal. Republicans were especially infuriated with the Federalist judges who had refused to review the Sedition Act under which Federalists had prosecuted critics of the Adams administration. At Jefferson's prompting, the House impeached (indicted) Federal District Judge John Pickering of New Hampshire, an elderly, emotionally disturbed alcoholic. He was an easy target, and in 1805 the Senate convicted him, removing him from office.

The day Pickering was ousted, the House impeached Supreme Court Justice Samuel Chase for judicial misconduct. A staunch Federalist, Chase had pushed for prosecutions under the Sedition Act, had

thirds. He then moved to reduce the national debt from $83 million to $57 million, as part of a plan to retire it altogether by 1817. If Alexander Hamilton had viewed the national debt as the engine of economic growth, Jefferson saw it as the source of government corruption. Jefferson even closed two of the nation's five diplomatic missions abroad—at The Hague and Berlin—to save money.

More than frugality, however, distinguished Democratic-Republicans from Federalists. Before Jefferson's election, opposition to the Alien and Sedition Acts of 1798 had helped unite Democratic-Republicans (see page 210). Jefferson now declined to use the acts against his opponents (as President Adams

actively campaigned for Adams in 1800, and repeatedly had denounced Jefferson's administration from the bench. The Democratic-Republicans, however, failed to muster the two-thirds majority of senators necessary to convict him. Chase's acquittal preserved the Court's independence at a critical time before the role of the judiciary as an equal branch of government had been established. In failing to remove Chase, the Senate established the precedent that criminal actions, not political disagreements, were the only proper grounds for impeachment. In his tenure as president, Jefferson appointed three new Supreme Court justices. Nonetheless, the Court remained a Federalist stronghold under Chief Justice John Marshall.

Jefferson and Marshall shared much in common. They were fellow Virginians, even distant cousins, and

John Marshall

Marshall was of the generation of Madison and Monroe, the bright young men who formed Jefferson's intellectual entourage. Jefferson, however, viewed Marshall as a traitor to republicanism after Marshall became a Federalist in the 1790s. President Adams had appointed him secretary of state and then, in his last weeks as a lame-duck president, named Marshall as chief justice. Though an autocrat by nature, Marshall possessed a grace and openness of manner that complemented the new Republican political style. As a justice he adopted republican dress, wearing a plain black gown rather than the British robes of scarlet and ermine or the colorful academic garb worn by other justices. Charles de Saint-Memin's portrait of Marshall in 1801 captures both his autocratic bearing and his direct manner. Under Marshall's domination, however, the Supreme Court retained a Federalist outlook even after Democratic-Republican justices achieved a majority in 1811. Throughout his tenure (1801–1835), the Court consistently upheld federal supremacy over the states and protected the interests of commerce and capital.

Marshall made the Court an equal branch of government in practice as well as theory. Judicial service became a coveted honor for ambitious and talented men. Previously people regarded it lightly, and justices had served only short terms. No judicial building was constructed in Washington; Congress considered it unessential, and the Court continued to meet in a chamber of the Capitol. Marshall unified the Court, influencing the justices to issue joint majority opinions rather than a host of individual concurring judgments. Marshall himself became the voice of the majority: from 1801 through 1805 he wrote twenty-four of the

John Marshall (1755–1835) was chief justice of the United States from 1801 to 1835. He posed for this portrait by the French artist Charles Balthazar Julien Fevret de Saint-Memin in 1801, the year he joined the Court. The artist captured the power and strength with which Marshall would dominate the Court. (Duke University Archives)

Court's twenty-six decisions; through 1810 he wrote 85 percent of the opinions, including every important one.

Marshall significantly increased the Supreme Court's power in the landmark case of *Marbury v. Madison* (1803), another skirmish in

Marbury v. Madison

war over the judiciary. William Marbury, one of Adams's midnight appointees, had been named a justice of the peace in the District of Columbia. James Madison, Jefferson's new secretary of state, declined to certify Marbury's appointment so that the president could instead appoint a Democratic-Republican. Marbury sued, requesting a writ of mandamus (a court order forcing the president to appoint him). The case presented a political dilemma. If the Supreme Court ruled in favor of Marbury and issued a writ of mandamus, the president probably would not comply with it, and the Court had no way to force him to do so. But if the Federalist-dominated bench refused to issue the writ, it would be handing the Democratic-Republicans a victory.

Marshall brilliantly recast the issue to avoid both pitfalls. Speaking for the Court, he ruled that Marbury had a right to his appointment but that the Supreme Court could not compel Madison to honor the appointment because the Constitution did not grant the Court power to issue a writ of mandamus. In the absence of any specific mention in the Constitution, Marshall ruled, the section of the Judiciary Act of 1789 that authorized the Court to issue such writs was unconstitutional. In *Marbury v. Madison*, the Supreme Court denied itself the power to issue writs of mandamus but established its far greater power to judge the constitutionality of laws passed by Congress.

In succeeding years Marshall fashioned the theory of judicial review, the power of the Supreme Court to decide the constitutionality of legislation and presidential acts. Since the Constitution was the supreme law, he reasoned, any federal or state act contrary to the Constitution must be null and void. The Supreme Court, whose duty it was to uphold the law, would decide whether or not a legislative act contradicted the Constitution. "It is emphatically the province and duty of the judicial department," Marshall ruled, "to say what the law is." The power of judicial review established in *Marbury v. Madison* permanently enhanced the independence of the judiciary and breathed life into the Constitution. "Marshall found the Constitution paper and made it power," President James A. Garfield later observed.

Louisiana and Lewis and Clark

Democratic-Republicans and Federalists divided sharply over more than just the Court; Jefferson's acquisition of the Louisiana Territory in 1803 was another point of contention. Jefferson shared with many other Americans the belief that the United States was destined to expand its "empire of liberty," and his presidency made western expansion a national goal.

Since American independence, Louisiana had held a special place in the young nation's expansionist dreams. Louisiana defined the western border of the United States, which stretched along the Mississippi River from the Gulf of Mexico to present-day Minnesota. Spain had acquired the Louisiana Territory from France in 1763, at the end of

Louisiana

the Seven Years War (see page 118). By 1800 hundreds of thousands of Americans in search of land had settled in the rich Mississippi and Ohio River valleys, intruding on Indian lands. These settlers floated their farm goods down the Mississippi and Ohio Rivers to New Orleans for export. Whoever controlled the port of New Orleans thus had a hand on the throat of the American economy. Americans preferred Spanish control of Louisiana to control by France, a much stronger power.

In secret pacts with Spain in 1800 and 1801, however, France had acquired the territory once again. The United States learned of the transfer only in 1802, when Napoleon seemed poised to rebuild a French empire in the New World. "Every eye in the United States is now focused on the affairs of Louisiana," Jefferson wrote to Robert R. Livingston, the American minister in Paris. American concerns intensified in October of that year when Spanish officials, on the eve of ceding control to the French, violated Pinckney's Treaty (see pages 205–206) by denying Americans the privilege of storing their products at New Orleans prior to transshipment to foreign markets. "The Mississippi," Secretary of State James Madison wrote, "is to them [western settlers] everything. It is the Hudson, the Delaware, the Potomac and all navigable rivers of the Atlantic States formed into one stream." Western farmers and eastern merchants thought a devious Napoleon had closed the port; they grumbled and talked war.

Jefferson personally took charge. To relieve the pressure for war and to win western farm support, Jefferson prepared for war while sending Virginia governor James Monroe as his personal envoy to join Robert Livingston in France. Their mission: to buy the port of New Orleans and as much of the Mississippi valley as possible. Meanwhile, Congress authorized the call-up of eighty thousand militiamen in case war became necessary. Arriving in Paris in April 1803, Monroe was astonished to learn that France already had offered to sell all 827,000 square miles of Louisiana to the United States for a mere $15 million. Napoleon had lost interest in the New World. Once he failed to recapture independent Haiti, the idea of a New World empire dissolved and Louisiana became superfluous. At the same time he needed money for renewed warfare against Britain. On April 30 Monroe and Livingston signed a treaty buying the vast territory whose exact borders were not yet mapped and whose land was uncharted (see Map 9.1).

Louisiana Purchase

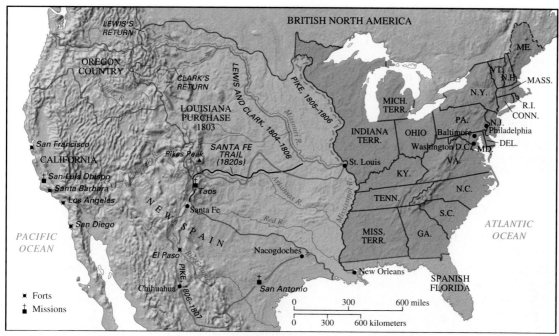

Map 9.1   Louisiana Purchase   The Louisiana Purchase (1803) doubled the area of the United States and opened the trans-Mississippi West for American settlement.

At one stroke of a pen, the Louisiana Purchase doubled the size of the nation and opened the way for continental expansion. It stood as the most popular achievement of Jefferson's presidency. But for Jefferson, the purchase presented a dilemma. For one thing, in purchasing Louisiana, Jefferson forgot his commitment to debt reduction. And some questioned Jefferson's power to make such a move. To be sure, the purchase promised fulfillment of his dream of a nation "with room enough for our descendants to the hundredth and thousandth generation." It provided a means to resolve Indian-settler conflict in the West by making available land to which eastern tribes could be forcibly removed. But was it constitutional? The Constitution nowhere authorized the president to acquire new territory and incorporate it into the nation.

Jefferson considered proposing a constitutional amendment to allow the purchase but decided against it. He believed that the president's implied powers to protect the nation justified the purchase. His longstanding interest in Louisiana and the West also allayed his constitutional concerns. As early as 1782, as an American envoy in France, Jefferson had suggested sending an exploratory mission across the continent to California. A naturalist and scientist, Jefferson seemed fascinated with every aspect of the West—its geography, people, plants, and animals; he had long wanted

to acquire, subdue, and exploit it. As secretary of state in the 1790s, he had been active in promoting a search for "the shortest & most convenient route of communications between the U.S. & the Pacific Ocean."

In 1803 Jefferson sent an expedition headed by Meriwether Lewis and William Clark to the Pacific coast via the Missouri and Columbia Rivers. The twenty-nine-year-old Lewis, a regular army officer in the 1790s, had exchanged rugged military life to be Jefferson's private secretary in 1801. As friend, teacher, leader, role model, and father figure, Jefferson gave Lewis a "crash course" on the botany and the environment of the West, and he proved an exceptional student. The thirty-year-old Clark was an explorer and former soldier who had fought against and negotiated with Native Americans. Aware of the risks as well as the scientific importance of their mission, both were eager for the commission. The expedition also had political import, for the publication of Alexander MacKenzie's *Voyages from Montreal* in 1801 described the first crossing of the continent in Canada in 1793. The publication raised fears that the British would dominate the Far West.

Lewis and Clark

Lewis and Clark officially started their journey in May 1804. They traveled up the Missouri River and wintered at Fort Mandan in present-day North

Western artist Charles Russell depicts a Hidatsa leader trying to rub the black pigment off York, William Clark's slave who was part of the "Corps of Discovery." Many Indians were astonished at York because they had not seen a black man before. (Courtesy of the Montana Historical Society. Gift of the Artist)

Dakota. Here they selected their twenty-nine-member corps and were joined by Indian guides. In April 1805 they resumed their journey, traveling through present-day Montana. In August, having reached the navigable limits of the Missouri, the party continued the journey with horses. With the help of a local Shoshone guide, they crossed the Bitterroot Mountains. Traversing the Rockies, "the most terrible mountains I ever beheld," according to Sergeant Patrick Gass's diary, proved their most dangerous and treacherous venture. At times they lost their way; tumbled down steep mountain trails; and slept in the snow, bone cold. Short of food, they had to kill a horse for meat. In November 1805 they reached the Pacific Ocean in present-day Oregon, where they wintered, and the following March began the return trek. Lewis and Clark split up to explore alternate routes and reunited in August 1806. They arrived home in St. Louis on September 23, 1806.

The original Corps of Discovery was a diverse group. It included army regulars and young adventurers from Kentucky who became soldiers when they joined the corps. Clark's slave York, whom he inherited in 1799 from his father, came along as did two men who were half-French and half-Omaha and another who was son of a French Canadian father and a Shawnee mother. Immigrants included an Irishman and a German. Later at the Mandan villages the French Canadian trader Toussaint Charbonneau and his pregnant fifteen-year-old Shoshone wife, Sacagawea, joined the expedition, Lewis and Clark took Charbonneau because they wanted Sacagawea, who knew the languages of the mountain Indians, and she proved invaluable as a guide and translator; she knew the land and the people better than anyone else. The youngest member of the group

Corps of Discovery

was the newborn Jean Baptiste Charbonneau, son of Sacagawea, born on February 11, 1805.

Headed by army officers, the expedition followed military rules. But it also was, at times, much more informal and democratic than army regulations or even civilian society allowed. When trouble arose, Lewis and Clark held courts-martial to discipline corps members for such infractions as drunkenness. Contrary to army rules, enlisted men sat on the court. In more serious cases when an accused corps member faced the death penalty, such as a sentry falling asleep or an enlisted man deserting, Lewis and Clark presided. When Sergeant Charles Floyd died of a ruptured appendix at the beginning of the journey, Lewis and Clark allowed the soldiers to elect Private Patrick Gass as his successor, a most unusual move. Later, in November 1805, when the expedition voted where to locate their winter quarters on the Pacific coast, all voted, including the slave York and the Indian woman Sacagawea. Yet issues of race and gender were present. Along the way Indians were astonished at York; many had not seen a black man before. They were curious of his skin color, his "short, curling hair," and his strength. At the end of the journey the names of York and Sacagawea did not appear on the roster Lewis submitted to the War Department. Neither received pay for their work though their assistance had been indispensable.

Although some Americans still believed that the lands in the West were uninhabited, Lewis and Clark knew better. They anticipated a crowded wilderness and hoped to cement U.S. relations with Indians. The explorers carried with them twenty-one bags of gifts for Native American leaders, both to establish goodwill and to stimulate interest in trading for American manufactured goods. They brought back stories not only of various peoples, but also of fauna and flora unknown to the western scientific community; they encountered the grizzly bear, bighorn sheep, and mountain goats. Lewis sent boxes of natural-history specimens to Jefferson, including plant and tree cuttings.

In time, the expedition became legendary and Lewis and Clark fabled American explorers. Many of the artifacts they brought back became relics. They mapped the West and, with their reports and specimens, furthered dreams of a continental empire. The corps members were well rewarded and basked in their renown. But one among them reaped few rewards from the expedition: the slave York. In 1808 York demanded his freedom from Clark as a reward for his service to the expedition. York's wife, a slave, lived in Louisville, Kentucky, and he wished to join her. Clark

let him visit her, and York proposed that he stay there, hiring himself out and sending money to Clark. Clark refused and in May 1809 York returned to Clark in St. Louis. Clark found York "insolent and sulky. I gave him a severe trouncing the other Day, and he has much mended" his ways.

Other explorations followed Lewis and Clark's and further publicized the land west of the Mississippi.

Exploration of the West

In 1805 and 1806 Lieutenant Zebulon Pike sought the source of the continent-cutting river and a navigable water route to the Far West. When Pike and his men wandered into Spanish territory to the south, the Spanish held them captive for several months in Mexico. After his release, Pike wrote an account of his experiences that set commercial minds spinning. He described a potential commercial market in southwestern Spanish cities as well as bountiful furs and precious minerals. Over the next few decades, Americans avidly read accounts of western exploration. The vision of a road to the Southwest became a reality with the opening of the Santa Fe Trail in the 1820s, and settlement followed the trail.

New Spain's *Tejas* (Texas) province bordered the Louisiana Territory. Provincial officials welcomed Americans interested in the land south of Louisiana, and American immigrants began to drift in. Some fought as volunteers with Indians and Mexican rebels in a twelve-year war with Spain that ended with Mexican independence in 1821. The establishment of an independent Mexico inspired these Americans to dream of an independent Texas nation—a place for Americans, not for Mexicans. It seems there was no place for people of color, including Mexicans—a mix of European, Indian, and African peoples—in the "empire of liberty."

Political Factionalism and Jefferson's Reelection

 Prior to the Republican victory in 1800, most Federalists had disdained popular campaigning. They believed in government by the "best" people—those whose education, wealth, and experience qualified them to be leaders. For candidates to debate their own merits in front of their inferiors—the voters—was utterly demeaning, they thought. No wonder the direct appeals of the Democratic-Republicans struck the Federalists as a subversion of the natural political order.

After the resounding Federalist defeat in 1800, however, a younger generation of Federalists began to imitate the Democratic-Republicans.

A New Style of Campaigning

Led by such men as Josiah Quincy, a Massachusetts congressman, the Younger Federalists campaigned for popular support. Quincy cleverly presented the Federalists as the people's party, attacking Democratic-Republicans as autocratic planters. "Jeffersonian Democracy," Quincy gibed in 1804, was "an Indian word, signifying 'a great tobacco planter who had herds of black slaves.'" In attacking frugal government, the Federalists played on fears of a weakened army and navy. Eastern merchants depended on a strong navy to protect ocean trade; westerners looked to the army to defend them as they encroached on the territory of Native Americans.

In states where both factions organized and ran candidates, people became more active in politics. In some states about 90 percent of the eligible voters cast ballots between 1804 and 1816. But the base of eligible voters—nearly all of whom were white males—remained restricted: property qualifications for voting and holding office persisted, and in 1804 six state legislatures still selected presidential electors. Fearing the divisiveness of partisanship, some Democratic-Republicans restrained their organizational efforts, and most leaders shied away from formal, cohesive political organizations.

Yet political competition and a vigorous partisan press prompted grassroots electioneering. Political barbecues symbolized the new style of campaign. In New York the factions roasted oxen; on the New England coast they baked clams; in Maryland they served oysters. Guests washed down their meals with beer and punch and sometimes competed in corn-shucking or horse-pulling contests. Voters demonstrated their allegiance by attending these events and displaying images of their party leaders. Oratory became a popular form of entertainment, and candidates delivered lengthy and uninhibited speeches wherever crowds gathered. They often made wild accusations, which—given the slow speed of communications—might go unanswered until after the election.

Grassroots Electioneering

The Federalists never mastered the art of campaigning. Older Federalists remained opposed to blatant campaigning. And though strong in Connecticut, Delaware, and a few other states, the Federalists were weak at the national level and never offered the Democratic-Republicans sustained competition. Divisions among Federalists often undermined their success, and the extremism of some Older Federalists discredited most of the rest. A case in point was Timothy Pickering, a Massachusetts congressman and former secretary of state. Pickering opposed the Louisiana Purchase, feared Jefferson's reelection, and urged the secession of New England in 1803 and 1804. He won some support, but most Federalists balked at his plan for secession. Ever the opportunist, Vice President Aaron Burr, intrigued with Pickering's idea of northeastern independence, fantasized about leading New York into secession, with other states following. But when Burr lost his bid to become governor of New York in 1804, dreams of a northern confederacy evaporated.

Where Federalists were too weak to pose a threat, Democratic-Republicans fought among themselves. Politics suffered from divisiveness and personal animosities that were as strong a force as ideology, and the controversies surrounding Burr illustrate the convergence of the political and the personal. The United States was just beginning to build a tradition of nonviolent politics, and it would be a long time before it took root. Indeed some historians have speculated that political parties helped contain violence by establishing alternate rituals for nonviolent expression. But in the nation's early years political disagreements did erupt into violence. The most famous was the Burr-Hamilton duel, involving a former vice president and a former secretary of the treasury.

The charismatic and ambitious Aaron Burr and Alexander Hamilton had long despised each other. Hamilton relentlessly blocked Burr's path. He thwarted Burr's attempt to steal the election of 1800 from Jefferson, and in the 1804 mudslinging New York gubernatorial race, Burr lost to a rival Democratic-Republican faction backed by the Federalist Hamilton. Both Burr and Hamilton held grudges, and when Hamilton made derogatory remarks about him, Burr challenged his nemesis to a duel. Hamilton accepted even though he found dueling repugnant; his son Philip had died in 1801 from dueling wounds. Because New York had outlawed dueling, the two men met across the Hudson River at Weehawken, New Jersey. Hamilton did not fire, and he paid for that decision with his life. But in killing Hamilton, Burr only added to his dishonor in the

Hamilton-Burr Duel

How do historians know...

that popular interest in elections was increasing early in the nineteenth century? Election data are not available, but paintings like John Lewis Krimmel's *Election Day in Philadelphia* (1815) convey that interest. Only white males could vote at the time, and the crowd is composed mostly of white men, although at least one African American and some women and children are present. The artist depicts a festive occasion. Citizens riding on a float in the background carry their own flag; they have created a parade. A holiday spirit seems to prevail as men cluster in groups talking, arguing, sharing jokes, and generally appearing to be enjoying themselves. Perhaps there is a hint of overindulgence as well. The man sitting in front of an overturned chair *(left foreground)*, with his hat on the ground behind him, seems to have fallen,

perhaps from too much drink—a common affliction in the party atmosphere of election day. Among the spectators are two women *(right foreground)*, one of whom is holding the hand of a little girl. They suggest a restraining force on the raucous scene. The woman dressed in white and her friend offer a common female image of the time: the woman as an emblem of republican virtue. The space between the female and male figures suggests that the women stand apart not only as nonvoters but also as symbols of virtue and seriousness absent in the male world. Overall, the painting depicts a popular event, mixing a party atmosphere with civic duty. From a sober exercise of democratic responsibility, voting had become a popular event. (Photo: Courtesy of Winterthur Museum)

public's eyes. He was indicted for murder in New York and New Jersey and faced immediate arrest if he returned to either state.

Jefferson was appalled that politics could lead to personal violence. In 1808 he advised his grandson, Thomas Jefferson Randolph, to avoid political arguments. The president had witnessed too many politicians "getting warm, becoming rude, and shooting one another." It was not just the deaths of Philip and Alexander Hamilton that Jefferson had in mind. In 1806 the president's son-in-law, Congressman Thomas Mann Randolph, and his distant cousin, former Jefferson ally and now fierce opponent, John Randolph, chairman of the House Ways and Means Committee, tangled. Nasty floor speeches led the two Randolphs to arrange a duel, but Thomas Mann Randolph's apology averted gunfire. The embers of mistrust smoldered, and the possibility of a duel remained. After the War of 1812 dueling became rarer in politics and was confined mostly to the South as a traditional means of defending one's personal or family honor.

Rather than preserving his honor, Burr's killing of Hamilton made him an outcast. His political career in ruins, Burr plotted to create in the Southwest a new empire carved out of the Louisiana Territory. With the collusion of General James Wilkinson, the U.S. commander in the Mississippi valley, Burr planned to raise a private army to grab land from the United States or from Spain (his exact plans remain unknown). Wilkinson switched sides and informed President Jefferson of Burr's devious intention. Jefferson personally assisted the prosecution in Burr's 1807 trial for treason, over which Chief Justice Marshall presided. The jury acquitted Burr, who fled to Europe.

Jefferson's Reelection

Campaigning for reelection in 1804, Jefferson took credit for the restoration of republican values and the acquisition of the Louisiana Territory. Jefferson and the Democratic-Republicans claimed they ended the Federalist threat to liberty by repealing the Alien and Sedition and Judiciary Acts. They also boasted that they had reduced the size of government by cutting spending. Despite his opponents' charges, Jefferson had demonstrated that Democratic-Republicans supported commerce and promoted free trade. American trade with Europe was flourishing. Federalists who earlier had criticized Jefferson for not seizing Louisiana now unwisely attacked the president for paying too much for it and for exceeding his powers in buying the territory.

Jefferson's opponent in 1804 was Charles Cotesworth Pinckney, a wealthy South Carolina lawyer and former Revolutionary War aide to George Washington. As Adams's vice-presidential running mate in 1800, Pinckney had inherited the Federalist leadership. Jefferson dumped the disloyal and unreliable Aaron Burr from the 1804 ticket, and he and his running mate, George Clinton of New York, swamped Pinckney and New Yorker Rufus King in the electoral college by 162 votes to 14, carrying fifteen of the seventeen states.

Indian Resistance

 Lewis and Clark's account testified to the Indian presence in the West, and most Americans viewed Native Americans, no matter where they lived, as obstacles to American settlement. Violations of treaties and coerced new ones, forcing Indians to cede ever more land to the United States, continually shrunk Indian territory. With less land, Indians found hunting and agriculture more difficult. Not only their traditional ways but also their independence and existence were threatened. Encroachment by whites and the periodic ravages of disease—smallpox, measles, and influenza—brought further misery.

In the early 1800s two Shawnee brothers, Prophet (1775–1837) and Tecumseh (1768–1813), led a revolt against further American encroachment by fostering a pan-Indian federation that stretched from the Old Northwest to the South. Prophet's early life typified the experiences of the Indians of the Old Northwest. Born in 1775 a few months after his father's death in battle, Prophet, called Lalawethika ("Noisemaker"), as a young man was expelled to Ohio along with other Shawnees under the 1795 Treaty of Greenville (see page 184), and he later moved to Indiana. Within Prophet and Tecumseh's own lifetimes the Shawnees had lost most of their Ohio land; by the 1800s they occupied scattered sites in Ohio and in the Michigan and Louisiana territories. Displacement left Lalawethika forlorn, and like many other Native Americans he turned to whiskey for escape. He also turned to traditional folk knowledge and remedies and in 1804 became a tribal medicine man. His medicine, however, could not stop the white man's diseases from ravaging his village.

Lalawethika emerged from his own battle with illness in 1805 as a new man, called Tenskwatawa ("the Open Door"), or "the Prophet." Claiming to have died

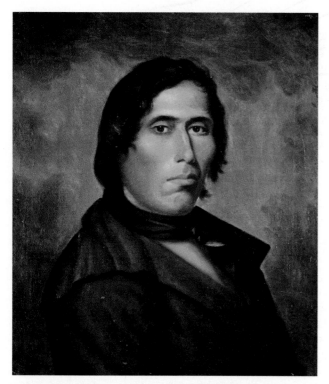

The Shawnee chiefs Tecumseh *(left)* and Prophet *(right).* The two brothers led a revival of traditional Shawnee culture and preached Native American federation against white encroachment. In the War of 1812 they allied themselves with the British, but Tecumseh's death at the Battle of the Thames (1813) and British indifference thereafter caused Native Americans' resistance and unity to collapse.   (Tecumseh: Field Museum of Natural History, Chicago, FMNH Neg. #A93851; Prophet: National Museum of American Art, Smithsonian Institution, Washington, D.C.)

The Prophet

and been resurrected, he traveled widely in the Ohio River valley as a religious leader, attacking the decline of moral values among Native Americans, warning of damnation for those who drank whiskey, condemning intertribal battles, and stressing harmony and respect for elders. He urged Indians to return to the old ways and abandon white customs: to hunt with bows and arrows, not guns; to stop wearing hats; and to refrain from eating bread and instead to cultivate corn and beans. Whiskey, he preached, was made for whites; the forest had been created for Indians.

Prophet was building a religious movement that offered reassurance to the Shawnees, Potawatomis, and other displaced western Indians. As a leader his power came from his eloquence, deep conviction, and performance of miracles. By timing his invocations to coincide with a solar eclipse, he even seemed to darken the sun. His outspoken opposition to federal Indian policy drew others into his camp, and as his message spread to southern tribes, the federal government and white settlers became alarmed.

By 1808 Prophet and his older brother Tecumseh talked less about spiritual renewal and more about resisting American aggression. Tecumseh was turning Prophet's religious movement into a political one. The British, who looked for alliances with Native Americans after renewed Anglo-American hostilities (see page 236), encouraged Indians to defy eviction from lands claimed by the U.S. government. In repudiating land cessions to the government under the Treaty of Fort Wayne (1809), Tecumseh told Indiana's governor William Henry Harrison at Vincennes in 1810 that "the only way to check and stop this evil is, for all the red men to unite in claiming a common and equal right in the land, as it was at first, and should be

Tecumseh

yet; for it . . . belongs to all, for the use of each. . . . No part has a right to sell, even to each other, much less to strangers."

Tecumseh, a towering six-foot warrior and charismatic orator, soon overshadowed his brother as Shawnee leader. He dressed as a chief from a century before, exchanging his European shirts and cloth trousers for soft deerskin suits with fringes. He replaced the bright beads and ribbons sold by whites with dyed porcupine quills. He returned to traditional diet as well, refusing foreign food. Younger Indians flocked to him. Warriors found his political visions more relevant than Prophet's spirituality in protecting themselves against the United States. Convinced that only an Indian federation could stop the advance of white settlement, Tecumseh sought to unify northern and southern Indians by traveling widely, preaching Indian resistance. And he warned Harrison that Indians would resist white occupation of the 2.5 million acres on the Wabash River that they had ceded in the Treaty of Fort Wayne.

American Neutrality Imperiled by a World at War

 "Peace, commerce, and honest friendship with all nations, entangling alliance with none," President Jefferson had proclaimed in his first inaugural address. Jefferson's efforts to stand aloof from European conflict were successful until 1805. Thereafter the United States could not escape the web of European hostilities, and protection of American commerce and foreign relations occupied nearly all of Jefferson's second administration. The easy victory over the Barbary states would not be repeated against the British.

After the Senate ratified the Jay Treaty in 1795 (see page 205), the United States and Great Britain appeared to reconcile their differences. Britain withdrew from its western forts and interfered less in American trade with France. Since the United States was Britain's best customer, and the British Empire in turn bought the bulk of American exports, both sides worked hard for good relations.

But in May 1803, two weeks after Napoleon sold Louisiana to the United States, renewal of the Napoleonic wars between France and Britain (and later Britain's continental allies, Prussia, Austria, and Russia) again trapped the United States between Britain and France on the high seas. For two years American commerce benefited from the conflict. As the world's largest neutral carrier, the United States became the chief supplier of food to Europe. American merchants also gained control of most of the West Indian trade.

But after defeating the French and Spanish fleets at the Battle of Trafalgar in October 1805, Britain's Royal Navy tightened its control of the oceans. Two months later Napoleon crushed the Russian and Austrian armies at Austerlitz. Stalemated, France and Britain launched a commercial war, blockading each other's trade. As a trading partner of both countries, the United States paid a high price.

All tension focused on the high seas, where Britain, commanding the world's largest navy, suffered a severe shortage of sailors. Too few men enlisted, and those in service frequently deserted, demoralized by harsh treatment. Some British sailors joined U.S. merchant ships, where conditions were better. The Royal Navy resorted to stopping American vessels and seizing British deserters, British-born naturalized American seamen, and other unlucky sailors suspected of being British. Perhaps six to eight thousand Americans were impressed in this way between 1803 and 1812. Moreover, alleged deserters—many of them American citizens—faced British courts-martial. Americans saw impressment as a direct assault on the independence of their new republic. The principle of "once a British subject, always a British subject" mocked U.S. citizenship and sovereignty.

Impressment of American Sailors

The British violated other American rights as well. They interfered with U.S. trade with the West Indies by blocking goods the United States believed were part of neutral trade. They also searched and seized U.S. vessels within American territory offshore.

In February 1806 Americans denounced British impressment as aggression and a violation of America's neutral rights. In protest, Congress passed the Non-Importation Act, barring British manufactured goods from entering American ports. Since the act exempted most cloth or metal articles, it had little impact on British trade; instead, it was a warning to the British of what to expect if they continued to violate American rights. In November Jefferson suspended the act temporarily while William Pinckney, a Baltimore lawyer, joined James Monroe in London to negotiate a settlement. But the treaty Monroe and Pinckney carried home violated their instructions—it did not so much as mention impressment—and Jefferson never submitted it to the Senate for ratification.

Anglo-American relations steadily deteriorated. Then in June 1807, the forty-gun frigate U.S.S. *Chesapeake* left Norfolk, Virginia, headed

Chesapeake Affair

to protect American ships in the Mediterranean. About 10 miles from shore, still inside American territorial waters, it met the fifty-gun British frigate *Leopard*. When the *Chesapeake* refused to be searched for deserters, the *Leopard* repeatedly fired its cannon broadside into the American ship. Three Americans were killed and eighteen wounded, including the ship's captain. The British seized four deserters from the Royal Navy—three of them American citizens; one of the deserters, British subject Jenkin Ratford, was hanged. Damaged and humiliated, the *Chesapeake* returned to port. Americans were outraged and united. "But one feeling pervades the nation," said a leading Democratic-Republican, former Congressman Joseph Nicholson. "All distinctions of Federalism and Democracy are banished." The *Chesapeake* affair not only intensified the emotional impact of impressment but also exposed American military weakness.

Had the United States been better prepared militarily, the ensuing howl of public indignation might have brought about a declaration of war. But the still-fledgling country was ill equipped to defend its neutral rights with force; it was certainly no match for the British navy. With Congress in recess, Jefferson was able to avoid hostilities, choosing instead what he called "peaceable coercion." In July the president closed American waters to British warships to prevent similar incidents, and soon thereafter he increased military and naval expenditures. In December 1807 Jefferson again put economic pressure on Great Britain by invoking the Non-Importation Act, followed eight days later by a new restriction, the Embargo Act.

The Embargo Act was intended to avoid war. Jefferson thought of it as a short-term measure to prevent confrontation between American merchant vessels and British and French warships and to put pressure on

A painting of the British frigate *Leopard* firing its guns into the U.S.S. *Chesapeake* when the U.S. ship refused to be searched for British deserters. The British boarded the subdued *Chesapeake* and seized four deserters, three of them American citizens. Americans were humiliated and angered by the British violation of American rights.   (Courtesy of William Gilkerson)

Embargo Act France and England by denying them American products. The embargo forbade all exports from the United States to any country. Foreign ships delivering goods left American ports with empty holds. U.S. exports dropped some 80 percent in 1808, but smuggling blossomed overnight.

Few American policies were as well intentioned and as unpopular and unsuccessful as Jefferson's embargo. Although "peaceable coercion" had been an enlightened concept in international affairs, some Democratic-Republicans felt uneasy about interfering with trade. Federalists opposed the embargo vociferously. Some feared its impact abroad. "If England [were to] sink," Federalist vice-presidential candidate Rufus King said in 1808, expressing Federalist pro-British sympathies, "her fall will prove the grave of our liberties." Mercantile New England, the heart of Federalist opposition to Jefferson, took the brunt of the resulting economic depression. In the winter of 1808–1809, talk of secession spread through New England port cities.

Although general unemployment soared, some individuals benefited from the embargo. Merchants with ships abroad (those not idled by the embargo) and merchants willing to risk the lax enforcement to trade illegally could garner enormous profits. U.S. manufacturers—the early textile mills, for instance—received a boost, since the domestic market became theirs exclusively.

The embargo actually had little impact on Britain. The British most severely hurt—West Indians and factory workers in England—had no voice in policy. English merchants actually gained because they took over the Atlantic carrying trade from the stalled American ships. And because of a successful British blockade of Europe, the embargo had little practical effect on the French. Indeed, it gave France an excuse to set privateers against American ships that had evaded the embargo and were, possibly, heading to British ports. The French cynically claimed that such ships were British ships in disguise because the embargo prevented American vessels from sailing.

In the election of 1808, the Democratic-Republicans faced not only the Federalists but also factional dissent and dissatisfaction in seaboard states hobbled by the embargo.

Election of 1808 Although nine state legislatures passed resolutions urging Jefferson to run again, the president followed Washington's lead in renouncing a third term. He supported James Madison, his secretary of state, as the Democratic-Republican standard-bearer. For the first time, however, the Democratic-Republican nomination was contested. Madison won the endorsement of the party's congressional caucus, but Virginia Democratic-Republicans put forth James Monroe, who later withdrew, and some easterners supported Vice President George Clinton.

Charles Cotesworth Pinckney and Rufus King again headed the Federalist ticket, but with new vigor. The Younger Federalists, led by Harrison Gray Otis and other Bostonians, made the most of the widespread disaffection with Republican policy, especially the embargo. Although Pinckney received only 47 electoral votes to Madison's 122, the Federalists offered genuine competition. Pinckney carried all of New England except Vermont, and he won Delaware and some electoral votes in two other states. Federalists also gained seats in Congress and captured the New York State legislature. The Federalist future looked promising.

Under the pressure of domestic opposition, the embargo eventually collapsed. In its place, the Non-Intercourse Act of 1809 reopened

Non-Intercourse Act trade with all nations except Britain and France, and it authorized the president to resume trade with Britain or France if either of them ceased to violate neutral rights. On leaving office in March, Jefferson expressed the weight of his failure: "Never did a prisoner, released from his chains," he wrote, "feel such relief as I in shaking off the shackles of power."

The new act solved only the problems created by the embargo; it did not prevent further British and French interference with American commerce. For one brief moment it appeared to work. In June 1809 President Madison reopened trade with England after the British minister to the United States assured him that Britain would repeal restrictions on American trade. His Majesty's government in London, however, repudiated the minister's assurances, and Madison reverted to nonintercourse.

When the Non-Intercourse Act expired in 1810, Congress substituted a variant, Macon's Bill Number 2, that exchanged the proverbial stick for a carrot. The bill reopened trade with both Great Britain and France but provided that when either nation stopped violating American commercial rights, the president could suspend American commerce with the other. Madison, eager to avoid war, fell victim to French duplicity. When Napoleon accepted the offer, Madison declared nonintercourse with Great Britain in 1811. Napoleon, however, tricked him. The French continued to seize

American ships, and nonintercourse failed a second time. But because the Royal Navy dominated the seas, Britain, not France, became the main focus of American hostility.

Commerce and Industry

 The economy of the early republic relied heavily on shipping, and the commercial fleet played a significant role in extending American trade around the world. American fishermen explored the Atlantic, while whalers hunted for prey in the Atlantic and Pacific Oceans. The United States became a major supplier to Europe, taking advantage of the disruption in food production caused by European conflicts. Americans also exported cotton, lumber, sugar, and other commodities to Europe, and brought back manufactured goods. The slave trade lured American sailing ships to Africa. Boston, Salem, and Philadelphia merchants opened trade with China, sending cloth and metal to swap for furs with Chinook Indians on the Oregon coast, then sailing to China to trade for porcelain, tea, and silk. Greater profits could be made by importing manufactured goods than by producing them at home.

After 1807 embargoes and war, however, boosted domestic manufacturing. The disruptions in commerce made domestic manufactures profitable, and merchants began to shift their capital from shipping to manufacturing. In 1807 there were twenty cotton and woolen mills in New England; by 1813 there were more than two hundred.

Factories were still new in America. Samuel Slater set up the first American textile mill in Rhode Island in the 1790s. It used water-powered spinning machines that English immigrant Slater had built from memorized British models. Though Federalists like Alexander Hamilton, through his *Report on Manufactures* (see page 202), had pushed the United States to promote manufacturing, Jefferson envisioned an "empire of liberty" that was agricultural and commercial, not industrial. Holding fast to frugal, limited government, the Democratic-Republican policy did not promote industry.

This contemporary painting shows the Boston Manufacturing Company's 1814 textile factory at Waltham, Massachusetts. All manufacturing processes were brought together under one roof, and the company built its first factories in rural New England to tap roaring rivers as a power source.   (Courtesy of Gore Place Society, Waltham, Mass.)

Construction of the first American power loom and the chartering of the Boston Manufacturing Company in 1813 radically transformed textile manufacturing. Francis Cabot Lowell and other Boston merchants capitalized the corporation at $400,000—ten times the amount behind the first Rhode Island mills. The owners erected their factories in Waltham, Massachusetts, bringing all the manufacturing processes to a single location. They employed a resident manager to run the mill, thus separating ownership from management. Workers received wages, and the cloth they produced was sold throughout the United States.

Waltham or Lowell System

The cloth was so inexpensive that many women began to purchase it rather than make their own. While spinning and especially weaving remained women's work in many rural homes, women who formerly had spun their own yarn now received yarn from the mills and returned finished cloth. The change was subtle but significant: although the work itself was familiar, women were operating their looms for wages and producing cloth for the market, not primarily for their families.

The managers could not find enough hands in rural Waltham to staff the mill, so they recruited New England farm daughters, accepting responsibility for their living conditions. As inducements they offered cash wages, company-run boarding houses, and cultural events such as evening lectures—none of which were available on the farm. This paternalistic approach, called the Waltham or Lowell system, spread to other mills erected alongside New England rivers.

The early mills, dependent on waterpower, sprung up in rural areas. By erecting dams and watercourses, mill owners diverted water from farmers and destroyed fishing, an important source of income and protein in rural and village America. To protect their customary rights, fishermen and farmers fought the manufacturers in New England state legislatures, but petitions from job seekers in the mill environs supported the manufacturers. The ensuing compromises promoted mill development.

The War of 1812

Though unprepared for war in 1812, the United States seemed unable to avoid it. Economic pressure had failed to protect American ships and sailors. Having exhausted all efforts to alter British policy, and fearing for the survival of American independence, the United States drifted toward war. The Democratic-Republican "War Hawks," elected to Congress in 1810, cried loudest for war. Britain's response was too little and too late. In spring 1812, the admiralty ordered British ships to avoid clashes with the American navy and to avoid searches and seizures of American ships. Then in June 1812, Britain reopened the seas to American shipping. Hard times had hit the British Isles: the Anglo-French conflict had blocked much British commerce to the European continent, and exports to the United States had fallen 80 percent. But two days after the change in British policy, before word of it had crossed the Atlantic, Congress declared war.

In his message to Congress on June 1, 1812, President Madison enumerated familiar grievances: impressment, interference with neutral commerce, and British alliances with western Indians. More generally, the Democratic-Republicans resolved to defend American independence and honor, and some Americans hoped to conquer and annex British Canada.

The war Congress was a partisan one. Most militant were the War Hawks, land-hungry southerners and westerners, all Democratic-Republicans, led by John C. Calhoun of South Carolina and first-term congressman and House Speaker Henry Clay of Kentucky. John Randolph of Roanoke, an opponent of war, charged angrily, "Agrarian cupidity, not maritime rights, urges war." He heard "but one word" in Congress: "Canada! Canada! Canada!" Most representatives from the coastal states opposed war because armed conflict with the Royal Navy would interrupt American shipping. On June 4, the House voted 79 to 49 for war; two weeks later the Senate followed suit 19 to 13. Republicans favored war by a vote of 98 to 23; Federalists opposed it 39 to 0. On June 19, President Madison signed the bill. The United States went to war with Britain.

The Vote for War

The war unfolded as a series of scuffles and skirmishes, for which the U.S. Army and Navy and the state militias were unprepared. Officers executed campaigns poorly, and full-scale battles happened rarely (see Map 9.2). But the Americans had the advantage of fighting close to home.

Jefferson's warning that "our constitution is a peace establishment—it is not calculated for war" proved true. Though the U.S. Navy had a corps of experienced officers who had proved their mettle in the Barbary War, it was no match for the Royal Navy. The

Map 9.2 Major Campaigns of the War of 1812 The land war centered on the U.S.-Canadian border, the Chesapeake Bay, and the Louisiana and Mississippi Territories.

Recruiting an Army

U.S. Army had neither an able staff nor an adequate force of enlisted men. By 1812 the U.S. Military Academy at West Point, founded in 1802, had produced only eighty-nine regular officers. The American army depended on political leaders and state militias to recruit volunteers, but not all states cooperated. The government offered enlistees a sign-up bonus of $16, monthly pay of $5, a full set of clothes, and a promise of three months' pay and rights to purchase 160 acres of western land upon discharge. Forty-two percent of the enlistees were illiterate.

At first, recruitment in the West went well. Civic spirit, desire for land, and strong anti-Indian sentiment stimulated thousands of enlistments from the Old Northwest, Kentucky, Tennessee, and the southern frontier. The army made itself more acceptable to new recruits by abolishing flogging as punishment in 1812. Within a year, however, frontier enlistments declined. Word spread that the War Department failed to meet its payroll on time. By fall 1814, the army lagged six to twelve months behind in paying soldiers. Nor were supplies adequate; troops often went without shoes, uniforms, or blankets and the rations they received were sometimes spoiled.

Raising an army proved even more difficult in New England, where many viewed the conflict as a Democratic-Republican affair—"Mr. Madison's War"—and Federalists discouraged enlistments. Even some New England Democratic-Republicans declined to raise volunteer companies. Those who accepted promised their men that they would serve only in a defensive role, as in Maine where they guarded the coastline. Indeed, the inability of the United States to mount a successful invasion of Canada was due in part to the army's failure to assemble an effective force. Militias in New England and New York often refused to fight outside their state borders.

Nonetheless, Canada was tempting, and seemed takeable. The mighty Royal Navy could not reach the Great Lakes separating the United

Invasion of Canada

States and Canada because there was no river access to them from the Atlantic. Canada's population of just one-half million was a fraction of the United States's 7.5 million. Canada had seven thousand regulars in uniform; the United States, 12,000. And Americans hoped that the French in Canada might welcome U.S. forces.

Begun with high hopes, the invasion of Canada ended in disaster. The American strategy concentrated on the West, aiming to split Canadian forces and isolate the pro-British Indians. At the outset of the war, Tecumseh joined the British, who promised him in return an Indian nation in the Great Lakes region. U.S. General William Hull, territorial governor of Michigan, marched his troops into Upper Canada, near Detroit. More experienced as a politician than as a soldier, Hull had surrounded himself with newly minted colonels as politically astute and militarily ignorant as he was. Although his forces in the area outnumbered the British and their Indian allies, Hull waged a timid campaign, retreating more than he attacked. His abandonment of Mackinac Island and Fort Dearborn in Chicago and his surrender of Fort Detroit left the entire Midwest exposed to the enemy. The only bright spot was the September 1812 defense of Fort Harrison in Indiana Territory by Captain Zachary Taylor, who

provided the Americans with their first land victory. By the winter of 1812–1813, the British controlled about half of the Old Northwest.

The United States had no greater success on the Niagara front, where New York borders Canada. At the Battle of Queenstown, Canada, north of Niagara, the U.S. Army met defeat because the New York militia refused to leave New York. This frustrating scenario was repeated near Lake Champlain, when the New York militia's refusal to cross the border into Canada foiled American plans to attack Montreal. And neither the French nor the American loyalists who had fled to Canada at the time of the American Revolution rose to welcome the Americans.

The navy provided the only good news in the first year of the war. The U.S.S. *Constitution*, the U.S.S. *Wasp*, and the U.S.S. *United States* all

Naval Battles

bested British warships on the Atlantic Ocean. The *Constitution*'s 1812 rout of H.M.S. *Guerrière* in the Atlantic emboldened the U.S. Navy and earned the American ship the nickname "Old Ironsides." In the first year of war the Americans lost 20 percent of their ships while in defeat the British lost just 1 percent of their vessels. The United States, however, could ill afford to lose *any* ships. Democratic-Republican frugality had left the navy with only seventeen ships in 1812. It could not fight the British in a general naval war and thus Britannia ruled the waves.

The Royal Navy blockaded the Chesapeake and Delaware Bays in December 1812, and by 1814 the blockade covered nearly all American ports along the Atlantic and Gulf coasts. After 1811, American trade overseas had declined nearly 90 percent, and the decline in revenues from customs duties threatened to bankrupt the federal government and prostrate New England.

The contest for control of the Great Lakes, the key to the war in the Northwest, evolved as a ship-building race. Under Master Com-

Great Lakes Campaign

mandant Oliver Hazard Perry and shipbuilder Noah Brown, the United States outbuilt the British on Lake Erie and defeated them at the bloody Battle of Put-in-Bay on September 10, 1813. With this costly victory, the Americans gained control of Lake Erie.

General William Henry Harrison then began the offensive that proved to be among the United States's most successful land campaigns in the war. A ragged group of Kentucky militia volunteers who had been drafted into the regular army marched 20 to 30 miles a day to join Harrison's forces in Ohio. They had received no training and were armed only with swords and knives. Now with forty-five hundred men, Harrison's force attacked and took Detroit. Then they crossed to Canada, pursuing and defeating the British, Shawnee, and Chippewa forces on October 5 at the Battle of the Thames. In victory the United States captured six hundred British troops and great amounts of war materiel; the United States regained control of the Old Northwest. Tecumseh died in the battle, and with his death expired Native American unity. Following the loss of their leader, some Indians joined the United States against Britain. After the Battle of the Thames, the Americans razed the Canadian capital of York (now Toronto). Though they did not have enough troops to hold the city, they looted and burned the Parliament building before withdrawing. The stunning land victory had the added effect of stopping the British on Lake Ontario and occupying British operations on Lake Erie.

After defeating Napoleon in Europe in April 1814, the British launched a land counteroffensive against the United States, concentrating on the Chesapeake Bay region. In retaliation for the burning of York—and to divert American troops from Lake Champlain, where the British planned a new offensive—royal troops occupied Washington, D.C., in August and set it ablaze, leaving the presidential mansion and parts of the city burning all night. Chaos ruled. The president and cabinet had planned to rendezvous in Frederick, Maryland, but Madison and his advisers fled to Virginia. First Lady Dolley Madison oversaw removing cabinet documents to safety.

The British intended the attack on the capital only as a diversion. The major battle occurred in Septem-

Andrew Jackson imposed the Treaty of Fort Jackson on the Creek nation, ending the campaign against the Red Sticks. The treaty required the Creeks to pay the costs of the war, which Jackson estimated as the equivalent of 20 million acres. In moving the Creeks out of what is now central Alabama, Jackson initiated the Indians' forced removal from the South. Ironically, of the thirty-five chiefs who made their mark on the treaty, part of which is shown here, only one was a member of the Creek nation.   (National Archives)

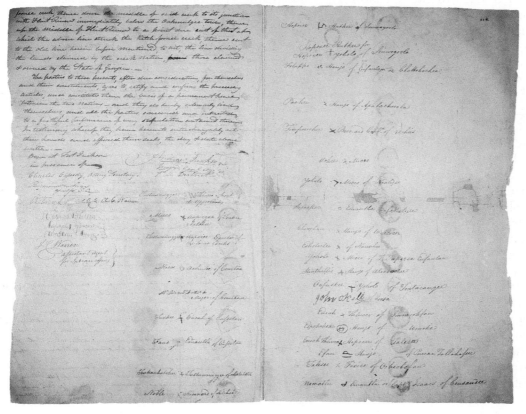

ber 1814 at Baltimore, where the Americans held firm. Francis Scott Key, detained on a British ship, watched the bombardment of Fort McHenry from Baltimore harbor and the next morning wrote the verses of "The Star-Spangled Banner" (which became the national anthem in 1931). Although the British inflicted heavy damage both materially and psychologically, they achieved little militarily. Their offensive at Lake Champlain proved equally unsuccessful when American ships turned back a British flotilla at Plattsburgh. The British halted their offense, and the war was stalemated.

The last campaigns of the war took place in the South, against the Creeks along the Gulf of Mexico and against the British around New Orleans (see Map 9.2). The Creeks had responded to the call of Tecumseh, whose mother was a Creek, to resist U.S. expan-

Campaign Against the Creeks

sion. Some had died in Indiana Territory, at Prophetstown on Tippecanoe Creek, when General Harrison's troops routed Shawnee forces there in 1811. In December 1812 General Andrew Jackson raised his Tennessee militia to fight the Creeks. By late 1813 his anti-Creek campaign stalled for lack of supplies. His men, who had signed up for a year, muttered about going home. Jackson refused to discharge them; they could not, he said, abandon their posts on enemy ground. Officers repeatedly threatened to shoot any man who left. Indeed, in March 1814 Jackson executed John Woods, a militiaman, for disobedience and mutiny. This act broke the opposition within the ranks, and Jackson's men defeated the Creek nation at the Battle of Horseshoe Bend in Mississippi Territory in March 1814.

Ballou's Pictorial Drawing-Room Companion depicts the Battle of New Orleans, the last campaign of the War of 1812. Andrew Jackson's troops—army regulars, Tennessee and Kentucky volunteers, and two companies of African American volunteers from New Orleans—held off the better-trained British troops in January 1815. The battle made Andrew Jackson a national hero.   (Historic New Orleans Collection)

The victory began Jackson's rise to political prominence. In the 1814 Treaty of Fort Jackson, the

**Battle of
New Orleans**

Creeks ceded two-thirds of their land and withdrew to the southern and western part of Mississippi Territory (what is now Alabama); the removal of Indians from the South had begun. Jackson became a major general in the regular army and continued south toward the Gulf of Mexico. To forestall a British invasion at Pensacola Bay, which guarded an overland route to New Orleans, Jackson seized Pensacola—in Spanish Florida—in November 1814. Then, after securing Mobile, he marched on to New Orleans to defend it against the British.

The Battle of New Orleans was the last campaign of the war. Early in December the British fleet landed fifteen hundred men east of the city, hoping to seize the mouth of the Mississippi River and thus strangle the lifeline of the American West. They faced American regulars, Tennessee and Kentucky volunteers, and two companies of free African American volunteers from New Orleans. For three weeks the British under Sir Edward Pakenham and the Americans led by Jackson played cat-and-mouse. Finally, on January 8, 1815, the two forces met head-on. In fortified positions, Jackson's poorly trained army held its ground against two frontal assaults from a British contingent of six thousand. At day's end, more than two thousand British soldiers lay dead or wounded; the Americans suffered only twenty-one casualties. Andrew Jackson emerged a national hero, and Americans memorialized the battle in song and paintings. The Battle of New Orleans actually took place two weeks after the end of the war. Unknown to the participants, a treaty had been signed in Ghent, Belgium, on December 24, 1814.

Peace and Consequences

The U.S. government had gone to war reluctantly and throughout the conflict probed for a diplomatic end to hostilities. In 1813 President Madison eagerly accepted a Russian offer to mediate, but Great Britain balked. Three months later, British foreign minister Lord Castlereagh suggested opening peace talks. It took more than ten months to arrange meetings, but in August 1814 a team of American negotiators, including John Quincy Adams and Henry Clay, began talks with the British in Ghent.

The Ghent treaty made no mention of the issues that had led to war. The United States received no satisfaction on impressment, blockades, or other maritime rights for neutrals. British demands for an independent Indian nation in the Northwest and territorial cessions from Maine to Minnesota likewise went unsatisfied. The Treaty of Ghent essentially restored the prewar status quo. It provided for an end to hostilities with the British and with Native Americans, release of prisoners, restoration of conquered territory, and arbitration of boundary disputes.

Why did the negotiators settle for so little? Events in Europe had made peace and the status quo acceptable at the end of 1814, as they had not been in 1812. Napoleon's defeat allowed the United States to abandon its demands, since peace in Europe made impressment and interference with American commerce moot issues. Similarly, war-weary Britain—its treasury nearly depleted—stopped pressing for a military victory.

The War of 1812 affirmed the independence of the American republic. Nearly three hundred thou-

**Consequences
of the War
of 1812**

sand troops had taken up arms to maintain independence; almost two thousand died for the cause, and four thousand were wounded. Although conflict with Great Britain over trade and territory continued, it never again led to war. The experience strengthened America's resolve to steer clear of European politics because the Anglo-French conflagration had drawn the United States into war. At the same time, with Indian resistance broken, U.S. expansion would spread south and west, not north to Canada.

The war carried disastrous results for most Native Americans. Although they were not a party to the Treaty of Ghent, the ninth article of the pact pledged the United States to end hostilities and to restore "all the possessions, rights, and privileges" that Indians had enjoyed before the war. Midwestern Indians signed more than a dozen treaties with the United States in 1815, but they had little meaning. With the death of Tecumseh, the Indians had lost their most powerful political and military leader; with the withdrawal of the British, they had lost their strongest ally. The Shawnees, Potawatomis, Chippewas, and others had lost the means to resist American expansion.

The war exposed weaknesses in defense and transportation at home. American generals had found U.S. roads inadequate to move troops and supplies. In the Northwest, General Harrison's troops had depended on homemade cartridges and gifts of clothing from Ohio residents; in Maine, troops had melted down spoons to make bullets. Improved transportation and a well-equipped army became national priorities; both were vital for westward expansion. In 1815 President Madison responded by centralizing control of the military and building a line of forts for coastal defense, and Congress voted a standing army of ten thousand men—one-third of the army's wartime strength but three times the size of the army during Jefferson's administration. In 1818 the National Road reached Wheeling, Virginia (now West Virginia), from its Cumberland, Maryland, beginning and carried settlers westward (see page 253).

Perhaps most important of all, the war stimulated economic growth. The embargo, the Non-Importation and Non-Intercourse Acts, and the war itself spurred the production of manufactured goods because New England capitalists began to invest in home manufactures. The effects of these changes were far-reaching (see Chapter 10).

Finally, the war sealed the fate of the Federalists. Realizing that they could not win a presidential election in wartime, the Federalists joined renegade Democratic-Republicans in supporting New York City mayor DeWitt Clinton in September 1812. Federalist organization peaked at the state level as the Younger Federalists campaigned hard. Clinton nevertheless lost to President Madison by 128 to 89 electoral votes; areas that favored the war (the South and West) remained solidly Democratic-Republican. The Federalists gained some congressional seats and carried many local elections, but extremism, in the form of the Hartford Convention, undermined them.

During the war Federalists had revived talk of secession. With the war stalemated, delegates from New

Hartford Convention

England met in Hartford, Connecticut, for three weeks in the winter of 1814–1815 to discuss revising the national compact or pulling out of the republic. Moderates prevented a resolution of secession, but convention members condemned the war and the embargo and endorsed radical changes in the Constitution. They wanted to restrict the presidency to one term and require a two-thirds congressional vote to admit new states to the Union. A barometer of their dissatisfaction was a proposal forbidding naturalized citizens from holding office. The delegates fruitlessly attempted to preserve New England Federalist political power as electoral strength shifted to the South and West and immigrants became politically active.

The timing of the Hartford Convention proved lethal. The victory at New Orleans and news of the peace treaty made the convention, with its talk of secession and constitutional amendments, look ridiculous if not treasonous. Rather than harassing a beleaguered wartime administration, the Federalists found themselves in retreat before a rising tide of nationalism. Though the Federalists survived in a handful of states until the 1820s, the faction dissolved. The War of 1812, at first a source of revival as opponents of war flocked to the Federalist banner, helped speed its demise.

Summary

The 1800 election marked the peaceful transition in power from the Federalists to the opposition Democratic-Republicans. Thomas Jefferson replaced John Adams as president and sought both to unify the nation and to solidify Democratic-Republican control of the government. Jeffersonians favored frugal government, and they cut the budget, military forces, and diplomatic missions.

The Supreme Court under Chief Justice John Marshall remained a Federalist bastion. Both parties fought over the judiciary, and Marshall would ensure, until 1835, the dominance of Federalist principle: federal supremacy over the states and the protection of commerce and capital. In *Marbury v. Madison* (1803), the Supreme Court established its great power of judicial review.

Jefferson considered the acquisition of Louisiana Territory and the commissioning of Lewis and Clark's expedition among his significant presidential accomplishments. In a single act the United States doubled its size. Increasingly Americans looked westward, and Lewis and Clark's Corps of Discovery practiced "buckskin diplomacy" while exploring the land, flora, fauna, and people west of the Mississippi. Americans quickly moved to absorb Louisiana.

With Jefferson and his successor James Madison, the Democratic-Republicans won every presidential election in this period. Though the electorate was limited only to males and mostly to whites, both the Federalists and the Democratic-Republicans competed at the grassroots level for popular support. Political conflict was bitter, divisions real. Sometimes they could prove fatal as in the Burr-Hamilton duel.

Despite internal divisions, the greatest threats came from abroad. In the war with the Barbary states, the United States sought to guard its commerce and ships on the high seas. The second war with Britain—the War of 1812—was fought for similar reasons but against a much more formidable power. The peace treaty reaffirmed American independence; thereafter the nation was able to settle disputes with Great Britain at the bargaining table. The war also dealt a serious blow to Indian resistance in the West and South. At the same time, embargoes and war forced Americans to look toward building domestic markets and jump-started American manufacturing. Military and diplomatic assertiveness brought Americans a sense of national identity and self-confidence.

LEGACY FOR A PEOPLE AND A NATION
The Peaceful Transfer of Power

Among those in attendance at Jefferson's inauguration on March 4, 1801, was novelist Margaret Bayard Smith. Afterward she wrote: "The changes of administration, which in every government and in every age have most generally been epochs of confusion, villainy and bloodshed, in this happy country take place without any species of distraction, or disorder." It need not have been so. Washington, D.C., still under construction, was full of revolutionaries. Alexander Hamilton, Thomas Jefferson, Aaron Burr, and Charles Pinckney had once risked their lives and fortunes for political ends.

John Adams, another revolutionary, was so bitter over his loss that he exited the city before sunrise that morning. Adams had lost by a narrow margin in the electoral college, but Aaron Burr, Jefferson's running mate, threw the election into turmoil when he unsuccessfully tried to grab the presidency for himself. The campaign of 1800 had been particularly nasty and personal, and candidates hinted that were their opponents elected, chaos would ensue.

Why didn't it? After all, what would plague most new states in the nineteenth and twentieth centuries was the unwillingness of regimes to hand over power peacefully to legitimate successors. Coups, bloodshed, and military rule seemed to be most common.

In later years Jefferson called his election to the presidency the "Revolution of 1800." He meant that the Federalists, in control of the government since its inception in 1789, were turned out and the republican principles of the Revolution were about to be restored.

The real revolution, however, was that the Federalists had relinquished power to the Democratic-Republicans, without confusion or villainy or bloodshed, as Margaret Bayard Smith observed. It established the precedent that political battles, with the exception of the Civil War, would be waged not in the streets but at the polls, in Congress, and before the courts. The developing party system itself would channel political disagreements within acceptable, peaceful means. The "revolution" of 1800 established a unique legacy for a people and a nation that would define governance in the United States: the transfer of governmental power based on the ballot, not on arms.

For Further Reading, see page A-11 of the Appendix. For Web resources, go to http://www.college.hmco.com.

THE OLD GRANITE STATE,

Judson.   Abby.   John.   Asa

A SONG,   *Price 50 Cts Nett.*

COMPOSED, ARRANGED AND SUNG, BY

THE HUTCHINSON FAMILY.

The Hutchinson Family, also known as the Tribe of Jesse, was the most popular singing group in nineteenth-century America. Abby, Asa, Jesse, John, and Judson Hutchinson—five of a family of sixteen children from rural New Hampshire—performed the patriotic, religious, and sentimental songs that had dominated popular music since the Revolution. They initiated new musical styles, wrote lyrics full of social commentary, and made entertainment a commodity, promoted and performed in the market economy.

Unlike most musical groups, the Tribe of Jesse not only sang but also presented well-rehearsed and elaborately produced performances. They used folk tunes that the audiences found familiar and enjoyed, but their lyrics explored controversial topics such as abolition and temperance. Their 1844 "Get Off the Track!" used imagery from railroads, the newest form of transportation, to hail the unstoppable power of the antislavery movement.

The Hutchinson Family traveled by rail, too, performing across the expanding United States, but drawing their largest audiences in the growing cities of the North. The family's fee for a single night in the 1840s reached $1,000, about 400 times a worker's daily wage. They had an entourage of managers, agents, and publishers. Hawkers sold sheet music, portraits, and songbooks at the Hutchinsons' concerts. The Hutchinson Family made a business of music and entertainment, selling nostalgia and reform.

The Hutchinsons' off-stage lives, too, bridged the old and the new. They had come from the farms of New Hampshire, they sang in "The 'Old Granite State.'" They left home, they explained in song, with the blessing of their "aged parents," to sing of liberty, traveling "round the World." Besides their musical talent, the Hutchinson Family offered their audiences reassurance in a time of rapid change. By setting their lyrics to familiar hymns (we are "good old fashioned singers"), they connected their advocacy of reform with the comfortable past. And by describing a bucolic future, they reassured their audiences that the present, with all its turmoil, would turn out well.

The Hutchinson Family celebrated their native rural New Hampshire in "The 'Old Granite State,'" their most popular song. They made a business of performing, and hawkers sold their sheet music at concerts. (Courtesy of Lynn Historical Society, hand-colored by Sandi Rygiel, Picture Research Consultants, Inc.)

10

NATIONALISM, EXPANSION, AND THE MARKET ECONOMY 1816–1845

The Hutchinsons' concert tours exemplified the market economy, in which goods and services sold in cash or credit transactions created a network of exchange that bound distant enterprises together. The family performed in western areas in the 1840s that had had no American settlements twenty years before. The canals and railroads that carried them also increasingly linked the nation's regions after the War of 1812. People moved inland from the seaboard, farmed the rich lands across the Appalachians, and sold their crops at home and abroad. Grain went east to coastal cities, cotton went to Europe, and ready-made men's garments from New York and Cincinnati sold across the nation. Increasingly, farmers turned to staple-crop agriculture and city people worked not for themselves but for others, for wages. These large-scale enterprises needed capital, and new financial institutions amassed and loaned it. Mechanization took hold; factories and precision-made machinery put home workshops and handcrafters out of business; on farms, horse-drawn reapers replaced farmhands. In turn, the increased specialization in plantation and commercial agriculture, manufacturing, transportation, and finance further fired the engines of the new nationwide, capitalist, market-oriented economy.

The end of the War of 1812 unleashed this growth. A new nationalist spirit encouraged the economy and promoted western expansion at home, trade abroad, and assertiveness throughout the Western Hemisphere. Economic growth and territorial expansion, however, generated new problems. Sectional conflicts over slavery and economic development created divisions. Migration, shifts in occupations, and changes in the ways people worked created new tensions. Not everyone profited in wealth and opportunity as the Hutchinson Family did. Journeyman tailors, displaced by retailers and cheaper labor, found their trades disappearing. New England farm daughters who became wage workers found their world changing no less radically. Moreover, boom-and-bust cycles, now on a national scale, wrenched livelihoods and lives. Mills, factories, roads, canals, and railroads altered or destroyed the landscape.

Everywhere Americans were on the move. Settlement, North and South, moved to the interior, and farms and cities, linked by rivers, then roads, canals, and railroads, stretched to the Ohio and Mississippi River valleys and beyond. The Indian inhabitants attempted to hold their ground but were in the end removed to the West, pushed off their lands by the same drive for profit, the same nationalist spirit, that was re-shaping American national politics and the dynamic American economy. ■

Postwar Nationalism

 Nationalism surged after the War of 1812. Self-confident, the nation asserted itself at home and abroad as Democratic-Republicans borrowed a page from the Federalists' agenda and encouraged economic growth. Though James Monroe would follow James Madison as the last of the presidents who had attended the Constitutional Convention, political power began to shift away from the founders of the republic. Congressional leaders Henry Clay and John C. Calhoun, and those who vied for the presidency in the 1820s—John Quincy Adams and Andrew Jackson—formed a new generation of political leaders who were nationalistic in outlook.

James Madison inspired the postwar wave of nationalism. In his December 1815 message to Congress, he recommended economic development and military expansion. His agenda included a national bank (the charter of the first bank had expired in 1811) and improved transportation. To raise government revenues and foster manufacturing, Madison called for a protective tariff—a tax on imported goods designed to protect American manufactures. Yet his program acknowledged Jeffersonian republicanism; only a constitutional amendment, Madison argued, could authorize the federal government to build local roads and canals.

Congressional leaders saw Madison's program as a way of unifying the country. Democratic-Republican John C. Calhoun of South Carolina and House Speaker Henry Clay of Kentucky believed that the tariff would stimulate industry. The agricultural South and West would sell cotton to the churning mills of New England and food to its millworkers. New roads and canals would transport the goods, and tariff revenues would provide money to build them. A national bank would handle the transactions.

Nationalist Program

In the last year of Madison's administration, the Democratic-Republican Congress enacted much of the nationalist program. In 1816 it chartered the Second Bank of the United States to assist the government and to issue currency. Like its predecessor, the bank mixed public and private ownership; the government provided one-fifth of the bank's capital and appointed one-fifth of its directors.

IMPORTANT EVENTS

1815	Madison proposes internal improvements
1816	Second Bank of the United States chartered
	Tariff of 1816 imposes first substantial duties
	Monroe elected president
1817	Rush-Bagot Treaty limits British and American naval forces on Lake Champlain and Great Lakes
1819	*McCulloch v. Maryland* establishes supremacy of federal over state law
	Adams-Onís Treaty with Spain gives Florida to U.S. and defines Louisiana territorial border
1819–1823	Hard times bring unemployment
1820	Missouri Compromise creates formula for admitting slave and free states
	Monroe reelected
1820s	New England textile mills expand
1823	Monroe Doctrine closes Western Hemisphere to European intervention
1824	*Gibbons v. Ogden* affirms federal over state authority in interstate commerce
	Monroe proposes Indian removal
1825	Erie Canal completed
1830	Railroad era begins
	Congress passes Indian Removal Act
1830s	McCormick reaper and Deere steel plow patented
1830s–1840s	Cotton production shifts to Mississippi valley
1831	Cherokees turn to courts to defend treaty rights in *Cherokee Nation v. Georgia*
1832	Marshall declares Cherokee nation a distinct political community in *Worcester v. Georgia*
1834	Women workers strike at Lowell textile mills
1835–1842	Seminoles successfully resist removal in Second Seminole War
1836	Second Bank of the United States closes
1837	*Charles River Bridge v. Warren Bridge* encourages new enterprises
1839–1843	Hard times strike again
1842	*Commonwealth v. Hunt* declares strikes lawful
1844	Government grant sponsors first telegraph line

Congress also passed a protective tariff to aid industries that had flourished during the War of 1812 but were now threatened by the resumption of overseas trade. The Tariff of 1816 levied taxes on imported woolens and cottons, and on iron, leather, hats, paper, and sugar, in effect raising their prices in the United States. Foreshadowing a growing trend, support for the tariff divided along sectional lines: New England and the western and Middle Atlantic states stood to benefit and applauded it, but the South did not.

The South did press for better transportation. It was Congressman Calhoun of South Carolina, not the president, who promoted roads and canals to "bind the republic together." However, on March 3, 1817, the day before he left office, Madison vetoed Calhoun's internal improvements bill as unconstitutional. The president *did* approve funds for extending the National Road to Ohio, deeming it a military necessity.

James Monroe, Madison's successor, continued Madison's domestic program, supporting tariffs and vetoing internal improvements.

James Monroe

Monroe was the third Virginian elected president since 1801. A former senator and twice governor of Virginia, he had served under Madison as secretary of state and of war and used his close association with Jefferson and Madison to attain the presidency.

Among the nation's founders, Monroe was a most ordinary and colorless man who rarely had an original idea. But in 1816 he easily defeated the last Federalist presidential nominee, Rufus King, and swept all the electoral votes except for the Federalist strongholds of Massachusetts, Connecticut, and Delaware. The American people were "one great family." A Boston newspaper dubbed this one-party period the "Era of Good Feelings."

Led by Federalist chief justice John Marshall, the Supreme Court became the bulwark of a nationalist point of view. In *McCulloch v. Maryland* (1819), the Court struck down a Maryland law taxing a branch of the federally chartered Second Bank of the United States. Maryland had imposed the tax in an effort to destroy the bank's Baltimore branch. The issue was thus one of state versus federal jurisdiction. Speaking for a unanimous Court, Marshall asserted the supremacy of the federal government over the states. "The Constitution and the laws thereof are supreme," he declared. "They control the constitution and laws of the respective states and cannot be controlled by them."

McCulloch v. Maryland

The Court went on to consider whether Congress could issue a bank charter. The Constitution did not spell out such power, but Marshall noted that Congress had the authority to pass "all laws which shall be necessary and proper for carrying into execution" the enumerated powers of the government. Marshall ruled that Congress could legally exercise "those great powers on which the welfare of the nation essentially depends." If the ends were legitimate and the means were not prohibited, Marshall ruled, a law was constitutional. The Constitution was, in Marshall's words, "intended to endure for ages to come, and consequently, to be adapted to the various causes of human affairs." The bank charter was declared legal.

McCulloch v. Maryland thus joined nationalism and economics. By asserting federal supremacy, Marshall protected the commercial and industrial interests that favored a national bank; this was federalism in the tradition of Alexander Hamilton (see page 200). The decision was only one in a series of rulings that cemented the federalist view. In *Fletcher v. Peck* (1810), the Court had voided a Georgia law that violated individuals' rights to make contracts. In *Dartmouth College v. Woodward* (1819), the Court nullified a New Hampshire act altering the charter of Dartmouth College. Marshall ruled that the charter was a contract, and in protecting such contracts he thwarted state interference in commerce and business. *Gibbons v. Ogden* (1824) confirmed federal supremacy in interstate commerce.

Monroe's secretary of state, John Quincy Adams, matched the self-confident Marshall Court in assertiveness and nationalism. A small, austere man once described by a British official as a "bulldog among spaniels," Adams, the son of John and Abigail Adams, was a superb diplomat who spoke six languages. From 1817 to 1825 he brilliantly managed the nation's foreign policy, stubbornly pushing for expansion, fishing rights for Americans in Atlantic waters, political distance from the Old World, and peace. An ardent expansionist, he nonetheless believed that it must come about through negotiations, not war, and that newly acquired territories must bar slavery. The United States, Adams said in an 1821 Fourth of July speech, "goes not abroad, in search of monsters to destroy. She is the well-wisher to the freedom and independence of all."

John Quincy Adams as Secretary of State

An Anglophobe, Adams nonetheless worked to strengthen the peace with Great Britain negotiated at Ghent (1814). In 1817 the two nations agreed in the Rush-Bagot Treaty to limit their naval forces to one ship each on Lake Champlain and Lake Ontario and to two ships each on the four other Great Lakes. This first disarmament treaty of modern times led to the demilitarization of the border between the United States

John Quincy Adams (1767–1848), architect of the Monroe Doctrine, was secretary of state from 1817 to 1825. Thomas Sully's portrait, painted in 1825, captured Adams's determination and stubbornness.   (New York State Office of Parks, Recreation, and Historic Preservation, Philipse Manor Hall State Historic Site)

and Canada. Adams then pushed for the Convention of 1818, which fixed the United States–Canadian border from Lake of the Woods in Minnesota westward to the Rockies along the 49th parallel (see Map 10.1). When agreement could not be reached on the territory west of the Rockies, Britain and the United States settled on joint occupation of Oregon for ten years (renewed indefinitely in 1827).

Adams's next moved to settle long-term disputes with Spain. Although the 1803 Louisiana Purchase had omitted reference to Spanish-ruled West Florida, the United States claimed the territory as far east as the Perdido River (the present-day Florida-Alabama border) but occupied only a small finger of the area. During the War of 1812 the United States had seized Mobile and the remainder of West Florida. After the war Adams took advantage of Spain's preoccupation with domestic and colonial troubles to negotiate for the purchase of East Florida. During the 1818 talks, General Andrew Jackson took it on himself to occupy much of present-day Florida on the pretext of suppressing Seminole raids against American settlements across the border. Adams was furious with Jackson but defended his brazen act.

The following year, Don Luís de Onís, the Spanish minister to the United States, agreed to cede

Adams-Onís Treaty

Florida to the United States without payment. The Adams-Onís, or Transcontinental, Treaty also defined the southwestern boundary of the Louisiana Purchase and set the southern border of Oregon at the 42nd parallel (see Map 10.1). (Spain retained present-day Texas, New Mexico, and California.) The U.S. government assumed $5 million of claims by American citizens against Spain and gave up its dubious claim to northern Mexico (Texas). Expansion was achieved at little cost and without war.

When the Spanish flag was last lowered over St. Augustine on July 10, 1821, and at Pensacola on July 17, Florida residents differed in how they greeted the United States and the American colonial governor, General Andrew Jackson. Some planter-slaveholders and traders welcomed the American flag, but Creeks and Seminoles, free blacks, runaway slaves, and Spanish-speaking town dwellers did not. Many feared Jackson, who had led raids against the Seminoles in Florida in 1814 and 1818. The Spanish encouraged residents to resettle in Mexico, Cuba, or Texas, but most stayed put though wary of the United States.

Conflict between the United States and European nations was temporarily resolved by the Rush-Bagot Treaty, the Convention of 1818, and the Adams-Onís Treaty, but events to the south still threatened American interests. John Quincy Adams's desire to insulate the United States and the Western Hemisphere from European conflict brought about his greatest achievement: the Monroe Doctrine.

The immediate issue was the recognition of new governments in Latin America. Between 1808 and 1822, the United Provinces of the

Independent States in Latin America

Río de la Plata (present-day northern Argentina, Paraguay, and Uruguay), Chile, Peru, Colombia, and Mexico all broke free from Spain. Monroe and Adams moved cautiously, seeking to avoid conflict with Spain and to be assured of the stability of the new regimes. Then in 1822, shortly after the Adams-Onís Treaty was signed and ratified, the United States became the first nation outside Latin America to recognize the new states, including Mexico.

Soon events in Europe again threatened the stability of the New World. Spain suffered a domestic revolt, and France, to bolster the weak Spanish monarchy against the rebels, occupied Spain. The United States feared that France would return the new Latin American states to colonial rule. Great Britain, similarly distrustful of France, proposed a joint United States–British declaration against European intervention in the Western Hemisphere and a joint disavowal of territorial ambitions in the region. Adams rejected the British overture. Following George Washington's admonition to avoid foreign entanglements, he insisted that the United States act independently.

Despite clamors to take joint action with Great Britain, Adams refused to budge. Those who favored a multilateral move believed the United States needed British naval power to prevent French or Russian expansion in the New World. But Adams won. "It would be more candid, as well as more dignified," he argued, "to avow our principles explicitly to Russia and France, than to come in as a cockboat in the wake of the British man-of-war." Adams interpreted the British disavowal of territorial ambitions as an attempt to thwart American expansion.

President Monroe presented the American position—the Monroe Doctrine—to Congress in December 1823. His message called for

Monroe Doctrine

noncolonization of the Western Hemisphere by European nations, a principle that addressed American anxiety not only about Latin America but also about Russian expansion beyond Alaska and its settlements in California. He also demanded nonintervention by Europe in the affairs of independent New World nations, and he pledged noninterference by the United States in European affairs, including those of Europe's existing New World colonies.

The Monroe Doctrine proved popular at home. It tapped American nationalism and anti-British and anti-European feelings, and it eventually became the foundation of American policy in the Western Hemisphere. Monroe's words, however, carried no force. Indeed, the policy could not have succeeded without the support of the British, who were committed to keeping other European nations out of the hemisphere to protect their dominance in the Atlantic trade. Europeans ignored the Monroe Doctrine; it was the Royal Navy they respected, not American policy.

While nationalism brought Americans together, the question of slavery divided them. Since the drafting of the Constitution, political leaders had tried to avoid the issue. The one exception was an act ending the foreign slave trade after January

"Fire Bell in the Night"

1, 1808, which passed without much opposition. The act followed the expiration of the constitutional ban (Article I, Section 9) on ending the slave trade before 1808. In 1819, however, slavery crept onto the political agenda when Missouri residents petitioned Congress for admission to the Union as a slave state. For two and a half years the issue dominated Congress. "This momentous question," wrote Thomas Jefferson, fearful for the life of the Union, "like a fire bell in the night, awakened and filled me with terror."

The debate transcended slavery in Missouri. The compromises that had kept the issue under wraps since the Constitutional Convention could collapse. Five new states had joined the Union since 1812: Louisiana (1812), Indiana (1816), Mississippi (1817), Illinois (1818), and Alabama (1819). Of these, Louisiana, Mississippi, and Alabama permitted slavery. Because Missouri was on the same latitude as free Illinois, Indiana, and Ohio (a state since 1803), its admission as a slave state would thrust slavery farther northward. It would also tilt the uneasy political balance in the Senate

Map 10.1 Missouri Compromise and the State of the Union, 1820 The compromise worked out by House Speaker Henry Clay established a formula that avoided debate over whether new states would allow or prohibit slavery. In the process, it divided the United States into northern and southern regions.

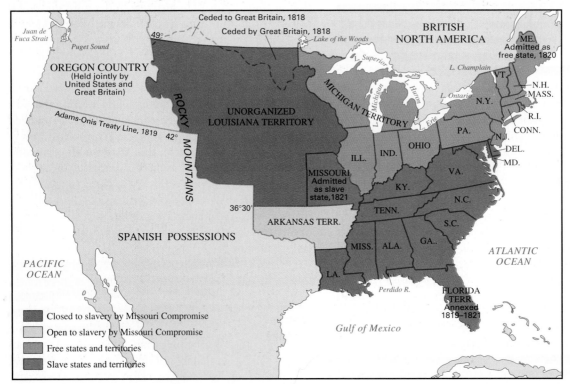

toward the slave states. In 1819 the Union consisted of eleven slave and eleven free states. If Missouri joined, slave states would have a one-vote edge in the Senate.

The moral issues made slavery an explosive question. Settlers from slave states—Kentuckians and Tennesseans—made up most of the new Missourians. But in the North slavery was slowly dying out, and many northerners had concluded that it was evil. When Representative James Tallmadge, Jr., of New York proposed gradual emancipation in Missouri, a passionate and sometimes violent debate ensued. Southerners accused the North of threatening to destroy the Union. "If you persist, the Union will be dissolved," Thomas W. Cobb of Georgia shouted at Tallmadge. "Seas of blood can only extinguish" the fire Tallmadge was igniting, Cobb warned. "Let it come," retorted Tallmadge. The House, which had a northern majority, passed the Tallmadge amendment, but the Senate rejected it. The two sides were deadlocked.

A compromise emerged in 1820 under pressure from House Speaker Henry Clay. Maine would enter

Missouri Compromise

as a free state, carved out of Massachusetts, while Missouri entered as a slave state. In the rest of the Louisiana Territory north of latitude 36°30' (Missouri's southern boundary), slavery was prohibited forever (see Map 10.1). The compromise carried, but the agreement almost unraveled in November when Missouri submitted a constitution that barred free blacks from entering the state. Opponents contended that the proposed state constitution violated the federal Constitution's provision that "the citizens of each State shall be entitled to all privileges and immunities of citizens in the several States." Proponents argued that many states, North and South, restricted black migrants from entering. In 1821 Clay produced a second compromise: Missouri guaranteed that none of its laws would discriminate against citizens of other states. (Once admitted to the Union, however, Missouri twice adopted laws banning free blacks.)

The Market Economy and Government's Economic Role

Increasingly in the years after the War of 1812, Americans became involved in the market economy—growing crops and producing goods specifically for cash sale and using the cash to purchase items produced by other people. Farms and slave plantations produced

crops for market sales. Plantations raised rice, tobacco, sugar, or cotton; farmers grew only one or two crops or raised animals for market. Farm women gave up spinning and weaving and purchased fabric made by wage-earning farm girls in Massachusetts textile mills. Nonfarm men and women sold not goods but their labor for cash, working for wages. Most free farmers and workers bought in stores, increasing the amount of goods produced in workshops and factories. Such a system encouraged specialization. It also energized transportation, as both goods and entertainment, like the Hutchinsons, circulated nationally.

Before canals and railroads, farmers had geared production to their own needs and to local and foreign, not national, markets. They lived in interdependent communities and exchanged labor and goods with their neighbors. Farm families produced much of what they needed—food, clothing, candles, soap, and the like—and traded for or purchased items they could not produce, such as cooking pots, horseshoes, coffee, tea, and sugar.

Mechanization, the division of labor, new methods of financing, and improvements in transportation all fueled the expansion of the economy. Goods and services multiplied. This growth, in turn, prompted new improvements and greater opportunities for wage labor. The effect was cumulative; by the 1840s the economy was growing faster than in the previous four decades. While per capita income increased 50 percent between 1800 and 1840, the price of manufactured goods and food fell.

The pace of economic growth, however, was uneven. Prosperity reigned during two long periods, from 1823 to 1835 and from 1843 to

Boom-and-Bust Cycles

1857. But there were long stretches of economic contraction as well. Contraction and deflation (decline in the general price level) occurred again during the hard times of 1819–1823 and 1839–1843. During these periods banks collapsed, businesses went under, wages and prices declined, and jobs were hard to find or to keep. Yet even during boom periods major industries like construction offered only cyclical employment. The boom-and-bust cycle was also seasonal and personal. Free laborers in Baltimore, for example, typically found steady work only from March through October, then unemployment and hunger from November through February.

In 1819 the postwar boom collapsed. Expansion had been built on easy credit; state banks had printed notes freely, fueling speculative buying of western land. Speculators had bought acreage to sell at a profit rather than to farm. When manufacturing fell in 1818, prices spiraled downward. The Second Bank of the United States cut back on loans, thus further shrinking the economy. With urban workers, farmers, and southern planters having less money to spend, the economy declined.

The contraction devastated workers and their families. As a Baltimore physician noted in 1819, working people felt hard times "a thousand fold more than the merchants." In the 1839 contraction in Baltimore, when hundreds of small manufacturers closed their doors, tailors, shoemakers, milliners, and shipyard and construction workers lost their jobs. Ninety miles to the north, Philadelphia took on an eerie aura. "The streets seemed deserted," Sidney George Fisher observed in 1842. "The largest [merchant] houses are shut up and to rent, there is no business . . . no money, no confidence." Only auctions boomed, as sheriffs sold off seized property at a quarter of pre-depression prices, a dismal scene as portrayed by artist E. Didier in *Auction in Chatham Street* in nearby New York (see the painting below). In Philadelphia and other cities, soup societies fed the hungry. In New York, bread lines and beggars crowded the sidewalks. In smaller cities like Lynn, Massachusetts, the poor became scavengers, digging for clams and harvesting dandelions.

What caused the boom-and-bust cycles that brought about such suffering? Generally speaking, they were a direct result of the mar-

Cause of the Boom-and-Bust Cycles

ket economy. As with the expansion following the War of 1812, prosperity stimulated demand for finished goods such as clothing and furniture. Increased demand in turn led not only to higher prices and still higher production but also, because of business optimism and expectation of higher prices, to speculation in land. Then, as with the hard times of 1819, production surpassed demand, causing prices and wages to fall; in response, land and stock values collapsed.

E. Didier painted *Auction in Chatham Street* in 1834. Auction houses in New York and other cities boomed during hard times. (Museum of the City of New York)

In the economic thinking of the time, some considered this process beneficial—a self-adjusting cycle that eliminated unprofitable economic ventures. In theory, people concentrated on the activities they did best, and the economy as a whole became more efficient. Advocates of the system also argued that it enhanced individual freedom, since theoretically each seller, whether of goods or labor, determined the price. But in fact the system tied workers to a perpetual roller coaster; they became dependent on wages—and on the availability of jobs—for their very existence. The cycles that governed the market economy influenced every corner of the country as even small localities became tied, or handcuffed, to regional and national markets.

The market economy also ushered in another type of boom-and-bust cycle: harvest and destruction. Canals and railroads spurred demand for distant resources, then accelerated the destruction of forests, natural waterways, and any landscape features that represented obstacles. Railroads made possible large-scale lumbering of pinewood forests in Michigan and Wisconsin. During the 1840s, lumber companies deforested millions of acres, leaving most of that land unfit even for agriculture. The process of harvest and destruction would eventually change the ecology of the United States.

The idea of a market economy drew on eighteenth-century republicanism. Advanced by members of the elite as well as by craftsmen, it emphasized economic liberty and individualism (see page 168). Limited, not activist, government, adherents argued, fostered economic expansion because individuals pursuing their own private interests benefited the nation as a whole.

Government Economic Role

Nonetheless, the federal government played an active role in technological and industrial growth. Federal arsenals pioneered new manufacturing techniques and helped to develop the machine-tool industry. The United States Post Office fostered the circulation of information, a critical element in a market economy. The number of post offices grew from three thousand in 1815 to fourteen thousand in 1845. The post office also played a brief but crucial role in the development of the telegraph, financing the first telegraph line, from Washington to Baltimore, in 1844. Invented by artist Samuel F. B. Morse, the telegraph allowed information to travel faster, almost instantaneously, over long distances. To create an atmosphere conducive to economic growth and individual creativity, the government protected inventions and domestic industries. Patent laws gave inventors a seventeen-year monopoly on their inventions, and tariffs protected American industry from foreign competition.

Government policy also fostered farm life. Republicanism associated farming with virtue, independence, and productivity, essential values in the new republic, and the federal government surveyed public land and opened it to settlement. Internal improvements such as harbors, roads, and canals—some underwritten by government—linked new farms in the West to markets in the East. When Indians got in the way of expansion, the federal government moved them across the Mississippi River (see pages 269–274).

The federal judiciary validated government promotion of the economy and encouraged business enterprise and risk taking. In *Gibbons v. Ogden* (1824), the Supreme Court overturned the New York State law that gave Robert Fulton and Robert Livingston a monopoly on the New York–New Jersey steamboat trade.

Legal Foundations of Commerce

Aaron Ogden, their successor, lost the monopoly when Chief Justice John Marshall ruled that the congressional prerogative of licensing new enterprises took precedence over New York's grant of monopoly rights to Fulton and Livingston. Marshall declared that Congress's power under the commerce clause of the Constitution extended to "every species of commercial intercourse," including transportation systems. Within a year, forty-three steamboats were plying Ogden's route.

In defining interstate commerce broadly, the Marshall Court expanded federal powers over the economy while restricting the ability of states to control economic activity within their borders. Its action was consistent with the earlier decision in *Dartmouth College v. Woodward* (1819), which protected the sanctity of contracts against interference by the states (see page 246). "If business is to prosper," Marshall wrote, "men must have assurance that contracts will be enforced."

Federal and state courts, in conjunction with state legislatures, also encouraged the proliferation of corporations—organizations entitled to hold property and transact business as if they were individuals. Corporation owners, called shareholders, were granted *limited liability*, or freedom from responsibility for the company's debts beyond their original investments. An attractive feature to potential investors, limited liability encouraged people to back

Corporations

The Marshall Court encouraged business competition by ending state-licensed monopolies on inland waterways. *Gibbons v. Ogden* (1824) opened up the New York–New Jersey trade to new lines, and within a short time dozens of steamboats were ferrying passengers and freight across the Hudson River.   (© Collection of The New-York Historical Society)

new business ventures. Shareholders elected managers who ran the corporation, though often managers controlled a majority of the voting stock. By 1817 the number of corporations in the United States had grown to two thousand, from three hundred in 1800. By 1830 the New England states alone had issued nineteen hundred charters, one-third to manufacturing and mining firms. At first each firm needed a special legislative act to incorporate, but after the 1830s applications became so numerous that states established routine procedures allowing firms to incorporate easily.

Though legislative action created corporations, the courts played a crucial role in extending their powers and protecting them. The

Charles River Bridge Case

Supreme Court in particular encouraged corporate development and free enterprise by ruling, in *Charles River Bridge v. Warren Bridge* (1837), that new enterprises could not be restrained by implied privileges under old charters. The case involved issues of great importance: should a new interest be allowed to compete against existing enterprises, and should the state protect existing privilege or encourage innovation and the growth of commerce through competition?

The Massachusetts legislature had chartered the Charles River Bridge Company in 1785 and six years later extended its charter for seventy years. In return for assuming the risk of building a bridge between Charlestown and Boston, the owners received the right to collect tolls. In 1828 the legislature chartered another company to build the Warren Bridge across the Charles nearby; the owner would have the right to collect tolls for six years, after which the bridge would be turned over to the state and be free of tolls. The Charles River Bridge Company sued in 1829, claiming that the new bridge breached the earlier charter and contradicted the principles in *Dartmouth College v. Woodward*.

Speaking for the Court majority, Marshall's successor Roger Taney declared that the original charter did not confer the privilege of monopoly and that exclusivity could not therefore be implied. Focusing on the question of corporate privilege rather than the law of contracts, Taney ruled that charter grants should be interpreted narrowly and that ambiguities would be decided in favor of the public interest. New enterprises should not be restricted by old charters, and economic growth would best be served by narrowing the application of the *Dartmouth College* decision. In this way the judiciary promoted individual enterprise and competition.

In promoting the economy, state governments far surpassed the federal government. From 1815 through

States' Support for the Economy the 1840s, for example, government money, mostly from the states, financed three-fourths of the nearly $200 million invested in canals. In the 1830s the states started to invest in rail construction. Though the federal government played a larger role in constructing railroads than in building canals, state and local governments provided more than half of the capital for southern rail lines. State governments also invested in corporate and bank stocks, providing corporations and banks with much-needed capital. In fact, states actually equaled or exceeded private enterprise in their investments.

Pennsylvania, encompassing a vast area from the Delaware River to beyond the Appalachians, developed the nation's most extensive program of internal improvements to stimulate settlement and economic growth. The state invested a total of $100 million in canals, railroads, banks, and manufacturing firms; its appointees sat on more than 150 corporate boards of directors. But Pennsylvania and other states did more than invest resources in industry. Through special acts and incorporation laws, they regulated the nature and activities of corporations and banks and used their licensing capacities to control industrial operations. Georgia, for example, regulated the grading and marketing of tobacco.

Largely as a result of these government efforts, the United States experienced uneven but sustained economic growth from the end of the War of 1812 until midcentury. Political controversy raged over questions of state versus federal activity—especially with regard to internal improvements and banking—but all parties agreed on the general goal of economic expansion. Indeed, during these years the major restraint on government action was not philosophical but financial: the public purse was small. As the private sector grew more vigorous, entrepreneurs looked less to government for financial support, and the states played less of a role in investment.

Transportation Links

Improved transportation was another factor facilitating economic growth. Northern, Middle Atlantic, and western states invested heavily in roads, canals, and railroads, with much of the financing borrowed from Europe. With regional and national financial institutions increasingly concentrated in New York, Boston, and Philadelphia, northeastern seaboard cities became the center of American commerce. New York financial and commercial houses dominated the American export trade, not only of New England textiles but also, through affiliates in southern port cities, of southern cotton. The South's staple crop was marketed to, and through, the North. The Deep South, with most of its capital invested in slave labor and land, built fewer canals, railroads, and factories and remained mostly rural.

Water routes provided the cheapest and most available transportation. Before the War of 1812 nearly all commerce moved on navigable rivers, and bulk shipments—cotton in the South and grain in the West—continued to move to ocean port cities by water. Increasingly, however, settlement extended beyond the river links, and the federal and state governments, followed by private corporations, invested heavily in alternative transportation modes.

In the 1820s new arteries opened up east-west travel. The National Road—a stone-based, gravel-topped highway originating in Cumberland, Maryland—reached Columbus, Ohio, in 1833. More important, the Erie Canal, completed in 1825, linked the Great Lakes with New York City and the Atlantic Ocean. The canal carried easterners and then immigrants to settle the Old Northwest and the frontier beyond; in the opposite direction, it transported western grain to the large and growing eastern markets. Railroads and later the telegraph would solidify these east-west links. Other than for carrying cotton, links between the Deep South and the North were rarer.

Canals The 363-mile-long Erie Canal was a visionary enterprise. When the state of New York authorized its construction in 1817, the longest American canal was only 28 miles long. Vigorously promoted by Governor DeWitt Clinton, the Erie cost $7 million, much of it borrowed from British investors. The canal shortened the journey between Buffalo and New York City from twenty to six days and reduced freight charges from $100 to $5 a ton. By 1835 traffic was so heavy that the canal had to be widened from 40 to 70 feet and deepened from 4 to 7 feet. Skeptics who had called the canal "Clinton's big ditch" had long since fallen silent.

The success of the Erie Canal triggered an explosion of canal building. By 1840 canals crisscrossed the Northeast and Midwest, and total canal mileage reached 3,300—an increase of more than 2,000 miles in a single decade (see Map 10.2). Unfortunately for investors, none of these canals enjoyed the financial

The town of Lockport, New York, owed its existence to the Erie Canal, and serving boats, freight, and passengers was its major industry. This view of the town was rendered in 1836, eleven years after the canal was opened.   (Library of Congress, hand-colored by Sandi Rygiel, Picture Research Consultants, Inc.)

success achieved by the Erie. As the high cost of construction combined with an economic contraction, investment in canals began to slump in the 1830s. By midcentury more miles were being abandoned than built, and the canal era had unmistakably ended.

Meanwhile, railroad construction boomed. The railroad era in the United States began in 1830 when

Railroads

Peter Cooper's locomotive, "Tom Thumb," first steamed along 13 miles of Baltimore and Ohio Railroad track. In 1833 the nation's second railroad ran 136 miles from Charleston to Hamburg in South Carolina. By 1850 the United States had nearly 9,000 miles of railroad track.

The earliest railroads connected nearby cities, such as Philadelphia and Baltimore; not until the 1850s did railroads offer long-distance service at reasonable rates. The early lines had to overcome technical problems. Locomotives heavy enough to climb steep grades and pull long trains required strong rails and resilient track beds. Engineers met those needs by replacing wooden tracks with iron rails and by supporting the rails with ties embedded in gravel. A new wheel alignment—the swivel truck—permitted heavy engines to hold the track on sharp curves. Other problems persisted: the lack of a standard gauge for the width of track thwarted development of a national system. Pennsylvania and Ohio railroads, for instance, had no fewer than seven different track widths. A journey from Philadelphia to Charleston, South Carolina, involved eight different gauges, which meant that passengers and freight had to change trains seven times. Only at Bowling Green, Kentucky, did northern and southern railroads connect directly with one another.

Technology and investments in transportation dramatically reduced travel time and shipping. Before

Reduction in Travel Time and Cost

1815 river transportation was the only feasible route for long-distance journeys. In 1815 a traveler took four days to go by stagecoach from New York City to Baltimore and nearly

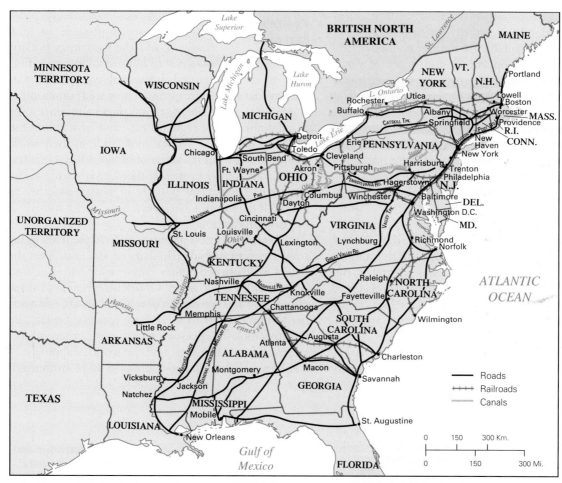

Map 10.2   Major Roads, Canals, and Railroads, 1850   A transportation network linked the seaboard to the interior. Settlers followed those routes westward, and they sent back grain, grain products, and cotton to the port cities.

four weeks to reach Detroit. By 1830 the New York–Baltimore journey took a day and a half, while the Erie Canal reduced the New York–Detroit journey to two weeks. Before the War of 1812 wagon transportation cost 30 to 70 cents per ton per mile. By midcentury railroads brought the cost of land transportation down 95 percent and reduced the journey to one-fifth the time.

Commercial Farming

Although manufacturing increased steadily, agriculture remained the backbone of the economy and American exports. But increasingly the market economy altered farming. Self-sufficient household and plantation economies gave way to market-oriented farming. Equally

important, the center of commercial farming moved westward. In the 1830s and after, the plantation South shifted to the Mississippi River valley, while commercial farming came to dominate the Old Northwest and the Ohio River valley, then moved even farther westward to the prairies.

After the 1820s, northeastern agriculture began to decline. Eastern farmers had already cultivated all the land available to them; expansion was impossible. Moreover, small New England farms with their uneven terrains did not lend themselves to the new labor-saving farm implements introduced in the 1830s—mechanical sowers, reapers, threshers, and balers. As a result, many northern farmers either moved west or gave up farming for jobs in the merchant houses and factories.

Northeastern Agriculture

But neither the countinghouse nor the factory depleted New England agriculture. The farmers who remained proved as adaptable on the farm as were their children working at copy desks and water-powered looms. By the 1850s many New England and Middle Atlantic farm families had abandoned the commercial production of wheat and corn and stopped tilling poor land. Instead, they improved their livestock, especially cattle, and specialized in vegetable and fruit production and dairy farming. They financed these initiatives through land sales and debt. In fact, their greatest potential profit was from increasing land values, not from farming itself.

Farm families everywhere gradually adjusted to market conditions. In 1820 about one-third of all food produced was intended for market. By 1850 the amount surpassed 50 percent. Middlemen specializing in the grain and food trades replaced the rural storekeepers who had once handled all transactions for local farmers, acting both as retailers and as marketing and purchasing agents.

Farm women had a distinctive role in the market economy aside from their work in fields and barn-

Women's Paid Labor

yards. Many sold eggs, dairy products, and garden produce in local markets, and their earnings became essential to household incomes. Butter and cheese making replaced spinning and weaving; farm women now sold commodities and bought cloth. The work was physically demanding and did not replace regular home and farm chores but added to them. Yet women took pride in their work, often gaining from it a sense of independence that was as valuable as their profits. Esther Lewis, a widow who sent from 75 to 100 pounds of butter monthly to Philadelphia in the 1830s, even hired other women to increase production.

Women's success at butter and cheese making led some farms to specialize in dairy production. After the Erie Canal opened, Ohio dairy farms had access to New York's export trade. Ohio entrepreneurs turned cheese into factory production in the 1840s, contracting to buy curd from local dairy farmers. Canals and railroads took the cheese to eastern ports, where wholesalers sold the cheese around the world, shipping it to California, England, and China. In 1844 Britain im-

Women tended cows and chickens and sold dairy products and eggs in the growing market economy. (Princeton University Library, Sinclair Hamilton Collection. Visual Materials Division, Department of Rare Books and Special Collections)

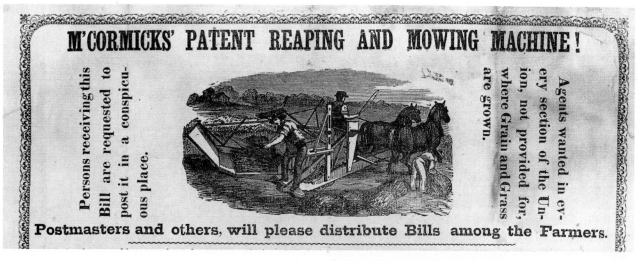

Cyrus McCormick invented the reaper in 1831, and midwestern farmers bought reapers as they mechanized their farms in the 1840s. Increased farm production fed the growing eastern cities and led to grain export.   (Chicago Historical Society)

ported more than 5 million pounds of cheese from the United States.

Most farm families welcomed the opportunities offered by the market economy. While continuing to take pride in self-sufficiency, they shifted toward specialization and market-oriented production. The rewards for such flexibility were great. Produce sold at market financed land and equipment purchases and made credit arrangements possible. Farm families who owned their land flourished.

Meanwhile, the economic distance widened between farm owners on the one hand and tenants and hired hands on the other. The rising cost of land and of farming made it harder to start up. By the 1840s it took more than ten years for a rural laborer to save enough money to farm for himself. Thus the number of tenant farmers increased. Previously farmers had relied mostly on the labor of unpaid family members or enslaved workers; now they had to secure waged farm labor.

Individually and collectively, Americans still valued agrarian life. State governments energetically promoted commercial agriculture to spur economic growth and sustain the values of an agrarian-based republic. Massachusetts in 1817 and New York in 1819 began to subsidize agricultural prizes and county fairs. New York required contestants to submit written descriptions of how they grew their prize crops; the state then published the essays to encourage new methods and specialization. The post office circulated farm journals that helped familiarize farmers with developments in agriculture.

Gradually the Old Northwest replaced the Northeast as the center of American family agriculture.

Mechanization of Agriculture

Farms in the Old Northwest were much larger, flatter, and better suited to the new mechanized farming implements than were their northeastern counterparts. Cyrus McCormick, a Virginia farmer, had invented the reaper in 1831. In one continuous motion, a revolving drum on the horse-drawn reaper positioned grain stalks in front of a blade and the cut grain fell onto a platform. Though ridiculed by the *London Times* as "a cross between a flying machine, a wheelbarrow, and an Astly chariot," the reaper was a great success. McCormick patented his machine in 1834 and built a factory in Chicago that by 1847 sold a thousand reapers a year. Midwestern farmers bought reapers on credit and paid for them with the profits from their high yields. Similarly, John Deere's steel plow, invented in 1837, replaced the traditional iron plow; steel blades kept the soil from sticking and were tough enough to break the roots of prairie grass.

And just in time. The Midwest was becoming one of the leading agricultural regions of the world. Midwestern farms fed the growing cities in the East, bursting with growing immigrant populations, and still produced enough to export to Europe.

At the end of the eighteenth century, southern agriculture was diverse. The South grew sufficient grain to feed itself. Although debt plagued Virginia's tobacco growers, farther south, along the coast, slaves grew rice and some indigo for the market. Cotton was profitable only for the Sea Island planters in South Carolina and Georgia, who grew the luxurious long and silky variety. Short-staple cotton, which grew readily in the interior and in all kinds of soil, was unmarketable because its sticky seeds lay tangled in the fibers. Then, in 1793, Eli Whitney invented the cotton gin (see pages 195–196). This machine, which separated the cotton from the seeds fifty times faster than by hand, made possible the expansion of cotton production at the very time that new textile mills in England and New England were increasing demand for cotton cloth. The result was a boom.

The Cotton South

After 1800 the cultivation of short-staple cotton spread rapidly. By the 1820s there were cotton plantations in the fertile lands of Louisiana, Mississippi, Alabama, Arkansas, and Tennessee. From 1820 to 1840, South Carolina sank from first to fifth in cotton production, and Mississippi rose to first. Each decade after 1820, the total crop doubled. By 1825 the South was the world's dominant supplier of cotton, and the white fibers were America's largest export. Southerners with capital bought more land and more slaves and planted ever more cotton.

No region was more tied to international markets than the South, yet the region seemed immune to its transforming power. It produced cotton exclusively as a market crop. Though some cotton production became mechanized, with steam engines used in place of horses to power gins and presses, most southern capital remained concentrated in land and slaves. It could not shift easily to support manufacturing and commerce. In many ways the cotton economy resembled a colonial economy. Planters depended on distant agents, some in southern cities, many in the North, and even some in Europe, to represent them and handle finances, which often included loans. Thus critical market decisions were made by bankers, financiers, and brokers, all outside the South. The South was engaged in the new market economy, but at a distance.

The cotton boom, dependent on slave labor, fixed the slave system to the land as it spread westward. Slaveholders sought profits, just as did commercial farmers, merchants, and entrepreneurs in the North. But they did not pay wages for labor; they bought laborers. Ultimately this "peculiar" system (see pages 332–338) would separate the South from the national economy and the nation.

The Rise of Manufacturing and Commerce

Though at first Americans imported machines or copied British designs, they soon built their own. Matthew Baldwin made steam engines in Philadelphia in the 1820s, but in 1834, with railroads expanding, Baldwin turned to making steam locomotives. By 1839 he had produced 140 of them, or 45 percent of all American-made locomotives. A visitor to his shop in 1838 found twelve engines in various states of construction. "Those parts of the engine, such as the cylinder, piston, valves . . . in which good fitting and fine workmanship are indispensable to the efficient action of the machine, were very highly finished," the British visitor reported. By 1840 the United States exported railroad engines to Russia, some German states, and even Britain.

British visitors to the 1851 London Crystal Palace Exhibition, the first modern world's fair, were equally impressed by American design and fine tooling of working parts. American companies displayed hundreds of American machines and wares—from farm tools to exotic devices such as the reaper and an ice-cream freezer—that astonished observers. American manufacturers returned home with dozens of medals. Most impressive to the Europeans were three simple machines: Alfred C. Hobb's unpickable padlocks, Samuel Colt's revolvers, and Robbins and Lawrence's rifles fashioned with completely interchangeable parts. Like Baldwin's locomotives, all were machine-tooled rather than handmade, products of what the British called the American system of manufacturing.

American System of Manufacturing

The American system of manufacturing used precision machinery to produce interchangeable parts that did not require individual adjustment to fit. Eli Whitney, a Yale graduate and inventor of the cotton gin, had promoted the idea of interchangeable parts in 1798 when he contracted with the federal government to make ten thousand rifles in twenty-eight months. By the 1820s the United States Ordnance Department had contracted with private firms to in-

In the 1830s an unknown artist painted *Middlesex Company Woolen Mills,* portraying the hulking mass of the mill buildings. The company organized all the manufacturing processes at a single location, in Lowell, Massachusetts, on the Merrimack River. (Museum of American Textile History)

troduce machine-made interchangeable parts for firearms. The American system quickly spread beyond the arsenals, giving birth to the machine-tool industry—the manufacture of machines for the purposes of mass production. One outcome was an explosion in consumer goods. Because the time and skill involved in manufacturing were greatly reduced, the new system permitted mass production at low cost: Waltham watches, Yale locks, and other goods became household items, inexpensive yet of uniformly high quality.

Even larger than the machine-tool industry was the textile industry. New England mills began processing and weaving southern cotton in the same decade that Whitney patented his gin. Boosted by embargo and war, then protected by the tariff, the textile industry boomed with the expansion of cotton cultivation after the war (see Map 10.3). By the 1840s a cotton mill resembled a modern factory and textiles were the most important industry in the

Textile Mills

nation. Cotton cloth production rose from 4 million yards in 1817 to 323 million in 1840. The industry employed around eighty thousand workers in the mid-1840s, more than half of them women.

The industry's great innovation was that the machines, not the women, spun the yarn and wove the cloth. Workers watched the machines and intervened to maintain the operation. When a thread broke, the machine stopped automatically; a worker then found the break, pieced the ends together, and restarted the machine. The mills increasingly used specialized machines. Their application of the American system of manufacturing enabled American firms to compete successfully with British cotton mills.

Textile manufacturing changed New England and had its greatest impact on Lowell, Massachusetts. The population of Lowell, the "city of spindles" and the prototype of early American industrialization, grew from twenty-five hundred to thirty-three thousand between 1826 and midcentury. The largest of the cotton-

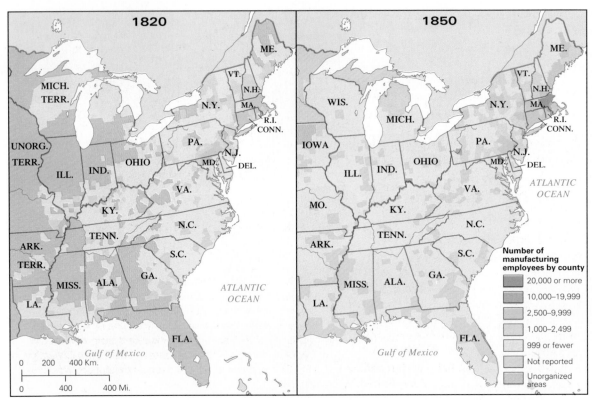

Map 10.3   U.S. Manufacturing Employment, 1820 and 1850   In 1820 manufacturing employment was concentrated mostly in the Northeast, where the first textile mills appeared. By 1850 the density of manufacturing in the Northeast had increased, but new manufacturing centers arose in Baltimore, Pittsburgh, and Cincinnati. (Source: *Historical Atlas of the United States,* 2d ed. [Washington, D.C.: National Geographic Society, 1993], p. 148. Reprinted by permission of National Geographic Maps/National Geographic Society Image Collection.)

mill towns and the front runner in technological change, Lowell boasted the biggest work force, the greatest output, and the most capital invested.

The success of the textile factories spawned the ready-made clothing industry. Before the 1820s, women sewed most clothing at home, and some people purchased used clothing. Tailors and seamstresses made wealthy men's and women's clothing to order. By the 1820s and 1830s, much clothing was mass-produced. Manufacturers used two methods, either separately or in combination. In one, the clothing was made in a factory; in the other, at home, through the putting-out system. In this arrangement, a journeyman tailor—a trained craftsman employed by a master tailor who owned the workshop—cut the fabric panels in the factory, and the masters "put out" the sewing at piece rates to women working in their own homes.

In 1832 Boston manufacturers employed three hundred journeyman tailors at $2 per day and thirteen

Ready-made Clothing

hundred women and one hundred boys at 50 cents a day. Apprentices, if used at all, were no longer learning a trade; they were a permanent source of cheap labor. Women learned their sewing skills at home, passed down from mother to daughter. In the 1840s as many as a dozen different pairs of hands contributed to making a single pair of pants under the putting-out system.

Most of the early mass-produced clothes, crudely made and limited to a few loose-fitting sizes, were produced for and purchased by men who lived in city boarding houses and rooming houses, far from the female kin who previously would have made their garments. Most women made their own clothes, but those who could afford to do so employed seamstresses. Improvements in fit and changes in men's fashion eventually made ready-to-wear apparel more acceptable to clerks and professional men. In the 1840s the short sack coat, which did not taper at the waist, began to replace the embroidered waistcoat. This forerunner of the modern suit jacket fit loosely and needed little custom tailoring. Now even upper-class men were willing to consider ready-made apparel.

Retail clothing stores well stocked with ready-made clothes appeared in the 1820s. T. S. Whitmarsh of Boston advertised in 1827 that

Retail Merchants

"he keeps constantly for Sale, from 5 to 10,000 Fashionable ready-made Garments." Such merchants often bought goods wholesale, though many manufactured shirts and trousers in their own factories. Lewis and Hanford of New York City boasted of cutting more than one hundred thousand garments in the winter of 1848–1849. The New York firm sold most of its clothing in the South and owned its own retail outlet in New Orleans. Paul Tulane, a New Orleans competitor, owned a New York factory that made goods for his Louisiana store. In the West, Cincinnati became the center of the new men's clothing industry. By midcentury, Cincinnati's ready-to-wear apparel industry employed fifteen hundred men and ten thousand women. As in Boston, most of the women did outwork.

Commerce expanded hand in hand with manufacturing. Cotton, for instance, had once been traded by plantation agents, who sold the raw

Specialization of Commerce

cotton and bought manufactured goods that they then sold to plantation owners, extending them credit when necessary. Cotton exports rose from 83 million pounds in 1815 to 298 million in 1830 to more than a billion pounds for the first time in 1849. Gradually, some agents came to specialize in finance alone: they were cotton brokers, who for a commission brought together buyers and sellers. Similarly, wheat and hog brokers sprang up in the West—in Cincinnati, Louisville, and St. Louis. The distribution of finished goods also became more specialized as wholesalers bought large quantities of particular items from manufacturers, and jobbers broke down the wholesale lots for retail stores and country merchants.

General merchants persisted longer in small towns than in cities. They continued to exchange some goods

General Merchants

with local farm women—trading flour or pots and pans for eggs or other produce. And local craftsmen continued to sell their own finished goods, such as shoes and clothing. In some rural areas and on the frontier, peddlers acted as general merchants. But as transportation improved and towns grew, even small-town merchants began to specialize.

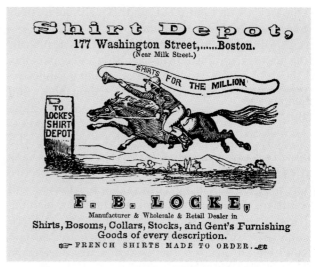

F. B. Locke adapted to the new market for ready-made clothing by becoming a manufacturer, wholesaler, and retailer of men's shirts. Although he continued to make shirts to order, the staple of his Shirt Depot was mass-produced shirts, as this advertisement from the *Boston Directory* for 1848–1849 indicates.   (Warshaw Collection of Business Americana, Smithsonian Institution, Washington, D.C.)

Commercial specialization transformed some traders in big cities, especially New York, into virtual merchant princes. After the Erie Canal opened, New York City became a stop on every major trade route from Europe, the southern ports, and the West. New York traders were the middlemen for southern cotton and western grain. Merchants in other cities played a similar role within their own regions. Some traders in turn invested their profits in factories, further stimulating urban manufacturing. Some cities specialized: Rochester became a milling center, and Cincinnati—"Porkopolis"—became the first meatpacking center.

Merchants who engaged in complex commercial transactions required large office staffs. Most of the all-male office staff worked on high stools, laboriously copying business forms and correspondence. At the bottom of the office hierarchy were messenger boys, often preteens, who delivered documents. Above them were the ordinary copyists, who hand-copied as many documents as needed. Clerks processed documents and shipping papers and did translations. Above them were the bookkeeper and the confidential chief clerk. Those seeking employment in such an office, called a countinghouse, often took a course from a writing master to acquire a "good hand." All hoped to rise someday to the status of partner, although their chances of doing so were slim.

Financial institutions, which played a significant role in the expansion of manufacturing and commerce, also became a leading industry.

Banking and Credit Systems

Banks, insurance companies, and corporations linked savers—those who deposited money in banks—with producers and speculators who wished to borrow money. After 1816, the Second Bank of the United States injected a national perspective into finance, but many farmers, local bankers, and politicians denounced the bank as a monster, blaming it for serving national, not local, interests. Western landowners suffered severe losses when the Second Bank reduced loans in the western states during the Panic of 1819. In 1836 critics finally succeeded in killing the bank (see page 292).

The closing of the Second Bank in 1836 caused a nationwide credit shortage, which, in conjunction with the Panic of 1837, led to fundamental reforms in banking. Michigan and New York introduced charter laws promoting what was called *free banking*. Many other states soon followed suit. Previously, every new bank needed a special legislative charter before it could open for business; thus each bank incorporation was in effect a political decision. Under the new laws, any proposed bank that met certain minimum conditions—amount of capital invested, number of notes issued, and types of loans to be offered—would receive a state charter automatically. Banks in Michigan, New York, and, soon, other states were thus freer to incorporate, although the legislatures placed some restrictions on their operations to reduce the risk of bank failure.

Free banking proved to be a significant stimulus to the economy in the late 1840s and 1850s. New banks sprang up everywhere, providing merchants and manufacturers with the credit they needed. The free-banking laws also served as a precedent for general incorporation statutes that allowed manufacturing firms to receive state charters without special acts of the state legislature.

Workers and the Workplace

Loud the morning bell is ringing,
   Up, up sleepers, haste away;
Yonder sits the redbreast singing,
   But to list we must not stay.

. . .

Sisters, haste, the bell is tolling,
   Soon will close the dreadful gate;
Then, alas! We must go strolling,
   Through the counting-room too late.

. . .

Now the sun is upward climbing,
   And the breakfast hour has come;
Ding, dong, ding, the bell is chiming,
   Hasten, sisters, hasten home.

The poet, writing in 1844 in the *Factory Girl's Garland*, uses the sound of the factory bell as a refrain to emphasize its incessant control, announcing when the workers are to wake, eat, begin work, stop work, and go to sleep. Night and day the millworkers felt the stress of factory schedules.

But the first generation of young single women who left New England villages and farms to work in the mills had come with great optimism. The mills offered steady work and good pay, plus airy boarding houses, prepared meals, and cultural activities. Though housekeepers enforced strict curfews, banned alcohol, and reported on workers' behavior and church attendance, mill work brought financial independence and friendship.

Sisters and cousins often worked in the same mill and lived in the same boarding house. They helped each other adjust, and their letters home drew kin to the mills. The benefits were not sufficient, however, to change their ambitions to be wives and mothers. Most arrivals were sixteen and stayed only about five years. When they left the mills to marry, other younger women interested in earning a wage took their places.

In the hard times from 1837 to 1842, demand for cloth declined, and most mills ran only part-time. Subsequently managers pressured workers by means of the speed-up, the stretch-out, and the premium system.

Boom and Bust in the Textile Mills

The speed-up increased the speed of the machines; the stretch-out increased the number of machines each worker had to operate; and premiums paid to the overseers whose departments produced the most cloth encouraged them to pressure workers for greater output. The result: between 1836 and 1850 the number of spindles and looms in Lowell increased 150 and 140 percent, respectively, while the number of workers increased by only 50 percent. The corporation's goal of building an industrial empire and maximizing profits took precedence over its paternalistic concern for workers' living conditions. In the race for profits, owners lengthened hours, cut wages, tightened discipline,

How do historians know...

that work in New England mills was regimented? This timetable from the Lowell Mills is among the rich sources historians consult to reconstruct workers' experiences in the mills. Textile factories were the first corporations to impose rigid work rules, necessitated by the size of the labor force, the management structure, and the organization of the work. Managers established exact times for beginning and ending work and for meals. Few workers carried a timepiece, so a system of bells regulated the lives of the factory community. For young mill women from the New England countryside, and later for Irish women, such regimentation must have seemed a world apart from the natural rhythms of rural life. (Photo: American Textile Museum)

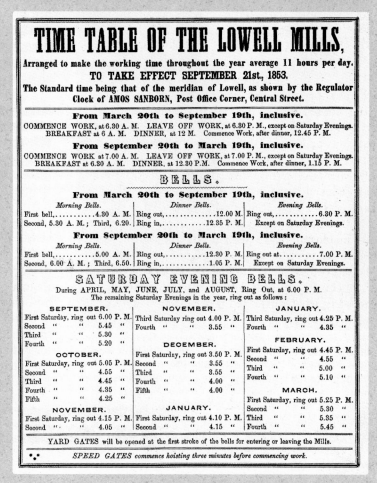

and packed the boarding houses. Some millworkers began to think of themselves as slaves.

New England millworkers responded to their deteriorating working conditions by organizing and striking. In 1834, in reaction to a 25

Protests

percent wage cut, they unsuccessfully "turned out" (struck) against the Lowell mills. Two years later, when boarding house fees increased, they turned out again. As conditions continued to worsen, workers adopted new methods of resistance. In the 1840s, strikes gave way to a concerted effort to shorten the workday. Massachusetts mill women and other workers joined forces to press for state legislation mandating a ten-hour day. Eliza R. Hemingway, a three-year veteran of two different Lowell mills, told a Massachusetts House of

Representatives committee in 1845 that workers' hours were too long. In the summer, work ran from 5:00 A.M. to 7:00 P.M., with time off for meals.

Women aired their complaints in worker-run newspapers: in 1842, the *Factory Girl* appeared in New Hampshire, the *Wampanoag and Operatives' Journal* in Massachusetts. Two years later they founded the *Factory Girl's Garland* and the *Voice of Industry*, nicknamed "the factory girl's voice." Even the *Lowell Offering*, the owner-sponsored paper that was the pride of millworkers and managers alike, became embroiled in controversy when workers charged its editors had suppressed articles criticizing working conditions.

The women's labor organizations were weakened by the short tenure of most workers. Few of the militant native-born millworkers stayed on to fight the managers

This young mill girl at Waltham or Lowell, probably in the late 1840s, posed for an early daguerreotype. Her swollen and rough hands contrast with her youth, neat dress, and carefully tied, beribboned hair. Her hands suggest that she worked, as did most twelve- and thirteen-year-olds, as a warper, straightening the strands of cotton or wool as they entered the looms.   (Courtesy of Jack Naylor)

and owners, and gradually there were fewer New England daughters to enter the mills. They were replaced, in the 1850s, by Irish immigrant women who lived at home. Technological improvements in the looms and other machinery had made the work less skilled and more routine. The mills could thus pay lower wages and draw from a reservoir of unskilled labor.

A growing gender division in the workplace, especially in the textile, clothing, and shoemaking industries, was one important outcome of large-scale manufacturing. Although women and men in traditional agricultural and artisan households tended to perform different tasks, they worked as a family unit. As wage work spread, however, men's and women's work cultures became increasingly separate. The women and girls who left home for jobs in textile mills worked

Gender Divisions in Work

and lived in a mostly female world. In the clothing and shoemaking industries, whose male artisans had once worked at home assisted by unpaid family labor, men began working outside the home while women continued to work at home through the putting-out system. Tasks and wages, too, became rigidly differentiated: women sewed, whereas men shaped materials and finished products, receiving higher wages in shops employing men only.

The market economy had an impact on unpaid household labor as well. As home and workplace became separate and labor came to be defined in terms of wages (what could be sold in the marketplace) rather than production (what could be made by hand), the unpaid labor of women was devalued. Cash exchanged was the measure, and as families increasingly recorded their incomes and expenditures in account books, there was no category for women's unpaid services. Yet those labors were extensive; indeed, the family depended on women's work within the household, ever more so as sons and even daughters sought wage work outside the home and had less time for household tasks. Thus gender defined household labor, and in the market economy it went unrecorded. Inevitably, it seemed to be worth little and was taken for granted.

The new textile mills, shoe factories, iron mills, and railroads were the antithesis of traditional workshop and household production. In factory workplaces authority was hierarchically organized. Factory workers lost their sense of autonomy as impersonal market forces seemed to dominate their lives. Their jobs were insecure, as competition frequently led to layoffs and replacement by cheaper, less-skilled workers or children. Moreover, the formal rules of the factory contrasted sharply with the more relaxed atmosphere of artisan shops and farm households. Journeymen recognized that the new system of manufacturing threatened them. When master craftsmen in shoemaking and textiles turned their workshops into small factories with themselves as managers, master and journeymen were distanced. In large factories, the distance was greater, as supervisors represented owners whom workers never saw. The division of labor and the use of machines narrowed the skills required. And the bell, the steam whistle, or the clock governed the flow of work, as the *Factory Girl's Garland* poem anxiously described.

Changes in the Workplace

One problem, of course, was the quickening pace of the work between the bells. Workers who at first sought factory jobs for higher wages changed their minds in the face of wage reductions, speed-ups, and stretch-outs. Other conditions were trying, too. Mill-workers had to tolerate the roar of the looms, and all workers on power machines risked accidents that could maim or even kill. Perhaps most demoralizing, opportunities for advancement in the new system were virtually nil.

As a sense of distance from their employers took hold, so did deep-seated differences among workers. Initially, mill women drew on kinship, village, and gender ties to build supportive networks in factories. But in the 1840s, as recently arrived Irish immigrant women entered the mills, many workers found themselves working with total strangers. Once employed, their only bases for friendship and mutual support were their work experiences. Wage workers felt distanced from traditional culture as well. As wage work became common, the republican virtues associated with independent craft traditions eroded. The rigid rules of factory work and the swings in employment brought on by boom-and-bust cycles restricted individual freedom. At every turn, workers were hemmed in by formidable forces.

In response, some workers organized to resist changes wrought by the market economy and factories and to regain control of their work and their lives. Women textile workers organized into unions and demonstrated for better wages and conditions or lobbied legislatures for relief. Male workers, like shoemakers, also organized and protested, but because they were eligible to vote, they also organized political parties. Labor parties formed in Pennsylvania, New York, and Massachusetts in the 1820s, and later spread to other states, advocated free public education and an end to imprisonment for debt and opposed banks and monopolies. The interests of workers' parties often coincided with those of middle-class reformers: temperance, observance of the Sabbath, and suppression of vice (see Chapter 11). Ironically, however, reform politics also tended to divide workers. Many reforms—moral education, temperance, Sabbath closings—served the interests of merchants and industrialists seeking a more disciplined work force. Temperance and Sabbath closings pitted Protestants against Catholics who celebrated Sunday at public beer gardens. Anti-immigrant and anti-Catholic movements further divided workers.

Organized labor's greatest achievement during this period was to gain relief from the threat of conspiracy

Labor Parties

Emergence of a Labor Movement

laws. When journeyman shoemakers organized during the first decade of the century, their employers accused them of criminal conspiracy. The cordwainers' (shoemakers') cases between 1806 and 1815 left labor organizations in a tenuous position. Although the courts acknowledged the journeymen's right to organize, judges ruled unlawful any coercive action by workers that would harm other businesses or the public. In other words, strikes were ruled illegal. Eventually a Massachusetts case, *Commonwealth v. Hunt* (1842), effectively reversed this status when Chief Justice Lemuel Shaw ruled that Boston journeyman bootmakers could strike "in such manner as best to subserve their own interests." Conspiracy laws no longer thwarted unionization.

Yet workers found permanent labor organizations difficult to sustain. Most workers outside the crafts were unskilled or semiskilled at best. Moreover, religion, race, ethnicity, and gender divided workers. The first unions arose among urban journeymen in printing, woodworking, shoemaking, and tailoring. These early unions tended to be local; the strongest resembled medieval guilds in that members sought to protect themselves against the competition of inferior workmen by regulating apprenticeship and establishing minimum wages. They also excluded women and African Americans. (Massachusetts mill women organized their own unions.) Umbrella organizations composed of individual craft unions, like the National Trades Union (1834), arose in several cities in the 1820s and 1830s. But the movement fell apart amid wage reductions and unemployment in the hard times of 1839–1843.

Labor organizations remained weak; individual producers—craftsmen, factory workers, and farmers—lost economic power; and workers increasingly forfeited control over their own work. While mill owners, corporate investors, large-scale landowners, and slave-holding planters reaped benefits from economic growth, workers' share of the national wealth declined after 1830.

Americans on the Move

Growth in the years following the War of 1812 was not economic only. The Louisiana Purchase (1803) doubled the land area of the United States and acquisitions in the 1840s nearly doubled it again. Population soared, increasing by a third in each decade. The U.S.

Map 10.4   Settled Areas of the United States, 1820 and 1840   Removal of Indians and a growing transportation network opened up land to white and black settlers in the West and in the Southeast, as the U.S. population grew from 9.6 million in 1820 to 17.1 million in 1840.

population grew by 10.6 million people between 1820 and 1845, and immigration accounted for only a small amount; 89 percent of the population growth was from natural increase. In 1845, 20.2 million people lived in the United States.

In land and population the United States expanded outward, mostly westward, from its original seaboard base (see Map 10.4). The admission of new states tells the story: Indiana (1816), Mississippi (1817), Illinois (1818), Alabama (1819), Maine (1820), and Missouri

Westward Movement

(1821) brought the union to twenty-four states in the 1820s. Arkansas (1836) and Michigan (1837) soon followed, as did Florida and Texas (1845), Iowa (1846), and Wisconsin (1848) in the following decade.

Southerner and easterner, cotton raiser and grain farmer, black and white, slave and free person, owner and renter, investor and speculator, and settler and transient marched across the Appalachians. In the first two decades of the century Americans poured into the Ohio River valley; then, starting in the 1820s they moved into the Mississippi River valley and beyond, doubling the population living beyond the Appalachi-

Women who traveled west with their husbands found their domestic skills in great demand. In this watercolor entitled *Laying Out of Karns' City, Minnesota* (1856), E. Whitefield shows a woman preparing a meal out of her lean-to kitchen for her husband and their guests.   (Chicago Historical Society)

ans. By midcentury two-thirds of Americans lived west of the Appalachians. Mostly young and hard-working, they had visions of establishing family farms and achieving economic security.

Some 5 to 10 percent of Americans moved each year, their travel made ever faster and easier by the expanding transportation networks. Restless, they settled only temporarily and then moved on. "There is more travelling in the United States than in any part of the world," observed a commentator in 1828. "Here the whole population is in motion, whereas, in old countries, there are millions who have never been beyond the sound of the parish bell." People tended to move short distances; thus long moves were made in stages. Though most people lived on farms, there was also a steady rural to urban migration.

After the 1820s the heart of cotton cultivation and the plantation system shifted from the coastal states to Alabama and the newly set-

The South

tled Mississippi valley—Tennessee, Louisiana, Arkansas, and Mississippi. Southerners brought their institu-

tions with them; slaves moved with planters to the newer areas of the South, and yeoman farmers followed.

The shift was dramatic. The population of Mississippi soared from 73,000 in 1820 to 607,000 in 1850, with African American slaves in the majority. Across the Mississippi River, the population of Arkansas went from 14,000 in 1820 to 210,000 in 1850. Indian removal made expansion possible.

The South and cotton continued westward into Texas. In 1830 the 7,000 American immigrants living in northwest Mexico outnumbered Mexicans there two to one. By 1835 the American population reached 35,000, including 3,000 slaves. The American settlers were restless for independence or U.S. annexation and chafed at Mexico's resistance toward Anglo domination in Texas. Independence in 1836 spurred further American immigration into Texas. By 1845 "Texas fever" had boosted the Anglo population to 125,000. Statehood that year opened the floodgates.

Not all moves were westward. A steady stream drifted from the Upper South to the Ohio valley, from

Moves North and South

slave to free states. Abraham Lincoln's family, for example, took this path in moving from Kentucky to Indiana Territory and, later, to Illinois. Though northern black people moved westward as well, thousands of free people of color moved to northern states and Canada in the 1830s following the adoption of black codes and mob violence in the South (see pages 325–326). Fugitives from slavery too went north. Hispanics in the Southwest continued to move north into areas of Texas and present-day New Mexico and Utah. Hispanics and Indians competed for control of the land, but when the U.S. Army suppressed the Comanches, Apaches, Navajos, and Utes, Hispanic migration spread. After the United States acquired Florida and attempted to colonize and suppress the Indian peoples there, southerners poured into the new territory.

Settlers needed land and credit. Reflecting the nationalist outlook, the federal government served as real

Land Grants and Sales

estate agent, transferring land to private hands, filling the West with non-Indian peoples, and promoting republican virtue. Some public lands were granted as rewards for military service; veterans of the War of 1812 received 160 acres. Until 1820 civilians could buy government land at $2 an acre (a relatively high price) on a liberal four-year payment plan, but the minimum purchase had been reduced in 1817 to 80 acres. After 1819 the government discontinued credit sales but reduced the price to an affordable $1.25 an acre.

Some eager pioneers settled land before it had been surveyed and offered for sale. Such illegal settlers, or squatters, then had to buy the land at auction and faced the risk of being unable to purchase it. In 1841, to facilitate settlement and end property disputes, Congress passed the Pre-emption Act, which legalized settlement prior to surveying.

Since most settlers needed to borrow money, private credit systems arose: banks, private investors,

Credit

country storekeepers, and speculators all loaned money to farmers. Nearly all economic activity in the West involved credit, from land sales to produce shipments to railroad construction. In 1816 and 1836 easy credit boosted land prices. When tight credit, high interest, low prices, or destructive weather squeezed farmers' income, land values collapsed, ending the speculative bubble. Mortgage bankers and speculators then purchased land cheaply. As a consequence, many farmers became renters instead of own-

Henry Lewis's *St. Louis in 1846* depicts a pioneer family stopping to view the great Missouri city across the river. The contrast between the towering city, surrounded by modern steamboats and dominating the Mississippi and Missouri Rivers, and the pioneer family, with their wagons and horses, highlights the role cities played in western settlement and growth. (St. Louis Art Museum, Eliza McMillan Fund)

ers of land; tenancy became more common in the West than it had been in New England.

From the start, newly settled western areas depended on their links with towns and cities. Ohio River cities—Louisville and Cincinnati—and the old French settlements—Detroit on the Great Lakes, St. Louis on the Mississippi River—predated and promoted the earliest western settlements. So too in the South, from New Orleans to Natchez to Memphis, towns spearheaded settlement and economic growth. Steamboats connected the river cities with eastern markets and ports, carrying grain east and returning with finished goods. Like cities in the Northeast, these western cities eventually developed into manufacturing centers as merchants shifted their investments from commerce to industry. Louisville, for instance, became a textile center. Smaller cities specialized in flour mills, and all produced consumer goods for the hinterlands. As commerce, urban growth, and industrialization overtook the farmers' frontier, the West was wed to the Northeast.

Frontier Cities

Native American Resistance and Removal

Indians were also on the move, but their migrations were more forced than voluntary. Indian removal made white expansion possible, but it uprooted the indigenous cultures of the eastern and southern woodlands. Perhaps 100,000 eastern and southern Indian people were removed between 1820 and 1850; about 30,000 died in the process. Those who remained became virtually invisible.

The U.S. Constitution acknowledged Indian distinctiveness by recognizing Indian sovereignty and by giving the federal government responsibility for dealing with Native Americans. In its relations with Indian leaders, the government followed international protocol. The federal government received Indian delegations with pomp and ceremony. They exchanged presents as tokens of friendships. Agreements between an Indian national and the United States were signed, sealed, and ratified like any other international treaty.

Treaty Making

In practice, however, treaty making and Indian sovereignty were fictions. Protocol appeared to signify mutual respect and independence, but treaty negotiations exposed the sham. The American government used treaty making as a tactic to acquire Indian land, as

in the Lower Mississippi. Instead of bargains struck by two equal nations, treaties often were imposed by the victor on the vanquished. Old treaties gave way to new ones requiring Native Americans to cede their traditional holdings in exchange for other land in the West. Whether through arms or economic pressure, the federal government forced Native Americans to sign and relinquish treaties.

Indians could delay but not prevent removal. Though Indian resistance persisted after the War of 1812, it only slowed the inevitable. In the 1820s native peoples in Ohio, southern Indiana and Illinois, southwestern Michigan, most of Missouri, central Alabama, and southern Mississippi ceded lands under federal pressure. They gave up nearly 200 million acres for pennies an acre.

To maintain independence and preserve their ways of life, many Indian nations tried to accommodate to the expanding market economy. In the first three decades of the century, the Choctaw, Chickasaw, and Creek peoples in the lower Mississippi responded to the growing cotton economy by becoming suppliers and traders. Under treaty provisions, Indian commerce took place through trading posts and stores that provided Indians with supplies and purchased or bartered Indian-produced goods. Indians exchanged hides, skins, and beeswax for cloth, ammunition, manufactured goods, and illegal liquor. The trading posts extended credit to chiefs, and increasingly they fell into debt. With pelt prices falling, the debts grew enormously and often could be paid off only by selling land to the federal government. The Choctaws, Creeks, and Chickasaws found themselves in a cycle of trade debt and land cessions. By 1822 the Choctaw nation had sold 13 million acres but still carried a debt of $13,000. The Indians struggled to adjust, increasing agriculture and hunting, working as farm hands and craftsman, and selling produce at market stalls in Natchez and New Orleans. Over time, however, they could not prevent the spread of the cotton economy that arose on their lands. With loss of land came dependency. The Choctaws came to rely on Europeans not only for manufactured goods but also for food.

Indians in the Market Economy

Dependency facilitated removal of Native American peoples to western lands. While the population of other groups increased by leaps and bounds, the Indian population fell. Alexis de Tocqueville noticed the contrast. "Not only have these wild tribes receded, but they are destroyed," Tocqueville concluded, after personally observing the tragedy of forced removal, "and as they give way or perish, an immense and increasing people fill their place. There is no instance upon record of so prodigious a growth or so rapid a destruction." War, forced removal, disease, especially smallpox, and malnutrition reduced many Indian nations by 50 percent. More than half of the Pawnees, Omahas, Otoes, Missouris, and Kansas died in the 1830s alone.

The wanderings of the Shawnees, the people of Prophet and Tecumseh (see pages 228–230), illustrate the uprooting of Indian people. After

Shawnees

giving up 17 million acres in Ohio in the 1795 Treaty of Greenville (see page 184), the Shawnees scattered to Indiana and eastern Missouri. After the War of 1812, Prophet's Indiana group withdrew to Canada under British protection. In 1822 other Shawnees sought Mexican protection and moved from Missouri to present-day eastern Texas. As the U.S. government promoted removal to Kansas, Prophet returned from Canada to lead a group to the new Shawnee lands in eastern Kansas in 1825. When Missouri achieved statehood in 1821, Shawnees living there were also forced to move to Kansas, where in the 1830s other Shawnees removed from Ohio or, expelled from Texas, joined them. By 1854 Kansas was open to white settlement, and the Shawnees had to cede seven-eighths of their land, or 1.4 million acres.

Removal had a profound impact on all Shawnees. The men lost their traditional role as providers; their methods of hunting and their knowledge of woodland animals were useless on the prairies of Kansas. As grain became the tribe's dietary staple, Shawnee women played a greater role as providers, supplemented by government aid under treaty provisions. (Typically, treaties required annual government distributions of grain, blankets, and cash payments.) Remarkably, the Shawnees preserved their language and culture in the face of these drastic changes. Although resistance proved incapable of protecting their lands, it did help maintain their culture.

Ever since the early days of European colonization, whites had sought the assimilation of Native Americans through education and

Assimilation and Education

Christianity (see page 53). This goal took on renewed urgency as the United States expanded westward. "Put into the hand of [Indian] children the primer and the hoe," the House Committee on Indian Affairs recommended in 1818, "and they will naturally, in time, take hold of the plough; and, as

their minds become enlightened and expand, the Bible will be their book, and they will grow up in habits of morality and industry . . . and become useful members of society." In 1819, in response to missionary lobbying, Congress appropriated $10,000 annually for "civilization of the tribes adjoining the frontier settlements." Protestant missionaries administered the "civilizing fund" and established mission schools.

Within five years thirty-two boarding schools enrolled Indian students. They substituted English for Native American languages and taught agriculture alongside the Christian Gospel. The emphasis on agriculture taught the value of private property, hard work, and adaptation to the market economy, and laid the basis for Christian communities. But to settlers eyeing Indian land, assimilation through education seemed too slow a process. At the program's peak, schools across the United States enrolled fewer than fifteen hundred students; at that rate it would take centuries to assimilate all the Indians. Thus wherever Native Americans lived, illegal settlers disrupted their lives. Though obligated to protect the integrity of treaty lands, the federal government did so only half-heartedly. With government supporting westward expansion, legitimate Indian claims had to give way to the advance of white civilization.

In the 1820s it became apparent that neither economic dependency, education, nor Christianity could persuade Native Americans to cede enough land to satisfy the expansionists. Attention focused on southeastern tribes—Cherokees, Creeks, Choctaws, Chickasaws, and Seminoles—because much of their land remained intact after the War of 1812 and because they aggressively resisted white encroachment. Possessing some formal political institutions, they were better organized than the northern tribes to resist.

In his last annual message to Congress in late 1824, President James Monroe suggested that all Indians be moved beyond the Mississippi River. Three days later he sent a spe-

Indian Removal as Federal Policy

cial message to Congress proposing removal. Monroe described his proposal as an "honorable" one that would protect Indians from invasion and provide them with independence for "improvement and civilization." Force would be unnecessary, he believed; Indians would willingly accept western land free from white encroachment.

Monroe's proposition targeted the Cherokees, Creeks, Choctaws, and Chickasaws, and they unanimously rejected it. Between 1789 and 1825 they had

Southern Indians attempted to remain in their ancestral lands in the South. Karl Bodmer's watercolor portrayed a Choctaw camp on the Mississippi River near Natchez, before the Indians were forced out of Mississippi and Alabama in 1830. (Joslyn Art Museum, Omaha, Nebraska)

negotiated thirty treaties with the United States, and they had reached their limits. Most wished to remain on what little was left of their ancestral land.

Pressure from Georgia had prompted Monroe's policy. Cherokees and Creeks lived in northwestern Georgia, and in the 1820s the state accused the federal government of not fulfilling its 1802 promise to remove the Indians in return for the state's renunciation of its claim to western lands. Georgia was satisfied neither by Monroe's removal messages nor by further cessions by the Creeks. In 1826, under federal pressure, the Creek nation ceded all but a small strip of its Georgia acreage. But Georgia still was not satisfied. Only the removal of the Georgia Creeks to the West could resolve the conflict between the state and the federal government.

For the Creeks the outcome was a devastating blow. In an ultimately unsuccessful attempt to hold fast to the remainder of their traditional lands, which were in Alabama, they radically altered their political structure. In 1829, at the expense of traditional village autonomy, they centralized tribal authority and forbade any chief from ceding land. In the end, they lost not only their land but also their traditional forms of social and political organization.

Adapting to American ways seemed no more successful than resistance in forestalling removal. No

Cherokees

people met the challenge of civilizing themselves by American standards more thoroughly than the Cherokees, whose traditional home centered on eastern Tennessee and northern Alabama and Georgia. Between 1819 and 1829 the tribe became economically self-sufficient and politically self-governing; during this Cherokee renaissance the twelve to fifteen thousand adult Cherokees came to think of themselves as a nation, not a collection of villages. In 1821 and 1822 Sequoyah, a self-educated Cherokee, devised an eighty-six-character phonetic alphabet that made possible a Cherokee-language Bible and a bilingual tribal newspaper, *Cherokee Phoenix* (1828). Between 1820 and 1823 the Cherokees created a formal government with a bicameral legislature, a court system, and a salaried bureaucracy. In 1827 they adopted a written constitution, modeled after that of the United States. Cherokee land laws, however, differed from U.S. law. The tribe collectively owned all Cherokee land and forbade land sales to outsiders. Nonetheless, the Cherokees assimilated American cultural patterns. By 1833 they held fifteen hundred black slaves whose legal status was the same as that of slaves held by southern whites. Moreover, missionaries had been so successful that the Cherokees could be considered a Christian community.

Although the Cherokees developed a political system similar to that of an American state, they failed to win respect or acceptance from southerners. In the 1820s, Georgia pressed them to sell the 7,200 square miles of land they held in the state. Congress appropriated $30,000 in 1822 to buy the Cherokee land in Georgia, but the Cherokees preferred to stay where they were. Impatient with their refusals to negotiate cession, Georgia annulled the Cherokees' constitution, extended the state's sovereignty over them, prohibited the Cherokee National Council from meeting except to cede land, and ordered their lands seized. The discovery of gold on Cherokee land in 1829 whetted Georgia's appetite for Cherokee territory.

Backed by sympathetic whites but not by the new president, Andrew Jackson, the Cherokees under Chief John Ross turned to the federal courts to defend their treaty with the United States and to disarm new

Cherokee Nation v. Georgia

threats by Georgia to seize their land. Their legal strategy reflected their growing political sophistication. In *Cherokee Nation v. Georgia* (1831), Chief Justice John Marshall ruled that under the federal Constitution an Indian tribe was neither a foreign nation nor a state and therefore had no standing in federal courts. Nonetheless, said Marshall, the Indians had an unquestionable right to their lands; they could lose title only by voluntarily giving it up. A year later, in *Worcester v. Georgia*, Marshall defined the Cherokee position more clearly. The Indian nation was, he declared, a distinct political community in which "the laws of Georgia can have no force" and into which Georgians could not enter without permission or treaty privilege. The Cherokees cheered. *Phoenix* editor Elias Boudinot called the decision "glorious news." But Georgia refused to comply.

Map 10.5   Removal of Native Americans from the South, 1820–1840   Over a twenty-year period, the federal government and southern states forced Native Americans to exchange their traditional homes for western land. Some tribal groups remained in the South, but most settled in the alien western environment.   (Acknowledgment is due to Martin Gilbert and George Weidenfeld and Nicholson Limited for permission to reproduce this map taken from *American History Atlas*)

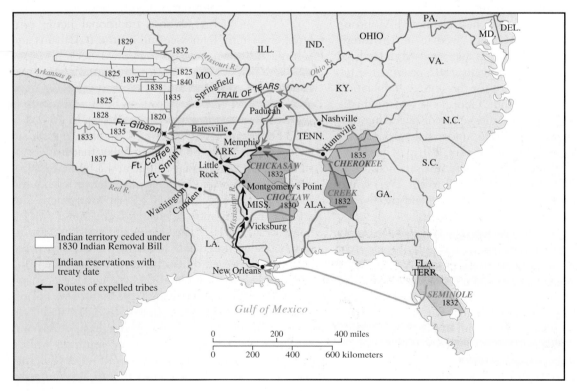

President Andrew Jackson, whose reputation had been built as an Indian fighter, refused to interfere because the case involved a state action. Newspapers widely reported that Jackson had said, "John Marshall has made his decision: now let him enforce it." Keen to open up new lands for settlement, Jackson favored expelling the Cherokees. In the Removal Act of 1830 Congress had provided Jackson with the funds he needed to negotiate new treaties and resettle the resistant tribes west of the Mississippi (see Map 10.5).

Trail of Tears

The Choctaws went first; they made the forced journey from Mississippi and Alabama to the West in the winter of 1831 and 1832. Alexis de Tocqueville was visiting Memphis when they passed through: "The wounded, the sick, newborn babies, and the old men on the point of death. . . . I saw them embark to cross the great river," he wrote, "and the sight will never fade from my memory. Neither sob nor complaint rose from that silent assembly. Their afflictions were of long standing, and they felt them to be irremediable." Other tribes soon joined the forced march. The Creeks in Alabama resisted removal until 1836, when the army pushed them westward. A year later the Chickasaws followed.

Having fought removal in the courts, the Cherokees were divided. Some believed that further resistance was hopeless and accepted removal as the only chance to preserve their civilization. The leaders of this minority agreed in 1835 to exchange their southern home for western land in the Treaty of New Echota. Most, though, wanted to stand firm. John Ross, with petitions signed by fifteen thousand Cherokees, lobbied the Senate against ratification of the treaty. They lost. But when the time for evacuation came in 1838, most Cherokees refused to move. President Martin Van Buren sent federal troops to round them up. About twenty thousand Cherokees were evicted, held in detention camps, and marched to Indian Territory in present-day Oklahoma under military escort. Nearly one-quarter of them died of disease and exhaustion on what came to be known as the Trail of Tears.

When the forced march to the West ended, the Indians had traded about 100 million acres east of the Mississippi for 32 million acres west of the river plus

The Trail of Tears, by twentieth-century Pawnee artist Brummet Echohawk. About twenty thousand Cherokees were evicted in 1838–1839, and about one-quarter of them died on the forced march to present-day Oklahoma.   (Thomas Gilcrease Institute of American History and Art)

$68 million. Only a few scattered remnants, among them the Seminoles in Florida and the Cherokees in the southern Appalachian Mountains, remained in the East and South.

Forced removal had a disastrous impact on the Cherokees and the other displaced tribes. In the West they encountered an alien environment; lacking traditional ties, few felt at peace with the land. The animals and plants they found were unfamiliar. Unable to live off the land, many became dependent on government payments for survival. Removal also brought new internal conflicts. The Cherokees in particular struggled over their tribal government. In 1839 followers of John Ross assassinated the leaders of the protreaty faction. Violence continued sporadically until a new treaty in 1846 imposed a temporary truce.

Conflicts also arose among migrating Native American groups from the South and East and Indians already living in the West, as they were forced to share land and scarce resources. Nearly one hundred thousand newcomers settled west of the Mississippi, and the existing game could not support them all. The Osages and Pawnees grittily fought the newcomers who, under U.S. Army escort, were invading their land and homes.

In Florida a small band of Seminoles continued to resist. Some Seminole leaders agreed in the 1832 Treaty of Payne's Landing to relocate to the West within three years, but others opposed the treaty, and some probably did not know it existed. A minority under Osceola, a charismatic leader, refused to vacate their homes and fought the protreaty group. When federal troops were sent to impose removal in 1835, Osceola waged a fierce guerrilla war against them.

Second Seminole War

The Florida Indians were a varied group that included many Creeks and mixed Indian–African Americans (ex-slaves or descendants of runaway slaves). The U.S. Army, however, considered them all Seminoles, subject to removal. General Thomas Jesup believed that the runaway slave population was the key to the war. "This, you may be assured, is a Negro, not an Indian war," he wrote a friend in 1836, "and if it be not speedily put down, the South will feel the effects of it on their slave population before the end of the next season."

Osceola was captured under a white flag of truce and died in an army prison in 1838, but the Seminoles fought on under Chief Coacoochee (Wild Cat) and other leaders. In 1842 the United States abandoned the removal effort. Most of Osceola's followers agreed to move west to Indian Territory in 1858, but many Seminoles remained in the Florida Everglades, proud of having resisted conquest.

Summary

 Nationalism and self-confidence accompanied the end of the War of 1812. Under the Democratic-Republicans the federal government fostered expansion and economic growth through internal improvements, tariffs, the Second Bank of the United States, land sales, and Indian removal. The Supreme Court and American diplomats, too, asserted nationalism. The Monroe Doctrine was among John Quincy Adams's finest achievements.

But sectionalism accompanied nationalism and geographical expansion. Conflicts over tariffs, economic hard times, and slavery brought discord. The Missouri Compromise was a stopgap measure to avoid the explosive issue of slavery.

From 1816 through 1845 the United States experienced explosive growth. Population increased sixfold, mostly from natural increase, and moved westward. New farms grew cotton and grain for the market, and cities followed. In the process, Indians and Hispanics were pushed aside.

Agriculture remained the dominant industry, though by midcentury a booming manufacturing sector challenged farming. And agriculture itself was becoming market-oriented and mechanized. The market economy brought sustained growth; it also ushered in cycles of boom and bust. Hard times and unemployment became frequent occurrences. The growing economy also meant larger-scale destruction of the environment: mills exploited New England waterways as a source of power.

Large-scale manufacturing also altered traditional patterns of production and consumption. Farm families began to purchase goods formerly made by wives and daughters, and geared production to faraway markets. Farm women increasingly contributed income from market sales to the household purse. In New England many young women left the family farm to become the first factory workers in the new textile industry. As workshops and factories replaced home-based production, and the master-journeyman-apprentice system faded away, workplace relations became more impersonal, working conditions grew harsher, and men's and women's work became increasingly dissimilar. Industrial jobs began to attract large numbers of immigrants, and some workers organized labor unions.

Americans turned to controlling, resisting, or advocating change in the home and public spheres, through reform and politics.

LEGACY FOR A PEOPLE AND A NATION
A Mixed Economy

How active should the U.S. government be? Should it run, regulate, or leave to the market system healthcare, Social Security and private pensions, corporate concentration, and stock trading and investments? In other words, to what degree should the government be responsible for the well-being of the economy and individuals?

The Articles of Confederation limited government, the Constitution empowered it, and the Bill of Rights restricted it in specific areas. While Americans have continuously debated the appropriate role of government, the United States has generally occupied a middle ground: a mixed economy.

In the early nineteenth century, government played an active role in economic and social expansion. Federal and state governments built roads and canals, developed harbors, and operated post offices and the early telegraph. More commonly the government intervened to stimulate and regulate the private sector. In chartering corporations and banks and in land sales and grants, the United States created an infrastructure that laid the way for the market economy and industrialization.

In the late nineteenth century advocates of laissez-faire or hands-off government challenged the pre–Civil War traditions of an active government. Laissez faire dominated briefly until the 1880s and 1890s when large corporations and trusts accumulated so much power that governments stepped in to regulate railroads and business concentration. After the turn of the century the federal government extended regulation to food, drugs, the environment, working conditions, and fair business practices. Probably the most innovative example of the mixed economy was the creation in 1913 of the Federal Reserve System—a public system for overseeing currency and banking that left control in private hands. After a revival of laissez faire in the 1920s, the crisis of the Great Depression of the 1930s and World War II would lead the federal government to establish the modern welfare state, which operates through a mixed public/private structure.

As the United States begins the twenty-first century, its people again debate the appropriate role of government. Conservatives view government as the problem rather than the solution, arguing that government regulation hampers individual freedom and distorts the law of supply and demand. Advocates of an activist government argue that only the government has the power and resources to check economic concentration and to protect health, safety, and the environment. The framework of this debate is a legacy from before the Civil War.

For Further Reading, see page A-12 of the Appendix. For Web resources, go to http://college.hmco.com.

"I proceed, Gentlemen, briefly to call your attention to the present state of Insane persons confined within this Commonwealth," Dorothea Dix petitioned the Massachusetts legislature in 1843, "in cages, closets, stalls, pens! Chained, naked, beaten with rods and lashed into obedience."

Dix revealed the netherworld she had uncovered in investigating the treatment of the insane during the previous two years. She found appalling conditions in Massachusetts: men and women in cages, chained to walls, in dark dungeons, brutalized and held in solitary confinement. In a visit to a Newburyport almshouse in the summer of 1842, Dix expressed her surprise at the comfortable conditions for the "one idiotic" and seven insane inhabitants. On the grounds she discovered, however, one man residing in a shed whose door opened to the local "dead room" or morgue; his only companions were corpses. Shocked, she heard from an attendant about another insane inmate of whom no one spoke openly: "a woman in a cellar."

Dix asked to see the woman. The superintendent warned Dix that the woman "was dangerous to be approached; that 'she had lately attacked his wife,' and was often naked." Dix pressed on. "If you will not go with me," she said, "give me the keys and I will go alone." They unlocked the doors and entered an underground cell. Beneath the staircase was a tiny door. In the shadows Dix saw "a female apparently wasted to a skeleton, partially wrapped in blankets." She was withered, wrote Dix, "not by age, but by suffering." When the inmate saw the visitors, she wailed with despair: "Why am I consigned to hell? dark—dark—I used to pray, I used to read the Bible—I have done no crime in my heart. I had friends; why have all forsaken me!—my God! my God! why hast thou forsaken me?"

Dix described in the most personal and vivid terms her visits to jails, almshouses, and private homes, and the cruel treatment of the insane. Her petition to the General Court of Massachusetts was so graphic and shocking that the legislature voted to reprint it as a government pamphlet: "Memorial to the Massachusetts Legislature" (1843). Part petition, part sermon, and part autobiography, it made riveting reading.

Dorothea Dix's powerful personal descriptions of the brutal treatment of the mentally ill propelled her from reform to politics. This early photograph of Dix portrays both her austere demeanor and her crusading spirit. (Boston Athenaeum)

11

REFORM AND POLITICS IN THE AGE OF JACKSON 1824–1845

The first-person narrative—"I tell what I have seen"—gave Dix's message power. She seemed, however, an unlikely herald. Reared in Massachusetts, she began teaching in Worcester at age fourteen in 1816. She wrote an elementary science text and published children's devotional verse and poetry. Her appearance was somber: she wore dark dresses with starched white collars and pulled her hair back tightly, making her face look more angular and austere. She never married and seemed aloof to other Bostonians, but she became an impassioned crusader for asylum reform, advocating hospitals for the mentally ill. In the 1840s she traveled more than 40,000 miles, exposing the inhumane treatment of the insane and petitioning state legislatures. From 1848 through 1856 she lobbied Congress annually to set aside 5 million acres to fund insane asylums. During the Civil War Dix recruited and supervised nurses for the federal government; afterward she resumed her efforts on behalf of the mentally ill. She died in 1887 in a hospital she had founded.

Dix epitomized much of early-nineteenth-century reform. She started with a religious belief in individual self-improvement and human perfectibility that led her to advocate collective responsibility, especially on behalf of those dependent on the kindness of others. She made reform her career, fearlessly entering the public arena at a time when women of her class were circumscribed to private life. In investigating asylums, in petitioning the Massachusetts legislature, and in lobbying other states and Congress, Dix moved from reform to politics, and she helped create a new public role for women, in the process broadening the base of political participation.

The religious and reform fervor of the period arose both as part of the spiritual renewal known as the Second Great Awakening and as a response to the enormous transformation that the United States experienced after the War of 1812. Immigration, the spread of a market economy, growing inequality, the westward advance of settlement, and territorial expansion all contributed to remaking the United States. Many Americans had difficulty keeping up with the rapid pace of change and felt they were no longer masters of their own fates.

Anxieties wrought by rapid change drove the impulse to reform society. Men and women organized to end the abuses of alcohol and prostitution, to improve conditions in prisons and asylums, to oppose secret and antidemocratic societies, to end slavery, and to achieve equal rights for women. Inevitably reform movements pushed men and women into politics, though only men voted. Opponents of reform, however, were equally concerned about social problems. What distinguished them from reformers was their skepticism about human perfectibility and their distrust of institutions and the exercise of power, both public and private. To them, government coercion was the greater evil. They sought to reverse, not shape, change.

Two issues in particular bridged reform and politics: the short-lived Antimasonry frenzy against secret societies; and the intense, uncompromising crusade for immediate emancipation. Though Antimasons organized the first third-party movement, abolition eventually overrode all other concerns. No single issue evoked the passion that slavery did. It pitted neighbor against neighbor and region against region.

The Jacksonians, too, saw themselves as reformers. They opposed special privileges and the Second Bank of the United States with the same vigor with which reformers opposed sin. President Jackson believed that a strong federal government restricted individual freedom by favoring one group over another. Social and religious reformers disagreed. Wanting a more active federal role, they rallied around the new Whig Party, which became the vehicle of humanitarian reform. Democrats and Whigs constituted a new party system, characterized by strong organizations, intensely loyal followings, and energetic religious and ethnic competition.

Both parties eagerly promoted expansionism during the prosperous 1840s. Democrats saw the agrarian West as an antidote to urbanization and industrialization; Whigs focused on the new commercial opportunities it offered. Expanding the nation all the way to the Pacific seemed to be the manifest destiny of the United States. Texas, California, and Oregon, unknown to most Americans in 1800, had become familiar places by the 1830s and 1840s, and to lay hold of them, the United States would challenge its neighbors to the north and south. ■

From Revival to Reform

Religion was probably the prime motivating force behind organized benevolence and reform. Beginning in the late 1790s religious revivals galvanized Protestants, especially women, into social action. The most famous was at Cane Ridge, Kentucky, in 1801, and it became legendary. One report estimated twenty-five thousand people attended the August meetings, at a time when

IMPORTANT EVENTS

1790s–1840s Second Great Awakening spreads religious fervor

1820s Reformers in New York and Pennsylvania establish model penitentiaries

1824 No presidential candidate wins a majority in the electoral college

1825 House of Representatives elects Adams president

1826 American Society for the Promotion of Temperance founded
Morgan affair is catalyst for Antimasonry movement

1828 Tariff of Abominations passed
Jackson elected president

1830 Webster-Hayne debate explores the nature of the Union

1830s–40s Democratic-Whig competition gels in second party system

1831 Garrison begins abolitionist newspaper *The Liberator*
First national Antimason convention

1832 Jackson vetoes rechartering of the Second Bank of the United States
Jackson reelected president

1832–33 South Carolina nullifies tariffs of 1828 and 1832, prompting nullification crisis

1836 Republic of Texas established after breaking from Mexico
Specie Circular ends credit purchase of public lands
Van Buren elected president

1837 *Caroline* affair sparks Anglo-U.S.-Canadian hostility
Financial panic ends boom of the 1830s

1838–39 United States and Canada mobilize their militias over Maine–New Brunswick border dispute

1839–43 Hard times spread unemployment and deflation

1840 Whigs win presidency under Harrison

1841 Tyler assumes the presidency after Harrison's death
"Oregon fever" attracts settlers to the Northwest and intensifies expansionism

1843 Dix petitions Massachusetts legislature regarding deplorable condition of insane asylums

1844 Polk elected president

1845 Texas admitted to the Union

1848 Woman's Rights Convention at Seneca Falls, New York, calls for women's suffrage

Kentucky's largest city, Lexington, had fewer than two thousand inhabitants. Revivals spread in waves, finding ready audiences in the frontier folk of the countryside. At camp meetings, sometimes lasting a week and attended by thousands of people, preachers exhorted sinners to repent and become genuine Christians. They offered salvation to all through personal conversion. At a time when only a minority could read and write, these itinerant evangelists were democratizing American religion, making it available to all.

Resembling the Great Awakening of the eighteenth century (see pages 110–111), the movement came to be called the Second Great Awakening. Under its influence, the role of churches and ministers in community life diminished as lay participation increased, and Chris-

Second Great Awakening

tians in all parts of the country tried to right the wrongs of the world. Visiting the United States in the 1830s, Alexis de Tocqueville noted that "there is no country in the world where the Christian religion retains greater influence" than in America.

In the South, huge numbers of people regularly attended revivals, but they especially drew women and African Americans, free and slave. The call to personal repentance and conversion invigorated Protestantism, giving southern churches an evangelical base and giving evangelicalism a southern accent. In essence, the Second Great Awakening turned the South into the Bible belt. In the North, New York lawyer Charles G. Finney led the revival movement. After his 1821 soul-shaking conversion, which he interpreted as "a retainer from the Lord Jesus Christ to plead his cause," Finney abandoned the law to convert souls, staging three- to four-day camp meetings in western New York towns.

Salvation could be achieved, Finney preached, through spontaneous conversion like his own. He mesmerized his audiences, evoking emotional responses. In everyday language, Finney preached that "God has made man a moral free agent." In other words, evil was avoidable: Christians were not doomed by original sin, and anyone could achieve salvation. Finney's brand of revivalism transcended sects, class, and race but had a particularly strong base among Baptists and Methodists. These denominations grew the most because their structure maximized democratic participation and they drew their ministers from ordinary folk.

The Second Great Awakening raised people's hopes for the Second Coming of the Christian messiah and the establishment of the Kingdom of God on earth. Revivalists resolved to speed the Second Coming by combating the forces of evil and darkness. Some revivalists even believed that the United States had a special mission in God's design and therefore a special role in eliminating evil. As the pace of social change quickened in the 1830s and 1840s, western New York experienced such continuous and heated waves of revivalism that it became known as "the burned-over district." Migration patterns spread not only religion but also the impulse for moral reform.

Regardless of theology, all revivalists shared a belief in individual self-improvement. The doctrine of perfectibility demanded that Christians actively organize and convert others. Thus the Second Great Awakening bred reform, and evangelical Protestants became missionaries for both religious and secular salvation. Wherever they preached, evangelists generated new religious groups and voluntary reform societies. New sects like the Mormons arose out of this ferment. So did associations to address the pressing issues of the day: temperance, education, Sabbath observance, dueling, and later slavery. Religious zeal led believers to support missionaries abroad, particularly in Asia and Africa. Collectively these groups constituted a national web of benevolent and moral-reform societies, and strengthened by numbers, the privately persuaded inevitably moved toward public action.

More women than men answered the call of Christianity, sustaining the Second Great Awakening and invigorating local churches. Pious middle-class women in Rochester, New York, for instance, responded to Finney by spreading

Role of Women

the word to other women during the day while their husbands were at work. Gradually women brought their families and sometimes their husbands into church and reform. Although many businessmen recruited their employees to benevolent work, women more than men tended to feel personally responsible for counteracting the increasingly secular orientation of the expanding market economy. The emotionally charged conversion experience could return women to what they believed was the right path. It also offered them communal ties with other women.

Everywhere prayer groups and female missionary societies motivated organized religious and benevolent activity on an unprecedented scale. For women and some men, reform represented their first political involvement at a time when women did not cast votes. In reform organizations women represented themselves; by participating directly in service activities, they pioneered new, visible, public roles for women. Within churches and society, they dissented and opposed traditional political leaders.

An exposé of prostitution in New York City illustrates how reform led to political action and dissent.

The Plight of Prostitutes

John R. McDowall, a divinity student, published a report in 1830 documenting the prevalence of prostitution in New York City. Philip Hone, a prominent civic leader (see pages 316–317), denounced McDowall's report as "a disgraceful document," and he and other New York businessmen and politicians defended the city's good name against "those base slanders." Women, moved by the plight of "fallen women," revived the fight against prostitution in 1834. But whereas male reformers made the prostitutes the target of their zeal, the newly organized Female Moral Reform Society focused on the men who victimized young women, publicizing the names of clients who entered brothels in New York City. They organized a shelter for refuge and an employment agency to find jobs for prostitutes.

During the 1830s, the New York society expanded its activities and geographical scope, calling itself the American Female Moral Reform Society. By 1840 it had 555 affiliated chapters across the nation. The society also entered the political sphere. In New York State in the 1840s, the movement successfully crusaded for criminal sanctions against the men who seduced women into prostitution, as well as against the prostitutes themselves.

One of the most successful reform efforts was the campaign against alcohol. Drinking was more wide-

Temperance

spread in the early nineteenth century than it is today. American men gathered in public houses and rural inns to gossip, talk politics, play cards, escape work and home, and to drink whiskey, rum, and hard cider. Contracts were sealed, celebrations commemorated, and harvests toasted with liquor. Respectable women did not drink in public, but many regularly tippled alcohol-based patent medicines promoted as cure-alls. Why then did temperance become such a vital issue? And why were women especially active in the movement? Like all nineteenth-century reform, temperance had a strong religious foundation.

Evangelicals considered drinking a sin; it created poverty, dependency, and crime. Moreover, in many denominations, forsaking alcohol was part of conversion. The sale of whiskey often violated the Sabbath, for workers commonly labored six days and spent Sunday at the public house drinking and socializing. Equally important, alcoholism destroyed families. In the early 1840s thousands of ordinary women formed Martha Washington societies to protect families by reforming alcoholics, raising children as teetotalers, and spreading the temperance message. Popular culture of the time was laced with domestic images of the damage alcohol left in its wake: abandoned wives, prodigal sons, drunken fathers. Timothy Shay Arthur dramatized all these evils in *Ten Nights in a Barroom* (1853), a classic American melodrama, as did Deacon Robert Peckham in his temperance paintings. Employers complained that drinkers took "St. Monday" as a holiday to recover from Sunday. In the new world of the factory, drinking was unacceptable.

Demon rum became a prime target of reformers. As the temperance movement gained momentum, its goal shifted from moderate use of alcohol to voluntary abstinence and finally to prohibition. The American Society for the Promotion of Temperance, organized in 1826 to sign drinkers to a pledge of abstinence, became a pressure group for state prohibition legislation. By the mid-1830s five thousand state and local temperance societies touted teetotalism, and more than a million people had taken the pledge. Several hundred thousand children, for instance, enlisted in the Cold Water Army.

Temperance Societies

The temperance movement's success was reflected in a sharp decline in alcohol use. Per capita consumption fell from 5 gallons in 1800 to below 2 gallons in the 1840s. Success bred more victories. Maine prohibited the manufacture and sale of alcohol except for medicinal purposes in 1851, and by 1855 similar laws

The evils of drinking and the bliss of temperance were a major theme in popular culture. Deacon Robert Peckham illustrated the contrast in two paintings from the 1840s: *The Woes of Liquor (Intemperance)* and *The Happy Abstemious Family (Temperance)*. (Worcester Historical Museum)

had been enacted throughout New England and in New York, Pennsylvania, and the Midwest.

Even as consumption was declining, opposition to alcohol was growing. From the 1820s on, many reformers expressed their prejudices by regarding alcohol as an evil introduced by Catholic immigrants. The Irish and Germans, the *American Protestant Magazine* complained in 1849, "bring the grog shops like the frogs of Egypt upon us." Rum and immigrants defiled the Sabbath; rum and immigrants brought poverty; rum and immigrants supported the feared papacy. Some Catholics took the pledge of abstinence and formed their own organizations, such as the St. Mary's Mutual Benevolent Total Abstinence Society in Boston. Even nondrinking Catholics tended to oppose state regulation of drinking, however; temperance seemed to them a question of individual choice. They favored self-control, not state coercion.

As the career of Dorothea Dix demonstrated, moral reform also stimulated the construction of asylums and other institutions to house prisoners, the mentally ill, orphans, delinquent children, and the poor.

Penitentiaries and Asylums

Such institutions were needed, reformers argued, to shelter victims of society's turbulence and impose on them a familial discipline. It was widely believed that criminals came from unstable families whose lack of restraint led to vice and drink. Idleness was both a symptom and a cause of crime; thus the clock governed a prisoner's day, and idleness was banished. Through discipline, inmates might become self-reliant and responsible. Even the most sinful could be redeemed.

In the 1820s New York and Pennsylvania developed competing models for reforming criminals. Both rejected incarceration simply to punish criminals or to remove them from society, advocating instead that disciplined regimens would rehabilitate them. New York's Auburn (1819–1823) and Ossining (1825) prisons isolated prisoners in individual cells but brought them together in common workshops. Pennsylvania's Pittsburgh (1826) and Philadelphia (1829) prisons isolated prisoners completely, forcing them to eat, sleep, and work in their individual cells, allowing them contact only with guards and visitors. Both systems sought to separate criminals from evil influences and to expose them to a regimen of order and discipline.

Similar approaches were employed in insane asylums, hospitals, and orphanages. Formerly the prescribed treatment removed disturbed individuals from society and isolated them among strangers; many were incarcerated with criminals. Dorothea Dix argued that

this treatment was inhumane. The new asylums were clean and orderly. In response to Dix's crusade and reform societies, twenty-eight of the thirty-three states had public institutions for the mentally ill by 1860.

Antimasonry

 More intense than the asylum movement but of shorter duration was the crusade against Freemasonry, a secret fraternity that had come to the United States from England in the eighteenth century. Sons of the Enlightenment such as Benjamin Franklin and George Washington were attracted to Masonry, with its emphasis on individual belief in a deity (as opposed to organized religion) and on brotherhood (as opposed to one church). In the early nineteenth century Freemasonry spread, attracting middle- and upper-class men prominent in commerce and civic affairs. For the ambitious, the Masons offered access to powerful community leaders. Monumental lodges called attention to the Mason's affluence and prominence.

Opponents of Masonry charged that the order's secrecy and appeal to elites were antidemocratic and antirepublican. Publications such as the *Anti Masonic Almanac* attacked Masonic initiation rites. Evangelicals labeled the order satanic. Antimasons argued that Masonry threatened the family because it excluded women and encouraged men to neglect their families for alcohol and ribald entertainments at Masonic lodges. As the temperance movement sought to liberate individuals from drink, Antimasons sought to liberate society from the grip of what they considered a powerful, antirepublican secret fraternity. Just as penitentiaries and asylums would rehabilitate the criminal and insane, so the Antimasons believed that the abolition of Masonry would reestablish communal moral discipline and harmony. The political arena quickly absorbed Antimasonry, and its short life illustrates the close association of politics and reform in the 1820s and after.

The catalyst for Antimasonry as an organized movement was the suspected murder of William Morgan, a disillusioned Mason who published an exposé in 1826, *The Illustration of Masonry, By One of the Fraternity Who Has Devoted Thirty Years to the Subject.* Even before the book appeared, a group of Masons abducted Morgan in Canandaigua, New York. It was widely believed that his kidnappers murdered him, though his body was never found.

Morgan Affair

Events seemed to confirm Masonry's antidemocratic character. Prosecutors who were Masons appeared to obstruct the investigation of Morgan's abduction. The public pressed for justice, and the series of notorious trials that ensued from 1827 through 1831 led many to suspect a conspiracy. The cover-up became as much of an issue as Masonry itself, and the movement spread to other states. Antimasonry coalesced overnight in the burned-over district of western New York, and it quickly became a political movement.

With a growing popular following and a call for public morality and republican principles, the Antimasons held conventions in 1827 to se-

Convention System

lect candidates to oppose Masons running for office. The next year the conventions supported the National Republican candidate, John Quincy Adams, and opposed Andrew Jackson because he was a Mason. The Antimasons held the first national political convention in Baltimore in 1831, and a year later they nominated William Wirt as their presidential candidate. Thus the Antimasons became a rallying point for those opposed to President Andrew Jackson. Their electoral strength lay in New England and New York: in Vermont the Antimasons became the dominant party for a brief time in 1833; in Massachusetts they replaced the Democrats as the second major party. Antimasonry found little support, however, in the slave South.

By the mid-1830s, Antimasonry had lost momentum as a moral and political phenomenon. A single-issue party, the Antimasons declined along with Freemasonry. Yet the movement left its mark on the politics of the era. As a moral crusade focused on public officeholders, it inspired broad participation in the political process. It drew new white voters into politics at a time when male suffrage was being extended, and it attracted the lower and middle classes by pitting them against the Masonic elite, exploiting their distrust of local political leaders. The Antimasons also changed party organization by pioneering the convention, rather than the caucus, for nominating candidates for office and by introducing the party platform.

Abolitionism and the Women's Movement

Antimasonry foreshadowed and had much in common with abolitionism. Indeed, as Antimasonry waned, the antislavery movement gathered momentum. Abolitionist William Lloyd Garrison at first ignored the frenzy over the Morgan affair but in 1832 he joined

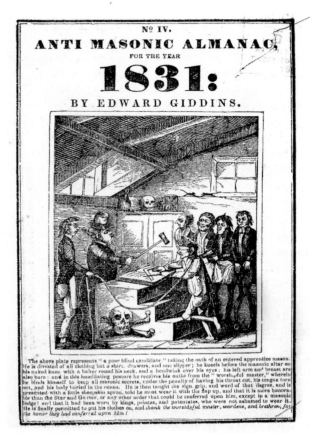

Nº IV.
ANTI MASONIC ALMANAC,
FOR THE YEAR
1831:
BY EDWARD GIDDINS.

Antimasonic publications, such as this 1831 almanac, made much of the allegedly sinister initiation rites that bound a new member "to keep all Masonic secrets, under the penalty of having his throat cut, his tongue torn out, and his body buried in the ocean."   (Print collection, Miriam and Ira D. Wallach Division of Art, Prints, and Photographs, New York Public Library, Astor, Lenox and Tilden Foundations)

the ranks of Antimasons. Echoing his stand on emancipation, Garrison wrote: "I go for the immediate, unconditional and total abolition of Freemasonry." In his eyes, both slavery and Masonry undermined republican values. Eventually the issue of slavery became so compelling that it consumed all other reforms and threatened the nation itself. Those who advocated immediate emancipation saw slavery as, above all, a moral issue—a flaw in the character of the American nation.

Before the 1830s few whites advocated the abolition of slavery. In the Northeast and Old Northwest, where by 1820 slavery had been virtually abolished (five states had gradual emancipation plans), whites took little interest in the issue. Antislavery sentiment appeared strongest in the Upper South, though north-

Women played an activist role in reform, especially in abolitionism. A rare daguerreotype from August 1850 shows women and men, including Frederick Douglass, on the podium at an abolitionist rally in Cazenovia, New York. (Collection of J. Paul Getty Museum, Los Angeles, California)

ern involvement grew after the War of 1812. The American Colonization Society, founded in 1816 in Washington, D.C., advocated gradual, voluntary emancipation and resettlement of former slaves in Africa, establishing the colony of Liberia for that purpose in the 1820s. Society members did not believe that free blacks had a place in the United States, and its members included Jefferson and other slaveholders, some evangelicals and Quakers, and (briefly) a few blacks. In the 1830s the immediatists—those who demanded immediate, complete, and uncompensated emancipation—surpassed the gradualists as the dominant strand of abolitionism.

At first only African Americans demanded an immediate end to slavery. David Walker's *Appeal . . . to the Colored Citizens* (1829) was a clarion call read by northern black people. Walker, a southern-born free black, was Boston's leading abolitionist until his death in 1830. When Walker died, there were fifty black abolitionist soci-

Black Abolitionists

eties in the United States assisting fugitive slaves, lobbying for emancipation, exposing the evils of slavery, and reminding the nation that its mission as defined in the Declaration of Independence remained unfulfilled. A free black press spread the word by fighting in print for suffrage and civil rights for free blacks. So did former slaves like Frederick Douglass and Sojourner Truth, whose writings and speeches of their personal experiences as slaves mobilized northerners. Douglass and Underground Railroad champion Harriet Tubman joined forces in the 1840s with white reformers in the American Anti-Slavery Society. Their militant and unrelenting campaign also won European support. "Brethren, arise, arise, arise!" Henry Highland Garnet commanded the 1843 National Colored Convention. "Strike for your lives and liberties. Now is the day and hour. Let every slave in the land do this and the days of slavery are numbered. Rather die freemen than live to be slaves."

In the 1830s a small number of white reformers, driven by moral urgency, also crusaded for immediate emancipation. The most prominent and uncompromising immediatist, though not the most representative, was the incendiary William Lloyd Garrison, a talented journalist who broke with moderate abolitionists in 1831. That year he began publishing *The Liberator*, which for thirty-five years would be his major weapon against slavery. He declared in its first issue, "I am in earnest—I will not equivocate—I will not excuse—I will not retreat a single inch—and *I will be heard.*"

William Lloyd Garrison

Garrison's staunch refusal to work with anyone who tolerated the delay of emancipation isolated him from other opponents of slavery. He even forswore political action on the grounds that it was government that permitted slavery. Garrison burned a copy of the Constitution on July 4, 1854, proclaiming, "So perish all compromises with tyranny." By his actions and rhetorical power, Garrison helped to push antislavery onto the agenda, though he had no specific plan for abolishing it. In essence, what Garrison called for was conversion of those who held slaves or cooperated with institutions that supported slavery; they must repent.

It is difficult to differentiate between those who became immediatists and those who did not. But immediatists like Garrison, Elizabeth Chandler, Amos Phelps, and Theodore Weld had much in common. They were young evangelicals active

Immediatists

How do historians know...

that African Americans and women played prominent roles in the abolitionist movement?

Abolitionists lived open lives. They used newspapers, pamphlets, speeches, and sermons to expose the evils of slavery, to mount a crusade for emancipation, and to build a movement. Weekly abolitionist newspapers, such as *The Liberator*, published by William Lloyd Garrison, printed their correspondence, their speeches, and minutes of their meetings.

The Liberator appeared from 1831 to 1866, and it recorded the activities of the immediatist aboli-

tionists. Under the banners "No Union with Slaveholders" and "The United States Constitution is a 'covenant with death, and an agreement with hell,'" it preached to the choir, printing passionate attacks on slavery and reports of local antislavery societies. *The Liberator*'s pages recorded the activities of black and women abolitionists, frequently in their own words. The subscription lists that have survived indicate that a majority of its subscribers probably were African Americans.   (Photo: Trustees of the Boston Public Library)

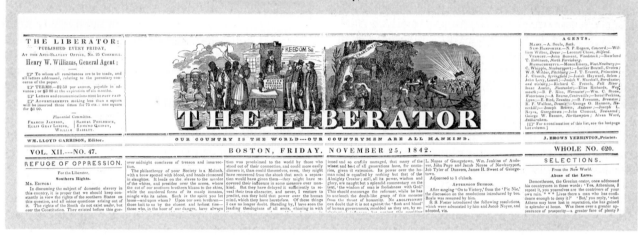

in benevolent societies in the 1820s; many became ordained ministers or started out intending ministry as a career; and many had personal contact with free blacks and were sympathetic to African American rights. They were convinced that slaveholding was a sin. Their common concern, in turn, made them more political: to abolish sin, they sought to change the institutions that harbored or fostered it. Finally, they shared great moral intensity. Because they were unwilling to compromise, their zeal made them forceful political activists. Their main organizational vehicle was the American Anti-Slavery Society, founded in 1833.

Most benevolent workers and reformers kept their distance from the immediatists. They shared with immediatists the view that slavery was a sin but believed in gradual emancipation. They feared that if they moved too fast, attacked sinners too harshly, or interfered too aggressively in time-honored customs and

beliefs, they would destroy the harmony and order they sought to bring about through peaceful reform. But peace was at a premium: unlike temperance, the antislavery movement faced fierce opposition, even mob violence.

Immediatists' greatest recruitment successes resulted from defending their own constitutional rights, not the rights of slaves. Wherever they went, immediatists found their civil rights, especially free speech, at risk, threatened by hostile crowds. At Utica, New York, in 1835, merchants and professionals broke up the state Anti-Slavery Convention that had welcomed blacks and women. Mob violence peaked that year with more than fifty riots aimed at abolitionists or African Americans. In 1837 in Alton, Illinois, a mob murdered abolitionist editor Elijah P. Lovejoy, who had been driven out of slaveholding Missouri, and rioters sacked his printing office. But

Opposition to Abolitionists

public outrage at Lovejoy's murder only broadened the base of antislavery support in the North.

In the South, mobs blocked the distribution of antislavery tracts. They destroyed pamphlets that the American Anti-Slavery Society sent out by the millions using new rotary printing presses. The state of South Carolina intercepted and burned abolitionist literature, and President Andrew Jackson proposed a law prohibiting the mailing of antislavery tracts. In 1835 proslavery assailants killed four abolitionists in South Carolina and Louisiana and forty supposed insurrectionists in Mississippi and Louisiana that summer. Riots in the South, unchecked by authorities, were violent and deadly.

At a rally in Boston's Faneuil Hall in 1835, former Federalist Harrison Gray Otis portrayed abolitionists as subversives. Attacking Garrison's American Anti-Slavery Society as "revolutionary," he accused it of having women "turn their sewing parties into abolition clubs." Soon, Otis charged, school primers would teach "that A stands for abolition." Abolitionists, he predicted, would turn to politics, causing unforeseeable calamity. "What will become of the nation?" Otis asked. "What will become of the union?"

But the furor between the abolitionists and their opponents was already being played out in the House of Representatives. Abolitionists

Gag Rule

were bombarding Congress with petitions to abolish slavery and the slave trade in the District of Columbia, which Congress governed. The House in 1836 adopted what abolitionists immediately labeled the "gag rule," which automatically tabled abolitionist petitions, effectively preventing debate on them. When the immediatists, in response, flooded Congress with nearly seven hundred thousand petitions, the gag rule gave new energy to the antislavery movement. In a dramatic defense of the right of petition, former president John Quincy Adams, now a representative from Massachusetts, took to the floor again and again to speak against the gag rule. (Its repeal in 1844 was anticlimactic.)

The Missouri Compromise, censorship of the mails, and the gag rule represented attempts to keep the issue of slavery out of the political arena. Yet the more national leaders, especially Democrats, worked to avoid the matter, the more they hardened the resolve of the antislavery forces. The unlawful and violent tactics used by opponents of abolition actually unified the movement by forcing factions to work together for mutual defense.

At the outset abolition was highly factionalized, and its adherents fought one another as often as they fought the defenders of slavery. They were divided over Garrison's emphasis on "moral suasion"—winning over the hearts of slaveowners rather than coercing them—versus the practical politics of James G. Birney, the Liberty Party's candidate for president in 1840 and 1844, who sought to end slavery by electing abolitionists. Abolitionists also disagreed about the place of free people of color in American society. And the movement split over support for other reforms, especially the rights of women.

Women had been prominent in the antislavery movement from the first. They joined local female antislavery societies through their

Women Abolitionists

churches as part of the network of moral reform. In 1833 women in Boston founded the Female Anti-Slavery Society, which disbanded seven years later over the issue of politics, but in many antislavery organizations women were as active and politically involved as men. Lydia Maria Child, Maria Chapman, and Lucretia Mott served on the American Anti-Slavery Society's executive committee; Child edited its official paper, the *National Anti-Slavery Standard*, from 1841 to 1843, and Chapman coedited it from 1844 until 1848. Garrison's moral suasion attracted many women because it gave them a platform from which to oppose slavery. Yet some politically active societies excluded women because they could not vote.

Opposition to women's prominent roles in reform movements led some women to reexamine their position in society at large. In the 1830s Angelina and Sarah Grimké challenged slavery and women's right to speak out. Born into a slaveholding family in Charleston, South Carolina, both sisters experienced conversion and independently became Quakers. When in 1834 they became activists, especially in abolitionism, they found in Garrison's immediatism a home. Yet they were soon attacked for speaking before mixed groups of men and women. Some New England Congregationalists, and even some abolitionists, joined in the criticism; one pastoral letter stated that women should obey, not lecture, men. This reaction turned the Grimkés' attention from slavery to women's condition. They attacked the concept of "subordination to man," insisting that men and women had the "same rights and same duties." Sarah Grimké's *Letters on the Equality of the Sexes and the Condition of Women* (1838) and her sister's *Letters to Catharine E. Beecher*, published the same year, were the opening volleys in the long war over the legal and social inequality of women.

It was only a matter of time before women involved with abolitionism crossed the path from pious and moral opposition against slavery

Women's Rights

to political engagement on behalf of women's rights. Eight years after their humiliation in London, Elizabeth Cady Stanton and Lucretia Mott, with Lucy Stone, organized the convention they had resolved to hold. In July 1848 three hundred women and men reformers gathered at the Woman's Rights Convention at Seneca Falls, New York, to demand political, social, and economic equality for women. They protested women's legal disabilities—inability to vote, limited property rights—and their social restrictions—exclusion from advanced schooling and from most occupations. Their Declaration of Sentiments, modeled after the Declaration of Independence, indicted the injustices suffered by women and launched the women's rights movement. "All men and women are created equal," the declaration proclaimed. If women had the vote, participants argued, they could protect themselves and realize their full potential as moral and spiritual leaders. What is important is that the women lobbying for suffrage created new public, political roles for women.

Advocates of women's rights were slow to garner support, especially from men, who held most of the political and legal power. In the 1840s the question of women's rights split the antislavery movement. Some men joined the ranks, notably Garrison and Frederick Douglass, but most men actively opposed the movement. Not everyone at Seneca Falls signed the resolution on women's suffrage. Of the one hundred who did, only two would live to see the passage of the Nineteenth Amendment to the Constitution seventy-two years later.

Jacksonianism and Party Politics

In the 1820s, reform pushed its way into politics. No less than reformers, politicians sought to control the direction of change in the expanding nation. The 1824 presidential election ignited a political barn fire that reformers, abolitionists, and expansionists would continuously stoke. By the 1830s, politics had become the great nineteenth-century American pastime.

The election of 1824, in which John Quincy Adams and Andrew Jackson faced off for the first time,

Elizabeth Cady Stanton posed in 1848 with two of her sons, Henry Jr., left, and Neil. Stanton, one of the organizers of the Seneca Falls Woman's Rights Convention, traveled widely and agitated for women's equality while raising five children.   (Collection of Rhoda Jenkins)

End of the Caucus System

heralded a more open political system. From 1800 through 1820 the system in which a congressional caucus (House and Senate members of the political party) chose Jefferson, Madison, and Monroe as the Democratic-Republican nominees had worked well. That it limited voters' involvement in choosing candidates was not an anomaly because in 1800 only five of the sixteen states selected presidential electors by popular vote. In most of the others, state legislatures selected the electors who voted for president. By 1824, however, eighteen out of twenty-four states chose electors by popular vote.

The Democratic-Republican caucus in 1824 chose William H. Crawford of Georgia, secretary of the treasury, as its presidential candidate. But other Democratic-Republicans, emboldened by the chance to appeal directly to voters, put themselves forward as sectional candidates. John Quincy Adams drew support from New England, while westerners backed

Presidential candidate Andrew Jackson is portrayed on a trinket or sewing box in 1824. This is an example of how campaigns entered popular culture and also illustrates the active role of women, excluded from voting, in politics. (Collection of David J. and Janice L. Frent)

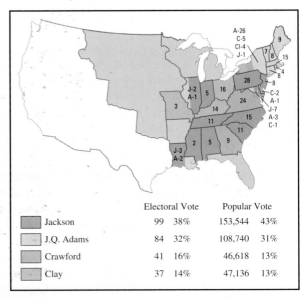

		Electoral Vote		Popular Vote	
	Jackson	99	38%	153,544	43%
	J.Q. Adams	84	32%	108,740	31%
	Crawford	41	16%	46,618	13%
	Clay	37	14%	47,136	13%

Map 11.1 Presidential Election, 1824 Andrew Jackson led in both electoral and popular votes but failed to win a majority of electoral college votes. The House elected John Quincy Adams president.

House Speaker Henry Clay of Kentucky. Secretary of War John C. Calhoun looked to the South for support and hoped to win Pennsylvania as well. The Tennessee legislature nominated Andrew Jackson, a popular military hero whose political views were unknown. Jackson had the most widespread support, but Crawford led in the party caucus. By boycotting the caucus and by attacking it as undemocratic, the four other candidates and their supporters ended the role of Congress in nominating presidential candidates.

In the four-way presidential election of 1824, Andrew Jackson led in both electoral and popular votes,

Election of 1824

but no candidate received a majority in the electoral college (see Map 11.1). Adams finished second, and Crawford and Clay trailed far behind (Calhoun had dropped out of the race before the election). As required by the Constitution, the House of Representatives, voting by state delegation, one vote to a state, selected the next president from among the leaders in electoral votes. Clay, who had received the fewest votes, was dropped. Crawford, who had a stroke after the election, never received serious consideration. The influential Clay—Speaker of the House and leader of the Ohio valley states—backed Adams, who received the votes of thirteen of the twenty-four state delegations to win. Clay then became Adams's secretary of state, the traditional steppingstone to the presidency.

Angry Jacksonians denounced the outcome of the election as a "corrupt bargain" that had stolen the office. Jackson's bitterness reinforced his opposition to elitism and fueled his later emphasis on the people's will. The Democratic-Republican Party split. The Adams wing emerged as the National Republicans, and the Jacksonians became the Democrats; they immediately began planning a reversal for 1828.

After taking the oath of office, Adams proposed a strong nationalist policy incorporating Henry Clay's "American System," a program of protective tariffs, a national bank, and internal improvements. Adams believed the federal government should take an activist role not only in the economy but also in education, science, and the arts. He proposed establishing a national university in Washington, D.C. Brilliant as a diplomat and secretary of state, Adams was an inept president. The political skills he had demonstrated in winning the office eluded him as chief executive. He underestimated the lingering effects of the Panic of 1819 and the resulting staunch opposition to a national bank and protective tariffs. Meanwhile, supporters of Andrew Jackson sabotaged Adams's administration at every opportunity.

The 1828 election pitted Adams against Jackson in a rowdy campaign. Voters displayed their enthusiasm

Election of 1828

for Jackson with badges, medals, and other campaign paraphernalia, which were mass-produced for the first time. The contest was also intensely personal. Mudslinging was the order of the day. Jackson's supporters accused Adams of stealing the 1824 election and, when he was envoy to Russia, of having secured prostitutes for the czar. Anti-Jacksonians published reports that Rachel Jackson had had an affair with Jackson and married the young officer before her first husband divorced her in 1793; she was, they sneered, an adulterer and a bigamist. In 1806 Jackson had killed John Dickinson in a Kentucky duel defending Rachel's integrity, and the cry of murderer was revived in the election. After the election Rachel Jackson discovered a pamphlet defending her, and she was mortified by the extent of the charges. In December 1828 she died of a heart attack. Jackson never forgave her "murderers."

Although Adams kept the states he won in 1824, the opposition was unified, and Jackson swamped him (see Map 11.2). Jackson polled 56 percent of the popular vote and won in the electoral college by 178 to 83 votes. He and his supporters believed that the will of the people had finally been served. Through a lavishly financed coalition of state parties, political leaders, and newspaper editors, a popular movement had elected the president, and an era had ended. The Democratic Party became the first well-organized national political party in the United States, and tight party organization became the hallmark of nineteenth-century American politics.

Nicknamed "Old Hickory" after the toughest of American hardwoods, Andrew Jackson was a rough-and-tumble, ambitious man. Born in

Andrew Jackson

South Carolina in 1767, he rose from humble beginnings to become a wealthy Tennessee planter and slaveholder. Jackson was the first American president from the West and the first born in a log cabin; he was at ease among both frontiersmen and southern planters. Though vindictive and given to violent displays of temper, he could charm opposition into assent. A natural leader, Jackson inspired immense loyalty. He had an instinct for politics and picked both issues and supporters shrewdly.

Few Americans have been as celebrated as Jackson. Having served in the Revolution as a boy, he claimed a connection to the founding generation. In the Tennessee militia General Jackson led the campaign to remove Creeks from the Alabama and Geor-

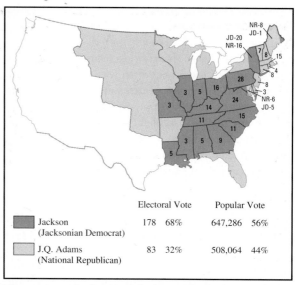

		Electoral Vote		Popular Vote	
■	Jackson (Jacksonian Democrat)	178	68%	647,286	56%
▢	J.Q. Adams (National Republican)	83	32%	508,064	44%

Map 11.2   Presidential Election, 1828   Andrew Jackson avenged his 1824 loss of the presidency, sweeping the election in 1828.

gia frontier (see page 238). He burst onto the national scene in 1815 as the great hero of the Battle of New Orleans, and in 1818 enhanced his glory in an expedition against Seminoles in Spanish Florida. Jackson also served as a congressman and senator from Tennessee, and as the first territorial governor of Florida (1821), before running for president in 1824.

Jackson and his supporters offered an alternative to the strong federal government advocated by John Quincy Adams. The Democrats rep-

Democrats

resented a wide range of views but shared a fundamental commitment to the Jeffersonian concept of an agrarian society. They distrusted a powerful central government as the enemy of individual liberty. The 1824 "corrupt bargain" had strengthened their suspicion of Washington politics. Jackson himself, a backwoodsman and farmer, symbolized simpler times.

Jacksonians feared the concentration of economic and political power. They believed that government intervention in the economy benefited special-interest groups and created corporate monopolies, which favored the rich. They sought to restore the independence of the individual—the artisan and the yeoman farmer—by ending federal support of banks and corporations and restricting the use of paper currency, which they distrusted. Their definition of the proper role of government tended to be negative, and Jackson's political power was largely expressed in negative acts. He exercised the veto more than all previous presidents combined.

Jackson and his supporters also opposed reform as a movement. Reformers eager to turn their programs into legislation called for a more activist government. But Democrats tended to oppose programs like educational reform and the establishment of a public education system. They believed, for instance, that public schools restricted individual liberty by interfering with parental responsibility and undermined freedom of religion by replacing church schools. Nor did Jackson share reformers' humanitarian concerns. He showed little sympathy for Native Americans, initiating the removal of the Cherokees along the Trail of Tears (see page 273).

Jacksonians considered themselves reformers in a different way. By restraining government and emphasizing individualism, they sought to restore traditional republican virtues, such as prudence and economy. No less zealous than reformers, Jackson sought to encourage self-discipline and self-reliance and to restore the harmony that he saw disrupted by economic and social change. In doing so, Jackson looked to Jefferson and the generation of the founders as models of traditional values. "My political creed," Jackson wrote to Tennessee congressman James K. Polk in 1826, "was formed in the old republican school."

Jacksonians as Reformers

Like Jefferson, Jackson strengthened the executive branch of government even as he weakened the federal role. Given his popularity and the strength of his personality, this concentration of power in the presidency was perhaps inevitable, but in combining the roles of party leader and chief of state, he centralized power in the White House. Jackson relied on political friends, his "Kitchen Cabinet," for advice; he rarely consulted his official cabinet. Enamored of power, Jackson never hesitated to confront his opponents with all the weapons at his disposal. He commanded enormous loyalty, and he rewarded his followers handsomely. Rotating officeholders, Jackson claimed, made government more responsive to the public will, but it allowed him to introduce a spoils system to appoint loyal Democrats to office. He removed fewer than one-quarter of the federal officeholders he inherited, but he used patronage to strengthen party organization and loyalty.

Jackson stressed rejection of elitism and special favors, rotation of officeholders, and belief in popular government. Time and again he declared that sovereignty resided with the people, not with the states or the courts. In this respect Jackson was a reformer; he returned government to majority rule. Yet it is hard to distinguish between Jackson's belief in himself as the instrument of the people and simple egotism and demagogic arrogance. After all, his opponents, too, claimed to represent the people.

Animosity grew year by year among President Jackson's supporters and opponents. Massachusetts senator Daniel Webster feared the men around the president; Henry Clay most feared Jackson himself. Rotation in office, they contended, corrupted government. Opponents mocked Jackson as "King Andrew I," charging him with abuse of power by ignoring the Supreme Court's ruling on Cherokee rights (see page 272), by using the spoils system, and by consulting his Kitchen Cabinet. Critics rejected his claim of restoring republican virtue and accused him of recklessly destroying the economy.

Amid all the agitation, Jackson pursued his agenda. He invigorated the philosophy of limited government. In 1830 he vetoed the Maysville Road bill—which would have funded construction of a 60-mile turnpike from Maysville to Lexington, Kentucky. A federally subsidized internal improvement confined to one state was unconstitutional, he charged; such projects were properly a state responsibility. The veto undermined Henry Clay's nationalist program and personally embarrassed Clay because the project was in his home district. Such federal-state issues were to loom even larger in the nullification crisis.

Federalism at Issue: The Nullification and Bank Controversies

Soon Jackson had to face directly the question of the proper division of sovereignty between state and central governments. The slave South feared federal power, no state more so than South Carolina, where the planter class was strongest and slavery most concentrated. Southerners also resented protectionist tariffs.

To protect manufactures, Congress in 1828 imposed high import duties on manufactured cloth and iron. But in protecting northern factories, the tariff raised the costs of these goods to southerners, who quickly labeled it the Tariff of Abominations.

Tariff of Abominations

To articulate their interests, South Carolina's political leaders turned to the doctrine of nullification, according to which a state had the right to overrule, or nullify, federal legislation. Nullification was based on the idea expressed in the Virginia and Kentucky resolutions of 1798 (see page 210)—that the states, representing the people, have a right to judge the constitutionality of federal actions. Jackson's vice president, John C. Calhoun of South Carolina, argued in his unsigned *Exposition and Protest* that, in any disagreement between the federal government and a state, a special state convention—like the conventions called to ratify the Constitution—should decide the conflict by either nullifying or affirming the federal law. Only the power of nullification, Calhoun asserted, could protect the minority against the tyranny of the majority.

In public, Calhoun let others take the lead in advancing nullification. As Jackson's running mate in 1828, he had avoided endorsing nullification and thus embarrassing the Democratic ticket; he also hoped to win Jackson's support as the Democratic presidential heir apparent.

Webster-Hayne Debate

Thus in early 1830 Calhoun presided silently over the Senate and its packed galleries when Senator Daniel Webster of Massachusetts and Senator Robert Y. Hayne of South Carolina debated states' rights. The debate started over a resolution to restrict western land sales and engaged the tariff issue by exploring sectional differences. It quickly turned to the nature of the Union, with nullification a subtext. With Vice President Calhoun nodding in agreement, Hayne charged that the North was threatening to bring disunity, as it had done fifteen years earlier at the Hartford Convention (see page 240). Hayne accused reformers of wanting in "the spirit of false philanthropy" to destroy the South.

For two days Webster eloquently defended New England and the republic, as he kept nullification on the defense. Though debating Hayne, he aimed his remarks at Calhoun. At the climax of the debate, Webster invoked two powerful images. One was the outcome of nullification: "states dissevered, discordant, belligerent; on a land rent with civil feuds, or drenched . . . in fraternal blood!" The other was a patriotic vision of a great nation flourishing under the motto "Liberty and Union, now and forever, one and inseparable."

Though sympathetic to states' rights and distrustful of the federal government, Jackson rejected the idea of state sovereignty. He strongly believed that sovereignty rested with the people. Deeply loyal to the Union, he shared Webster's dread of nullification. Soon after the Webster-Hayne debate, the president made his position clear at a Jefferson Day dinner with the toast "Our Federal Union, it must and shall be preserved." Vice President Calhoun, when his turn came, toasted "The Federal Union—next to our liberty the most dear." Thus Calhoun revealed his adherence to states' rights. Calhoun and Jackson grew apart, and Jackson looked to Secretary of State Martin Van Buren, not Calhoun, as his successor.

Nullification Crisis

Tensions did not subside when Congress passed a new tariff in 1832 reducing some duties but retaining high taxes on imported iron, cottons, and woolens. Though a majority of southern representatives supported the new tariff, South Carolinians refused to go along. In their eyes, the constitutional right to control their own destiny had been sacrificed to the demands of northern industrialists. More than the duties, they feared that the act could set a precedent for congressional legislation on slavery. In November 1832 a South Carolina state convention nullified both tariffs, making it unlawful for federal officials to collect duties in the state.

Old Hickory was quick to respond. Privately he threatened to invade South Carolina and hang Vice President Calhoun; publicly he took measured steps. In December Jackson issued a proclamation opposing nullification. He moved troops to federal forts in South Carolina and prepared U.S. marshals to collect the required duties. At Jackson's request, Congress passed the Force Act, which gave the president authority to call up troops but also offered a way to avoid using force by collecting duties before foreign ships reached Charleston's harbor. At the same time, Jackson extended an olive branch by recommending tariff reductions.

Calhoun, disturbed by South Carolina's drift toward separatism, resigned as vice president and soon won election to represent South Carolina in the U.S. Senate. There he worked with Henry Clay to draw up the compromise Tariff of 1833. Quickly passed by Congress and signed by the president, the new tariff lengthened the list of duty-free items and reduced duties over nine years. Satisfied, South Carolina's convention repealed its nullification law. In a final salvo, it also nullified Jackson's Force Act. Jackson ignored the gesture.

Nullification offered a genuine debate on the nature and principles of the republic. Each side believed it was upholding the Constitution. Both sides felt they were opposing special privilege and subversion of republican values. South Carolina opposed the tyranny of the federal government and manufacturers who sought tariff protection. Jackson fought the tyranny of South Carolina, whose refusal to bow to federal authority threatened to split the republic. Neither side won a clear victory, though both claimed to have done so. It took another crisis, over a central bank, to define the powers of the federal government more clearly.

At stake was survival of the Second Bank of the United States, whose twenty-year charter was scheduled to expire in 1836. Like its predecessor, the bank served as a depository for federal funds and was an important source of credit for businesses. Its bank notes circulated as currency throughout the country; they could be readily exchanged for gold, and the federal government accepted them as payment in all transactions. Through its twenty-five branch offices, the Second Bank acted as a clearing-house for state banks, keeping them honest by refusing to accept bank notes of any state bank without sufficient gold in reserve. Most state banks resented the central bank's police role: by presenting a state bank's notes for redemption all at once, the Second Bank could easily ruin a state bank. Moreover, with less money in reserve, state banks found themselves unable to compete on an equal footing with the Second Bank.

Second Bank of the United States

Many state governments also regarded the national bank as unresponsive to local needs. Westerners and urban workers remembered with bitterness the bank's conservative credit policies during the Panic of 1819 (see page 249). As a private, profit-making institution, its policies reflected the interest of its owners, especially its president, Nicholas Biddle, who controlled the bank completely. An eastern patrician, Biddle symbolized all that westerners found wrong with the bank.

Rechartering was a volatile issue in the 1832 presidential campaign. The bank's charter was valid until 1836, but Henry Clay, the National Republican presidential candidate, persuaded Biddle to ask Congress to approve an early rechartering. This strategy was designed to pressure Jackson to sign the rechartering bill or to override his veto of it. The plan backfired, however. The president vetoed the bill, and the Senate failed to override. Jackson's veto message was an emotional attack on the undemocratic nature of the bank. "It is to be regretted," he wrote, "that the rich and powerful too often bend the acts of government to their selfish purposes."

The bank thus became the prime issue in the presidential campaign of 1832, with Jackson denouncing special privilege and economic power. With every state but South Carolina now choosing electors by popular vote, the Jacksonians used their party organization to mobilize voters by advertising the presidential election as the focal point of the political system. When the Antimasons adopted a party platform, the first in the nation's history, the Democrats and the National Republicans quickly followed suit. The Democratic convention nominated Jackson and Martin Van Buren, Jackson's first secretary of state and then American minister to Great Britain; the National Republican convention selected Clay and John Sergeant. South Carolina nominated its own candidate, John Floyd. Jackson was reelected easily in a Democratic Party triumph.

After his sweeping victory and second inauguration, Jackson moved in 1833 to dismantle the Second Bank of the United States. He deposited federal funds in state-chartered banks (critics called them his "pet banks"). Without federal money, the Second Bank shriveled. When its federal charter expired in 1836, it became just another Pennsylvania-chartered private bank. Five years later it closed its doors.

Jackson's Second Term

In conjunction with the demise of the Bank of the United States, Congress passed the Deposit Act of 1836 with Jackson's support. The act authorized the secretary of the treasury to designate one bank in each state and territory to provide the services formerly performed by the Bank of the United States. The act provided that the federal surplus in excess of $5 million be distributed to the states as interest-free loans beginning in 1837. These loans were never repaid—a fitting Jacksonian restraint on the federal purse.

The surplus had derived from wholesale speculation in public lands: speculators borrowed money to purchase public land, used the land as collateral for credit to buy additional acreage, and repeated the cycle. Between 1834 and 1836 federal receipts from land sales rose from $5 million to $25 million. The state banks providing the loans issued bank notes. Jackson, an opponent of paper money, feared that the speculative craze threatened the stability of state banks and undermined the interests of settlers, who could not compete with speculators in bidding for the best land.

Specie Circular

In keeping with his hard-money instincts and opposition to paper currency, the president ordered Treasury Secretary Levi Woodbury to issue the Specie Circular. It provided that after August 1836 only

An 1832 anti-Jackson cartoon depicts Andrew Jackson and three rivals playing a game of brag, a bluffing card game. The stakes: the 1832 election. Henry Clay, on the left, reveals what the cartoonist presents as the winning hand: the cards for "U.S. Bank," "Internal Improvements," and "Domestic Manufactures." In the foreground, John C. Calhoun folds his hand of "Nullification" and "Anti-Tariff," which cannot match Clay's. Former Attorney General William Wirt "bolts" with his "Anti-Masonic" card, a loser. A decrepit Jackson has the weakest cards: "Intrigue," "Corruption," and "Imbecility," which have no value once his bluff is called. In the election, however, Jackson followed through in bragging of strength; he easily won reelection.   (Library Company of Philadelphia)

specie—gold or silver—or Virginia scrip (paper money) would be accepted as payment for land. By ending credit sales, it significantly reduced purchases of public land and the federal budget surplus. As a result the government suspended payments to the states soon after they began.

The policy was a disaster. Although federal land sales were sharply reduced, speculation continued as available land for sale became scarce. The increased demand for specie squeezed banks, and many suspended the redemption of bank notes for specie. Credit contracted further as banks issued fewer notes and made fewer loans. Jackson aggravated the situation by instinctively pursuing a tight money policy. More important, the Specie Circular was similar to a bill defeated in the Senate just three months earlier. Jackson's opponents thus saw King Andrew at work. In the waning days of Jackson's administration, Congress voted to repeal the circular, but the president pocket-vetoed the bill by holding it unsigned until Congress adjourned. Finally in mid-1838, a joint resolution of Congress overturned the circular. Restrictions on land sales ended, but the speculative fervor was over.

From George Washington to John Quincy Adams, the first six presidents had vetoed nine bills; Jackson alone vetoed twelve. Previous presidents believed that vetoes were justified only on constitutional grounds, but Jackson considered policy disagreement legitimate grounds as well. He made the veto an effective weapon for controlling Congress, since representatives and senators had to consider the possibility of a presidential veto in their deliberations on any bill. In effect, Jackson made the executive for the first time a rival branch of government, equal in power to Congress.

Use of the Veto

The Whig Challenge and the Second Party System

 Most historians view the 1830s and 1840s as an age of reform and popularly based political parties. Only when the passions of reformers and abolitionists spilled over into politics did party differences become paramount and party loyalties solidify. For the first time in American history, grassroots political groups, organized from the bottom up, set the tone of political life. And both parties were national, drawing voters and winning counties in every region.

Opponents of the Democrats, including remnants of the National Republican Party, found shelter under a common umbrella, the Whig Party, in the 1830s. Resentful of Jackson's domination of Congress, the Whigs borrowed the name of the British party that had opposed the tyranny of Hanoverian monarchs in the eighteenth century. From 1834 through the 1840s, the Whigs and the Democrats competed on a nearly equal footing. They fought at the city, county, state, and national levels and achieved a stability previously unknown in American politics. The political competition of this period—known as the second party system—was more intense and well organized than that of the first party system of Democratic-Republicans versus Federalists.

Reform and the party system changed politics. As political participation broadened, the electoral process opened up. By the 1830s only a handful of states significantly restricted adult white male suffrage. Some even allowed immigrants who had taken out citizenship papers to vote. Hotly contested elections further stimulated public interest in politics. The net effect was a sharp increase in the number of votes cast in presidential elections. Between 1824 and 1828 that number increased threefold, from 360,000 to over 1.1 million. In 1840, 2.4 million men cast votes. The proportion of eligible voters who cast ballots also increased, from about 27 percent in 1824 to more than 80 percent in 1840.

Increasingly the parties diverged. Whigs favored economic expansion through an activist government, Democrats through limited central government. Whigs supported corporate charters, a national bank, and paper currency; Democrats were opposed to all three. Whigs also favored more humanitarian reforms than did Democrats, including public schools, abolition of capital

Whigs and Reformers

punishment, prison and asylum reform, and temperance. Whigs were more optimistic than Democrats, generally speaking, and more enterprising. They did not object to helping a specific group if doing so would promote the general welfare. The chartering of corporations, they argued, expanded economic opportunity for everyone, laborers and farmers alike. Democrats, distrustful of concentrated economic power and of moral and economic coercion, held fast to the Jeffersonian principle of limited government.

Religion and ethnicity, not economics and class, most influenced party affiliation. The Whigs' support for energetic government and humanitarian and moral reform won the favor of evangelical Protestants, especially those involved in religious revival. Methodists and Baptists were overwhelmingly Whigs, as were the small number of free black voters. Democrats, by contrast, tended to be foreign-born Catholics and nonevangelical Protestants, both of whom preferred to keep religion and politics separate.

The Whig Party was the vehicle of revivalist Protestantism. In many locales the membership rolls of reform societies overlapped those of the party. Indeed, Whigs practiced a kind of political revivalism. Their rallies resembled camp meetings; in their speeches they employed pulpit rhetoric; their programs embodied the perfectionist beliefs of reformers. This potent blend of religion and politics—"intimately united" in America, according to Tocqueville—greatly intensified political loyalties.

In their appeal to evangelicals, Whigs alienated members of other faiths. The evangelicals' ideal Christian state had no room for Catholics, Mormons, Unitarians, Universalists, or religious freethinkers. Those groups opposed Sabbath laws and temperance legislation in particular and state interference in moral and religious questions in general. As a result, more than 95 percent of Irish Catholics, 90 percent of Reformed Dutch, and 80 percent of German Catholics voted Democratic.

Vice President Martin Van Buren, handpicked by Jackson, headed the Democratic ticket in the 1836 presidential election. Van Buren was a shrewd politician who had built a political machine—the Albany Regency—in New York and then left to join Jackson's cabinet in 1829. Having helped found the Democratic Party, Van Buren was a professional politician; he made his career in party politics.

Election of 1836

Because the Whigs in 1836 had not yet coalesced into a national party, they entered three sectional candidates: Daniel Webster of New England, Hugh White of the South, and William Henry Harrison of the West. By splintering the vote, they hoped to throw the election into the House of Representatives. Van Buren, however, comfortably captured the electoral college even though he had only a 25,000-vote edge out of a total of 1.5 million votes cast. No vice-presidential candidate received a majority of electoral votes, and for the only time in American history the Senate decided a vice-presidential race, selecting Democratic candidate Richard M. Johnson of Kentucky.

Van Buren and Hard Times

Van Buren took office just weeks before the American credit system collapsed. In response to the impact of the Specie Circular, New York banks stopped redeeming paper currency with gold in mid-1837. Soon all banks suspended payments in hard coin. Thus began a downward economic spiral that curtailed bank loans and strangled business confidence. Credit contraction made things worse; after a brief recovery, hard times persisted from 1839 until 1843.

Ill advisedly, Van Buren followed Jackson's hard-money policies. He cut federal spending, which caused prices to drop further, and he opposed a national bank, which would have expanded credit. Even worse, the president proposed a new regional treasury system for government deposits. The proposed treasury branches would accept and pay out only gold and silver coin; they would not accept paper currency or checks drawn on state banks. Van Buren's independent treasury bill became law in 1840. By increasing the demand for hard coin, it deprived banks of gold and further accelerated price deflation. Whigs and Democrats faced off at the state level over these issues. Whigs favored new banks, more paper currency, and readily available corporate and bank charters. As the party of hard money, Democrats favored eliminating paper currency altogether. Increasingly the Democrats became distrustful even of state banks, and by the mid-1840s a majority favored eliminating all bank corporations.

With the nation in the grip of hard times, the Whigs prepared confidently for the election of 1840.

William Henry Harrison and the Election of 1840

Their strategy was simple: hold on to loyal supporters and win over independents by blaming hard times on the Democrats. The Whigs rallied behind a military hero, General William Henry Harrison, conqueror of the Shawnees at Tippecanoe

Creek in 1811 (see page 238). The Democrats renominated President Van Buren at a somber convention.

Harrison, or "Old Tippecanoe," and his running mate, John Tyler of Virginia, ran a "log cabin and hard cider" campaign—a people's crusade—against the aristocratic president in "the Palace." Though descended from a Virginia plantation family, Harrison presented himself as an ordinary farmer. The Whigs wooed supporters and independents alike with huge rallies, parades, songs, posters, campaign mementos, and a party newspaper, *The Log Cabin*. Harrison took a position above the issues, earning himself the nickname "General Mum," but party hacks bluntly blamed the hard times on the Democrats. In a huge turnout, 80 percent of eligible voters cast ballots. Harrison won the popular vote by a narrow margin but swept the electoral college by 234 to 60.

Immediately after taking office in 1841, President Harrison convened a special session of Congress to pass the Whig program: repeal of the independent treasury system, a new national bank, and a higher protective tariff. But the sixty-eight-year-old Harrison caught pneumonia and died within a month of his inauguration. His successor, John Tyler, was a former Democrat who had left the party to protest Jackson's nullification proclamation.

In office, Tyler turned out to be more of a Democrat than a Whig. As critical of the Whigs' economic nationalism as he had been of Jackson's use of executive power, Tyler consistently opposed his own party's congressional agenda. He repeatedly vetoed Henry Clay's protective tariffs, internal improvements, and bills aimed at reviving the Bank of the United States. The only important measures that became law during his term were repeal of the independent treasury system and passage of a higher tariff. Two days after Tyler's second veto of a bank bill, the entire cabinet except Secretary of State Daniel Webster resigned; Webster, busy negotiating a new treaty with Great Britain, left shortly thereafter. Tyler became a president without a party, and the Whigs lost the presidency without losing an election. Disgusted Whigs referred to Tyler as "His Accidency."

Anglo-American Tensions

Hard times in the late 1830s and early 1840s deflected attention from a renewal of Anglo-American tensions that had multiple sources: northern commercial rivalry with Britain, the default of state governments and corporations on British-held debts during the Panic of 1837, rebellion in Canada, boundary disputes, southern

Using techniques that look familiar to politicians today, General William Henry Harrison in 1840 ran a "log cabin and hard cider" campaign against Jackson's heir, President Martin Van Buren. The campaign handkerchief shows Harrison welcoming two of his comrades to his log cabin, with a barrel of cider outside. *The Log Cabin,* a newspaper edited by Horace Greeley, was the voice of the Harrison campaign, and it reached eighty thousand partisans.   (Handkerchief: © Collection of The New-York Historical Society; Newspaper: Division of Political History, Smithsonian Institution, Washington, D.C.)

alarm over West Indian emancipation, and American expansionism.

One of the most troublesome disputes arose from the *Caroline* affair. A U.S. citizen, Amos Durfee, had been killed when Canadian militia set afire the privately owned steamer *Caroline* in the Niagara River. (The *Caroline* had supported an unsuccessful uprising against Great Britain in 1837.) Britain refused to apologize, and American newspapers called for revenge. Fearing that popular support for the Canadian rebels would ignite war, President Van Buren posted troops at the border to discourage raids. Tensions subsided in late 1840 when Alexander McLeod, a Canadian deputy sheriff, was arrested in New York for the murder of Durfee. McLeod eventually was acquitted. Had he been found guilty and executed, Lord Palmerston, the British foreign minister, might have sought war.

At almost the same time an old border dispute between Maine and New Brunswick disrupted Anglo-American relations. Great Britain had accepted an 1831 arbitration decision fixing a new boundary, but the U.S. Senate rejected it. Thus when Canadian lumbermen cut trees in the disputed region in the winter of 1838–1839, the citizens of Maine attempted to expel them. The lumbermen captured the Maine land agent and posse, both sides mobilized their militias, and Congress authorized a call-up of fifty thousand men. Ultimately, no blood was spilled. General Winfield Scott, who had patrolled the border during the *Caroline* affair, was dispatched to Aroostook, Maine, where he arranged a truce. The two sides compromised on their conflicting land claims in the Webster-Ashburton Treaty (1842).

These border disputes with Great Britain prefigured the conflicts that were to erupt in the 1840s over the expansion of the United States. With Tyler's succession to power in 1841 and James K. Polk's Democratic victory in the presidential election of 1844, federal activism in the domestic sphere ended for the rest of the decade, as attention turned to territorial expansion. Reform, however, was not dead. Its passions would resurface before the decade was over in the debate about slavery in the territories.

Manifest Destiny and Expansionism

 The belief that American expansion westward and southward was inevitable, just, and divinely ordained was first labeled manifest destiny by John L. O'Sullivan, editor of the *United States Magazine and Domestic Review*. The annexation of Texas, O'Sullivan wrote in 1845, was "the fulfillment of our manifest destiny to overspread the continent allotted by Providence for the free development of our yearly multiplying millions." Armed with such sentiments, expansionism reached a new fervor in the 1840s.

Since colonial days Americans had hungered for more land. Acquisition of the Louisiana Territory (1803) and Florida (1819) had set the process in motion (see Map 9.1 on page 223). As the proportion of Americans living west of the Appalachians grew from one-quarter to one-half between 1830 and 1860, both national parties joined the popular clamor for expansion. Agrarian Democrats sought western land to balance urbanization. Enterprising Whigs looked to the new commercial opportunities the West offered. Southerners envisioned the extension of slavery and more slave states.

Fierce national pride spurred the quest for land. Subdued during hard times, it reasserted itself after 1843 when the economy recovered. Americans were convinced that theirs was the greatest country on earth, with a special role to play in the world. As reform sought to perfect American society, so too expansionism promised to extend the benefits of America's republican system of government to the unfortunate and the inferior.

In part, racism contributed to manifest destiny as well. The impulse to colonize and develop the West was based on the belief that Euro-Americans could use the land more productively than Native Americans or Hispanics. Euro-Americans viewed Native Americans and Hispanics as inferior peoples, best controlled or conquered. Thus the same racial attitudes that justified discrimination against black people and slavery supported expansion in the West.

The desire to secure the nation from perceived external threats also fed expansionist fever. The internal enemies of the 1830s—banks, corporations, paper cur-

rency, alcohol—seemed pale in comparison to the opportunities Americans saw along their borders in the 1840s. Expansion, some believed, was necessary to preserve American independence.

Among the long-standing objectives of expansionists was Texas, which in addition to present-day Texas

Republic of Texas

included parts of Oklahoma, Kansas, Colorado, Wyoming, and New Mexico (see Map 11.3). After winning its independence from Spain in 1821, Mexico encouraged the development of its remote northern province, offering large tracts of land virtually free to U.S. settlers called *empresarios*. The settlers in turn agreed to become Mexican citizens, adopt the Catholic religion, and bring hundreds of American families into the area. Moses and Stephen Austin, who had helped to formulate the policy, responded eagerly.

By 1835 thirty-five thousand Americans, including many slaveholders, lived in Texas. As the new settlers' numbers and power grew, they tended to ignore their commitments to the Mexican government. In response, the dictatorship of General Antonio López de Santa Anna tightened control over the region. In turn,

Texans believed that their war for independence paralleled the Revolutionary War. The lady of liberty on this banner, carried by Texans in 1836, brings to mind similar images that stirred patriots during the American Revolution. (Archives Division, Texas State Library)

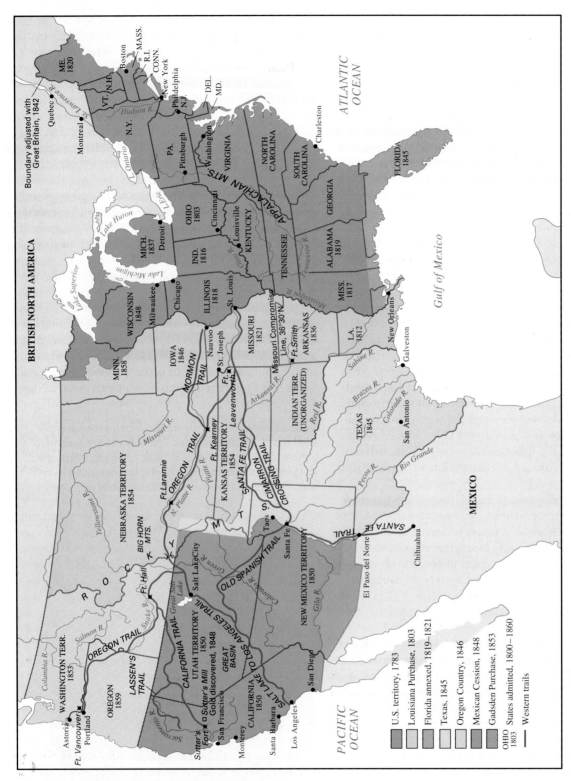

Map 11.3 Westward Expansion, 1800–1860 Through exploration, purchase, war, and treaty, the United States became a continental nation, stretching from the Atlantic to the Pacific.

the Anglo immigrants and *Tejanos*—Mexicans living in Texas—rebelled. At the Alamo mission in San Antonio in 1836, fewer than two hundred Texans made a heroic but unsuccessful stand against three thousand Mexicans under General Santa Anna. "Remember the Alamo" became the Texans' rallying cry. By the end of the year the Texans had won independence, delighting most Americans. Some saw the victory as a triumph of Protestants over Catholic Mexico; others cheered that proslavery Texans had defeated antislavery Mexicans.

Texas established the independent Lone Star Republic but soon sought annexation to the United States. Sam Houston, president of the Texas republic, opened negotiations with Washington, but the issue quickly became politically explosive. Southerners favored annexing proslavery Texas; abolitionists, many northerners, and most Whigs opposed annexation. In recognition of the political dangers, President Jackson reneged on his promise to recognize Texas, and President Van Buren ignored annexation. Rebuffed by the United States, Texans talked about closer ties with the British and extending their republic to the Pacific coast. With Britain controlling Canada, the prospect of a rival republic to the south caused some Americans to fear encirclement. If Texas reached the ocean and became an English ally, would not American independence be threatened?

President Tyler, committed to expansion, pushed for annexation. Eager to gain the 1844 Democratic nomination, Tyler hoped his position would build a political base in the South. Southerners also pressed for annexation; they lobbied former president Jackson, who responded that the United States must have Texas, "peacefully if we can, forcibly if we must." But the Senate rejected annexation in 1844. A letter from Secretary of State Calhoun to the British minister, justifying annexation to protect slavery, so outraged senators that the treaty was defeated 16 to 35.

Just as southerners sought expansion to the Southwest, so northerners looked to the Northwest. "Oregon fever" struck thousands in 1841.

Oregon Fever

Lured by the glowing reports of missionaries who seemed as enthusiastic about the Northwest's riches and beauty as about conversion of Indians, migrants in wagon trains took to the Oregon Trail. Their enthusiasm was tempered by apprehension. Lavinia Porter feared that her husband did not have "the training to make a living on the plains of the West or the crossing of the continent in an ox team a successful venture." The 2,000-mile journey took six months or more, but within a few years five thousand settlers had arrived in the fertile Willamette valley south of the Columbia River.

Britain and the United States had jointly occupied the disputed Oregon Territory since the Convention of 1818 (see pages 246–247). Beginning with the administration of President John Quincy Adams, the United States had tried to fix the boundary at the 49th parallel, but Britain was determined to maintain access to Puget Sound and the Columbia River. Time only increased the American appetite. In 1843 a Cincinnati convention of expansionists demanded the entire Oregon Country for the United States, up to its northernmost border at latitude 54°40'. Soon "Fifty-four Forty or Fight" became the rallying cry of American expansionists.

Expansion into Oregon and rejection of the annexation of Texas, both favored by antislavery forces, worried southern leaders. Anxious

James K. Polk and the Election of 1844

about their diminishing ability to control the debate over slavery, they persuaded the 1844 Democratic convention to adopt a rule requiring the presidential nominee to receive two-thirds of the convention votes. In effect, the southern states acquired a veto, and they wielded it to block Van Buren as the nominee; most southerners objected to his opposition to slavery and Texas annexation. Instead, the party chose "Young Hickory," House Speaker James K. Polk, a hard-money Jacksonian, avid expansionist, and slaveholding cotton planter from Tennessee. The Whig leader Henry Clay, who opposed annexation, won his party's nomination handily. The Democratic platform called for occupation of the entire Oregon Territory and annexation of Texas. The Whigs, while favoring annexation, argued that the Democrats' belligerent nationalism would lead the nation into war with Great Britain or Mexico or both. Clay favored expansion through negotiation.

With a well-organized campaign, Polk and the Democrats won the election by 170 electoral votes to 105. (They won the popular vote by just 38,000 out of 2.7 million votes cast.) Polk won New York's 36 electoral votes by just 6,000 popular votes. Abolitionist James G. Birney, the Liberty Party candidate, had drawn almost 16,000 votes away from Clay, handing New York and the election to Polk. Abolitionist forces thus unwittingly brought about the choice of a slaveholder as president, but they viewed Polk as more moderate than Clay on slavery and thus the lesser of two evils.

An unknown artist depicted, in rich detail, the election campaign of 1844. A team of Polk supporters offers a campaign handbill to the seated voter. Passions were so high and party organization was so extensive that door-to-door politicking became the norm. (Courtesy, Nathan Liverant & Son)

Interpreting Polk's victory as a mandate for annexation, President Tyler proposed in his final days in office that Texas be admitted by joint resolution of Congress. The usual method of annexation, by treaty negotiation, required a two-thirds vote in the Senate—which expansionists clearly did not have, since there were sufficient opponents to slavery who would vote against annexation. Joint resolution required only a simple majority in each house. The resolution passed the House by 120 to 98 and the Senate by 27 to 25. Three days before leaving office, Tyler signed the measure. Mexico, which had never recognized Texas independence, immediately broke relations with the United States. In October the citizens of Texas ratified annexation, and Texas joined the Union in December 1845.

Summary

 Religion, reform, and expansionism shaped politics from 1824 through the 1840s. As the Second Great Awakening spread through villages and towns, the converts, especially women, organized to reform a rapidly changing society. Religion imbued men and women with zeal to right the wrongs of American society and the world. Reformers pursued perfectionism and republican virtue by battling with the evils of slavery, prostitution, and alcohol. As reformers, they sought to improve insane asylums and penitentiaries. In the process, women entered public arenas as advocates of reform. Two issues elicited particular intensity: the comet of Antimasonry and the smoldering fire of abolitionism. The passions that both aroused were so potent, and success so elusive, that Antimasons and abolitionists transformed their moral crusades into political movements. Women's rights and nationalism contributed to the brew, and the new mixture made politics far more important and critical than just voting at elections.

Reform remade politics and politics remade public discourse. So too did American nationalism and economic cycles. As did reformers, President Adams raised expectations about an expanded governmental role. The organized parties of the 1820s and the struggles between the National Republicans and the Democrats, then between the Democrats and the Whigs, stimulated even greater interest in campaigns and political issues. The Democrats, who rallied around Andrew Jackson, and Jackson's opponents, who found shelter under the Whig tent, competed almost equally for the loyalty of voters. Both parties built strong organizations that faced off in national and local elections. And both parties favored economic expansion. Their world-views, however, were fundamentally different. Whigs were more optimistic and favored greater centralized government initiative. Democrats harbored a deep-seated belief in limited government. The controversies over the Second Bank of the United States and nullification allowed Americans to debate the principles of the republic. Jackson, however, did not hesitate to use presidential authority, and his opponents called him King Andrew.

No less than reform and politics, American people and communities experienced dramatic change in this period. As the nation became larger and its inhabitants more diverse, its manifest destiny divided rather than united, for along with expanding territories went the issue of slavery.

LEGACY FOR A PEOPLE AND A NATION
The Bible Belt

Had an eighteenth-century visitor to North America asked for the Bible belt, she would have been directed to New England, whose colonies were all founded for religious purposes. Early southerners tended to be more secular than religious. By the 1830s, however, the South was the most churched region, and southerners were the most devout. The Second Great Awakening, beginning with the Cane Ridge revival in 1801, spread like wildfire through the South. By the 1830s more than half of whites and one-quarter of

black southerners had undergone a conversion experience, and religion and the South formed a common identity. Embracing the Bible as the revealed word of God, it became known as the Bible belt.

Religion helped define southern distinctiveness. Southern Protestant liturgy and cadences were as much African as European; thus southern and northern denominations grew apart. They formally separated in the 1840s when Southern Baptists and Methodists withdrew from the national organizations that had barred slaveowners from church offices. Presbyterians withdrew later. After the Civil War evangelical denominations remained divided in northern and southern organizations.

Southern religion maintained tradition and resisted modern ways. Protestantism dominated, making the South more religiously homogeneous than other regions. Mostly evangelical, southern religion emphasized conversion and a personal battle against sin. By the twentieth century, fundamentalism, which stressed a literal reading of the Bible, reinforced resistance to modernism. Yet southern Protestantism lost ground as a political force in opposing evolution and in alliances with nativist groups.

But evangelicalism rose again in the 1960s, especially after a Catholic—John F. Kennedy—won the Democratic nomination for president. Many evangelicals began to vote their religion, moving to the Republican Party, and in 1964 Republican Barry Goldwater won the Bible belt states, breaking up the solid Democratic block. His conservative rhetoric resonated with southerners concerned about desegregation and erosion of religious values. *Time* called 1976 the "Year of the Evangelical" when born-again Southern Baptist Jimmy Carter was elected president.

In the 1980s and 1990s the Bible belt became the base of mobilized evangelical political action led by the Moral Majority. Religious and cultural issues rallied southern evangelicals: defending the traditional family and advocating prayer in schools, and opposing abortion, the Equal Rights Amendment, and gay rights legislation. In their own eyes, fundamentalist evangelical Protestants were defending biblical principles.

Thus the revivals that began in Kentucky in 1801 have rippled in ever wider circles across the South for two centuries, shaping the distinctive southern blend of culture and politics.

For Further Reading, see page A-13 of the Appendix. For Web resources, go to http://college.hmco.com.

"I hope that things will get better," Anna Maria Klinger wrote from New York to her family in Württemberg, Germany, in March 1849. She felt "lonely and forlorn in a foreign land." Twenty-eight-year-old Anna Maria had crossed the Atlantic among strangers, but her religious faith kept her going. "The dear Lord is my shield and refuge," she wrote home.

Anna's passage to America had taken fifteen weeks, including seven docked in Plymouth, England, while the ship was fitted. Three other young women migrants to America proved unsuitable as traveling companions. They "started behaving so badly" with young men, Anna Maria wrote her parents, that "I got annoyed because I couldn't stand such loose behavior."

Her luck improved in New York. She quickly found work as a domestic servant with a German family at $4 a day. New York was so large, she reported in letters home, that she could not walk around it in one day. She was the first in her immediate family to come to America, though two cousins had preceded her years before. Soon after arriving in New York, she met her future husband, Franz Schano, a deserter from the Bavarian army. Over the next decade she and Schano brought five of her siblings to New York: Babett, Gottlieb, Katharina, Daniel, and finally in 1858 the youngest, Rosina.

Finding work could be difficult—Franz, a stone-cutter, was unemployed for a time—but teenagers like Babett and Katharina found jobs as servants. Babett, who came in 1852, adjusted quickly. She now called herself Barbara and adopted the New York custom of wearing a hat. "If I were to run into you," she wrote her parents, "none of you would recognize me with my hat on." With her earnings as a servant, first for an English family then for a French family, Barbara repaid her sister for her fare to America.

Within a year of Barbara's arrival, Franz wrote home that she had taken up with a young man whom "we could see from the start would not be to her advantage." They "tried everything to dissuade her, but to no use." She soon gave birth to a baby son, "for whom she has a father all right but no husband, and when we noticed that she was expecting, we urged him to marry her but then he said he had never promised to

In 1851 the *Cornelius Grinnell* brought Irish immigrants from Liverpool to New York. John A. Rolph's 1851 ink wash caught the families taking fresh air, a relief from the miserable conditions below deck. (© J. Welles Henderson Collection)

PEOPLE AND COMMUNITIES IN THE NORTH AND WEST 1830–1860

marry her and he wouldn't ever marry her." He provided a cash settlement of $80 to Barbara.

Anna Maria, assisted by Franz, guided the family, keeping them together by sheer force of will. But the siblings' lives diverged. In 1855 Anna Maria and Franz moved to Albany, where Franz opened his own business and they bought a house for $1,000. Barbara went west, leaving her son with Anna Maria and Franz. Settled in Indiana, married, and living in a log cabin on a 40-acre homestead, Barbara complained that rural Indiana was boring. In 1861 her son joined her. Widowed and remarried again, she raised seven "Christian children" on her Indiana farm.

In 1860 Franz Schano died of consumption. Thirteen months later Anna Maria married Adam Plantz, a Prussian-born blacksmith; he, too, died of consumption only five weeks after. Then brother Gottlieb assumed the role of head of the family. Gottlieb and Daniel settled in Albany near Anna Maria and rode the roller coaster of the economy, prospering in good times, unemployed in hard times. Gottlieb ran a saloon, lost it, then worked in a piano factory and later as a wood carver. Daniel worked as a teamster. Eventually, they lost touch with two of their sisters. After Katharina, a widow, married a prosperous New York grocer, they no longer heard from her. They also lost contact with Rosina, who had moved to Canada. Years later they heard she was living again in New York and had "a whole brood of children" with her tinsmith husband.

The Klingers represented both the old values of traditional culture and the new values of the market system. Anna Maria worked hard, saved money, and found success in Albany even though widowhood twice threatened her security. Barbara, an unwed mother, lived a hardscrabble life. She reestablished herself 700 miles from New York, eventually finding peace in a German American rural community. Ambitious Katharina spent most of her income on herself, saving very little; her siblings complained of her selfishness. Even after years in the United States, the Klinger siblings were only partially Americanized. They always lived in German neighborhoods, and they socialized almost exclusively with family and fellow immigrants from Württemberg. Despite jealousies and conflicts, they helped one another and regularly sent money to their parents.

The Klinger family's experiences were similar to those of many immigrants. From the 1830s through the 1850s, millions of Europeans arrived on America's shores. Immigration added to the rapidly growing population and transformed the nation's character.

Within large cities and in the countryside, whole districts became enclaves of ethnic and religious groups.

What it meant to be an American was obviously changing. The Revolution and early nation building diminished as sources of American identity. European immigrants, slaves, free people of color, Hispanics, and Native Americans had cultural traditions different from those of the American colonial past. Increasingly some white Americans came to see the differences as racial rather than cultural. Free people of color in the North established the institutions and communities that would be the basis of modern African American life, but they found themselves as the black "other," racial outsiders like Hispanics in the Southwest. Immigrants, too, experienced antipathy. White native-born Americans rioted against them. In a society growing ever more diverse and complex, conflict became common.

The market economy both energized and accentuated the differences among Americans. In the nation's cities, opulent mansions rose within sight of notorious slums, and both wealth and poverty reached extremes unknown in agrarian communities. As in the past, Americans sought community in their neighborhoods, not in the nation, but ethnic background, race, religion, and class divided Americans. Farm families attempted to maintain cohesive, rural villages, while utopians and groups like the Mormons sought to create self-governing communal havens.

The market economy altered family life too. With the growth of commerce and industry, the home began to lose its function as a workplace. Goods formerly made at home were now mass-manufactured in factories and bought in stores. Public schools took over much of the family's traditional role as prime educator. Leisure, too, became a commodity to be purchased by those who could afford it. Families shrank in size, and more people lived outside family units. In the North and West the market economy, urban growth, and immigration challenged economic and social conventions. ■

Country Life

 Rural life changed significantly in the first half of the nineteenth century. Established rural communities lost population as families went west in search of more fertile and cheaper land. New communities in the West arose almost overnight, linked by the new transportation networks to the markets of the East. European immigrants and free people of color from the East and

IMPORTANT EVENTS

1827 *Freedom's Journal*, first African American newspaper, appears

1830 Smith founds Mormon Church
First National Negro Convention

1830s–50s Urban riots commonplace

1832 Rice debuts in New York minstrel show

1835 Arkansas passes first women's property law

1837 Emerson delivers "The American Scholar" address
Boston employs paid policemen

1837–48 Mann heads the Massachusetts Board of Education

1838 Mormons driven out of Missouri

1841–47 Brook Farm combines spirituality, work, and play in a utopian rural community

1842 Knickerbocker baseball club formed

1844 Nativist riots peak in Philadelphia
Smith brothers murdered in Illinois

1845 Irish potato blight begins
Narrative of the Life of Frederick Douglass appears

1846–47 Mormon trek to the Great Salt Lake

1847–57 Immigration at peak pre–Civil War levels

1848 Abortive revolution in German states
U.S. acquires Alta California in Treaty of Guadalupe Hidalgo
Gold discovered in California

1849 California gold rush transforms the West Coast

1852 Stowe's *Uncle Tom's Cabin* published

1854 Railroad reaches the Mississippi River
Large-scale Chinese immigration begins

1855 New York establishes Castle Garden as immigrant center

Upper South joined the population stream seeking farmland in the prairies. Religious fervor following from the Second Great Awakening inspired some to seek spiritual regeneration, rather than cash-crop profits, through the establishment of utopian communities.

In the 1850s, western settlement, technological improvements, competition, economic recovery, and a desire for national unity prompted development of regional and, eventually, national rail networks. By 1853 rail lines linked Chicago to eastern cities, and a year later track reached the Mississippi River. By 1860 rails stretched as far west as St. Joseph, Missouri, as railroad track tripled during the 1850s, reaching 30,600 miles in 1860.

Railroads

The farm village, with its churches, post office, general store, railroad or wagon depot, and tavern, remained the center of rural life and linked farmers with the world. Communal values still ruled. Families gathered on one another's farms to accomplish as a community what they could not manage individually. Barn-raisings regularly brought people together. A farm family with the help of an itinerant carpenter would prepare the walls.

Farm Communities

The neighbors would come by buggy to help the family raise walls into position and build a roof. Afterward everyone celebrated with a hearty communal feast and sang, danced, and played games. They might compete in foot races, wrestling, or marksmanship, and on occasion they raced horses. Similar gatherings took place at harvest time and on special occasions.

Farm men and women had active social lives. Men met frequently at general stores, weekly markets, and taverns, and hunted and fished together. Some women also attended market, especially those engaged in dairy farming. More typically they met at after-church dinners, prayer groups, sewing and corn-husking bees, and quilting parties. These were cherished opportunities to exchange experiences, thoughts, and spiritual support, and to swap letters, books, and news.

Irene Hardy, who grew up in rural Ohio in the 1840s, left a memoir of the gatherings she had attended as a girl. Fifty years later she recalled apple bees at which neighbors gathered to make apple butter or preserves. After the day's work, Hardy recalled, the elders gossiped while the youngsters joked and teased each other and flirted. "Then came supper, apple and pumpkin pies, cider, doughnuts, cakes, cold chicken and turkey," Hardy wrote,

Bees

The Lackawanna Valley (1855) by George Inness. Hired by the Lackawanna Railroad to paint a picture showing the company's new roundhouse at Scranton, in northeastern Pennsylvania, Inness combined landscape and locomotive technology into an organic whole. Industrialism, Inness seems to say, belonged to the American landscape; it would neither overpower nor obliterate the land.   (Gift of Mrs. Huttleston Rogers, © Board of Trustees, National Gallery of Art, Washington, D.C.)

"after which games, 'Forfeits,' 'Building a Bridge,' 'Snatchability,' even 'Blind Man's Bluff' and 'Pussy Wants a Corner.'" Traditional country bees had their town counterparts. Fredrika Bremer, a Swedish visitor, described a sewing bee in Cambridge, Massachusetts, in 1849, at which neighborhood women made clothes for "a family who had lost all their clothing by fire." Yet town bees were not the all-day family affairs of the countryside, and when the Hardy family moved to the town of Eaton, Ohio, Irene missed the country gatherings. The families of Eaton seldom held bees; instead, they purchased the goods country people made. They were wage earners and consumers, and the market economy shaped and controlled their daily lives.

Americans were increasingly conscious of such changes, and a few resisted, seeking to avoid the untamed growth of cities and, in utopian rural communities, to restore traditional work tasks and social cohesion. The religious ferment of the Second Great Awakening (see pages 279–280) promoted new religious communities as well. Virtually all these communities broke with tradition by experimenting with communal living, innovative (sometimes shocking) family arrangements, and more egalitarian gender roles in a cooperative rather than competitive environment.

The Shakers, the largest of the communal utopian experiments, reached their peak between 1820 and 1860. In those years six thousand members lived in twenty settlements in eight states. Shaker communities emphasized agriculture and handcrafts; most managed to become self-sufficient and profitable enterprises. Shaker furniture became famous for its simplicity, excellent construction, and beauty of design.

Shakers

The Shakers had been established in England a half-century earlier. Founder Ann Lee brought the phenomenon to America in 1774. Named for the way they danced at worship services, the Shakers believed that the end of the world was near and that sin entered the world through sexual intercourse. They considered existing churches too worldly and viewed the Shaker community as the instrument of salvation.

Though economically conservative, the Shakers were social radicals. They abolished individual families; each colony was one large family. They also elected women to lead. During its period of greatest growth, a woman, Lucy Wright, headed the Shaker ministry. The sect's practice of celibacy, however, led it to depend on enlisting new recruits, and its strict rules proved unattractive to many Americans, especially as interest in utopian communities faded.

The most successful communitarian group was the Church of Jesus Christ of Latter-day Saints, known

Mormon Community of Saints

as the Mormons. During the religious ferment of the 1820s, Joseph Smith, a young farmer in western New York, reported that an angel called Moroni had visited him and given him engraved divine gold plates. Smith published his revelations as the *Book of Mormon* and

organized a church in western New York in 1830. The next year they moved west to Ohio to build a "New Jerusalem" to await the second coming of Jesus.

Violence stalked the Mormons; angry mobs drove them from Ohio, and they settled in Missouri. Still, their rapid growth created antagonism, as did their claim that only Mormons would be saved upon Jesus' return. Anti-Mormons charged that Mormonism was fraudulent, a scam by Joseph Smith. Opponents also feared Mormon political power. In 1838 the governor of Missouri charged Smith with fomenting insurrections and gathered evidence to indict Smith and other leaders for treason.

Joseph Smith and his followers resettled in Nauvoo, Illinois. The state legislature gave them a city charter, which made them self-governing, and authorized a local militia. After 1841, when Smith introduced the practice of polygamy, allowing men to have several wives at once, opponents, who now included some ex-Mormons, became furious. In 1842 Smith became mayor, and this consolidation of religious and political power antagonized opponents further. They faced their worst fears when in 1843 Nauvoo petitioned the federal government to be a self-governing territory. Schisms within Mormonism added to the controversies. In 1844 the authorities indicted Smith and

Violence stalked the Mormons until they found safety in the Great Salt Lake valley. Here a Mormon family—a father, three wives, and five children—poses for a photographer in the 1850s in Salt Lake City. (Church of Jesus Christ of Latter-Day Saints)

others with plotting to murder their opponents, but the Nauvoo courts released them. Then Joseph and his brother Hyrum were arrested for treason and jailed in Carthage, Illinois. The militia from Warsaw, Nauvoo's neighbor, stormed the jail and killed the two brothers. The next year the Mormons began a trek westward to find security in the wilderness. They found a home in the Great Salt Lake valley, in unorganized territory. There, under Brigham Young, head of the Twelve Apostles (the Mormons' governing body), they established a patriarchal, cooperative "community of saints." They found in the distant desert West both religious freedom and political autonomy.

In Utah the Mormons distributed agricultural land according to family size. An extensive irrigation system, constructed by men who contributed their labor in proportion to the quantity of land they received and the amount of water they expected to use, transformed the arid valley into a rich oasis. As the colony developed, the church elders gained control of water, trade, industry, and eventually the territorial government of Utah.

Religious conviction fortified the Latter-day Saints to withstand persecution. The Mormons offered success and community in this world and salvation in the next to anyone who would join. Indeed, many recruits were poor and uneducated. To those who rejected existing churches, the Mormons also offered fellowship and religious certainty within a tight-knit society and cooperative economic system.

Not all utopian communities gravitated to the wilderness. The Brook Farm cooperative in West Roxbury, Massachusetts, near Boston, had a lasting impact although its achievements were more artistic than economic. Inspired by transcendentalism—the belief that the physical world is secondary to the spiritual realm, which human beings can know by ignoring custom and experience and relying instead on intuition—Brook Farm's members rejected materialism in favor of rural communalism, combining spirituality, manual labor, intellectual life, and play. Founded in 1841 by the Unitarian minister George Ripley, a literary critic and friend of transcendentalist lecturer and essayist Ralph Waldo Emerson, Brook Farm attracted farmers, craftsmen, and writers, among them the novelist Nathaniel Hawthorne. Indeed, the fame of Brook Farm rested on the intellectual achievements of its members. Its school drew students from outside the community, and its residents contributed regularly to the *Dial*, the leading

Brook Farm

transcendentalist journal. In 1845 Brook Farm's hundred members organized themselves into model phalanxes (working-living units) suggested by French utopian Charles Fourier. Rigid regimentation replaced individualism, and membership dropped. After a disastrous fire in 1846, the experiment collapsed in 1847.

Though short-lived, Brook Farm played a significant role in the flowering of a national literature. During these years Hawthorne, Emerson, and *Dial* editor Margaret Fuller joined Henry David Thoreau, Herman Melville, and others in a literary outpouring known today as the American Renaissance. In philosophical intensity and moral idealism, their work was both distinctively American and an outgrowth of the European romantic movement. Their themes were universal, their settings and characters American. Hawthorne, for instance, used Puritan New England as a backdrop, and Melville wrote of great spiritual quests as seafaring adventures.

The essayist Ralph Waldo Emerson was the prime mover of the American Renaissance and a pillar of the transcendental movement. Emerson had followed his father and grandfather into the ministry but quit his Boston Unitarian pulpit in 1831. After a two-year sojourn in Europe, he returned to lecture and write, preaching individualism and self-reliance. "We live in succession, in division, in parts, in particles," Emerson wrote. "We see the world piece by piece, as the sun, the moon, the animal, the tree; but the whole, of which these are the shining parts, is the soul." Intuitive experience of God is attainable, insisted Emerson, because "the Highest dwells" within every individual in the form of the "Over-soul." What gave Emerson's writings force was, for his times, a simple, direct prose. In his first book, *Nature* (1836), and in "The American Scholar" (1837), a Phi Beta Kappa address at Harvard, Emerson explored human nature and American culture. Widely admired, he influenced Thoreau, Fuller, Hawthorne, and other members of Brook Farm.

Ralph Waldo Emerson

Whether intellectual, spiritual, or economic in their origins, utopian communities can be seen as attempts to recapture the cohesiveness of traditional agricultural and artisan life in reaction to the competitive pressures of the market economy and urbanization. Utopians resembled Puritan perfectionists; like the Separatists of seventeenth-century New England (see page 49), they sought to begin anew in their own colonies.

The West

In the 1840s a trickling stream of migrants followed the Oregon Trail to the West Coast. Then, in 1848, gold was discovered in California. The next year a pioneer observed that the Oregon Trail "bore no evidence of having been much traveled." Traffic flowed south instead, and California became the new population center on the Pacific slope. One measure of this shift was the overland mail routes. In the 1840s the Oregon Trail had been the main communications link between the Midwest and the Pacific. Ten years later the post office routes terminated in California, not Oregon; in fact, in the 1850s there was no mail route north of Sacramento.

When the United States acquired Alta California from Mexico in the 1848 Treaty of Guadalupe Hidalgo

Discovery of Gold

(see page 364), the province was inhabited mostly by Indians, with some Mexicans living on large estates. A chain of small settlements surrounded military forts (*presidios*) and missions. That changed almost overnight after James Marshall, a carpenter, spotted gold particles in the millrace at Sutter's Mill (now Coloma, California, northwest of Sacramento) in January 1848. Word of the discovery spread and Californians rushed to scrabble for instant fortunes. When the military explorer John C. Frémont reached San Francisco five months later, he found that "all, or nearly all, its male inhabitants had gone to the mines." The town, "which a few months before was so busy and thriving, was then almost deserted."

By 1849 the news had sped around the world, and hundreds of thousands of fortune seekers, mostly

The discovery of gold in California brought tens of thousands to participate in "Nature's Great Lottery scheme." This daguerreotype captured a group of black and white miners sifting for gold traces at Spanish Flats in 1852 California. (California State Library)

young men, streamed in from Mexico, England, Germany, France, Ireland, and from all over the United States, including some African Americans. They mined the lodes and washed away the surface soil with hydraulic works, leaving the land unsuitable for anything after they abandoned it.

Gold mining seemed to offer instant riches, and indeed, some made fortunes. In 1848 a California male servant earned $2,000 mining for gold and returned to Monterey a rich man. Peter Brown, a black man from Ste. Genevieve, Missouri, went to California alone, as did most "forty-niners." He wrote his wife in 1851 that "California is the best country in the world to make money. It is also the best place for black folks on the globe." He had earned $300 in two months.

Most "forty-niners," however, never found enough gold to pay their expenses. "The stories you hear frequently in the States," one gold seeker wrote home, "are the most extravagant lies imaginable—the mines are a humbug." Another gold seeker called gold mining "Nature's Great Lottery scheme." Many found work in California's cities and agricultural districts more profitable. Meanwhile, enterprising merchants rushed to supply, feed, and clothe the new settlers. One such merchant was Levi Strauss, a German Jewish immigrant, whose tough mining pants found a ready market among the prospectors.

San Francisco, the former *presidio* and mission of Yerba Buena, had in 1848 been a small settlement of about a thousand Mexicans, Anglos, soldiers, friars, and Indians. As the West Coast gateway to the interior, it now became an instant city, ballooning to thirty-five thousand people in 1850. Ships bringing people and supplies continuously jammed the harbor. A French visitor in that year wrote, "At San Francisco, where fifteen months ago one found only a half dozen large cabins, one finds today a stock exchange, a theater, churches of all Christian cults, and a large number of quite beautiful homes."

The forty-niners had their eyes on gold nuggets, but they had to be fed. Thus began the great California agricultural boom. Farmers

Farming

preferred wheat; it required minimal investment, was easily planted, and offered a quick return at the end of a relatively short growing season. California farmers eagerly imported horse-drawn machines, since labor was scarce (and expensive). By the mid-1850s, California exported wheat and had become firmly linked, through commerce, to the rest of the United States. Farmers on the West Coast cleared the land and constructed log cabins. Success often depended on their access to water, and they sought to divert the streams and rivers of the West to irrigate their land.

In contrast to the Midwest, where family farms were the basic unit of production, in California men

Women Settlers

dominated mining, grazing, and large-scale wheat farming. Most men came alone, drawn by a sense of adventure and personal opportunity. Women who accompanied their husbands—only one-seventh of the travelers on the overland trails were women—experienced the migration differently. Their lives drastically changed as they left behind networks of friends and kin to journey, often with children, along an unknown and hazardous path to a strange environment. Yet in the West their domestic skills were in great demand. They received high fees for cooking, laundering, and sewing, and they ran boarding houses and hotels (men shunned domestic work).

City Life

When Anna Maria Klinger arrived in America in 1849, she first settled in New York City. She and other immigrants as well as migrants from New England and the Middle Atlantic states poured into New York and other cities in the 1830s, 1840s, and 1850s. Cities, especially northern ones, expanded geometrically. The nation's population increased during this period from 12.9 million to 31.4 million. Europeans spread westward, and small rural settlements quickly became towns. In 1830 the nation had only 23 cities with 10,000 or more people and only 7 with more than 25,000. By 1860, 93 towns exceeded 10,000, 35 towns had more than 25,000, and 9 exceeded 100,000 (see Map 12.1). The Northeast was most heavily urban, and the percentage of people living in urban areas there grew from 14 to 35 percent between 1830 and 1860.

Some cities became great metropolitan centers. By 1830 New York City had been the nation's most populous city and major commercial center for twenty years. At midcentury Baltimore and New Orleans dominated the South, and San Francisco was the leading West Coast city. In the Midwest, the new lake cities (Chicago, Detroit, and Cleveland) began to pass the frontier river cities (Cincinnati, Louisville, and Pittsburgh) founded a generation earlier. The largest cities of the North anchored a nationwide network linked by canals, roads, railroads, and the telegraph (see Chapter 10).

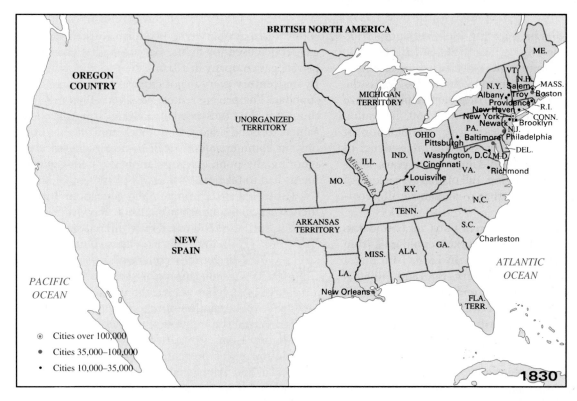

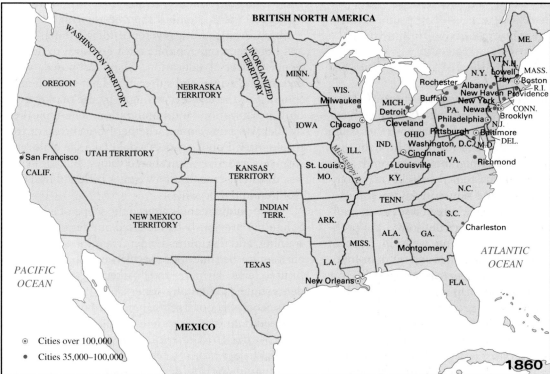

Map 12.1 Major American Cities in 1830 and 1860 The number of Americans who lived in cities increased rapidly between 1830 and 1860, and the number of large cities grew as well. In 1830 only New York City had a population exceeding one hundred thousand; thirty years later, eight more cities had surpassed that level.

As the nation's premier city, New York grew from 202,000 people in 1830 to over 814,000 in 1860. The

New York City

immigrant port city was mostly Irish and German by the 1850s. Across the East River, Brooklyn tripled in size between 1850 and 1860, becoming the nation's third-largest city, with a population of 279,000. Many people were short-term residents of the two cities; the majority did not stay ten years. Thus New York was ever changing, full of energy, reeking of sweat, horse dung, and garbage—and above all, teeming with people.

New York City literally had burst its boundaries around 1830. Until then New Yorkers could walk from one end to the other in an hour. In 1825, 14th Street was the city's northern boundary. By 1860, 400,000 people lived above that divide, and 42nd Street was the city's northern limit. Gone were the cow pastures, kitchen gardens, and orchards of the eighteenth century. George Templeton Strong, a New York lawyer, recorded in his diary in 1856 that he had attended a party on 37th Street: "It seems but the other day that thirty-seventh Street was an imaginary line running through a rural district and grazed over by cows." Mass transit made city expansion possible. Horse-drawn omnibuses appeared in New York in 1827, and the Harlem Railroad, completed in 1832, ran the length of Manhattan. By the 1850s all big cities had horse-drawn streetcars.

By modern standards nineteenth-century cities were disorderly, unsafe, and unhealthy. Expansion oc-

Urban Problems

curred so rapidly that few cities could handle the problems it brought. For example, migrants from rural areas were accustomed to relieving themselves outside and throwing refuse in any vacant area. In the city, such waste smelled, spread disease, and polluted water. New York City partially solved the problem in the 1840s by abandoning wells in favor of reservoir water piped into buildings and outdoor fountains. In some districts, scavengers and refuse collectors carted away garbage and human waste, but in much of the city it just rotted on the ground. Only one-quarter of New York City's streets had sewers by 1857.

New York and other cities lacked adequate taxing power to provide services for all. The best the city could do was to tax property adjoining new sewers, paved streets, and water mains. Thus new services and basic sanitation depended on residents' ability to pay. As a result, those most in need of services got them last. Another solution was to charter private compa-

nies to sell basic services. This plan worked well with gas service used for lights. Baltimore first chartered a private gas company in 1816; New York did so in 1842. By midcentury every major city was lit by a private gas supplier. The private sector, however, failed to supply the water the cities needed. Private firms lacked the capital to build adequate systems, and they laid pipe only in commercial and well-to-do residential areas, ignoring the poor. As population grew, city governments had to take over.

Cities led in offering public education. In 1800 there were no public schools outside New England; by

Horace Mann and Public Schools

1860 every state offered some public education to whites. Under Horace Mann, secretary of the state board of education from 1837 to 1848, Massachusetts led the way. It established a minimum school year of six months and formalized the training of teachers.

Mann was an evangelist for public education and school reform; his preaching on behalf of free, state-sponsored education changed schooling throughout the nation. "If we do not prepare children to become good citizens," Mann argued, "if we do not develop their capacities, . . . imbue their hearts with the love of truth and duty, and a reverence for all things sacred and holy, then our republic must go down to destruction." Universal education, Mann proposed, would end misery, crime, and suffering. Mann and others responded to the changes wrought by the market economy, urbanization, and immigration. The typical city dweller was a newcomer, whether from abroad or from the country. Public schools would take the children of strangers and give them shared values. But the system was distinctly racialized; few states included free black children in public schools.

Free public schools altered the scope of education. Schooling previously had focused on literacy, religious training, and discipline. Under Mann's leadership, the curriculum became more secular and appropriate for future clerks, farmers, and workers of America. Students studied geography, American history, arithmetic, and science. Schools retained moral education, but they dropped direct religious indoctrination. Nonetheless, primers like *McGuffey's Eclectic Readers* still used Protestant Scripture to teach children to accept their positions in society. A good child, *McGuffey* taught, does not envy the rich: "It is God who makes some poor and others rich." *McGuffey* further preached that "the rich have troubles which we know nothing of; and . . . the poor, if they are good, may be very happy."

Catholics, immigrants, blacks, and working-class people sought to control their own schools, but the state legislatures established secular statewide standards under Protestant educators. Catholics in New York responded by building their own educational system over the next half-century. When Los Angeles became a city in 1850, it attempted to establish bilingual Spanish-English instruction. Trained bilingual teachers could not be found, however, and when the schools opened, they offered only English instruction.

Towns and cities created new patterns of leisure as well as work. In rural society, as Irene Hardy recalled, both social activities and work often

Leisure took place at home. But in cities, dedicated spaces—streets, theaters, sports fields—constituted a social sphere where people could come together away from home. Through the sale of admission tickets or membership in associations, leisure became a commodity to be purchased. As the population became more diverse, leisure associations reflected ethnic, racial, and class divisions.

Traditional rural pursuits continued in the city. Men frequented taverns and spent spare time drinking and playing games of skill and strength—arm wrestling, ninepins, and pitching coins. Though city dwellers had less opportunity than their rural counterparts to ride and hunt, fishing remained popular among both men and women. Churches continued to serve as social centers and the Second Great Awakening increased women's involvement. Church clubs combined socializing with good works.

Americans not only played more but read more. Thanks to the expansion of public education, the vast majority of native-born white Ameri-

Reading cans were literate by the 1850s. In cities, urban newspapers and magazines proliferated and bookstores spread. Power printing presses and better transportation made possible wide distribution of books and periodicals. The religious press—of both traditional sects and dissenters—produced pamphlets, hymnals, Bibles, and religious newspapers. Americans also read secular publications. Newspapers and magazines—political organs, literary journals, and the voices of specialized groups like millworkers—abounded in the 1830s and after. In Brookfield, Massachusetts, in 1798, the mails brought one weekly newspaper; fifty years later, in 1848, fifty different newspapers and another fifty-five monthly magazines regularly arrived on subscribers' doorsteps.

Fiction and autobiographies competed with religious tracts as popular literature. Newspapers and magazines printed fiction, and bookstores and stationers in large cities sold novels and autobiographies. Frederick Douglass's powerful attack on slavery in the *Narrative of the Life of Frederick Douglass, an American Slave, Written by Himself* (1845) sold widely. Many popular novels, some written by women, often for women, were set in the home and upheld Christian values. They reflected growing gender differences in American society in their exploration of the divisions between home and work, between emotion and authority, and between sentimentality and power. Yet in their support of traditional female moral roles, they also can be read as a challenge to prevailing values. Although Susan Warner's *The Wide, Wide, Wide World* (1850), Nathaniel Hawthorne's *The House of the Seven Gables* (1851), and Fanny Fern's *Ruth Hall* (1855) did not challenge women's traditional domestic roles, they gave women a special moral bearing. In giving a positive cast to notions of community and republican virtue, they implicitly criticized the growing market economy. By the 1850s popular fiction circulated widely. Harriet Beecher Stowe's antislavery novel, *Uncle Tom's Cabin, or Life Among the Lowly* (1852), which appeared serially in 1851–1852, sold 300,000 copies in book form in its first year.

A major attraction, theater provided a social sphere in which both men and women gathered. A theater was often the second public

Theater building constructed in a town—after a church. Large cities boasted two or more theaters catering to different classes. In New York City the Park Theater enjoyed the patronage of the carriage trade, the Bowery drew the middle class, and the Chatham attracted workers. Some plays cut across class lines. Shakespeare was performed so often and appreciated so widely that even illiterate theatergoers knew his plays well. In the 1840s musical and dramatic presentations took on a more professional tone; like the Hutchinson Family (see pages 243–244), newly popular minstrel shows and traveling circuses offered carefully rehearsed routines. Dancing and music remained popular and took new forms, as in blackfaced minstrelsy.

By the 1840s hundreds of traveling minstrel troupes performed a complete evening's entertainment in American theaters. Minstrel acts

Minstrel Show had first appeared twenty or thirty years earlier, when white men, in burnt cork makeup, imitated African Americans in song, dance, and patter. In the early 1830s Thomas D. Rice of New York became famous for his role as Jim Crow, an old southern slave. In ill-fitting patched clothing and torn shoes, the blackface Rice shuffled, danced, and sang on stage. Another stereotyped image soon joined him: Zip Coon, a black Bowery Boy. What minstrels presented was a European version of African American culture.

Minstrelsy combined contradictory elements. At one level, performers masked as people of color told jokes mocking economic and political elites. At the same time the actors stereotyped black people by exaggerating physical features. They also presented blacks as sensual and lazy, thus stoking the fires of racism with ridicule. In blending black culture with white humor, African dance with English folktunes, and the African banjo with the Irish fiddle, minstrelsy seemed to represent the new urban potpourri. In portraying foils to sexual purity and work discipline, minstrelsy also constituted a resistance to the moral demands and factory regimens of the era. Ultimately, minstrelsy furthered growing racial divisions in the United States. The fictional representation of blacks on stage not only defined "blackness" but also defined "whiteness." Whiteness as a racial category took on meaning as laughing white audiences distinguished themselves from the black characters.

Increasingly, urban recreation and sports became more formal commodities to be purchased. One had to

Sports

buy a ticket to go to the theater, the circus, P. T. Barnum's American Museum in New York City, the racetrack, or the ballpark.

Spectator sports became increasingly popular. From 1831 enthusiasts could read the all-sports newspaper, *Spirit of the Times*. By 1849 news of boxing was so much in demand that a round-by-round account of a Maryland boxing match was telegraphed throughout the East. Horseracing, walking races, and, in the 1850s, baseball began to attract large urban male crowds.

Organized leagues replaced spontaneity. A group of Wall Street office workers formed the Knickerbocker Club in 1842 and in 1845 drew up rules for the game of baseball. Their rules were widely adopted and continue to serve as the basis for the game.

Ironically, public leisure soon developed a private dimension. Exclusive private clubs and associations

City Culture

arose to provide space and occasions for leisure set apart from the crowds and rowdiness of public events. As cities grew, their populations seemed

increasingly fragmented. Finding people similar to oneself required more of a conscious effort. The new associations that evolved served as a bulwark against the cultures of other groups—immigrants, migrants, blacks, and artisans. Middle- and upper-class New Yorkers who felt alienated in the city of their birth founded exclusive clubs. Some joined the Masonic order, which offered everything the bustling, chaotic city did not: an elaborate hierarchy, an orderly code of deference between ranks, harmony, and shared values. Members knew one another. Masons played a political role as well: they recruited officeholders and marched in the parades that were a regular feature of the city's political life.

Ethnic, racial, and religious groups seeking to socialize and preserve similar shared traditions formed their own clubs and societies. The Irish formed the Hibernian Society and the Sons of Erin; Germans brought Turnvereine physical-cultural clubs from across the Atlantic; Jews founded B'nai B'rith as a men's club; and African Americans had chapters of the Prince Hall Masons in their communities. Women, too, organized their own associations, ranging from social organizations to benevolent societies. Americans of all sorts—native- and foreign-born, black and white—also formed churches and church-associated clubs. Associations brought together like people, but they also formalized divisions among groups.

Divisions seemed to occur naturally on city streets. In the 1840s, a youth culture developed on the Bowery, one of New York's entertainment strips. In the evenings the lamp-lit promenade, lined with theaters, dance halls, and cafés, became an urban midway. Older New Yorkers feared the "Bowery boys and gals," whose ostentatious dress and behavior seemed threatening to them. Around 1847 artist Nicholino Calyo depicted three Bowery boys in a watercolor painting (see page 315). A Bowery boy had long hair, often greased into a roll. He wore a broad-brimmed black hat, an open shirt collar, a black frock coat that reached below the knee, and as much jewelry as he could afford. His swaggering gait, especially when he had a girlfriend on his arm, frightened many in the middle class. Equally disturbing to old New Yorkers were the young working women who strolled the Bowery. They came in groups to enjoy each other's company and to meet Bowery boys. Unlike more genteel ladies who wore modest veils or bonnets, Bowery "gals" drew attention to themselves with outlandish costumes and ornate hats.

Nicholino Calyo's watercolor *Soap-Locks, or Bowery Boys* (c. 1847) captured the bold body language and showy dress of the youths who controlled the sidewalks of the Bowery. (© Collection of The New-York Historical Society)

Much more than on the stage, racial, ethnic, and class divisions were played out on city streets. Most working people spent much of their lives outdoors; they worked in the streets as laborers, shopped in open markets, paraded on special occasions, and socialized in all these places. Young people courted, neighbors argued, and ethnic and racial groups defended their turf on the streets. Increasingly, urban streets served as a political arena as crowds formed to listen to speakers, to respond and to demonstrate, and sometimes to take mob action.

Economic, political, social, racial, and ethnic conflict erupted on city streets. In the 1830s riots became commonplace as professionals, merchants, craftsmen, and laborers vented their rage against political and economic rivals. "Gentlemen of property and standing," unnerved by antislavery proponents, sacked abolitionist and antislavery organizations, even murdering newspaper editor Elijah Lovejoy in Alton, Illinois, in 1837. In the 1840s "respectable" citizens drove the Mormons out of Missouri and Illinois. In Philadelphia native-born workers attacked Irish weavers in 1828, and whites and blacks fought on the docks in 1834 and 1835. Residents of

Urban Riots

North Philadelphia took to the streets continuously from 1840 to 1842 until the construction of a railroad through their neighborhood was abandoned. These disturbances came to a head in the Philadelphia riots of 1844, in which mostly Protestant skilled workers attacked Irish Catholics. Smaller cities, too, became battlegrounds as nativist riots peaked in the 1850s; Louisville, for instance, witnessed an anti-German riot in 1855. By 1840 more than 125 people had died in urban riots, and by 1860 fatalities exceeded 1,000.

As public disorder spread, Boston hired uniformed policemen in 1837 to supplement its part-time watchmen and constables, and New York in 1845 established a uniformed force. Nonetheless, middle-class city dwellers did not venture out alone at night. The police tried to control and suppress street activity, as did local ordinances that regulated street vendors. Local laws against vagrancy and disturbing the peace often were used against free blacks and immigrants. The continuing inflow of immigrants to the cities worsened social tensions by pitting groups against one other in the contest for jobs, housing, and street space. In the midst of so much noise, crime, and conflict, the lavish uptown residences of the very rich rose like an affront to those struggling to survive.

Extremes of Wealth

 The French nobleman Alexis de Tocqueville and other observers characterized the United States before the Civil War as primarily a place of equality and opportunity for white males. Tocqueville and his companion Gustave de Beaumont traveled 4,000 miles and visited all twenty-four states over a nine-month period in 1831 and 1832. Tocqueville opened *Democracy in America*, his classic analysis of the American people and nation, with this observation: "No novelty in the United States struck me more vividly during my stay there than the equality of conditions."

Tocqueville attributed American equality—the relative fluidity of the social order—to Americans' mobility and restlessness. Geographic mobility, he felt, offered people a chance to start anew regardless of where they came from or who they were. Wealth and family mattered little; a person could be known by deeds alone. Indeed, Americans seemed driven by an itch to move and ambition. "An American will build a house in which to pass his old age," Tocqueville wrote, "and sell it before the roof is on; he will plant a garden and rent it just as the trees are coming into bearing; he will clear a field and leave others to reap the harvest; he will take up a profession and leave it, settle in one place and soon go off elsewhere with his changing desires."

Others disagreed with the egalitarian view of American life. *New York Sun* publisher Moses Yale Beach believed a new aristocracy based on wealth and power was forming. Author of twelve editions of *Wealth* and *Biography of the Wealthy Citizens of New York City*, Beach listed 750 New Yorkers with assets of $100,000 or more in 1845. John Jacob Astor, with a fortune of $25 million, led the list of nineteen millionaires. Ten years later, Beach reported more than a thousand New Yorkers worth $100,000, among them twenty-eight millionaires. Combining gossip-column items with wild guesses at people's wealth, Beach's publications suggest the enormous wealth of New York's upper class. Tocqueville himself, sensitive to conflicting trends in American life, had described the new industrial wealth. The rich and well educated "come forward to exploit industries," Tocqueville wrote, and become "more and more like the administrators of a huge empire.... What is this if not an aristocracy?"

Wealth throughout the United States was becoming concentrated in the hands of a relatively small

"If Not an Aristocracy"

number of people. In New York City between 1828 and 1845, the richest 4 percent of the city's population increased their holdings from an estimated 63 percent to 80 percent of all individual wealth. Meanwhile, the holdings of many ordinary people virtually disappeared. In Brooklyn between 1810 and 1841, the share of wealth held by the bottom two-thirds of families decreased from 10 percent to almost nothing. By 1860 the top 5 percent of American families owned more than half of the nation's wealth, and the top 10 percent owned nearly three-quarters.

A cloud of uncertainty hovered over working men and women. Anxious that hard times were always imminent, many resented the competition of immigrants and goods produced by slave labor. They dreaded poverty, chronic illness, disability, old age, widowhood, and desertion. Women feared raising a family without a spouse. And they had good reason: few women could find a job that paid enough to support a family. Fear of poverty prompted the Klinger sisters, for instance, to marry again and again.

Urban Poverty

Poverty dogged the urban working class. Newly arrived immigrants, free blacks, the working poor, and thieves, beggars, and prostitutes eked out a living in urban slums. New York City's Five Points, a few blocks from City Hall, lacked running water and sewers and was notorious for its squalor. Dominated by the Old Brewery, which had been converted to housing in 1837, the neighborhood was predominantly immigrant Irish and recently freed black people. Contemporaries estimated that more than a thousand people lived in the Old Brewery's rooms, cellars, and subcellars. Throughout the city, workers' housing was at a premium. Houses built for two families often held four; tenements built for six families held twelve. Families took in lodgers to help pay the rent.

A world apart from Five Points and the people of the streets, though only a short walk away, lived the upper-class elite society of Philip Hone, one-time mayor of New York. Hone's diary, meticulously kept from 1826 until his death in 1851, records the life of an American aristocrat. On February 28, 1840, for instance, Hone attended a masked ball at the Fifth Avenue mansion of Henry Breevoort, Jr., and Laura Carson Breevoort. The ball began at the fashionable hour of 10 P.M., and the five hundred invited ladies and gentlemen wore costumes adorned with ermine and gold. For more than a week, Hone believed, the affair "occupied the minds of people of all stations,

The Urban Elite

A visible sign of urban poverty in the 1850s was the homeless and orphaned children, most of them immigrants, who wandered the streets of New York City. The Home for the Friendless Orphanage, at Twenty-ninth Street and Madison Avenue, provided shelter for some of the orphan girls. (© Collection of The New-York Historical Society)

ranks, and employments." Similar parties were held in Boston, Philadelphia, Baltimore, and Charleston.

Hone regularly attended elegant dinner parties graced by fine cuisine and imported wines. The New York elite who filled the pages of Hone's diary—the 1 percent of the population who owned half of the city's wealth—lived in mansions attended by servants. Country estates, ocean resorts, mineral spas, and grand tours of Europe offered relief from the winter and spring social seasons and escape from the heat and smells of the summer.

Much of this wealth was inherited. For every John Jacob Astor who made millions in the western fur trade or George Law who left a farm to become a millionaire contractor and investor, ten others had inherited or married money. Andrew H. Mickle, a poor Irish immigrant who became a millionaire and mayor of New York City, derived his fortune from marrying the daughter of his employer. Many of the wealthiest New Yorkers bore the names of the colonial commercial elite: Breevoort, Roosevelt, Van Rensselaer, and Whitney. These rich New Yorkers were not idle; they worked at increasing their fortunes and power. Urban capitalists like Philip Hone and the fashionable society, like their Boston counterparts who founded the Boston Manufacturing Company, invested in and profited enormously from commerce and manufacturing. Wealth begat wealth, and marriage cemented upper-crust family ties.

Meanwhile, a distinct middle class appeared on the urban scene. Small in number, they were the city businessmen, traders, and professionals in the market economy. The growth and specialization of trade rapidly increased their numbers. Middle-class families enjoyed the new consumer items: wool carpeting, fine wallpaper, and rooms full of furniture replaced the bare floors, whitewashed walls, and relative sparseness of eighteenth-century homes. Houses were large, often having from four to six rooms. Middle-class children slept one to a bed, and by the 1840s and 1850s middle-class families used indoor toilets. When Philadelphia publishing agent Joseph Engles died in 1861, an inventory of his estate indicated that his parlor contained two sofas, thirteen chairs, three card tables, a fancy table, a piano,

The Middle Class

John Lewis Krimmel painted this portrait of himself and his sister-in-law and her children around 1812. It shows a prosperous middle-class Philadelphia German family that had been in the United States around five years. The dress and home of the Krimmel children stand in sharp contrast to the homeless and orphaned children of New York City. (The Warner Collection of Gulf States Paper Corporation, Tuscaloosa, Alabama. Photo courtesy of The Schwarz Gallery, Philadelphia)

a mirror, and a fine carpet. Other rooms were similarly furnished.

Middle-class families formed the backbone of the clubs and societies that Tocqueville had observed in America. They filled the family pews in church on Sundays; their children pursued whatever educational opportunities were available. They were as distant from Philip Hone's world as they were from the milieu of the working class and the poor. Increasingly they looked to the family and home as the core of middle-class life.

Women, Families, and the Domestic Ideal

 Once primarily an economic unit, urban families in the nineteenth century lost their role as producers (see Chapter 10). As manufacturing left the home, so did wage workers. One result was specialization of roles by gender and by life stage.

Men dominated American families. English common law gave husbands absolute control over the family. The men owned their wives' personal property; they were legal guardians of the children; and they owned whatever family members produced or earned. A father still had the legal authority to oppose his daughter's choice of husband. Nonetheless, most American women, with their parents' blessing, chose their own marriage partners.

Marriage and family life were the central adult experiences of most women. Although married women still had limited legal rights and standing, they made modest gains in property and spousal rights from the 1830s on. Arkansas in 1835 passed the first married women's property law, and by 1860 sixteen more states had followed suit. In those states, women—single, married, or widowed—could own and convey property. When a wife inherited, earned, or acquired property, it was hers, not her husband's; and she could write a will. In the 1830s states began to liberalize divorce, adding cruelty and desertion as grounds for divorce. Nonetheless divorce was rare.

As the urban workplace and home became separate entities, men worked for wages outside the home,

Supporting Families

and so did their offspring. In New England daughters left farms to work in textile mills, sons to work in urban commerce. In the 1840s the new urban department stores hired young women as clerks and cash runners. Many women worked for a time as teachers, usually for two to five years. Paid employment typically represented a brief stage in women's lives before they left their parental households and entered their marital households.

Working-class women—the poor, widows, and free blacks—worked to support themselves and their families. Leaving their parental homes as early as age twelve, they earned wages most of their lives, with only short respites for bearing and rearing children. But unlike men and New England farm daughters, most of these women did not work in the new shops and factories. Instead, they sold their domestic skills for wages outside their own households. Unmarried girls and women worked as domestic servants in other women's homes; married and widowed women worked as laundresses, seamstresses, and cooks. Some hawked food and wares on city streets; others did piecework sewing at home, earning wages in the putting-out system; and some became prostitutes. Few of these occupations enabled them to support themselves or a family at a respectable level.

Most women continued to perform unpaid labor in the home. As the urban family lost its role in the production of goods, household upkeep and child rearing claimed women's full-time attention. Religion, morality, domestic arts, and music and literature filled the void left by the decline in the economic functions of the family; these realms came to be known as woman's sphere. A woman who achieved mastery in these areas lived up to the middle-class ideal of the cult of domesticity.

Middle-class Americans idealized the family as a moral institution characterized by selflessness and co-

Idealizing the Family

operation. The world of work—the market economy—was seen as an arena of conflict increasingly identified with men and dominated by base self-interest. In a rapidly changing world, the family represented stability and traditional values. The domestic ideal restricted the range of paying jobs available to middle-class women. One occupation was considered consonant with the genteel female role: teaching. In 1823 the Beecher sisters, Catharine and Mary, established the Hartford Female Seminary

Rebecca Lukens pioneered in an unusual role for a woman in early-nineteenth-century America: she ran the Lukens Steel Company in eastern Pennsylvania from 1825 until she died in 1854. The deaths of her father in 1823 and of her husband in 1825 left her with the mill and large debts. She revived the steel company and soon was shipping iron plates as far away as Europe. (Courtesy of Lukens, Inc., Coatesville, Pa.)

and offered history and science in addition to the traditional women's curriculum of domestic arts and religion. A decade later Catharine Beecher successfully campaigned for teacher-training schools for women. By 1850 school teaching had become a woman's profession. "Females govern with less resort to physical force," Horace Mann asserted, "and exert a more kindly, humanizing and refining influence upon the dispositions and manners of their pupils." Most urban teachers were unmarried women, who earned about half the salary of male teachers.

Meanwhile, family size was shrinking. In 1830 American women bore an average of five or six children; by 1860 the figure had dropped to five. This decline occurred even though many immigrants with

Decline in Family Size

large-family traditions were settling in the United States; thus the birth rate among native-born women declined even more steeply. Although rural families remained larger than their urban counterparts, birth rates among both groups declined comparably.

A number of factors reduced family size. Small families were viewed as increasingly desirable in an economy in which the family was a unit of consumption rather than production. Children in smaller families would have greater opportunities: parents could give them more attention, better education, and more financial help. Evidence suggests many wives and husbands made deliberate decisions to limit the size of families. Where farmland was relatively expensive in eastern states, for instance, family size was smaller than in cheaper agricultural districts to the west. In urban areas, children tended to become an economic burden rather than an asset as the family lost its role as a producer of goods.

Limiting Families

How did men and women limit their families in the early nineteenth century? Average age at marriage rose, thus shortening the period of potential childbearing. Women also bore their last child at a younger age, dropping from around forty in the mid-eighteenth century to around thirty-five in the mid-nineteenth. This change suggests family planning. Many couples used traditional forms of birth control, such as coitus interruptus (withdrawal of the male before completion of the sexual act) and breast-feeding, which makes some women temporarily infertile. Medical devices, however, were beginning to compete with these ancient and imperfect practices. Although animal-skin condoms imported from France were too expensive for popular use, cheap rubber condoms became available in the 1850s. Some couples used the rhythm method—attempting to confine intercourse to a woman's infertile periods. Awareness of the "safe period," however, was uncertain, even among physicians.

Abortion

If all else failed, women resorted to abortions, especially after 1830. Ineffective folk methods of self-induced abortion had been around for centuries, but in the 1830s abortionists, mostly women, advertised surgical services in large cities. To protect women from unqualified abortionists, and in response to reformers opposed to abortion, states began to regulate the procedure. Between 1821 and 1841, ten states and one territory either restricted late-term abortions or prohibited abortion altogether; by 1860 twenty states had adopted such restrictions.

Significantly, the birth-control methods that women themselves controlled—the rhythm method, abstinence, and abortion—became increasingly common. The new emphasis on domesticity encouraged women's autonomy in the home and by extension gave them greater control over their own bodies. Women ruled the household, including the bedroom, with refinement and purity. As one woman put it, "Woman's duty was to subdue male passions, not to kindle them."

Smaller families and fewer births changed women's lives. At one time birth and infant care had occupied nearly the entire span of women's adult lives, and few mothers lived to see their youngest child reach maturity. Smaller families also allowed women to devote more time to their older children, and childhood gradually came to be perceived as a distinct period in the life span. The expansion of public education in the 1830s and the policy of grouping schoolchildren by age reinforced this trend.

Single Men and Women

Urban life always offered a place for men outside families. Rooming and boarding houses provided them with places to live. The expansion of cities and the market economy offered independence for women outside families as well. Single women departed from the centuries-old pattern in which a woman moved from her father's to her husband's household. Louisa May Alcott (1832–1888), the author of *Little Women* (1868) who lived most of her life in Massachusetts, sought independence and financial security for herself. Her father, the philosopher Bronson Alcott, never adequately supported his family. Not even the family's participation in a utopian cooperative put enough food on the table. Alcott worked as a seamstress, governess, teacher, and housemaid before her writing brought her success. "I think I shall come out right, and prove that though an Alcott, I can support myself," she wrote her father in 1856. "I like the independent feeling; and though not an easy life, it is a free one, and I enjoy it. I can't do much with my hands; so I will make a battering-ram of my head and make a way through this rough-and-tumble world."

Louisa May Alcott forswore marriage. She and other unmarried women pursued careers and lives defined by female relationships. Given the difficulty women had finding ways to support themselves, they undertook independence at great risk. Nonetheless, the proportion of single women in the population increased significantly in the nineteenth century. In Massachusetts in 1850, 17 percent of native-born women never married—a far larger percentage than in colonial days. Independent white women, in sum, were taking advantage of new opportunities offered by the market economy and urban expansion.

Immigrant Lives in America

 The United States continued to be a nation of newcomers. The 5 million immigrants who came to the United States between 1830 and 1860 outnumbered the entire population of the country recorded in the first census in 1790. The vast majority were European (see Figure 12.1). During the peak period of pre–Civil War immigration, from 1847 through 1857, 3.3 million immigrants entered the United States; 1.3 million were from Ireland and 1.1 million, like the Klingers, came from the German states. By 1860, 15 percent of the white population was foreign-born.

This massive migration had been set in motion decades earlier. At the turn of the nineteenth century, the Napoleonic wars gave rise to one of the greatest population shifts in history; ultimately it lasted more than a century. War, revolution, famine, religious persecution, and the lure of industrialization led many Europeans to leave home. From the other side of the

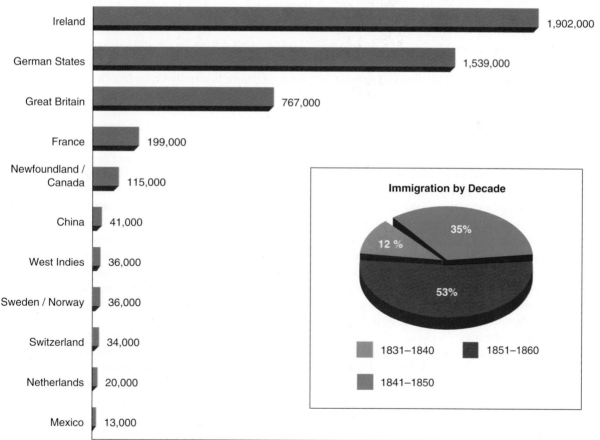

Number of Immigrants per Country, 1831–1860

Ireland	1,902,000
German States	1,539,000
Great Britain	767,000
France	199,000
Newfoundland / Canada	115,000
China	41,000
West Indies	36,000
Sweden / Norway	36,000
Switzerland	34,000
Netherlands	20,000
Mexico	13,000

Immigration by Decade

- 35%
- 12%
- 53%
- 1831–1840
- 1851–1860
- 1841–1850

Figure 12.1   Major Sources of Immigration to the United States, 1831–1860   Most immigrants came from two areas: Great Britain, of which Ireland was a part, and the German states. These two areas sent more immigrants between 1830 and 1860 than the inhabitants of the United States enumerated at the first census in 1790. By 1860, 15 percent of the white population was of foreign birth.   (Source: Data from Stephan Thernstrom, ed., *Harvard Encyclopedia of American Ethnic Groups* [Cambridge, Mass., and London: Harvard University Press, 1980], 1047.)

world, Chinese immigration to the United States was just beginning; 41,000 Chinese, nearly all men, entered the United States from 1854 through 1860 to work mostly in heavy construction. The United States attracted immigrants as its economy offered jobs and its Constitution protected religious freedom.

The market economy needed workers. Large construction projects and massive mining operations sought strong young men, and textile mills sought young women. To fill these jobs both private firms and governments recruited European immigrants. Midwestern and western states lured potential settlers to promote economic growth. Two transplanted New Yorkers, Augustus and Joe Kirby Allen, for instance, in 1836 set themselves up in what became Houston, Texas, and advertised in newspapers for settlers. In the 1850s Wisconsin appointed a commissioner of emigration, who advertised the state's advantages in European newspapers. Wisconsin also opened an office in New York and hired European agents to compete with other states and with firms like the Illinois Central Railroad in recruiting immigrants. Europeans' awareness of the United States grew as employers, states, and shipping companies promoted opportunities across the Atlantic. Often the message was stark: work and prosper in America or starve in Europe. The price of a ticket on the regularly scheduled sailing ships crossing the ocean after 1848 was within easy reach of millions of Europeans.

Promotion of Immigration

As the experience of the Klinger family exemplifies, success in America stimulated further emigration. "I wish, and do often say that we wish you were all in this happy land," wrote shoemaker John West of Germantown, Pennsylvania, to his kin in Corsley, England, in 1831, adding: "A man nor woman need not stay out of employment one hour here." John Down, a weaver from Frome, England, who immigrated to New York without his family, described for his wife in 1830 the bountiful meals he shared with a farmer's family. The farm hands sat at the same table with their masters and ate a banquet of puddings, pies, fruits and vegetables of the season, and preserves. Though Down sorely missed his family, he wrote, "I do not repent of coming, for you know that there was nothing but poverty before me." Such testimonials to the success of pauper immigrants in America circulated widely in Europe.

Letters Home

They endured the hardships of travel and of living in a strange land. The average transatlantic crossing took six weeks; in bad weather it could take three months. Disease spread unchecked among people packed together like cattle in steerage. More than seventeen thousand immigrants, mostly Irish, died from "ship fever" in 1847. On arrival, con artists and swindlers preyed on the newcomers. Boarding house and employment agents tried to lure them from their chosen destinations. In response, New York State established Castle Garden as an immigrant center in 1855. There, at the tip of Manhattan Island, the major port for European entry, immigrants were somewhat sheltered from fraud. Authorized transportation companies maintained offices in the large rotunda and assisted new arrivals with their travel plans.

Most immigrants gravitated toward cities, and many stayed in New York City itself. By 1855, 52 percent of its 623,000 inhabitants were immigrants, 28 percent from Ireland and 16 percent from the German states. Boston, another major entry port for the Irish, took on a European tone; throughout the 1850s the city was about 35 percent foreign-born, of whom more than two-thirds were Irish. In the West, St. Louis's population was 61 percent foreign-born and San Francisco had a foreign-born majority.

Settling In

Only a few immigrants had farming experience or the means to purchase land, but those who did settled in rural areas. German, Dutch, and Scandinavian farmers, in particular, headed toward the Midwest. Greater percentages of Scandinavians and Netherlanders took up farming than did other nationalities; both groups came mostly as religious dissenters and migrated in family units. The Dutch who founded colonies in Michigan and Wisconsin, for instance, had seceded from the official Reformed Church of the Netherlands, fleeing persecution in their native land to establish new and more pious communities such as Holland and Zeeland in Michigan.

Not all immigrants found success in the United States; hundreds of thousands returned to their homelands disappointed. Before the famines of the late 1840s hit Ireland, American recruiters had lured many Irish to swing picks and shovels on American canals and railroads and to work in construction. The promise that "he should soon become a wealthy man" lured Michael Gaugin, who had worked for thirteen years as an assistant engineer in the construction of a Dublin canal. The Irish agent for a New York firm convinced him to quit his job, which included a house and an acre of ground, to

Immigrant Disenchantment

come to America. But Gaugin landed in New York City during the financial panic of 1837. He could not find work, and within two months he was broke, struggling to find the means to return to Ireland.

Before the great famine, caused by a blight that turned the potato crop—Ireland's food staple—rotten and inedible, there had been a small

Irish Immigrants

but steady stream of migration from Ireland to the United States. From 1845 to 1849, death from starvation, malnutrition, and typhus spread in Ireland. In all, 1 million died and about 1.5 million fled, two-thirds of them to the United States. Ireland's major export became its people. At the peak of Irish immigration, from 1847 to 1854, 1.2 million Irish men and women entered the United States. In every year but one between 1830 and 1854, the Irish constituted the largest group of immigrants. By the end of the nineteenth century there would be more Irish in the United States than in Ireland.

Most of the new immigrants from Ireland were young, female, poor, from rural counties, and Roman Catholic. In America, the women found work in textile mills and households. Young Irishmen worked in transportation and construction. The Irish supported their families back home and in Irish enclaves in cities, built Catholic churches and schools, and established networks of charitable and social organizations.

This wave of Irish immigrants, descended from the ancient Celts who spoke Gaelic, differed greatly

Racial Ideas

from the Irish who had migrated earlier to the American colonies. In the eighteenth century (see page 90), the Protestant Scots-Irish predominated; they were considered British. But the Celts were considered inferior. The British had thought them barbaric, and colonists carried those views to America. Dr. Robert Knox of the Edinburgh College of Surgeons believed the British stood for liberty, whereas "the source of all evil lies in the race, the Celtic race of Ireland." "Race is everything," he declared in an 1850 study published in Philadelphia; "literature, science, art, in a word, civilization, depends upon it." Many Americans agreed, describing Irish immigrants in negative, racial terms. They talked about Celtic racial characteristics: a small upturned nose, high forehead, and black tint of skin. As scientists like Knox began to classify peoples into biological types, scientific theory buttressed the developing notion of race.

With the immigration of new groups to the United States—Celts, Jews, and Catholics, for instance—with

Though the popular slogan "No Irish Need Apply" excluded Irish immigrants from jobs and housing, it was used by Kathleen O'Neil to attack such exclusion in her lyrics and spirited melody. In the song the Irishman meets discrimination head on, and "No Irish Need Apply" is banished.   (Special Collections, Milton S. Eisenhower Library, The Johns Hopkins University)

the black population expanding, and with territorial expansion bringing Hispanics and more Indians into the United States as well, native-born white Americans were increasingly confronted with people who did not look like them. Many considered these non-British, non-European, non-Protestant people separate races, distinct from their own. Ralph Waldo Emerson, while rejecting the extremes of Dr. Knox's argument, asserted the importance of race in *English Traits* (1856). To Emerson, as a son inherits his ancestors' "every mental and moral property," so too does a race pass on to its members its physical, intellectual, and moral characteristics. "Race avails . . . that all Celts are Catholics," Emerson wrote. "Race is a controlling influence in the Jew. . . . Race in the negro (sic) is of appalling importance. The French in Canada, cut off from all intercourse with the parent people, have held their national traits."

Were the Irish part of the white majority? In the 1840s and 1850s native-born white Americans and British and German immigrants often treated Irish men and women as if they were nonwhites. Posting placards warning "No Irish Need Apply," they excluded the Irish from many occupations. The Irish immigrants who lived with blacks in Five Points seemed to many observers to be much closer to black than white.

Anti-Catholicism

Closely related to racial stereotyping in its causes and nasty effects was anti-Catholicism, which became strident in the 1830s and was most overt and cruel in Boston, where a great many Irish had settled. Anti-Catholic riots were almost commonplace. In Charlestown, Massachusetts, a mob burned a convent in 1834; in Philadelphia a crowd attacked priests and nuns and vandalized churches in 1844; and in Lawrence, Massachusetts, a mob leveled the Irish neighborhood in 1854.

The native-born whites who rejected the Irish and hated Catholics were motivated in part by economic competition and anxiety. Competition was stiffest among the lowest paid and least desirable jobs, from women's textile millwork and domestic service to men's day-laboring jobs. To apprehensive workers, racializing the Irish as Celts was a way of keeping them out of the running. Irish-Catholics were also blamed for nearly every social problem, from immorality and alcoholism to poverty and economic upheaval. Impoverished native-born workers complained to the Massachusetts legislature in 1845 that the Irish displaced "the honest and respectable laborers of the State . . . and from their manner of living . . . work for much less per day . . . being satisfied with food to support the animal existence alone." American workers, they claimed, "not only labor for the body but for the mind, the soul, and the State."

In emphasizing "the soul, and the State," native-born workers added a political dimension to their racial expression. Republicanism depended on broad participation and the consent of the governed, and it seemed to American nativists that the Irish, a nonwhite, non-British "race," were not fit to participate.

German Immigrants

The experience of German immigrants differed from that of the Irish. By and large Americans viewed most Germans, especially the majority Protestant group, as white. They shared a racial stock with the English, who according to Emerson, "come mainly from the Germans." Americans stereotyped Germans as hard working, self-reliant, and intelligent, attributes also applied to white people. Many believed that Germans fit more easily into American culture.

In the ten years from 1846 to 1855, 977,000 immigrants from the German states entered the United States, including the Klinger family. In 1854 Germans replaced the Irish as the largest group of new arrivals. Potato blight also prompted emigration from the German states in the 1840s; other hardships added to the steady stream. Many people came from regions where small landholdings made it hard to eke out a living. Craftsmen displaced by the industrial revolution sought jobs in the American expanding market economy. Political refugees—liberals, freethinkers, socialists, communists, and anarchists—fled to the United States after the abortive revolutions of 1848.

Germans shared a German language, though neither a single German state nor a common culture united them. While New York's sizable German population made it the world's third largest German-speaking city—after Vienna and Berlin—Germans settled elsewhere in the United States as well. In the South they were peddlers and merchants; in the North and West they worked as farmers, urban laborers, and businessmen. Their tendency to migrate as families and groups helped them maintain German customs and institutions. Many settled in small towns and rural areas where they could preserve their language and regional German cultures. In larger cities immigrants from the same German states tended to cluster together. Their presence transformed the tone of cities like Cincinnati and Milwaukee, as they became major producers of German beer and sausage and built shops and factories based on German crafts skills, from cigar making to tool works.

Non-Protestant Germans did not fare so well, frequently encountering hostility fed by religious and racial prejudice. A significant number of German immigrants were Jewish, and Jews were considered a separate race. Anti-Catholics attacked the German immigrants who were Catholic. The Sunday tradition of urban German families gathering at beer gardens to eat and drink, to dance and sing, and sometimes to play cards outraged Protestants, who viewed this behavior as violating the sanctity of the Lord's day.

Hispanics

From Florida to Texas and the Southwest to California, Hispanic inhabitants of the borderlands became "immigrants" without actually moving; treaties placed them in the United States. Some Mexicans were unhappy to find themselves in a new country, while others welcomed the political self-government that the United States seemed to promise.

But reality did not live up to promise. In Nueces County, Texas, at the time of the Texas Revolution (1836), Mexicans held all the land; twenty years later, they had lost it. The new Anglo owners produced crops for the market economy; *rancheros* and *vaqueros*—cowboys—became obsolete. Although many Mexicans, called *Tejanos*, had fought for Texas's independence, new Anglo settlers tended to treat them as inferiors and foreigners. They became second-class citizens on land where they had lived for generations. Still they retained their culture. They held fast to their language, Roman Catholic religion, and cultural traditions. San Antonio, Mexican from 1821 to 1836 and thereafter a Texas city, illustrates *Tejano* persistence. The church, free public schools (established in 1827), newspapers, mutual aid societies, public holidays, and celebrations of life-cycle events from baptism to marriage to funerals all perpetuated *Tejano* culture.

In California—unlike in Texas, New Mexico, and Arizona—Hispanic society and political power quickly gave way to American and European culture. *Californios*, the Mexican population, numbered 10,000 in 1848, or two-thirds of the non-Indian population. By the end of the century the Hispanic population was 15,000 out of 1.5 million, and Hispanic culture was only a remnant, though Mexican immigrants would reestablish it in the twentieth century.

White Americans considered Hispanics, a group descended from Indians and Spaniards, as a separate, nonwhite race. Anglo-Americans also inherited the British view of Spaniards as sneaky, cowardly, lazy, and decadent, stereotypes they applied to Hispanics. Racializing Hispanics helped to justify the attitudes and actions of aggressive whites, who pushed aside any who stood in the way of expansion and settlement.

This painting (c. 1840) of Saint Isadore of Madrid, patron saint of farmers, is attributed to Rafael Aragon. Hispanic farmers in the Southwest sought the aid of Saint Isadore as they struggled to raise crops and preserve their culture. (Courtesy of Dr. and Mrs. Ward Alan Minge)

Free People of Color

 African Americans were the most visible nonwhite group in the early nineteenth century. As their numbers grew, from 2.3 million in 1830 to 4.4 million in 1860, they were increasingly viewed solely as a racial group, a people racially apart from English and other European groups. In law and society most black people found themselves as outsiders in the land of their birth.

The free African American population rose from 320,000 in 1820 to almost 500,000 in 1860. Nearly half lived in the North, some in rural settlements but far more in cities such as Philadelphia, New York, and

Cincinnati. Baltimore, in the border state of Maryland, had the largest community. An estimated 60,000 free blacks lived in Canada as exiles from the United States. Despite differences in occupation, wealth, education, religion, and social status, the necessity of self-defense promoted solidarity among free blacks.

Ex-slaves constantly increased the ranks of free people of color. Some, like Frederick Douglass and Harriet Tubman, were fugitives. Douglass, a Baltimore ship caulker, escaped in 1838 by bluffing his way to Philadelphia and freedom. Tubman, a slave in Maryland, escaped to Philadelphia in 1849 when it was rumored that she would be sold out of the state. Over the next two years she returned twice to free her two children, her sister, her mother, and her brother and his family. Some slaves received freedom in owners' wills when masters sought, at death, to rid themselves of the stain of owning slaves. Some owners released elderly slaves rather than support them in old age. Others freed their children, offspring of liaisons and forced relations with slaves.

Free people of color forged cohesive communities and created autonomous institutions within them.

African American Communities

Swept up by the Second Great Awakening, blacks turned to religion and reform. The African Methodist Episcopal Church, founded in Philadelphia in 1816, run by and for free people of color, led the way, and other churches soon followed, many of them evangelical. Black churches were the center of community life, and pastors became political leaders. Pastors taught religious and secular classes, and their chapels and social halls functioned as town halls, housing schools, political forums and conventions, protest meetings, and benevolent and self-help associations.

Black churches—especially the African Methodist Episcopal Church, run by and for free people of color—were central in the communal and religious life of free people of color. Mrs. Juliann Jane Tillman, an AME minister in Philadelphia, was a popular preacher. Peter S. Duval printed this 1844 life drawing of Tillman by Alfred Hoffy. (Library of Congress)

A network of voluntary associations became the hallmark of black communities. Besides the churches, men and women organized fraternal and benevolent associations, literary societies, and schools. In Philadelphia in the 1840s, more than half of the black population belonged to mutual beneficiary societies, and female benevolent societies and schools flourished. The Prince Hall Masons had more than fifty lodges in seventeen states by 1860. Many black leaders believed that these mutual aid societies would encourage thrift, industry, and morality, thus assisting their members to improve their lot. But no amount of effort could counteract the burden of white racism, which impinged on every aspect of their lives. For example, blacks in effect paid double for education: their taxes supported white public schools, which excluded black children; then they raised additional funds to educate their own children.

In the majority of states where free blacks were excluded from the ballot, they formed protest organizations to fight for equal rights. Among the early efforts to organize for self-defense was the Negro Convention movement. From 1830 to 1835, and irregularly thereafter, free blacks held national conventions with delegates drawn from city and state organizations. Under the leadership of the small black middle class, which included the Philadelphia sail manufacturer James Forten and the orator Reverend Henry Highland Garnet, the convention movement served as a forum to attack slavery and agitate for equal rights. Militant new black newspapers joined the struggle. *Freedom's Journal*, the first black weekly, appeared in 1827; in 1837 the *Weekly Advocate* began publication in New York City. Both papers circulated throughout the North, disseminating African American political analysis and promoting activism.

Activists fought the relegation of blacks to second-class status. The Constitution acknowledged slavery but the Bill of Rights seemed to apply to free African Americans. The Fifth Amendment specified that "no person shall . . . be deprived of life, liberty, or property, without due process of law." But eighteenth-century political theory had defined the republic as being for whites only (see page 173), and early federal legislation excluded blacks from common rights. The first naturalization law in 1790 limited citizenship to "free white persons." It implied that black people were not fit for self-government. Thus from the start legislation excluded free people of color from citizenship rights. When Congress created militias in 1792, they included only whites. After the admission of Missouri

How do historians know...

that African Americans were intensively engaged in political thought and activism in the early nineteenth century? One important source is publications of black institutions like the National Negro Conventions, first held in 1830. Free people of color held at least eleven national conventions and almost forty state conventions between 1830 and 1860. Bishop Richard Allen of the African Methodist Episcopal Church presided over the first national convention, in Philadelphia. The delegates called for pursuing "all legal means for the speedy elevation of ourselves and brethren to the scale and standing of men" and discussed emigration to Canada. The reports of the conventions document the involvement of African Americans in the reforms of the times and the importance they placed on education and equal rights. In the 1850s the conventions turned more nationalistic.

The convention movement was democratic. Most communities elected their delegates to the national conventions at public meetings or at local and state conventions. Although the minutes reveal a wide range of opinion within black communities, delegates universally agreed on abolishing slavery, immediate emancipation, and equal rights for free people of color.   (Photo: Title page for the Minutes of the Proceedings of the National Negro Convention, 1831)

CONSTITUTION OF THE AMERICAN SOCIETY OF FREE PERSONS OF COLOUR, FOR IMPROVING THEIR CONDITION IN THE UNITED STATES; FOR PURCHASING LANDS; AND FOR THE ESTABLISHMENT OF A SETTLEMENT IN UPPER CANADA. ALSO THE PROCEEDINGS OF THE CONVENTION, WITH THEIR ADDRESS TO THE FREE PERSONS OF COLOUR IN THE UNITED STATES.

PHILADELPHIA: PRINTED BY J. W. ALLEN, NO 26, STRAWBERRY-ST. 1831.

in 1821, every new state admitted until the Civil War, free and slave, banned blacks from voting. When Congress organized the Oregon and New Mexico Territories, it reserved public land grants for whites. Clearly free people of color were defined as an alien race; they could not participate in the republican ideal that government rested on the consent of the governed.

Even in the North, states attempted to exclude African Americans. While southern states, which found the existence of free people of color incompatible with slavery, restricted black rights as a way of encouraging free blacks to leave their states, these people were not welcome in most northern and western states either. Many states barred free blacks or required them to post bonds ranging from $500 to $1,000 to guarantee their good conduct, as did Illinois (1819), Michigan (1837), and Oregon (1857). Only in Massachusetts, New Hampshire, Vermont, and Maine could blacks vote on an equal basis with whites throughout the early nineteenth century. In 1842 African Americans gained the right to vote in Rhode Island (where all voters faced restrictive property qualifications), but they had lost it earlier in Pennsylvania and Connecticut. Only Massachusetts permitted blacks to serve on juries. Four midwestern states and California did not allow African Americans to testify against whites. In

Oregon blacks could not own real estate, make contracts, or sue in court. The laws were meant to render African Americans powerless.

Throughout the United States white social custom became more rigid in excluding or segregating free people of color. Hotels and

Racial Exclusion and Segregation

restaurants barred them, as did most theaters and white churches. Abolitionist Frederick Douglass was repeatedly turned away from public facilities during a speaking tour of the North in 1844.

Economic discrimination solidified social segregation. Black people were banned from the jobs opening up in the expanding market economy. The jobs available were consistent with white views of blacks as an inferior race, fit only for hard physical labor or servile work. Countinghouses, retail stores, and factories refused to hire black men except as janitors and handymen. New England mills hired only whites. Except for a small professional and skilled elite, free black men in the North found steady work elusive; most toiled as unskilled daily laborers.

African American women found jobs more easily than men did. Their domestic skills were in great demand in the cities; they worked

African American Women

as servants, cooks, laundresses, and seamstresses, and kept boarding houses. Unlike their white counterparts, these women did not view paid employment as a temporary phase in their lives; around 40 percent of black women worked for wages during their child-rearing years.

But gender roles also restricted black women. In religious organizations they participated regularly but rarely held leadership positions. Besides holding paid work outside the home, they were expected to perform domestic duties, which included responsibility for education. A number of black women participated in abolitionist as well as literary societies, but they, like their white sisters, were discouraged from speaking in public. Black women also had to deal with black men's needs to be strong and protect women, roles men found impossible in slavery and difficult in freedom. Both men and women carried the burden of refuting racial stereotypes, but black women bore the additional burden of gender stereotypes.

The mood of free blacks turned pessimistic in the late 1840s and 1850s. Many felt frustrated by the failure of the abolitionist movement and angered by the passage of the stringent Fugitive Slave Act of 1850 (see

Black Nationalism

page 368). Some fled to Canada, others became more militant, and a few joined John Brown in his plans for a slave uprising (see page 380). Many more were swept up in a wave of black nationalism that stressed racial solidarity, self-help, and a growing interest in Africa. Before this time, efforts to send African Americans "back to Africa" had originated with whites seeking to rid the United States of blacks. But in the 1850s blacks held emigrationist conventions of their own under the leadership of abolitionists Henry Bibb and Martin Delany. Delany led an exploration party to the Niger valley as the emissary of a black convention, there signing a treaty with Yoruba rulers allowing him to settle American blacks in their African kingdom.

Nothing illustrates the poignant position of free blacks in the United States better than the flight of black Americans to Canada and Africa in search of freedom while millions of European migrants were flooding to the United States for liberty and opportunity. With the coming of the Civil War, the status of blacks would move onto the national political agenda, and African Americans would focus on their position at home.

Summary

The American people and communities in the North and West were far more diverse and turbulent in the 1850s than they had been in the 1820s. The market economy and westward movement altered farm life, city life, and class structure; heavy immigration, growing racial ideas, and the anguished position of free people of color added to the tensions. Inequality increased as did the gap between the haves and the have-nots. As the nation grew more populous and the market economy upset work and social relations, many felt a loss of tradition and community. Some longed to return to old values. Utopians like the Shakers, Mormons, and Brook Farmers sought to counter isolation and individualism.

Increasingly cities became the center of American life, with New York the predominant metropolis. Growing populations brought new problems, however, and cities struggled to provide adequate public health and safety and education for their residents. Large cities offered rich leisure activities, from entertainment to sporting events. Increasingly, however, people divided along class, ethnic, and racial lines.

Whether formal, as in the Masonic order, or informal as in the youth culture of the Bowery, divisions became more rigid. The gap between rich and poor widened.

In the midst of these changes, middle-class families sought to insulate their homes from the competition of the market economy. Many wives and mothers found fulfillment in the domestic ideal; others found "woman's sphere" confining. Middle-class urban women became associated with nurturing roles, first in homes and schools, then in churches and reform societies. Working-class women had more modest goals: escaping poverty and winning respect. Most Americans found some comfort in religion.

Famine and oppression in Europe propelled millions of people across the Atlantic, most from Ireland and the German states. American expansion added Hispanics to the nation. Diversity, competition, and religious and scientific thought fueled racial ideas. Many European descendants began to view the Irish, Hispanics, and African Americans as inferior races rather than as cultural groups. Racism justified second-class citizenship for Hispanics and black people.

LEGACY FOR A PEOPLE AND A NATION

White Fascination with and Appropriation of Black Culture

White Americans' fascination with and appropriation of black culture blossomed in the early nineteenth century. Whites performed songs and dances from blackface minstrel reviews, while urban young people imitated black language, dress, and hairstyles. In the 1850s white songwriter Stephen Foster's "Old Folks at Home," "Susanna," and "Camptown Races" were enormously popular. Whites believed they were traditional black folk songs, though they romanticized the slave South.

American popular culture combined African, European, and African American traditions. Its emphasis on performance, improvisation, strong rhythms, vernacular language, multiple meanings, and integration into everyday life is evident of strong African ties. These elements appealed to whites because of their ex-

pressive powers. Whites also believed that black cultural forms were "exotic" and offered "natural" forms of expression.

Black traditions continue to influence twentieth-century popular culture. Minstrelsy turned into vaudeville and Broadway theater, which gave birth to American popular music. Popular dance and music, performed mostly by whites, drew heavily on black gospel, slave spirituals, the blues, and jazz, and spread through live performance, recorded music, and later radio and television. Black traditions influenced the swing bands of the 1930s, and after World War II, they shaped rhythm and blues, rock 'n' roll, and, later, rap, hip-hop, and ska.

Until recently, most whites experienced black culture as appropriated by whites. Minstrels in blackface and Stephen Foster's songs modified black culture for white audiences. But in the late twentieth century, a synthesis of black and white traditions became notable. In the early 1950s Bill Haley and the Comets, a white country-western group, combined black rhythm and blues with white country and western music. Their 1954 sensation, "Shake, Rattle & Roll," for instance, was a sanitized version of Big Joe Turner's rhythm and blues hit. White audiences responded enthusiastically, and when Haley and the Comets played "Rock Around the Clock" in the 1955 movie *Blackboard Jungle*, rock 'n' roll took off. Elvis Presley too synthesized rhythm and blues and gospel with country music and middle-of-the-road popular music. Rap and hip-hop built on the talking blues, call and response, and urban black and Chicano/a dance styles of the 1970s. White suburban youth made them dominant popular forms.

Popular music and dance, with its African American roots, is uniquely American. Young people fostered this popular culture and used its expressive elements to define themselves. Thus African American culture has given the people and nation a unique cultural legacy.

For Further Reading, see page A-15 of the Appendix. For Web resources, go to http://www.college.hmco.com

A slaveholder in debt was a dangerous man. Pierce Butler was broke. It was late winter of 1859, fear of disunion dominated national life, and Butler's slave auction had all of coastal Georgia and South Carolina talking. Butler was the grandson of Major Pierce Butler, a framer of the Constitution, a senator from South Carolina, and a wealthy planter. Butler the younger divided his time between the family's ostentatious home in Philadelphia and 1,500 acres of cotton plantations on Butler Island and St. Simons Island in Georgia, worked by eight hundred slaves. His marriage to the famous British actress Fanny Kemble had ended in divorce; she could not bear the realities of slavery on her husband's cotton plantations, and he could not bear her protests. By 1859 Butler had squandered a fortune of $700,000 through speculation and gambling. Allegedly, he blew $25,000 on one hand of cards.

Most of Butler's properties and possessions in Philadelphia were sold to satisfy his creditors. Then came the largest slave auction in American history. In the last week of February, 436 Butler slaves were taken to Savannah by railroad and steamboat. They were housed for several days in horse-and-carriage sheds at the Ten Broeck racetrack. People of all ages—infants, husbands, wives, children, grandparents—huddled in fearful expectation. Joseph Bryan, a slave broker and auctioneer, managed the sale. Among the planters and speculators who were there to buy was an undercover *New York Tribune* reporter. The auction, held in the racecourse's grandstand, lasted an agonizing two days in a driving rainstorm.

If possible, families were sold intact for group prices; thus the old and infirm could still be liquidated, while the closest kin stayed together. A seventeen-year-old "Prime woman" named Dorcas and her three-month-old son, Joe, went for $2,200. A nineteen-year-old "prime young man," Abel, netted $1,295. Some families of four, such as Goin and Cassander and their two daughters, Emiline and Judy, brought only $1,600 together. At the end of the second day of what blacks

Thomas S. Noble's painting *The Last Sale of Slaves* depicts the public drama and family horror of slave auctions. Noble's work stimulated a heated newspaper debate in St. Louis over its abolitionist message. The sight of people treated as property, and bills of sale signed on the table, leave slavery's most haunting images. (Missouri Historical Society)

13

PEOPLE AND COMMUNITIES IN A SLAVE SOCIETY: THE SOUTH 1830–1860

in the region called the "weeping time," Butler had amassed $303,850 by selling 436 human beings. It would have been impossible to convince the numbed and despairing African Americans who traveled away from Savannah in wagons or railcars that slavery did not cause the war that would soon follow. Their sorrow was soon the nation's as well.

Many northerners remained undisturbed during the antebellum era by the growth of human bondage, even its worst elements such as the Butler auction. But a growing number came to see it as threatening and immoral. By the 1830s the North was an emerging market economy embarking on an industrial revolution.

Meanwhile, the South, with a different kind of growth and prosperity, also participated in the market revolution. New lands were settled and new states peopled, and steadily the South emerged as the world's most extensive and vigorous slave economy, linked to an international cotton trade and textile industry. Slavery had a far-reaching influence on the whole society. The Old South's wealth came from export crops, land, and slaves; and its population was almost wholly rural. In the land where cotton became king, racial slavery affected not only economics but values, customs, laws, and the region's relationship to the nation. ■

The "Peculiar" South?

The South, the section composed of the slaveholding states from the Chesapeake region to Missouri and from Florida to Texas, has often been considered America's most distinctive region. Historians have long asked the "old perennial" question: how was the Old South like or unlike the rest of the nation? Was the South behind national economic growth and development? Or, put most directly, was the South "backward" in comparison to the industrializing North?

There has long been a tendency to equate certain American values such as materialism, individualism, and faith in progress with the North in the nineteenth century, and to equate values such as tradition, conservatism, and family loyalty to the South. The South, so the stereotype has it, was static, and the North dynamic in the decades leading up to the Civil War. Indeed, the great fact of secession and the Confederacy will always give the South a distinct place in American history. But there are many measures of just how different South was from North in the antebellum era. It depends on which measures one chooses.

The South was peculiar because of its commitment to slavery, but it was also much like the rest of the

New Orleans, the South's largest city and a major port, was a wealthy hub of a thriving market economy, rooted in cotton and woven together by river trade. This view from 1860 shows hundreds of cotton bales and dozens of steamboats waiting to receive them. (Chicago Historical Society)

IMPORTANT EVENTS

1810–20 137,000 slaves are forced to move from North Carolina and the Chesapeake to Alabama, Mississippi, and other western regions

1822 Vesey's plot is discovered in South Carolina

1831 Turner leads a violent slave rebellion in Virginia

1832 Virginia holds last serious debate in South about the future of slavery
Publication of Dew's proslavery tract, "Abolition of Negro Slavery"

1832 and after Legislators in several states increase restrictions on slaves

1830s Class tensions lead to electoral reforms in much of the South
The cotton trade provides much of the export capital to finance northeastern economic growth

1836 Arkansas gains admission to the Union

1839 Mississippi's Married Women's Property Act gives married women some property rights

1840s Southern slave economy prospers, but northern, urban economic growth is less dependent on it

1845 Florida and Texas gain admission to the Union
Publication of Douglass's *Narrative of the Life of Frederick Douglass, An American Slave*

1850–60 Of some 300,000 slaves who migrate from Upper to Lower South, 60–70% go by outright sale

1857 Helper denounces the slave system in *The Impending Crisis*
Publication of Fitzhugh's "Southern Thought," an aggressive defense of slavery

South-North Similarity

nation. The geographic sizes of the South and the North were roughly the same. By the 1830s southerners shared a heritage from the era of the American Revolution, the same heroes and political ideology, with their fellow free citizens in the North. With varying accents, southerners spoke the same language and worshiped the same Protestant God as northerners. White Americans in the South lived under the same cherished Constitution as northerners, and they shared a common mixture of nationalism and localism in their attitudes toward government. Down to the 1840s, northerners and southerners invoked the doctrine of states' rights against federal authority with nearly equal frequency. A faith in the future fueled by a sense of American mission and the dreams inspired by the westward movement were as much a part of southern as of northern experience.

Indeed, some of the most eloquent visions of America as a land of independent, self-sufficient farmers expanding westward had come from a southerner, Thomas Jefferson. Jefferson believed that "virtue" rested in those who tilled the soil, that farmers made the best citizens. In 1804 Jefferson declared his "moral and physical preference of the agricultural over the

manufacturing man." But as slavery and the plantation economy expanded (see Map 13.1), the South did not become a land of individual opportunity in quite the same manner as the North.

During the thirty years before the Civil War, the South shared in the nation's economic booms and busts. Research has shown that despite its enormous cruelties, slavery was a profitable labor system for planters. In purely economic measures, slavery was not a drag on the South's prosperity. Southerners and northerners shared an expanding capitalist economy. As it grew, the slave-based economy of money-crop agriculture reflected the rational choices of planters. More land and more slaves generally converted into more wealth. By the eve of the Civil War in 1860, the distribution of wealth and property in the two sections was almost identical: 50 percent of free adult males owned only 1 percent of real and personal property, while the richest 1 percent owned 27 percent of the wealth. One study comparing Texas and Wisconsin in 1850 shows that the richest 2 percent of families in each state owned 31 to 32 percent of the wealth. So, both North and South had ruling classes, even if their wealth was invested in different kinds of property. Entrepreneurs in both sections, whether forging plantations out

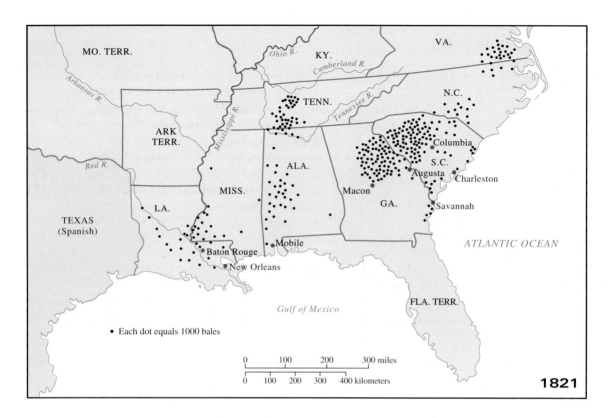

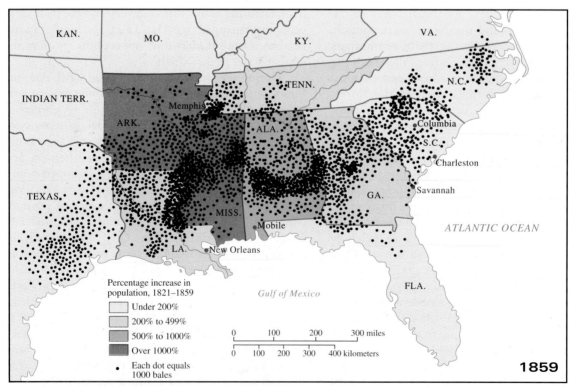

Map 13.1   Cotton Production in the South   These two maps reveal the rapid westward expansion of cotton production and its importance to the antebellum South.

of Mississippi Delta land or shoe factories and textile mills in New England river towns, sought their fortunes in an expanding market economy.

But there were also important differences between the North and the South. The South's climate and longer growing season gave it an unmistakable rural and agricultural destiny. Its people, white and black, developed an intense attachment to place, to the ways people were related to the land and to one another. It developed as a biracial society of brutal inequality, where the liberty of one race directly depended on the enslavement of another.

South-North Dissimilarity

In this agrarian society, cotton growers spread out over as large an area as possible to maximize production and income. Population density was low in the older plantation states and extremely low in the frontier areas. By 1860 there were only 2.3 people per square mile in vast and largely unsettled Texas, 15.6 in Louisiana, and 18.0 in Georgia. By contrast, population density in the nonslaveholding states east of the Mississippi River was almost three times higher. The Northeast had an average of 65.4 people per square mile. Massachusetts had 153.1 people per square mile, and New York City compressed 86,400 people into each square mile. When in the 1850s young Frederick Law Olmsted of Connecticut, later renowned as a landscape architect, toured the South as a journalist, he traveled mostly on horseback along primitive trails. Between Columbus, Georgia, and Montgomery, Alabama, Olmsted found "a hilly wilderness, with a few dreary villages, and many isolated cotton farms." For the designer of Central Park in New York City, this was just too much ruralness.

Where people were scarce, it was difficult to finance and operate schools, churches, libraries, or even inns and restaurants. Southerners were strongly committed to their churches, and some believed in the importance of universities, but all such institutions were far less developed than those in the North. Factories

Eastman Johnson's *Fiddling His Way* (1866) depicts rural life by representing the visit of an itinerant black musician to a farm family. Expressions and gestures suggest remarkable ease between the races at the yeoman level of southern society.   (The Chrysler Museum of Art, Norfolk, Virginia. Bequest of Walter P. Chrysler, Jr.)

were rare because planters invested most of their capital in slaves. A few southerners did invest in iron or textiles on a small scale. But the largest southern "industry" was lumbering, and the largest factories used slave labor to make cigars. More decisively, the South was slower than the North to develop a unified market economy and a regional transportation network. Despite concerted efforts, the South had only 35 percent of the nation's railroad mileage in 1860.

The South lagged way behind the North in nearly any measure of industrial growth. It always had its reformist voices, however, who advocated commercial development. The South did have urban centers, especially ports like New Orleans and Charleston, which became bustling crossroads of commerce and small-scale manufacturing. But slavery slowed urban growth. As a system of labor and racial control, slavery did not work well in cities. As one historian has said, southern urban centers were small market towns, dependent on agricultural trade—"urbanization without cities." Likewise, the South did not attract immigrants as readily as the North. By 1860 only 13 percent of the nation's foreign-born population lived in the slave states.

Like northerners, antebellum southerners were adherents to evangelical Christianity. Americans from all regions held in common a faith in a personal God and in conversion and piety as the means to salvation. But southern evangelicalism was distinct from its northern practice. In the South, Baptists and Methodists concentrated on personal rather than social improvement. By the 1830s in the North, evangelicalism was a major wellspring of reform movements (see Chapter 11); but in the states where blacks were so numerous and unfree, and where the very social structure was under increasingly aggressive attacks from abolitionists, religion, as one scholar has written, preached "a hands-off policy concerning slavery." Although blacks themselves began to convert to Christianity in the early-nineteenth-century South, many southern whites feared a reform impulse that would foster what one historian has called an "interracial communion" in their churches and in their communities. The only reform movements that did take hold in the emerging Bible belt of the South, such as temperance, focused on personal behavior, not social reform.

When antebellum southerners built prisons or hospitals, these institutions tended to fit into a conservative social structure. Southern law restricted the authority of the courts, reinforcing a tradition of planter control. Penitentiaries tended to house only white prisoners, as most blacks were under the authority of personal masters. Law-breaking in the South tended to be crimes of violence rather than crimes against property. Similarly, the rural character of the South and the significance of the plantation as a self-sufficient social unit meant that the section put few resources into improving disease control and public health. So, in a host of ways, the South was distinct.

Perhaps in no way was the South more peculiar than in its embrace of a particular world-view, a system

A Southern World-View and the Proslavery Argument

of thought and meaning held especially by the planter class, but also influencing all groups of whites. Like those of all people, southerners' values, beliefs, and habits and their rationalizations for slavery were not so different from those of any civilization trying to defend the institutions it inherits. But at the heart of the proslavery argument was a deep and abiding racism. The persistence of modern racism in all sections of the United States is all the more reason to comprehend antebellum southerners' justifications for human slavery, from whence so many modern racial assumptions are derived.

By 1830 white southerners defended slavery as a "positive good," and not merely a "necessary evil." They used the Bible and its many references to slaveholding, as well as the ancient roots of slavery, to foster a historical argument for bondage. They arrayed a variety of assumptions about the superiority and inferiority of races in support of slavery as the natural status of blacks. Whites were the more intellectual race and blacks the race more inherently physical, and therefore destined for labor. Proslavery writers did not mince words. In a proslavery tract written in 1851, John Campbell confidently declared that "there is as much difference between the lowest tribe of negroes and the white Frenchman, Englishman, or American, as there is between the monkey and the negro."

Some southerners defended slavery in practical terms; they simply saw their bondsmen as economic necessity and as symbols of their quest of prosperity. Others, such as James Henry Hammond of South Carolina, in 1845, argued that slaveholding was essentially a matter of property rights. He spoke for many southerners in his unwillingness to "deal in abstractions" about the "right and wrong" of slavery: property was sacred and slaves were legal property—end of argument.

The deepest root of the proslavery argument was a conservative, hierarchical view of human relations, a concern for social order as slavery's defenders believed God or nature had prescribed it. Southerners cherished stability, duty, and honor, believing social change

Most slaveowners lived in comfortable country homes rather than in stately mansions. This rare daguerreotype, dating from about 1853, shows a family in front of their home. Notice the presence of a male slave in the left background. (The J. Paul Getty Museum, Los Angeles, California)

should come only in slow increments, if at all. As the Virginia legislature debated the gradual abolition of slavery in 1832, in the wake of a major slave rebellion, Thomas R. Dew contended, "There is a time for all things, and nothing in this world should be done before its time."

Southern defenders of slavery held views decidedly different from those of northern reformers on the concept of freedom, progress, and equality. They turned natural law doctrine to their favor, arguing that the natural state of mankind was inequality of ability and condition, not equality. A former U.S. senator in South Carolina, William Harper, charged in 1837 that Jefferson's famous dictum about equality in the Declaration of Independence was no more than a "sentimental phrase." "Is it not palpably nearer the truth to say that no man was ever born free," Harper argued, "and that no two men were ever born equal?" Proslavery writers believed that people were born to certain stations or purposes in life; they stressed dependence over autonomy, and duty over rights, as the human condition. As the Virginia writer George Fitzhugh put it in 1854, "men are not born entitled to equal rights. It would be far nearer the truth to say, that some were born with saddles on their backs, and others booted and spurred to ride them."

Hence, however differently their slaves may have interpreted the relationship, many slaveholders believed that their ownership of people bound them, by honor, to a set of paternal obligations. They saw themselves as guardians of a familial relationship between masters and slaves given to them by fate and heritage. Although contradicted by countless examples of slave resistance and escape, planters needed to believe in, and exerted great energy in constructing, the idea of the faithful, contented slave. Slaveholders had come to understand, and needed to endlessly justify, how much the freedom of whites depended on the slavery of blacks. All these ideas about honor and mutual dependency were, of course, weighed against profits.

What the South had become by the 1830s, and grew even more fully into by 1860, was not merely a society with slaves, but a slave society (see page 72). In this way, the region was most distinct within the larger American nation. Slavery and race affected everything in the Old South. Whites and blacks alike grew up, were socialized, married, reared children, worked, invested their incomes or conceived of property, and honed their most basic habits of behavior under the influence of slavery. This was true of slaveholding and nonslaveholding whites, as well as of blacks who were slave and free. Slavery shaped the social structure of the South, fueled almost anything meaningful in its economy, and came to dominate its politics.

A Slave Society

This does not mean that the Old South did not share a common culture, political system, and economy with the North, and with Europe. The South was interdependent with the North and the West in a growing capitalist market system. Southerners relied on northern banks, northern steamship companies working the great western rivers, and northern merchants to keep the cotton trade flowing. But there were elements of that system that southerners increasingly rejected during the antebellum era, especially urbanism, the wage labor system, a broadening right to vote, and any threats to the racial and class order on which they so depended. Although enmeshed in a national economy, the Old South became antimodern, disdainful of some of the very changes that increasingly made it different and eventually overwhelmed it.

In the antebellum era, as later, there were many Souths, depending on whether one considered the South Carolina low country or the Appalachian highlands of east Tennessee, the Mississippi Delta or the piney woods regions of the same state. But Americans have always been determined to define what one historian called the "Dixie difference." "The South is both American and something different," writes another historian, "at times a mirror or magnifier of national traits and at other times a counterculture." This was most acutely true in the decades before the Civil War.

Just how peculiar the South was will always be debated. Culturally, the South developed a proclivity to tell its own story. Its ruralness and its sense of tradition may have given southerners a special habit of telling tales. "Southerners . . . love a good tale," says Mississippi writer Eudora Welty. "They are born reciters, great memory retainers, diary keepers, letter exchangers, and letter savers, history tracers, and debaters, and—outstaying all the rest—great talkers." The South's tragic and distinct story begins in the Old South. The story was peculiar and national all at once.

Free Southerners: Farmers, Planters, and Free Blacks

A large majority of white southern families (three-quarters in 1860) owned no slaves. Some lived in towns and ran stores or businesses, but most were yeoman farmers who owned their own land and grew their own food. The social distance between different groups of whites was great. Still greater was the distance between whites and blacks.

These farmers were individualistic and hard working. Unlike their northern counterparts, their lives were not being transformed by improvements in transportation. They could be independent thinkers as well, but their status as a numerical majority did not mean that they set the political or economic direction of the slave society. Often isolated, always absorbed in the work of their farms, they operated both apart from and within the slave-based staple-crop economy. They valued their self-reliance and freedom from others' control.

Yeoman Farmers

Yeomen pioneered the southern wilderness, moving into undeveloped regions and building log cabins. After the War of 1812 they moved in successive waves down the southern Appalachians into new Gulf lands, first as herders of livestock and then as farmers. In large sections of the South, especially inland from the coast and away from large rivers, small, self-sufficient farms that grew staple crops were the norm. Lured by stories of good land, many men uprooted their wives and children repeatedly. So many shared the excitement over new lands that one North Carolinian wrote in alarm, "The Alabama Fever rages here with great violence. . . . I am apprehensive if it continues to spread as it has done, it will almost depopulate the country."

On the southern frontier men worked hard to clear fields and establish farms, while their wives labored in the household economy and patiently re-created the social ties—to relatives, neighbors, fellow churchgoers—that enriched everyone's experience. Women seldom shared the men's excitement about moving. They dreaded the isolation and loneliness of the frontier. "We have been [moving] all our lives," lamented one woman. "As soon as ever we git comfortably settled, it is time to be off to something new."

Some yeomen acquired large tracts of level land, purchased slaves, and became planters. These people made up part of the new wealth of the boom states of Mississippi and Louisiana, the region to which the southern political power base shifted by the 1840s and 1850s. Others clung to familiar mountainous areas or kept moving as independent farmers because, as one frontiersman put it, he disliked "seeing the nose of my neighbor sticking out between the trees."

The yeomen enjoyed a folk culture based on family, church, and local region. Their speech patterns and inflections recalled their Scots-Irish and Irish backgrounds. They flocked to religious revivals called camp meetings, and in between they got together for

Yeoman Folk Culture

house-raisings, logrollings, quilting bees, corn-shuckings, and hunting for both food and sport. Such occasions combined work with fun, offering food in abundance, and usually liquor as well. They also provided welcome fellowship to isolated rural dwellers.

A demanding round of work and family responsibilities shaped women's lives in the home. At harvest they helped in the fields, and throughout the year the care and preparation of food consumed much of their time. Household tasks continued during frequent pregnancies and childcare. Primary nursing and medical care also fell to the mother, who might have a book of remedies to aid her but often relied on folk wisdom.

Among the men there were many who aspired to wealth, eager to join the race for slaves and cotton profits.

Yeoman Livelihoods

North Carolinian John F. Flintoff kept a diary of his struggle for success. At age eighteen in 1841, Flintoff went to Mississippi to seek his fortune. Like other aspiring yeomen, he worked as an overseer of slaves but often found it impossible to please his employers. At one point he gave up and returned to North Carolina, where he married and lived for a while in his parents' house. But Flintoff was "impatient to get along in the world," so he tried Louisiana next and then Mississippi again.

Flintoff's health suffered in the Gulf region and, routinely, "first rate employment" alternated with "very low wages." Moreover, as a young man working on isolated plantations, Flintoff often felt lonely. Even a revival meeting in 1844 proved "an extremely cold time" with "little warm feeling." His uncle and other employers found fault with his work, and in 1846 Flintoff concluded in despair that "managing negroes and large farms is soul destroying."

But a desire to succeed at this very economic proposition kept him going. At twenty-six, even before he owned any land, Flintoff bought his first slave, "a negro boy 7 years old." Soon he had purchased two more children, the cheapest slaves available. Conscious of his status as a slaveowner, Flintoff resented the low wages he was paid. In 1853, with nine young slaves and a growing family, Flintoff faced "the most unhappy time of my life." Fired by his uncle, he returned to North Carolina, sold some of his slaves, and purchased 124 acres with help from his in-laws. Flintoff grew corn, wheat, and tobacco and earned extra cash hauling wood. By 1860 he owned three horses, twenty-six hogs, ten head of cattle, and several slaves

and was paying off his debts. As the Civil War approached, he looked forward to freeing his wife from labor, and possibly sending his sons to college. Although Flintoff demonstrated that a farmer could move in and out of the slaveholding class, his path had been wrenching, and he never achieved the cotton planter status he desired.

Probably more typical of the southern yeoman was Ferdinand L. Steel, who as a young man moved from North Carolina to Tennessee to work as a river boatman but eventually took up farming in Mississippi. Steel rose every day at five and worked until sundown. With the help of his family he raised corn, wheat, pork, and vegetables. Cotton was his cash crop: he sold five or six bales (about 2,000 pounds) a year to obtain money for sugar, coffee, salt, calico, gunpowder, and a few other store-bought goods.

Thus Steel entered the market economy as a small farmer, but with mixed results. He picked his own cotton and complained that cotton cultivation was brutal work. He felt like a serf in cotton's kingdom. When cotton prices fell, a small grower like Steel could be driven into debt and lose his farm. In fact, he wanted to grow less cotton. "We are too weak handed" to manage it, he noted in his diary. "We had better . . . raise corn and keep out of debt and we will have no necessity of raising cotton."

Steel's life in Mississippi in the 1840s retained much of the flavor of the frontier. He made all the family's shoes; his wife and sister sewed dresses, shirts, and "pantiloons." The Steel women also rendered their own soap and spun and wove cotton into cloth; the men hunted game. Steel doctored his illnesses with boneset tea and other herbs. As the nation fell deeper into crisis over the future of free or slave labor, this independent southern farmer never came close to owning a slave.

The focus of Steel's life was family and religion. Family members prayed together daily, and he studied Scripture for an hour after lunch. "My Faith increases, & I enjoy much of that peace which the world cannot give," he wrote in 1841. Seeking to prepare himself for Judgment Day, Steel borrowed histories, Latin and Greek grammars, and religious books from his church. Eventually he became a traveling Methodist minister. "My life is one of toil," he reflected, "but blessed be God that it is as well with me as it is."

Toil with even less security was the lot of two other groups of free southerners: landless whites and free blacks. A sizable minority of white southern workers—from 25 to 40 percent, depending on the state—

Landless Whites were unskilled laborers who owned no land and worked for others in the countryside and towns. Their property consisted of a few household items and some animals—usually pigs—that could feed themselves on the open range. The landless included some immigrants, especially Irish, who did heavy and dangerous work such as building railroads and digging ditches.

In the countryside, white farm laborers struggled to purchase land in the face of low wages or, if they rented, unpredictable market prices for their crops. By scrimping and saving and finding odd jobs, some managed to climb into the ranks of yeomen. When James and Nancy Bennitt of North Carolina succeeded in their ten-year struggle to buy land, they decided to avoid the unstable market in cotton; thereafter they raised extra corn and wheat as sources of cash. People like the Bennitts were both participants in and victims of an economy dominated by cotton producers who relied on slave labor.

Herdsmen who viewed pigs and livestock as a major economic asset always had a desperate struggle to succeed. By 1860, as the South anticipated war to preserve its society, between 300,000 and 400,000 white people in the four states of Virginia, North and South Carolina, and Georgia lived in genuine poverty, approximately one-fifth of the total white population. Their lives were harsh to say the least. An early antebellum traveler in central South Carolina described the white folk he encountered in the countryside: "The people looked yellow, poor, and sickly. Some of them lived the most miserably I ever saw any poor people live." In many ways the cotton boom only made the poor poorer.

For the nearly quarter-million free blacks in the South in 1860, conditions were generally worse than the yeoman's and often little better than the slave's. **Free Blacks** The free blacks of the Upper South were usually descendants of men and women manumitted by their owners in the 1780s and 1790s. A remarkable number of slaveholders in Virginia and the Chesapeake region had freed their slaves because of religious principles and revolutionary ideals in the wake of American independence (see Chapter 7). Many also became free as runaways, especially by the 1830s, disappearing into the southern population or making their way northward.

White southerners were increasingly desperate to restrict this growing free black presence in their midst in the antebellum years. "It seems the number of free Negroes," complained a Virginia slaveholder, "always exceeds the number of Negroes freed." Some free blacks made substantial progress in towns or cities, but most lived in rural areas and struggled to survive. They usually did not own land and had to labor in someone else's fields, often beside slaves. By law free blacks could not own a gun, buy liquor, violate curfew, assemble except in church, testify in court, or (throughout the South after 1835) vote. Despite these obstacles, a minority bought land, and others found jobs as skilled craftsmen.

A few free blacks prospered and bought slaves, most of them purchasing their own wives and children (whom they could not free, since laws required newly emancipated blacks to leave their states). In 1830 there were 3,775 free black slaveholders in the South; 80 percent lived in the four states of Louisiana, South Carolina, Virginia, and Maryland, and approximately one-half of the total lived in the two cities of New Orleans and Charleston. Hundreds of petitions survive in which black slaveholders asked to be exempted from antimanumission laws passed in most southern states. At the same time, a few mulattos in New Orleans were active slave traders in its booming market.

In the cotton and Gulf regions, a large proportion of free blacks were mulattos, the privileged offspring of wealthy white planters. Not all **Free Black Communities** planters freed their mixed-race offspring, but those who did often recognized a moral obligation and gave their children a good education and financial backing. In a few cities like New Orleans, Charleston, and Mobile, extensive interracial sex, as well as migrations from the Caribbean, had produced a mulatto population that was recognized as a distinct class.

In many southern cities by the 1840s, free black communities formed, especially around an expanding number of churches. By the late 1850s, Baltimore had fifteen churches, Louisville nine, and Nashville and St. Louis four each, and most of them were African Methodist Episcopal. Class and race distinctions were important to southern free blacks, but outside a few cities, which developed fraternal orders of skilled craftsmen and fellowships of light-skinned people, most mulattos experienced more disadvantages than benefits. In the United States, "one drop" of black "blood" made them black, and potentially enslaveable.

At the top of the southern social pyramid were slaveholding planters. As a group they lived well and enjoyed luxuries. But most lived in comfortable farmhouses, not on the opulent scale that legend suggests.

Planters

The grand plantation mansions, with fabulous gardens and long rows of outlying slave quarters, are an enduring symbol of the Old South. But a few statistics tell the fuller story: in 1850, 50 percent of southern slaveholders had fewer than five slaves; 72 percent had fewer than ten; 88 percent had fewer than twenty. Thus the average slaveholder was not a wealthy aristocrat but an aspiring farmer, usually a person of humble origins, with little formal education.

Consider the Louisiana cotton planter Bennet Barrow, a newly rich planter of the 1840s who was preoccupied with moneymaking. He worried constantly over his cotton crop, filling his diary with weather reports and gloomy predictions of his yields. Yet Barrow also strove to appear above such worries. Barrow hunted frequently and had a passion for racing horses and raising hounds. He could report the loss of a slave without feeling, but emotion broke through his laconic manner when illness afflicted his sporting animals. "Never was a person more unlucky than I am," he mourned. "My favorite pup never lives." His strongest feelings surfaced when his horse Jos Bell—equal to "the best Horse in the South"—"broke down running a mile . . . ruined for Ever." The same day the

This grand portrait (1851) by William Frye of Minor Winn Gracey and his wife, Mourning Smith Gracey, of Alabama, celebrates the planter class's wealth and status in the artifacts surrounding the couple. (Loaned by William M. Spencer III, Birmingham Museum of Art)

distraught Barrow gave his field hands a "general Whipping." In 1841 diary entries he worried about a rumored slave insurrection. He gave a "severe whipping" to several of his slaves when they disobediently killed a hog. And when a slave named Ginney Jerry "sherked" his cotton-picking duties and was rumored "about to run off," Barrow whipped him one day, and the next, recorded matter-of-factly: "took my gun found him in the Bayou behind the Quarter, shot him in his thigh—etc. raining all around."

The richest planters used their wealth to model genteel sophistication. Extended visits, parties, and balls to which women wore the latest fashions provided opportunities for friendship, courtship, and display. Such parties were held during the Christmas holidays, but also on such occasions as a molasses stewing, a Bachelor's Ball, a horse race, or the crowning of the May Queen. These entertainments were especially important as diversions for plantation women. Young women relished social events to break the monotony of their domestic lives. In 1826 a Virginia girl was ecstatic about the "week . . . I was in Town." "There were five beaux and as many belles in the house constantly," she declared, and all she and her companions did was "eat, visit, romp, and sleep. . . ."

Some old Virginia and South Carolina families were represented among the proud new "cotton snobs" of Alabama and Mississippi, but most of the planters in these cotton boom states were newly rich by the 1840s. As one historian put it, "a number of men mounted from log cabin to plantation mansion on a stairway of cotton bales, accumulating slaves as they climbed." And many did not live like rich men. Some lived for decades in their original log cabins, improved only by clapboards or a frame addition. They put their new wealth into cotton acreage and slaves even as they sought refinement and high social status.

William Faulkner immortalized the new wealthy planter in a fictional character, Thomas Sutpen, in his novel *Absalom, Absalom!* (1936). Sutpen arrives in a Mississippi county in the 1830s, buys a huge plantation he calls Sutpen's Hundred, and with his troop of slaves converts it into a wealthy enterprise. Sutpen marries a local girl, and although he is always viewed as a mysterious outsider by many earlier residents of the county, he becomes a pillar of the slaveholding class. Sutpen eventually serves as an officer in the Confederate Army, but he achieves his status largely because he was a self-made man of indomitable will and slave-based wealth. Although his ambition is ultimately his undoing, one of the earliest lessons Sutpen had learned

about success in the South he migrated into was, as he says, that "you got to have land and niggers and a fine house. . . ."

The cotton boom in the Mississippi valley created one-generation aristocrats. A nonfictional case in point is Greenwood Leflore, a Chocktaw chieftain who owned a plantation in Mississippi with four hundred slaves. After selling his cotton on the world market, he spent $10,000 in France to furnish one room of his mansion. The floor was covered with a handwoven Aubusson carpet, and the furniture was all Louis XIV period pieces, upholstered in crimson and gold leaf. A table and cabinet were ornamented with tortoise-shell inlay and brasswork, and the room also featured a variety of mirrors and paintings, and a clock and candelabra in brass and ebony completed Leflore's conspicuous display of wealth.

Southern Paternalism

Slaveholding men dominated society and, especially among the wealthiest and oldest families, justified their dominance through a paternalistic ideology. Instead of stressing the profitable aspects of commercial agriculture, they focused on their *obligations*, viewing themselves as custodians of the welfare of society in general and of the black families they owned in particular. The paternalistic planter saw himself not as an oppressor but as the benevolent guardian of an inferior race. He developed affectionate feelings toward his slaves (as long as they knew their place) and was genuinely shocked at criticism of his behavior. Even yeomen who moved in and out of the slaveowning class shared this attitude of racial paternalism.

Paul Carrington Cameron, who was North Carolina's largest slaveholder, exemplifies this mentality. After a period of sickness among his one thousand North Carolina slaves (he had hundreds more in Alabama and Mississippi), Cameron wrote, "I fear the Negroes have suffered much from the want of proper attention and kindness under this late distemper . . . no love of lucre shall ever induce me to be cruel. . . ." On another occasion he described to his sister the sense of responsibility he felt: "Do you remember a cold & frosty morning, during [our mother's] illness, when she said to me 'Paul my son the people ought to be shod' this is ever in my ears, whenever I see any ones shoes in bad order; and in my ears it will be, so long as I am master."

It was comforting to rich planters to see themselves in this way, and slaves—accommodating to the realities of power—encouraged their masters to think their benevolence was appreciated. Paternalism also served as a defense against abolitionist criticism. Still, paternalism was often a matter of style, covering harsher assumptions. As talk of paternalistic duties increased, theories about the complete and permanent inferiority of blacks multiplied. In reality, paternalism grew as a give-and-take relationship between masters and slaves, each extracting from the other as much as they could of what they desired—labor from the bondsmen, a measure of autonomy and living space from the slaveowners. But it also evolved as a theory of black slavery and white dominance. As one historian has argued, paternalism "grew out of the necessity to discipline and morally justify a system of exploitation, . . . a fragile bridge across the intolerable contradictions inherent" in a slave society dependent on "the willing reproduction and productivity of its victims."

Even Paul Cameron's benevolence vanished with changed circumstances. After the Civil War, he bristled at African Americans' efforts to be free and made sweeping economic decisions without regard to their welfare. Writing on Christmas Day 1865, Cameron showed little Christian charity (but a healthy profit motive) when he declared, "I am convinced that the people who gets rid of the free negro first will be the first to advance in improved agriculture. Have made no effort to retain any of mine [and] will not attempt a crop beyond the capacity of 30 hands." With that he turned off his land nearly a thousand black people, rented his fields to several white farmers, and invested in industry.

Relations between men and women in the planter class were similarly paternalistic. The upper-class southern woman was raised and educated to be a wife, mother, and subordinate companion to men. South Carolina's Mary Boykin Chesnut wrote of her husband, "He is master of the house. To hear is to obey. . . . All the comfort of my life depends upon his being in a good humor." In a social system based on the coercion of an entire race, women were not allowed to challenge society's rules on sexual or racial relations.

Plantation Mistresses

Planters' daughters usually attended one of the South's rapidly multiplying boarding schools. There they formed friendships with other girls and received an education that emphasized grammar, composition, penmanship, geography, literature, and languages. Typically the young woman could entertain suitors whom her parents approved. But very soon she had to choose a husband and commit herself for life to a man whom she generally had known for only a brief time. Young women were often alienated and emotionally unfulfilled. They had to follow the wishes of their families, especially fathers. "It was for me best that I yielded to the wishes of papa," wrote a young North Carolinian in 1823. "I wonder when my best will cease to be painful and when I shall begin to enjoy life instead of enduring it."

Upon marriage, a planter class woman ceded to her husband most of her legal rights, becoming part of his family. Most of the year she was isolated on a large plantation, where she had to oversee the cooking and preserving of food, manage the house, supervise care of the children, and attend sick slaves. All these realities were more rigid and confining on the frontier, where isolation was even greater. Women sought refuge in their extended families and associations with other women. In 1821 a Georgia woman wrote to her brother of the distress of a cousin's wife: "They are living . . . in the frontiers of the state and [a] perfectly uncivilized place. Cousin W. gets a good practice [the husband]—but she is almost crazy to get to Alabama where one of her sisters is living." Men on plantations could occasionally escape into the public realm—to town, business, or politics. Women could retreat from rural plantation culture only into kinship.

It is not surprising that a perceptive young woman sometimes approached marriage with anxiety. Women could hardly help viewing their wedding days, as one put it in 1832, as "the day to fix my fate." Lucy Breckinridge, a wealthy Virginia girl of twenty, lamented the autonomy she surrendered at the altar. In her diary she recorded this unvarnished observation on marriage: "If [husbands] care for their wives at all it is only as a sort of servant, a being made to attend to their comforts and to keep the children out of the way. . . . A woman's life after she is married, unless there is an immense amount of love, is nothing but suffering and hard work."

Marriage and Family

Lucy loved young children but knew that childbearing often involved grief, poor health, and death. In 1840 the birth rate for white southern women in their childbearing years was almost 30 percent higher than the national average. The average southern white woman could expect to bear eight children in 1800; by 1860 the figure had decreased to only six, with one or more miscarriages likely. For those women who wanted to plan their families, methods of contraception and medical care were uncertain. Complications of childbirth were a major cause of death, occurring twice as often in the hot, humid South as in the Northeast.

Slavery was another source of problems that white women had to endure but were not supposed to notice. "Violations of the moral law . . . made mulattoes as common as blackberries," protested a woman in Georgia, but wives had to play "the ostrich game." "A magnate who runs a hideous black harem," wrote Mrs. Chesnut, ". . . poses as the model of all human virtues to these poor women whom God and the laws have given him. From the height of his awful majesty, he scolds and thunders at them, as if he never did wrong in his life."

Southern men tolerated little discussion by women of the slavery issue. In the 1840s and 1850s, as abolitionist attacks on slavery increased, southern men published a barrage of articles stressing that women should restrict their concerns to the home. The *Southern Quarterly Review* declared, "The proper place for a woman is at home. One of her highest privileges, to be politically merged in the existence of her husband."

But some southern women were beginning to seek a larger role. A study of women in Petersburg, Virginia, a large tobacco-manufacturing town, revealed behavior that valued financial autonomy. Over several decades before 1860, the proportion of women who never married, or did not remarry after the death of a spouse, grew to exceed 33 percent. Likewise the number of women who worked for wages, controlled their own property, and ran millinery or dressmaking businesses increased. In managing property, these and other women benefited from legal changes; to protect families from the husband's indebtedness during business panics and recessions, reforms gave married women some property rights.

Slave Life and Labor

 For African Americans, slavery was a burden that destroyed some people and forced others to develop modes of survival. Slaves knew a life of poverty, coercion, toil, and resentment. They provided the physical strength, and much of the know-how, to build a burgeoning agricultural empire. But their daily lives embodied the nation's most basic contradiction: in the world's model republic, they were on the wrong side of a brutally unequal power relationship between masters and slaves.

Southern slaves enjoyed few material comforts beyond the bare necessities. Although they generally had

Slaves' Everyday Conditions

enough to eat, their diet was plain and monotonous. Clothing too was plain, coarse, and inexpensive. Few slaves received more than one or two changes of clothing for hot and cold seasons and one blanket each winter. Children of both sexes ran naked in hot weather and wore long cotton shirts in winter. Many slaves had to go without shoes until December, even as far north as Virginia. The shoes they received were frequent objects of complaint—uncomfortable brass-toed brogans or stiff wraparounds made from tanned leather. The bare feet of slaves were often symbolic of their status, and one reason why, after freedom, many black parents were so concerned to provide their children with shoes.

Summer and winter, slaves typically lived in small one-room cabins, possibly with a window opening but no glass. Some of the richer plantations provided more substantial houses, but the average slave lived in crude accommodations, where dirt was the only floor. The gravest drawback of slave cabins was not lack of comfort but their unhealthfulness. Each small cabin housed one or two entire families. Crowding and lack of sanitation fostered the spread of infection and contagious diseases such as typhoid fever, malaria, and dysentery.

Hard work was the central fact of slaves' existence. The long hours and large work gangs that characterized Gulf Coast cotton districts oper-

Slaves' Work Routines

ated almost like factories in the field. Overseers rang the morning bell before dawn—so early that some slaves remembered being "afraid to start work for fear that they would cover the cotton plants with dirt because they couldn't see clearly." Slaves who cultivated tobacco in the Upper South worked long hours picking the sticky, sometimes noxious, tobacco leaves under harsh discipline. And, as one woman recalled when interviewed in the 1930s, "it was way after sundown 'fore they could stop that field work. Then they had to hustle to finish their night work [such as watering livestock or cleaning cotton] in time for supper, or go to bed without it."

Working "from sun to sun" became a norm in much of the South. Long hours and hard work were among the advantages that slave labor gave southern planters. As one planter put it, slaves were the best la-

George Fuller, an itinerant painter from Massachusetts, worked from 1856 to 1858 in Alabama, where he made this sketch in ink and pencil of a mistress joining her slave at work on washday.   (Pocumtuck Valley Memorial Association)

bor because "you could command them and make them do what was right." Profit took precedence over paternalism. Slave women did heavy fieldwork, often as much as the men and even during pregnancy. Old people—of whom there were few—were kept busy caring for young children, doing light chores, or carding, ginning, and spinning cotton. Children had to gather kindling, carry water to the fields, or sweep the yard. The black abolitionist orator Frances Ellen Watkins captured this grinding economic reality of slavery in an 1857 speech, charging that slaveholders had "found out a fearful alchemy by which . . . blood can be transformed into gold. Instead of listening to the cry of agony, they listen to the ring of dollars and stoop down to pick up the coin."

Different jobs, talents, and circumstances created variations in status and rivalries among slaves. But only one-quarter of all slaves lived on plantations of fifty or more blacks, so few experienced a wide chasm separating house servants and lowly field hands. Many slaves did both housework and fieldwork, depending on their age and the season, and this arrangement helped create a sense of group unity.

But incentives had to be part of the labor regime and the master-slave relationship as well. Planters in the South Carolina and Georgia low country used a task system whereby slaves were assigned measured amounts of work to be performed in a given amount of time. So much cotton on a daily basis was to be picked from a designated field; so many rows hoed or plowed in a particular slave's specified section. When the task system worked best, slaves and masters alike embraced it, fostering a degree of reciprocal trust.

By the 1830s slaveowners found that labor could be regulated and motivated by the clock. When their task and "clock time" was up, slaves' time was their own, for working in garden plots, tending to hogs, or even hiring out their own extra labor. The system's incentives afforded many slave families life-sustaining material and psychological benefits. From this experience and personal space, many slaves developed their own sense of property ownership.

Slaves could not demand autonomy too much, of course, because the owner enjoyed a monopoly on force and violence. Whites throughout the South believed that slaves "can't be governed except with the whip." One South Carolinian frankly explained to a northern journalist that he whipped his slaves regularly, "say once a fort-

Violence Against Slaves

night; . . . the fear of the lash kept them in good order." Evidence suggests that whippings were less frequent on small farms than on large plantations. But beatings symbolized authority to the master and tyranny to the slaves, who made them a benchmark for evaluating a master. In the words of former slaves, a good owner was one who did not "whip too much," whereas a bad owner "whipped till he's bloodied you and blistered you."

As these reports suggest, terrible abuses could and did occur. The master wielded virtually absolute authority on his plantation, and courts did not recognize the word of chattel. Slaveholders rarely had to answer to the law or to the state. Pregnant women were whipped, and there were burnings, mutilations, tortures, and murders. Yet physical cruelty may have been less prevalent in the United States than in other slave-holding parts of the New World. In sugar-growing operations in Brazil and mining regions in Peru in the 1800s, slaves were regarded as an expendable resource to be replaced after several years. Especially in some of the sugar islands of the Caribbean, treatment was so poor and death rates were so high that the heavily male slave population shrank in size. In the United States, by contrast, the slave population experienced a steady natural increase as births exceeded deaths and each generation grew larger. Indeed, the North American slave population was the only one in the New World to naturally reproduce itself.

The worst evil of American slavery was not its physical cruelty but the nature of slavery itself: coercion, lack of freedom, belonging to another person, virtually no hope for mobility or change. Recalling their time in bondage, some former slaves emphasized the physical abuse, or the "bullwhip days," as one woman described her past. But memories of physical punishment focused on the tyranny of whipping as much as the pain. Delia Garlic made the essential point: "It's bad to belong to folks that own you soul an' body. I could tell you 'bout it all day, but even then you couldn't guess the awfulness of it." Thomas Lewis put it this way: "There was no such thing as being good to slaves. Many people were better than others, but a slave belonged to his master and there was no way to get out of it." To be a slave was to be the object of another person's will and material gain, to be owned, as the saying went, "from the cradle to the grave."

As these comments reveal, the great majority of American slaves retained their mental independence and self-respect despite their bondage. Contrary to popular belief at the time, they were not loyal partners in their own oppression. They had to be subservient and speak honeyed words to their masters, but they talked and behaved quite differently among themselves. The evidence of their resistant attitudes comes from their actions and their own life stories. In his *Narrative* (1845), Frederick Douglass wrote that most slaves, when asked about "their condition and the character of their masters, almost universally say they are contented, and that their masters are kind." Slaves did this, said Douglass, because they were governed by the maxim that "a still tongue makes a wise head," especially in the presence of unfamiliar people. Because they were "part of the human family," slaves often quarreled over who had the best master. But at the end of the day, Douglass remarked, when one had a bad master, he sought a better master; and when he had a better one, he wanted to "be his own master."

Some former slaves remembered warm feelings between masters and slaves, but the prevailing attitudes were distrust and antagonism.

Slave-Master Relationships

Slaves saw through acts of kindness. One woman said her mistress was "a mighty good somebody to belong to" but only "'cause she was raisin' us to work for her." A man recalled that his owners took good care of their slaves, "and Grandma Maria say, 'Why shouldn't they—it was their money.'" Slaves also resented being used as beasts of burden. One man observed that his master "fed us reg'lar on good, 'stantial food, just like you'd tend to your horse, if you had a real good one." Another recalled his master eyeing the slave children and saying, "'That one will be worth a thousand dollars.' . . . You see, it was just like raisin' young mules."

Slaves were alert to the thousand daily signs of their degraded status. One man recalled the general rule that slaves ate cornbread and owners ate biscuits. If blacks did get biscuits, "the flour that we made the biscuits out of was the third-grade sorts." A former slave recalled, "Us catch lots of 'possums," but "the white folks ate 'em. Our mouths would water for some of that 'possum, but it wasn't often they let us have none." If the owner took his slaves' garden produce to town and sold it for them, the slaves often suspected him of pocketing part of the profits.

Suspicion often grew into hatred. When a yellow fever epidemic struck in 1852, many slaves saw it as God's retribution. An elderly ex-slave named Minnie Fulkes cherished the conviction that God was going to punish white people for their cruelty to blacks. She described the whippings that her mother had to endure, and then she exclaimed, "Lord, Lord, I hate white people and the flood waters goin' to drown some more."

On the plantation, of course, slaves had to keep such thoughts to themselves. Often they expressed one feeling to whites, another within their own households. In their daily lives slaves created many ways to survive and to sustain their humanity in this world of repression.

Slave Culture

A people is always "more than the sum of its brutalization," wrote the African American novelist Ralph Ellison in 1967. What people create in the face of hard luck and oppression is what provides hope. The resource that enabled slaves to maintain such defiance was their culture: a body of beliefs, values, and practices born of their past and maintained in the present. As best they could, they built a community knitted together by sto-

ries, music, a religious world-view, leadership, the smells of their cooking, the sounds of their own voices, and the tapping of their feet. "The values expressed in folklore," wrote the African American poet Sterling Brown, provided a "wellspring to which slaves . . . could return in times of doubt to be refreshed."

Slaves had few of the basic hopes one generation wishes to transmit to the next that were not denied. That they endured and found loyalty and strength among themselves is a tribute to their courage and triumph of the human spirit.

Slave culture changed significantly after 1800, as fewer and fewer slaves were African-born. For a few years South Carolina reopened the international slave trade, but after 1808 Congress banned further importations. By the 1830s, the vast majority of slaves in the South were native-born Americans. Many blacks, therefore, can trace their American ancestry back farther than many white Americans.

African Cultural Survival

In addition to the heavy labor required on southern plantations, slaves also performed work of fine craftsmanship in furniture making, needlework, and other areas. This dining room corner cupboard is walnut veneer on pine and cedar and was built around 1840. The quilt, emblazoned with chalice cups to celebrate the annual visit of an Anglican bishop, was made around 1860. Both are from Texas.   (Cupboard: Courtesy of the Witte Museum and the San Antonio Museum Association, San Antonio, Texas; Quilt: The American Museum in Britain, photo courtesy of The Museum of the Confederacy)

How do historians know...

that the slaves' daily feelings, yearnings, crises, or hardships were reflected in their songs? In the slave narratives, autobiographies written by ex-slaves after their escapes, former bondsmen and bondswomen left many clues to the meanings of slave culture. In *Narrative of the Life of Frederick Douglass, An American Slave* (1845), the most famous black abolitionist gave many answers to the riddles of the slaves' psychological world. Slaves interpreted their experience from a sacred world-view in which God and the spirit could enter daily life at any time. It was also a world of paradoxes and ironic reversals. Douglass's discussion of slave life constantly moves between the slaves' endurance of dehumanization and their ability to fashion creative resistance. He argues that the slaves' humanity manifests itself in a cunning accommodation to, and subversion of, evil authority.

Douglass, seen here when he was in his early thirties, anticipates modern historians' treatment of slave culture most directly in his discussion of slave music (see excerpt below). Through imagination, he invites the future scholar into the piney woods around the Wye River plantation (the "Great House Farm") on the slaves' "allowance day" (when food and clothing were distributed), and there, in silence, to "analyze the sounds that shall pass through the chambers of

his soul." *Analyze the sounds:* Since the 1960s, in the study of folklore, especially the lyrics of the spirituals, this is precisely what historians of slave culture have done. By coming to understand the form and substance of slave music, folktales, and religious practices, scholars have been able to better comprehend the psychological and spiritual survival of American bondspeople. They have come to see that cultural behavior is how all people find self-definition and resist those elements of life that threaten to control their souls. In many studies of slave communities, scholars have taken Douglass up on his invitation. (Photo: Metropolitan Museum of Art, The Rubel Collection, Promised Gift of William Rubel [L.1997.84.8])

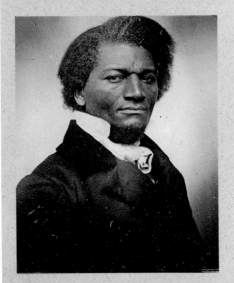

The slaves selected to go to the Great House Farm, for the monthly allowance for themselves and their fellow-slaves, were peculiarly enthusiastic. While on their way, they would make the dense old woods, for miles around, reverberate with their wild songs, revealing at once the highest joy and the deepest sadness. They would compose and sing as they went along, consulting neither time nor tune. . . . They would . . . sing most exultingly the following words:—

> *I am going away to the Great House Farm!*
> *O, yea! O, yea! O!*

This they would sing, as a chorus, to words to which to many would seem unmeaning jargon, but which, nevertheless, were full of meaning to themselves. I have sometimes thought that the mere hearing of those songs would do more to impress some minds with the horrible character of slavery, than the reading of whole volumes of philosophy on the subject could do.

I did not, when a slave, understand the deep meaning of those rude and apparently incoherent songs. I was myself within the circle; so that I neither saw nor heard as those without might see and hear. They told a tale of woe which was then altogether beyond my feeble comprehension; they were tones loud, long, and deep; they breathed the prayer and complaint of souls boiling over with the bitterest anguish. Every tone was a testimony against slavery, and a prayer to God for deliverance from chains. The hearing of those wild notes always depressed my spirit, and filled me with ineffable sadness, I have frequently found myself in tears while hearing them. . . . Those songs still follow me, to deepen my hatred of slavery, and quicken my sympathies for my brethren in bonds. If any one wishes to be impressed with the soul-killing effects of slavery, let him go to Colonel Lloyd's plantation, and, on allowance-day, place himself in the deep pine woods, and there let him, in silence, analyze the sounds that shall pass through the chambers of his soul. . . .

The songs of the slave represent the sorrows of his heart; and he is relieved by them, only as an aching heart is relieved by its tears. . . .

Despite lack of firsthand memory, African influences remained strong, especially in appearance and forms of expression. Some slave men plaited their hair into rows and fancy designs; slave women often wore their hair "in string"—tied in small bunches secured by a string or piece of cloth. A few men and many women wrapped their heads in kerchiefs of the styles and colors of West Africa. Some could remember the names of African ancestors passed on to them by family lore. In burial practices, slaves used jars and other glass objects to decorate graves, following similar African traditions.

Music, religion, and folktales were parts of daily life for most slaves. Borrowing partly from their African background, as well as forging new American folkways, they developed what scholars have called a "sacred world-view," which affected all aspects of work, leisure, and self-understanding. Slaves made musical instruments with carved motifs that resembled African stringed instruments. Their drumming and dancing followed African patterns that made whites marvel. One visitor to Georgia in the 1860s described a ritual dance of African origin: "A ring of singers is formed. . . . They then utter a kind of melodious chant, which gradually increases in strength, and in noise, until it fairly shakes the house, and it can be heard for a long distance." This observer of the "ring shout" also noted the agility of the dancers and the African call-and-response pattern in their chanting.

Many slaves continued to believe in spirit possession. Whites, too, believed in ghosts and charms, but the slaves' belief resembled the African concept of the living dead—the idea that deceased relatives visit the earth for many years until the process of dying is complete. Slaves also practiced conjuration, voodoo, and quasi-magical root medicine. By the 1850s the most notable conjurers and root doctors were reputed to live in South Carolina, Georgia, Louisiana, and other isolated coastal areas with high slave populations. But even in Maryland, a young Frederick Douglass carried a special root that had to be positioned "always on the right side," given him by an "old advisor" who lived alone in the woods.

These cultural survivals provided slaves with a sense of their separate past and their own special ways. Such practices and beliefs were not static "Africanisms" or mere "retentions." They were cultural adaptations, living traditions reformed in the Americas in response to new experience.

As they became African Americans, slaves also developed a sense of racial identity. In the colonial period, Africans had arrived in America from many different states and kingdoms, represented in distinctive languages, body markings, and traditions. Planters had used ethnic differences to create occupational hierarchies. By the early antebellum period, however, old ethnic identities gave way as American slaves increasingly saw themselves as a single group unified by race. Africans had arrived in the New World with virtually no concept of "race"; by the antebellum era, their descendants had learned through bitter experience that race was now the defining feature of their lives. They were a transplanted and transformed people.

As African culture gave way to a maturing African American culture, more and more slaves adopted Christianity. But they fashioned Christianity into an instrument of support and resistance. Theirs was a religion of justice and deliverance, quite unlike their masters' religious propaganda directed at them as a means of control. "You ought to have heard that preachin'," said one man. "'Obey your master and mistress, don't steal chickens and eggs and meat,' but nary a word about havin' a soul to save." Slaves believed that Jesus cared about their souls and their plight. In their interpretations of biblical stories, as one historian has said, they were "literally willing themselves reborn." They rejected the idea that in heaven whites would have "the colored folks . . . there to wait on 'em." Instead, slaveholders would be "broilin' in hell for their sin" when God's justice came.

Slaves' Religion and Music

For slaves, Christianity was a religion of personal and group salvation. Devout men and women worshiped every day, "in the field or by the side of the road," or in special "prayer grounds" that afforded privacy. Some slaves held fervent secret prayer meetings that lasted far into the night. Many slaves nurtured an unshakable belief that God would enter history and end their bondage. This faith—and the joy and emotional release that accompanied worship—sustained them.

Slaves also adapted Christianity to African practices. In West African belief, devotees are possessed by a god so thoroughly that the god's own personality replaces the human personality. In the late antebellum era, Christian slaves experienced possession by the Protestant "Holy Spirit." The combination of shouting, singing, and dancing that seemed to overtake black worshipers formed the heart of their religious faith. "The old meeting house caught fire," recalled an ex-slave preacher. "The spirit was there. . . . God saw our need and came to us. I used to wonder what made people shout but now I don't. There is a joy on the inside and it wells up so strong that we can't keep still. It is fire in the bones. Any time that fire touches a man, he will jump." Out in brush arbors or in meetinghouses, slaves took in the presence of God and sang away their woes. Some travelers observed "bands" of "Fist and Heel Worshippers." "He who could sing loudest and longest led the 'Band,'" said a suspicious black bishop from the North who opposed emotional religion, "a handkerchief in hand with which he kept time, while his feet resounded on the floor like the drumsticks of a bass drum." Many post-slavery black choirs could not perform properly without a good wooden floor to use as their "drum."

Rhythm and physical movement were crucial to slaves' religious experience. In their own preachers' chanted sermons, which reached out to gather the sinner into a narrative of meanings and cadences along the way to conversion, an American tradition was born. The chanted sermon was both a message from Scripture and a patterned form that required audience response punctuated by "yes sirs!" and "amens!" But it was in song that the slaves left their most sublime gift to American culture.

Through the spirituals, slaves tried to impose order on the chaos of their lives. Many themes run through the lyrics of slave songs. Often referred to later as the "sorrow songs," they also anticipate imminent rebirth. Sadness could give way immediately to joy: "Did you ever stan' on a mountain, wash yo hands in a cloud?" Rebirth was at the heart as well of the famous hymn "Oh, Freedom": "Oh, Oh, Freedom / Oh, Oh, Freedom over me— / But before I'll be a slave, / I'll be buried in my grave, / And go home to my Lord, / And Be Free!"

This tension and sudden change between sorrow and joy animates many songs: "Sometimes I feel like a motherless chile . . . / Sometimes I feel like an eagle in the air, / Spread my wings and fly, fly, fly!" Many songs also express a sense of intimacy and closeness with God. Some songs display an unmistakable rebelliousness, such as the enduring "He said, and if I had my way / If I had my way, if I had my way, / I'd tear this building down!" And some spirituals reached for a collective sense of hope in the black community as a whole:

> O, gracious Lord! When shall it be,
> That we poor souls shall all be free;
> Lord, break them slavery powers—

> Will you go along with me?
> Lord break them slavery powers,
> Go sound the jubilee!

In many ways, American slaves converted the Christian God to themselves. They sought an alternative world to live in—a home other than the one fate had given them on earth. In a thousand variations on the 'Brer Rabbit folktales, in which power and success could be reversed, and in the countless refrains of their songs, they fashioned survival and resistance out of their own cultural imagination.

The main source of support for individuals was the family, which faced severe pressures. Many families were separated by the forced migration and sale of an estimated 2 million slaves between 1820 and 1860 into the region extending from western Georgia to eastern Texas. When the Union Army registered thousands of black marriages in Mississippi and Louisiana in 1864 and 1865, fully 25 percent of the men over forty reported that they had been forcibly separated from a previous wife. Thousands of black families were disrupted every year to serve the needs of the expanding cotton economy.

The Slave Trade and Separation

Many antebellum white southerners made their livings from the slave trade. In South Carolina alone by the 1850s, there were over one hundred slave-trading firms selling an annual average of approximately 6,500 slaves to southwestern states. Although southerners often denied it, vast numbers of slaves moved west by outright sale and not by migrating with their owners. A typical trader's advertisement read: "NEGROES WANTED. I am paying the highest cash prices for young and likely NEGROES, those having good front teeth and being otherwise sound."

Slave traders were practical, roving businessmen. They were sometimes considered degraded by white planters, but many became prominent citizens, and whatever their status, many slaveowners did business with them. Market forces, as the Butler auction indicates, drove this commerce in humanity. At slave "pens" in cities such as New Orleans, traders promoted a "a large and commodious showroom . . . prepared to accommodate over 200 Negroes for sale." Traders did their utmost to make their slaves appear young, healthy, and happy, cutting gray whiskers off men, using "paddles" as discipline so as not to scar their merchandise, and forcing people to dance and sing as buyers arrived for an auction. When trans-

A slave coffle on the march toward
newly settled states of the Southwest.
(Collection of William Loren Katz)

ported to the southwestern markets, slaves were often
chained together in "coffles," which made journeys of
500 miles or more on foot.

The complacent mixture of racism and business
among traders is evident in their own language. "I refused a girl 20 year[s] old at 700 yesterday," one trader
wrote to another in 1853. "If you think best to take her
at 700 I can still get her. She is very badly whipped but
good teeth." Some sales were transacted at owners' requests. "Bought a cook yesterday that was to go out of
state," wrote a trader; "she just made the people mad
that was all." Some traders demonstrated how deeply
slavery and racism were intertwined. "I have bought
the boy Isaac for 1100," wrote a trader in 1854 to his
partner. "I think him very prime. . . . He is a . . . house
servant . . . first rate cook . . . and splendid carriage driver. He is also a fine painter and varnisher and . . . says
he can make a fine panel door. . . . Also he performs
well on the violin. . . . He is a genius and its strange to
say I think he is smarter than I am."

But separation did not mean that slave families
could not endure. American slaves clung tenaciously

The Black Family in Slavery

to the personal relationships that
gave meaning to life. Although American law did not recognize slave families, masters permitted them; in fact,
slaveowners expected slaves to form
families and have children. As a result, even along the
rapidly expanding edge of the cotton kingdom, there
was a normal ratio of men to women, young to old.
Studies have shown that on some of the largest cotton
plantations of South Carolina, when masters allowed
their slaves increased autonomy working on the task
system, the property accumulation thus fostered led to
more stable and healthier families.

Following African kinship traditions, African Americans avoided marriage between cousins (commonplace among aristocratic slaveowners). Adapting West
African customs, they did not condemn unwed mothers but did expect a young woman to enter a monoga-
mous relationship after one pregnancy, if not before.
By naming their children after relatives of past generations, African Americans emphasized their family
histories. If they chose to bear the surname of a slave-

This photograph of five generations of a slave family, taken in Beaufort, South Carolina, in 1862, is silent but powerful testimony to the importance that enslaved African Americans placed on their ever-threatened family ties.   (Library of Congress)

owner, it was often the name not of their current master but of the owner under whom their family had begun their bondage in America.

Sexual abuse and rape by white masters of slave women were ever-present threats. Harriet Jacobs, who spent much of her youth and early adult years dodging her owner's relentless sexual pursuit, described this circumstance as "the war of my life." In recollecting her desperate effort to protect her children and help them find a way north to freedom, Jacobs asked a haunting question that many slave women carried with them to their graves: "Why does the slave ever love? Why allow the tendrils of the heart to twine around objects which may at any moment be wrenched away by the hand of violence?"

Slaves hated interference in their family lives. Indeed, some individuals refused separations and struggled for years to keep their children together and reestablish contact with lost loved ones. Kinship networks, indeed, were often what held family life together in many slave communities.

Slave Resistance and Rebellion

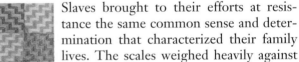Slaves brought to their efforts at resistance the same common sense and determination that characterized their family lives. The scales weighed heavily against overt revolution, and the slaves knew it. But they seized opportunities to alter their work conditions. They sometimes slacked off when they were not being watched. Thus owners complained that slaves "never would lay out their strength freely." One exasperated Virginia planter voiced his irritation (and the racism nurtured by slavery) when he said, "You can make a nigger work, *but you cannot make him think.*" These attitudes made many whites disbelievers in the prospect of black free labor after the Civil War.

Daily discontent and desperation were also manifest in sabotage of equipment, in wanton carelessness about work, in theft of food, livestock, or crops, or in getting drunk on stolen liquor. Some slaves who were

Strategies of Resistance

hired out for as much as a year away from their families might show their anger by hoarding their earnings. Or, they might just fall into recalcitrance. "I have a boy in my employ called Jim Archer," complained a Vicksburg, Mississippi, slaveholder in 1843. "Jim does not want to be under anyones control and says . . . he wants to go home this summer." A woman named Ellen, hired as a cook in Tennessee in 1856, quietly put mercury poison into a roasted apple for her unsuspecting mistress.

Many male, and some female, slaves acted out their defiance by violently attacking overseers or even their owners. Southern court records and newspapers are full of accounts of these resistant slaves who gave the lie to the syrupy image of the docile bondsmen. The price they paid was high. Such lonely rebels were customarily secured and flogged, sold away, or hanged. One Louisiana planter reported strapping two especially uncooperative slaves to a stake and delivering 150 lashes to one and 175 to the other.

Many individual slaves attempted to run away to the North, and some received assistance from the loose network known as the Underground Railroad (see page 369). But it was more common for slaves to run off temporarily to hide in the woods. Fear, disgruntlement over treatment, family separation, and a hundred other complaints might motivate slaves to try to stay at large in the Upper South states for weeks or months at a time. Only a minority of those who tried such escapes ever made it to freedom in the North, but these fugitives made slavery a very insecure institution by the 1850s.

American slavery produced some fearless revolutionaries. Gabriel's Rebellion involved as many as a thousand slaves when it was discovered in 1800, just before it exploded in Richmond, Virginia (see pages 213–214). A similar conspiracy in Charleston in 1822, led by a free black named Denmark Vesey, involved many of the prominent whites' most trusted slaves. Born a slave, Vesey won a lottery of $1,500 in 1800 and bought his own freedom. As a literate religious leader, he struck terror into South Carolina as he combined biblical teachings with revolutionary, natural rights ideology to justify his conspiracy to overthrow the slaveholding regime. The Vesey plot began in 1821 when white authorities closed a black church founded three years earlier in a split between white and black Methodists. Betrayed by whites and blacks alike, the Vesey rebellion and its potential horrors deeply un-

nerved official white South Carolina. When the arrests and trials were over, thirty-seven conspirators were executed and more than three dozen others were banished from the state.

The most famous rebel of all, Nat Turner, struck for freedom in Southampton County, Virginia, in 1831.

Nat Turner's Insurrection

The son of an African woman who passionately hated her enslavement, Nat Turner was a precocious child who learned to read when he was very young. Encouraged by his first owner to study the Bible, he enjoyed certain privileges but also endured hard work and changes of masters. His father successfully escaped to freedom.

Eventually young Nat became a preacher with a reputation for eloquence and a tendency toward mysticism. After nurturing his plan for several years, Turner led a band of rebels from farm to farm in the predawn darkness of August 22, 1831. The group severed limbs and crushed skulls with axes or killed their victims with guns. Before alarmed planters stopped them, Nat Turner and his followers had slaughtered sixty whites of both sexes and all ages in forty-eight hours. The rebellion was soon put down, and in retaliation, whites killed slaves at random all over the region, including in adjoining states. Turner was eventually caught and then hanged. As many as two hundred African Americans, including innocent victims of marauding whites, lost their lives as a result of the rebellion.

Nat Turner remains one of the most haunting symbols in America's unresolved history with racial slavery and discrimination. While in jail awaiting execution, Turner was interviewed by a Virginia lawyer and slaveholder, Thomas R. Gray. Their intriguing, collaborative creation, *The Confessions of Nat Turner*, became a bestseller within a month of Turner's hanging. Turner told of his early childhood, his religious visions, his zeal to be free; Gray called the rebel a "gloomy fanatic," but in a manner that made him fascinating and produced one of the most remarkable documents in the annals of American slavery. In the wake of Turner's insurrection, many states passed stiffened legal codes against black education and religious practice.

Most importantly, in 1832 the state of Virginia, shocked to its core, held a full-scale legislative and public debate over gradual emancipation as a means of ridding itself of slavery and of blacks. The plan debated would not have freed any slaves until 1858, and it provided that eventually all blacks would be colonized outside Virginia. Fear and anti-black sentiments drove this debate. In the end, Virginia opted out of this pivotal moment by doing nothing except reinforcing its own moral and economic defenses of slavery. When the House of Delegates finally voted, the motion favoring gradual abolition lost by 73 to 58. Ironically, if the Virginia debate had gone the other way, Nat Turner's Rebellion would have succeeded in destroying slavery because racism had triumphed. At the very least, Turner got the nation's attention.

Harmony and Tension in a Slave Society

From 1830 to 1860, slavery impinged on laws and customs, individual values, and, increasingly, every aspect of southern politics. In all things, from their workaday movements to Sunday worship, slaves fell under the supervision of whites. State courts held that a slave "has no civil right" and could not hold property "except at the will and pleasure of his master." Revolts like Nat Turner's tightened the legal straitjacket even more. As political conflicts between North and South deepened, fears of slave revolt grew, and restrictions on slaves increased accordingly.

State and federal laws aided the capture of fugitive slaves and required nonslaveholders to support the slave system. All white male citizens had a legal duty to participate in slave patrols. Ship captains, harbor masters, and other whites in strategic positions in both North and South were required to scrutinize the papers of African Americans who might be attempting to escape bondage.

Slavery, Wealth, and Social Standing

Slavery deeply affected southern values precisely because it was the main determinant of wealth. Ownership of slaves guaranteed the labor to produce cotton and other crops on a large scale. Slaves were therefore vital to the acquisition of a fortune. Beyond that, they were a commodity and an investment, much like gold; people bought them on speculation, hoping for a steady rise in their market values. Across the South, variations in wealth from county to county corresponded very closely to variations in slaveholding.

Wealth in slaves also translated into political power: a solid majority of political officeholders were slaveholders, and the most powerful were usually large-scale planters. Lawyers and newspaper editors were sometimes influential, but they were dependent on planters for business and support.

Slavery's influence spread throughout the social system until even the values and mores of nonslaveholders bore its imprint. The availability of slave labor tended to devalue free labor: where strenuous work under supervision was reserved for an enslaved race, few free people relished it. When Alexis de Tocqueville crossed from Ohio into Kentucky in his celebrated travels of 1831, he observed "the effect that slavery produces on society. On the right bank of the Ohio [River] everything is activity, industry; labor is honoured; there are no slaves. Pass to the left bank and the scene changes so suddenly that you think yourself on the other side of the world; the enterprising spirit is gone. There, work is not only painful; it is shameful. . . ." Tocqueville's own class impulses found a home in the South, however. There he found a "veritable aristocracy which . . . combines many prejudices with high sentiments and instincts."

The values of the aristocrat—lineage, privilege, pride, and refinement of person and manner—commanded respect throughout the South. Many of those qualities were in short supply, however, in the recently settled portions of the cotton kingdom, where frontier values of courage and self-reliance ruled. Thus independence and defense of one's honor became highly valued traits for planter and frontier farmer alike.

Aristocratic Values and Frontier Individualism

Instead of gradually disappearing as it did in the North, dueling, which required men to defend their honor through violence, lasted much longer in the South. In North Carolina in 1851 a wealthy planter named Samuel Fleming responded to a series of disputes with the lawyer William Waightstill Avery by "cowhiding" (whipping) him on a public street. According to the code, Avery had two choices: to redeem his honor violently or to brand himself a coward through inaction. Three weeks later Avery shot Fleming dead at point-blank range during a session of Burke County Superior Court, with Judge William Battle and numerous spectators looking on. A jury later took only ten minutes to find Avery not guilty, and the spectators gave him a standing ovation. Though Judge Battle was troubled by this outcome, most white males seemed satisfied.

Other aristocratic values of the planter class were less acceptable to the average voter. Planters believed they were better than other people. In their pride, they expected not only to wield power but to receive deference from poorer whites. Independent and proud, the yeoman class resented infringements of their rights, and many belonged to evangelical faiths that exalted values of simplicity that were alien to the planters' love of wealth. Also conscious of national democratic ideals, yeomen sometimes challenged or rejected the aristocratic pretensions of planters.

Class tensions emerged in the western, nonslaveholding parts of the seaboard states by the 1830s.

Yeoman Demands for Political Reform

There yeoman farmers resented their underrepresentation in state legislatures and the corruption in local government. After vigorous debate, the reformers won many battles. Voters in more recently settled areas—Alabama, Mississippi, Tennessee, Arkansas, and Texas—adopted white manhood suffrage and other electoral reforms, including popular election of governors, legislative apportionment based on white population only, and locally chosen county government. Kentucky, Georgia, Florida, Louisiana, Maryland, and North Carolina adopted most or some of these measures. Only South Carolina and Virginia effectively defended property qualifications for office, legislative malapportionment, and selection of the governor by state legislatures. The structure of southern government thus became more democratic than planters wished.

Slaveowners knew that a more open government structure could permit troubling issues to arise. In Virginia, it was nonslaveholding westerners who petitioned and initiated the debate over abolition in the wake of Nat Turner's Rebellion in 1832, the last public debate on slavery in the antebellum South.

Given such tensions, it was perhaps remarkable that slaveholders and nonslaveholders did not experience more overt conflict. Why were

Antebellum White Class Relations

class confrontations among whites so infrequent? Historians have given several answers. One of the most important factors was race. The South's racial ideology stressed the superiority of all whites to blacks. Thus slavery became the basis of equality among whites, and racism inflated the status of poor whites and gave them a common interest with the rich. Moreover, family ties linked some nonslaveholders to wealthy planters, especially on the expanding frontier.

The "Old South" was a new and mobile society in which many people rose in status by acquiring land or

A bill of sale documents that this slave woman, Louisa, was owned by the young child whom she holds on her lap. In the future Louisa's life would be subject to the child's wishes and decisions.   (Missouri Historical Society, St. Louis)

slaves, and those who did not wished they could. Even in cotton-rich Alabama in the 1850s, fewer than half of the richest families in a typical county belonged to its elite ten years later. Most did not die or lose their wealth; they merely moved on to some new state. This constant mobility in an expanding plantation economy meant that southern society did not settle into an utterly rigid social pattern.

Most importantly, in their daily lives yeomen and slaveholders were seldom in conflict. Before the Civil War most yeomen were able to pursue unhindered their independent lifestyle. They worked their farms, avoided debt, and marked progress for their families that in their rural habitats was unrelated to slaveholding. Likewise, slaveholders pursued their goals quite independently of yeomen. Planters farmed for the market but also for themselves. Thus the planter did not depend on the nonslaveholder as a producer of food crops.

Suppression of dissent also played an increasing role. After 1830 white southerners who criticized the slave system out of moral conviction or class resentment were intimidated, attacked, or legally prosecuted. (Some, like James Birney, went north and joined the antislavery movement. Two sisters from Charleston, Angelina and Sarah Grimké, became leading advocates of both abolition and women's rights—see page 286.) By the 1850s the defense of slavery's interests exerted an ever more powerful influence on southern politics and society.

Still, there were signs that the relative lack of conflict between slaveholders and nonslaveholders was coming to an end in the late antebellum period. As cotton lands filled up, nonslaveholders saw their opportunities beginning to narrow; meanwhile, wealthy planters enjoyed expanding profits. The risks of entering cotton production were becoming too great and the cost of slaves too high for many yeomen to rise in society. From 1830 to 1860 the percentage of white southern families holding slaves declined steadily from 36 to 25 percent. At the same time, the monetary gap between the classes was widening. Although slaveowners accounted for this smaller portion of the population, planters' share of the South's agricultural wealth remained at between 90 and 95 percent.

Hardening of Class Lines

Urban artisans and mechanics felt the pinch acutely. Their numbers were few and in bad times they were often the first to lose work as markets collapsed. Moreover, they faced stiff competition from urban slaves, whose masters wanted to hire them out to practice trades. White workers in the port cities of Charleston and Wilmington and elsewhere staged protests demanding that economic competition from slaves be forbidden, but they were ignored. The angry protests of white workers resulted in harsh restrictions on free African American laborers and craftsmen, who had no powerful allies to defend their interests. On the eve of the Civil War, many successful free blacks actually felt compelled to leave Charleston for fear of being reenslaved.

Pre–Civil War politics reflected these tensions as well. Anticipating possible secession and the prospect of a war to defend slavery, slaveowners expressed growing fear about the loyalty of nonslaveholders. Schemes to widen the ownership of slaves were discussed, including reopening the African slave trade. In North Carolina, a prolonged and increasingly bitter controversy erupted over the combination of high taxes on land and low taxes on slaves. When nonslaveholder Hinton R. Helper denounced the slave system in *The Impending Crisis*, published in 1857, discerning planters feared the eruption of such controversies in every southern state.

But for the moment slaveowners stood secure. In the 1850s they occupied from 50 to 85 percent of the seats in state legislatures and a similarly high percentage of the South's congressional seats. Planters had established their point of view in all the other major social institutions. Professors who criticized slavery had been dismissed from colleges and universities; schoolbooks that contained "unsound" ideas had been replaced. And almost all the Methodist and Baptist clergy had become slavery's most vocal defenders.

Summary

During the thirty years before the Civil War the South grew as part of America's westward expansion. Ideologically and economically, the southern states developed in many distinctive ways; at the same time, they were also deeply enmeshed in the nation's heritage and political economy. Far more than the North, the antebellum South was a biracial society; whites grew up directly influenced by black folkways and culture, and blacks, the vast majority of whom were slaves, became predominantly native-born Americans and the co-builders with whites of a rural, agricultural society.

With the sustained thirty- to forty-year cotton boom, the South grew fatefully into a much larger slave society than it had been early in the century. The coercive influence of slavery affected virtually every element of southern life and politics, and increasingly produced a leadership determined to preserve a conservative, hierarchical social and racial order. Despite the white supremacy that united them, the democratic values of yeomen often clashed with the profit motives of aristocratic planters. The benevolent self-image and paternalistic ideology of slaveholders had to ultimately stand the test of the slaves' own judgments. African American slaves responded by fashioning over time a rich expressive folk culture and a religion of personal and group deliverance. Their experiences could be profoundly different from one region and kind of labor to another. Some blacks were crushed by bondage;

many others transcended it in an epic of survival and resistance.

From the Old South on to modern times, white and black southerners have always shared a tragic, mutual history. By 1850, through their own wits and on the backs of African labor, white southerners had aggressively built one of the last profitable, expanding slave societies on earth. North of them, deeply intertwined with them in the same nation, market economy, constitutional system, and history, a different kind of society had grown even faster—one driven by industrialism and individualistic free labor. The clash of these two deeply connected, yet mutually fearful and divided societies was about to explode in political storms over how the nation would define its future.

LEGACY FOR A PEOPLE AND A NATION
The Black Family

In the late 1830s Virginia slaveholder Robert Bruce prepared a list of the slaves on his plantation. He noted that three maternal grandmothers performed the primary care of small children whose mothers either were dead or had been sold away. Bruce made no mention of slave fathers.

Bruce's list illustrates one of slavery's deepest legacies—its impact on family life. The questions are still with us. Can poverty and broken families since emancipation be attributed to the slave experience? Does slavery's heritage require persistent redistributive justice in our current society? And who or what is responsible for continuing disparities in the family stability of blacks and whites: history (the nation's policies) or individuals (personal behavior)?

Slavery put unbearable pressures on black family life, and ever since emancipation, popular lore supported the idea that a nuclear family could not survive the masters' economic and sexual power. In 1939 the black sociologist E. Franklin Frazier argued that "no social organization" survived from African heritage among American slaves, and that the family "went to pieces." In the 1960s Daniel Patrick Moynihan conducted a study that concluded that blacks had plunged into urban poverty because of a set of behaviors drawn from the past that eroded stable families. The values alleged to cause this "culture of poverty" are self-indulgence, low educational aspiration, and lack of thrift. This analysis thrives on the image of the black male adult's absence from familial responsibilities.

Historians challenged the "damage" thesis in the 1970s, revealing evidence of strong families during and after slavery. Moreover, sociologists argued that the fact of poverty, not a "culture" developed from it, severs marriages and families. But even these new theses are challenged by studies of widespread family separation during slavery, the women-centered character of slave life, and the ravages of sharecropping and segregation.

Much damage was done by slavery to black family life. Exactly what the long-term effects are may never produce a consensus. But this question drives nearly every policy debate Americans face over the relationships among race, history, and social welfare. Many single black women raise well-adjusted children; and kin networks are still crucial in African American family life. But troubling facts remain: a majority of black children still live in families that include their mothers but not their fathers, whereas about four of five white children under eighteen live with both parents.

For Further Reading, see page A-16 of the Appendix. For Web resources, go to http://college.hmco.com.

JOHN C. FREMONT.
THE REPUBLICANS CHOICE FOR PRESIDENT

WM L. DAYTON.
VICE PRESIDENT FROM 1857 TO 1861.

AND

Entered according to Act of Congress in the Year 1856 by N.Currier, in the Clerk's Office of the District Court of the Southern Dist of N.Y.

GRAND NATIONAL REPUBLICAN BANNER.
FREE LABOR, FREE SPEECH, FREE TERITORY.

As the delegates filed into the Musical Fund Hall in Philadelphia on June 17, 1856, they knew they had created something special in American politics. The first national nominating convention of the Republican Party met to approve a platform and select their presidential ticket. Formed just two years earlier, the party drew together a broad coalition of northern politicians who opposed the expansion of slavery, as well as the growing power of the South in the federal government. Most American political conventions in those years were raucous affairs; but at this gathering, according to a journalist, there was only "a slight quantity of liquor consumed, very little profane swearing . . . and . . . intense propriety." Republicans had come to Philadelphia for the solemn business of offering the American electorate a genuinely antislavery national future.

Their coalition combined men who had been former Democrats; men who had been founding members of the American Party, a group that wanted to prohibit foreigners, especially Catholics, from settling in the United States; and many former Whigs, whose party had been shattered by the crisis over slavery and its expansion. They consisted of conservatives, moderates, and radicals; some believed slavery and all its influences a moral evil, while others saw it as a political problem.

At this convention, a radical temper prevailed. The convention was only minutes old when the temporary chairman, Robert Emmet of New York, brought the delegates to their feet by using the Declaration of Independence to label slavery a great political danger to the nation's future. Permanent chairman Henry S. Lane of Indiana followed by declaring the "vital principle of the Republican party" to be "no more slave states," an aim he rooted in the "natural rights of man." Speaker after speaker declared that their party would render "freedom national" and "slavery sectional" by using the power of Congress to outlaw human bondage in all western territories.

Born as an antislavery coalition out of the controversy over the spread of slavery into the West, the Republican Party nominated John C. Frémont for president and William L. Dayton for vice president at its first national convention in Philadelphia in June 1856. The Republicans altered America's political landscape nearly overnight; southern slaveholders feared them, and a broad base of northerners flocked to their free-soil vision of the nation's future.   (Collection of Janice L. and David J. Frent)

SLAVERY AND AMERICA'S FUTURE: THE ROAD TO WAR 1845–1861

The convention's platform committee was fittingly chaired by David Wilmot, a former Democrat who was no friend of black civil and political rights. But Wilmot, like others, was firmly opposed to slavery's expansion and just as firmly endorsed the protection of free white men's labor and land ownership across the continent. The platform denounced the South's interest in the acquisition of Cuba, supported the building of a transcontinental railroad, and nodded gently against nativism. But these were all "like a tail to the antislavery kite," as one historian put it. At the heart of the platform was the short, direct credo calling upon Congress to "prohibit in the territories those twin relics of barbarism—polygamy and slavery."

The Republicans nominated the famous western explorer and former California senator, John C. Frémont, for president. In the election that followed, Americans began to vote by section and not by party as never before. The Republican coalition began to unify the North around keeping the West free and alarmed the South, which now saw the future of its slave society endangered by a political movement determined to limit if not destroy slavery. Frémont would lose the 1856 election, but Republicans made the best showing ever in American history of a newly born party in its first presidential bid.

As the Republicans engaged in their near miss at winning the presidency in 1856, a larger drama of conflict and violence had begun to envelop the nation. In Kansas territory, open warfare had exploded between proslavery and antislavery settlers. On the floor of the U.S. Senate a southern representative beat a northern senator senseless. A new fugitive slave law sent thousands of blacks fleeing into Canada in fear for their liberty and their lives. The tradition of compromise on political problems related to slavery teetered on the brink of complete collapse. Within a year the Supreme Court had issued a dramatic decision about slavery, its constitutionality in westward expansion, and the status of African American citizenship—to the delight of most southerners and the dread of most northerners. And abolitionist John Brown was planning a raid into Virginia to start a slave rebellion.

The political culture of the American republic, now under the leadership of Americans born after the passing of the Revolutionary War generation, was disintegrating. As the 1850s advanced, slavery pulled Americans, North and South, into a maelstrom of dispute that its best statesmen, ultimately, could not subdue. The prosperous, model republic, riven by stark contradictions, was on the road to a terrible war.

Divergent economic and political aims, which had long been held in check, now flew apart over the issue of slavery. The old nationwide political parties fractured, and a realignment that reinforced sectional interests took their place. The means for compromise steadily slipped from the nation's grasp.

Slavery had aroused passions that could be neither contained nor resolved. What began as a dark cloud over the territories became a storm engulfing the nation. Between 1845 and 1853 the United States added Texas, California, Oregon Country, and the Southwest to its domain and launched the settlement of the Great Plains. During the administration of President James K. Polk alone (1845–1849), the nation increased its land mass by two-thirds. Each time the nation expanded, it confronted a thorny issue: should new territories and states be slave or free?

The ensuing political storms gave rise to a feeling in both North and South that America's future was at stake—the character of its economy, its labor system, its definition of liberty under the Constitution, and its racial self-definition. The new Republican Party believed that America's future depended on the unbounded labor of free men, whose rights were protected by a government devoted to liberty. They charged southerners with using the power of the federal government to make slavery legal throughout the Union. Southern leaders defended slavery and charged the North with unconstitutional efforts to destroy it. To these southerners enslavement of blacks was the foundation of civilization and equality among whites; a government that failed to protect slavery was unworthy of their loyalty.

For blacks, the growing dispute brought hope and despair. They could take heart that the country's political strife over slavery might somehow lead to their liberation. But in a nation now trying to define its future, blacks had to wonder whether they had a future at all in America. In 1855 Frederick Douglass spoke for slaves and former slaves when he wrote that "the thought of only being a creature of the present and the past, troubled me, and I longed to have a future—a future with hope in it." In those words, Douglass spoke as well to the nation's central dilemma. ■

The War with Mexico and Its Consequences

In the 1840s, territorial expansion surged forward under the leadership of President James K. Polk of North Carolina. The annexation of Texas (see page 300) just be-

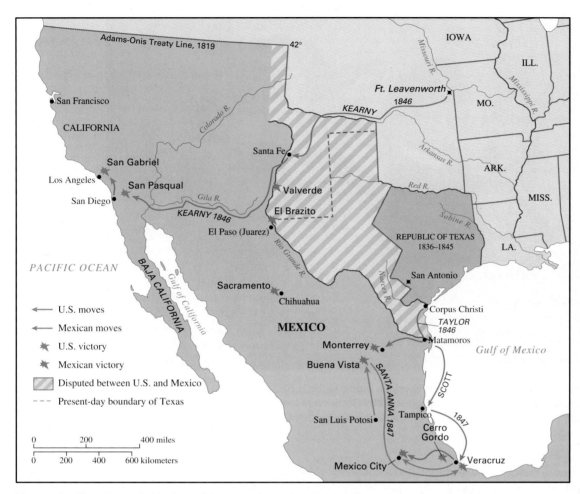

Map 14.2　The War with Mexico　This map shows the territory disputed between the United States and Mexico. After U.S. gains in northeastern Mexico and in New Mexico and California, General Winfield Scott captured Mexico City in the decisive campaign of the war.

man swallows arsenic, which brings him down in turn. Mexico will poison us." Even proslavery spokesman John C. Calhoun saw the perils of expansionism. Mexico, he said, was "the forbidden fruit; the penalty of eating it would be to subject our institutions to political death."

Early in the war U.S. forces made significant gains. The troops proved unruly and undisciplined, and their politically ambitious commanders often quarreled among themselves. Nevertheless, progress was steady. In May 1846 Polk ordered Colonel Stephen Kearny and a small detachment to invade the remote and thinly populated provinces of New Mexico and California. Taking Santa Fe without opposition, Kearny pushed into Cal-

Conquest

ifornia, where he joined forces with rebellious American settlers led by Captain John C. Frémont and with a couple of U.S. naval units. General Zachary Taylor's forces attacked and occupied Monterrey, which surrendered in September, securing northeastern Mexico (see Map 14.2). American soldiers soon established dominion over distant California before the end of 1846.

Because losses on the periphery of their large country had not broken Mexican resistance, General Winfield Scott carried the war to the enemy's heartland. Landing at Veracruz, he led fourteen thousand men toward Mexico City. This daring invasion proved the decisive campaign of the war. Scott's men, outnumbered and threatened by yellow fever, encountered a series of formidable Mexican defenses, but engineers repeatedly discovered flanking routes around

Enthusiastic publishers vied to furnish the American public with up-to-date news of the War with Mexico. This is one of three lithographs issued by Currier and Ives in 1846 to celebrate U.S. forces' capture of Mexico's General La Vega during the Battle of Resaca de la Palma, fought near the border of Texas and Mexico.   (Amon Carter Museum, Fort Worth, Texas)

their foes. After a series of hard-fought battles, U.S. troops captured the Mexican capital.

Representatives of both countries signed the Treaty of Guadalupe Hidalgo in February 1848. The United States gained California and New Mexico (including present-day Nevada, Utah, and Arizona, and parts of Colorado and Wyoming) and recognition of the Rio Grande as the southern boundary of Texas. In return, the American government agreed to settle the claims of its citizens against Mexico ($3.2 million) and to pay Mexico a mere $15 million (before the war Polk had been prepared to pay up to $40 million).

Treaty of Guadalupe Hidalgo

The costs of the war included the deaths of thirteen thousand Americans (mostly from disease) and fifty thousand Mexicans, plus Mexican American enmity that endured into the twentieth century. The domestic cost to the United States was even higher. Public opinion was sharply divided, despite widespread hostility toward Mexicans. Southwesterners were enthusiastic about the war, as were most southern planters; New Englanders strenuously opposed it.

Whigs in Congress charged that Polk, a Democrat, had "provoked" an unnecessary war and "usurped the power of Congress." The aged John Quincy Adams denounced the war; and a tall, young, Illinois Whig named Abraham Lincoln called Polk's justifications the "half insane mumbling of a fever-dream." Abolitionists and a small minority of antislavery Whigs charged that the war was no less than a plot to extend slavery. Congressman Joshua Giddings of Ohio charged that Polk's purpose was "to render slavery secure in Texas" and to extend slavery's dominion over vast expanses of new territory.

These charges fed northern fear of the so-called Slave Power. Abolitionists had long warned of a slaveholding oligarchy that intended to dominate the nation through its hold on federal power. These dangerous aristocrats had gained control of the South by persecuting critics of slavery and suppressing dissent. They had forced the gag rule on Congress in 1836 (see page 286) and threatened northern liberties. To many white northerners, even those who saw nothing wrong with slavery, it was

"Slave Power Conspiracy"

the battle over free speech and the right of petition that first made the idea of a Slave Power credible. The War with Mexico deepened such fears. Why, asked antislavery northerners, had claims to part of Oregon been abandoned and a questionable war begun for vast, new slave territory?

Northern opinion on slavery expansion began to shift, but the impact of events on southern opinion was even more dramatic. At first some southern leaders criticized the War with Mexico. Southern Whigs attacked the Democratic president for causing the war, and few southern congressmen saw defense of slavery as the paramount issue. Even John C. Calhoun—despite his earlier schemes to annex Texas for slavery—strongly opposed the seizure of large amounts of land from Mexico. Many whites in both North and South feared that large land seizures would bring thousands of nonwhite Mexicans into the United States and upset the racial order. An Indiana politician did not want "any mixed races in our Union, nor men of any color except white, unless they be slaves." And the *Charleston Mercury* of South Carolina asked if the nation expected "to melt into our population eight millions of men, at war with us by race, by language, by religion, manners and laws." Despite their racism, many statesmen soon saw other prospects in the outcomes of a war of conquest in the Southwest.

The War with Mexico proved generally popular with southern voters, and no southern Whig could oppose it once slavery became the central issue. That happened in August 1846, when David Wilmot, a Pennsylvania Democrat, proposed an amendment, or proviso, to a military appropriations bill: that "neither slavery nor involuntary servitude shall ever exist" in any territory gained from Mexico. Although the proviso never passed both houses of Congress, its repeated introduction by northerners transformed the debate.

Wilmot Proviso

Southerners suddenly circled their wagons to protect the future of a slave society. Alexander H. Stephens, only recently "no defender of slavery," now declared that slavery was based on the Bible and above moral criticism, and John C. Calhoun asserted a radical new southern position. The territories, Calhoun insisted, belonged to all the states, and the federal government could do nothing to limit the spread of slavery there. Southern slaveholders had a constitutional right rooted in the Fifth Amendment, Calhoun claimed, to take their slaves (as property) anywhere in the territories.

This position, often called "state sovereignty," which quickly became a test of orthodoxy among southern politicians, was a radical reversal of history. In 1787 the Confederation Congress had excluded slavery from the Northwest Territory (see pages 182–183); Article IV of the federal Constitution had authorized Congress to make "all needful rules and regulations" for the territories; and the Missouri Compromise had barred slavery from most of the Louisiana Purchase. Now, however, southern leaders demanded protection and future guarantees for slavery.

In the North, the Wilmot Proviso became a rallying cry for abolitionists. Eventually the legislatures of fourteen northern states endorsed it—and not because all its supporters were abolitionists. David Wilmot, significantly, was neither an abolitionist nor an antislavery Whig. He denied having any "squeamish sensitiveness upon the subject of slavery" or "morbid sympathy for the slave." Instead, his goal was to defend "the rights of white freemen" and to obtain California "for free white labor." Wilmot sought opportunity for "the sons of toil, of my own race and own color." His involvement in antislavery controversy is a measure of the remarkable ability of the territorial issue to alarm northerners of many viewpoints.

As Wilmot demonstrated, it was possible, however, to be both a racist and an opponent of slavery. The vast majority of white northerners were not active abolitionists, and their desire to keep the West free from slavery was often matched by their desire to keep blacks from settling there. Fear of the Slave Power was thus building a potent antislavery movement that united abolitionists and antiblack voters. The latter's concern was to protect from the Slave Power an abiding version of the American Dream: the free, individual, immigrant farmer's access to social mobility through acquisition of land and jobs in the West. This sacred ideal of free labor, and its dread of concentrated power, fueled a new political persuasion in America. Opposition to slavery's extension and fear of a conspiratorial Slave Power were growing. And as northerners became increasingly antislavery, southern slaveholders felt deep alarm.

The slavery question divided northerners and southerners in both parties and could not be kept out of national politics. After Polk renounced a second term as president, the Democrats nominated Senator Lewis Cass of Michigan for president and General William Butler of Kentucky for vice president. Cass, a party loyalist who had served in Jackson's cabinet, had

The Election of 1848 and Popular Sovereignty

devised in 1847 the idea of "popular sovereignty" for the territories—letting residents in the territories decide the question of slavery for themselves. His party's platform declared that Congress lacked the power to interfere with slavery and criticized those who pressed the question. The Whigs nominated General Zachary Taylor, a southern slaveholder and war hero; Congressman Millard Fillmore of New York was his running mate. The Whig convention similarly refused to assert that Congress had power over slavery in the territories.

But the issue would not stay in the background. Many southern Democrats distrusted Cass and eventually voted for Taylor because he was a slaveholder. Among northerners, concern over slavery led to the formation of a new party. New York Democrats committed to the Wilmot Proviso rebelled against Cass and nominated former president Martin Van Buren. Antislavery Whigs and former supporters of the Liberty Party then joined them to organize the Free-Soil Party, with Van Buren as its candidate (see Table 14.1). This party, whose slogan was "Free Soil, Free Speech, Free Labor, and Free Men," won almost 300,000 northern votes. For a new third party to win 10 percent of the national vote was a signal achievement. Taylor polled 1.4 million votes to Cass's 1.2 million and won the White House, but the results were more ominous than decisive. The War with Mexico made the political issue of slavery expansion into a moral issue. Politics split along sectional lines as never before. Religious denominations, too, were splitting into northern and southern wings. Judgments about slavery in America rarely lacked a religious dimension in these years; many Protestants, North and South, began to fear that God had an appointment with America, either to destroy the national sin of slavery or to help the South defend it as part of his divine order.

The conflicts of 1848 would dominate politics throughout the 1850s, as slavery in the territories colored every other national issue. The nation's uncertain attempts to deal with economic and social change gave way to more pressing questions about the nature of the Union itself.

1850: Compromise or Armistice?

 The first sectional battle of the new decade involved California. More than eighty thousand Americans flooded into California during the gold rush of 1849 (see page 309). With Congress unable to agree on a formula to govern the territories, President Taylor urged these settlers to apply directly for admission to the Union. They promptly did so, proposing a state constitution that did not allow for slavery. Because California's admission as a free state would upset the sectional balance of power in the Senate (the ratio of slave to free states was 15 to 15), southern politicians wanted to postpone admission and make California a slave territory, or at least to extend the Missouri Compromise line west to the Pacific. Representatives from nine southern states, meeting in Nashville, asserted the South's right to part of the territory.

Henry Clay, the venerable Whig leader, sensed that the Union was in peril. Twice before—in 1820 and 1833—Clay, the "Great Pacificator," had taken the lead in shaping sectional compromise; now he struggled one last time to preserve the nation. To hushed Senate galleries Clay presented a series of compromise measures in the winter of 1850. At one point Clay held up what he claimed was a piece of George Washington's coffin as a means of inspiring unity. Over the weeks that followed, he and Senator Stephen A. Douglas of Illinois, the "Little Giant," steered their omnibus bill, or compromise package, through debate and amendment.

Table 14.1 New Political Parties			
Party	**Period of Influence**	**Area of Influence**	**Outcome**
Liberty Party	1839–1848	North	Merged with other antislavery groups to form Free-Soil Party
Free-Soil Party	1848–1854	North	Merged with Republican Party
Know-Nothings (American Party)	1853–1856	Nationwide	Disappeared, freeing most to join Republican Party
Republican Party	1854–present	North (later nationwide)	Became rival of Democratic Party and won presidency in 1860

The problems to be solved were numerous and difficult. Would California, or part of it, become a free state? How should the territory acquired from Mexico be organized? Texas, which allowed slavery, claimed large portions of the new land as far west as Santa Fe, so that claim, too, had to be settled. Southerners complained that fugitive slaves were not being returned as the Constitution required, and northerners objected to the sale of human beings in the nation's capital. Eight years earlier, in *Prigg v. Pennsylvania* (1842), the Supreme Court had ruled that enforcement of the fugitive slave clause in the Constitution was a federal obligation, thus fueling southern desires to bring this issue to a head. But most troublesome of all was the status of slavery in the territories.

Clay and Douglas hoped to avoid a specific formula, for Lewis Cass's idea of popular sovereignty possessed what one historian called the "charm of ambiguity" that appealed to practical politicians. Ultimately Congress would have to approve statehood for a territory, but "in the meantime," said Cass, it should allow the people living there "to regulate their own concerns in their own way."

Those simple words proved all but unenforceable. When could settlers prohibit slavery? To avoid dissension within their party, northern and southern Democrats explained Cass's statement to their constituents in two incompatible ways. Southerners claimed that neither Congress nor a territorial legislature could bar slavery. Only late in the territorial process, when settlers were ready to draft a state constitution, could they take that step, thus allowing time for slavery to take root. Northerners, however, insisted that Americans living in a territory were entitled to local self-government and thus could outlaw slavery at any time, especially early in the process.

The cause of compromise gained a powerful supporter when Senator Daniel Webster committed his prestige and eloquence to Clay's bill. "I wish to speak today," Webster declaimed on March 7 in a scene of high drama, "not as a Massachusetts man, nor as a Northern man, but as an American. I speak today for the preservation of the Union. Hear me for my cause." Abandoning his earlier support for the Wilmot Proviso, Webster urged northerners not to "taunt or reproach" the South with antislavery measures. To southern firebrands he issued a warning that disunion inevitably would cause violence and destruction. For his efforts at compromise, Webster was condemned by many former abolitionist friends in New England who accused him of going over to the "devil."

Only three days earlier, with equal drama, Calhoun was carried from his sickbed to deliver a speech opposing the compromise. Unable to stand and speak, his address was read for him by Senator James Mason of Virginia. Grizzled and dying, the South's intellectual defender warned that the "cords which bind these states" were "already greatly weakened." Calhoun did not address the specific measures in the bill; he predicted disunion if southern demands were not met, thereby frightening some into support of compromise.

Yet Webster's influence and rising fear were not enough. After months of labor, Clay and Douglas finally brought their legislative package to a vote, and lost. But the determined Douglas would not give up. With Clay sick and absent from Washington, Douglas reintroduced the compromise measures one at a time. Though there was no majority for compromise, Douglas shrewdly realized that different majorities might be created for the separate measures. Because southerners favored some bills and northerners the rest, the small bloc for compromise could vote first with one section and then with the other. The strategy worked, and Douglas's resourcefulness salvaged a positive result from more than eight months of congressional crisis. The Compromise of 1850 became law.

Compromise of 1850

The compromise had five essential measures: California became a free state; the Texas boundary was set at its present limits (see Map 14.3 on page 372) and the United States paid Texas $10 million in compensation for the loss of New Mexico territory; the territories of New Mexico and Utah were organized on a basis of popular sovereignty; the fugitive slave law was strengthened; and the slave trade was abolished in the District of Columbia. Jubilation greeted passage of the compromise; crowds in Washington and other cities celebrated the happy news. "On one glorious night," records a modern historian, "the word went abroad that it was the duty of every patriot to get drunk. Before the next morning many a citizen had proved his patriotism."

In reality, there was less cause for celebration than people hoped. At best, the Compromise of 1850 was an artful evasion. As one historian has argued, the legislation was more an "armistice," delaying greater conflict, than a compromise. Douglas had found a way to pass the five proposals without convincing northerners and southerners to agree on fundamentals. The compromise bought time for the nation, but it did not provide a real settlement of the territorial questions.

Furthermore, the compromise had two basic flaws. The first concerned the ambiguity of territorial legislation: how exactly was popular sovereignty to be enforced? During debate, southerners insisted there would be no prohibition of slavery during the territorial stage, and northerners declared that settlers could bar slavery whenever they wished. The compromise even allowed for the appeal of a territorial legislature's action to the Supreme Court. One witty politician remarked that the legislators had enacted a lawsuit instead of a law.

The second flaw lay in the Fugitive Slave Act, which gave new—and controversial—protection to

Fugitive Slave Act

slavery. The law empowered slaveowners to go into court in their own states to present evidence that a slave who owed them service had escaped. The resulting transcript and a description of the fugitive would then serve as legal proof of a person's slave status, even in free states and territories. Specially appointed court officials adjudicated the identity of the person described, not whether he or she was indeed a slave. Penalties made it a felony to harbor fugitives, and the law stated that northern citizens could be summoned to hunt fugitives. The fees paid to U.S. marshals favored slaveholders: $10 if the alleged fugitive was returned to the slaveowner, $5 if not returned.

Abolitionist newspapers quickly attacked the Fugitive Slave Act as a violation of fundamental American rights. Why, in a land of freedom, were alleged fugitives denied a trial by jury? Why were they given no chance to present evidence or cross-examine witnesses? Why did the law give authorities a financial incentive to send suspected fugitives into bondage? These arguments convinced some northerners that free blacks could be sent into slavery with no means to defend themselves. Protest meetings were held all over the North, especially in staunchly abolitionist communities.

Between 1850 and 1854, violent resistance to slave catchers occurred in dozens of northern towns. Sometimes a captured fugitive was broken out of jail or from the clutches of slave agents by abolitionists, as in the case of Shadrach Minkins in 1851 in Boston, who was spirited by a series of wagons and trains across Massachusetts, up through Vermont, to Montreal, Canada. Also in 1851, a fugitive named Jerry McHenry was freed by an abolitionist mob in Syracuse, New York, and hurried into Canadian freedom. That same year as well, the small black community in Lancaster County, Pennsylvania, rose up in arms to defend four escaped slaves from a federal posse charged with reenslaving them. At this "Christiana riot," the fugitives shot and killed Edward Gorsuch, the Maryland slaveowner who sought the return of his "property." Amid increasing border warfare over fugitive slaves, a headline reporting the Christiana affair screamed "Civil War, The First Blow Struck!"

Many abolitionists became convinced by their experience of resisting the Fugitive Slave Act that violence was a legitimate means of opposing slavery. In an 1854 column entitled "Is It Right and Wise to Kill a Kidnapper?" Frederick Douglass said that the only way to make the fugitive slave law "dead letter" was to make a "few dead slave catchers."

At this point a novel portrayed the humanity and suffering of slaves in a way that touched millions of northerners. Harriet Beecher Stowe,

Uncle Tom's Cabin

whose New England family had produced many prominent ministers, wrote *Uncle Tom's Cabin* out of deep moral conviction. Her story, serialized in 1851 and published as a book in 1852, conveyed the agonies faced by slave families and described a mother's dash to freedom with her child across the frozen Ohio River. Stowe also portrayed slavery's evil effects on slaveholders, indicting the institution itself more harshly than she indicted the southerners caught in its web. Moreover, Stowe exposed northern racism and complicity with slavery by making the worst slaveholder a man of New England birth, and a visiting relative on a plantation a squeamish Vermont woman who could hardly cope with the near presence of blacks.

In nine months the book sold over three hundred thousand copies, by mid-1853 over a million. Countless people saw *Uncle Tom's Cabin* performed as a stage play or heard the story in dramatic readings or read similar novels inspired by it. Stowe brought home the evil of slavery to many who had never given it much thought. Indeed, for generations, the characters in *Uncle Tom's Cabin*—Eliza, George, Little Eva, Simon Legree, Miss Ophelia, Augustine St. Clair, and Uncle Tom himself—became touchstones of the American imagination about the entire era of slavery and the Civil War.

The popularity of *Uncle Tom's Cabin* alarmed anxious southern whites. In politics and now in popular literature they saw threats to their way of life. Behind the South's aggressive claims about territorial rights lay the fear that if nearby areas became free soil, they would be used as bases from which to spread abolitionism into the slave states. To most white southerners, a moral condemnation of slaveholding anywhere meant the same thing everywhere.

To protect slavery in the arena of ideas, southerners needed to counter indictments of the institution as a moral wrong. Accordingly, some fifteen to twenty proslavery novels were published in the 1850s as responses to *Uncle Tom's Cabin*. Most of these anti–Uncle Tom books paled in comparison to Mrs. Stowe's masterpiece, but southern writers continued to defend their system as more humane than wage labor, and they blamed the slave trade on the "outside interference" of Yankee speculators. In awkward stories such as J. W. Page's *Uncle Robin in His Cabin and Tom Without One in Boston*, slaves were induced to run away by visiting abolitionists, and then all but starved in northern cities.

In reality, slaveholders were especially disturbed by the 1850s over what was widely called the Underground Railroad. This loose, illegal network of abolitionist stations all over the border state region (the area all along the Ohio River and the boundaries between Pennsylvania and Maryland and Virginia), spiriting runaways to freedom in safe houses, secret hideouts, and wagons, had never been very organized. Thousands of slaves did escape by these routes but largely through their own wits and courage, and through the assistance of black vigilance committees in some northern cities. Lewis Hayden in Boston, David Ruggles in New York, William Still in Philadelphia, John Parker in Ripley, Ohio, and Jacob Gibbs in Washington, D.C., were only some of the many black abolitionists who managed fugitive slave escapes through their regions.

The Underground Railroad

Moreover, Harriet Tubman, herself an escapee in 1848, returned to her native Maryland and to Virginia nearly twenty times, and through clandestine measures helped as many as three hundred slaves to freedom, some of them her own family members. Maryland planters were so outraged at her heroic success that they offered a $40,000 reward for her capture.

In Ohio numerous white abolitionists, often Quakers, joined with blacks as agents of slave liberation at various points along the river border between slavery and freedom. In the wake of the Fugitive Slave Act, an estimated twenty thousand blacks, most of them fugitive slaves, moved from the northern states into Canada seeking security. The Underground Railroad also had numerous maritime routes, as coastal slaves escaped aboard ship out of Virginia or the Carolinas, or from a major port like New Orleans. This constant, dangerous flow of humanity was a testament to human courage, good luck, and the will for free-

The Webb Family toured the North, presenting dramatic readings of *Uncle Tom's Cabin*. Performances by the Webbs and others deepened the already powerful impact of Harriet Beecher Stowe's novel. (Harriet Beecher Stowe Center, Hartford, Conn.)

dom. It never reached the scale that some angry slaveholders believed, but in reality and in legend it applied pressure to the slavery crisis and served as a symbol and a national conscience against oppression.

The 1852 election gave southern leaders hope that slavery would be secure under the administration of a new president. Franklin Pierce, a Democrat from New Hampshire, won an easy victory over the Whig presidential nominee, General Winfield Scott. Pierce defended each section's rights as essential to the nation's unity, and southerners hoped that his firm support for the Compromise of 1850 might end the season of crisis. Because Scott's views on the compromise had been unknown and the Free-Soil candidate, John P. Hale of New Hampshire, had openly rejected it, Pierce's victory suggested widespread support for the compromise.

Election of 1852 and the Collapse of Compromise

Pierce's victory, however, derived less from his strengths than from the Whig Party's weakness. The

In *Still Life of Harriet Tubman with Bible and Candle,* we see the youthful, calm, determined leader of the Underground Railroad. Appearing gentle, Tubman was in her own way a revolutionary who liberated nearly three hundred of her people.   (© 2000 Louis Psihoyos/Matrix)

Whigs were a congressional and state-based party that never had achieved much success in presidential politics. Sectional discord was splitting the party in two, further undermining its national competitiveness, and the deaths of President Taylor, Daniel Webster, and Henry Clay had deprived Whigs of decisive leadership. In 1852 the Whig Party was all but dead.

President Pierce's embrace of the compromise appalled many northerners. His vigorous enforcement of the Fugitive Slave Act provoked outrage and fear of the Slave Power, especially in the case of the fugitive slave Anthony Burns. Burns had fled Virginia by stowing away on a ship. In Boston, thinking he was safe in a city known for abolitionism, Burns began a new life. But in 1854 federal marshals found and placed him under guard in Boston's courthouse. An interracial crowd of abolitionists attacked the courthouse, killing a jailor, in an unsuccessful attempt to free Burns, whose case attracted nationwide attention.

Pierce moved decisively to enforce the Fugitive Slave Act. He telegraphed local officials to "incur any expense to insure the execution of the law" and sent marines, cavalry, and artillery to Boston. When Burns's owner seemed willing to sell his property, the U.S. attorney blocked the sale and won a decision that Anthony Burns must return to slavery. U.S. troops marched Burns to Boston harbor through streets draped in black and hung with American flags at half-mast. At a cost of $100,000, a single black man was returned to slavery through the power of federal law.

The national will to sustain the future of slavery was now tested at every turn. This demonstration of federal support for slavery radicalized opinion, even among many conservatives. Textile manufacturer Amos A. Lawrence observed that "we went to bed one night old fashioned, conservative, Compromise Union Whigs & waked up stark mad Abolitionists." Juries refused to convict the abolitionists who had stormed the courthouse, and New England states began to pass personal-liberty laws designed to impede or block federal enforcement. Before the end of the 1850s, nine northern states passed such laws. Where northerners now saw evidence of a dominating Slave Power, outraged slaveholders saw the legal defense of their rights.

Pierce seemed unable to avoid sectional conflict in other arenas as well. His proposal for a transcontinental railroad derailed when congressmen fought over its location, North or South. His attempts to acquire foreign territory stirred more trouble. An annexation treaty with Hawai'i failed because southern senators would not vote for another free state, and efforts to acquire slaveholding Cuba angered northerners. Events in the Pacific also caused division at home. With two orchestrated landings in the Bay of Tokyo, in 1853 and 1854, Commodore Matthew Perry established U.S. intentions to trade with Japan, whether that country sought such contact or not. Offended and intrigued, the Japanese were impressed with Perry's steam-powered warships, the first such black smoke-belching floating machines they had seen. Perry's Treaty of Kanagawa in March 1854 negotiated two ports as coaling stations for American ships. The much sought-after trading arrangements were slow in coming, although this did not stop merchants and bankers from lavishing on Perry a hero's honors when he returned to the United States. In his meetings with the Japanese, the pompous Perry had given his hosts, whom he considered an inferior people, a telegraph system, a quarter-scale railroad train, a bound history of the War with Mexico, and 100 gallons of Kentucky whiskey.

Soon back home another territorial bill threw Congress and the nation into even greater turmoil and the Compromise of 1850 fell into complete collapse.

Slavery Expansion and Collapse of the Party System

The new controversy began in a surprising way. Stephen A. Douglas, one of the architects of the Compromise of 1850, introduced a bill to establish the Kansas and Nebraska Territories. Talented and ambitious, Douglas was known for compromise, not sectional quarreling. But he did not view slavery as a fundamental problem, and he was willing to risk some controversy to win economic benefits for Illinois, his home state. A transcontinental railroad would encourage settlement of the Great Plains and stimulate the economy of Illinois; but no company would build such a railroad before Congress organized the territories it would cross. Thus interest in promoting the construction of such a railroad drove Douglas to introduce a bill that inflamed sectional passions.

The Kansas-Nebraska bill exposed the first flaw of the Compromise of 1850—the conflicting interpretations of popular sovereignty. Douglas's

The Kansas-Nebraska Bill

bill left "all questions pertaining to slavery in the Territories . . . to the people residing therein." Northerners and southerners, however, still disagreed violently over what territorial settlers could constitutionally do. Moreover, the Kansas and Nebraska Territories lay within the Louisiana Purchase, and the Missouri Compromise prohibited slavery in all that land from latitude 36°30' north to the Canadian border. If popular sovereignty were to mean anything in Kansas and Nebraska, it had to mean that the Missouri Compromise was no longer in effect and that settlers could establish slavery there.

Southern congressmen, anxious to establish slaveholders' right to take slaves into any territory, pressed Douglas to concede this point. They demanded an explicit repeal of the 36°30' limitation as the price of their support. During a carriage ride with Senator Archibald Dixon of Kentucky, Douglas debated the point at length. Finally he made an impulsive decision: "By God, Sir, you are right. I will incorporate it in my bill, though I know it will raise a hell of a storm."

Perhaps Douglas underestimated the storm because he believed that conditions of climate and soil would keep slavery out of Kansas and Nebraska. Nev-

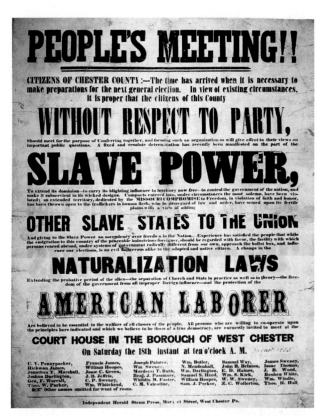

Throughout the North the Kansas-Nebraska Act kindled fires of alarm over the Slave Power's "determination to extend its dominion" and "control the government of the nation." Public meetings like the one announced here, held in West Chester, Pennsylvania, aided the new Republican Party.   (American Antiquarian Society)

ertheless, his bill threw open to slavery land from which it had been prohibited for thirty-four years. Opposition from Free-Soilers and antislavery forces was immediate and enduring; many considered this turn of events a betrayal of a sacred trust. The titanic struggle in Congress lasted three and a half months. Douglas won the support of President Pierce and eventually prevailed: the bill became law in May 1854 by a vote that demonstrated the dangerous sectionalization of American politics (see Map 14.3 and Table 14.2).

But the storm was just beginning. Abolitionists charged sinister aggression by the Slave Power, and northern fears of slavery's influence deepened. Opposition to the Fugitive Slave Act grew dramatically; between 1855 and 1859 Connecticut, Rhode Island, Massachusetts, Michigan, Maine, Ohio, and Wisconsin passed personal-liberty laws. These laws enraged southern leaders by providing counsel for alleged fugitives and requiring trial by jury. More important was

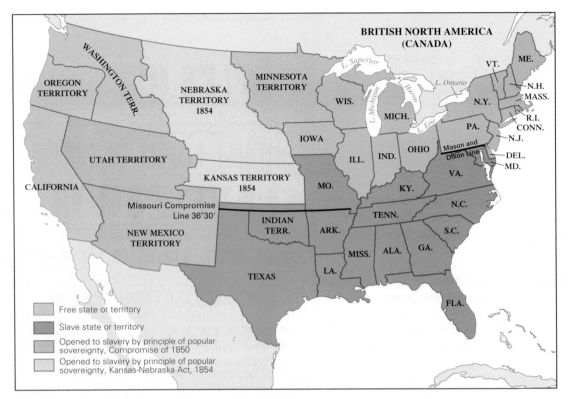

Map 14.3 The Kansas-Nebraska Act and Slavery Expansion, 1854 The vote on the Kansas-Nebraska Act (see also Table 14.2) in the House of Representatives demonstrates the sectionalization of American politics due to the slavery question.

the devastating impact of the Kansas-Nebraska Act on political parties. The weakened Whig Party broke apart into northern and southern wings that could no longer cooperate nationally. One of the two foundations of the second party system (see pages 294–295) was now gone. The Democrats survived, but their support in the North fell drastically in the 1854 elections. Northern Democrats lost sixty-six of their ninety-one congressional seats and lost control of all but two free-state legislatures.

The beneficiary of northern voters' wrath was a new political party. During debate on the Kansas-Nebraska bill, six congressmen had published an "Appeal of the Independent Democrats." Joshua Giddings, Salmon Chase, and Charles Sumner—the principal authors of this protest—attacked Douglas's legislation as a "gross violation of a sacred pledge" (the Missouri Compromise) and a "criminal betrayal of precious rights" that would make free territory a "dreary region of despotism." Their appeal tapped a reservoir of deep concerns in the North, cogently expressed by Illinois's Abraham Lincoln.

Although Lincoln did not personally condemn southerners—"They are just what we would be in their

Birth of the Republican Party

situation"—he exposed the meaning of the Kansas-Nebraska Act. Denying "that there can be moral right in the enslaving of one man by another," Lincoln argued that the founders, from love of liberty, had banned slavery from the Northwest Territory, kept the word *slavery* out of the Constitution, and treated it overall as a "cancer" on the republic. Rather than encouraging liberty, the Kansas-Nebraska Act put slavery "on the high road to extension and perpetuity," and that constituted a "moral wrong and injustice." America's future, Lincoln warned, was being mortgaged to slavery and all its influences.

Thousands of ordinary northerners agreed. During the summer and fall of 1854, antislavery Whigs and Democrats, Free-Soilers, and other reformers throughout the Old Northwest met to form the new Republican Party, dedicated to keeping slavery out of the territories. The influence of the Republicans rapidly spread to the East, and they won a stunning victory in the 1854 elections. In their first appearance on the ballot, Republicans captured a majority of northern House seats. Antislavery sentiment had created a new party and caused roughly a quarter of northern Democrats to desert their party.

For the first time, too, a sectional party had gained significant power in the political system. Now the

Table 14.2   The Vote on the Kansas-Nebraska Act

The vote was 113–100 in favor.

	Aye	Nay
Northern Democrats	44	42
Southern Democrats	57	2
Northern Whigs	0	45
Southern Whigs	12	7
Northern Free-Soilers		4

Whigs were gone, and only the Democrats struggled to maintain national membership. The Republicans absorbed the Free-Soil Party and grew rapidly in the North. Indeed, the emergence of the Republican coalition of antislavery interests is the most rapid transformation in party allegiance and voter behavior in American history. This fact alone attests to the centrality of slavery expansion in the causation of the Civil War.

And Republicans were not the only new party. For a brief period, an anti-immigrant organization, the American Party, blossomed. This party, popularly known as the Know-Nothings (because its first members kept their purposes secret, answering "I know nothing" to all questions), exploited nativist fear of foreigners and Catholics. Between 1848 and 1860, nearly 3.5 million immigrants entered the United States—proportionally the heaviest inflow of foreigners ever in American history (see pages 321–323). Democrats courted the votes of these new citizens, but many native-born, Anglo-Saxon Protestants believed that Irish and German Catholics would owe primary allegiance to the Pope in Rome and not to the American nation.

Know-Nothings

In 1854 anti-immigrant fears gave the Know-Nothings spectacular success in some northern states. They triumphed especially in Massachusetts, electing 11 congressmen, a governor, all state officers, all state senators, and all but 2 of 378 state representatives. The temperance movement also gained new strength early in the 1850s with its promises to stamp out the evils associated with liquor and immigrants (a particularly anti-Irish campaign). In this context the Know-Nothings strove to reinforce Protestant morality and restrict voting and officeholding to the native-born. As the Whig Party faded from the scene, the Know-Nothings temporarily filled the void. But their terror tactics against immigrant voters drove many potential supporters away. And, like the Whigs, the Know-Nothings could not keep their northern and southern wings together, and they dissolved after 1856. The growing Republican coalition wooed the nativists with temperance ordinances and laws postponing suffrage for naturalized citizens (see Table 14.1 on page 366).

With nearly half of the old electorate up for grabs, the demise of the Whig Party ensured a major realignment of the political system. To win over these homeless Whigs, the remaining parties made appeals to various segments of the electorate. Immigration, temperance, homestead bills, the tariff, internal improvements—all played important roles in attracting voters during the 1850s. The Republicans appealed strongly to those interested in the economic development of the West. Commercial agriculture was booming in the Ohio–Mississippi–Great Lakes area, but residents of that region desired more canals, roads, and river and harbor improvements to reap the full benefit of their labors. Because credit was scarce, a homestead program attracted voters: its proponents argued that western land should be made available free to individual farmers. Seizing their opportunity, the Republicans added internal improvements and land-grant planks to their platform. They also backed higher tariffs as an enticement to industrialists and businessmen, whose interest in tariff protection grew after a financial panic in 1857.

Party Realignment and the Republicans' Appeal

Partisan ideological appeals became the currency of the realigned political system. As Republicans preached "Free Soil, Free Labor, Free Men," they captured a self-image of many northerners. These phrases resonated with traditional ideals of equality, liberty, and opportunity under self-government—the heritage of republicanism. Invoking that heritage also undercut charges that the Republican Party was radical and unreliable.

"Free Soil, Free Labor, Free Men" seemed an appropriate motto for a northern economy that was energetic, expanding, and prosperous. Thousands of farmers had moved west to establish productive farms and growing communities. Midwesterners multiplied their yields by using new machines such as disk harrows and mechanical reapers. Railroads were carrying their crops to urban markets. And industry was beginning to perform wonders of production, making available goods that only recently had been beyond the reach of the average person. As northerners surveyed the general growth and prosperity, they thought they saw a reason for it.

The key to progress appeared, to many people, to be free labor—the dignity of work and the incentive of opportunity. Any hard-working and virtuous man, it was thought, could improve his condition and achieve economic independence by seizing opportunities that the country had to offer. Republicans argued that the South, with little industry and its slave labor system, was backward and retrograde by comparison, and their arguments captured much of the spirit of the age in the North.

Republican Ideology

Traditional republicanism hailed the virtuous common man as the backbone of the country. In Abraham Lincoln, a man of humble origins who had become a successful lawyer and political leader, Republicans had a symbol of that tradition. They portrayed their party as the guardian of economic opportunity, giving individuals a chance to work, acquire land, and attain success. In the words of an Iowa Republican, the United States was thriving because its "door is thrown open to all, and even the poorest and humblest in the land, may, by industry and application, gain a position which will entitle him to the respect and confidence of his fellow-men."

At stake in the enveloping crises of the 1850s were thus two competing definitions of "liberty": southern planters' claims to protection of their liberty in the possession and transport of their slaves anywhere in the land, and northern workers' and farmers' claims to protection of their liberty to seek a new start on free land, unimpeded by a system that defined labor as slave and black. Thus, a growing number of northerners expressed the fear that the rising political storm was an "irrepressible conflict."

Opposition to the extension of slavery had brought the Republicans into being, but party members carefully broadened their appeal by adopting the causes of other groups. Their coalition ideology consisted of many elements: resentment of southern political power, devotion to unionism, antislavery based on free labor arguments, moral revulsion to slavery, and racial prejudice. As the *New York Tribune* editor Horace Greeley wrote in 1856, "It is beaten into my bones that the American people are not yet anti-slavery." Four years later, Greeley again observed that "an Anti-Slavery man per se cannot be elected." But, he added, "a Tariff, River-and-Harbor, Pacific Railroad, Free Homestead man, may succeed although he is Anti-Slavery." As these elements joined the Republican Party, they also grew to fear slavery even more.

In the South, the disintegration of the Whig Party had left many southerners at loose ends politically; they

Southern Democrats

included a good number of wealthy planters, smaller slaveholders, and urban businessmen. Some gravitated to the American Party, but not for long. In the increasingly tense atmosphere of sectional crisis, these people were highly susceptible to strong states' rights positions and defense of slavery. The security of their own communities seemed to be at stake. In the 1850s, Democratic leaders managed to convert most of the formerly Whig slaveholders, who responded to their class interests.

Most southern Democrats, however, were not slaveholders. Since Andrew Jackson's day, small farmers had been the heart of the Democratic Party. Democratic politicians, though often slaveowners themselves, lauded the common man and argued that their policies advanced his interests. According to the southern version of republicanism, white citizens in a slave society enjoyed liberty and social equality because black people were enslaved. As Jefferson Davis put it in 1851, in other societies distinctions were drawn "by property, between the rich and the poor." But in the South, slavery elevated every white person's status and allowed the nonslaveholder to "stand upon the broad level of equality with the rich man." To retain the support of ordinary whites, southern Democrats emphasized this appeal to racism. The issue in the sectional crisis, they warned, was "shall negroes govern white men, or white men govern negroes?"

Southern leaders also portrayed sectional controversies as matters of injustice and insult to the South. The rights of all southern whites were in jeopardy, they argued, because antislavery and Free-Soil forces threatened an institution protected in the Constitution. The stable, well-ordered South was the true defender of constitutional principles, the rapidly changing North their destroyer.

Racial fears and traditional political loyalties helped keep the political alliance between yeoman farmers and planters largely intact through the 1850s. Across class lines, white southerners joined together in the interest of community security against what they perceived as the Republican Party's capacity to cause slave unrest in their midst. Potential conflicts between slaveholders and nonslaveholders were not discussed, and no viable party emerged to replace the Whigs. The result was a one-party system that emphasized sectional issues and loyalty. In the South as in the North, political realignment sharpened sectional identities.

Political leaders of both sections used race in their arguments about opportunity, but northerners and southerners saw different futures. The *Montgomery* (Alabama) *Mail* warned southern whites in 1860 that the Republicans intended "to free the negroes and force amalgamation between them and the children of the poor men of the South. The rich will be able to keep out of the way of the contamination." Republicans warned northern workers that if slavery entered the territories, the great reservoir of opportunity for ordinary citizens would be poisoned.

In the territory of Kansas a succession of events, like hammer blows, deepened the conflict. The Kansas-Nebraska Act spawned hatred and violence as land-hungry claim jumpers and partisans in the sectional struggle clashed repeatedly in Kansas Territory. Abolitionists and religious groups sent in armed Free-Soil settlers; southerners sent in their reinforcements to establish slavery and prevent "northern hordes" from stealing Kansas away. Conflicts led to bloodshed, and soon the whole nation was talking about "Bleeding Kansas."

Bleeding Kansas

Politics in the territory resembled war more than democracy. During elections for a territorial legislature in 1855, thousands of proslavery Missourians—known as Border Ruffians—invaded the polls and ran up a large but fraudulent majority for slavery candidates. The resulting legislature legalized slavery, and in response Free-Soilers held an unauthorized convention at which they cre-

ated their own government and constitution. In the spring of 1856, a proslavery posse sent to arrest the Free-Soil leaders sacked the Kansas town of Lawrence, killing several people. In revenge John Brown, a radical abolitionist who saw himself as God's instrument to destroy slavery, murdered five proslavery settlers living along Pottawatomie Creek. Soon, armed bands of guerrillas roamed the territory, battling over land claims as well as slavery.

These passions brought violence to the U.S. Senate in May 1856, when Charles Sumner of Massachusetts denounced "the Crime against Kansas." Radical in his antislavery views, Sumner bitterly assailed the president, the South, and Senator Andrew P. Butler of South Carolina. Soon thereafter Butler's cousin, Representative Preston Brooks, approached Sumner at the latter's Senate desk, raised his cane, and began to beat Sumner on the head. Trapped behind his desk, which was bolted in place, Sumner tried to rise, eventually wrenching the desk free before he collapsed, bleeding, on the floor.

Shocked northerners recoiled from what they saw as another southern assault on free speech and the South's readiness to use violence to have its way. William Cullen Bryant, editor of the *New York Evening Post*, asked, "Has it come to this, that we must speak with bated breath in the presence of our southern masters?" As if in reply, the *Richmond Enquirer* denounced "vulgar Abolitionists in the Senate" who "have been

The Border Ruffians, depicted in this pen-and-ink drawing, were proslavery Missourians who periodically invaded Kansas to vote and help establish slavery there. Conflicts over land claims further complicated the violence in Bleeding Kansas.   (Yale University Art Gallery, Mabel Brady Garvan Collection)

Slavery and America's Future: The Road to War, 1845–1861

suffered to run too long without collars. They must be lashed into submission." Popular opinion in Massachusetts strongly supported Sumner; South Carolina voters reelected Brooks and sent him dozens of commemorative canes. The country was becoming polarized.

The election of 1856 showed how extreme that polarization had become. When Democrats met to select a nominee, they shied away from prominent leaders whose views on the territories were well known. Instead, they chose James Buchanan of Pennsylvania, whose chief virtue was that for the past four years he had been ambassador to Britain, uninvolved in territorial controversies. This anonymity and superior party organization helped Buchanan win 1.8 million votes and the election, but he owed his victory to southern support. Hence, he was tagged with the label "a northern man with southern principles." Eleven of sixteen free states voted against him, and Democrats did not regain ascendancy in those states for decades. The Republican candidate, John C. Frémont, won those eleven free states and 1.3 million votes; Republicans had become the dominant party in the North after only two years of existence. The Know-Nothing candidate, Millard Fillmore, won almost 1 million votes, but this election was to be his party's last hurrah. The coming battle would pit a sectional Republican Party against an increasingly divided Democratic Party.

Slavery and the Nation's Future

For years the issue of slavery in the territories had convulsed Congress, and for years Congress had tried to settle the issue with vague formulas. In 1857 a different branch of government stepped into the fray. The Supreme Court took up this emotionally charged subject and attempted to silence controversy with a definitive verdict.

A Missouri slave named Dred Scott had sued his owner for his freedom. Scott based his claim on the fact that his former owner, an army surgeon, had taken him for several years into Illinois, a free state, and into the Wisconsin Territory, from which slavery had been barred by the Missouri Compromise. Scott first won and then lost his case as it moved on appeal through the state courts, into the federal system, and finally after eleven years to the Supreme Court.

Dred Scott Case

Normally Supreme Court justices were reluctant to inject themselves into political issues, and it seemed

likely that the Court would stay out of this one. An 1851 decision had declared that state courts determined the status of Negroes who lived within their jurisdictions. The Supreme Court had only to follow this precedent to avoid ruling on substantive, and very controversial, issues: Was a black person like Dred Scott a citizen of the United States and thus eligible to sue in federal court? Had residence in a free state or territory made him free? Did Congress have the power to prohibit slavery in a territory or to delegate that power to a territorial legislature?

Initially the Supreme Court seemed ready to dispose of *Dred Scott v. Sanford* by following the 1851 precedent. The chief justice even assigned one justice the task of writing such an opinion. Then, for a number of reasons, the Court decided to rule on the Missouri Compromise after all. Two northern justices indicated that they would dissent from the assigned opinion and argue for Scott's freedom and the constitutionality of the Missouri Compromise. Their decision emboldened southerners on the Court, who were growing eager to declare the 1820 geographical restriction on slavery unconstitutional. Southern sympathizers in Washington were pressing for a proslavery verdict, and several justices simply felt they should try to resolve sectional strife once and for all.

In March 1857, Chief Justice Roger B. Taney of Maryland delivered the majority opinion of a divided Court. Taney declared that Scott was not a citizen of either the United States or Missouri; that residence in free territory did not make Scott free; and that Congress had no power to bar slavery from any territory. The decision not only overturned a sectional compromise that had been honored for years; it also invalidated the basic ideas of the Wilmot Proviso and probably popular sovereignty as well.

The Slave Power seemed to have won a major constitutional victory. African Americans were especially dismayed, for Taney's decision asserted that the founders had never intended for black people to be citizens. At the nation's founding, the chief justice wrote, blacks had been regarded "as beings of an inferior order" with "no rights which the white man was bound to respect." Taney was mistaken, however. African Americans had been citizens in several of the original states. Nevertheless, the ruling seemed to shut the door permanently on their hopes for justice and equal rights. Blacks, after 1857, lived in the land of the *Dred Scott* decision.

Northern whites who rejected the decision's content were suspicious of the circumstances that produced it. Five of the nine justices were southerners;

Dred Scott, a slave who brought suit in Missouri for his freedom, and Chief Justice Roger Taney, a descendant of Maryland's slaveholding elite, were principal figures in the most controversial Supreme Court decision of the nineteenth century. (Scott: Missouri Historical Society; Taney: Maryland Historical Society, Baltimore)

three of the northern justices actively dissented or refused to concur in crucial parts of the decision. The only northerner who supported Taney's opinion, Justice Robert Grier of Pennsylvania, was known to be close to President Buchanan. In fact, Buchanan had secretly brought to bear improper but effective influence.

A storm of angry reaction broke in the North. The decision seemed to confirm every charge against the aggressive Slave Power. "There is such a thing as the slave power," warned the *Cincinnati Daily Commercial*. "It has marched over and annihilated the boundaries of the states. We are now one great homogenous slaveholding community." The *Cincinnati Freeman* asked, "What security have the Germans and the Irish that their children will not, within a hundred years, be reduced to slavery in this land of their adoption?" "Where will it end?" asked the *Atlantic Monthly*. "Is the success of this conspiracy to be final and eternal?" The poet James Russell Lowell expressed the anxieties of poor northern whites when he had his Yankee character Ezekiel Biglow say:

> Wy, it's just ez clear ez figgers,
> Clear ez one an' one make two,
> Chaps thet make black slaves o' niggers,
> Want to make wite slaves o' you.

Republican politicians used these fears to strengthen their antislavery coalition. Abraham Lincoln stressed that the territorial question affected every citizen. "The whole nation," he had declared as

Abraham Lincoln on the Slave Power

early as 1854, "is interested that the best use shall be made of these Territories. We want them for homes of free white people. This they cannot be, to any considerable extent, if slavery shall be planted within them." The territories must be reserved, he insisted, "as an outlet for free white people everywhere" so that immigrants could come to America and "find new homes and better their condition in life."

More importantly, Lincoln warned of slavery's increasing control over the nation. The founders had created a government dedicated to freedom, Lincoln insisted. Admittedly they had recognized slavery's existence, but the public mind, he argued in 1858, had always rested in the belief that slavery would die either naturally or by legislation. The next step in the unfolding Slave Power conspiracy, Lincoln alleged, would be a Supreme Court decision "declaring that the Constitution does not permit a State to exclude slavery from its limits. . . . We shall lie down pleasantly, dreaming that the people of Missouri are on the verge of making their State free; and we shall awake to the reality instead, that the Supreme Court has made Illinois a slave State." This charge was not pure hyperbole, for lawsuits soon challenged state laws that freed slaves brought within their borders.

Lincoln's most eloquent statement against the Slave Power was his famous "House Divided" speech, delivered as he announced his campaign for the U.S.

How do historians know...

that Abraham Lincoln despised slavery? Lincoln, of course, was a politician who made many public addresses and statements. Later, as president, he mastered the form of the public letter sent to leading newspapers. Lincoln paid close attention to his understanding of public opinion on the issues of slavery and emancipation, and when the war came, he put saving the Union ahead of freeing slaves as a matter of policy, until the two causes became interdependent. But before he received the Republican nomination for president in 1860, he was long on record as a leading voice of his party's intention to put slavery on a "course of ultimate extinction." This photograph was taken in Chicago in 1859, the year before the Illinois lawyer was elected president.

Lincoln also produced many private writings. The page reproduced here comes from a notebook in which he recorded his reactions to a proslavery book, *Slavery Ordained of God*, by Reverend Fred A. Ross. Criticizing Ross, Lincoln revealed his dislike of privilege and exposed the self-interest of those who would exploit others: "Dr. Ross sits in the shade, with gloves on his hands, and subsists on the bread that Sambo is earning in the burning sun" rather than "delv[ing] for his own bread." Lincoln was no radical abolitionist, and his various stands on slavery represented both his pragmatic politics and his personal views. But there can be no doubt that, when it came to his own convictions, he hated slavery as an idea and as an institution.   (Photos: Notebook: Courtesy of the Illinois State Historical Library; Lincoln: Chicago Historical Society)

Senate in 1858. Using biblical metaphor and extraordinary grace, he declared:

> 'A house divided against itself cannot stand.' I believe this government cannot endure, permanently half slave and half free. I do not expect the Union to be dissolved—I do not expect the House to fall—but I do expect it to cease to be divided. It will become all one thing or all the other. Either the opponents of slavery will arrest the further spread of it, and place it where the public mind shall rest in the belief that it is in the course of ultimate extinction; or its advocates will push it forward, till it shall become alike lawful in all the States, old as well as new, North as well as South.

Lincoln warned repeatedly that the latter possibility was real, and events convinced countless northerners that slaveholders were nearing their goal of making slavery a national institution. And southerners never forgot Lincoln's use of the direct words "ultimate extinction."

Politically, these forceful Republican arguments offset the difficulties that the *Dred Scott* decision posed. By endorsing the South's doctrine of state sovereignty, the Court had in effect declared that the central position of the Republican Party—no extension of slavery—was unconstitutional. Republicans could only repudiate the decision, appealing to a "higher law," or hope to change the personnel of the Court. They did both and gained politically as fear of the Slave Power grew. But fear also grew among free blacks, as they wondered if they had any future in America. Frederick Douglass continued to try to fashion hope among his people, but concluded a speech in the wake of the *Dred Scott* decision bleakly: "I walk by faith, not by sight."

For northern Democrats like Stephen Douglas, the Court's decision posed an awful dilemma. Northern voters were alarmed by the prospect that the territories would be opened to slavery. To retain their support, Douglas had to find some way to reassure them. Yet, given his ambitions to lead the national Democratic Party and become president, Douglas could not afford to alienate southern Democrats.

The Lecompton Constitution

Douglas chose to stand by his principle of popular sovereignty, even if the result angered southerners. In 1857 Kansans voted on a proslavery constitution that had been drafted at Lecompton. It was defeated by more than ten thousand votes. The evidence was overwhelming that Kansans did not want slavery, yet President Buchanan tried to force the Lecompton Constitution through Congress in an effort to hastily organize the territory.

Never had the Slave Power's influence over the government seemed more blatant; the Buchanan administration and southerners demanded a proslavery outcome, contrary to the popular will of the majority in Kansas. Breaking with the administration, Douglas threw his weight against the Lecompton Constitution. He gauged opinion in Kansas correctly, for in 1858 voters there rejected the constitution again. But his action infuriated southern Democrats. After the *Dred Scott* decision, southerners like Senator Albert G. Brown of Mississippi believed that slavery was protected in the territories: "The Constitution as expounded by the Supreme Court awards it. We demand it; we mean to have it."

Douglas further alienated the southern wing of his party in his well-publicized debates with Abraham

Stephen Douglas and the Freeport Doctrine

Lincoln, who challenged him for the Illinois Senate seat in 1858. Speaking at Freeport, Illinois, Douglas attempted to revive the concept of popular sovereignty with some tortured arguments. Asserting that the Supreme Court had ruled only on the powers of Congress, not on the powers of a territorial legislature, Douglas claimed that citizens in a territory could still bar slavery either by passing a law against it or by doing nothing. Without the patrol laws and police regulations that supported slavery, he reasoned, the institution could not exist. This argument, called the Freeport Doctrine, temporarily shored up Douglas's crumbling position in the North. But it gave southern Democrats further evidence that Douglas was unreliable, and many turned viciously against him. Many southerners studied the trend in northern opinion and concluded that southern rights and slavery would be safe only in a separate nation.

Such feelings were not new. As early as 1838, the Louisiana planter Bennet Barrow had written in his diary: "Northern States meddling with slavery . . . openly speaking of the sin of Slavery in the southern states . . . must eventually cause a separation of the Union." In 1856 a calmer, more polished Georgian named Charles Colcock Jones, Jr., rejoiced at James Buchanan's defeat of Republican John C. Frémont for the presidency. The result guaranteed four more years of peace and prosperity, wrote Jones, but "beyond that period . . . we scarce dare expect a continuance of our present relations." Increasingly, slaveowners lived with a sense of crisis about the fate of the Union.

The immediate consequence for politics, however, was the likelihood of a split in the Democratic Party. Northern Democrats could not support the territorial protection for slavery that southern Democrats insisted was theirs as a constitutional right. Thus, in the North and in the South the issue of slavery in the territories continued to destroy moderation and promote militancy.

Disunion

It is worth remembering that in the late 1850s most Americans were not caught up daily in the slavery crisis. They were preoccupied with personal affairs, especially coping with the effects of the economic panic that had begun in the spring of 1857. They were worried about widespread unemployment, a sick cow, the plummeting price of wheat, the declining wages at a textile mill, or a son who wanted to marry and needed land. In the Midwest, clerks, mechanics, domestics, railroad hands, and lumber camp workers lost jobs by the thousands. Bankers were at a loss for what to do about a weak credit system caused by frenzied western land speculation that began early in the decade. In parts of the South, such as Georgia, the panic intensified class divisions between upcountry yeomen and coastal slaveholding planters. Farmers blamed the tight money policies of Georgia's budding commercial banking system on wealthy planters who controlled the state's Democratic Party.

By 1858 Philadelphia had 40,000 unemployed workers, and New York City nearly 100,000. Fear of bread riots and class warfare gripped many cities in the North. True to form, blame for such economic woe became sectionalized, as southerners saw their system justified by the temporary collapse of industrial prosperity, and northerners feared even more the incursions of the Slave Power on an insecure future.

The earliest known photograph of John Brown, probably taken in 1846 in Massachusetts, shows him pledging his devotion to an unidentified flag, possibly an abolitionist banner. Already Brown was aiding runaway slaves and pondering ways to strike at slavery. (Ohio Historical Society)

Soon, however, the entire nation's focus would be thrown again on a new dimension of the slavery question—armed rebellion. Born in Connecticut in 1800, John Brown had been raised by staunchly religious and antislavery parents. Between 1820 and 1855, he engaged in some twenty business ventures, including farming, nearly all of them failures. But Brown had a distinctive vision of abolitionism, though he never joined any antislavery organizations. He relied on an Old Testament conception of justice—"an eye for an eye"—and he had a puritanical obsession with the wickedness of others, especially southern slaveowners. Brown believed that slavery was an "unjustifiable" state of war conducted by one group of people against another. He also believed that violence in a righteous cause was a holy act, even a rite of purification for those who engaged in it. To Brown, the destruction of slavery in America required revolutionary ideology and revolutionary acts.

John Brown's Raid on Harpers Ferry

On October 16, 1859, Brown led a small band of whites and blacks (eighteen men in all) in an attack on the federal arsenal at Harpers Ferry, Virginia. Hoping to trigger a slave rebellion, Brown failed miserably and was quickly captured. In a celebrated trial in November, and a highly guarded but widely publicized execution in December, in Charles Town, Virginia, Brown became one of the most enduring martyrs, as well as villains, of American history. His attempted insurrection struck fear into the South.

Then it became known that Brown had received financial backing from several prominent abolitionists. When northern intellectuals such as Emerson and Henry David Thoreau praised Brown as a holy warrior who "would make the gallows as glorious as the cross," and as "an angel of light," white southerners' outrage multiplied. The South almost universally interpreted Brown's attack at Harpers Ferry as the act of midnight terrorism, as the fulfillment of their long-stated dread of "abolition emissaries" who would infiltrate the region to incite slave rebellion.

Perhaps most telling of all was the fact that the pivotal election of 1860 was less than a year away when Brown went so eagerly to the gallows, handing a note to his jailer with the famous prediction: "I John Brown am now quite certain that the crimes of this guilty land will never be *purged away, but with blood.*" Most troubling to southerners, perhaps, was their awareness that while Republican politicians condemned Brown's crimes, they did so in a way that deflected attention onto the still greater crime of slavery.

Many Americans believed that the election of 1860 would decide the fate of the Union. Only the Democratic Party remained as an organization that was truly national in scope. "One after another," wrote a Mississippi editor, "the links which have bound the North and South together, have been severed . . . [but] the Democratic party looms gradually up . . . and waves the olive branch over the troubled waters of politics." But at its 1860 convention in Charleston, South Carolina, the Democratic Party split.

Election of 1860

Stephen A. Douglas wanted his party's presidential nomination, but he could not afford to alienate northern voters by accepting the southern position on the territories. Southern Democrats, however, insisted on recognition of their rights—as the *Dred Scott* decision had defined them—and they moved to block Douglas's nomination. When Douglas obtained a majority for his version of the platform, delegates from the five Gulf states plus South Carolina, Georgia, and Arkansas walked out of the convention. After efforts at compromise failed, the Democrats presented two nominees: Douglas for the northern wing, and Vice President John C. Breckinridge of Kentucky for the southern.

The Republicans nominated Abraham Lincoln at a rousing convention in Chicago. Lincoln's choice reflected the growing power of the Midwest, and he was perceived as more moderate on slavery than the early front runner, Senator William H. Seward of New York. A Constitutional Union Party, formed to preserve the nation but strong only in the Upper South, nominated John Bell of Tennessee.

Bell's only issue in the ensuing campaign was the urgency of preserving the Union, and Douglas desperately wanted to hold his northern and southern supporters together. Even Breckinridge quickly backed away from the appearance of extremism, and his supporters in several states stressed his unionism. Although Lincoln and the Republicans denied any intent to interfere with slavery in the states where it existed, they stood firm against the extension of slavery into the territories.

The election of 1860 was sectional in character, and the only one in American history in which the losers refused to accept the result. Lincoln won, but Douglas, Breckinridge, and Bell together received most of the votes. Douglas had broad-based support but won few states. Breckinridge carried nine southern states, all in the Deep South. Bell won pluralities in Virginia, Kentucky, and Tennessee. Lincoln prevailed in the North, but in the four border states that ultimately remained loyal to the Union (Missouri, Kentucky, Maryland, and Delaware) he gained only a plurality, not a majority (see Table 14.3). Lincoln's victory was won in the electoral college. He polled only 40 percent of the total vote and was not even on the ballot in ten slave states.

Opposition to slavery's extension was the core issue of the Republican Party, and Lincoln's alarm over slavery's growing political power was genuine. Moreover, abolitionists and supporters of free soil in the North worked to keep the Republicans from compromising on their territorial stand. Meanwhile in the South, proslavery advocates and secessionists whipped up public opinion and demanded that state conventions assemble to consider secession.

Lincoln made the crucial decision not to soften his party's position on the territories. He wrote of the necessity of maintaining the bond of faith between voter and candidate and of declining to set "the minority over the majority." But Lincoln's refusal to compromise derived both from conviction and from concern for the unity of the Republican Party. Although many conservative Republicans—eastern businessmen and former Whigs who did not feel strongly about slavery—hoped for a compromise, the original and most

Table 14.3   Presidential Vote in 1860 (by State)

Lincoln (Republican)	Carried all northern states and all electoral votes except 3 in New Jersey
Breckinridge (Southern Democrat)	Carried all slave states except Virginia, Kentucky, Tennessee, and Missouri
Bell (Constitutional Union)	Carried Virginia, Kentucky, Tennessee
Douglas (Northern Democrat)	Carried only Missouri

Lincoln received only 26,000 votes in the entire South and was not even on the ballot in ten slave states. Breckinridge was not on the ballot in three northern states.

committed Republicans—antislavery voters and "conscience Whigs"—were adamant for free soil. Lincoln chose to stand firm against slavery's extension.

In the winter of 1860–1861, southern leaders in the Senate were willing, conditionally, to accept a compromise drawn up by Senator John J. Crittenden of Kentucky. Hoping to don the mantle of Henry Clay and avert disunion, Crittenden proposed that the two sections divide the territories between them at latitude 36°30'. But the southerners would agree to this only if the Republicans did, too, for they wanted no less and knew that extremists in the South would demand much more. When Lincoln ruled out concessions on the territorial issue, Crittenden's peacemaking effort, based on old and discredited measures, collapsed.

Meanwhile, the Union was being destroyed. On December 20, 1860, South Carolina passed an ordinance of secession amid jubilation and cheering. This

On February 18, 1861, in Montgomery, Alabama, Jefferson Davis took an oath as president of the Confederate States of America. Davis later recalled that he foresaw "troubles innumerable" but was committed to seek independence as his paramount goal.   (Boston Athenaeum)

Secession

step marked the inaugural success of a strategy favored by secessionists: separate-state secession. Recognizing the difficulty of persuading all the southern states to challenge the federal government simultaneously, secessionists concentrated their efforts on the most extreme proslavery state. They hoped South Carolina's secession would induce other states to follow, with each decision building momentum for disunion.

The strategy proved effective. By reclaiming its independence, South Carolina raised the stakes in the sectional confrontation. No longer was secession an unthinkable step; the Union was broken. Secessionists now argued that other states should follow South Carolina and that those who favored compromise could make a better deal outside the Union than in it. Moderates found it difficult to dismiss such arguments, since most of them—even those who felt deep affection for the Union—were committed to defending southern rights and the southern way of life.

The Confederate States of America

Southern extremists soon got their way in the Deep South. Overwhelming their opposition, they called separate state conventions and passed secession ordinances in Mississippi, Florida, Alabama, Georgia, Louisiana, and Texas. By February 1861 these states had joined South Carolina to form a new government in Montgomery, Alabama: the Confederate States of America. The delegates at Montgomery chose Jefferson Davis as their president, and the Confederacy began to function independently of the United States.

This apparent unanimity of action was deceiving. Confused and dissatisfied with the alternatives, many southerners who in 1860 had voted in the U.S. presidential election stayed home a few months later rather than vote for delegates who would decide on secession. Even so, in some state conventions the vote to secede was close, with secession decided by overrepresentation of plantation districts. Furthermore, the conventions were noticeably unwilling to let voters ratify their acts. Four states in the Upper South—Virginia, North Carolina, Tennessee, and Arkansas—flatly rejected secession and did not join the Confederacy until after fighting had begun. In the border states, popular sentiment was deeply divided; minorities in Kentucky and Missouri tried to secede, but these slave states ultimately came under Union control, along with Maryland and Delaware (see Map 14.4).

Such misgivings were not surprising. Secession posed new and troubling issues for southerners, espe-

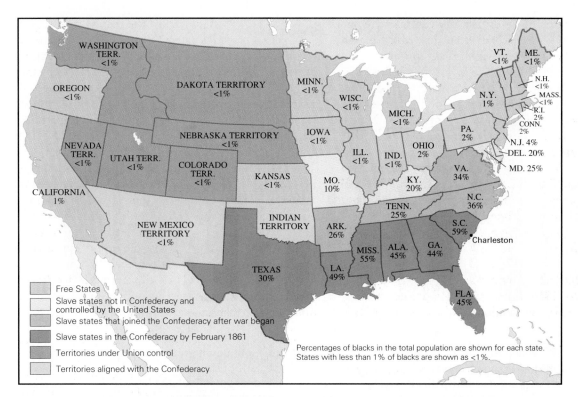

Map 14.4 The Divided Nation—Slave and Free Areas, 1861 After fighting began, the Upper South joined the Deep South in the Confederacy. How does the nation's pattern of division correspond to the distribution of slavery and the percentage of blacks in the population?

cially the possibility of war, where it would be fought, and who would die. Analysis of election returns from 1860 and 1861 indicates that slaveholders and non-slaveholders were beginning to part company politically. Heavily slaveholding counties strongly supported secession. But nonslaveholding areas that had favored Breckinridge in the presidential election proved far less willing to support secession: most counties with few slaves took an antisecession position or were staunchly Unionist (see Figure 14.1). Large numbers of yeomen also sat out the election. With war on the horizon, non-slaveholders were beginning to consider their class interests and to ask themselves how far they would go to support slavery and slaveowners.

After Alabama's convention approved secession, one delegate wrote: "Here I set & from my window see the nasty little thing [flag] flaunting in the breeze which has taken the place of that glorious banner which has been the pride of millions of Americans and the boast of freemen the wide world over." Although such sentiments presented problems for the Confederacy, they were not sufficiently developed to prevent secession.

The dilemma facing President Lincoln on inauguration day in March 1861 was how to maintain the authority of the federal government without provoking war. Proceeding cautiously, he sought only to hold on to forts in the states that had left the Union, reasoning that in this way he could assert federal sovereignty while waiting for a restoration of relations. But Jefferson Davis, who could not claim to lead a sovereign nation if the Confederate ports were under foreign (that is, United States) control, was unwilling to be so patient. A collision was inevitable.

Fort Sumter and Outbreak of War

It arrived in the early morning hours of April 12, 1861, at Fort Sumter in Charleston harbor. A federal garrison there ran low on food, and Lincoln notified the South Carolinians that he was sending a ship to resupply the fort. For the Montgomery government, the alternatives were to attack the fort or to acquiesce to Lincoln's authority. After the Confederate cabinet met, the secretary of war ordered local commanders to obtain a surrender or attack the fort. After two days of

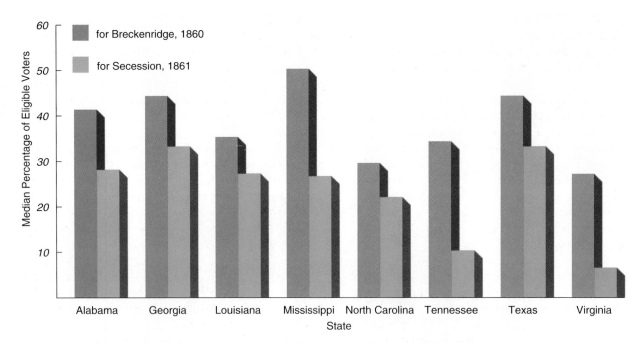

Figure 14.1 **Voting Returns of Counties with Few Slaveholders, Eight Southern States, 1860 and 1861** This graph depicts voting in counties whose percentage of slaveholders ranked them among the lower half of the counties in their state. How does voters' support for secession in 1861 compare with support for John Breckinridge, the southern Democratic candidate in 1860? Why was their support for secession so weak? At this time counties with many slaveholders were giving increased support to secession.

heavy bombardment, the federal garrison finally surrendered. No one died in battle, though an accident during postbattle ceremonies killed two Union soldiers. Confederates permitted the U.S. troops to sail away on unarmed vessels while Charlestonians celebrated wildly. The Civil War—the bloodiest war in America's history—had begun.

Summary

 Throughout the 1840s and 1850s many able leaders had worked diligently to avert this outcome. Most people, North and South, had hoped to keep the nation together. As late as 1858 even Jefferson Davis had declared, "This great country will continue united," saying that "to the innermost fibers of my heart I love it all, and every part." Secession dismayed northern editors and voters, and it also plunged some planters into depression. Paul Cameron, the largest slaveowner in North Carolina, confessed that he was "very unhappy. I love the Union." Many blacks, however, shared Frederick Douglass's outlook. "The contest

must now be decided," he wrote in March 1861, "and decided forever, which of the two, Freedom or Slavery, shall give law to this Republic. Let the conflict come."

Why had war broken out? Why had all efforts to prevent it failed? The conflict slavery generated was fundamental and beyond adjustment. The emotions bound up in attacking and defending it were too powerful, and the interests it affected too vital, for compromise. Because it was deeply entwined with major policy questions of the present and the foreseeable future, each section ultimately regarded slavery as too important to be put aside.

Even if one excludes extreme views, North and South had fundamentally different attitudes toward the institution. The logic of Republican ideology tended in the direction of abolishing slavery, even though Republicans denied any such intention. The logic of southern arguments led toward establishing slavery everywhere, though southern leaders too denied such a motive. Lincoln put these facts succinctly. In a postelection letter to his old friend Alexander Stephens of Georgia, soon to be vice president of the Confederacy, Lincoln offered assurance that Republicans would not attack slavery in the states where it existed. But Lincoln continued, "You think slavery is right and ought to be expanded; while we think it is wrong and ought to be restricted. That I suppose is the rub."

A nation may face unresolvable issues yet manage to get past them. New events can capture people's attention; time can alter interests and attitudes—this is why historians always remind us of the importance of "contingency" in human affairs. That is precisely what the advocates of compromise hoped for. They tried to contain conflict and buy time for the nation, to avoid issues that could not be settled, and to preserve areas of consensus among Americans. But their efforts were doomed to failure.

Territorial expansion generated disputes so frequently that the nation never enjoyed a breathing space. Every southern victory increased fear of the Slave Power, and each new expression of Free-Soil sentiment made alarmed slaveholders more insistent in their demands. Eventually even those opposed to war could see no way to avoid it. In the profoundest sense, slavery was the root of the war. But as the fighting began, this, the war's central issue, was shrouded in confusion. How would the Civil War affect slavery, its place in the law, and African Americans' place in society? Would the institution survive a short war, but not a long war? As a people and a nation, Americans had reached the most fateful turning point in their history. Answers would now come from the battlefield and from the mobilization of two societies to wage war on a scale they had not imagined.

LEGACY FOR A PEOPLE AND A NATION
Revolutionary Violence

The greatest significance of John Brown's raid on Harpers Ferry in 1859 rests in its long aftermath in American memory. "Men consented to his death," wrote Frederick Douglass of Brown, "and then went home and taught their children to honor his memory." Brown is as important as a symbol as he is for his deeds. He has been at once one of the most beloved and most loathed figures in American history. In the song that bears his name, "John Brown's Body," a popular marching tune during the Civil War, his "soul goes marching on." As the poet Stephen Vincent Benet wrote: "You can weigh John Brown's body well enough, / But how and in what balance weigh John Brown?"

In the wake of his execution, in painting, song, and poetry, people constructed a John Brown mythology. Was he the Christ-like figure who died for the nation's sins, who had to commit crimes in order to expose the nation's larger crime? Or was he the terrorist thief, who murdered in the name of his own peculiar vision of God's will? Brown can be disturbing and inspiring, majestic and foolish, a monster or a warrior saint. He represented the highest ideals and ruthless deeds. He killed for justice. Perhaps Brown was one of the avengers of history who does the work the rest of us won't, couldn't, or shouldn't.

Brown forces us to ask when and how revolutionary violence—violence in the name of a political or spiritual end—is justified. The 1850s and the turn of the twenty-first century are two different contexts. But in today's world, terrorist, revolutionary violence is commonplace in our weekly news: an airliner is blown up over Lockerbie, Scotland; buses are strafed in Jerusalem; a federal building explodes in Oklahoma City; the Irish Republican Army plants bombs in London subways; American embassies are attacked in Africa and Europe—a truck bomb here, a car bomb there. Many organizations over the years have adopted John Brown as their justifying symbol, from left-wing students opposing American foreign policy to current anti-abortion groups who target clinics and doctors. The story of John Brown's raid in 1859 forces us to confront the question of when revolutionary violence is right or wrong.

For Further Reading, see page A-17 of the Appendix. For Web resources, go to http://college.hmco.com.

He was an ordinary twenty-seven-year-old store clerk from a New England town. But he went off, as though directed by a manly compass, to seek the extraordinary experiences of comradeship and war. In the spring of 1861, Charles Brewster, a member of a militia unit in Northampton, Massachusetts, left his mother and two sisters behind and joined Company C of the Tenth Massachusetts Volunteers. At that moment, Brewster had no idea of his capacity for leadership or his ability to uphold such values as courage and manliness. But the war released him from the boredom and failure of his life.

On April 18, only three days after the surrender of Fort Sumter, a mustering of Company C turned into a large public rally where forty new men enlisted. By April 24 seventy-five Northampton women committed their labor to sew uniforms for the company. Some women worked at home, while others sewed in the town hall. Local poets came to the armory to recite patriotic verses to the would-be soldiers. Yesterday farmers, clerks, and mechanics, today they were the heroes who would "whip secesh." By June 10, after weeks of drilling, Brewster's company attended a farewell ball, and four days later they strode down Main Street amid a cheering throng of spectators. Flags waved everywhere, several brass bands competed, and Brewster and his company boarded a train going south. En route the soldiers continued the joyous fervor of the day by singing "patriotic airs" to the accompaniment of a lone accordion.

Before their three-year enlistment ended, the Tenth Massachusetts participated in nearly every major battle fought by the Army of the Potomac from early 1862 to the summer of 1864. When the survivors of the Tenth were mustered out, only 220 of the nearly 1,000 in the original regiment were still on active duty. Their summer outing had transformed into the bloodiest war in history. They had seen thousands die of disease, practiced war upon civilians and the southern landscape, and loyally served the cause as variously defined, trying their best to fulfill their communities' expectations. In more than two hundred sometimes

Transforming Fire: The Civil War 1861–1865

War drastically altered the lives of millions of Americans. Many young men found in soldiering a combination of comradeship, devotion, boredom, and horror. Winslow Homer gave the ironic title *Home, Sweet, Home* to this painting of Union soldiers in camp about 1863. (Private Collection, photograph courtesy of Hirschl and Adler Galleries, New York)

lyrical letters to his mother and sisters, Brewster, who rose to lieutenant and adjutant of his regiment, left a trove of commentary on the meaning of war, the character of slavery and why it had to be destroyed, and especially the values of common, mid-nineteenth-century American men.

Brewster was as racist as many southerners in his perceptions of blacks. He was no "desperate hero" about battlefield courage, and he nearly died of dysentery more than once. He was personally eager for rank and recognition, and he eventually held only contempt for civilians who stayed at home. He was often miserably lonely and homesick, and he described battlefield carnage with an honest realism. The early romantic was transformed into a mature veteran by what he called the "terrible, terrible business" of war.

Most tellingly, Brewster grew in his attitudes about race. In 1862 he defied orders and took in a seventeen-year-old ex-slave as his personal servant, patronizingly clothing him with his own old pants sent from home. In 1864, after surviving some of the worst battles of the war in Virginia, which destroyed his regiment, and frightened of civilian life, Brewster reenlisted to be a recruiter of black troops. In this new role, Brewster worked from an office in Norfolk, Virginia, where his principal job was writing "love letters" for illiterate black women to their soldier husbands at the front. In imagining Brewster sitting at a table with a lonely freedwoman, swallowing his prejudices toward blacks and women, and repeatedly writing or reciting the phrases "give my love to . . ." and "your Husband untall Death," we can glimpse the enormous potential for human transformation at work in this war.

The Civil War brought astonishing, unexpected changes not only to Charles Brewster but everywhere in both North and South. Countless southern soldiers experienced similar transformations. But they, and their families, also experienced what few other groups of Americans have—utter defeat. For some Americans, wealth changed to poverty and hope to despair; for others, the suffering of war spelled opportunity. Contrasts abounded, between noble and crass motives and between individuals seeking different goals. Even the South's slaves, who hoped that they were witnessing God's "Holy War"—the "coming of the jubilee"—encountered unsympathetic liberators. When a Yankee soldier ransacked a slave woman's cabin, stealing her best quilts, she denounced him as a "nasty, stinkin' rascal" who had betrayed his cause of freedom. Angrily the soldier contradicted her, saying, "I'm fightin' for $14 a month and the Union."

Northern troops were not the only ones to feel anger over their sacrifices. Impoverished by the war, one southern farmer had endured inflation, taxes, and shortages to support the Confederacy. Then an impressment agent arrived to take still more from him—grain and meat, horses and mules, and wagons. In return, the agent offered only a certificate promising repayment sometime in the future. Bitter and disgusted, the farmer spoke for many by declaring, "The sooner this damned Government falls to pieces, the better it will be for us."

Many northern businessmen, however, viewed the economic effects of the war with optimistic anticipation. The conflict ensured vast government expenditures, a heavy demand for goods, and lucrative federal contracts. *Harper's Monthly* reported that an eminent financier expected a long war—the kind of war that would mean huge purchases, paper money, active speculation, and rising prices. "The battle of Bull Run," predicted the financier, "makes the fortune of every man in Wall Street who is not a natural idiot."

For millions, the Civil War was a life-changing event. It obliterated the normal patterns and circumstances of life. Millions of men were swept away into training camps and battle units. Armies numbering in the hundreds of thousands marched over the South, devastating once-peaceful countrysides. Families struggled to survive without their men; businesses tried to cope with the loss of workers. Women in both North and South took on extra responsibilities in the home and moved into new jobs in the work force. Many women joined the ranks of nurses and hospital workers. No sphere of life was untouched.

Change was most drastic in the South, where the leaders of the secession movement had launched a conservative revolution for their section's national independence. Born of states' rights doctrine, their break with the Union now had to be transformed into a centralized nation to fight a vast war. Never were men more mistaken: their revolutionary means were fundamentally incompatible with their conservative purpose. Southern whites had feared that a peacetime government of Republicans would interfere with slavery and upset the routine of plantation life. Instead their own actions led to a war that turned southern life upside down and imperiled the very existence of slavery. Jefferson Davis, president of the Confederate States of America, devised policies more objectionable to the elite than any proposed by President-elect Lincoln. Life in the Confederacy proved to be a shockingly unsouthern experience.

IMPORTANT EVENTS

1861 Battle of Bull Run
McClellan organizes Union Army
Union blockade begins
U.S. Congress passes first confiscation act
Trent affair
Some slaves admitted to Union lines as
"contraband" of war

1862 Union captures Fort Henry and
Fort Donelson
U.S. Navy captures New Orleans
Battle of Shiloh shows the war's
destructiveness
Confederacy enacts conscription
McClellan's Peninsula Campaign fails
to take Richmond
U.S. Congress passes second confiscation
act, initiating emancipation
Confederacy mounts offensive in Maryland
and Kentucky
Battle of Antietam ends Lee's drive into
Maryland in September
British intervention in the war on
Confederate side is averted by events
and northern diplomacy

1863 Emancipation Proclamation takes effect
U.S. Congress passes National Banking Act
Union enacts conscription
African American soldiers join Union Army
Food riots occur in southern cities

Battle of Chancellorsville ends in
Confederate victory but Jackson's death
Union wins key victories at Gettysburg
and Vicksburg
Draft riots take place in New York City
Battle of Chattanooga leaves South vulnerable
to Sherman's march into Georgia

1864 Battles of the Wilderness and Spotsylvania
produce heavy casualties on both sides in
the effort to capture and defend Richmond
Battle of Cold Harbor continues carnage in
Virginia
Lincoln requests Republican Party plank
abolishing slavery
Sherman captures Atlanta
Confederacy begins to collapse on the home
front, as southern hardship destroys morale
Lincoln wins reelection, eliminating any Con-
federate hopes for a negotiated end to war
Jefferson Davis proposes emancipation within
the Confederacy
Sherman marches through Georgia to the sea

1865 Sherman marches through Carolinas
U.S. Congress approves Thirteenth
Amendment
Lee abandons Richmond and Petersburg
Lee surrenders at Appomattox Court House
Lincoln assassinated
Death toll in war reaches 620,000

War altered the North as well, but less sharply. Because most of the fighting took place on southern soil, northern farms and factories remained virtually unscathed. The drafting of workers and the changing need for products slowed the pace of industrialization somewhat, but factories and businesses remained busy. Workers lost ground to inflation, but the economy hummed. A new pro-business atmosphere dominated Congress, where the seats of southern representatives were empty. To the alarm of many, the powers of the federal government and of the president increased during the war.

The war created social strains in both North and South. Disaffection was strongest in the Confederacy, where poverty and class resentment fed a lower-class antagonism to the war that threatened the Confederacy from within as federal armies assailed it from without. In the North, dissent also flourished, and antiwar sentiment occasionally erupted into violence.

Ultimately, the Civil War forced on the nation a social and political revolution regarding race. Its greatest effect was to compel leaders and citizens to deal directly with the issue they had struggled over but had been unable to resolve: slavery. This issue, in complex and indirect ways, had caused the war. Now the scope and demands of the war forced reluctant Americans to confront it. And blacks themselves embraced what was for them the most fundamental turning point in their experience as Americans. ■

America Goes to War, 1861–1862

 Few Americans understood what they were getting into when the war began. The onset of hostilities sparked patriotic sentiments, optimistic speeches, and joyous ceremonies in both North and South. Northern communities, large and small, raised companies of

In *Departure of the Seventh Regiment* (1861), flags and the spectacle of thousands of young men from New York marching off to battle give a deceptively gay appearance to the beginning of the Civil War. (Museum of Fine Arts, Boston; M. and M. Karolik Collection)

volunteers eager to save the Union and sent them off with fanfare (a scene captured in the painting *Departure of the Seventh Regiment*). In the South, confident recruits boasted of whipping the Yankees and returning home at least before Christmas. Southern women sewed dashing uniforms for men who soon would be lucky to wear drab gray or butternut homespun. Americans went to war in 1861 with decidedly romantic notions of what they would experience.

Through the spring of 1861 both sides scrambled to organize and train their undisciplined armies. On July 21, 1861, the first battle took place outside Manassas Junction, Virginia, near a stream called Bull Run. General Irvin McDowell and 30,000 Union troops attacked General P. G. T. Beauregard's 22,000 southerners (see Map 15.1 on page 394). As raw recruits struggled amid the confusion of their first battle, federal forces began to gain ground. Then they ran into a line of Virginia troops under General Thomas Jackson. "There is Jackson standing like a stone wall," shouted one Confederate. "Stonewall" Jackson's line held, and the arrival of 9,000 Confederate reinforcements won the day for the South. Union troops fled back to Washington and shocked northern congressmen and spectators,

First Battle of Bull Run

who had watched the battle from a point 2 miles away; a few of them were actually captured for their folly.

The unexpected rout at Bull Run gave northerners their first hint of the nature of the war to come. While the United States enjoyed an enormous advantage in resources, victory would not be easy. Pro-Union feeling was growing in western Virginia, and loyalties were divided in the four border slave states—Missouri, Kentucky, Maryland, and Delaware. But the rest of the Upper South, the states of North Carolina, Virginia, Tennessee, and Arkansas, had joined the Confederacy in the wake of the attack on Fort Sumter. Moved by an outpouring of regional loyalty, half a million southerners volunteered to fight, so many that the Confederate government could hardly arm them all. The United States therefore undertook a massive mobilization of troops around Washington, D.C.

Lincoln gave command of the army to General George B. McClellan, an officer who proved to be better at organization and training than at fighting. McClellan put his growing army into camp and devoted the fall and winter of 1861 to readying a formidable force of a quarter-million men whose mission would be to take Richmond, established as the Confederate capital by July 1861. "The vast preparation of the enemy," wrote one southern soldier, produced a "feeling of despondency" in the South for the first time. But southern morale remained high early in the war.

While McClellan prepared, the Union began to implement other parts of its overall strategy, which

Grand Strategy called for a blockade of southern ports and eventual capture of the Mississippi River. Like a constricting snake, this "Anaconda plan" would strangle the Confederacy (see Map 15.2 on page 412). At first the Union Navy had too few ships to patrol 3,550 miles of coastline and block the Confederacy's avenues of commerce and supply. Gradually, however, the navy increased the blockade's effectiveness, though it never stopped southern commerce completely.

Confederate strategy was essentially defensive. A defensive posture was not only consistent with the South's claim of independence, but acknowledged the North's advantage in resources (see Figure 15.1). Furthermore, communities all across the South demanded their defense. Jefferson Davis, however, wisely rejected a static or wholly defensive strategy. The South would pursue an "offensive defensive," taking advantage of opportunities to attack and using its interior lines of transportation to concentrate troops at crucial points. In its war aims, the Confederacy did not need to conquer the North; the Union effort, however, as time would tell, required conquest of the South.

Strategic thinking on both sides slighted the importance of "the West," that vast expanse of territory between Virginia and the Mississippi River. When the war began, both sides were unprepared for large-scale operations in the West, but before the end of the war they would prove to be decisive. Guerrilla warfare broke out in 1861 in the politically divided state of

Missouri, and key locations along the Mississippi and other major rivers in the West would prove to be crucial prizes in the North's eventual victory. In the Far West, beyond the Mississippi River, the Confederacy hoped to gain an advantage by negotiating treaties with the Creeks, Choctaws, Chickasaws, Cherokees, Seminoles, and smaller tribes of Plains Indians. Although early strategy evolved haphazardly, both sides would soon know they were in a war the scale of which few people had ever imagined.

The last half of 1861 brought no major land battles, but the North made gains by sea. Late in the

Union Naval Campaign summer Union naval forces captured Cape Hatteras and then seized Hilton Head, one of the Sea Islands off Port Royal, South Carolina. A few months later, similar operations secured vital coastal points in North Carolina, as well as Fort Pulaski, which defended Savannah. Federal naval operations established significant beachheads along the Confederate coastline (see Map 15.2).

The coastal victories off South Carolina foreshadowed a revolution in slave society. At the federal gunboats' approach, frightened planters abandoned their lands and fled. For a while, Confederate cavalry tried to round up slaves and move them to the interior as well. But thousands of slaves greeted what they hoped to be freedom with rejoicing and broke the hated cotton gins. Some entered their masters' homes and absconded with clothing and furniture, which they conspicuously displayed. Their jubilation and the growing stream of runaways who poured into the Union lines eliminated any doubt about which side slaves would support, given the opportunity. Unwilling at first to

Figure 15.1 Comparative Resources, Union and Confederate States, 1861 The North had vastly superior resources. Although the North's advantages in manpower and industrial capacity proved very important, the South still had to be conquered, its society and its will crushed. (Source: *The Times Atlas of World History.* Time Books, London, 1978. Used with permission.)

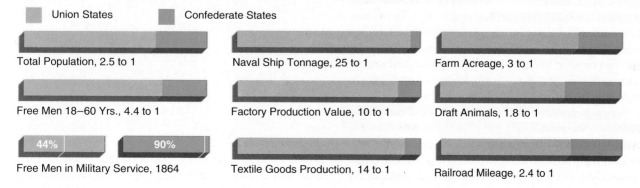

wage a war against slavery, the federal government did not acknowledge the slaves' freedom—though it began to use their labor in the Union cause. This swelling tide of emancipated slaves, defined by many Union officers as "contraband" of war (confiscated enemy property), forced first a bitter and confused debate within the Union Army and government over how to treat the freedmen, and then a forthright attempt to harness their power.

The coastal incursions worried southerners, but the spring of 1862 brought even stronger evidence of the war's gravity. In March two ironclad ships—the *Monitor* (a Union warship) and the *Merrimack* (a Union ship recycled by the Confederacy)—fought each other for the first time; their battle, though indecisive, ushered in a new era in naval design. In April Union ships commanded by Admiral David Farragut smashed through log booms blocking the Mississippi River and fought their way upstream to capture New Orleans. Farther west three full Confederate regiments were organized, mostly of Cherokees, from Indian Territory, but a Union victory at Elkhorn Tavern, Arkansas, shattered southern control of Indian Territory. Thereafter, dissension within Native American groups and a Union victory the following year at Honey Springs, Arkansas, reduced Confederate operations in Indian Territory to guerrilla raids.

In February 1862 land and river forces in northern Tennessee won significant victories for the Union.

Grant's Tennessee Campaign and the Battle of Shiloh

A hard-drinking Union commander named Ulysses S. Grant saw the strategic importance of Fort Henry and Fort Donelson, the Confederate outposts guarding the Tennessee and Cumberland Rivers. If federal troops could capture these forts, Grant realized, they would open two prime routes into the heartland of the Confederacy. In just ten days he seized the forts, cutting off the Confederates so completely that he demanded unconditional surrender of Fort Donelson. A path into Tennessee, Alabama, and Mississippi now lay open before the Union Army. Grant's achievement of such a surrender from his former West Point roommate, Confederate commander Simon Bolivar Buckner, inspired northern public opinion that spring.

Grant moved on into southern Tennessee and the first of the war's shockingly bloody encounters, the Battle of Shiloh. On April 6 Confederate general Albert Sidney Johnston caught federal troops with their backs to the water awaiting reinforcements along the Tennessee River. The Confederates attacked early in the morning and inflicted heavy damage all day. Close to victory, General Johnston was shot from his horse and killed. Southern forces almost achieved a breakthrough, but Union reinforcements arrived that night. The next day the tide of battle turned, and after ten hours of terrible combat, Grant's men forced the Confederates to withdraw.

Neither side won a victory at Shiloh, yet the losses were staggering. Northern troops lost 13,000 men (killed, wounded, or captured) out of 63,000; southerners sacrificed 11,000 out of 40,000. Total casualties in this single battle exceeded those in all three of America's previous wars combined. Now both sides were beginning to sense the true nature of the war. "I saw an open field," Grant recalled, "over which Confederates had made repeated charges . . . , so covered with dead that it would have been possible to walk across the clearing, in any direction, stepping on dead bodies, without a foot touching the ground." Shiloh utterly changed Grant's thinking about the war. He had hoped that southerners soon would be "heartily tired" of the conflict. After Shiloh, "I gave up all idea of saving the Union except by complete conquest." Memories of Shiloh battlefield, and many others to come, would haunt the soldiers who survived for the rest of their lives. Herman Melville's "Shiloh, A Requiem" captures the pathos of that spring day when armies learned the truth about war.

> Skimming lightly, wheeling still,
>   The swallows fly low
> Over the field in clouded days,
>   The forest-field of Shiloh—
> Over the field where April rain
> Solaced the parched ones stretched in pain
> Through the pause of night
> That followed the Sunday fight
>   Around the church of Shiloh—
> The church so lone, the log-built one,
> That echoed to many a parting groan
>   And natural prayer
>   Of dying foemen mingled there—
> Foemen at morn, but friends at eve—
>   Fame or country least their care:
> (What like a bullet can undeceive!)
>   But now they lie low,
> While over them the swallows skim,
>   And all is hushed at Shiloh.

Meanwhile, on the Virginia front, President Lincoln had a different problem. General McClellan was

Both armies experienced religious revivals during the war. This photograph shows members of a largely Irish regiment from New York celebrating Mass at the beginning of the war. Notice the presence of some female visitors in the left foreground. (Library of Congress)

McClellan and the Peninsula Campaign

slow to move. Only thirty-six, McClellan had already achieved notable success as an army officer and railroad president. Keenly aware of his historic role, he did not want to fail and insisted on having everything in order before he attacked. Habitually overestimating the size of enemy forces, McClellan called repeatedly for reinforcements and ignored Lincoln's directions to advance. McClellan advocated war of limited aims that would lead to a quick reunion. He intended no disruption of slavery, nor any war on noncombatants. McClellan's conservative vision of the war was practically outdated before he ever moved his army into Virginia. Finally he chose to move by a water route, sailing his troops down the Chesapeake, landing them on the peninsula between the York and James Rivers, and advancing on Richmond from the east (see Map 15.1).

After a bloody but indecisive battle at Fair Oaks on May 31–June 1, the federal armies moved to within 7 miles of the Confederate capital. They could see the spires on Richmond churches. The Confederate commanding general, Joseph E. Johnston, was badly wounded at Fair Oaks, and President Jefferson Davis placed his chief military adviser, Robert E. Lee, in command. The fifty-five-year-old Lee was an aristocratic Virginian, a life-long military officer, and a veteran of distinction from the War with Mexico. Although he opposed secession and found slavery distasteful, Lee loyally gave his allegiance to his state. He soon foiled McClellan's legions.

First, he sent Stonewall Jackson's corps of 17,000 northwest into the Shenandoah valley behind Union forces, where they threatened Washington, D.C., and with rapid-strike mobility drew some federal troops away from Richmond to protect their own capital. Further, in mid-June, in an extraordinary four-day ride around the entire Union Army, Confederate cavalry under J. E. B. Stuart, a self-styled Virginia cavalier, with red cape and plumed hat, confirmed the exposed position of a major portion of McClellan's army north of the rain-swollen Chickahominy River. Then, in a series of engagements known as the Seven Days Battles, June 26–July 1, Lee struck at McClellan's army. Lee never managed to close his pincers around the retreating Union forces, but the daring move of taking the majority of his army northeast and attacking the Union right flank, while leaving only a small force to

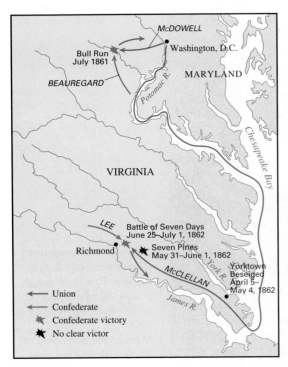

Map 15.1 McClellan's Campaign The water route chosen by McClellan to threaten Richmond during the peninsular campaign.

defend Richmond, forced McClellan (always believing he was outnumbered) to retreat toward the James River.

During the sustained fighting of the Seven Days, the Union forces suffered 20,614 casualties, and the Confederates 15,849. After repeated rebel assaults against entrenched positions on high ground at Malvern Hill, an officer concluded: "It was not war, it was murder." By August 3 McClellan withdrew his army back to the Potomac and the environs of Washington. Richmond remained safe for almost two more years.

Buoyed by these results, Jefferson Davis conceived an ambitious plan to turn the tide of the war and gain recognition of the Confederacy by European nations. He ordered a gen-

Confederate Offensive in Maryland and Kentucky

eral offensive, sending Lee north into Maryland and Generals Kirby Smith and Braxton Bragg into Kentucky. Calling on residents of Maryland and Kentucky to make a separate peace with his government, Davis also invited northwestern states like Indiana, which sent much of their trade down the Mississippi to New Orleans, to leave the Union. This was a coordinated effort to take the war to the North, to contest the allegiance of the border states, and to try to force a decisive turning point.

The plan was promising, but every part of the offensive failed. In the bloodiest day of the entire war, September 17, 1862, McClellan turned Lee back from Sharpsburg, Maryland. In the Battle of Antietam 5,000 men died (3,500 had died at Shiloh), and another 18,000 were wounded. Lee was lucky to escape destruction, for McClellan had intercepted a lost battle order, wrapped around cigars for each Confederate corps commander and inadvertently dropped by a courier. But McClellan moved slowly, failed to use his larger forces in simultaneous attacks all along the line, and allowed Lee's stricken army to retreat to safety across the Potomac. In the wake of Antietam, Lincoln removed McClellan from command.

In Kentucky Generals Smith and Bragg secured Lexington and Frankfurt, but their effort to force the Yankees back to the Ohio River was stopped at the Battle of Perryville on October 8. Bragg's army retreated back into Tennessee where, on December 31, 1862, to January 2, 1863, they fought an indecisive but much bloodier battle at Murfreesboro. Casualties exceeded even those of Shiloh and many lives were sacrificed on a bitter winter landscape.

Confederate leaders had marshaled all their strength for a breakthrough but had failed. Outnumbered and disadvantaged in resources, the South could not continue the offensive. Profoundly disappointed, Davis admitted to a committee of Confederate representatives that southerners were entering "the darkest and most dangerous period we have yet had." Tenacious defense and stoic endurance now seemed the South's only long-range hope.

But 1862 also brought painful lessons to the North. Confederate general J. E. B. Stuart executed a daring cavalry raid into Pennsylvania in October. Then on December 13 Union general Ambrose Burnside, now in command of the Army of the Potomac, unwisely ordered his soldiers to attack Lee's army, which held fortified positions on high ground at Fredericksburg, Virginia. Lee's men performed so coolly and controlled the engagement so thoroughly that Lee was moved to say, "It is well that war is so terrible. We should grow too fond of it." Burnside's repeated assaults up Marye's Heights shocked even the opponents. "The Federals had fallen like the steady dripping of rain from the eaves of a house," remarked Confederate general James Longstreet. And a Union officer observed the carnage of 1,300 dead and 9,600

In October 1862 in New York City, photographer Mathew Brady opened an exhibition of photographs from the Battle of Antietam. Although few knew it, Brady's vision was very poor, and this photograph of Confederate dead was actually made by his assistants, Alexander Gardner and James F. Gibson. (Library of Congress)

wounded Union soldiers: "The whole plain was covered with men, prostrate and dropping. . . . I had never before seen fighting like that—nothing approaching it in terrible uproar and destruction . . . the next brigade coming up in succession would do its duty, and melt like snow coming down on warm ground."

The rebellion was far from being suppressed. Both sides were learning that they would have to pay a terrible price. And people on both home fronts had now to decide just what they would endure to win a war of one society against the other.

War Transforms the South

 The war caused tremendous disruptions in civilian life and altered southern society beyond all expectations. One of the first traditions to fall was the southern preference for local and limited government. States' rights had been a formative ideology for the Confederacy, but state governments were weak and sketchy operations. The average citizen, on whom the hand of gov-

ernment had rested lightly, probably knew county authorities best. To withstand the massive power of the North, however, the South needed to centralize; like the colonial revolutionaries, southerners faced a choice of join together or die separately. No one saw the necessity of centralization more clearly than Jefferson Davis. If the states of the Confederacy insisted on fighting separately, said Davis, "we had better make terms as soon as we can."

Promptly Davis moved to bring all arms, supplies, and troops under his control. But by early 1862 the scope and duration of the conflict required something more. Tens of thousands of Confederate soldiers had volunteered for just one year's service, planning to return home in the spring to plant their crops. To keep southern armies in the field, the War Department encouraged reenlistments and called for new volunteers. However, as one official admitted, "the spirit of volunteering had died out." Three states threatened or instituted a draft. Finally, faced with a critical shortage of troops, in April

The Confederacy and Centralization of Power

This Confederate soldier, like thousands of his comrades, took advantage of an opportunity to pose with his wife and brother. As the death toll mounted and suffering increased, southern women grew less willing to urge their men into battle. (Collection of Larry Williford)

1862 the Confederate government enacted the first national conscription (draft) law in American history. Thus the war forced unprecedented change on states that had seceded out of fear of change.

Jefferson Davis was a strong chief executive. He adopted a firm leadership role toward the Confederate Congress, which raised taxes and later passed a tax-in-kind—paid in farm products. Almost three thousand agents dispersed to collect the tax, assisted by almost fifteen hundred appraisers. Where opposition arose, the government suspended the writ of habeas corpus (which prevented individuals from being held without trial) and imposed martial law. In the face of political opposition that cherished states' rights, Davis proved unyielding. This tax system, however, proved inadequate to the South's war effort.

To replace the food that men in uniform would have grown, Davis exhorted farmers to switch from cash crops to food crops; he encouraged the states to require them to do so. But the army remained short of food and labor. In emergencies the War Department resorted to impressing slaves to work on fortifications, and after 1861 the government relied heavily on con-

fiscation of food to feed the troops. Officers swooped down on farms in the line of march and carted away grain, meat, wagons, and draft animals.

Soon the Confederate administration in Richmond gained virtually complete control over the southern economy. Because it controlled the supply of labor through conscription, the administration could compel industry to work on government contracts and supply the military's needs. The Confederate Congress also gave the central government almost complete control of the railroads. New statutes even limited corporate profits and dividends. A large bureaucracy sprang up to administer these operations: over seventy thousand civilians staffed the Confederate administration. By the war's end, the southern bureaucracy was larger in proportion to population than its northern counterpart. Early in the war, Davis hoped that such centralization would inspire a new national loyalty across the South.

Clerks and subordinate officials crowded the towns and cities where Confederate departments set up their offices. The sudden population booms that resulted overwhelmed the housing supply and stimulated new construction. The pressure was especially great in Richmond, whose population increased 250 percent. Mobile's population jumped from 29,000 to 41,000; Atlanta began to grow; and 10,000 people poured into war-related industries in little Selma, Alabama.

Wartime Southern Cities and Industry

As the Union blockade disrupted imports of manufactured products, the traditionally agricultural South forged industries. Many planters shared Davis's hope that industrialization would bring "deliverance, full and unrestricted, from all commercial dependence" on the North or the world. Indeed, beginning almost from scratch, the Confederacy achieved tremendous feats of industrial development. Chief of Ordnance Josiah Gorgas increased the capacity of Richmond's Tredegar Iron Works and other factories to the point that by 1865 his Ordnance Bureau was supplying all Confederate small arms and ammunition. Meanwhile, the government constructed new railroad lines to improve the efficiency of the South's transportation system. Much of the labor on railroads and ironworks consisted of slaves relocated from farms and plantations.

White women, restricted to narrow roles in antebellum society, gained substantial new responsibilities in wartime. The wives and mothers of soldiers now headed households and performed men's work, including raising crops and tending animals. Women in non-

Changing Roles of Women

slaveowning families cultivated fields themselves, while wealthier women suddenly had to manage field hands unaccustomed to female overseers. In the cities, white women—who had been virtually excluded from the labor force—found a limited number of respectable new paying jobs. Clerks had always been males, but the war changed that, too. "Government girls" staffed the Confederate bureaucracy, and female schoolteachers appeared in the South for the first time.

Some women gained confidence from their new responsibilities. Among these was Janie Smith, a young North Carolinian. Raised in a rural area by prosperous parents, she now faced grim realities as the war reached her farm and troops turned her home into a hospital. "It makes me shudder when I think of the awful sights I witnessed that morning," she wrote to a friend. "Ambulance after ambulance drove up with our wounded. . . . Under every shed and tree, the tables were carried for amputating the limbs. . . . The blood lay in puddles in the grove; the groans of the dying and complaints of those undergoing amputation were horrible." But Janie Smith learned to cope with crisis. She ended her account with the proud words, "I can dress amputated limbs now and do most anything in the way of nursing wounded soldiers."

Patriotic sacrifice appealed to some women, but others resented their new burdens. Many among the wealthy found their war-imposed tasks difficult and their changed situation distasteful. A Texas woman who had struggled to discipline slaves pronounced herself "sick of trying to do a man's business." Others grew angry over shortages and resented cooking and unfamiliar contact with lower-class women. Some women grew scornful of the war and demanded that their men return to help provide for families.

For millions of ordinary southerners change brought privation and suffering. Mass poverty descended for the first time on a large minority of the white population.

Human Suffering, Hoarding, and Inflation

Many yeoman families had lost their breadwinners to the army. As a South Carolina newspaper put it, "The duties of war have called away from home the sole supports of many, many families. . . . Help must be given, or the poor will suffer." The poor sought help from relatives, neighbors, friends, anyone. Sometimes they pleaded their cases to the Confederate government. "In the name of humanity," begged one woman, "discharge my husband he is not able to do your government much good and he might do his children some good . . . my poor children have no home nor no Father." To the extent that the South eventually lost the will to fight in the face of defeat, women played a key role in bringing the war to an end.

Other factors aggravated the effect of the labor shortage. The South was in many places so sparsely populated that the conscription of one skilled craftsman could work a hardship on the people of an entire county. Often they begged in unison for the exemption or discharge of the local miller or the neighborhood tanner, wheelwright, or potter. Physicians also were in short supply. Most serious, however, was the loss of a blacksmith. As a petition from Alabama explained, "Our Section of County [is] left entirely Destitute of any man that is able to keep in order any kind of Farming Tules."

The blockade of Confederate shipping created shortages of common but important items—salt, sugar, coffee, nails—and speculation and hoarding made the shortages worse. Greedy businessmen cornered the supply of some commodities; prosperous citizens stocked up on food. The *Richmond Enquirer* criticized a planter who purchased so many wagonloads of supplies that his "lawn and paths looked like a wharf covered with a ship's loads." "This disposition to speculate upon the yeomanry of the country," lamented the *Richmond Examiner*, "is the most mortifying feature of the war." North Carolina's Governor Zebulon Vance worried about "the cry of distress . . . from the poor wives and children of our soldiers. . . . What will become of them?"

Inflation raged out of control, fueled by the Confederate government's heavy borrowing and inadequate taxes, until prices had increased almost 7,000 percent. Inflation particularly imperiled urban dwellers without their own sources of food. As early as 1861 and 1862, newspapers reported that "want and starvation are staring thousands in the face," and troubled officials predicted that "women and children are bound to come to suffering if not starvation." Some families came to the aid of their neighbors, and "free markets," which disbursed goods as charity, sprang up in various cities. But other people would not cooperate: "It is folly for a poor mother to call on the rich people about here," raged one woman. "Their hearts are of steel they would sooner throw what they have to spare to the dogs than give it to a starving child." Private charity, as well as a rudimentary relief program organized by the Confederacy, failed to meet the need.

As their fortunes declined, people of once-modest means looked around and found abundant evidence that all classes were not sacrificing equally. And they noted that the Confederate government enacted policies that favored the upper class.

Inequities of the Confederate Draft

Until the last year of the war, for example, prosperous southerners could avoid military service by hiring substitutes. Prices for substitutes skyrocketed until it cost a man $5,000 or $6,000 to send someone to the front in his place. Well over 50,000 upper-class southerners purchased such substitutes. Mary Boykin Chesnut knew of one young aristocrat who "spent a fortune in substitutes. . . . He is at the end of his row now, for all able-bodied men are ordered to the front. I hear he is going as some general's courier." The rich traded on their social connections to avoid danger. "It is a notorious fact," complained an angry Georgian, that "if a man has influential friends—or a little money to spare—he will never be enrolled." A Confederate senator from Mississippi, James Phelan, informed Jefferson Davis that apparently "nine tenths of the youngsters of the land whose relatives are conspicuous in society, wealthy, or influential obtain some safe perch where they can doze with their heads under their wings."

Anger at such discrimination exploded in October 1862 when the Confederate Congress exempted from military duty anyone who was supervising at least twenty slaves. "Never did a law meet with more universal odium," observed one representative. "Its influence upon the poor is most calamitous." Protests poured in from every corner of the Confederacy, and North Carolina's legislators formally condemned the law. Its defenders argued, however, that the exemption preserved order and aided food production, and the statute remained on the books. The twenty-slave law is indicative of the racial fears many Confederates felt as the war threatened to overturn southern society.

Dissension spread and alert politicians and newspaper editors warned of class warfare. The bitterness of letters to Confederate officials suggests the depth of the people's anger. "If I and my little children suffer [and] die while there Father is in service," threatened one woman, "I invoke God Almighty that our blood rest upon the South." Another woman swore to the secretary of war that unless help was provided to poverty-stricken wives and mothers "an allwise god . . . will send down his fury and judgment in a very grate manar . . . [on] those that are in power." War magnified existing social tensions in the Confederacy, and created a few new ones.

Wartime Northern Economy and Society

With the onset of war, a tidal wave of change rolled over the North as well. Factories and citizens' associations geared up to support the war, and the federal government and its executive branch gained new powers. The energies of an industrializing, capitalist society were harnessed to serve the cause of the Union. Idealism and greed flourished together, and the northern economy proved its awesome productivity. Northern factories ran overtime, and unemployment was low. Northern farms and factories came through the war unharmed, whereas most of the South suffered extensive damage. To Union soldiers on the battlefield, sacrifice was a grim reality, but northern civilians experienced the bustle and energy of wartime production.

At first the war was a shock to business. Northern firms lost their southern markets, and many companies had to change their products and find new customers in order to remain open. Southern debts became uncollectible, jeopardizing not only northern merchants but also many western banks. In farming regions, families struggled with an aggravated shortage of labor. A few enterprises never pulled out of the tailspin caused by the war. Cotton mills lacked cotton; construction declined; shoe manufacturers sold few of the cheap shoes that planters had bought for their slaves.

Northern Business, Industry, and Agriculture

But certain entrepreneurs, such as wool producers, benefited from shortages of competing products, and soaring demand for war-related goods swept some businesses to new success. To feed the hungry war machine, the federal government pumped unprecedented sums into the economy. The Treasury issued $3.2 billion in bonds and paper money called greenbacks, and the War Department spent over $360 million in revenues from new taxes, including a broad excise tax and the nation's first income tax. Government contracts soon totaled more than $1 billion.

Secretary of War Edwin M. Stanton's list of the supplies needed by the Ordnance Department indicates the scope of government demand: "7,892 cannon, 11,787 artillery carriages, 4,022,130 small-arms, . . . 1,022,176,474 cartridges for small-arms, 1,220,555,435 percussion caps, . . . 26,440,054 pounds of gunpowder, 6,395,152 pounds of niter, and 90,416,295 pounds of lead." Stanton's list covered only weapons; the government also purchased huge quantities of uniforms, boots, food, camp equipment, saddles, ships, and other necessities. War-related spending revived business in many northern states. In 1863 a merchants' magazine examined the effects of the war in Massachusetts: "Seldom, if ever, has the business of Massachusetts been more active or profitable than during the past year. . . . In every department of labor the government has been, directly or indirectly, the chief employer and paymaster." Government contracts saved Massachusetts shoe manufacturers from ruin.

Nothing illustrated the wartime partnership between business and government better than the work of Jay Cooke, a wealthy New York financier. Cooke threw himself into the marketing of government bonds to finance the war effort. With imagination and energy, he convinced both large investors and ordinary citizens to invest enormous sums, in the process earning hefty commissions for himself. But the financier's profit served the Union cause, as the interests of capitalism and government, finance and patriotism, merged. The booming economy, the Republican alliance with business, and the frantic wartime activity combined to create a new pro-business atmosphere in Washington.

War aided some heavy industries in the North, especially iron and steel production. Although new railroad construction slowed, repairs helped the manufacture of rails to increase. Of considerable significance for the future was the railroad industry's adoption of a standard gauge (width) for track, which eliminated the unloading and reloading of boxcars and created a unified transportation system.

The northern economy also grew because of a complementary relationship between agriculture and industry. Mechanization of agriculture had begun before the war. Wartime recruitment and conscription, however, gave western farmers an added incentive to purchase labor-saving machinery. The shift from human labor to machines created new markets for industry and expanded the food supply for the urban industrial work force. The boom in the sale of agricultural tools was tremendous. Cyrus and William McCormick built an industrial empire in Chicago from the sale of their reapers. Between 1862 and 1864 the manufacture of mowers and reapers doubled to 70,000 yearly; even so, manufacturers could not satisfy the demand. By the end of the war, 375,000 reapers were in use, triple the number in 1861. Large-scale commercial agriculture had become a reality. As a result, northern farm families whose breadwinners went to

Despite initial problems, the task of supplying a vast war machine kept the northern economy humming. This photograph shows businesses on the west side of Hudson Street in New York City in 1865. (© Collection of The New-York Historical Society)

war did not suffer as much as their counterparts did in the South. "We have seen," one magazine observed, "a stout matron whose sons are in the army, cutting hay with her team . . . and she cut seven acres with ease in a day, riding leisurely upon her cutter."

Northern industrial and urban workers did not fare as well. After the initial slump, jobs became plen-

New Militancy Among Northern Workers

tiful, but inflation ate up much of a worker's paycheck. The price of coffee had tripled; rice and sugar had doubled; and clothing, fuel, and rent had all climbed. Between 1860 and 1864 consumer prices rose at least 76 percent, while daily wages rose only 42 percent. Workers' families consequently suffered a substantial decline in their standards of living.

As their real wages shrank, industrial workers lost job security. To increase production, some employers were replacing workers with labor-saving machines. Other employers urged the government to promote immigration to secure cheap labor. Workers responded by forming unions and sometimes by striking. Skilled craftsmen organized to combat the loss of their jobs and status to machines; women and unskilled workers, who were excluded by the craftsmen, formed their own unions. In recognition of the increasingly national scope of business activity, thirteen occupational groups—including tailors, coal miners, and railway engineers—formed national unions during the Civil War, and the number of strikes climbed steadily.

Employers reacted with hostility to this new labor independence. Manufacturers viewed labor activism as a threat to their freedom of action and accordingly formed statewide or craft-based associations to cooperate and pool information. These employers shared blacklists of union members and required new workers to sign "yellow dog" contracts (promises not to join a union). To put down strikes, they hired strikebreakers from among blacks, immigrants, and women, and sometimes used federal troops to break the will of unions.

Despite the unions' emerging presence, they did not prevent employers from making profits, nor from profiteering on government contracts. Unscrupulous businessmen took advantage of the suddenly immense demand for army supplies by selling clothing and blankets made of "shoddy"—wool fibers reclaimed from rags or worn cloth. Shoddy goods often came apart in the rain; most of the shoes purchased in the early months of the war were worthless. Contractors sold

inferior guns for double the usual price and passed off tainted meat as good. Corruption was so widespread that it led to a year-long investigation by the House of Representatives. A group of contractors who had demanded $50 million for their products dropped their claims to $17 million as a result of the findings of the investigation. Those who romanticize the Civil War era rarely learn of these historical realities.

Legitimate enterprises also made healthy profits. The output of woolen mills increased so dramatically

Government and Business Partnership

that dividends in the industry nearly tripled. Some cotton mills made record profits on what they sold, even though they reduced their output. Brokerage houses worked until midnight and earned unheard-of commissions. Railroads carried immense quantities of freight and passengers, increasing their business to the point that railroad stocks doubled and tripled in value. The price of Erie Railroad stock rose from $17 to $126 a share during the war.

Railroads also were a leading beneficiary of government largesse. With the South absent from Congress, the northern, rather than southern, route of the transcontinental railroad quickly prevailed. In 1862 and 1864 Congress chartered two corporations, the Union Pacific Railroad and the Central Pacific Railroad, and assisted them financially in connecting Omaha, Nebraska, with Sacramento, California. For each mile of track laid, the railroads received a loan of from $16,000 to $48,000 in government bonds plus 20 square miles of land along a free 400-foot-wide right of way. Overall, the two corporations gained approximately 20 million acres of land and nearly $60 million in loans.

Other businessmen benefited handsomely from the Morrill Land Grant Act (1862). To promote public

Economic Nationalism

education in agriculture, engineering, and military science, Congress granted each state 30,000 acres of federal land for each of its congressional districts. The states could sell the land, as long as they used the income for the purposes Congress had intended. The law eventually fostered sixty-nine colleges and universities, but one of its immediate effects was to enrich a few prominent speculators. Hard-pressed to meet wartime expenses, some states sold their land cheaply to wealthy entrepreneurs. At the same time, the Homestead Act of 1862 offered cheap, and sometimes free, land to people who would settle the West and improve their property.

Before the war, there was no national banking, taxation, or currency. Banks operating under state charters issued no fewer than seven thousand different kinds of notes, which were difficult to distinguish from forgeries. During the war, Congress and the Treasury Department established a national banking system empowered to issue national bank notes. At the close of the war in 1865, Congress forced most state banks to join the national system by means of a prohibitive tax. This process created sounder currency, but also inflexibility in the money supply and an eastern-oriented financial structure that, later in the century, pushed farmers in need of credit and cash to revolt.

In response to the war, the Republicans created an activist federal government. They converted the sale of war bonds into a crusade, affirming that the country could absorb any level of debt or expense for the cause of union. Indeed, with agricultural legislation, the land grant colleges, higher tariffs, and railroad subsidies, the federal government entered the economy forever. Moreover, Republican economic policies bonded people to the nation as never before. As freeing the slaves became a fundamental war aim, this economic nationalism would loom important as a buttress for a controversial cause.

The powers of the federal government and the president grew steadily during the crisis. Abraham Lincoln, like Jefferson Davis, found that war required active presidential leadership. At the beginning of the conflict, Lincoln launched a major shipbuilding program without waiting for Congress to assemble. The lawmakers later approved his decision, and Lincoln continued to act in advance of Congress when he deemed such action necessary. In one striking exercise of executive power, Lincoln suspended the writ of habeas corpus for everyone living between Washington, D.C., and Philadelphia. There was scant legal justification for this act, but the president's motive was practical: to ensure the loyalty of Maryland, which surrounded the capital on three sides. Later in the war, with congressional approval, Lincoln repeatedly suspended habeas corpus and invoked martial law, mainly in the border states but elsewhere as well. Between fifteen and twenty thousand U.S. citizens were arrested on suspicion of disloyal acts. These measures have led some to claim that Lincoln achieved "dictatorial" powers as a wartime president.

On occasion Lincoln used his wartime authority to bolster his own political fortunes. He and his gener-

Expansion of Presidential Power

als proved adept at furloughing soldiers so they could vote in close elections; those whom Lincoln furloughed, of course, usually voted Republican. He also came to the aid of other officeholders in his party. When the Republican governor of Indiana, who was battling Democrats in his legislature who sought a negotiated end to the war, ran short of funds, Lincoln had the War Department supply $250,000. This procedure lacked constitutional sanction, but it advanced the Union cause.

In thousands of self-governing towns and communities, northern citizens felt a personal connection to representative government. Secession threatened to destroy their system, and northerners rallied to its defense. Secular and church leaders supported the cause, and even ministers who preferred to separate politics and pulpit denounced "the iniquity of causeless rebellion." In the first two years of the war, northern morale remained remarkably high for a cause that today may seem abstract—the Union—but at the time meant the preservation of a social and political order that people cherished.

The Union Cause

But social attitudes on the northern home front evolved in directions that would have shocked the soldiers in the field. In the excitement of moneymaking, an eagerness to display one's wealth flourished in the largest cities. *Harper's Monthly* reported that "the suddenly enriched contractors, speculators, and stock-jobbers . . . are spending money with a profusion never before witnessed in our country, at no time remarkable for its frugality. . . . The men button their waistcoats with diamonds . . . and the women powder their hair with gold and silver dust." The *New York Herald* summarized that city's atmosphere: "Not to keep a carriage, not to wear diamonds, . . . is now equivalent to being a nobody. This war has entirely changed the American character. . . . The individual who makes the most money—no matter how—and spends the most—no matter for what—is considered the greatest man."

Yet idealism coexisted with ostentation. Many churches endorsed the Union cause as God's cause. One Methodist newspaper described the war as a contest between "equalizing, humanizing Christianity" and "disunion, war, selfishness, [and] slavery." Abolitionists campaigned to turn the war into a crusade against slavery. Free black communities and churches both black and white responded to the needs of slaves who flocked to the Union lines, sending clothing, ministers, and teachers to aid the freedpeople. Indeed, northern blacks gave wholehearted support to the war, volunteering by the thousands at first and drilling their own militia units in spite of the initial rejection they received from the Lincoln administration.

Northern women, like their southern counterparts, took on new roles. Those who stayed home organized over ten thousand soldiers' aid societies, rolled bandages, and raised $3 million to aid injured troops. Women were instrumental in pressing for the first trained ambulance corps in the Union armies, and they formed the backbone of the U.S. Sanitary Commission, a civilian agency officially recognized by the War Department in 1861. The Sanitary Commission provided crucial nutritional and medical aid to soldiers. Although most of its officers were men, the bulk of its volunteers who ran its seven thousand auxiliaries were women. Women organized elaborate "Sanitary Fairs" all across the North to raise money and awareness for soldiers' health and hygiene.

Northern Women

Approximately 3,200 women also served as nurses in frontline hospitals, where they pressed for better care of the wounded. Yet women were only about one-quarter of all nurses, and they had to fight for a chance to serve at all. The professionalization of medicine

Walt Whitman, now America's most celebrated wartime poet. His *Drum Taps* series, part of his evolving masterpiece *Leaves of Grass,* left some of the most haunting and moving poetic images of both the death and new life wrought by the war. (National Portrait Gallery, Smithsonian Institution, Washington, D.C.)

since the Revolution had created a medical system dominated by men, and many male physicians did not want women's aid. Even Clara Barton, famous for her persistence in working in the worst hospitals at the front, was ousted from her post in 1863. But with Barton, women such as the stern Dorothea Dix (see page 277), well-known for her efforts to reform asylums for the insane, and an Illinois widow, Mary Ann Bickerdyke, who served tirelessly in Sherman's army in the West, established a heroic tradition for Civil War nurses. They also advanced the professionalization of nursing as several schools of nursing were established in northern cities during or after the war.

The poet Walt Whitman left a record of his experiences as a volunteer nurse in Washington, D.C. As he dressed wounds and tried to comfort suffering and lonely men, Whitman found "the marrow of the tragedy concentrated in those Army Hospitals." But despite "indescribably horrid wounds," he also found inspiration in such suffering and a deepening faith in American democracy. Whitman celebrated the "incredible dauntlessness" and sacrifice of the common soldier who fought for the Union. As he had written in the preface to his great work *Leaves of Grass* (1855), "The genius of the United States is not best or most in its executives or legislatures, but always most in the common people." Whitman worked this idealization of the common man into his poetry, which also explored homoerotic themes and rejected the lofty meter and rhyme of European verse to strive for a "genuineness" that would appeal to the masses.

Walt Whitman's War

In "The Wound Dresser," Whitman meditated unforgettably on the deaths he witnessed on both sides:

> On, on I go, (open doors of time! open hospital doors!)
> The crush'd head I dress, (poor crazed hand tear not
>   the bandage away,)
> The neck of the cavalry-man with the bullet through
>   and through I examine,
> Hard the breathing rattles, quite glazed already the eye,
>   yet life struggled hard,
> (Come sweet death! be persuaded O beautiful death!
>   In mercy come quickly.)

Whitman mused for millions in the war who suffered the death of a husband, brother, father, or friend. Indeed, the scale of death in this war shocked many Americans into believing that this conflict had to be for purposes larger than themselves.

Thus northern society embraced strangely contradictory tendencies. Materialism and greed flourished alongside idealism, religious conviction, and self-sacrifice. While some soldiers risked their lives willingly out of a desire to preserve the Union or extend freedom, many others openly sought to avoid service. Under the law, a draftee could stay at home by providing a substitute or paying a $300 commutation fee. Many wealthy men chose these options, and in response to popular demand, clubs, cities, and states provided the money for others to escape conscription. In all, 118,000 substitutes were provided and 87,000 commutations paid before Congress ended the commutation system in 1864. Naturally, in decades to come Americans would commemorate and build monuments to soldiers' sacrifice and idealism, not to opportunism.

The Advent of Emancipation

Despite the sense of loyalty to cause that animated soldiers and civilians on both sides, the governments of the United States and the Confederacy lacked clarity about the purpose of the war. Throughout the first several months of the struggle, both Davis and Lincoln studiously avoided references to slavery. Davis realized that emphasis on the issue could increase class conflict in the South. To avoid identifying the Confederacy only with the interests of slaveholders, he articulated a broader, traditional ideology. Davis told southerners that they were fighting for constitutional liberty: northerners had betrayed the founders' legacy, and southerners had seceded to preserve it. As long as Lincoln also avoided making slavery an issue, Davis's line seemed to work.

Lincoln had his own reasons for not mentioning slavery. It was crucial at first not to antagonize the Union's border slave states, whose loyalty was tenuous. Also for many months Lincoln hoped that a pro-Union majority would assert itself in the South. It might be possible, he thought, to coax the South back into the Union and stop the fighting, short of what he later called "the result so fundamental and astounding"—emancipation. Raising the slavery issue would severely undermine both goals. Powerful political considerations also dictated Lincoln's reticence. The Republican Party was a young and unwieldy coalition. Some Republicans burned with moral outrage over slavery; others were frankly racist, dedicated to protecting free whites from the Slave Power and the competition of cheap slave labor. A forthright stand by Lincoln on the subject of slavery could split the party, gratifying some groups and alienating others. No northern consensus on what to do about slavery existed early in the war.

The president's hesitancy ran counter to some of his personal feelings. Lincoln was a compassionate man whose humility and moral anguish during the war were evident in his speeches and writings. But as a politician, Lincoln distinguished between his own moral convictions and his official acts. His political positions were studied and complex, calculated for maximum advantage.

Lincoln, the Gradual Emancipator

Many blacks furiously attacked Lincoln during the first year of the war for his refusal to convert the struggle into an "abolition war." When Lincoln countermanded General John C. Frémont's order of liberation for slaves owned by disloyal masters in Missouri in September 1861, the *Anglo-African* declared that the president, by his actions, "hurls back into the hell of slavery thousands . . . rightfully set free." As late as July 1862, Frederick Douglass condemned Lincoln as a "miserable tool of traitors and rebels," and characterized administration policy as reconstruction of "the old union on the old and corrupting basis of compromise, by which slavery shall retain all the power that it ever had." Douglass wanted the old union destroyed and a new one created in the crucible of a war that would destroy slavery and rewrite the Constitution in the name of human equality. To his own amazement, within a year, just such a profound result began to take place.

Lincoln first broached the subject of slavery in a substantive way in March 1862, when he proposed that the states consider emancipation on their own. He asked Congress to promise aid to any state that decided to emancipate, appealing especially to border state representatives. What Lincoln proposed was gradual emancipation, with compensation for slaveholders and colonization of the freed slaves outside the United States. To a delegation of free blacks he explained that "it is better for us both . . . to be separated."

Until well into 1864 Lincoln's administration promoted a wholly impractical scheme to colonize blacks in Central America or the Caribbean. Lincoln saw colonization as one option among others in dealing with the impending freedom of America's 4.2 million slaves. As yet, he was unconvinced that America had any prospect as a truly biracial society, and he desperately feared that white northerners might not support a war for black freedom. Led by Frederick Douglass, black abolitionists vehemently opposed these machinations by the Lincoln administration.

Other politicians had much greater plans for a struggle against slavery. A group of Republicans in Congress, known as the Radicals and led by men such as George Julian, Charles Sumner, and Thaddeus Stevens, dedicated themselves to a war for emancipation. They were instrumental in creating a special House-Senate committee on the conduct of the war, which investigated Union reverses, sought to make the war effort more efficient, and prodded the president to take stronger measures. Early in the war these Radicals, with widening support, turned their attention to slavery.

In August 1861, at the Radicals' instigation, Congress passed its first confiscation act. Designed to punish the Confederates, the law

Confiscation Acts

confiscated all property used for "insurrectionary purposes." Thus if the South used slaves in a hostile action, those slaves were declared seized and liberated as contraband of war. A second confiscation act (July 1862) went much further: it confiscated the property of anyone who supported the rebellion, even those who merely resided in the South and paid Confederate taxes. Their slaves were declared "forever free of their servitude." The logic behind these acts was that the insurrection—as Lincoln termed it— required strong measures to stop it. Let the government use its full powers, free the slaves, and crush the insurrection, urged the Radicals.

Lincoln refused to adopt that view in the summer of 1862. He stood by his proposal of voluntary gradual emancipation by the states and made no effort to enforce the second confiscation act. His stance provoked a public protest from Horace Greeley, editor of the powerful *New York Tribune*. In an open letter to the president entitled "The Prayer of Twenty Millions," Greeley pleaded with Lincoln to "execute the laws" and declared, "On the face of this wide earth, Mr. President, there is not one disinterested, determined, intelligent champion of the Union cause who does not feel that all attempts to put down the Rebellion and at the same time uphold its inciting cause are preposterous and futile." Lincoln's reply was an explicit statement of his calculated approach to the question. He disagreed, he said, with all those who would make the maintenance or destruction of slavery the paramount issue of the war. "I would save the Union," announced Lincoln. "If I could save the Union without freeing any slave I would do it, and if I could save it by freeing all the slaves I would do it; and if I could save it by freeing some and leaving others alone I would also do that.

What I do about slavery, and the colored race, I do because I believe it helps to save the Union." Lincoln closed with a personal disclaimer: "I have here stated my purpose according to my view of official duty; and I intend no modification of my oft-expressed personal wish that all men everywhere could be free."

When he wrote those words, Lincoln had already decided to boldly issue a presidential Emancipation Proclamation. He was waiting, however, for a Union victory so that it would not appear to be an act of desperation. Yet the letter to Greeley was not simply an effort to stall; it was an integral part of Lincoln's approach to the future of slavery, as the text of the Emancipation Proclamation would show. Lincoln was concerned to condition public opinion as best he could for the coming social revolution.

On September 22, 1862, shortly after Union success at the Battle of Antietam, Lincoln issued the first part of his two-part proclamation.

Emancipation Proclamations

Invoking his powers as commander-in-chief of the armed forces, he announced that on January 1, 1863, he would emancipate the slaves in the states "in rebellion against the United States." Lincoln made plain that he would judge a state to be in rebellion in January if it lacked bona fide representatives in the U.S. Congress. Thus his September proclamation was less a declaration of the right of slaves to be free than a threat to southerners: unless they put down their arms and returned to Congress, they would lose their slaves. "Knowing the value that was set on the slaves by the rebels," said Garrison Frazier, a black Georgia minister, "the President thought that his proclamation would stimulate them to lay down their arms . . . and their not doing so has now made the freedom of the slaves a part of the war." Lincoln had little expectation that southerners would give up their effort, but he was careful to offer them the option, thus trying to put the onus of emancipation on them.

In the fateful January 1 proclamation, Lincoln excepted (as areas in rebellion) every Confederate county or city that had fallen under Union control. Those areas, he declared, "are, for the present, left precisely as if this proclamation were not issued." Nor did Lincoln liberate slaves in the border slave states that remained in the Union. "The President has purposely made the proclamation inoperative in all places where . . . the slaves [are] accessible," charged the anti-administration *New York World*. "He has proclaimed emancipation only where he has notoriously no power to execute it." Partisanship aside, even Secretary of

State Seward, a moderate Republican, said sarcastically, "We show our sympathy with slavery by emancipating slaves where we cannot reach them and holding them in bondage where we can set them free." A British official, Lord Russell, commented on the "very strange nature" of the document, noting that it did not declare "a principle adverse to slavery." Russell may have missed the point.

Lincoln was worried about the constitutionality of his acts. Making the liberation of the slaves "a fit and necessary war measure" raised a variety of legal questions. How long did a war measure remain in force? Did it expire with the suppression of a rebellion? The proclamation did little to clarify the status or citizenship of the freed slaves, although it did open the possibility of military service for blacks. How indeed would this change the character and purpose of the war?

Thus the Emancipation Proclamation was an ambiguous document that said less than it seemed to say. But if as a legal document it was wanting, as a moral and political document it had great meaning. Because the proclamation defined the war as a war against slavery, radicals could applaud it, even if the president had not gone as far as Congress. Yet at the same time it protected Lincoln's position with conservatives, leaving him room to retreat if he chose and forcing no immediate changes on the border slave states. It was a delicate balancing act, but one from which there was no real turning back.

Most important, though, thousands of slaves had already reached Union lines in various sections of the South. They had "voted with their feet" for emancipation, as many said, well before the proclamation. And now, every advance of federal forces into slave society was a liberating step. This Lincoln knew in taking his own initially tentative, and then forthright, steps toward emancipation.

Across the North and in Union-occupied sections of the South, blacks and their white allies celebrated the Emancipation Proclamation with unprecedented fervor. Full of praise songs, these celebrations demonstrated that whatever the fine print of the proclamation, black folks knew that they had lived to see a new day. At a large "contraband camp" in Washington,

A group of "contrabands" (liberated slaves), photographed at Cumberland Landing, Virginia, May 14, 1862, at a sensitive point in the war when their legal status was still not fully determined. The faces and generations of the women, men, and children represent the human drama of emancipation.   (Library of Congress)

D.C., some six hundred black men, women, and children gathered at the superintendent's headquarters on New Year's Eve and sang through the night. In chorus after chorus of "Go Down, Moses," they announced the magnitude of their painful but beautiful exodus. One newly supplied verse concluded with "Go down, Abraham, away down in Dixie's land, tell Jeff Davis to let my people go!"

The need for men soon convinced the administration to recruit northern and southern blacks for the Union Army. By the spring of 1863, African American troops were answering the call of a dozen or more black recruiters barnstorming the cities and towns of the North. Lincoln came to see black soldiers as "the great available and yet unavailed of force for restoring the Union." African American leaders hoped that military service would secure equal rights for their people. Once the black soldier had fought for the Union, wrote Frederick Douglass, "there is no power on earth which can deny that he has earned the right of citizenship in the United States." If black soldiers turned the tide, asked another man, "would the nation refuse us our rights?"

In June 1864 Lincoln gave his support to a constitutional ban on slavery. Reformers such as Elizabeth Cady Stanton and Susan B. Anthony were pressing for an amendment that would write emancipation into the Constitution. On the eve of the Republican national convention, Lincoln called the party's chairman to the White House and instructed him to have the party "put into the platform as the keystone, the amendment of the Constitution abolishing and prohibiting slavery forever." The party promptly called for the Thirteenth Amendment. Republican delegates probably would have adopted such a plank without his urging, but Lincoln demonstrated his commitment by lobbying Congress for quick approval of the measure. The proposed amendment passed in early 1865 and was sent to the states for ratification. The war to save the Union had also become the war to free the slaves.

It has long been debated whether Abraham Lincoln deserved the label (one he never claimed for himself) of "Great Emancipator." Was Lincoln ultimately a reluctant emancipator, following rather than leading Congress and public opinion? Or did Lincoln give essential presidential leadership to the most transformative and sensitive aspect of the war by going slow on emancipation, but once moving, never backpedaling on the main issue—black freedom. Once he had realized the total character of the war and decided to prosecute it to the

Who Freed the Slaves?

unconditional surrender of the Confederates, Lincoln made the destruction of slavery central to the war's purpose.

Others have argued, however, that the slaves themselves are the central story in the achievement of their own freedom. When they were in proximity to the war zones, or had opportunities as traveling laborers, slaves fled for their freedom by the thousands. Some worked as camp laborers for the Union armies, and eventually more than 180,000 black men served in the Union Army and Navy. Sometimes freedom came as a combination of confusion, fear, and joy in the rural hinterlands of the South. Some found freedom as individuals in 1861, and some not until 1865 as members of trains of refugees. Some slaves remained supportive of their masters' welfare until the war was over. Some freedmen traversed great distances to reach contraband camps.

However freedom came to individuals, emancipation was a historical confluence of two essential forces: one, a policy directed by and dependent on the military authority of the president in his effort to win the war; and two, the will and courage necessary for acts of self-emancipation. In his annual message in December 1862, Lincoln asserted that "in *giving* freedom to the slave, we *assure* freedom to the free." Likewise, most blacks understood the long-term meaning in those words—in the midst of total war they comprehended their freedom as both given and taken.

Before the war was over, the Confederacy, too, addressed the issue of emancipation. Jefferson Davis himself offered a proposal for black freedom of a kind. He was dedicated to independence, but late in the war he was willing to sacrifice slavery to achieve that goal. Davis concluded late in 1864 that the military situation of the Confederacy was so desperate that independence with emancipation was preferable to defeat with emancipation. He proposed that the Confederate government purchase forty thousand slaves to work for the army as laborers, with a promise of freedom at the end of their service. Soon Davis upgraded the idea, calling for the recruitment and arming of slaves as soldiers, who likewise would gain their freedom at war's end. The wives and children of these soldiers, he made plain, must also receive freedom from the states. Davis and his advisers envisioned an "intermediate" status for ex-slaves of "serfage or peonage." Thus at the bitter end, a few southerners were willing to sacrifice some of the racial, if not class, destiny for which they had launched their revolution.

A Confederate Plan of Emancipation

How do historians know...

that ex-slaves fully embraced their new freedom? Jourdon Anderson was a former slave from Tennessee. Residing in Dayton, Ohio, with his family in August 1865, four months after the war ended, Anderson received a letter from his former owner, Colonel P. H. Anderson, asking him to return to the old place. "I have often felt uneasy about you," Anderson told his old master. As for the "good chance . . . you propose," Anderson said to the former slaveholder, "we have concluded to test your sincerity by asking you to send us our wages for the time we served you." With remarkable wit and irony, Anderson described the dignity with which he and his family lived in freedom (his children were in school and his wife was called "Mrs. Anderson"). Published in the *Cincinnati Commercial* and the *New York Tribune*, this astonishing letter, dictated by Anderson, demonstrates that freedom meant everything to the freedpeople: a free public identity, choice, education, and, not least, the "justice" represented by wages. (Photo: *New York Daily Tribune*, August 22, 1865)

Dayton, Ohio, August 7, 1865

To My Old Master, Colonel P. H. Anderson,
Big Spring, Tennessee

Sir: I got your letter and was glad to find you had not forgotten Jourdon, and that you wanted me to come back and live with you again, promising to do better for me than anybody else can. I have often felt uneasy about you. I thought the Yankees would have hung you long before this for harboring Rebs they found at your house. . . . Although you shot at me twice before I left you, I did not want to hear of your being hurt, and am glad you are still living. It would do me good to go back to the dear old home again and see Miss Mary and Miss Martha and Allen, Esther, Green, and Lee. Give my love to them all, and tell them I hope we will meet in the better world, if not in this. . . .

I want to know particularly what the good chance is you propose to give me. I am doing tolerably well here; I get $25 a month, with victuals and clothing; have a comfortable home for Mandy (the folks here call her Mrs. Anderson), and the children, Milly, Jane and Grundy, go to school and are learning well; the teacher says Grundy has a head for a preacher. . . . Now, if you will write and say what wages you will give me, I will be better able to decide whether it would be to my advantage to move back again.

As to my freedom, which you say I can have, there is nothing to be gained on that score, as I got my free-papers in 1864. . . . Mandy says she would be afraid to go back without some proof that you are sincerely disposed to treat us justly and kindly—and we have concluded to test your sincerity by asking you to send us our wages for the time we served you. This will make us forget and forgive old scores, and rely on your justice and friendship in the future. I served you faithfully for thirty-two years and Mandy twenty years. At $25 a month for me, and $2 a week for Mandy, our earnings would amount to $11,680. Add to this the interest for the time our wages has been kept back and deduct what you paid for our clothing and three doctor's visits to me, and pulling a tooth for Mandy, and the balance will show what we are in justice entitled to. Please send the money by Adams Express, in care of V. Winters, esq, Dayton, Ohio. If you fail to pay us for faithful labors in the past we can have little faith in your promises in the future. We trust the good Maker has opened your eyes to the wrongs which you and your fathers have done to me and my fathers, in making us toil for you for generations without recompense. Here I draw my wages every Saturday night, but in Tennessee there was never any pay day for the negroes any more than for the horses and cows. . . .

In answering this letter please state if there would be any safety for my Milly and Jane, who are now grown up and both good-looking girls. You know how it was with poor Matilda and Catherine. I would rather stay here and starve and die if it comes to that than have my girls brought to shame by the violence and wickedness of their young masters. You will also please state if there has been any schools opened for the colored children in your neighborhood, the great desire of my life now is to give my children an education, and have them form virtuous habits.

P.S.—Say howdy to George Carter, and thank him for taking the pistol from you when you were shooting at me.

From your old servant,
Jourdon Anderson

Letter from a Freedman to his Old Master.

The following is a genuine document. It was dictated by the old servant, and contains his ideas and forms of expression. [Cincinnati Commercial.

DAYTON, Ohio, August 7, 1865.
To my Old Master, Col. P. H. ANDERSON, Big Spring, Tennessee.

SIR: I got your letter and was glad to find that you had not forgotten Jordan, and that you wanted me to come back and live with you again, promising to do better for me than anybody else can. I have often felt uneasy about you. I thought the Yankees would have hung you long before this for harboring Rebs, they found at your house. I suppose they never heard about your going to Col. Martin's to kill the Union soldier that was left by his company in their stable. Although you shot at me twice before I left you, I did not want to hear of your being hurt, and am glad you are still living. It would do me good to go back to the dear old home again and see Miss Mary and Miss Martha and Allen, Esther, Green and Lee. Give my love to them all, and tell them I hope we will meet in the better

Bitter debate over Davis's plan resounded through the Confederacy. When the Confederate Congress approved slave enlistments without the promise of freedom in March 1865, Davis insisted on more. He issued an executive order to guarantee that owners would emancipate slave soldiers, and his allies in the states started to work for emancipation of the soldiers' families.

The war ended before much could come of these desperate policy initiatives on the part of the Confederacy. By contrast, Lincoln's Emancipation Proclamation stimulated a vital infusion of forces into the Union armies. Before the war was over, 134,000 slaves (and 52,000 free African Americans) had fought for freedom and the Union. Their participation aided northern victory while it discouraged recognition of the Confederacy by foreign governments, especially Great Britain, which had freed the slaves in its empire thirty years earlier. As both policy and process, emancipation had profound practical and moral implications for the new nation to be born out of the war.

The Soldiers' War

The intricacies of policymaking and social revolutions were far from the minds of most ordinary soldiers. Military service completely altered their lives. Enlistment took young men from their homes and submerged them in large organizations whose military discipline ignored their individuality. Army life meant tedium, physical hardship, and separation from loved ones. Yet the military experience had powerful attractions as well. It molded men on both sides so thoroughly that they came to resemble one another far more than they resembled civilians back home. Many soldiers forged amid war a bond with their fellows and a connection to a noble purpose that they cherished for years afterward.

Union soldiers may have sensed most clearly the massive scale of modern war. Most were young; the average soldier was between eighteen and twenty-one. Many went straight from small towns and farms into large armies supplied by extensive bureaucracies. By late 1861 there were 640,000 volunteers in arms, a stupendous increase over the regular army of 20,000 men. Many soldiers found adapting to camp life and military discipline daunting.

Soldiers benefited from certain new products, such as canned condensed milk, but blankets, clothing, and arms were often of poor quality. Vermin abounded. Hospitals were badly managed at first.

Hospitals and Camp Life

Rules of hygiene in large camps were scarcely enforced; latrines were poorly made or carelessly used. One investigation turned up "an area of over three acres, encircling the camp as a broad belt, on which is deposited an almost perfect layer of human excrement." Water supplies were unsafe and typhoid epidemics common. About 57,000 men died from dysentery and diarrhea; in fact, 224,000 Union troops died from disease or accidents, far more than the 140,000 who died as a result of battle. Confederate troops were less well supplied, especially in the latter part of the war, and they had no sanitary commission. Still, an extensive network of hospitals, aided by many white female volunteers and black women slaves, sprang up to aid the sick and wounded.

On both sides troops quickly learned that soldiering was far from glorious. "The dirt of a camp life knocks all its poetry into a cocked hat," wrote a North Carolina volunteer in 1862. One year later he marveled at his earlier innocence. Fighting had taught him "the realities of a soldier's life. We had no tents after the 6th of August, but slept on the ground, in the woods or open fields, without regard to the weather. . . . I learned to eat fat bacon raw, and to like it. . . . Without time to wash our clothes or our persons, and sleeping on the ground all huddled together, the whole army became lousy more or less with body lice." Union troops "skirmished" against lice by boiling their clothes or holding them over a hot fire, but, reported one soldier, "I find some on me in spite of all I can do."

Few had seen violent death before, but war soon exposed them to the blasted bodies of their friends and comrades. "Any one who goes over a battlefield after a battle," wrote one Confederate, "never cares to go over another. . . . It is a sad sight to see the dead and if possible more sad to see the wounded—shot in every possible way you can imagine." Many men died gallantly; there were innumerable striking displays of courage. But far more often soldiers gave up their lives in mass sacrifice, in tactics that made little sense.

Advances in technology made the Civil War particularly deadly. By far the most important were the rifle and the "minie ball." Bullets fired from a smoothbore musket tumbled and wobbled as they flew through the air and thus were not accurate at distances over 80 yards. Cutting spiraled grooves inside the barrel gave the projectile a spin and much greater accuracy, but rifles remained

The Rifled Musket

Union soldiers in camp, posing for a photograph, with black servants. The drudgery of camp life never prohibited soldiers from displaying their individuality.   (National Archives)

difficult to load and use until the Frenchman Claude Minie and the American James Burton developed a new kind of bullet. Civil War bullets were sizable lead slugs with a cavity at the bottom that expanded upon firing so that the bullet "took" the rifling and flew accurately. With these bullets, rifles were accurate at 400 yards and useful up to 1,000 yards.

This meant, of course, that soldiers assaulting a position defended by riflemen were in greater peril than ever before. Even though Civil War rifles were cumbersome to load (relatively few of the new, untried, breechloading and repeating rifles were ordered), the defense gained a significant advantage. While artillery now fired from a safe distance, there was no substitute for the infantry assault or the popular turning movements aimed at an enemy's flank. Thus advancing soldiers had to expose themselves repeatedly to accurate rifle fire. Because medical knowledge was rudimentary, even minor wounds often led to amputation, and to death through infection. Never before in Europe or America had such massive forces pummeled each other with weapons of such destructive power. As losses mounted, many citizens wondered at what Union soldier (and future Supreme Court justice) Oliver Wendell Holmes, Jr., called "the butcher's bill."

Still, Civil War soldiers developed deep commitments to each other and to their task. As campaigns dragged on, fighting and dying with their comrades became their reality, and most soldiers who did not desert grew determined to see the struggle through. "We now, like true Soldiers go determined not to yield one inch," wrote a New York corporal. When at last the war was over, "it seemed like breaking up a family to separate," one man observed. Another admitted, "We shook hands all around, and laughed and seemed to make merry, while our hearts were heavy and our eyes ready to shed tears."

The bonding may have been most dramatic among officers and men in the northern black regiments, for there white and black troops took their first steps toward bridging a deep racial divide. Racism in the Union Army was strong. Most white soldiers wanted nothing to do with black people and regarded them as inferior. "I never came out here for to free the black devils," wrote one soldier, and another objected to fighting beside African Americans because, "We are a too superior race for that." For many, acceptance of black troops grew only because they could do heavy labor and "stop Bullets as well as white people." A

The Black Soldier's Fight for Manhood

popular song celebrated "Sambo's Right to Be Kilt" as the only justification for black enlistments.

But among some a change occurred. While recruiting black troops in Virginia in late 1864, Charles Brewster sometimes denigrated the very men he sought to enlist. But he was delighted at the sight of a black cavalry unit because it made the local "secesh" furious, and he praised black soldiers who "fought nobly" and filled hospitals with "their wounded and mangled bodies." White officers who volunteered to lead black units only to gain promotion found that experience altered their opinions. After just one month with black troops, a white captain informed his wife, "I have a more elevated opinion of their abilities than I ever had before. I know that many of them are vastly the superiors of those . . . who would condemn them all to a life of brutal degradation." One general reported that his "colored regiments" possessed "remarkable aptitude for military training," and another observer said, "They fight like fiends."

Black troops created this change through their own dedication. They had a mission to destroy slavery and demonstrate their equality. "When Rebellion is crushed," wrote a black volunteer from Connecticut, "who will be more proud than I to say, 'I was one of the first of the despised race to leave the free North with a rifle on my shoulder, and give the lie to the old story that the black man will not fight.'" Corporal James Henry Gooding of Massachusetts's black Fifty-fourth Regiment explained that his unit intended "to live down all prejudice against its color, by a determination to do well in any position it is put." After an engagement he was proud that "a regiment of white men gave us three cheers as we were passing them," because "it shows that we did our duty as men should."

Through such experience under fire the blacks and whites of the Fifty-fourth Massachusetts forged deep bonds. Just before the regiment launched its costly assault on Fort Wagner in Charleston harbor, in July 1863, a black soldier called out to abolitionist Colonel Robert Gould Shaw, who would perish that day, "Colonel, I will stay by you till I die." "And he kept his word," noted a survivor of the attack. "He has never been seen since." Indeed, the heroic assault on Fort Wagner was celebrated for demonstrating the valor of black men. This bloody chapter in the history of American racism proved many things, not least of which was that black men had to die in battle to be acknowledged as men.

Such valor emerged despite persistent discrimination. Off-duty black soldiers were sometimes attacked by northern mobs; on duty, they did most of the "fa-

Company E, 4th U.S. Colored Infantry, photographed at Fort Lincoln, Virginia, in 1864. Nothing so symbolized the new manhood and citizenship among African Americans in the midst of the war as such young black men in blue.   (Chicago Historical Society)

tigue duty," or heavy labor. The Union government, moreover, paid white privates $13 per month plus a clothing allowance of $3.50, whereas black privates earned only $10 per month less $3 for clothing. Outraged by this injustice, several regiments refused to accept any pay whatsoever, and Congress eventually remedied the inequity. In this instance, at least, the majority of legislators agreed with a white private that black troops had "proved their title to manhood on many a bloody field fighting freedom's battles."

1863: The Tide of Battle Turns

 The fighting in the spring and summer of 1863 did not settle the war, but it began to suggest the outcome. The campaigns began in a deceptively positive way for Confederates, as their Army of Northern Virginia performed brilliantly in the Battle of Chancellorsville.

For once, a large Civil War army was not slow and cumbersome but executed tactics with speed and precision. On May 2 and 3, west of Fredericksburg, Virginia, some 130,000 members of the Union Army of the Potomac bore down on fewer than 60,000 Confederates. Boldly, as if they enjoyed being outnumbered, Lee and Stonewall Jackson divided their forces, ordering 30,000 men under Jackson on a day-long march westward to gain position for a flank attack. This classic turning movement was boldly carried out in the face of great numerical disadvantage. Arriving at their position late in the afternoon, Jackson's seasoned "foot cavalry" found unprepared Union troops laughing, smoking, and playing cards. The Union soldiers had no idea they were under attack until frightened deer and rabbits bounded out of the forest, followed by gray-clad troops. The Confederate attack drove the entire right side of the Union Army back in confusion. Eager to press his advantage, Jackson rode forward with a few officers to study the ground. As they returned at twilight, southern troops mistook them for federals and fired, fatally wounding their commander. The next day Union forces left in defeat. Chancellorsville was a remarkable southern victory but costly because of the loss of Stonewall Jackson.

July brought crushing defeats for the Confederacy in two critical battles—Vicksburg and Gettysburg—that severely damaged Confederate hopes for independence. Vicksburg was a vital western citadel, the last major fortification on the Mississippi River in

Battle of Chancellorsville

Siege of Vicksburg

southern hands (see Map 15.2). After months of searching through swamps and bayous, General Ulysses S. Grant found an advantageous approach to the city. He laid siege to Vicksburg in May, bottling up the defending army of General John Pemberton. If Vicksburg fell, Union forces would control the river, cutting the Confederacy in two and gaining an open path into its interior. To stave off such a result, Jefferson Davis gave command of all other forces in the area to General Joseph E. Johnston and beseeched him to go to Pemberton's aid. Meanwhile, at a council of war in Richmond, General Robert E. Lee proposed a Confederate invasion of the North. Although such an offensive would not relieve Vicksburg directly, it could stun and dismay the North and, if successful, possibly even lead to peace. By invading the North a second time, Lee hoped to take the war out of war-weary Virginia, garner civilian support in Maryland, win a major victory on northern soil, threaten major cities, and thereby force a Union capitulation on his terms.

Lee's troops streamed through western Maryland and into Pennsylvania, threatening both Washington and Baltimore. As his emboldened army advanced, the possibility of a major battle near the Union capital became more and more likely. Confederate prospects along the Mississippi, however, darkened. Davis repeatedly wired General Johnston, urging him to concentrate his forces and attack Grant's army. Johnston, however, did little, telegraphing back, "I consider saving Vicksburg hopeless." Grant's men, meanwhile, were supplying themselves from the abundant crops of the Mississippi River valley and could continue their siege indefinitely. Their rich meat-and-vegetables diet became so tiresome, in fact, that one day, as Grant rode by, a private looked up and muttered, "Hardtack," referring to the dry biscuits that were the usual staple of soldiers' diets. Soon a line of soldiers was shouting "Hardtack! Hardtack!" demanding respite from turkey and sweet potatoes.

In such circumstances the fall of Vicksburg was inevitable, and on July 4, 1863, its commander surrendered. The same day a battle that had been raging for three days concluded at Gettysburg, Pennsylvania (see Map 15.3). On July 1 Confederate forces hunting for a supply of shoes had collided with part of the Union Army. Heavy fighting on the second day over two steep hills left federal forces in possession of high ground along

Battle of Gettysburg

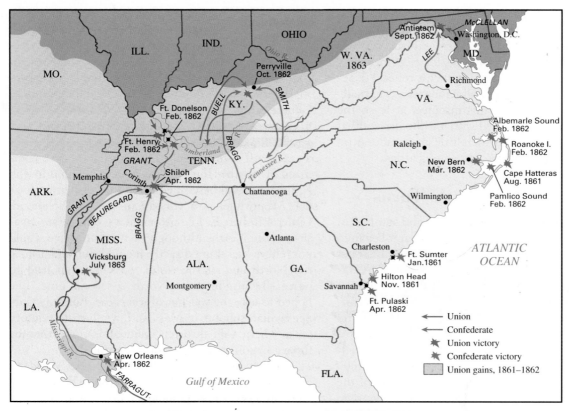

Map 15.2   War in the West, 1861–1863   Here is an overview of the Union's successful campaigns in the west and its seizure of key points on the Mississippi River, as well as along the Atlantic coast in 1862 and 1863. These actions were decisive in paving the way for ultimate northern victory.

Cemetery Ridge, running more than a mile south of the town. There they enjoyed the protection of a stone wall and a clear view of their foe across almost a mile of open field.

Undaunted, Lee believed his reinforced troops could break the Union line, and on July 3 he ordered a direct assault. Full of foreboding, General James Longstreet warned Lee that "no 15,000 men ever arrayed for battle can take that position." But Lee stuck to his plan. Virginians under General George E. Pickett and North Carolinians under General James Pettigrew methodically marched up the slope in a doomed assault known as Pickett's Charge. For a moment a few hundred Confederates breached the enemy's line, but most fell in heavy slaughter. On July 4 Lee had to withdraw, having suffered almost 4,000 dead and about 24,000 missing and wounded. The Confederate general reported to President Davis that "I am alone to blame" and offered to resign. Davis replied that to find a more capable commander was "an impossibility."

The Confederacy had reached what many consider its "high water mark" on that ridge at Gettysburg.

Southern troops displayed unforgettable courage and dedication at Gettysburg, and the Union Army, which suffered 23,000 casualties (nearly one-quarter of the force), under General George G. Meade exhibited the same bravery in stopping the Confederate invasion. But the results there and at Vicksburg were disastrous for the South. The Confederacy was split in two; west of the Mississippi General E. Kirby Smith had to operate on his own, virtually independent of Richmond. Moreover, the heartland of Louisiana, Tennessee, and Mississippi lay exposed to invasion, and Lee's defeat spelled the end of major southern offensive actions. Too weak to prevail in attack, the Confederacy henceforth would have to conserve its limited resources and rely on a prolonged defense. By refusing to be beaten, and wearing down northern morale, the South might yet win, but its prospects were darker than ever before.

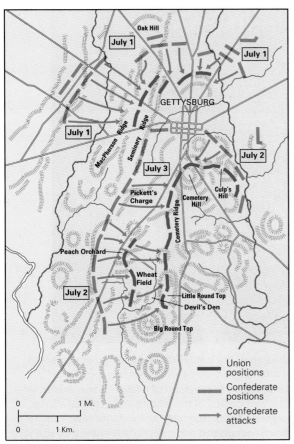

Map 15.3 Battle of Gettysburg In the war's greatest battle, fought around a small market town in southern Pennsylvania, Lee's invasion of the North was repulsed. Union forces had the advantage of high ground, shorter lines, and superior numbers. The casualties for the two armies—dead, wounded, and missing—exceeded 50,000 men.

Disunity, South and North

Both northern and southern governments waged the final two years of the war in the face of increasing opposition at home. Dissatisfactions that had surfaced earlier grew more intense and sometimes violent. The gigantic costs of a *civil* war that neither side seemed able to win fed the unrest. But protest also arose from fundamental stresses in the social structures of North and South.

The Confederacy's problems were both more serious and more deeply rooted than the North's. Vastly disadvantaged in industrial capacity, natural resources,

Disintegration of Confederate Unity

and labor, southerners felt the cost of the war more quickly, more directly, and more painfully than northerners. But even more fundamental were the Confederacy's internal problems; crises that were integrally connected with the southern class system threatened the Confederate cause.

One ominous development was the planters' increasing opposition to their own government. Not only did the Richmond government impose new taxes and the tax-in-kind, but Confederate military authorities also impressed slaves to build fortifications. And when Union forces advanced on plantation areas, Confederate commanders burned stores of cotton that lay in the enemy's path. Such interference with plantation routines and financial interests was not what planters had expected of their government, and they complained bitterly.

Nor were the centralizing policies of the Davis administration popular. The increasing size and power of the Richmond government startled and alarmed planters who had condemned federal usurpations. In fact, the Confederate constitution had granted substantial powers to the central government, especially in time of war. But many planters assumed with R. B. Rhett, editor of the *Charleston Mercury*, that the Confederate constitution "leaves the States untouched in their Sovereignty, and commits to the Confederate Government only a few simple objects, and a few simple powers to enforce them." Governor Joseph E. Brown of Georgia took a similarly inflated view of the importance of the states. During the brief interval between Georgia's secession from the Union and its admission to the Confederacy, Brown sent an ambassador to Europe to seek recognition for the sovereign republic of Georgia from Queen Victoria, Napoleon III, and the king of Belgium.

Years of opposition to the federal government within the Union had frozen southerners in a defensive posture. Now they erected the barrier of states' rights as a defense against change, hiding behind it while their capacity for creative statesmanship atrophied. Planters sought, above all, a guarantee that their plantations and their lives would remain untouched; many were not deeply committed either to building a southern nation or to winning independence. If the Confederacy had been allowed to depart from the Union in peace and continue as a semideveloped cotton-growing region, they would have been content. When secession revolutionized their world, they could not or would not adjust.

WHO IS HE?—On the field of Gettysburg, after the battles, the dead body of a Union soldier was found, holding in his clasped hands an ambrotype picture of three children, a girl and two boys, aged apparently about nine, seven and five years. In the picture, the youngest child, a boy, is seated in a high chair, between his elder brother and his sister, while the dresses of the two latter are made of the same material. The soldier was buried on the field where he fell, and his grave is marked, but his name could not be ascertained. It is hoped, however, that he may yet be identified by means of the ambrotype of the children found in his hands when his body was discovered. The picture is now in possession of Dr. Bourns, 1104 Spring Garden street, Philadelphia, who can be called upon or addressed in reference to it.

These "children of the battlefield" aroused great interest in the North after a burial detail at Gettysburg found this ambrotype clutched in the hand of a fallen Union soldier. After thousands of copies of the picture were circulated, the wife of Sergeant Amos Humiston of the 154th New York Infantry *(above)* recognized her children and knew that she was a widow.   (The C. Craig Caba Gettysburg Collection, from *Gettysburg.* Larry Sherer © 1991 Time-Life Books, Inc.)

Confused and embittered planters struck out at Jefferson Davis. Conscription, thundered Governor Brown, was "subversive of [Georgia's] sovereignty, and at war with all the principles for the support of which Georgia entered into this revolution." Searching for ways to frustrate the law, Brown bickered over draft exemptions and ordered local enrollment officials not to cooperate with the Confederacy. The *Charleston Mercury* told readers that "conscription . . . is . . . the very embodiment of Lincolnism, which our gallant armies are today fighting." In a gesture of stubborn selfishness, Robert Toombs of Georgia, a former U.S. senator, refused to switch from cotton to food crops, defying the wishes of the government, the newspapers, and his neighbors' petitions. His action bespoke the inflexibility of the southern elite at a crucial point in the Confederacy's struggle to survive.

The southern courts ultimately upheld Davis's power to conscript. Despite his cold formality and inability to disarm critics, Davis possessed two important virtues: iron determination and total dedication to independence. These qualities kept the Confederacy afloat. But his actions earned him the hatred of most influential and elite citizens.

Meanwhile, for ordinary southerners, the dire predictions of hunger and suffering were becoming a reality.

Food Riots in Southern Cities

Food riots occurred in the spring of 1863 in Atlanta, Macon, Columbus, and Augusta, Georgia, and in Salisbury and High Point, North Carolina. On April 2 a crowd assembled in Richmond to demand relief. A passerby, noticing the excitement, asked a young girl, "Is there some celebration?" "We celebrate our right to live," replied the girl. "We are starving. As soon as enough of us get together we are going to the bakeries and each of us will take a loaf of bread." Soon they did just that, sparking a riot that Davis himself had to quell at gunpoint.

Throughout the rural South, ordinary people resisted more quietly—by refusing to cooperate with conscription, tax collection, and impressments of food. "In all the States impressments are evaded by every means which ingenuity can suggest, and in some openly resisted," wrote a high-ranking commissary officer. Farmers who did provide food for the army refused to accept payment in certificates of credit or government bonds, as required by law. Conscription officers increasingly found no one to draft—men of draft age were hiding out in the forests. "The disposition to avoid military service is general," observed one of Georgia's senators in 1864. In some areas tax agents were killed in the line of duty.

Jefferson Davis was ill equipped to deal with such discontent. Austere and private by nature, he failed to communicate with the masses. Often he buried himself in military affairs or administrative details. His class perspective also distanced him from the sufferings of the common people. While his social circle in Richmond dined on duck and oysters, ordinary southerners recovered salt from the drippings on their smokehouse floors and went hungry. State governors who responded to people's needs won the public's loyalty, but Davis failed to reach out to the plain folk and thus lost their support.

Such discontent was certain to affect the Confederate armies. "What man is there that would stay in the army and no that his family is

Desertions from the Confederate Army

sufring at home?" an angry citizen wrote anonymously to the secretary of war. Worried about their loved ones and resentful of what they saw as a rich man's war, large numbers of men did indeed leave the armies. Their friends and neighbors gave them support. Mary Boykin Chesnut observed a man being dragged back to the army as his wife looked on. "Desert agin, Jake!" she cried openly. "You desert agin, quick as you kin. Come back to your wife and children."

Desertion did not become a serious problem for the Confederacy until mid-1862, and stiffer policing solved the problem that year. But from 1863 on, the number of men on duty fell rapidly as desertions soared. By mid-1863, John A. Campbell, the South's assistant secretary of war, wondered whether "so general a habit" as desertion could be considered a crime. Campbell estimated that 40,000 to 50,000 troops were absent without leave and that 100,000 were evading duty in some way. Furloughs, amnesty proclamations, and appeals to return had little effect; by November 1863 Secretary of War James Seddon admitted that one-third of the army could not be accounted for. The situation would worsen.

The defeats at Gettysburg and Vicksburg dealt a heavy blow to Confederate morale. When the news

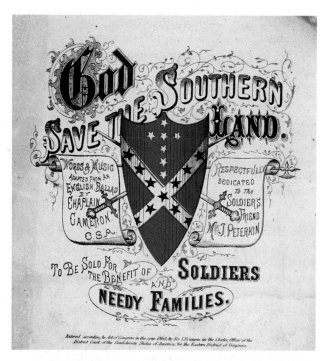

The impoverishment of nonslaveholding white families was a critical problem for the Confederacy. The sale of this sheet music was intended not only to boost morale but also to raise money that could be used to aid the hungry and needy. This effort and larger government initiatives, however, failed to solve the problem. (Chicago Historical Society)

reached Josiah Gorgas, the genius of Confederate ordnance operations, he confided to his diary, "Today absolute ruin seems our portion. The Confederacy totters to its destruction." In desperation President Davis and several state governors resorted to threats and racial scare tactics to drive southern whites to further sacrifice. Defeat, Davis warned, would mean "extermination of yourselves, your wives, and children." Governor Charles Clark of Mississippi predicted "elevation of the black race to a position of equality—aye, of superiority, that will make them your masters and rulers."

From this point on, the internal disintegration of the Confederacy quickened. A few newspapers began to call openly for peace. "We are for peace," admitted the *Raleigh* (North Carolina) *Daily Progress*, "because there has been enough of blood and carnage, enough of widows and orphans." A neighboring journal, the *North Carolina Standard*, tacitly admitted that defeat was inevitable and called for negotiations. Similar proposals were made in several state legislatures, though they were presented as plans for independence on honorable terms. Confederate leaders began to realize that they were losing the support of the common people. Governor Zebulon Vance of North Carolina wrote privately that victory would require more "blood and misery . . . and our people will not pay this price I am satisfied for their independence."

In North Carolina a peace movement grew under the leadership of William W. Holden, a popular Democratic politician and editor. Over

Southern Peace Movements

one hundred public meetings took place in the summer of 1863 in support of peace negotiations, and many seasoned political observers believed that Holden had the majority of the people behind him. In Georgia early in 1864, Governor Brown and Alexander H. Stephens, vice president of the Confederacy, led a similar effort. Ultimately, however, these movements came to naught. The lack of a two-party system threw into question the legitimacy of any criticism of the government; even Holden and Brown could not entirely escape the taint of dishonor and disloyalty. That the movement existed at all demonstrates deep disaffection.

The results of the 1863 congressional elections strengthened dissent in the Confederacy. Everywhere secessionists and supporters of the administration lost seats to men not identified with the government. Many of the new representatives were former Whigs who opposed the Davis administration or publicly favored peace. In the last years of the war, Davis's support in the Confederate Congress dwindled. Davis used the government bureaucracy and the army to enforce his unpopular policies. A few editors and a core of courageous, determined soldiers kept the Confederacy alive in spite of disintegrating popular support.

By 1864 much of the opposition to the war had moved entirely outside the political sphere. Southerners were simply giving up the struggle and withdrawing their cooperation from the government. Deserters dominated whole towns and counties. Secret societies favoring reunion, such as the Heroes of America and the Red Strings, sprang up. Active dissent was particularly common in upland and mountain regions. "The condition of things in the mountain districts of North Carolina, South Carolina, Georgia, and Alabama," admitted Assistant Secretary of War Campbell, "menaces the existence of the Confederacy as fatally as either of the armies of the United States." The government was losing the support of its citizens.

In the North opposition to the war was similar but less severe. Alarm intensified over the growing cen-

Antiwar Sentiment in the North

tralization of government, and by 1863 war-weariness was widespread. Resentment of the draft sparked protest, especially among poor citizens, and the Union Army struggled with a desertion rate as high as the Confederates'. But the Union was so much richer than the South in human resources that none of these problems ever threatened the effectiveness of the government. Fresh recruits were always available, especially after black enlistments began, and there were no shortages of food and other necessities.

Also, Lincoln possessed a talent that Davis lacked: he knew how to stay in touch with the ordinary citizen. Through letters to newspapers and to soldiers' families, he reached the common people and demonstrated that he had not forgotten them. The daily carnage, the tortuous political problems, and the ceaseless criticism weighed heavily on him. But this president—a self-educated man of humble origins—was able to communicate his suffering. His moving words helped to contain northern discontent, though they could not remove it.

Much of the wartime protest in the North was political in origin. The Democratic Party fought to regain power by blaming Lincoln for the war's death toll, the expan-

Peace Democrats

sion of federal powers, inflation and the high tariff, and the emancipation of blacks. Appealing to tradition, its leaders called for an end to the war and reunion on the basis of "the Constitution as it is and the Union as it was." The Democrats denounced conscription and martial law and defended states' rights and the interests of agriculture. They charged repeatedly that Republican policies were designed to flood the North with blacks, depriving white males of their status, their jobs, and their women. These claims appealed to southerners who had settled north of the Ohio River, to conservatives, to many poor people, and to some eastern merchants who had lost profitable southern trade. In the 1862 congressional elections, the Democrats made a strong comeback, and peace Democrats—who would go much further than others in their party to end the war—had influence in New York State and majorities in the legislatures of Illinois and Indiana.

Led by outspoken men like Representative Clement L. Vallandigham of Ohio, the peace Democrats made themselves highly visible. Vallandigham criticized Lincoln as a dictator who had suspended the writ of habeas corpus without congressional authority and had arrested thousands of innocent citizens. Like other Democrats, he condemned both conscription and emancipation and urged voters to use their power at the polls to depose "King Abraham." Vallandigham stayed carefully within legal bounds, but his attacks seemed so damaging to the war effort that military authorities arrested him for treason after Lincoln suspended habeas corpus. Lincoln wisely decided against punishment—and martyr's status—for the Ohioan and exiled him to the Confederacy. (Eventually Vallandigham returned to the North through Canada.)

Lincoln believed that antiwar Democrats were linked to secret organizations that harbored traitorous ideas. These societies, he feared, encouraged draft resistance, discouraged enlistment, sabotaged communications, and plotted to aid the Confederacy. Likening such groups to a poisonous snake, Republicans sometimes branded them—and by extension the peace Democrats—as "Copperheads." Though Democrats were connected with these organizations, most engaged in politics rather than treason. And though some saboteurs and Confederate agents were active in the North and Canada, they never genuinely threatened the Union war effort.

More violent opposition to the government arose from ordinary citizens facing the draft, which became

New York City Draft Riots

law in 1863. The urban poor and immigrants in strongly Democratic areas were especially hostile to conscription. Federal enrolling officers made up the lists of eligibles, a procedure open to personal favoritism and prejudice. Many men, including some of modest means, managed to avoid the army by hiring a substitute or paying commutation, but the poor viewed the commutation fee as discriminatory, and many immigrants suspected (wrongly, on the whole) that they were called in disproportionate numbers. (Approximately 200,000 men born in Germany and 150,000 born in Ireland served in the Union Army.)

As a result, there were scores of disturbances and melees. Enrolling officers received rough treatment in many parts of the North, and riots occurred in New Jersey, Ohio, Indiana, Pennsylvania, Illinois, and Wisconsin. By far the most serious outbreak of violence occurred in New York City in July 1863. The war was unpopular in that Democratic stronghold, and racial, ethnic, and class tensions ran high. Shippers had recently broken a longshoremen's strike by hiring black strikebreakers to work under police protection.

Mobs in the New York City draft riots directed much of their anger at African Americans. Rioters burned an orphanage for black children and killed scores of blacks. This wood engraving, which appeared in the *Illustrated London News* on August 8, 1863, depicts a lynching in Clarkson Street. (Chicago Historical Society)

Working-class New Yorkers feared an inflow of black labor from the South and regarded blacks as the cause of the war. Poor Irish workers resented being forced to serve in the place of others who could afford to avoid the draft.

Military police officers came under attack first, and then mobs crying "Down with the rich" looted wealthy homes and stores. But blacks became the special target. Those who happened to be in the rioters' path were beaten; soon the mob rampaged through African American neighborhoods, destroying an orphan asylum. At least seventy-four people died in the violence, which raged out of control for three days. Only the dispatch of army units fresh from Gettysburg ended the episode.

Discouragement and war-weariness reached a peak in the summer of 1864, when the Democratic Party nominated the popular General George B. McClellan for president and inserted a peace plank into its platform. The plank, written by Vallandigham, condemned "four years of failure to restore the Union by the experiment of war," called for an armistice, and spoke vaguely about preserving the Union. Lincoln, running with Tennessee's Andrew Johnson on a "National Union" ticket, concluded that it was "exceedingly probable that this Administration will not be reelected." During a publicized interchange with Confederate officials sent to Canada, Lincoln insisted that the terms for peace include reunion and "the abandonment of slavery." A wave of protest arose in the North from voters who were weary of war and dedicated only to reunion. Lincoln quickly backtracked, denying that his offer meant "that nothing *else* or *less* would be considered, if offered." He would insist on freedom only for those slaves (about 134,000) who had joined the Union Army under his promise of emancipation. Lincoln's action showed his political weakness, but the fortunes of war soon changed the electoral situation.

1864–1865: The Final Test of Wills

During the final year of the war, the Confederates could still have won their version of victory if military stalemate and northern antiwar sentiment had forced a negotiated settlement to end the war. But events, northern determination, and Lincoln's insistence on the unconditional surrender of Confederate forces prevailed as Americans endured the bloodiest nightmare in their history.

Northern Diplomatic Strategy

The North's long-term diplomatic strategy succeeded in 1864. From the outset, the North had pursued one paramount goal: to prevent recognition of the Confederacy by European nations. Foreign recognition would belie Lincoln's claim that the United States was fighting an illegal rebellion and would open the way to the financial and military aid that could ensure Confederate independence. The British elite, however, felt considerable sympathy for southern planters, whose aristocratic values were similar to their own. And both England and France stood to benefit from a divided and weakened America. Thus to achieve their goal, Lincoln and Secretary of State Seward needed to avoid both serious military defeats and controversies with the European powers.

Aware that the textile industry employed one-fifth of the British population directly or indirectly, southerners banked on British recognition of the Confederacy. But at the beginning of the war, British mills had a 50 percent surplus of cotton on hand; later on, new sources of supply in India, Egypt, and Brazil helped to meet Britain's needs. And throughout the war, some southern cotton continued to reach Europe, despite the Confederacy's embargo on cotton production, an ill-fated policy initiative aimed at securing British sup-

port. Refusing to be stampeded into recognition of the Confederacy, the British government kept its eye on the battlefield. France, though sympathetic to the South, was unwilling to act independently of Britain. Confederate agents managed to purchase valuable arms and supplies in Europe and obtained loans from European financiers, but they never achieved a diplomatic breakthrough.

More than once the Union strategy nearly broke down. An acute crisis occurred in 1861 when the overzealous commander of an American frigate stopped the British steamer *Trent* and removed two Confederate ambassadors, James Mason and John Slidell, sailing to Britain. They were imprisoned in Boston after being brought ashore. This action was cheered in the North, but the British interpreted it as a violation of freedom of the seas and demanded the prisoners' release. Lincoln and Seward waited until northern public opinion cooled and then released the two southerners. Soon forgotten, the incident nevertheless strained U.S.-British relations at a sensitive early stage in the war.

Then the sale to the Confederacy of warships constructed in England sparked vigorous protest from U.S. ambassador Charles Francis Adams. A few English-built ships, notably the *Alabama*, reached open water to serve the South. Over a period of twenty-two months, without entering a southern port (because of the Union blockade), the *Alabama* destroyed or captured more than sixty U.S. ships. But the British government, as a neutral power, soon barred delivery of warships such as the Laird rams (built by a private company), formidable vessels whose pointed prows were designed to end the blockade by battering the Union ships.

On the battlefield, the northern victory was far from won in 1864. General Nathaniel Banks's Red River campaign, designed to capture more of Louisiana and Texas, quickly fell apart, and the capture of Mobile Bay in August did not cause the fall of Mobile. Union general William Tecumseh Sherman commented that the North had to "keep the war South until they are not only ruined, exhausted, but humbled in pride and spirit." Sherman soon brought total war to the southern heartland. On the eastern front during the winter of 1863–1864, the two armies in Virginia settled into a stalemate awaiting yet another spring offensive by the North.

Battlefield Stalemate and a Union Strategy for Victory

Military authorities throughout history have agreed that deep invasion is very risky: the farther an

Both General Grant *(left)* and General Lee *(right)* were West Point graduates and had served in the U.S. Army during the War with Mexico. Their bloody battles against each other in 1864 stirred northern revulsion to the war even as they brought its end in sight.   (National Archives)

army penetrates enemy territory, the more vulnerable its own communications and supply lines. Moreover, observed the Prussian expert Karl von Clausewitz, if the invader encountered a "truly national" resistance, his troops would be "everywhere exposed to attacks by an insurgent population." Thus if southerners mounted such a "truly national" resistance, their defiance and the South's vast size could make a northern victory improbable.

General Grant, by now in command of all the federal armies, decided to test these conditions—and southern will—with a strategic innovation of his own: raids on a massive scale. Grant, less tied to tradition and maneuver by the book than most other Union commanders, proposed to use whole armies, not just cavalry, to destroy Confederate railroads, thus ruining the enemy's transportation and damaging the South's economy. Abandoning their lines of support, Union troops would live off the land while laying to waste all resources useful to the military and to the civilian population of the Confederacy. After General George H. Thomas's troops won the Battle of Chattanooga in

November 1863 by ignoring orders and charging up Missionary Ridge, the heartland of Georgia lay open. Moving to Virginia, Grant entrusted General Sherman with 100,000 men for an invasion deep into the South, toward the rail center of Atlanta.

Jefferson Davis countered by positioning the army of General Joseph E. Johnston in Sherman's path.

Atlanta

Davis's entire political strategy for 1864 was based on demonstrating Confederate military strength and successfully defending Atlanta. The U.S. presidential election of 1864 was approaching, and Davis hoped that southern resolve would lead to the defeat of Lincoln and the election of a president who would sue for peace. When General Johnston slowly but steadily fell back toward Atlanta, Davis grew anxious and sought assurances that Atlanta would be held. From a purely military point of view, Johnston maneuvered skillfully, but the president of the Confederacy could not take a purely military point of view. When Johnston provided no information and continued to retreat, Davis replaced him with the one-legged

General John Hood, who knew his job was to fight. "Our all depends on that army at Atlanta," wrote Mary Boykin Chesnut. "If that fails us, the game is up."

For southern morale, the game was up. Hood attacked but was beaten, and Sherman's army occupied Atlanta on September 2, 1864. The victory buoyed northern spirits and ensured Lincoln's reelection. "There is no hope," Mary Chesnut acknowledged; and a government clerk in Richmond wrote, "Our fondly-cherished visions of peace have vanished like a mirage of the desert." Davis exhorted southerners to fight on and win new victories before the federal elections, but he had to admit that "two-thirds of our men are absent . . . most of them absent without leave." In a desperate diversion, Hood's army marched north to cut Sherman's supply lines and force him to withdraw, but Sherman began to march sixty thousand of his men straight to the sea, planning to live off the land and destroying Confederate resources as he went (see Map 15.4).

Sherman's army was an unusually formidable force, composed almost entirely of battle-tested veterans and officers who had risen through the ranks from

Sherman's March to the Sea

the midwestern states. Before the march began, army doctors weeded out any men who were weak or sick. Tanned, bearded, tough, and unkempt, the remaining veterans were determined, as one put it, "to Conquer this Rebelien or Die." They believed "the South are to blame for this war" and were ready to make the South pay. Although many harbored racist attitudes, most had come to support emancipation because, as one said, "Slavery stands in the way of putting down the rebellion." Confederate General Johnston later commented, "There has been no such army since the days of Julius Caesar."

As Sherman's men moved across Georgia, they cut a path 50 to 60 miles wide and more than 200 miles long. The totality of the destruction they caused was awesome. A Georgia woman described the "Burnt Country" this way: "The fields were trampled down and the road was lined with carcasses of horses, hogs, and cattle that the invaders, unable either to consume or to carry with them, had wantonly shot down to starve our people and prevent them from making their crops. The stench in some places was unbearable."

Map 15.4 Sherman's March to the Sea The West proved a decisive theater at the end of the war. From Chattanooga, Union forces drove into Georgia, capturing Atlanta. Then General Sherman embarked on his march of destruction through Georgia to the coast and then northward through the Carolinas.

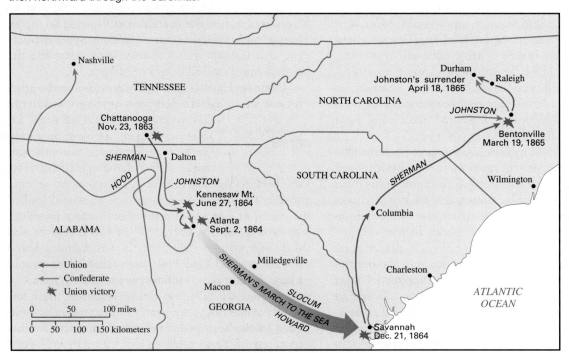

Such devastation diminished the South's material resources and sapped its will to resist.

After reaching Savannah in December, Sherman marched his armies north into the Carolinas. To his soldiers, South Carolina was "the root of secession." They burned and destroyed as they moved through, encountering little resistance. The opposing army of General Johnston was small, but Sherman's men should have been prime targets for guerrilla raids and harassing attacks by local defense units. The absence of both led South Carolina's James Chesnut, Jr. (a politician and the husband of Mary Chesnut), to write that his state "was shamefully and unnecessarily lost. . . . We had time, opportunity and means to destroy him. But there was wholly wanting the energy and ability required by the occasion." The South put up no "truly national" resistance; its people had lost the will to continue the struggle.

Sherman's march drew additional human resources to the Union cause. In Georgia alone as many as nineteen thousand slaves gladly took the opportunity to escape bondage and join the Union troops as they passed through the countryside. Others remained on the plantations to await the end of the war, either from an ingrained wariness of whites or negative experiences with federal soldiers. The destruction of food harmed slaves as well as white rebels, and many blacks lost livestock, clothing, crops, and other valuables to their liberators. In fact, the brutality of Sherman's troops shocked these veterans of the whip. "I've seen them cut the hams off of a live pig or ox and go off leavin' the animal groanin'," recalled one man. "The master had 'em kilt then, but it was awful."

It was awful, too, in Virginia, where the path to victory proved protracted and ghastly. Throughout the spring and summer of 1864, intent on capturing Richmond, Grant hurled his troops at Lee's army in Virginia and suffered appalling losses: almost 18,000 casualties in the Battle of the Wilderness, where skeletons poked out of the shallow graves dug one year before; more than 8,000 at Spotsylvania; and 12,000 in the space of a few hours at Cold Harbor (see Map 15.5).

Virginia's Bloody Soil

Before the assault at Cold Harbor (which Grant later admitted was a grave mistake), Union troops pinned scraps of paper bearing their names and addresses to their backs, certain they would be mowed down as they rushed Lee's trenches. In four weeks in May and June, Grant lost as many men as were enrolled in Lee's entire army. From early May until July,

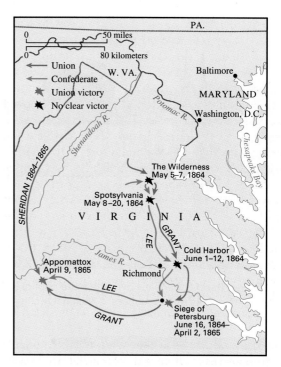

Map 15.5 The War in Virginia, 1864–1865 At great cost, Grant hammered away at Lee's army until the weakened southern forces finally surrendered at Appomattox Court House.

when Union forces had marched and fought all the way from forests west of Fredericksburg to Petersburg, south of Richmond, which they besieged, the two armies engaged each other nearly every day, often in full-scale battles. The war had reached a horrible modern scale. Wagon trains carrying thousands of Union wounded crawled back toward Washington. "It was as if war," wrote historian Bruce Catton, "the great clumsy machine for maiming people, had at last been perfected. Instead of turning out its grist spasmodically, with long waits between each delivery, it was at last able to produce every day, without any gaps at all."

Undaunted, Grant kept up the pressure, saying, "I propose to fight it out along this line if it takes all summer." Though costly, and testing northern morale to its limits, these battles prepared the way for eventual victory: Lee's army shrank until offensive action was no longer possible, while Grant's army kept replenishing its forces with new recruits. The siege of Petersburg, with the armies facing each other in miles of trenches, lasted throughout the winter of 1864–1865.

At the war's end, the U.S. flag flew over the state capitol in Richmond, Virginia, which bore many marks of destruction.   (National Archives)

The end finally came in the spring of 1865. Grant kept battering Lee, who tried but failed to break through the Union line. With the numerical superiority of Grant's army now greater than two to one, Confederate defeat was inevitable. On April 2 Lee abandoned Richmond and Petersburg. On April 9, hemmed in by Union troops, short of rations, and with fewer than thirty thousand men left, Lee surrendered at Appomattox Court House. Grant treated his rival with respect and paroled the defeated troops, allowing cavalrymen to keep their horses and take them home. The war was over at last. Within weeks, Confederate forces under Johnston surrendered and Davis, who had fled Richmond but wanted the war to continue, was captured in Georgia. The North rejoiced, and most southerners fell into despair, expecting waves of punishment. In the profound relief and stillness of the surrender field at Appomattox, no one could know the tasks of healing and justice that lay ahead.

Surrender at Appomattox

With Lee's surrender, Lincoln knew that the Union had been preserved, yet he lived to see but a few days of war's aftermath. On the evening of Good Friday, April 14, he accompanied his wife to Ford's Theatre in Washington to enjoy a popular comedy. There John Wilkes Booth, an embittered southern sympathizer, shot the president in the head at point-blank range. Lincoln died the next day. Twelve days later, troops tracked down and killed Booth. The Union had lost its wartime leader, and millions publicly mourned the martyred chief executive along the route of the funeral train that took his body home to Illinois. Relief at the war's end mingled hauntingly with a renewed sense of loss and anxiety about the future. Millions never forgot where they were and how they felt at the news of Lincoln's assassination.

Property damage and financial costs were enormous, though difficult to tally. U.S. loans and taxes during the conflict totaled almost $3 billion, and interest on the war debt was $2.8 billion. The Confederacy borrowed over $2 billion but lost far more in the destruction of homes, crops, livestock, and other property. As an example of the wreckage that attended four years of conflict on southern soil, the number of hogs in South Carolina plummeted from 965,000 in 1860 to approximately 150,000 in 1865, leaving many families without their primary source of meat.

Financial Tally

In southern war zones the landscape was desolated. Over wide regions fences and crops were destroyed; houses, barns, and bridges burned; and fields abandoned and left to erode. Union troops had looted factories and put two-thirds of the South's railroad system out of service. Visitors to the countryside were struck by how empty and impoverished it looked.

Estimates of the total cost of the war exceed $20 billion—five times the total expenditures of the federal government from its creation to 1861. The northern government increased its spending by 700 percent in the first full year of the war; by the last year its spending had soared to twenty times the prewar level. By 1865 the federal government accounted for over 26 percent of the gross national product.

Many of these changes were more or less permanent. In the 1880s, interest on the war debt still accounted for approximately 40 percent of the federal budget and Union soldiers' pensions for as much as 20 percent. The federal government had used its power to support manufacturing and business interests by means of tariffs, loans, and subsidies, and wartime measures left the government more deeply involved in the banking and transportation systems. If southerners had hoped to remove government from the economy, the war had now irrepressibly bound them together.

The human costs of the Civil War were especially staggering. The total number of military casualties on

Death Toll

both sides exceeded 1 million—a frightful toll for a nation of 31 million people. Approximately 360,000 Union soldiers died, 110,000 of them from wounds suffered in battle. Another 275,175 Union soldiers were wounded but survived. On the Confederate side, an estimated 260,000 lost their lives, and almost as many suffered wounds. More men died in the Civil War than in all other American wars combined until Vietnam. Of an estimated 194,743 northerners in southern prisons, 30,218 died, compared with 25,976 of 214,865 southerners who died in northern prisons. The prison story from the war is one in which neither side could claim pride, although it caused embittered debate in war memory for decades.

These unprecedented losses flowed from fundamental strife over the nature of the Union and the liberty of black people. Both sides saw vital interests in the struggle. As Julia Ward Howe wrote in her famous "Battle Hymn," they had heard "the trumpet that shall never call retreat." And so the war took its horrifying course. The first great legacy of the war in the lives of its survivors was, therefore, death itself. Although precise figures on enlistments are impossible to obtain, it appears that 700,000 to 800,000 men served in the Confederate armies. Far more, possibly 2.3 million, served in the Union armies. All these men were taken from home, family, and personal goals; their lives, if they survived at all, were disrupted in ways that were never repaired.

Summary

The Civil War altered American society forever. During the war, in both North and South, women had taken on new roles. Industrialization and large economic enterprises grew in power. Ordinary citizens found that their futures were increasingly tied to huge organizations. The character and extent of government power changed markedly. Under Republican leadership, the federal government had expanded its

The death of President Lincoln caused a vast outpouring of grief in the North. As this Currier and Ives print shows, on its way to Illinois, his funeral train stopped at several cities to allow local services to be held. (Anne S. K. Brown Military Collection, John Hay Library, Brown University)

power not only to preserve the Union but also to extend freedom. A social revolution and government authority emancipated the slaves, and Lincoln had called for "a new birth of freedom" in America. A republic desperately divided against itself had survived, yet in new constitutional forms yet to take shape under tremendous political strife during Reconstruction.

It was unclear, however, how or whether the nation would use its power to protect the rights of the former slaves. Secession was dead, but whether Americans would continue to embrace a centralized nationalism remained to be seen. How would white southerners, embittered and impoverished, respond to efforts to reconstruct the nation? How long would military occupation last in the South, and who would rule its civil society? How would the country care for the maimed, the orphans, the farming women without men to work their land, and all the dead who had to be properly found and buried? And of central importance: what would be the place of black men and women in American life? Black veterans and former slaves eagerly sought an answer. They would find it during Reconstruction.

In the Civil War Americans had undergone an epic of destruction and survival. White southerners had experienced defeat as few other Americans have ever faced. Blacks were walking proudly but anxiously from slavery to freedom. White northerners were, by and large, self-conscious victors in a massive war for the nation's existence and for new definitions of what freedom meant in America. The war, including all its drama, sacrifice, and social and political changes, left a compelling memory in American hearts and minds for generations.

LEGACY FOR A PEOPLE AND A NATION
The Confederate Battle Flag

The most widespread and controversial symbol to emerge from the Civil War era is the Confederate flag. Rather than the official flag of the Confederacy, it was a battle flag that soldiers carried to mark the center of a unit's position in the confusion of combat. Over time, this flag has taken on powerful emotional meanings.

At Confederate veterans' reunions and parades from the 1870s well into the twentieth century, the flag was an emblem of the South's Lost Cause. After extended controversy, many captured Confederate flags were returned by the federal government to southern states in 1905 as a gesture of reconciliation. Increasingly, Confederate remembrance merged with white supremacy at the turn of the twentieth century and African Americans resented the flag's appearance.

In the late 1940s the flag became a fixture of popular culture with heightened racial meanings. In 1948 it was a symbol of the States' Rights ("Dixiecrat") Party. By the 1950s waving the Confederate flag became a demonstration of defiance among southern whites against the civil rights revolution. With the spread of American popular culture abroad, the Confederate flag can now be found all over the world.

What does this flag mean as a symbol? Some southern whites argue that it is merely a marker of regional pride and identity. Some stress the flag's countercultural value as a symbol of rebellion against the establishment, or "political correctness." But to most blacks and to many whites, it expresses racism. The flag is loaded with coded meanings that can be interpreted in opposite ways. Some claim it represents the "nobility" of southern military tradition; others conclude that it stands for the hatred embodied in the history of the Ku Klux Klan.

In recent times, the Confederate flag has been the center of legal and political controversy. Disputes have emanated from city councils, high schools, and universities over public and private uses of the flag. Most visible of all have been the debates in the states of Georgia, South Carolina, and Alabama over whether to cease flying the Confederate flag at official sites. The debate over the meaning and legacy of the Confederate flag may never end. At issue are important questions and traditions: free speech, equal protection under law, perception versus reality, official government endorsement of collective symbols, the significance of race and racism in our national memory, and the meaning of the Civil War itself.

For Further Reading, see page A-18 of the Appendix. For Web resources, go to http://college.hmco.com.

In 1861 Robert Smalls was a slave in South Carolina, while Wade Hampton was a South Carolina legislator and one of the richest planters in the South. The events of the next fifteen years turned each man's world upside down more than once.

Robert Smalls became a Union hero in 1862 when he escaped from slavery by stealing a Confederate ship from Charleston harbor and piloting it to the blockading federal fleet. Thereafter, Smalls guided Union gunboats and toured the North recruiting black troops. Though he enjoyed celebrity status, Smalls encountered racial discrimination in the North and found in 1865 that neither his heroism nor his freedom entitled him to vote. But by 1868 that, too, had changed, and he began a career in politics. Smalls helped write his state's constitution, served in the legislature, and won election to Congress. There he denounced white violence and worked for educational and economic opportunity for his people. But Smalls was helpless to prevent the return of white control in South Carolina in 1877.

Wade Hampton joined the Confederate Army in 1861 and soon became a general. The South's defeat profoundly shocked him; and as Union forces closed in, he spoke wildly of "forc[ing] my way across the Mississippi" with "a devoted band of Cavalry" and continuing to fight. The postwar years brought further painful changes, including forced bankruptcy. In 1867 Hampton surprised other privileged whites by supporting suffrage for a few educated and propertied former slaves. By 1876, though, Hampton's fortunes were again on the rise: Democrats nominated him for governor, promising that he would "redeem" South Carolina from Republican misrule. Among Hampton's white supporters were the paramilitary Red Shirts who pledged to "control the vote of at least one Negro, by intimidation, purchase," or other means. Hampton won the governor's chair, then a seat in the U.S. Senate, and eventually an honored place as a distinguished Confederate veteran.

As the careers of Smalls and Hampton suggest, Reconstruction was revolutionary, but revolutions can

On January 6, 1874, Congressman Robert B. Elliott of South Carolina made an eloquent defense of the proposed civil rights bill. After a review of legal issues, he called on Congress to ignore the opposition of southerners, who he said had tried to destroy the nation, and deal justly with the Negro race, which had faithfully defended the Union. (Chicago Historical Society)

RECONSTRUCTION: AN UNFINISHED REVOLUTION 1865–1877

go backward. Robert Smalls rose from bondage to experience glory, emancipation, political power, and, ultimately, disappointment. Wade Hampton fell from privilege to endure defeat, failure, bankruptcy, and, eventually, a return to leadership in his state. Unprecedented changes took place in American society, but the underlying realities of economic power, racial prejudice, and judicial conservatism limited Reconstruction's revolutionary potential.

Nowhere was the turmoil of Reconstruction more evident than in national politics. Lincoln's successor, Andrew Johnson, fought bitterly with Congress over the shaping of a plan for Reconstruction. Though a southerner, Johnson had always been a foe of the South's wealthy planters, and his first acts as president suggested that he would be tough on "traitors." Before the end of 1865, however, Johnson's policies changed direction, and he became the friend and protector of southern interests. Jefferson Davis stayed in prison for two years, but Johnson quickly pardoned other rebel leaders and allowed them to occupy high offices. He also ordered the return of plantations to their original owners, including abandoned coastal lands on which forty thousand freed men and women had settled by order of General William Tecumseh Sherman early in 1865. Burdened by a train of thousands of black refugees following his army on the march to the sea, Sherman issued special Field Order Number 15 in February 1865. The order set aside 400,000 acres of land in the Georgia and South Carolina Sea Islands region for the exclusive settlement of the freedpeople. Hope swelled among ex-slaves as 40-acre plots, mules, and "possessary titles" were promised to them. But President Johnson ordered them removed in October and returned the land to its original owners under army protection.

Johnson imagined a lenient and rapid "restoration" of the South to the Union rather than the fundamental "reconstruction" that Republican congressmen favored. Between 1866 and 1868, the president and the Republican leadership in Congress engaged in a bitterly antagonistic power struggle over how to put the United States back together again.

Before these struggles were over, Congress had impeached the president, enfranchised the freed men, and given them a role in reconstructing the South. The nation also adopted the Fourteenth and Fifteenth Amendments, ushering equal protection of the law, a definition of citizenship, and universal manhood suffrage into the Constitution. Yet some underlying realities never changed. Little was done to open the doors of economic opportunity to black southerners, and throughout this period of upheaval, the cause of equal rights for African Americans as the central aim of Reconstruction rose and fell.

By 1869 the Ku Klux Klan employed extensive violence and terror to thwart Reconstruction and undermine black freedom. As white Democrats in the South recaptured state governments, undoing the political revolution, they encountered little opposition from the North. Voters had grown weary and suspicious of the use of federal power to prop up failing Republican governments. Moreover, as the 1870s advanced, industrial growth accelerated, creating new opportunities and raising new priorities. A new economic depression after 1873 refocused northerners' attention. Political corruption became a nationwide scandal, bribery a way of doing business. "Money has become the God of this country," wrote one disgusted observer, "and men, otherwise good men, are almost compelled to worship at her shrine."

Thus Reconstruction became a revolution eclipsed. The white South's desire to take back control of their states and of race relations overwhelmed the national interest in stopping them. But Reconstruction left enduring legacies the nation has struggled with ever since. ■

Wartime Reconstruction

Civil wars leave immense challenges of healing, justice, and physical rebuilding. Anticipating that process, Reconstruction of the Union was an issue as early as 1863, well before the war ended. Many key questions loomed on the horizon when and if the North succeeded on the battlefield. How would the nation be restored? How would southern states and leaders be treated? As errant brothers, or as traitors? What was the constitutional basis for readmission of states to the Union and where, if anywhere, could American statesmen look for precedence or guidance? More specifically, four vexing problems compelled early thinking and would haunt the Reconstruction era throughout. One, *who* would rule in the South once it was defeated? Two, *who* would rule in the federal government, Congress or the president? Three, what were the dimensions of *black freedom*, and what rights under law would the freedmen enjoy? And four, would Reconstruction be a preservation of the *old* republic, or a second revolution, a re-invention of a *new* republic?

IMPORTANT EVENTS

1865 Johnson begins rapid and lenient Reconstruction
Confederate leaders regain power
White southern governments pass restrictive black codes
Congress refuses to seat southern representatives
Thirteenth Amendment ratified

1866 Congress passes Civil Rights Act and renewal of Freedmen's Bureau over Johnson's veto
Congress approves Fourteenth Amendment
Most southern states reject Fourteenth Amendment
In *Ex parte Milligan* the Supreme Court reasserts its influence
In congressional elections, Republicans win more than two-thirds majority, a renunciation of Johnson's plan of Reconstruction

1867 Congress passes Reconstruction Act and Tenure of Office Act
Secretary of State William Seward arranges purchase of Alaska
Constitutional conventions called in southern states

1868 House impeaches Johnson; Senate acquits him
Most southern states gain readmission to the Union under Radical plan
Fourteenth Amendment ratified
Grant elected president

1869 Congress approves Fifteenth Amendment (ratified in 1870)

1870 Congress passes first Enforcement Act

1871 Congress passes second Enforcement Act and Ku Klux Klan Act
Treaty with England settles *Alabama* claims

1872 Amnesty Act frees almost all remaining Confederates from restrictions on holding office
Liberal Republicans organize and oppose Grant
Debtors urge government to keep greenbacks in circulation
Grant reelected

1873 *Slaughter-House* cases limit power of Fourteenth Amendment
Panic of 1873 sends economy into extended depression, leading to widespread unemployment and labor strife

1874 Grant vetoes increase in supply of paper money
Democrats win majority in House of Representatives

1875 Several Grant appointees indicted for corruption
Congress passes weak Civil Rights Act
Congress requires that after 1878 greenbacks be convertible into gold
Democratic Party continues to "redeem" control of southern states with white supremacy campaigns

1876 *U.S. v. Cruikshank* and *U.S. v. Reese* further weaken Fourteenth Amendment
Presidential election disputed

1877 Congress elects Hayes president
Exodusters migrate to Kansas
"Home rule" returns to three remaining southern states not yet controlled by Democrats; Reconstruction considered over

Abraham Lincoln had never been antisouthern, though he had grown to become the leader of an antislavery war. He lost three brothers-in-law killed in the war on the Confederate side. His worst fear was that the war would collapse at the end into guerrilla warfare across the South, with surviving bands of Confederates carrying

Lincoln's 10 Percent Plan

on resistance. Lincoln insisted that his generals give lenient terms to southern soldiers once they surrendered. He planned early for a swift and moderate Reconstruction process. In his Second Inaugural Address, delivered only a month before his assassination, Lincoln promised "malice toward none; with charity for all," as Americans strove to "bind up the nation's wounds."

In his "Proclamation of Amnesty and Reconstruction," issued in December 1863, Lincoln proposed to replace majority rule with "loyal rule" as a means of reconstructing southern state governments before hostilities ended. He envisioned Reconstruction as a process of experimentation. He proposed pardons to all ex-Confederates except the highest ranking military and civilian officers. Then, as soon as 10 percent of the voting population in the 1860 election had taken an oath and established a government, it would be recognized. Lincoln did not consult Congress in these plans, and "loyal" assemblies (known as "Lincoln governments") were created in Louisiana, Tennessee, and Arkansas in 1864, states largely occupied by Union troops. These governments were weak and dependent on northern armies for survival.

Congress responded with great hostility to Lincoln's moves to readmit southern states in what seemed

Congress and the Wade-Davis Bill

such a premature manner. Many Radical Republicans, strong proponents of emancipation and aggressive prosecution of the war against the South, considered the 10 percent plan a "mere mockery" of democracy. Led by Thaddeus Stevens of Pennsylvania in the House and Charles Sumner of Massachusetts in the Senate, congressional Republicans locked horns with Lincoln and proposed a longer and harsher approach to Reconstruction. Stevens advocated a "conquered provinces" theory, and Sumner, recovered from his beating at the hands of Preston Brooks (see page 375), employed an argument of "state suicide." Both contended that southerners had organized as a foreign nation to make war on the United States and, by secession, had destroyed their status as states. They therefore must be treated as "conquered foreign lands" and reverted to the status of "unorganized territories" before any process of readmission could be entertained (by Congress).

In July 1864, the Wade-Davis bill, named for its sponsors, Senator Benjamin Wade of Ohio and Congressman Henry W. Davis of Maryland, emerged from Congress with three specific conditions for southern readmission: one, it demanded a "majority" of white male citizens participating in the creation of a new government; two, to vote or be a delegate to constitutional conventions, men had to take an "iron-clad" oath (declaring they had never aided the Confederate war effort); and three, all officers above the rank of lieutenant, and all civil officials in the Confederacy,

would be disfranchised and deemed "not a citizen of the United States." The Confederate states were to be defined as "conquered enemies," said Davis, and the process of readmission was to be harsh and slow. Lincoln, ever the adroit politician, pocket-vetoed the bill and issued a conciliatory proclamation of his own announcing that he would not be inflexibly committed to any "one plan" of Reconstruction.

The timing of this exchange came during Grant's bloody campaign in Virginia against Lee. The outcome of the war and Lincoln's reelection were still in doubt. Radical members of his own party, indeed, were organizing a dump-Lincoln campaign for the 1864 election. On August 5, Radical Republicans issued the "Wade-Davis Manifesto" to newspapers, which contained an unprecedented attack on a sitting president by members of his own party. They accused Lincoln of usurpation of presidential powers and disgraceful leniency toward an eventually conquered South. What emerged in 1864–1865 was a clear-cut debate and a potential constitutional crisis. Lincoln saw Reconstruction as a means of weakening the Confederacy and winning the war; the Radicals saw it as a longer-term transformation of the political and racial order of the country.

In early 1865, Congress and Lincoln joined in passing two important measures that recognized slavery's centrality to the war. On Janu-

Thirteenth Amendment and the Freedmen's Bureau

ary 31, with strong administration backing, Congress passed the Thirteenth Amendment, which had two provisions. It abolished involuntary servitude everywhere in the United States and declared that Congress shall have power to enforce this outcome by "appropriate legislation." When the measure passed by 119 to 56, a mere two votes more than the necessary two-thirds, unprecedented rejoicing broke out in Congress. A Republican recorded in his diary: "Members joined in the shouting and kept it up for some minutes. Some embraced one another, others wept like children. I have felt ever since the vote, as if I were in a new country."

Potentially as significant, on March 3, 1865, Congress created the Bureau of Refugees, Freedmen, and Abandoned Lands—the Freedmen's Bureau, an unprecedented agency of social uplift, necessitated by the ravages of the war. Americans had never engaged in federal aid to citizens on such a scale. With thousands of refugees, white and black, displaced in the South, the government continued what private freedmen's aid societies had started as early as 1862. In the mere four years of its existence, the Freedmen's Bureau supplied food and medical services, built several thousand schools and some colleges, negotiated several hundred thousand employment contracts between freedmen and their former masters, and tried to manage confiscated land.

The Bureau would be a controversial aspect of Reconstruction, within the South where whites generally hated it, and within the federal government where politicians divided over its constitutionality. Some Bureau agents were devoted to freedmen's rights, while others were opportunists who exploited the chaos of the postwar South. The war had forced into the open an eternal question of republics: What are the social welfare obligations of the state toward its people, and what do people owe their governments in return? Apart from their conquest and displacement of the eastern Indians, Americans were relatively inexperienced at the Freedmen's Bureau's task—social reform through military occupation.

The Meanings of Freedom

 Black southerners entered into life after slavery with hope and circumspection. A Texas man recalled his father telling him, even before the war was over, "Our forever was going to be spent living among the Southerners, after they got licked." Expecting hostility, freed men and women tried to gain as much as they could from their new circumstances. Often the changes they valued the most were personal—alterations in location, employer, or living arrangements.

For America's former slaves, Reconstruction had one paramount meaning: a chance to explore freedom.

The Feel of Freedom

A southern white woman admitted in her diary that the black people "showed a natural and exultant joy at being free." Former slaves remembered singing far into the night after federal troops, who confirmed rumors of their emancipation, reached their plantations. The slaves on a Texas plantation shouted for joy, their leader proclaiming,

Post-emancipation society in the South brought about the renegotiation of old relationships, as in the scene depicted in Winslow Homer's *A Visit From the Old Mistress* (1876).   (National Gallery of American Art/Art Resource)

"We is free—no more whippings and beatings." A few people gave in to the natural desire to do what had been impossible before. One angry grandmother dropped her hoe and ran to confront her mistress. "I'm free!" she yelled. "Yes, I'm free! Ain't got to work for you no more! You can't put me in your pocket [sell me] now!" Another man recalled that he and others "started on the move," either to search for family members or just to exercise the human right of mobility.

Many freed men and women reacted more cautiously and shrewdly, taking care to test the boundaries of their new condition. "After the war was over," explained one man, "we was afraid to move. Just like terrapins or turtles after emancipation. Just stick our heads out to see how the land lay." As slaves they had learned to expect hostility from white people, and they did not presume it would instantly disappear. Life in freedom might still be a matter of what was allowed, not what was right. "You got to say master?" asked a freedman in Georgia. "Naw," answered his fellows, but "they said it all the same." One sign of this shrewd caution was the way freed people evaluated potential employers. "Most all the Negroes that had good owners stayed with 'em, but the others left. Some of 'em come back and some didn't," explained one man. After considerable wandering in search of better circumstances, a majority of blacks eventually settled as agricultural workers back on their former farms or plantations. But they relocated their houses and did their utmost to control the conditions of their labor.

Former slaves concentrated on improving their daily lives. Throughout the South they devoted themselves to reuniting their families, separated during slavery by sale or hardship, and during the war by dislocation and the emancipation process. The search for family members who had been sold away during slavery was awe inspiring. With only shreds of information to guide them, thousands of freed people embarked on odysseys in search of a husband, wife, child, or parent. By relying on the black community for help and information, and placing ads in black newspapers that continued to appear well into the 1880s, some succeeded in their quest, sometimes almost miraculously. Others trudged through several states and never found loved ones.

Reunion of African American Families

Husbands and wives who had belonged to different masters established homes together for the first time, and parents asserted the right to raise their own children. A mother bristled when her old master claimed a right to whip her children. She informed him that "he warn't goin' to brush none of her chilluns no more." The freed men and women were too much at risk to act recklessly, but, as one man put it, they were tired of punishment and "sure didn't take no more foolishness off of white folks."

Blacks' Search for Independence

Many black people wanted to minimize contact with whites because, as Reverend Garrison Frazier told General Sherman in January 1865, "There is a prejudice against us . . . that will take years to get over." To avoid contact with overbearing whites who were used to supervising them, blacks abandoned the slave quarters and fanned out to distant corners of the land they worked. "After the war my stepfather come," recalled Annie Young, "and got my mother and we moved out in the piney woods." Others described moving "across the creek to [themselves]" or building a "saplin house . . . back in the woods." Some rural dwellers established small all-black settlements that still exist today along the back roads of the South.

Even once-privileged slaves desired such independence and social separation. One man turned down the master's offer of the overseer's house and moved instead to a shack in "Freetown." He also declined to let the former owner grind his grain for free because it "make him feel like a free man to pay for things just like anyone else." One couple, a carriage driver and trusted house servant during slavery, passed up the fine cooking of the "big house" to move "in the colored settlement."

African Americans' Desire for Land

In addition to a fair employer, what freed men and women most wanted was the ownership of land. Land represented their chance to farm for themselves, to enjoy the independence that self-sufficient farmers value. It represented compensation for generations of travail in bondage.

A northern observer noted that slaves freed in the Sea Islands of South Carolina and Georgia made "plain, straight-forward" inquiries as they settled the land set aside for them by Sherman. They wanted to be sure the land "would be theirs after they had improved it." Everywhere, blacks young and old thirsted for homes of their own.

But how much of a chance would whites give to blacks? Most members of both political parties opposed genuine land redistribution to the freedmen. Even northern reformers who with Lincoln's encouragement had administered the Sea Islands during the war showed little sympathy for black aspirations. The former Sea Island slaves wanted to establish small, self-sufficient farms. Northern soldiers, officials, and missionaries of both races brought education and aid to the freedmen but also insisted that they grow cotton. They emphasized profit, cash crops, and the values of competitive capitalism.

"The Yankees preach nothing but cotton, cotton!" complained one Sea Island black. "We wants land," wrote another, but tax officials "make the lots too big, and cut we out." Indeed, the U.S. government sold thousands of acres in the Sea Islands for nonpayment of taxes, but 90 percent of the land went to wealthy investors from the North. At a protest against evictions from a contraband camp in Virginia in 1866, freedman Bayley Wyatt made black desires and claims clear: "We has a right to the land where we are located. For why? I tell you. Our wives, our children, our husbands, has been sold over and over again to purchase the lands we now locates upon; for that reason we have a divine right to the land."

Ex-slaves reached out for valuable things in life that had been denied them. One of these was education. Blacks of all ages hungered for the knowledge in books that had been permitted only to whites. With freedom, they started schools and filled classrooms both day and night. On log seats and dirt floors, freed men and women studied their letters in old almanacs and discarded dictionaries. Young children brought infants to school with them, and adults attended at night or after "the crops were laid by." Many a teacher had "to make herself heard over three other classes reciting in concert" in a small room. The desire to escape slavery's ignorance was so great that, despite their poverty, many blacks paid tuition, typically $1 or $1.50 a month. These small amounts constituted major portions of a person's agricultural wages and added up to more than $1 million by 1870.

The federal government and northern reformers of both races assisted this pursuit of education. In its brief life the Freedmen's Bureau founded over four thousand schools, and idealistic men and women from the North established and staffed others founded by private northern philanthropy. The Yankee schoolmarm—dedicated, selfless, and religious—became an agent of progress in many southern communities. Thus did African Americans seek a break from their pasts through learning. The results included the beginnings of a public school system in each southern

The Black Embrace of Education

African Americans of all ages eagerly pursued the opportunity in freedom to gain an education. This young woman in Mt. Meigs, Alabama, is helping her mother learn to read. (Smithsonian Institute, photo by Rudolf Eickemeyer)

state and the enrollment of over six hundred thousand African Americans in elementary school by 1877.

Blacks and their white allies also saw the need for colleges and universities to train teachers, ministers, and professionals for leadership. The American Missionary Association founded seven colleges, including Fisk and Atlanta Universities, between 1866 and 1869. The Freedmen's Bureau helped to establish Howard University in Washington, D.C., and northern religious groups such as the Methodists, Baptists, and Congregationalists supported dozens of seminaries and teachers' colleges. By the late 1870s black churches had joined in the effort, founding numerous colleges despite limited resources.

During Reconstruction, African American leaders often were highly educated individuals; many of them came from the prewar elite of free people of color. This group had benefited from its association with wealthy whites, many of whom were blood relatives; some planters had given their mulatto children an outstanding education. Francis Cardozo, who held various offices in South Carolina, had attended universities in Scotland and England. P. B. S. Pinchback, who became lieutenant governor of Louisiana, was the son of a planter who had sent him to school in Cincinnati. Both of the two black senators from Mississippi, Blanche K. Bruce and Hiram Revels, possessed privileged educations. Bruce was the son of a planter who had provided tutoring at home; Revels was the son of free North Carolina mulattos who had sent him to Knox College in Illinois. These men and many self-educated former slaves brought to political office their experience as artisans, businessmen, lawyers, teachers, and preachers.

Freed from the restrictions and regulations of slavery, blacks could build their own institutions as they saw fit. The secret churches of slavery came into the open; in countless communities throughout the South, ex-slaves "started a brush arbor." A brush arbor was merely "a sort of . . . shelter with leaves for a roof," but the freed men and women worshiped in it enthusiastically. "Preachin' and

Growth of Black Churches

shouting sometimes lasted all day," they recalled, for the opportunity to worship together freely meant "glorious times."

Within a few years independent branches of the Methodist and Baptist denominations had attracted the great majority of black Christians in the South. By 1877, in South Carolina alone, the African Methodist Episcopal Church had 1,000 ministers, 44,000 members, and its own school of theology, while the A.M.E. Zion Church had 45,000 members. In the rapid growth of churches, some of which became the wealthiest and the most autonomous institutions in black life, the freedpeople demonstrated their most secure claim on freedom as they created enduring communities.

The desire to gain as much independence as possible also shaped the former slaves' economic arrangements. Since most of them lacked money to buy land, they preferred the next best thing: renting the land they worked. But the South had a cash-poor economy with few sources of credit, and few whites would consider renting land to blacks. Most blacks had no means to get cash before the harvest, and thus other alternatives had to be tried.

Rise of the Sharecropping System

Churches became a center of African American life, for social and political purposes as well as for worship. This engraving, which appeared in *Harper's Weekly* in 1874, shows the minister of the First African Baptist Church of Richmond, Virginia, preaching to the congregation from an elevated pulpit.   (The Valentine Museum, Richmond, Virginia)

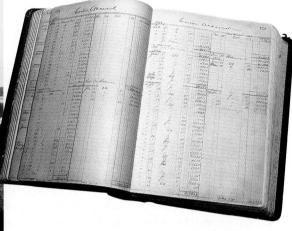

Sharecropping became an oppressive system in the postwar South. At plantation stores like this one, photographed in Mississippi in 1868, merchants recorded in their ledger books debts that few sharecroppers were able to repay. (Recordbook: Smithsonian Institute, Division of Community Life; Plantation store: Amistad Foundation Collection at the Wadsworth Athenaeum, Hartford, Connecticut)

Black farmers and white landowners therefore turned to sharecropping, a system in which farmers kept part of their crop and gave the rest to the landowner while living on his property. The landlord or a merchant "furnished" food and supplies needed before the harvest, and he received payment from the crop. Republican laws gave laborers the first lien, or legal claim, on the crop, enhancing their sense of ownership. Although landowners tried to set the laborers' share at a low level, black farmers had some bargaining power, at least at first. Sharecroppers would hold out, or move and try to switch employers from one year to another.

The sharecropping system, which materialized as early as 1868 in parts of the South, originated as a desirable compromise. It eased landowners' problems with cash and credit, and provided them a permanent, dependent labor force; blacks accepted it because it gave them more freedom from daily supervision. Instead of working under a white overseer, as in slavery, they farmed a plot of land on their own in family groups. But sharecropping later proved to be a disaster. Owners and merchants developed a monopoly of control over the agricultural economy, as sharecroppers found themselves riveted into ever-increasing debt (see pages 563–564).

The fundamental problem, however, was that southern farmers as a whole still concentrated on cotton, a crop with a bright past and a dim future. During the Civil War, India, Brazil, and Egypt had begun to supply cotton to Britain, and the South lost markets as well as income. In freedom, black women, like their white counterparts, often stayed away from the fields. Black families placed greater value on human dignity than on reaching higher levels of production. By 1878 the South had recovered its prewar share of British cotton purchases. But even as southerners grew more cotton, their reward diminished. Cotton prices began a long decline, as world demand fell off.

Overdependence on Cotton

In these circumstances overspecialization in cotton was a mistake, but for most southern farmers there was no alternative. Landowners required sharecroppers to grow the salable cash crop. Thus southern agriculture slipped deeper and deeper into depression. Black sharecroppers struggled under a growing burden of debt that reduced their independence and bound them to landowners and to furnishing merchants almost as oppressively as slavery had bound them to their masters. Many white farmers became debtors, too, and gradually lost their land. This economic transformation took place as the nation struggled to put its political house back in order.

Johnson's Reconstruction Plan

 When Reconstruction began under President Andrew Johnson, many expected his policies to be harsh. Throughout his career in Tennessee he had criticized the wealthy planters and championed the small farmers. When an assassin's bullet thrust Johnson into the presidency, many former slaveowners shared the dismay of a North Carolina woman who wrote, "Think of Andy Johnson [as] the president! What will become of us— 'the aristocrats of the South' as we are termed?" Northern Radicals also had reason to believe that Johnson would deal sternly with the South. When one of them suggested the exile or execution of ten or twelve leading rebels to set an example, Johnson replied, "How are you going to pick out so small a number? . . . Treason is a crime; and crime must be punished."

Like his martyred predecessor, Johnson followed a path in antebellum politics from obscurity to power.

Who Was Andrew Johnson? With no formal education, he became a tailor's apprentice. But from 1829, while in his early twenties, he held nearly every office in Tennessee politics: alderman, state representative, congressman, two terms as governor, and U.S. senator by 1857. Although elected as a southern Democrat, Johnson was the only senator from a seceded state who refused to follow his state out of the Union. Lincoln appointed him war governor of Tennessee in 1862, and hence, his symbolic place on the ticket in the president's bid for reelection in 1864.

Johnson's political beliefs made him look a little like a Republican, but at heart he was an old Jacksonian Democrat. And as they said in the mountainous region of east Tennessee, where Johnson established a reputation as a stump speaker, "Old Andy never went back on his 'raisin." Although a staunch Unionist, he was also an ardent states' rightist. Before the war, Johnson had supported tax-funded public schools and homestead legislation, fashioning himself as a champion of the common man. Although he vehemently opposed secession, Johnson advocated limited government. Above all, when it came to race, Johnson was a thoroughgoing white supremacist. He shared none of the Radicals' expansive conception of federal power. Johnson accepted emancipation as a result of the war, but he did not favor black civil and political rights. His philosophy toward Reconstruction may be summed up in the slogan he adopted: "The Constitution as it is, and the Union as it was."

Through 1865 Johnson alone controlled Reconstruction policy, for Congress recessed shortly before he became president and did not reconvene until December. In the following eight months, Johnson put into operation his own plan, forming new state governments in the South by using his power to grant pardons. Johnson followed Lincoln's leniency by extending even easier terms to southerners. But which southerners would be allowed to vote?

Johnson's Leniency and Racial Views

Johnson held that black suffrage could never be imposed on a southern state by the federal government. His racism put him on a collision course with the Radicals. Johnson held what one politician called "unconquerable prejudices against the African race." In perhaps the most blatantly racist official statement ever delivered by an American president, Johnson declared in his annual message of 1867 that blacks possessed less "capacity for government than any other race of people. No independent government of any form has ever been successful in their hands; . . . wherever they have been left to their own devices they have shown a constant tendency to relapse into barbarism."

This racial conservatism had an enduring effect on Johnson's policies. Where whites were concerned, however, Johnson seemed to be pursuing changes in class relations. He proposed rules that would keep the wealthy planter class at least temporarily out of power. White southerners were required to swear an oath of loyalty as a condition of gaining amnesty or pardon, but Johnson barred several categories of people from taking the oath: former federal officials, high-ranking Confederate officers, and political leaders or graduates of West Point or Annapolis who had violated their oaths to support the United States by aiding the Confederacy. To this list Johnson added another important group: all southerners who aided the rebellion and whose taxable property was worth more than $20,000. These individuals had to apply personally to the president for pardon and restoration of their political rights.

Thus it appeared that the leadership class of the Old South would be removed from power, for virtually all the rich and powerful whites of prewar days needed Johnson's special pardon. The president, it seemed, meant to take revenge on the haughty

Johnson's Pardon Policy

aristocrats and thereby promote a new leadership of deserving yeomen.

Johnson appointed provisional governors who began the Reconstruction process by calling constitutional conventions. The delegates chosen for these conventions had to draft new constitutions that eliminated slavery and invalidated secession. After ratification of these constitutions, new governments could be elected, and the states would be restored to the Union with full congressional representation. But only those southerners who had taken the oath of amnesty and been eligible to vote on the day the state seceded could participate in this process. Thus unpardoned whites and former slaves were not eligible.

If Johnson intended to strip the old elite of its power, he did not hold to his plan. The old white leadership proved resilient and influential; prominent Confederates (a few with pardons but many without) won elections and turned up in various appointive offices. Then, surprisingly, Johnson helped to subvert his own plan: he started pardoning aristocrats and leading rebels who should not have been in office. He hired additional clerks to write out the necessary documents and then began to issue pardons to large categories of people. By September 1865 hundreds were being issued in a single day. These pardons, plus the rapid return of planters' abandoned lands, restored the old elite to power and quickly gave Johnson the image as the South's champion. He further gained southern loyalty with his hostility to the Freedmen's Bureau.

Why did Johnson allow the planters to regain power? Perhaps vanity betrayed his judgment. Too long an isolated outsider, Johnson may have succumbed to the attention and flattery of the pardon seekers. He was also determined upon a rapid Reconstruction in order to deny the Radicals the opportunity for the more thorough racial and political changes they desired in the South. And, given Johnson's need for southern support in the 1866 elections, he decided to endorse the new governments and declare Reconstruction complete only eight months after Appomattox. Thus in December 1865 many Confederate congressmen traveled to Washington to claim seats in the U.S. Congress. Even Alexander Stephens, vice president of the Confederacy, returned to Capitol Hill as a senator-elect.

The election of such prominent rebels troubled many northerners. So did other results of Johnson's program. Some of the state conventions were slow to repudiate secession; others admitted only grudgingly that slavery was dead. Two refused to take any action

Combative and inflexible, President Andrew Johnson contributed greatly to the failure of his own Reconstruction program.   (Library of Congress)

to repudiate the large Confederate debt, which northerners felt should not be paid. Even Johnson admitted that these acts showed "something like defiance, which is all out of place at this time."

Furthermore, to define the status of freed men and women and control their labor, some legislatures merely revised large sections of the slave codes by substituting the word *freedmen* for *slaves*. The new black codes compelled the former slaves, now supposedly free, to carry passes, observe a curfew, live in housing provided by a landowner, and give up hope of entering many desirable occupations. Stiff vagrancy laws and restrictive labor contracts bound supposedly free laborers to plantations, and "anti-enticement" laws punished anyone who tried to lure these workers to other employment. State-supported schools and orphanages excluded blacks entirely.

Black Codes

It seemed to northerners that the South was intent on returning African Americans to servility and that

Johnson's Reconstruction policy held no one responsible for the terrible war. But memories of the war—not yet a year over—were still raw, and would dominate political behavior for several elections to come. Thus the Republican majority in Congress decided to call a halt to the results of Johnson's plan. On reconvening, the House and Senate considered the credentials of the newly elected southern representatives and decided not to admit them. Instead, they bluntly challenged the president's authority and established a joint committee to study and investigate a new direction for Reconstruction.

The Congressional Reconstruction Plan

 Northern congressmen were hardly unified, but they did not doubt their right to shape Reconstruction policy. The Constitution mentioned neither secession nor reunion, but it gave Congress the primary role in the admission of states. Moreover, the Constitution declared that the United States shall guarantee to each state a republican form of government. This provision, legislators believed, gave them the authority to devise policies for Reconstruction.

They soon found that other constitutional questions affected their policies. What, for example, had rebellion done to the relationship between southern states and the Union? Lincoln had always insisted that states could not secede—they had engaged in an "insurrection"—and that the Union remained intact. Not even Andrew Johnson, however, accepted the southern position that state governments of the Confederacy could simply reenter the nation. Johnson argued that the Union had endured, though individuals had erred—thus the use of his power to grant or withhold pardons. Congressmen who favored vigorous Reconstruction measures argued that the war had broken the Union, and that the South was subject to the victor's will. Moderate congressmen held that the states had forfeited their rights through rebellion and thus had come under congressional supervision.

These theories mirrored the diversity of Congress itself. Northern Democrats, weakened by the war most of them had opposed in its final year, denounced any idea of racial equality and supported Johnson's policies. Conservative Republicans, despite their party loyalty, favored a limited federal role in Reconstruction. The Radical Republicans, led by

The Radicals

Thaddeus Stevens, Charles Sumner, and George Julian, wanted to transform the South. Although they were a minority within their party, they had the advantage of a clearly defined goal. They believed it was essential to democratize the South, establish public education, and ensure the rights of freed people. They favored black suffrage, often supported land confiscation and redistribution, and were willing to exclude the South from the Union for several years if necessary to achieve their goals. Born of the war and its outcome, the Radicals brought a new civic vision to American life; they wanted to create an activist federal government and the beginnings of racial equality. A large group of moderate Republicans did not want to go as far as the Radicals but believed some reworking of Johnson's policies was necessary.

One overwhelming political reality faced all four groups: the 1866 elections were approaching in the fall. Having questioned Johnson's program, Congress needed to develop an alternative plan and avoid going before the voters empty-handed. Ironically, Johnson and the Democrats sabotaged the possibility of a conservative coalition. They refused to cooperate with conservative or moderate Republicans and insisted that Reconstruction was over, that the new state governments were legitimate, and that southern representatives should be admitted to Congress. To devise a Republican program, conservative and moderate elements in the party had to work with the Radicals, whose influence grew in proportion to Johnson's intransigence.

Trying to work with Johnson, Republicans believed a compromise had been reached in the spring of 1866. Under its terms Johnson would agree to two modifications of his program: extension of the life of the Freedmen's Bureau for another year and passage of a civil rights bill to counteract the black codes. This bill would force southern courts to practice equality before the law by allowing federal judges to remove from state courts cases in which blacks were treated unfairly. Its provisions applied to public, not private, acts of discrimination. The civil rights bill of 1866 was the first statutory definition of the rights of American citizens.

Congress Wrests Control from Johnson

Johnson destroyed the compromise, however, by vetoing both bills (they later became law when Congress overrode the president's veto). Denouncing any change in his program, the president condemned Congress's action and revealed his own racism. Because the civil rights bill defined U.S. citizens as native-born

How do historians know...

that the Radical Republican vision of Reconstruction had a popular base and was not solely the creation of a few ambitious politicians? How do we understand and evaluate the contending wills and bitterness that existed in North and South as Reconstruction policies developed? Moreover, why did the Republicans take back control of the Reconstruction process from President Andrew Johnson in late 1865 and throughout 1866? This excerpt from a letter by Brigadier General James S. Brisbin on December 29, 1865, to Congressman Thaddeus Stevens (the principal architect of Radical Reconstruction) indicates both practical and philosophical reasons why many northerners supported a harsher plan for bringing the South back into the Union than Johnson had put in place. Brisbin had just read Stevens's speech on Reconstruction in Congress, in which the congressman had called for a halt to the seating of any representatives elected by the "Johnson governments" and proposed a lengthy investigation of southern conditions. Brisbin speaks as soldier and citizen, fearing that "the fruits of our toils and battles and sieges were to be bartered away and treason made as honorable as loyalty." Brisbin, who was commanding occupation troops in Arkansas, encouraged Stevens in his effort to slow down Reconstruction. "These people are not loyal," he writes; "they are only conquered." The letter anticipates much of what soon occurred in the bitter struggle to bind up sectional hatreds and respond to the profound challenges of emancipation and reunion. If Stevens needed any encouragement or justification in leading Congress in taking control of Reconstruction, he received it in this letter. This photograph of Congressman Thaddeus Stevens was taken during the early years of Reconstruction. (Photo: National Archives)

After four years of war during which we suffered all that men could suffer and after finally beating the rebles in battle we began to fear that the fruits of our toils our battles and seiges were to be bartered away and treason made as honorable as loyalty. For the assurance that rebles whose hands red with the blood of our brothers, are not just yet to be allowed to set themselves up to rule over us, thousands of loyal soldiers will thank you. . . .

These people are not loyal; they are only conquered, I tell you there is not as much loyalty in the South to day as there was the day Lee surrendered to Grant. The moment they lost their cause in the field they set about to gain by politics what they had failed to obtain by force of arms. . . .

My God can any sane man look at the men who fill their so called state Legislatures and then say the states are loyal. . . .

The bones of our dead brothers, falling in the great struggle lie buried in the soil of every Southern state and at least until they have returned to dust and their graves grown green we should not shake the bloody hands of the men who robbed them of life. The immodest haste (and it should be called brazen impudence) of the Southern people in attempting to get their delegations into Congress should be sufficient to arouse the suspicions of every Northern man that they were not sincere. . . .

These people are most anxious to renew their practical relations with the Federal Govt because . . . then they can go to work in earnest in their state Legislatures to pass vagrant laws and reduce the blacks to a slavery worse than that from which they have just escaped. Loyal men will not be elected to office in the South until the blacks are allowed to vote and I hope you will not allow any Southern member of his seat until he comes there elected by a majority of all the people of his District. I am no politician but what I see I know and I tell you you are right in what you said on re-construction. . . .

In 1866, as Congress reviewed the progress of Reconstruction, news from the South had a considerable impact. Violence against black people, like the riot in Memphis depicted here, helped convince northern legislators that they had to modify President Johnson's policies. (Library of Congress)

persons who were taxed, Johnson claimed it discriminated against "large numbers of intelligent, worthy, and patriotic foreigners . . . in favor of the negro." The bill, he said, operated "in favor of the colored and against the white race."

All hope of presidential-congressional cooperation was now dead. In 1866 newspapers reported daily violations of blacks' rights in the South and carried alarming accounts of antiblack violence—notably in Memphis and New Orleans, where police aided brutal mobs in their attacks. In Memphis forty blacks were killed and twelve schools burned by white mobs, and in New Orleans the toll was thirty-four African Americans dead and two hundred wounded. Such violence convinced Republicans, and the northern public, that more needed to be done. A new Republican plan took the form of a proposed amendment to the Constitution, forged out of a compromise between radical and conservative elements of the party. The Fourteenth Amendment, passed and sent to the states in June 1866, was Congress's alternative to Johnson's program of Reconstruction.

Of the four parts of the Fourteenth Amendment, the first would have the greatest legal significance in later years. It conferred citizenship on the freedmen

The Fourteenth Amendment

and prohibited states from abridging their constitutional "privileges and immunities" (see the Constitution in this book's Appendix). It also barred any state from taking a person's life, liberty, or property "without due process of law" and from denying "equal protection of the laws." These resounding phrases became powerful guarantees of African Americans' civil rights—indeed, of the rights of all citizens—in the twentieth century.

Nearly universal agreement emerged among Republicans on the amendment's second and third provisions. The second declared the Confederate debt null and void and guaranteed the war debt of the United States. Northerners rejected the notion of paying taxes to reimburse those who had financed a rebellion, and business groups agreed on the necessity of upholding the credit of the U.S. government. The third provision barred Confederate leaders from holding state and federal office. Only Congress, by a two-thirds vote of each house, could remove the penalty. The amendment thus guaranteed a degree of punishment for the leaders of the Confederacy.

The fourth part of the amendment dealt with representation and embodied the compromises that produced the document. Northerners disagreed about whether black citizens should have the right to vote. As a citizen of Indiana wrote to a southern relative, there was strong feeling in favor of "humane and liberal laws for the government and protection of the colored population." But there was prejudice, too. "Although there is a great deal [of] profession among us for the relief of the darkey yet I think much of it is far from being sincere. I guess we want to compel you to do right by them while we are not willing ourselves to do so." Those arched words are indicative of not only how revolutionary Reconstruction had become, but also how far the public will lagged behind the enactments that became new constitutional cornerstones.

Republican congressmen shied away from confronting this ambivalence, but political reality required them to do something. Emancipation made every former slave a full rather than three-fifths of a person, which would increase southern representation. Thus the postwar South stood to gain power in Congress, and if white southerners did not allow blacks to vote, former secessionists would derive the political benefit from emancipation. That was more irony than most northerners could bear. So Republicans determined that if a southern state did not grant black men the vote, their representation would be reduced proportionally. If they did enfranchise black men, their representation would be increased proportionally. This compromise avoided a direct enactment of black suffrage, but would deliver future black voters to the Republican Party.

The Fourteenth Amendment paved the way for black male suffrage but ignored female citizens, black and white. For this reason it provoked a strong reaction from the women's rights movement. Advocates of women's equality had worked with abolitionists for decades, often subordinating their cause to that of the slaves. During the drafting of the Fourteenth Amendment, however, female activists demanded to be heard. When legislators defined women as nonvoting citizens, prominent leaders such as Elizabeth Cady Stanton and Susan B. Anthony decided that it was time to end their alliance with abolitionists and fight more determinedly for themselves. Thus the amendment infused new life into the women's rights movement and caused considerable strife among old allies. Many male former abolitionists, white and black, were willing to delay the day of woman suffrage in favor of securing freed men the right to vote in the South.

In 1866, however, the major question in Reconstruction politics was how the public would respond to the congressional initiative. Johnson did his best to

The South's and Johnson's Defiance, 1866

block the Fourteenth Amendment in both North and South. Condemning Congress for its refusal to seat southern representatives, the president urged state legislatures in the South to vote against ratification. Every southern legislature except Tennessee's rejected the amendment by a wide margin. In three other states the amendment received no support at all.

To present his case to northerners, Johnson organized a National Union Convention and took to the stump himself. In an age when active personal campaigning was rare for a president, Johnson boarded a special train for a "swing around the circle" that carried his message deep into the Northeast, the Midwest, and then back to Washington. In city after city, he criticized the Republicans in a ranting, undignified style. Increasingly, audiences rejected his views and hooted and jeered at him. In this whistle-stop tour, Johnson began to hand out American flags with thirty-six rather than twenty-five stars, declaring that the Union was already restored. At many towns he likened himself to a "persecuted" Jesus who might now be martyred "upon the cross" for his magnanimity toward the South. And, repeatedly, he labeled the Radicals "traitors" for their efforts to take over Reconstruction. Johnson was shouted down and forced from the stage in Pittsburgh.

The elections of 1866 were a resounding victory for Republicans in Congress. Radicals and moderates whom Johnson had denounced won reelection by large margins, and the Republican majority grew to two-thirds of both houses of Congress. The North had spoken clearly: Johnson's policies were prematurely giving the advantage to rebels and traitors. Although the Radicals may have been out ahead of public opinion, most northerners feared for "the future peace and safety of the Union" if Johnson's approach to Reconstruction prevailed. Thus Republican congressional leaders won a mandate to pursue their Reconstruction plan.

But, thanks to Johnson and southern intransigence, that plan had reached an impasse. Nothing could be accomplished as long as the "Johnson governments" existed and the southern electorate remained exclusively white. Republicans resolved to form new state governments in the South and enfranchise the freedmen. The unavoidable logic of the situation forced the majority to accept the Radical plan. (See Table 16.1.)

After some embittered debate in which Republicans and the remaining Democrats in Congress argued

Table 16.1   Plans for Reconstruction Compared

	Johnson's Plan	Radicals' Plan	Fourteenth Amendment	Reconstruction Act of 1867
Voting	Whites only; high-ranking Confederate leaders must seek pardons	Give vote to black males	Southern whites may decide but can lose representation if they deny black suffrage	Black men gain vote; whites barred from office by Fourteenth Amendment cannot vote while new state governments are being formed
Officeholding	Many prominent Confederates regain power	Only loyal white and black males eligible	Confederate leaders barred until Congress votes amnesty	Fourteenth Amendment in effect
Time out of Union	Brief	Several years; until South is thoroughly democratized	Brief	3–5 years after war
Other change in southern society	Little; gain of power by yeomen not realized; emancipation grudgingly accepted, but no black civil or political rights	Expand public education; confiscate land and provide farms for freedmen; expansion of activist federal government	Probably slight, depending on enforcement	Considerable, depending on action of new state governments

The Reconstruction Acts of 1867–1868

over the meaning and memory of the Civil War itself, the First Reconstruction Act passed in March 1867. This plan, under which the southern states were actually readmitted to the Union, incorporated only a part of the Radical program. Union generals, commanding small garrisons of troops and charged with supervising all elections, assumed control in five military districts in the South (see Map 16.1). Confederate leaders designated in the Fourteenth Amendment were barred from voting until new state constitutions were ratified. The act guaranteed freedmen the right to vote in elections for state constitutional conventions and in subsequent elections. In addition, each southern state was required to ratify the Fourteenth Amendment, to ratify its new constitution by majority vote, and to submit it to Congress for approval.

Thus African Americans gained an opportunity to fight for a better life through the political process, and ex-Confederates were given what they interpreted as a bitter pill to swallow in order to return to the Union. The Second, Third, and Fourth Reconstruction Acts, passed between March 1867 and March 1868, provided for the details of operation for voter registration boards, the adoption of constitutions, and the administration of "good faith" oaths on the part of white southerners.

In the words of one historian, the Radicals succeeded in "clipping Johnson's wings." But they had hoped Congress could do much more. Thaddeus Stevens, for example, argued that economic opportunity was essential to the freedmen. "If we do not furnish them with homesteads from forfeited and rebel property," Stevens declared, "and hedge them around with protective laws . . . we had better left them in bondage." Stevens therefore drew up a plan for extensive confiscation and redistribution of land. Only one-tenth of the land affected by his plan was earmarked for freedmen, in 40-acre plots. The rest was to be sold to generate money for Union veterans' pensions, compensation to loyal southerners for damaged property, and payment of the federal debt.

The Failure of Land Redistribution

By these means Stevens hoped to win support for a basically unpopular measure. But he failed, and in general the Radicals were not able to generate public support. Northerners were accustomed to a limited role for government, and the business community staunchly opposed any interference with private property rights, even for former Confederates. Thus black

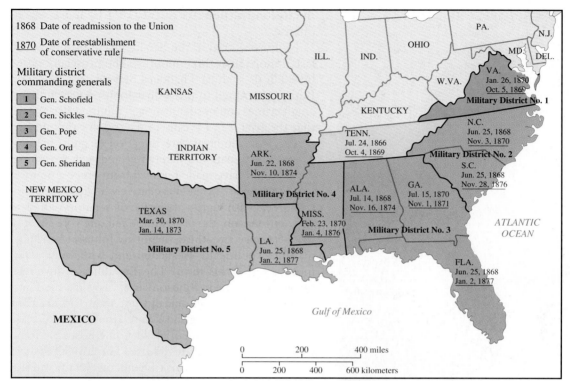

Map 16.1 **The Reconstruction** This map shows the five military districts established when Congress passed the Reconstruction Act of 1867. As the dates within each state indicate, conservative Democratic forces quickly regained control of government in four southern states. So-called Radical Reconstruction was curtailed in most of the others as factions within the weakened Republican Party began to cooperate with conservative Democrats.

farmers were forced to seek work in a hostile environment in which landowners opposed their acquisition of land, even as renters.

Congress's role as the architect of Reconstruction was not quite over, for its quarrels with Andrew Johnson were growing more bitter. To

Constitutional Crisis

restrict Johnson's influence and safeguard its plan, Congress passed a number of controversial laws. First, it set the date for its own reconvening—an unprecedented act, for the president traditionally summoned legislators to Washington. Then it limited Johnson's power over the army by requiring the president to issue military orders through the General of the Army, Ulysses S. Grant, who could not be dismissed without the Senate's consent. Finally, Congress passed the Tenure of Office Act, which gave the Senate power to approve changes in the president's cabinet. Designed to protect Secretary of War Stanton, who sympathized with the Radicals, this law violated the tradition that a president controlled appointments to his own cabinet.

All of these measures, as well as each of the Reconstruction Acts, were passed by a two-thirds override of presidential vetoes. The situation led some to believe that the federal government had reached a stage of "congressional tyranny," and others to conclude that Johnson had become an obstacle to the legitimate will of the people in reconstructing the nation on a just and permanent basis.

Johnson took several belligerent steps of his own. He issued orders to military commanders in the South limiting their powers and increasing the powers of the civil governments he had created in 1865. Then he removed military officers who were conscientiously enforcing Congress's new law, preferring commanders who allowed disqualified Confederates to vote. Finally, he tried to remove Secretary of War Stanton. With that attempt the confrontation reached its climax.

Impeachment is a political procedure provided for in the Constitution. It is a remedy for crimes or serious abuses of power by presidents, federal judges, and other high officials in the government. Those who are impeached (judged or politically indicted) in the

Thomas Waterman Wood, who had painted portraits of society figures in Nashville before the war, sensed the importance of Congress's decision in 1867 to enfranchise the freedmen. This oil painting, one of a series on suffrage, emphasizes the significance of the ballot for the black voter.   (Cheekwood Museum of Art, Nashville, Tennessee)

Impeachment of President Johnson

House are then tried in the Senate. Historically, this power has generally not been used as a means to investigate and judge the private lives of presidents, although in recent times it was used in this manner in the case of President Bill Clinton.

Twice in 1867, the House Judiciary Committee had considered impeachment of Johnson, rejecting the idea once and then recommending it by only a 5-to-4 vote. That recommendation was decisively defeated by the House. After Johnson tried to remove Stanton, however, a third attempt to impeach the president carried easily. The indictment concentrated on his violation of the Tenure of Office Act, though modern scholars regard his efforts to impede enforcement of the Reconstruction Act of 1867 as a far more serious offense.

Johnson's trial in the Senate began promptly and lasted more than three months. The prosecution, led by Radicals such as Thaddeus Stevens and Benjamin Butler, attempted to prove that Johnson was guilty of "high crimes and misdemeanors." But they also argued that the trial was a means to judge Johnson's performance, not a judicial determination of guilt or innocence. The Senate ultimately rejected such reasoning, which could have made removal from office a political weapon against any chief executive who disagreed with Congress. Although a majority of senators voted to convict Johnson, the prosecution fell one vote short of the necessary two-thirds majority. Johnson remained in office, politically weakened and with only a few months left in his term. The Republicans, in effect, managed the vote in Johnson's trial; they had their eyes on the 1868 election and did not want to hurt their prospects of regaining the White House.

Election of 1868

In the 1868 presidential election Ulysses S. Grant, running as a Republican, defeated Horatio Seymour, a New York Democrat. Grant was not a Radical, but his platform supported congressional Reconstruction and endorsed black suffrage in the South. (Significantly, Republicans stopped short of endorsing it in the North.) The Democrats, meanwhile, vigorously denounced Reconstruction and thus renewed the sectional conflict. Indeed, in the 1868 election, the Democrats conducted the most openly white supremacist campaign to that time in American history. Both sides waved the "bloody shirt," accusing each other as the villains of the war's sacrifices. By associating themselves with rebellion and with Johnson's repudiated program, the Democrats went down to defeat in all but eight states, though the popular vote was fairly close. Participating in their first presidential election ever on a wide scale, blacks decisively voted en masse for General Grant.

In office Grant acted as an administrator of Reconstruction but not as its enthusiastic advocate. He vacillated in his dealings with the southern states, sometimes defending Republican regimes and sometimes currying favor with Democrats. On occasion Grant called out federal troops to stop violence or enforce acts of Congress. But he never imposed a true military occupation on the South. Rapid demobilization had reduced a federal army of more than 1 million to 57,000 within a year of the surrender at Appomattox. Thereafter the number of troops in the South continued to fall, until in 1874 there were only 4,000

A Republican Party brass band in action during the 1868 election campaign in Baton Rouge, Louisiana. The Union regimental colors and soldier caps demonstrate the strong federal presence in the South at this pivotal moment in radical Reconstruction. (Andrew D. Lytle Collection, Louisiana and Lower Mississippi Valley Collections, LSU Libraries, Louisiana State University, Baton Rouge, La.)

in the southern states outside Texas. Throughout Reconstruction, the strongest federal units were in Texas and the West, fighting Indians, not white southerners. The later legend of "military rule," so important to southern claims of victimization during Reconstruction, was steeped in myth.

In 1869, in an effort to write democratic principles into the Constitution, the Radicals passed the Fifteenth

Fifteenth Amendment

Amendment. This measure forbade states to deny the right to vote "on account of race, color, or previous condition of servitude." Such wording did not guarantee the right to vote. It deliberately left states free to restrict suffrage on other grounds so that northern states could continue to deny suffrage to women and certain groups of men—Chinese immigrants, illiterates, and those too poor to pay poll taxes.

Ironically, the votes of four uncooperative southern states—compelled by Congress to approve the amendment as an added condition to rejoining the Union—proved necessary to impose even this language on parts of the North. Although several states outside the South refused to ratify, three-fourths of the states approved the measure, and the Fifteenth Amendment became law in 1870. It too had been a political compromise, and though African Americans rejoiced all across the land at its enactment, it left open the possi-

bility for states to create countless qualification tests to obstruct voting in the future.

With passage of the Fifteenth Amendment, many Americans, especially supportive northerners, considered Reconstruction essentially completed. "Let us have done with Reconstruction," pleaded the *New York Tribune* in April 1870. "The country is tired and sick of it. . . . Let us have Peace!" But some northerners, like radical abolitionist Wendell Phillips, worried. "Our day," he warned, "is fast slipping away. Once let public thought float off from the great issue of the war, and it will take . . . more than a generation to bring it back again."

Reconstruction Politics in the South

From the start, Reconstruction encountered the resistance of white southerners. In the black codes and in private attitudes, many whites stubbornly opposed emancipation, and the former planter class proved especially unbending. In 1866 a Georgia newspaper frankly observed that "most of the white citizens believe that the institution of slavery was right, and . . . they will believe that the condition, which comes nearest to slavery, that can now be established will be the best."

Thomas Nast, in this 1868 cartoon, pictured the combination of forces that threatened the success of Reconstruction: southern opposition and the greed, partisanship, and racism of northern interests. (Library of Congress)

Fearing loss of control over their slaves, some planters attempted to postpone freedom by denying or misrepresenting events. Former slaves

White Resistance

reported that their owners "didn't tell them it was freedom" or "wouldn't let [them] go." Agents of the Freedmen's Bureau reported that "the old system of slavery [is] working with even more rigor than formerly at a few miles distant from any point where U.S. troops are stationed." To hold onto their workers, some landowners claimed control over black children and used guardianship and apprentice laws to bind black families to the plantation.

Whites also blocked blacks from acquiring land. A few planters divided up plots among their slaves, but most condemned the idea of making blacks landowners. A Georgia woman whose family was known for its support of religious education for slaves was outraged that two property owners planned to "rent their lands

to the Negroes!" Such action was, she declared, "injurious to the best interest of the community."

Adamant resistance by propertied whites soon manifested itself in other ways, including violence. In one North Carolina town a local magistrate clubbed a black man on a public street, and bands of "Regulators" terrorized blacks in parts of that state and in Kentucky. Such incidents were predictable in a defeated society in which many planters believed, as a South Carolinian put it, that blacks "can't be governed except with the whip."

After President Johnson encouraged the South to resist congressional Reconstruction, white conservatives worked hard to capture the new state governments. Many whites also boycotted the polls in an attempt to defeat Congress's plans; by sitting out the elections, whites might block the new constitutions, which had to be approved by a majority of registered voters. This tactic was tried in North Carolina and succeeded in Alabama, forcing Congress to base ratification of the Fourteenth Amendment and of new state constitutions on a majority of "votes cast" (the provision of the Fourth Reconstruction Act).

Very few black men stayed away from the polls. Enthusiastically and hopefully, they voted Republican.

Black Voters and Emergence of a Southern Republican Party

Most agreed with one man who felt he should "stick to the end with the party that freed me." Illiteracy did not prohibit blacks (or uneducated whites) from making intelligent choices. Although Mississippi's William Henry could read only "a little," he testified that he and his friends

had no difficulty selecting the Republican ballot. "We stood around and watched," he explained. "We saw D. Sledge vote; he owned half the county. We knowed he voted Democratic so we voted the other ticket so it would be Republican." Women, who could not vote, encouraged their husbands and sons, and preachers exhorted their congregations to use the franchise. With such group spirit, zeal for voting spread through the entire black community.

Thanks to a large black turnout and the restrictions on prominent Confederates, a new southern Republican Party came to power in the constitutional conventions of 1868–1870. Republican delegates consisted of a sizable contingent of blacks (265 out of the total of just over 1,000 delegates throughout the South), some northerners who had moved to the South, and native southern whites who favored change. Together these Republicans brought the South into line with progressive reforms adopted earlier in the rest of the nation. The new constitutions were more democratic. They eliminated property qualifications for voting and holding office, and they turned many appointed offices into elective posts. They provided for public schools and institutions to care for the mentally ill, the blind, the deaf, the destitute, and the orphaned.

The conventions broadened women's rights in property holding and divorce. Usually, the goal was not to make women equal with men but to provide relief to thousands of suffering debtors. In families left poverty-stricken by the war and weighed down by debt, it was usually the husband who had contracted the debts. Thus giving women legal control over their own property provided some protection to their families. The goal of some delegates, however, was to elevate women. Blacks in particular called for laws to provide for woman suffrage, but they were ignored by their white colleagues.

Under these new constitutions the southern states elected Republican-controlled governments. For the

Triumph of Republican Governments

first time, the ranks of state legislators in 1868 included some black southerners. It remained to be seen now how much social change these new governments would bring about. Contrary to what white southerners would later claim, the Republican state governments did not disfranchise ex-Confederates as a group. The vexing questions of land reform and the assurance of racial equality all but overwhelmed the "radical" governments.

These new biracial regimes appreciated the realities of power and the depth of racial enmity. In most states, whites were in the majority and former slave-owners controlled the best land and other sources of economic power. James Lynch, a leading black politician from Mississippi, explained why African Americans shunned the "folly" of disfranchisement. Unlike northerners who "can leave when it becomes too uncomfortable," landless former slaves "must be in friendly relations with the great body of the whites in the state. Otherwise . . . peace can be maintained only by a standing army." Despised and lacking economic or social power, southern Republicans strove for acceptance and legitimacy.

Blacks also believed in the principle of universal suffrage and the Christian goal of reconciliation. Far from being vindictive toward the race that had enslaved them, they treated leading rebels with generosity and appealed to white southerners to adopt a spirit of fairness and cooperation. In this way the South's Republican Party condemned itself to defeat if white

voters would not cooperate. Within a few years Republicans were reduced to the embarrassment of making futile appeals to whites while ignoring the claims of their strongest supporters, blacks. But for a time both Republicans and their opponents, who called themselves Conservatives or Democrats, moved to the center and appealed for support from a broad range of groups. Some propertied whites accepted congressional Reconstruction as a reality and declared themselves willing to compete under the new rules. All sides found an area of agreement in economic policies.

Reflecting northern ideals and southern necessity, the Reconstruction governments enthusiastically pro-

Industrialization

moted industry. Confederates had seen how industry aided the North during the war. Accordingly, Reconstruction legislatures encouraged investment with loans, subsidies, and exemptions from taxation for periods up to ten years. The southern railroad system was rebuilt and expanded, and coal and iron mining made possible Birmingham's steel plants. Between 1860 and 1880, the number of manufacturing establishments in the South nearly doubled.

This emphasis on big business, however, produced higher state debts and taxes, drew money away from schools and other programs, and multiplied possibilities for corruption. It also locked Republicans into a conservative strategy. In courting elite whites who never joined the Republican Party, Republicans lost the opportunity of building support among poorer whites.

Policies appealing to African American voters never went beyond equality before the law. In fact, the

Republican Policies on Racial Equality

whites who controlled the southern Republican Party were reluctant to allow blacks a share of offices proportionate to their electoral strength. Aware of their weakness, black leaders did not push very far for revolutionary economic or social change. In every southern state, they led efforts to establish public schools, although they did not press for integrated facilities. In 1870 South Carolina passed the first comprehensive school law in the South. By 1875, 50 percent of black school-age children in that state were enrolled in school, and approximately one-third of the three thousand teachers were black.

Some African American politicians did fight for civil rights and integration. Most were mulattos from cities such as New Orleans or Mobile, where large populations of light-skinned free blacks had existed before the war. Their experience in such communities

One notable success in Reconstruction efforts to stimulate industry was Birmingham, Alabama. Here workers cast molten iron into blocks called pigs.   (Birmingham Public Library)

had made them sensitive to issues of status, and they spoke out for open and equal public accommodations. Laws requiring equal accommodations won passage throughout the Deep South, but they often went unenforced or required an injured party to bring expensive legal action for enforcement.

Economic progress was uppermost in the minds of most freed people and black representatives from rural districts. Black southerners needed land, but only a few promoted confiscation. In fact, much land did fall into state hands for nonpayment of taxes and was offered for sale in small lots. But most freedmen had too little cash to bid against investors or speculators, and few acquired land in this way. South Carolina established a land commission, but it could help only those with money to buy. Any widespread redistribution of land had to arise from Congress, which never supported such action. The lack of genuine land redistribution remained the significant lost opportunity of Reconstruction.

Within a few years, as centrists in both parties met with failure, white hostility to congressional Reconstruction began to dominate. Some conservatives had always desired to fight Reconstruction through pressure and racist propaganda. They put

The Myth of "Negro Rule"

economic and social pressure on blacks: one black Republican reported that "my neighbors will not employ me, nor sell me a farthing's worth of anything." Charging that the South had been turned over to ignorant blacks, conservatives deplored "black domination," which became a rallying cry for a return to white supremacy.

Such attacks were inflammatory propaganda, and part of the growing myth of "Negro rule," which would serve as a central theme in battles over the memory of Reconstruction. African Americans participated in politics but hardly dominated or controlled events. They were a majority in only two out of ten state constitutional writing conventions (transplanted northerners were a majority in one). In the state legislatures, only in the lower house in South Carolina did blacks ever constitute a majority; among officeholders, their numbers generally were far fewer than their proportion in the population. Sixteen blacks won seats in Congress before Reconstruction was over, but none was ever elected governor. Only eighteen served in a high state office such as lieutenant governor, treasurer, superintendent of education, or secretary of state. In all, some four hundred blacks served in political office during the Reconstruction era. Although they never dominated the process, they established a rich tradition of government service and civic activism. Elected officials, such as Robert Smalls in South Carolina, labored tirelessly for cheaper land prices, better healthcare, access to schools, and the enforcement of civil rights for their people. The black politicians of Reconstruction are lost in the mists, the forgotten heroes of this seedtime of America's long civil rights movement.

Conservatives also assailed the allies of black Republicans. Their propaganda denounced whites from the North as "carpetbaggers," greedy crooks planning to pour stolen tax revenues into their sturdy luggage made of carpet material. Immigrants from the North, who held the largest share of Republican offices, were all tarred with this brush.

Carpetbaggers and Scalawags

In fact, most northerners who settled in the South had come seeking business opportunities or a warmer climate and never entered politics. Those who did enter politics generally wanted to democratize the South and to introduce northern ways, such as industry, public education, and the spirit of enterprise. Carpetbaggers' ideals were tested by hard times and ostracism by white southerners.

In addition to tagging northern interlopers as carpetbaggers, Conservatives invented the term *scalawag* to discredit any native white southerner who cooperated with the Republicans. A substantial number of southerners did so, including some wealthy and prominent men. Most scalawags, however, were yeoman farmers, men from mountain areas and nonslaveholding districts who had been restive under the Confederacy. They saw that they could benefit from the education and opportunities promoted by Republicans. Banding together with freedmen, they pursued common class interests and hoped to make headway against the power of long-dominant planters. Cooperation even convinced a few scalawags that "there is but little if any difference in the talents of the two races," as one observed, and that all should have "an equal start." Yet this black-white coalition was vulnerable to the race issue, and most scalawags did not support racial equality. Republican tax policies also cut into upcountry yeoman support because reliance on the property tax hit many small landholders hard.

Taxation was a major problem for the Reconstruction governments. Republicans wanted to maintain prewar services, repair the war's destruction, stimulate industry, and support important new ventures such as public schools. But the Civil War had destroyed much of the South's tax base. One category of valuable property—slaves—had disappeared entirely. And hundreds

Albion Winegar Tourgee, a former Union soldier severely wounded at the Battle of Bull Run in 1861, became a carpetbagger and was elected a district judge in North Carolina during Reconstruction. In 1879 he published a best-selling novel, *A Fool's Errand,* which told his own story of travail as a Yankee immigrant in the South confronting the Ku Klux Klan and implementing freedmen's rights.   (Chautauqua County Historical Society, Westfield, N.Y.)

Tax Policy and Corruption as Political Wedges

of thousands of citizens had lost much of the rest of their property—money, livestock, fences, and buildings—to the war. Thus an increase in taxes was necessary even to maintain traditional services, and new ventures required still higher taxes. Inevitably, Republican tax policies aroused strong opposition, especially among the yeomen.

Corruption was another serious charge levied against the Republicans. Unfortunately, it often was true. Many carpetbaggers and black politicians engaged in fraudulent schemes, sold their votes, or padded expenses, taking part in what scholars recognize was a nationwide surge of corruption in an age ruled by "spoilsmen" (see pages 554–556). Corruption carried no party label, but the Democrats successfully pinned the blame on unqualified blacks and greedy carpetbaggers among southern Republicans.

All these problems hurt the Republicans, whose leaders also allowed factionalism along racial and class lines to undermine party unity. But in many southern states the deathblow came through violence. The Ku Klux Klan, a secret veterans' club that began in

Ku Klux Klan

Tennessee in 1866, spread through the South and rapidly evolved into a terrorist organization. Violence against African Americans occurred from the first days of Reconstruction but became far more organized and purposeful after 1867. Klansmen rode to frustrate Reconstruction and keep the freedmen in subjection. Nighttime harassment, whippings, beatings, and murder became common, and terrorism dominated some counties and regions.

Although the Klan persecuted blacks who stood up for their rights as laborers or individuals, its main purpose was political. Lawless nightriders made active Republicans the target of their attacks. Leading white and black Republicans were killed in several states. After freedmen who worked for a South Carolina scalawag started voting, terrorists visited the planta-

Members of the Ku Klux Klan devised ghoulish costumes to heighten the terror inspired by their acts. This photograph shows the costume of a Mississippi Klansman from 1871.   (Courtesy of Mr. Herbert Peck, Jr.)

tion and, in the words of one victim, "whipped every nigger man they could lay their hands on." Klansmen also attacked Union League clubs—Republican organizations that mobilized the black vote—and schoolteachers who were aiding the freedmen.

Klan violence was not a spontaneous outburst of racism; very specific social forces shaped and directed it. In North Carolina, for example, Alamance and Caswell Counties were the sites of the worst Klan violence. Slim Republican majorities there rested on cooperation between black voters and white yeomen, particularly those whose Unionism or discontent with the Confederacy had turned them against local Democratic officials. Together, these black and white Republicans had ousted officials long entrenched in power. The wealthy and powerful men in Alamance and Caswell who had lost their accustomed political control were the Klan's county officers and local chieftains. They organized a deliberate campaign of terror, recruiting members and planning atrocities. By whipping up racism or intimidating enough Republicans, the Ku Klux Klan weakened the Republican coalition and restored a Democratic majority.

Klan violence injured Republicans across the South. No fewer than one-tenth of the black leaders who had been delegates to the 1867–1868 state constitutional conventions were attacked, seven fatally. In one judicial district of North Carolina the Ku Klux Klan was responsible for twelve murders, over seven hundred beatings, and other acts of violence, including rape and arson. A single attack on Alabama Republicans in the town of Eutaw left four blacks dead and fifty-four wounded. In South Carolina five hundred masked Klansmen lynched eight black prisoners at the Union County jail, and in nearby York County the Klan committed at least eleven murders and hundreds of whippings. According to historian Eric Foner, the Klan "made it virtually impossible for Republicans to campaign or vote in large parts of Georgia."

Thus a combination of difficult fiscal problems, Republican mistakes, racial hostility, and terror brought down the Republican regimes. In most southern states, "Radical Reconstruction" lasted only a few years (see Map 16.1). The most enduring failure of Reconstruction, however, was not political; it was social and economic. Reconstruction failed to alter the South's social structure or its distribution of wealth and power. Without land of their own, freed men and women were dependent on white landowners who could and did use their economic power to compromise blacks' political freedom.

Failure of Reconstruction

Armed only with the ballot, freed men in the South had little chance to effect major changes.

To reform the southern social order, Congress would have had to redistribute land, but most lawmakers opposed an attack on private property. Radical Republicans like Albion Tourgée, a former Union soldier who moved to North Carolina and was elected a judge, condemned Congress's timidity. Turning the freedman out on his own without protection, said Tourgée, constituted "cheap philanthropy." Indeed, African Americans who had to live with the consequences of Reconstruction considered it a failure, for the North "threw all the Negroes on the world without any way of getting along." Moreover, without careful supervision by Congress, the situation of the freed men and women deteriorated. Whenever the North lost interest, Reconstruction would collapse.

Reconstruction Reversed

Northerners had always been more interested in suppressing rebellion than in aiding southern blacks, and by the early 1870s the North's commitment to bringing about change in the South was weakening. Criticism of the southern governments grew, new issues captured public attention, and sentiment for national reconciliation gained popularity in politics. In one southern state after another, Democrats regained control, and they threatened to defeat Republicans in the North as well. Whites in the old Confederacy referred to this decline of Reconstruction as "southern redemption," and by the 1870s, "redeemer" Democrats claimed to be the saviors of the South from alleged "black domination" and "carpetbag rule." And for one of only a few times in American history, violence and terror emerged as a tactic in normal politics.

In 1870 and 1871 the violent campaigns of the Ku Klux Klan forced Congress to pass two Enforcement Acts and an anti-Klan law. These

Political Implications of Klan Terrorism

laws made actions by individuals against the civil and political rights of others a federal criminal offense for the first time. They also provided for election supervisors and permitted martial law and suspension of the writ of habeas corpus to combat murders, beatings, and threats by the Klan. Federal prosecutors used the laws rather selectively. In 1872 and 1873 Mississippi and the Carolinas saw many prosecutions; but in other states where violence flourished, the laws were virtually ignored. Southern juries sometimes refused to convict Klansmen; out of a total of 3,310 cases, only 1,143 ended in convictions. Though many Klansmen (roughly two thousand in South Carolina alone) fled their states to avoid prosecution, and the Klan officially disbanded, the threat of violence did not end. Paramilitary organizations known as Rifle clubs and Red Shirts often took the Klan's place.

Klan terrorism openly defied Congress, yet even on this issue there were ominous signs that the North's commitment to racial justice was fading. Some conservative but influential Republicans opposed the anti-Klan laws. Rejecting other Republicans' arguments that the Thirteenth, Fourteenth, and Fifteenth Amendments had made the federal government the protector of the rights of citizens, these dissenters echoed an old Democratic charge that Congress was infringing on states' rights. Senator Lyman Trumbull of Illinois declared that the states remained "the depositories of the rights of the individual." If Congress could punish crimes like assault or murder, he asked, "what is the need of the State governments?" For years Democrats had complained of "centralization and consolidation"; now some Republicans seemed to agree with them. This opposition foreshadowed a more general revolt within Republican ranks in 1872.

Disenchanted with Reconstruction, a group calling itself the Liberal Republicans bolted the party in

The Liberal Republican Revolt

1872 and nominated Horace Greeley, the well-known editor of the *New York Tribune*, for president. The Liberal Republicans were a varied group, including civil service reformers, foes of corruption, and advocates of a lower tariff. Normally such disparate elements would not cooperate with one another, but two popular and widespread attitudes united them: distaste for federal intervention in the South and an elitist desire to let market forces and the "best men" determine events, both in the South and in Washington.

The Democrats also gave their nomination to Greeley in 1872. The combination was not enough to defeat Grant, who won reelection, but it reinforced Grant's desire to avoid confrontation with white southerners. Greeley's campaign for North-South reunion, for "clasping hands across the bloody chasm," was a bit premature to win at the polls, but a harbinger of the future of American politics. Organized Blue-Gray fraternalism (gatherings of Union and Confederate veterans) began as early as 1874 in some states. Grant continued to use military force sparingly and in 1875 refused a desperate request for troops from the governor of Mississippi to quell racial and political terrorism in that state.

Dissatisfaction with Grant's administration grew during his second term. Strong-willed but politically naive, Grant made a series of poor appointments. His secretary of war, his private secretary, and officials in the Treasury and Navy Departments were involved in bribery or tax-cheating scandals. Instead of exposing the corruption, Grant defended some of the culprits. In 1874, as Grant's popularity and his party's prestige declined, the Democrats recaptured the House of Representatives. This stunning turnabout signaled the beginning of the end of the old Radical Republican vision of Reconstruction. The Republican Party faced more unfavorable publicity in 1875, when several of Grant's appointees were indicted for corruption.

The effect of Democratic gains in Congress was to weaken legislative resolve on southern issues. Congress had already lifted the political disabilities of the Fourteenth Amendment from many former Confederates. In 1872 it had adopted a sweeping Amnesty Act, which pardoned most of the remaining rebels and left only five hundred barred from political officeholding. In 1875 Congress passed a Civil Rights Act, partly as a tribute to the recently deceased Charles Sumner, purporting to guarantee black people equal accommodations in public places, such as inns and theaters, but the bill was watered down and contained no effective provisions for enforcement. (The Supreme Court later struck down this law; see page 562.)

A General Amnesty

Democrats regained power in the South rather quickly, redeeming control of state governments in four states before 1872 and in a total of eight by January 1876 (see Map 16.1). In the North Democrats successfully stressed the failure and scandals of Reconstruction governments. As opinion shifted, historian Brooks Adams, the grandson and great-grandson of presidents, published an article condemning the enfranchisement of blacks as "a wholesale creation of the most ignorant mass of voters to be found in the civilized world." Many Republicans sensed that their constituents were tiring of southern issues and the legacies of the war. Despite the consequences for the freedpeople, sectional reconciliation now seemed crucial for commerce. The nation was expanding westward rapidly, and the South was a new frontier for investment.

Both industrialization and immigration were surging, hastening the pace of change in national life. Within only eight years, postwar industrial production

Reconciliation and Industrial Expansion

increased by an impressive 75 percent. For the first time, nonagricultural workers outnumbered farmers, and only Britain's industrial output was greater than that of the United States. Government financial policies did much to bring about this rapid growth. Soon after the war Congress used a portion of tax revenues to pay off the interest-bearing war debt: the debt fell from $2.33 billion in 1866 to only $587 million in 1893, and every dollar repaid was a dollar injected into the economy for potential reinvestment. Low taxes on investment and high tariffs on manufactured goods also aided industrialists. With such help, the northern economy quickly recovered its prewar rate of growth.

Between 1865 and 1873, 3 million new immigrants entered the country, most of them joining the labor force of industrial cities in the North and West. As the number of immigrants rose, a corresponding revival of suspicion and hostility among native-born Americans took place. Also prominent was the question of how Utah's growing Mormon community, which practiced polygamy, could be reconciled to American law.

Then the Panic of 1873 ushered in over five years of economic contraction. Three million people lost their jobs, and the clash between labor and capital became the major issue of the day (see Chapter 18). Class attitudes diverged, especially in the large cities. Debtors and the unemployed sought easy money policies to spur economic expansion (workers and farmers desperately needed cash). Businessmen, disturbed by the widespread strikes and industrial violence that accompanied the panic, became increasingly concerned about the defense of property.

Class conflict fueled a monetary issue: whether paper money—the Civil War greenbacks—should be kept in circulation. In 1872 Democratic farmers and debtors urged this policy to expand the money supply and raise prices, but businessmen, bankers, and creditors overruled them. Now hard times swelled the ranks of the "greenbackers"—voters who favored easy money.

Greenbacks Versus Sound Money

Congress voted in 1874 to increase the number of greenbacks in circulation, but Grant vetoed the bill in deference to the opinions of financial leaders. The next year, "sound money" interests prevailed in Congress, winning passage of a law requiring that greenbacks be convertible into gold after 1878. The chasm between farmers and workers and wealthy industrialists grew even wider.

In international affairs, there was renewed pressure for, and controversy about, expansion (see Chapter 22).

Foreign Expansion

In 1867 Secretary of State William H. Seward arranged a vast addition of territory to the national domain through the purchase of Alaska from the Russian government for $7.2 million. Opponents ridiculed Seward's venture, calling Alaska Frigidia, the Polar Bear Garden, and Walrussia. But Seward convinced important congressmen of Alaska's economic potential, and other lawmakers favored the dawning of friendship with Russia.

Also in 1867 the United States took control of the Midway Islands, a thousand miles from Hawai'i. And in 1870 President Grant tried unsuccessfully to annex the Dominican Republic. Seward and his successor, Hamilton Fish, also resolved troubling Civil War grievances against Great Britain. Through diplomacy they arranged a financial settlement of claims on Britain for damage done by the *Alabama* and other cruisers built in England and sold to the Confederacy (see page 616).

Meanwhile, the Supreme Court played its part in the northern retreat from Reconstruction. During the

Judicial Retreat from Reconstruction

Civil War the Court had been cautious and inactive. Reaction to the *Dred Scott* decision (1857) had been so violent, and the Union's wartime emergency so great, that the Court avoided interference with government actions. The justices breathed a collective sigh of relief, for example, when legal technicalities prevented them from reviewing the case of Clement Vallandigham, a Democratic opponent of Lincoln's war effort, who had been convicted by a military tribunal of aiding the enemy. But in 1866 a similar case, *Ex parte Milligan*, reached the Court through proper channels.

Lambdin P. Milligan of Indiana had plotted to free Confederate prisoners of war and overthrow state governments. For these acts a military court sentenced Milligan, a civilian, to death. Milligan challenged the authority of the military tribunal, claiming that he had a right to a civil trial. The Supreme Court declared that military trials were illegal when civil courts were open and functioning, and its language indicated that the Court intended to reassert its authority.

In the 1870s the Court successfully renewed its challenge to Congress's actions when it narrowed the meaning and effectiveness of the Fourteenth Amendment. The *Slaughter-House* cases (1873) began in 1869, when the Louisiana legislature granted one company a monopoly on the slaughtering of livestock in New Orleans. Rival butchers in the city promptly sued. Their attorney, former Supreme Court justice John A. Campbell, argued that Louisiana had violated the rights of some of its citizens in favor of others. The Fourteenth Amendment, Campbell contended, had revolutionized the constitutional system by bringing individual rights under federal protection. Campbell thus articulated an original goal of the Republican Party: to nationalize civil rights and guard them from state interference.

But in the *Slaughter-House* decision, the Supreme Court dealt a stunning blow to the scope and vitality of the Fourteenth Amendment. Refusing to accept Campbell's argument, it interpreted the "privileges and immunities" of citizens so narrowly that it reduced them almost to trivialities. State citizenship and national citizenship were separate, the Court declared. National citizenship involved only matters such as the right to travel freely from state to state and to use the navigable waters of the nation, and only these narrow rights were protected by the Fourteenth Amendment.

The Supreme Court also concluded that the butchers who sued had not been deprived of their rights or property in violation of the due-process clause of the amendment. Shrinking from a role as "perpetual censor upon all legislation of the States, on the civil rights of their own citizens," the Court's majority declared that the framers of the recent amendments had not intended to "destroy" the federal system, in which the states exercised "powers for domestic and local government, including the regulation of civil rights." Thus the justices severely limited the amendment's potential for securing and protecting the rights of black citizens—its original intent.

The next day the Court decided *Bradwell v. Illinois*, a case in which Myra Bradwell, a female attorney, had been denied the right to practice law in Illinois on account of her gender. Pointing to the Fourteenth Amendment, Bradwell's attorneys contended that the state had unconstitutionally abridged her "privileges and immunities" as a citizen. The Supreme Court rejected her claim, alluding to women's traditional role in the home.

In 1876 the Court weakened the Reconstruction era amendments even further by emasculating the enforcement clause of the Fourteenth Amendment and revealing deficiencies inherent in the Fifteenth Amendment. In *U.S. v. Cruikshank* the Court overruled the conviction under the 1870 Enforcement Act of Louisiana whites who had attacked a meeting of blacks and conspired to deprive them of their rights. The justices ruled that the Fourteenth Amendment did not give the federal government power to act against these whites. The duty of protecting citizens' equal rights, the Court said, "rests alone with the States." Such judicial conservatism had profound impact down through the next century, as the revolutionary potential in the Civil War amendments was blunted, if not destroyed.

As the 1876 elections approached, most political observers saw that the North was no longer willing to pursue the goals of Reconstruction. The results of a disputed presidential election confirmed this fact. Samuel J. Tilden, the Democratic governor of New York, ran strongly in the South and needed only one more electoral vote to triumph over Rutherford B. Hayes, the Republican nominee. Nineteen electoral votes from Louisiana, South Carolina, and Florida (the only southern states yet "unredeemed" by Democratic rule) were disputed; both Democrats and Republicans claimed to have won

Disputed Election of 1876 and the Compromise of 1877

Map 16.2 **Presidential Election of 1876 and the Compromise of 1877** In 1876 a combination of solid southern support and Democratic gains in the North gave Samuel Tilden the majority of popular votes, but Rutherford B. Hayes won the disputed election in the electoral college, after a deal satisfied Democratic wishes for an end to Reconstruction.

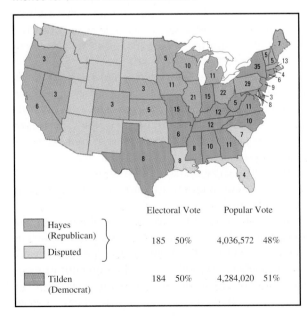

	Electoral Vote		Popular Vote	
Hayes (Republican)	185	50%	4,036,572	48%
Disputed				
Tilden (Democrat)	184	50%	4,284,020	51%

in those states despite fraud committed by their opponents. One vote from Oregon was undecided because of a technicality (see Map 16.2).

To resolve this unprecedented situation, on which the Constitution gave little guidance, Congress established a fifteen-member electoral commission. In the interest of impartiality, membership on the commission was to be balanced between Democrats and Republicans. But one independent Republican, Supreme Court Justice David Davis, refused appointment in order to accept his election as a senator. A regular Republican took his place, and the Republican Party prevailed 8 to 7 on every attempt to count the returns, along strict party lines. Hayes would become president if Congress accepted the commission's findings.

Congressional acceptance was not certain. Democrats controlled the House and could filibuster to block action on the vote. Many citizens worried that the nation had entered a major constitutional crisis and would slip once again into civil war, as some southerners vowed "Tilden or Fight." The crisis was resolved when Democrats acquiesced in the election of Hayes based on a "deal" cut in a Washington hotel. Negotiations took place between Hayes's supporters and southerners who wanted federal aid to railroads, internal improvements, federal patronage, and removal of troops from southern states. Neither party was well enough organized to implement and enforce the various parts of this bargain between the sections. Northern and southern Democrats simply decided they could not win and did not contest the election of a Republican who was not going to continue Reconstruction. Thus Hayes became president, inaugurated privately inside the White House to avoid any threat of violence, southerners relished their promises of economic aid, and Reconstruction was unmistakably over.

Southern Democrats rejoiced, but African Americans grieved over the betrayal of their hopes for equality. Tens of thousands considered leaving the South, where real freedom was no longer a possibility. "[We asked] whether it was possible we could stay under a people who had held us in bondage," said Henry Adams, who led a migration to Kansas. In South Carolina, Louisiana, Mississippi, and other southern states, thousands gathered up their possessions and migrated to Kansas. They were known as Exodusters, disappointed people still searching for their share in the American dream. Even in Kansas they met disillusionment, as the welcome extended by

Betrayal of Black Rights and the Exodusters

These cartoons reveal the North's readiness to give up on a strong Reconstruction policy. According to the images on the left, only federal bayonets could support the "rule or ruin" carpetbag regimes that oppressed the South. What do the background and foreground of the cartoon on the right suggest will be the results of President Hayes's "Let 'Em Alone Policy"?   (Library of Congress)

the state's governor soon gave way to hostile public reactions.

Blacks now had to weigh their options, which were not much wider than they had ever been. The Civil War had brought emancipation, and Reconstruction had guaranteed their rights under law. But events and attitudes in larger white America were foreboding. In a Fourth of July speech in Washington, D.C., in 1875, Frederick Douglass anticipated this predicament. He reflected anxiously on the American centennial to be celebrated the following year. The nation, Douglass feared, would "lift to the sky its million voices in one grand Centennial hosanna of peace and good will to all the white race . . . from gulf to lakes and from sea to sea." Douglass looked back on fifteen years of unparalleled change for his people and worried about the hold of white supremacy on America's historical memory: "If war among the whites brought peace and liberty to the blacks, what will peace among the whites bring?" Douglass's question would echo down through American political culture for decades.

Summary

Reconstruction left a contradictory record. It was an era of tragic aspirations and failures, but also of unprecedented legal, political, and social change. The Union victory brought about an increase in federal power, stronger nationalism, sweeping federal intervention in the southern states, and landmark amendments to the Constitution. But northern commitment to make these changes endure had eroded, and the revolution remained unfinished.

By 1876 in South Carolina, Wade Hampton ran successfully for governor, relying on a campaign of terror and intimidation carried out by his "Red Shirt" followers, crushing the black vote in many counties and ending Republican rule. Robert Smalls, however, managed to stay in office despite Democratic Party efforts to oust him. He won his final congressional election in 1884 against the viciously racist "Pitchfork" Ben Tillman. After leaving Congress, Smalls served from 1890 until 1913 as customs collector in his native Beaufort.

The North embraced emancipation, black suffrage, and constitutional alterations strengthening the central government. But it did so to defeat the rebellion and secure the peace. As the pressure of these crises declined, strong underlying continuities emerged and placed their mark on Reconstruction. The American people and the courts maintained a preference for state authority and a distrust of federal power. The ideology of free labor dictated that property should be respected and that individuals should be self-reliant. Racism endured and transformed into the even more virulent forms of Klan terror and theories that freedom would send blacks as a race back toward "barbarism." Concern for the human rights of African Americans was strongest when their plight threatened to undermine the interests of whites, and reform frequently had less appeal than moneymaking in an individualistic, enterprising society.

A host of other issues had arisen from industrialization. How would the country develop its immense resources in an increasingly interconnected national economy? How would farmers, industrial workers, immigrants, and capitalists fit into the new social system? Industrialization not only promised a higher standard of living but wrought increased exploitation of labor. Moreover, industry increased the nation's power and laid the foundation for an enlarged American role in international affairs. The American imagination again turned to the conquest of new frontiers.

In the wake of the Civil War Americans faced two profound tasks—the achievement of healing and the dispensing of justice. Both had to occur, but they never developed in historical balance. Making sectional reunion compatible with black freedom and equality overwhelmed the imagination in American political culture, and the nation still faced much of this dilemma more than a century later.

LEGACY FOR A PEOPLE AND A NATION
The Fourteenth Amendment

Before the Civil War, no definition of civil rights existed in America. Reconstruction legislation, especially the Fourteenth Amendment, changed that forever. Approved by Congress in 1866, the Fourteenth Amendment enshrined in the Constitution the ideas of birthright citizenship and equal rights. The Fourteenth Amendment was designed to secure and protect the rights of the freedpeople. But over time, the "equal protection of the law" clause became one of the most important and malleable provisions in the Constitution. It has been used at times to support the rights of states, cities, corporations, immigrants, women, religious organizations, gays and lesbians, students, and labor unions. It has advanced both tolerance and intolerance, affirmative action and anti-affirmative action programs. It provides the legal wellspring for the generations-old civil rights movement in the United States.

The amendment as originally written required individuals to pursue grievances through private litigation, alleging state denial of a claimed federal right. At first the Supreme Court interpreted it conservatively, especially on racial matters, and by 1900 the idea of color-blind liberty in America was devastated by Jim Crow laws, disfranchisement, and unpunished mob violence.

But Progressive reformers used the equal protection clause to advocate government support of health, union organizing, municipal housing, a progressive income tax, and the protection of woman and child laborers. In the 1920s and 1930s, a judicial defense of civil liberties and free speech took hold, especially from Justice Louis Brandeis. The Supreme Court expanded the amendment's guarantee of equality by a series of decisions upholding the rights of immigrant groups to resist "forced Americanization," especially Catholics in their creation of parochial schools. And, from its inception in 1910, the NAACP waged a long campaign to reveal the inequality of racial segregation in schooling and every other kind of public facility. Led by Charles Houston and Thurgood Marshall, this epic legal battle culminated in the *Brown v. Board of Education* desegregation decision of 1954. In the multilayered Civil Rights Act of 1964, the equal protection tradition was reenshrined into American law. Since 1964 Americans have lived in a society where the Fourteenth Amendment's legacy is the engine of expanded liberty for women and all minorities, as well as a political battleground for defining the nature and limits of human equality, and for redistributing justice long denied.

For Further Reading, see page A-20 of the Appendix. For Web resources, go to http://college.hmco.com.

APPENDIX

Suggestions for Further Reading

Chapter 1

General

Noble D. Cook, *Born to Die: Disease and New World Conquest, 1492–1650* (1998); Alfred W. Crosby, *The Columbian Exchange: Biological and Cultural Consequences of 1492* (1972); Alfred W. Crosby, *Ecological Imperialism: The Biological Expansion of Europe, 800–1900* (1986); John R. Elliott, *The Old World and the New* (1970); Bernard Lewis, *Cultures in Conflict: Christians, Muslims, and Jews in the Age of Discovery* (1995); D. W. Meinig, *Atlantic America, 1492–1800* (1986); Herman Viola and Carolyn Margolis, eds., *Seeds of Change: Five Hundred Years Since Columbus* (1991); Eric Wolf, *Europe and the People Without History* (1982).

Mesoamerican Civilizations

Inga Clendinnen, *Aztecs: An Interpretation* (1991); Michael Coe, *Mexico from the Olmecs to the Aztecs* (1994); Brian Fagan, *Kingdoms of Gold, Kingdoms of Jade: The Americas Before Columbus* (1991); John S. Henderson, *The World of the Ancient Maya* (1997); Eduardo Matos Moctezuma and David Carrasco, *Moctezuma's Mexico: Visions of the Aztec World* (1992); Linda Schele and David Friedel, *A Forest of Kings* [on the Mayas] (1990).

North American Indians

Kathleen Bragdon, *Native People of Southern New England, 1500–1650* (1996); Brian Fagan, *Ancient North America: The Archaeology of a Continent* (1991); Brian Fagan, *The Great Journey: The Peopling of Ancient America* (1987); Francis Jennings, *The Founders of America: From the Earliest Migrations to the Present* (1993); Alvin Josephy, Jr., ed., *America in 1492* (1992); Mark Mehrer, *Cahokia's Countryside: Household Archaeology, Settlement Patterns, and Social Power* (1995); Elsa Redmond, ed., *Chiefdoms and Chieftaincy in the Americas* (1999); Lynda N. Shaffer, *Native Americans Before 1492: The Moundbuilding Centers of the Eastern Woodlands* (1992); Colin F. Taylor, ed., *The Native Americans: The Indigenous People of North America* (1992); David Hurst Thomas, *Exploring Ancient Native America: An Archaeological Guide* (1999); Bruce Trigger and Wilcomb Washburn, eds., *The Cambridge History of the Native Peoples of the Americas*, vol. 1: *North America* (1996).

Africa

Jacob Ade Ajayi and Michael Crowder, *History of West Africa* (1985); Paul Bohannon and Philip Curtin, *Africa and Africans* (1988); Basil Davidson, *Africa in History*, rev. ed. (1991); Philip Curtin et al., eds., *African History: From Earliest Times to Independence*, rev. ed. (1995); John Iliffe, *Africans: The History of a Continent* (1996); Robert July, *A History of the African People* (1992); Paul Lovejoy, *Transformations in Slavery: A History of Slavery in Africa* (1983); Roland Oliver and J. D. Fage, *A Short History of Africa* (1988); John Thornton, *Africa and Africans in the Making of the Atlantic World, 1400–1680* (1992).

Europe in the Age of Discovery

Christopher Allmand, *The Hundred Years' War: England and France at War, ca. 1300–ca. 1450* (1988); Fernand Braudel, *The Mediterranean and the Mediterranean World in the Age of Philip II*, 2 vols., 2d ed. (1977); Roger Chartier, ed., *A History of Private Life*, vol. 3: *Passions of the Renaissance* (1989); G. R. Elton, ed., *The Reformation* (1990); Anthony Grafton, *New Worlds, Ancient Texts: The Power of Tradition and the Shock of Discovery* (1992); Denys Hay, *Europe in the Fourteenth and Fifteenth Centuries*, 2d ed. (1989); H. G. Koenigsberger et al., *Europe in the Sixteenth Century*, 2d ed. (1989); Robert S. Lopez, *The Commercial Revolution of the Middle Ages, 950–1350* (1971); Anthony Pagden, *Lords of All the World: Ideologies of Empire in Spain, Britain and France, 1500–1800* (1995); J. R. S. Phillips, *The Medieval Expansion of Europe* (1988); Philip Ziegler, *The Black Death* (1982).

Exploration and Discovery

Emerson Baker et al., eds., *American Beginnings: Exploration, Culture, and Cartography in the Land of Norumbega* (1994); Fredi Chiappelli et al., eds., *First Images of America: The Impact of the New World on the Old*, 2 vols. (1976); Felipe Fernández-Armesto, *Before Columbus: Exploration and Colonization from the Mediterranean to the Atlantic, 1229–1492* (1987); Felipe Fernández-Armesto, *Columbus* (1991); Charles Hudson, *Knights of Spain, Warriors of the Sun: Hernando de Soto and the South's Ancient Chiefdoms* (1997); Jerald T. Milanich, *Florida Indians and the Invasion from Europe* (1995); Jerald T. Milanich and Susan Milbrath, eds., *First Encounters: Spanish Explorations in the Caribbean and the United States,*

1492–1570 (1989); Samuel Eliot Morison, *The European Discovery of America: The Northern Voyages,* A.D. *1500–1600* (1971); Samuel Eliot Morison, *The European Discovery of America: The Southern Voyages,* A.D. *1492–1616* (1974); J. H. Parry, *The Age of Reconnaissance* (1963); J. H. Parry, *The Discovery of the Sea* (1974); William and Carla Phillips, *The Worlds of Christopher Columbus* (1992); David B. Quinn, *North America from Earliest Discovery to First Settlements* (1977); Irving Rouse, *The Tainos: Rise and Decline of the People Who Greeted Columbus* (1992); P. E. Russell, *Portugal, Spain, and the African Atlantic* (1995); Kirsten Seaver, *The Frozen Echo: Greenland and the Exploration of North America, ca.* A.D. *1000–1500* (1995); Roger C. Smith, *Vanguard of Empire: Ships of Exploration in the Age of Columbus* (1993).

Early European Conquest and Settlements

Kenneth Andrews, *Trade, Plunder and Settlement: Maritime Enterprise and the Genesis of the British Empire, 1480–1630* (1984); Nancy Farriss, *Maya Society Under Colonial Rule* (1984); Charles Gibson, *Spain in America* (1966); Ross Hassig, *Mexico and the Spanish Conquest* (1994); Paul E. Hoffman, *A New Andalucia and a Way to the Orient: The American Southeast during the Sixteenth Century* (1990); Karen O. Kupperman, *Roanoke, the Abandoned Colony* (1984); Miguel León-Portilla, ed., *The Broken Spears: The Aztec Account of the Conquest of Mexico* (1992); James Lockhart, ed. and trans., *We People Here: Nahuatl Accounts of the Conquest of Mexico* (1993); James Lockhart, *The Nahuas after the Conquest: A Social and Cultural History of the Indians of Central Mexico, Sixteenth Through Eighteenth Centuries* (1992); A. J. R. Russell-Wood, *A World on the Move: The Portuguese in Africa, Asia, and America, 1415–1808* (1993); Hugh Thomas, *Conquest: Montezuma, Cortés, and the Fall of Old Mexico* (1993); David J. Weber, *The Spanish Frontier in North America* (1992).

Chapter 2

General

David Hackett Fischer, *Albion's Seed: Four British Folkways in America* (1989); Karen O. Kupperman, ed., *America in European Consciousness, 1493–1750* (1995); D. W. Meinig, *Atlantic America, 1492–1800* (1986); Gary B. Nash, *Red, White, and Black: The Peoples of Early America,* 4th ed. (2000); Mary Beth Norton, *Founding Mothers & Fathers: Gendered Power and the Forming of American Society* (1996); John E. Pomfret, *Founding the American Colonies, 1583–1660* (1970); Paula Treckel, *To Comfort the Heart: Women in Seventeenth-Century America* (1996); Alden T. Vaughan, *Roots of American Racism* (1994).

New Spain, New Netherland, New France, and the Caribbean

Karen Anderson, *Chain Her by One Foot: The Subjugation of Native Women in Seventeenth-Century New France* (1991);

Charles R. Boxer, *The Dutch Seaborne Empire, 1600–1800* (1965); Denys Delâge, *Bitter Feast: Amerindians and Europeans in Northeastern North America, 1600–64* (1993); Richard S. Dunn, *Sugar and Slaves: The Rise of the Planter Class in the English West Indies, 1624–1713* (1972); William J. Eccles, *France in America,* rev. ed. (1990); Carol Hoffecker et al., eds., *New Sweden in America* (1995); Jonathan Israel, *Dutch Primacy in World Trade, 1585–1740* (1989); Donna Merwick, *Possessing Albany, 1630–1710* (1990); Sidney Mintz, *Sweetness and Power: The Place of Sugar in Modern History* (1985); Marc Simmons, *The Last Conquistador: Juan de Oñate and the Settling of the Far Southwest* (1991); David J. Weber, *The Spanish Frontier in North America* (1992).

England

Susan Dwyer Amussen, *An Ordered Society: Gender and Class in Early Modern England* (1988); Carl Bridenbaugh, *Vexed and Troubled Englishmen, 1590–1642,* rev. ed. (1976); Patrick Collinson, *The Religion of Protestants: The Church in English Society, 1559–1625* (1982); A. G. Dickens, *The English Reformation,* 2d. ed. (1989); Ralph Houlbrooke, *The English Family, 1450–1700* (1984); Peter Laslett, *The World We Have Lost,* 3d ed. (1984); J. P. Sommerville, *Politics and Ideology in England, 1603–1640* (1986); Keith Wrightson, *English Society, 1580–1680* (1982).

Early Contact Between Europeans and Indians

James Axtell, *The Invasion Within: The Contest of Cultures in Colonial North America* (1985); Philip Barbour, *Pocahontas and Her World* (1970); Alfred Cave, *The Pequot War* (1997); William Cronon, *Changes in the Land: Indians, Colonists, and the Ecology of New England* (1983); Frederic W. Gleach, *Powhatan's World and Colonial Virginia: A Conflict of Cultures* (1997); Francis Jennings, *The Invasion of America: Indians, Colonialism, and the Cant of Conquest* (1975); Karen O. Kupperman, *Settling with the Indians: The Meeting of English and Indian Cultures in America, 1580–1640* (1980); Patrick Malone, *The Skulking Way of War: Technology and Tactics Among the Indians of New England* (1991); Kenneth Morrison, *The Embattled Northeast: The Elusive Ideal of Alliance in Abnaki-Euroamerican Relations* (1984); Daniel Richter, *The Ordeal of the Longhouse: The Peoples of the Iroquois League in the Era of European Colonization* (1992); Helen C. Rountree, *Pocahontas's People: The Powhatan Indians of Virginia Through Four Centuries* (1990); Neal Salisbury, *Manitou and Providence: Indians, Europeans, and the Making of New England, 1500–1643* (1982); Bernard Sheehan, *Savagism and Civility: Indians and Englishmen in Colonial Virginia* (1980); Timothy Silver, *A New Face on the Countryside: Indians, Colonists, and Slaves in South Atlantic Forests, 1500–1800* (1990); Alden T. Vaughan, *The New England Frontier: Puritans and Indians, 1620–1675,* rev. ed. (1979); Peter Wood et al., eds., *Powhatan's Mantle: Indians in the Colonial Southeast* (1989).

Chesapeake Society and Politics

Lois Green Carr et al., *Robert Cole's World: Agriculture and Society in Early Maryland* (1991); David Galenson, *White Servitude in Colonial America: An Economic Analysis* (1981); James Horn, *Adapting to a New World: English Society in the Seventeenth-Century Chesapeake* (1994); Ivor Noël Hume, *The Virginia Adventure: Roanoke to James Towne* (1994); A. J. Leo Lemay, *The American Dream of Captain John Smith* (1991); Gloria L. Main, *Tobacco Colony: Life in Early Maryland, 1650–1720* (1983); Edmund S. Morgan, *American Slavery, American Freedom: The Ordeal of Colonial Virginia* (1975); James Perry, *The Formation of a Society on Virginia's Eastern Shore, 1615–1655* (1990); Darrett Rutman and Anita Rutman, *A Place in Time: Middlesex County, Virginia, 1650–1750* (1984); Alden T. Vaughan, *American Genesis: Captain John Smith and the Founding of Virginia* (1975).

New England Communities, Politics, and Religion

David Grayson Allen, *In English Ways: The Movement of Societies and the Transferral of English Law and Custom to Massachusetts Bay in the 17th Century* (1981); Virginia DeJohn Anderson, *New England's Generation: The Great Migration and the Formation of Society and Culture in the 17th Century* (1991); Charles Cohen, *God's Caress: The Psychology of Puritan Religious Experience* (1986); Philip Gura, *A Glimpse of Sion's Glory: Puritan Radicalism in New England, 1620–1660* (1984); David D. Hall, *Worlds of Wonder, Days of Judgment: Popular Religious Belief in Early New England* (1989); Stephen Innes, *Creating the Commonwealth: The Economic Culture of Puritan New England* (1995); Stephen Innes, *Labor in a New Land: Economy and Society in 17th-Century Springfield* (1983); Sydney V. James, *Colonial Rhode Island* (1975); George Langdon, *Pilgrim Colony: A History of New Plymouth, 1620–1691* (1966); Kenneth A. Lockridge, *A New England Town: The First Hundred Years (Dedham, Massachusetts, 1636–1736)* (1970); John Frederick Martin, *Profits in the Wilderness: Entrepreneurship and the Founding of New England Towns in the 17th Century* (1991); Edmund S. Morgan, *The Puritan Dilemma: The Story of John Winthrop* (1958); Darrett Rutman, *Winthrop's Boston* (1965).

New England Women and Family Life

David Cressy, *Coming Over: Migration and Communication Between England and New England in the Seventeenth Century* (1987); John P. Demos, *A Little Commonwealth: Family Life in Plymouth Colony* (1970); Philip J. Greven, Jr., *Four Generations: Population, Land, and Family in Colonial Andover, Massachusetts* (1970); Lyle Koehler, *A Search for Power: The "Weaker Sex" in Seventeenth-Century New England* (1980); Edmund S. Morgan, *The Puritan Family*, rev. ed. (1966); Amanda Porterfield, *Female Piety in Puritan New England* (1992); Roger Thompson, *Sex in Middlesex: Popular Mores in a Massachusetts County, 1649–1699* (1986); Laurel Thatcher Ulrich, *Good Wives: Image and Reality in the Lives of Women in Northern New England, 1650–1750* (1982).

Chapter 3

General

Colin Calloway, *New Worlds for All: Indians, Europeans, and the Remaking of Early America* (1997); Wesley Frank Craven, *The Colonies in Transition, 1660–1713* (1968); W. J. Eccles, *France in America*, rev. ed. (1990); Jack P. Greene and J. R. Pole, eds., *Colonial British America* (1984); John J. McCusker and Russell R. Menard, *The Economy of British America, 1607–1789* (1985).

New Netherland and the Restoration Colonies

Edwin Bronner, *William Penn's "Holy Experiment": The Founding of Pennsylvania, 1681–1701* (1962); Wesley Frank Craven, *New Jersey and the English Colonization of North America* (1964); Joyce Goodfriend, *Before the Melting Pot: Society and Culture in Colonial New York City, 1664–1730* (1992); Donna Merwick, *Death of a Notary: Conquest and Change in Colonial New York* (1999); Donna Merwick, *Possessing Albany, 1630-1710: The Dutch and English Experiences* (1990); Oliver Rink, *Holland on the Hudson: An Economic and Social History of Dutch New York* (1986); Robert C. Ritchie, *The Duke's Province: A Study of Politics and Society in Colonial New York, 1660–1691* (1977); Robert M. Weir, *Colonial South Carolina: A History* (1983).

Imperial Trade and Administration

Robert M. Bliss, *Revolution and Empire: English Politics and the American Colonies in the Seventeenth Century* (1991); Lawrence W. Harper, *The English Navigation Laws: A Seventeenth-Century Experiment in Social Engineering* (1939); Marcus Rediker, *Between the Devil and the Deep Blue Sea: Merchant Seamen, Pirates, and the Anglo-American Maritime World, 1700–1750* (1987); Robert C. Ritchie, *Captain Kidd and the War Against the Pirates* (1986); I. K. Steele, *Politics of Colonial Policy: The Board of Trade in Colonial Administration* (1968); Stephen Saunders Webb, *Lord Churchill's Coup: The Anglo-American Empire and the Glorious Revolution Reconsidered* (1995); Stephen Saunders Webb, *1676: The End of American Independence* (1984); Stephen Saunders Webb, *The Governors-General: The English Army and the Definition of the Empire, 1569–1681* (1979).

Africa and the Slave Trade

Robin Blackburn, *The Making of New World Slavery: From the Baroque to the Modern, 1492–1800* (1997); Jay Coughtry, *The Notorious Triangle: Rhode Island and the African Slave Trade, 1700–1807* (1981); Philip D. Curtin, *The Atlantic Slave Trade: A Census* (1969); Joseph Inikori and Stanley Engerman, eds., *The Atlantic Slave Trade* (1992); Herbert Klein,

The Middle Passage (1978); Robin Law, *The Slave Coast of West Africa, 1550–1750: The Impact of the Atlantic Slave Trade on an African Society* (1991); Daniel C. Littlefield, *Rice and Slaves: Ethnicity and the Slave Trade in Colonial South Carolina* (1981); James Rawley, *The Transatlantic Slave Trade: A History* (1981); Barbara Solow, ed., *Slavery and the Rise of the Atlantic System* (1991).

Africans in America

Ira Berlin, *Many Thousands Gone: The First Two Centuries of Slavery in North America* (1998); T. H. Breen and Stephen Innes, *"Myne Owne Ground": Race and Freedom on Virginia's Eastern Shore, 1640–1676* (1980); Douglas Deal, *Race and Class in Colonial Virginia: Indians, Englishmen, and Africans on the Eastern Shore During the Seventeenth Century* (1993); Michael A. Gomez, *Exchanging Our Country Marks: The Transformation of African Identities in the Colonial and Antebellum South* (1998); Graham R. Hodges, *Root & Branch: African Americans in New York and East Jersey, 1613–1863* (1999); Allan Kulikoff, *Tobacco and Slaves: The Development of Southern Cultures in the Chesapeake, 1680–1800* (1986); Jane Landers, *Black Society in Spanish Florida* (1999); Edgar J. McManus, *Black Bondage in the North* (1973); Edmund S. Morgan, *American Slavery, American Freedom: The Ordeal of Colonial Virginia* (1975); Lorena S. Walsh, *From Calabar to Carter's Grove: The History of a Virginia Slave Community* (1997); Betty Wood, *The Origins of American Slavery* (1997); Peter H. Wood, *Black Majority: Negroes in Colonial South Carolina from 1670 Through the Stono Rebellion* (1974).

European–Native American Relations in the North

Russell Bourne, *The Red King's Rebellion: Racial Politics in New England, 1675–1678* (1991); John Demos, *The Unredeemed Captive: A Family Story from Early America* (1994); Matthew Dennis, *Cultivating a Landscape of Peace: Iroquois-European Encounter in Seventeenth-Century America* (1993); Francis Jennings, *The Ambiguous Iroquois Empire* (1984); Jill Lepore, *The Name of War: King Philip's War and the Origins of American Identity* (1998); Peter Mancall, *Deadly Medicine: Indians and Alcohol in Early America* (1995); Michael Puglisi, *Puritans Beseiged: The Legacies of King Philip's War in the Massachusetts Bay Colony* (1991); Daniel Richter, *The Ordeal of the Longhouse: The Peoples of the Iroquois League in the Era of European Colonization* (1992); Daniel Richter and James Merrell, eds., *Beyond the Covenant Chain: The Iroquois and Their Neighbors in Indian America, 1600–1800* (1987); Richard White, *The Middle Ground: Indians, Empires, and Republics in the Great Lakes Region, 1650–1815* (1991).

European–Native American Relations in the South and West

David H. Corkran, *The Creek Frontier, 1540–1783* (1967); Verner W. Crane, *The Southern Frontier, 1660–1732* (1929);

Carl Ekberg, *French Roots in the Illinois Country: The Mississippi Frontier in Colonial Times* (1998); Ramón Gutiérrez, *When Jesus Came, the Corn Mothers Went Away: Marriage, Sexuality, and Power in New Mexico, 1500–1846* (1991); Elizabeth A. H. John, *Storms Brewed in Other Men's Worlds: The Confrontation of Indians, Spanish, and French in the Southwest, 1540–1795* (1975); Andrew Knaut, *The Pueblo Revolt of 1680* (1995); James Merrell, *The Indians' New World: Catawbas and Their Neighbors from European Contact through the Era of Removal* (1989); Daniel H. Usner, Jr., *Indians, Settlers, and Slaves in a Frontier Exchange Economy: The Lower Mississippi Valley before 1783* (1992).

Colonial Politics

Patricia U. Bonomi, *The Lord Cornbury Scandal: The Politics of Reputation in British America* (1998); Lois Green Carr and David W. Jordan, *Maryland's Revolution of Government, 1689–1692* (1974); Richard P. Johnson, *Adjustment to Empire: The New England Colonies, 1675–1715* (1981); David S. Lovejoy, *The Glorious Revolution in America* (1972); Jack M. Sosin, *English America and Imperial Inconstancy: The Rise of Provincial Autonomy, 1696–1715* (1985); Jack M. Sosin, *English America and the Restoration Monarchy of Charles II* (1980); Jack M. Sosin, *English America and the Revolution of 1688* (1982).

New England

Bernard Bailyn, *The New England Merchants in the Seventeenth Century* (1955); Richard Bushman, *From Puritan to Yankee: Character and the Social Order in Connecticut, 1690–1765* (1967); Christine Heyrman, *Commerce and Culture: The Maritime Communities of Colonial Massachusetts, 1690–1750* (1984); Richard Melvoin, *New England Outpost: War and Society in Colonial Deerfield* (1990); Amanda Porterfield, *Female Piety in Puritan New England* (1991); Laurel Thatcher Ulrich, *Good Wives: Image and Reality in the Lives of Women in Northern New England, 1650–1750* (1982).

New England Witchcraft

Paul Boyer and Stephen Nissenbaum, *Salem Possessed: The Social Origins of Witchcraft* (1974); Elaine Breslaw, *Tituba, Reluctant Witch of Salem: Devilish Indians and Puritan Fantasies* (1996); John Demos, *Entertaining Satan: Witchcraft and the Culture of Early New England* (1982); Richard Godbeer, *The Devil's Dominion: Magic and Religion in Early New England* (1992); Peter Hoffer, *The Devil's Disciples: Makers of the Salem Witchcraft Trials* (1996); Carol Karlsen, *The Devil in the Shape of a Woman: Witchcraft in Early New England* (1987); Bernard Rosenthal, *Salem Story: Reading the Witch Trials of 1692* (1993); Richard Weisman, *Witchcraft, Magic, and Religion in 17th-Century Massachusetts* (1984).

Chapter 4

General

Carol R. Berkin, *First Generations: Women in Colonial America* (1996); Jack P. Greene, *Pursuits of Happiness: The Social Development of the Early Modern British Colonies and the Formation of American Culture* (1988); Richard Hofstadter, *America at 1750: A Social Portrait* (1971); Peter C. Mancall, *Deadly Medicine: Indians and Alcohol in Early America* (1995); D. W. Meinig, *Atlantic America, 1492–1800* (1986); Stephanie G. Wolf, *As Various as Their Land: The Everyday Lives of 18th Century Americans* (1992).

New France and New Spain

Ramón Gutiérrez, *When Jesus Came, the Corn Mothers Went Away: Marriage, Sexuality, and Power in New Mexico, 1500–1846* (1991); Gwendolyn Midlo Hall, *Africans in Colonial Louisiana: The Development of Afro-Creole Culture in the Eighteenth Century* (1992); Dale Miquelon, *New France, 1701–1744* (1987); G. F. G. Stanley, *New France, 1744–1760* (1968); Daniel H. Usner, Jr., *Indians, Settlers, and Slaves in a Frontier Exchange Economy: The Lower Mississippi Valley Before 1783* (1992); David J. Weber, *The Spanish Frontier in North America* (1992); Richard White, *The Middle Ground: Indians, Empires, and Republics in the Great Lakes Region, 1650–1815* (1991).

Anglo-American Society

T. H. Breen, *Tobacco Culture* (1985); Carl Bridenbaugh, *Cities in Revolt: Urban Life in America, 1743–1776* (1955); Lois Green Carr et al., eds., *Colonial Chesapeake Society* (1988); David Conroy, *In Public Houses: Drink and the Revolution of Authority in Colonial Massachusetts* (1995); Rhys Isaac, *The Transformation of Virginia, 1740–1790* (1982); Christopher Jedrey, *The World of John Cleaveland: Family and Community in Eighteenth-Century New England* (1979); Sung Bok Kim, *Landlord and Tenant in Colonial New York: Manorial Society, 1664–1775* (1978); Peter C. Mancall, *Valley of Opportunity: Economic Culture Along the Upper Susquehanna, 1700–1800* (1991); Gary B. Nash, *The Urban Crucible: Social Change, Political Consciousness, and the Origins of the American Revolution* (1979); Michael Rozbicki, *The Complete Colonial Gentleman: Cultural Legitimacy in Plantation America* (1998); David S. Shields, *Civil Tongues and Polite Letters in British America* (1997); Michael Zuckerman, *Peaceable Kingdoms: New England Towns in the Eighteenth Century* (1970).

American Economic Development

Richard Bushman, *The Refinement of America: Persons, Houses, Cities* (1992); Cary Carson et al., eds., *Of Consuming Interests: The Style of Life in the Eighteenth Century* (1994); Marc Egnal, *New World Economies: The Growth of the Thirteen Colonies and Early Canada* (1999); David Hancock, *Citizens of the World: London Merchants and the Integration of the British Atlantic Community, 1735–1785* (1995); Stephen Innes, ed., *Work and Labor in Early America* (1988); Alice Hanson Jones, *Wealth of a Nation to Be: The American Colonies on the Eve of the Revolution* (1980); Cathy Matson, *Merchants and Empire: Trading in Colonial New York* (1998); John J. McCusker and Russell R. Menard, *The Economy of British America, 1607–1789* (1985); Margaret E. Newell, *From Dependency to Independence: Economic Revolution in Colonial New England* (1998); Edwin J. Perkins, *The Economy of Colonial America* (1980); Gary M. Walton and James F. Shepherd, *The Economic Rise of Early America* (1979).

Anglo-American Politics

Bernard Bailyn, *The Origins of American Politics* (1968); Patricia U. Bonomi, *A Factious People: Politics and Society in Colonial New York* (1971); Richard Bushman, *King and People in Provincial Massachusetts* (1985); Edward M. Cook, Jr., *The Fathers of the Towns: Leadership and Community Structure in Eighteenth-Century New England* (1976); Jack P. Greene, *The Quest for Power: The Lower Houses of Assembly in the Southern Royal Colonies, 1689–1776* (1963); John Gilman Kolp, *Gentleman and Freeholders: Electoral Politics in Colonial Virginia* (1998).

Immigration to British America

Bernard Bailyn, *The Peopling of British North America* (1986); Bernard Bailyn, *Voyagers to the West* (1986); Bernard Bailyn and Philip Morgan, eds., *Strangers Within the Realm* (1991); Marilyn Baseler, *"Asylum for Mankind": America 1607–1800* (1998); Jon Butler, *The Huguenots in America* (1983); R. J. Dickson, *Ulster Immigration to Colonial America, 1718–1775* (1966); David Dobson, *Scottish Immigration to Colonial America, 1607–1785* (1994); A. Roger Ekirch, *Bound for America: The Transportation of British Convicts to the Colonies, 1718–1775* (1987); Colin Kidd, *British Identities before Nationalism: Ethnicity and Nationhood in the British Atlantic World, 1600–1800* (1999); Ned Landsman, *Scotland and Its First American Colony* (1985); A. G. Roeber, *Palatines, Liberty, and Property: German Lutherans in Colonial British America* (1993); Marianne Wokeck, *Trade in Strangers: The Beginnings of Mass Migration to North America* (1999).

African Americans

Ira Berlin, *Many Thousands Gone: The First Two Centuries of Slavery in North America* (1998); Ira Berlin and Philip Morgan, eds., *Cultivation and Culture: Labor and the Shaping of Slave Life in the Americas* (1993); Thomas J. Davis, *A Rumor of Revolt: The "Great Negro Plot" in Colonial New York* (1985); Michael A. Gomez, *Exchanging Our Country Marks: The Transformation of African Identities in the Colonial and Ante-*

bellum South (1998); Graham R. Hodges, *Root & Branch: African Americans in New York and East Jersey, 1613–1863* (1999); Marvin L. Michael Kay and Lorin Lee Cary, *Slavery in North Carolina, 1748–1775* (1995); Allan Kulikoff, *Tobacco and Slaves: The Development of Southern Cultures in the Chesapeake, 1680–1800* (1986); Philip D. Morgan, *Slave Counterpoint: Black Culture in the Eighteenth-Century Chesapeake and Low Country* (1998); Gerald [Michael] Mullin, *Flight and Rebellion: Slave Resistance in Eighteenth-Century Virginia* (1972); Michael Mullin, *Africa in America: Slave Acculturation and Resistance in the American South and the British Caribbean, 1736–1834* (1992); William Pierson, *Black Yankees: The Development of an Afro-American Subculture in Eighteenth-Century New England* (1988); Mechal Sobel, *The World They Made Together: Black and White Values in Eighteenth-Century Virginia* (1987); Betty Wood, *Women's Work, Men's Work: The Informal Slave Economies of Low Country Georgia* (1995); Anne Yentsch, *A Chesapeake Family and Their Slaves* (1994).

Anglo-American Women, Men, and Families

Kathleen M. Brown, *Good Wives, Nasty Wenches, and Anxious Patriarchs: Gender, Race, and Power in Colonial Virginia* (1996); Cornelia Hughes Dayton, *Women Before the Bar: Gender, Law, and Society in Connecticut, 1639–1789* (1995); Philip J. Greven, *The Protestant Temperament: Patterns of Child-Rearing, Religious Experience, and the Self in Early America* (1977); Joan Gundersen, *To Be Useful to the World: Women in Eighteenth-Century America* (1996); Barry J. Levy, *Quakers and the American Family* (1988); June Namias, *White Captives: Gender and Ethnicity on the American Frontier* (1993); Marylynn Salmon, *Women and the Law of Property in Early America* (1986); Daniel Blake Smith, *Inside the Great House: Planter Family Life in Eighteenth-Century Chesapeake Society* (1980); Merril D. Smith, *Breaking the Bonds: Marital Discord in Pennsylvania, 1730–1830* (1992); Lisa Wilson, *Ye Heart of a Man: The Domestic Life of Men in Colonial New England* (1999).

Anglo-American Education, Science, and the Enlightenment

Patricia Cline Cohen, *A Calculating People: The Spread of Numeracy in Early America* (1982); Lawrence A. Cremin, *American Education: The Colonial Experience, 1607–1783* (1970); Richard Beale Davis, *Intellectual Life in the Colonial South, 1585–1763* (1978); Brooke Hindle, *The Pursuit of Science in Revolutionary America* (1956); Kenneth Lockridge, *Literacy in Colonial New England* (1974); Henry F. May, *The Enlightenment in America* (1976); Amy R. W. Meyers and Margaret Beck Pritchard, eds., *Nature's Empire: Mark Catesby's New World Vision* (1998); Thomas P. Slaughter, *The Natures of John and William Bartram* (1996); William Sloan and Julie Williams, *The Early American Press, 1690–1783* (1994); Raymond P. Stearns, *Science in the British Colonies of America* (1970).

Religion and the Great Awakening

Catherine Brekus, *Strangers and Pilgrims: Female Preaching in America, 1740–1845* (1998); Patricia U. Bonomi, *Under the Cope of Heaven: Religion, Society, and Politics in Colonial America* (1986); J. M. Bumstead and John E. Van de Wetering, *What Must I Do to Be Saved? The Great Awakening in Colonial America* (1976); Jon Butler, *Awash in a Sea of Faith: Christianizing the American People* (1990); Michael Crawford, *Seasons of Grace: Colonial New England's Revival Tradition in Its British Context* (1991); Alan E. Heimert, *Religion and the American Mind: From the Great Awakening to the Revolution* (1966); Frank Lambert, *Inventing the "Great Awakening"* (1999); David S. Lovejoy, *Religious Enthusiasm in the New World* (1985); Harry S. Stout, *The Divine Dramatist: George Whitefield and the Rise of Modern Evangelicalism* (1991); Patricia Tracy, *Jonathan Edwards, Pastor* (1980).

Chapter 5

General

Ian R. Christie and Benjamin W. Labaree, *Empire or Independence, 1760–1776: A British-American Dialogue on the Coming of the American Revolution* (1976); Barbara DeWolfe, ed., *Discoveries of America: Personal Accounts of British Emigrants to North America during the Revolutionary Era* (1997); Marc Egnal, *A Mighty Empire: The Origins of the American Revolution* (1988); Merrill Jensen, *The Founding of a Nation: A History of the American Revolution, 1763–1776* (1968); John Phillip Reid, *The Constitutional History of the American Revolution* (1995); Robert W. Tucker and David C. Hendrickson, *The Fall of the First British Empire: Origins of the War of American Independence* (1982).

Colonial Warfare and the British Empire

Fred Anderson, *A People's Army: Massachusetts Soldiers and Society in the Seven Years' War* (1984); Frank W. Brecher, *Losing a Continent: France's North American Policy, 1753–1763* (1998); Lawrence Henry Gipson, *The British Empire Before the American Revolution* (1936–1970); Douglas Leach, *Roots of Conflict: British Armed Forces and Colonial Americans, 1677–1763* (1986); Robert C. Newbold, *The Albany Congress and Plan of Union of 1754* (1955); William Pencak, *War, Politics, and Revolution in Provincial Massachusetts* (1981); Alan Rogers, *Empire and Liberty: American Resistance to British Authority, 1755–1763* (1974); John Shy, *Toward Lexington: The Role of the British Army in the Coming of the American Revolution* (1965); Ian K. Steele, *Warpaths: Invasions of North America* (1994); James Titus, *The Old Dominion at War: Society, Politics, and Warfare in Late Colonial Virginia* (1991).

British Politics and Policy

Colin Bonwick, *English Radicals and the American Revolution* (1977); James E. Bradley, *Popular Politics and the American*

Revolution in England (1986); John Brewer, *Party Ideology and Popular Politics at the Accession of George III* (1976); John Brooke, *King George III* (1972); John L. Bullion, *A Great and Necessary Measure: George Grenville and the Genesis of the Stamp Act, 1763–1765* (1981); Michael Kammen, *A Rope of Sand: The Colonial Agents, British Politics, and the American Revolution* (1968); Nancy F. Koehn, *The Power of Commerce: Economy and Governance in the First British Empire* (1994); P. D. G. Thomas, *Tea Party to Independence* (1991); P. D. G. Thomas, *The Townshend Duties Crisis* (1987); P. D. G. Thomas, *British Politics and the Stamp Act Crisis* (1975).

Native Americans and the West

Richard Aquila, *The Iroquois Restoration: Iroquois Diplomacy on the Colonial Frontier, 1701–1754* (1983); Andrew Cayton and Fredrika Teute, eds., *Contact Points: American Frontiers from the Mohawk Valley to the Mississippi, 1750–1830* (1998); David H. Corkran, *The Cherokee Frontier: Conflict and Survival, 1740–1762* (1962); Gregory Dowd, *A Spirited Resistance: The North American Indian Struggle for Unity, 1745–1815* (1992); Tom Hatley, *The Dividing Paths: Cherokees and South Carolinians through the Revolutionary Era* (1995); Francis Jennings, *Empire of Fortune: Crowns, Colonies and Tribes in the Seven Years' War in America* (1988); Howard H. Peckham, *Pontiac and the Indian Uprising* (1947); Jack M. Sosin, *Whitehall and the Wilderness: The Middle West in British Colonial Policy, 1760–1775* (1961); Richard White, *The Middle Ground: Indians, Empires and Republics in the Great Lakes Region, 1650–1815* (1991).

Political and Economic Thought

Bernard Bailyn, *The Ideological Origins of the American Revolution* (1967); J. C. D. Clark, *The Language of Liberty, 1660–1832: Political Discourse and Social Dynamics in the Anglo-American World* (1994); J. E. Crowley, *This Sheba, Self: The Conceptualization of Economic Life in Eighteenth-Century America* (1974); Jay Fliegelman, *Prodigals and Pilgrims: The American Revolution Against Patriarchal Authority, 1750–1800* (1982).

American Resistance

T. H. Breen, *Tobacco Culture: The Mentality of the Great Tidewater Planters on the Eve of the Revolution* (1985); Joseph Albert Ernst, *Money and Politics in America, 1755–1775: A Study in the Currency Act of 1764 and the Political Economy of Revolution* (1973); David Conroy, *Drink and the Revolution of Authority in Colonial Massachusetts* (1995); Dirk Hoerder, *Crowd Action in Revolutionary Massachusetts, 1765–1780* (1977); Woody Holton, *Forced Founders: Indians, Debtors, Slaves, and the Making of the American Revolution in Virginia* (1999); Benjamin W. Labaree, *The Boston Tea Party* (1964); Pauline R. Maier, *The Old Revolutionaries: Political Lives in the Age of Samuel Adams* (1980); Pauline R. Maier, *From Resistance to Revolution: Colonial Radicals and the Development of American*

Opposition to Britain, 1765–1776 (1972); Edmund S. Morgan and Helen M. Morgan, *The Stamp Act Crisis: Prologue to Revolution* (1953); Gary B. Nash, *The Urban Crucible: Social Change, Political Consciousness, and the Origins of the American Revolution* (1979); Bruce A. Ragsdale, *A Planters' Republic: The Search for Economic Independence in Revolutionary Virginia* (1996); Richard Ryerson, *The Revolution Has Now Begun: The Radical Committees of Philadelphia, 1765–1776* (1978); Peter Shaw, *American Patriots and the Rituals of Revolution* (1981); Peter Thompson, *Rum Punch & Revolution: Taverngoing & Public Life in Eighteenth-Century Philadelphia* (1999); Joseph Tiedemann, *Reluctant Revolutionaries: New York City and the Road to Independence, 1763–1776* (1997); John W. Tyler, *Smugglers and Patriots: Boston Merchants and the Advent of the American Revolution* (1986); Richard Walsh, *Charleston's Sons of Liberty: A Study of the Artisans, 1763–1789* (1959); Hiller B. Zobel, *The Boston Massacre* (1970).

Chapter 6

General

Benson Bobrick, *Angel in the Whirlwind: The Triumph of the American Revolution* (1997); Colin Bonwick, *The American Revolution* (1991); Edward Countryman, *The American Revolution* (1985); Theodore Draper, *A Struggle for Power: The American Revolution* (1996); Robert Middlekauff, *The Glorious Cause: The American Revolution, 1763–1783* (1982); Harry M. Ward, *The American Revolution: Nationhood Achieved, 1763–1788* (1995); Alfred F. Young, ed., *Beyond the American Revolution* (1993); Alfred F. Young, ed., *The American Revolution: Explorations in the History of American Radicalism* (1976).

Continental Congress, Committees, and the Declaration of Independence

David Ammerman, *In the Common Cause: American Response to the Coercive Acts of 1774* (1974); Richard D. Brown, *Revolutionary Politics in Massachusetts: The Boston Committee of Correspondence and the Towns, 1772–1774* (1970); Jay Fliegelman, *Declaring Independence: Jefferson, Natural Language, & the Culture of Performance* (1993); Pauline Maier, *American Scripture: Making the Declaration of Independence* (1997); Jerrilyn Marston, *King and Congress: The Transfer of Political Legitimacy, 1774–1776* (1987); Garry Wills, *Inventing America: Jefferson's Declaration of Independence* (1978); Ann Withington, *Toward a More Perfect Union: Virtue and the Formation of American Republics* (1992).

Military Affairs

Jeremy Black, *War for America: The Fight for Independence, 1775–1783* (1991); Richard Buel, *In Irons: Britain's Naval Supremacy and the American Revolutionary Economy* (1999); E. Wayne Carp, *To Starve the Army at Pleasure: Continental Army Administration and American Political Culture, 1775–*

1783 (1984); Stephen Conway, *The War of American Independence, 1775–1783* (1995); Don Higginbotham, *The War of American Independence: Military Attitudes, Policies, and Practice, 1763–1789* (1971); Ronald Hoffman and Peter Albert, eds., *Arms and Independence: The Military Character of the American Revolution* (1984); Richard Ketchum, *Saratoga: Turning Point of America's Revolutionary War* (1997); Piers Mackesy, *The War for America, 1775–1783* (1964); James K. Martin, *Benedict Arnold, Revolutionary Hero* (1997); James K. Martin and Mark Lender, *"A Respectable Army": The Military Origins of the Republic, 1763–1789* (1982); Charles Niemeyer, *America Goes to War: A Social History of the Continental Army* (1997); Charles Royster, *A Revolutionary People at War: The Continental Army and American Character, 1775–1783* (1980); John Shy, *A People Numerous and Armed: Reflections on the Military Struggle for American Independence*, rev. ed. (1990).

Local and Regional Studies

Michael Bellesiles, *Revolutionary Outlaws: Ethan Allen and the Struggle for Independence on the Early American Frontier* (1993); Richard Buel, *Dear Liberty: Connecticut's Mobilization for the Revolutionary War* (1980); Edward Countryman, *A People in Revolution: The American Revolution and Political Society in New York, 1760–1790* (1981); Elaine Crane, *A Dependent People: Newport, Rhode Island, in the Revolutionary Era* (1985); Jeffrey Crow and Larry Tise, eds., *The Southern Experience in the American Revolution* (1978); Thomas Doerflinger, *A Vigorous Spirit of Enterprise: Merchants and Economic Development in Revolutionary Philadelphia* (1986); John Mack Faragher, *Daniel Boone* (1992); David Hackett Fischer, *Paul Revere's Ride* (1994); Craig T. Friend, ed., *The Buzzel about Kentuck: Settling the Promised Land* (1999); Robert A. Gross, *The Minutemen and Their World* (1976); Ronald Hoffman, *A Spirit of Dissension: Economics, Politics, and the Revolution in Maryland* (1973); Ronald Hoffman, Thad W. Tate, and Peter Albert, eds., *An Uncivil War: The Southern Backcountry During the American Revolution* (1985); Jean B. Lee, *The Price of Nationhood: The American Revolution in Charles County* (1994); Stephen Rosswurm, *Arms, Country, and Class: The Philadelphia Militia and the "Lower Sort" During the American Revolution* (1988); John Selby, *The Revolution in Virginia, 1775–1783* (1988).

Indians and African Americans

Colin Calloway, *The American Revolution in Indian Country* (1995); Sylvia Frey, *Water from the Rock: Black Resistance in a Revolutionary Age* (1991); Barbara Graymont, *The Iroquois in the American Revolution* (1972); Isabel T. Kelsey, *Joseph Brant, 1743–1807: Man of Two Worlds* (1984); James H. O'Donnell III, *Southern Indians in the American Revolution* (1973); Anthony F. C. Wallace, *The Death and Rebirth of the Seneca* (1969).

Loyalists

Bernard Bailyn, *The Ordeal of Thomas Hutchinson* (1974); Robert McCluer Calhoon, *The Loyalists in Revolutionary America, 1760–1781* (1973); Mary Beth Norton, *The British-Americans: The Loyalist Exiles in England, 1774–1789* (1972); Janice Potter, *The Liberty We Seek: Loyalist Ideology in Colonial New York and Massachusetts* (1983); Paul H. Smith, *Loyalists and Redcoats: A Study in British Revolutionary Policy* (1964); James W. St. G. Walker, *The Black Loyalists: The Search for a Promised Land in Nova Scotia and Sierra Leone, 1783–1870* (1976).

Women

Richard Buel and Joy Buel, *The Way of Duty: A Woman and Her Family in Revolutionary America* (1984); Ronald Hoffman and Peter Albert, eds., *Women in the Age of the American Revolution* (1989); Linda K. Kerber, *Women of the Republic: Intellect and Ideology in Revolutionary America* (1980); Holly Mayer, *Belonging to the Army: Camp Followers and Community during the American Revolution* (1996); Mary Beth Norton, *Liberty's Daughters: The Revolutionary Experience of American Women, 1750–1800* (1980).

Foreign Policy

Jonathan Dull, *A Diplomatic History of the American Revolution* (1985); Ronald Hoffman and Peter Albert, eds., *Peace and the Peacemakers: The Treaty of 1783* (1986); Ronald Hoffman and Peter Albert, eds., *Diplomacy and Revolution: The Franco-American Alliance of 1778* (1981); Lawrence Kaplan, ed., *The American Revolution and a "Candid World"* (1977); Jan Willem Schulte Nordholt, *The Dutch Republic and American Independence* (1982); Richard W. Van Alstyne, *Empire and Independence: The International History of the American Revolution* (1965).

Patriot Leaders

Fawn M. Brodie, *Thomas Jefferson: An Intimate History* (1974); Richard Brookhiser, *Founding Father: Rediscovering George Washington* (1996); Joseph Ellis, *American Sphinx: The Character of Thomas Jefferson* (1997); John E. Ferling, *The First of Men: A Life of George Washington* (1988); Eric Foner, *Tom Paine and Revolutionary America* (1976); Norman Risjord, *Thomas Jefferson* (1994); John Rhodehamel, *The Great Experiment: George Washington and the American Republic* (1998); Charles Royster, *Light-Horse Harry Lee and the Legacy of the American Revolution* (1981); Peter Shaw, *The Character of John Adams* (1976); Sheila Skemp, *Benjamin and William Franklin: Father and Son, Patriot and Loyalist* (1994); Esmond Wright, *Franklin of Philadelphia* (1986).

Chapter 7

General

Richard Beeman et al., eds., *Beyond Confederation: Origins of the Constitution and American National Identity* (1987); Andrew Burstein, *Sentimental Democracy: The Evolution of America's Romantic Self-Image* (1999); John E. Crowley, *The Privileges of Independence: Neomercantilism and the American Revolution* (1993); Ronald Hoffman et al., eds., *The Economy of Early America: The Revolutionary Period, 1763–1790* (1988); Ronald Hoffman and Peter Albert, eds., *The Transforming Hand of Revolution: Reconsidering the American Revolution as a Social Movement* (1995); Mark E. Kann, *A Republic of Men: The American Founders, Gendered Language, and Patriarchal Politics* (1998); Cathy Matson and Peter S. Onuf, *A Union of Interests: Political and Economic Thought in Revolutionary America* (1990); Forrest McDonald, *Novus Ordo Seclorum: The Intellectual Origins of the Constitution* (1985); Edmund S. Morgan, *Inventing the People: The Rise of Popular Sovereignty in England and America* (1988); David Waldstreicher, *In the Midst of Perpetual Fetes: The Making of American Nationalism, 1776–1820* (1997); Gordon S. Wood, *The Radicalism of the American Revolution* (1992); Gordon S. Wood, *The Creation of the American Republic, 1776–1787* (1969); Alfred F. Young et al., eds., *We the People: Voices and Images of the New Nation* (1993); Rosemarie Zagarri, *The Politics of Size: Representation in the United States, 1776–1850* (1988).

Continental Congress and Articles of Confederation

E. James Ferguson, *The Power of the Purse: A History of American Public Finance, 1776–1790* (1961); H. James Henderson, *Party Politics in the Continental Congress* (1974); Merrill Jensen, *The New Nation: A History of the United States During the Confederation, 1781–1789* (1950); Richard B. Morris, *The Forging of the Union, 1781–1789* (1987); Peter S. Onuf, *Statehood and Union: A History of the Northwest Ordinance* (1987); Jack N. Rakove, *The Beginnings of National Politics: An Interpretive History of the Continental Congress* (1979).

State Politics

Willi Paul Adams, *The First American Constitutions: Republican Ideology and the Making of the State Constitutions in the Revolutionary Era* (1980); Robert Gross, ed., *In Debt to Shays* (1992); Ronald Hoffman and Peter Albert, eds., *Sovereign States in an Age of Uncertainty* (1981); Donald Lutz, *Popular Consent and Popular Control: Whig Political Theory in the Early State Constitutions* (1980); Jackson Turner Main, *Political Parties Before the Constitution* (1973); Jackson Turner Main, *The Sovereign States, 1775–1783* (1973); David P. Szatmary, *Shays' Rebellion: The Making of an Agrarian Insurrection* (1980).

The Constitution

Thornton Anderson, *Creating the Constitution: The Convention of 1787 and the First Congress* (1993); Lance Banning, *The Sacred Fire of Liberty: James Madison and the Founding of the Federal Republic* (1995); Roger H. Brown, *Redeeming the Republic: Federalists, Taxation, and the Origins of the Constitution* (1993); Saul Cornell, *Anti-Federalism & the Dissenting Tradition in America, 1788-1828* (1999); Christopher Duncan, *The Anti-Federalists and Early American Political Thought* (1995); Jackson Turner Main, *The Anti-Federalists: Critics of the Constitution, 1781–1788* (1961); Frederick W. Marks III, *Independence on Trial: Foreign Affairs and the Making of the Constitution* (1973); Jack N. Rakove, *Original Meanings: Politics and Ideas in the Making of the Constitution* (1996); Robert A. Rutland, *The Ordeal of the Constitution: The Antifederalists and the Ratification Struggle of 1787–88* (1966); Abraham Sofaer, *War, Foreign Affairs, and Constitutional Power,* vol. 1: *The Origins* (1976).

Education and Culture

Cathy N. Davidson, *Revolution and the Word: The Rise of the Novel in America* (1987); Joseph M. Ellis, *After the Revolution: Profiles of Early American Culture* (1979); Carl F. Kaestle, *Pillars of the Republic: Common Schools and American Society, 1780–1860* (1983); Russel B. Nye, *The Cultural Life of the New Nation, 1776–1803* (1960); Kenneth Silverman, *A Cultural History of the American Revolution* (1976).

Women

Edith Gelles, *Portia: The World of Abigail Adams* (1992); Ronald Hoffman and Peter Albert, eds., *Women in the Age of the American Revolution* (1989); Susan Juster, *Disorderly Women: Sexual Politics and Evangelicalism in Revolutionary New England* (1994); Linda K. Kerber, *Women of the Republic: Intellect and Ideology in Revolutionary America* (1980); Mary Beth Norton, *Liberty's Daughters: The Revolutionary Experience of American Women, 1750–1800* (1980); Sheila Skemp, *Judith Sargent Murray* (1998); Rosemarie Zagarri, *A Woman's Dilemma: Mercy Otis Warren and the American Revolution* (1995).

African Americans and Slavery

Ira Berlin, *Many Thousands Gone: The First Two Centuries of Slavery in North America* (1998); Ira Berlin and Ronald Hoffman, eds., *Slavery and Freedom in the Age of the American Revolution* (1983); Patricia Bradley, *Slavery, Propaganda, and the American Revolution* (1998); David Brion Davis, *The Problem of Slavery in the Age of Revolution, 1770–1823* (1975); Paul Finkelman, *Slavery and the Founders: Race and Liberty in the Age of Jefferson* (1996); Carol V. R. George, *Segregated Sabbaths: Richard Allen and the Emergence of Independent Black*

Churches, 1760–1840 (1973); Michael A. Gomez, *Exchanging Our Country Marks: The Transformation of African Identities in the Colonial and Antebellum South* (1998); Graham R. Hodges, *Root & Branch: African Americans in New York and East Jersey, 1613–1863* (1999); Winthrop Jordan, *White over Black: American Attitudes Toward the Negro, 1550–1812* (1968); Duncan J. Macleod, *Slavery, Race, and the American Revolution* (1974); Gary Nash, *Forging Freedom: The Formation of Philadelphia's Black Community, 1720–1840* (1988); Donald L. Robinson, *Slavery in the Structure of American Politics, 1765–1820* (1971); Shane White, *Somewhat More Independent: The End of Slavery in New York City, 1770–1810* (1991); Arthur Zilversmit, *The First Emancipation: The Abolition of Slavery in the North* (1967).

Indians

Harvey L. Carter, *The Life and Times of Little Turtle* (1987); Gregory E. Dowd, *A Spirited Resistance: The North American Indian Struggle for Unity, 1745–1815* (1992); Dorothy Jones, *License for Empire: Colonialism by Treaty in Early America* (1982); Wiley Sword, *President Washington's Indian War: The Struggle for the Old Northwest, 1790–1795* (1985); Anthony F. C. Wallace, *The Death and Rebirth of the Seneca* (1969); Richard White, *The Middle Ground: Indians, Empires, and Republics in the Great Lakes Region, 1650–1815* (1991).

Chapter 8

National Government and Administration

Kenneth Bowling, *The Creation of Washington, D.C.* (1991); Ralph Adams Brown, *The Presidency of John Adams* (1975); William Casto, *The Supreme Court in the Early Republic: The Chief Justiceships of John Jay and Oliver Ellsworth* (1995); Stanley Elkins and Eric McKitrick, *The Age of Federalism, 1788–1800* (1993); Morton Frisch, *Alexander Hamilton and the Political Order* (1991); Ronald Hoffman and Peter J. Albert, eds., *Launching the "Extended Republic": The Federalist Era* (1998); Richard Kohn, *Eagle and Sword: The Federalists and the Creation of the Military Establishment in America, 1783–1802* (1975); Tadahisa Kuroda, *The Origins of the Twelfth Amendment: The Electoral College in the Early Republic, 1787–1804* (1994); Forrest McDonald, *Alexander Hamilton* (1979); Forrest McDonald, *The Presidency of George Washington* (1974); John R. Nelson, Jr., *Liberty and Property: Political Economy and Policymaking in the New Nation, 1789–1812* (1987); James R. Sharp, *American Politics in the Early Republic: The New Nation in Crisis* (1993); Garry Wills, *Cincinnatus: George Washington and the Enlightenment* (1984).

Partisan Politics

Lance Banning, *The Jeffersonian Persuasion: Evolution of a Party Ideology* (1978); Richard Buel, *Securing the Revolution: Ideology in American Politics, 1789–1815* (1972); Joseph Charles, *The Origins of the American Party System* (1956); Noble E. Cunningham, *The Jeffersonian Republicans: The Formation of Party Organization, 1789–1801* (1957); Manning J. Dauer, *The Adams Federalists* (1953); Richard Hofstadter, *The Idea of a Party System: The Rise of Legitimate Opposition in the United States, 1780–1840* (1970); Thomas Slaughter, *The Whiskey Rebellion* (1986); John Zvesper, *Political Philosophy and Rhetoric: A Study of the Origins of American Party Politics* (1977).

Economics in Thought and Practice

Joyce Appleby, *Capitalism and a New Social Order: The Republican Vision of the 1790s* (1984); Christopher Clark, *The Roots of Rural Capitalism: Western Massachusetts, 1780–1860* (1990); Paul Gilje, ed., *Wages of Independence: Capitalism in the Early American Republic* (1997); James A. Henretta, *The Origins of American Capitalism* (1991); Allan Kulikoff, *The Agrarian Origins of American Capitalism* (1992); Curtis Nettels, *The Emergence of a National Economy, 1775–1815* (1962); Winifred Rothenberg, *From Market-Places to Market Economy: The Transformation of Rural Massachusetts, 1750–1850* (1992) .

Foreign Relations

Harry Ammon, *The Genêt Mission* (1973); Samuel F. Bemis, *Jay's Treaty*, 2d ed. (1962); Samuel F. Bemis, *Pinckney's Treaty*, 2d ed. (1960); Jerald A. Combs, *The Jay Treaty* (1970); Alexander DeConde, *The Quasi-War: Politics and Diplomacy of the Undeclared War with France, 1797–1801* (1966); Alexander DeConde, *Entangling Alliance: Politics and Diplomacy Under George Washington* (1958); Felix Gilbert, *To the Farewell Address: Ideas of Early American Foreign Policy* (1961); Reginald Horsman, *The Diplomacy of the New Republic, 1776–1815* (1985); Lawrence Kaplan, *"Entangling Alliances with None": American Foreign Policy in the Age of Jefferson* (1987); Conor Cruise O'Brien, *The Long Affair: Thomas Jefferson and the French Revolution, 1785–1800* (1996); Bradford Perkins, *The First Rapprochement: England and the United States, 1795–1805* (1967); Matthew Spalding and Patrick J. Garrity, *A Sacred Union of Citizens: George Washington's Farewell Address and American Character* (1996); William Stinchcombe, *The XYZ Affair* (1981); William E. Weeks, *Building the Continental Empire: American Expansion from the Revolution to the Civil War* (1996).

Civil Liberties

Ronald Hoffman and Peter Albert, eds., *The Bill of Rights: Government Proscribed* (1997); Leonard W. Levy, *Emergence of a Free Press* (1985); Leonard W. Levy, *Origins of the Fifth Amendment* (1968); Robert A. Rutland, *The Birth of the Bill of Rights, 1776–1791*, rev. ed. (1983); James Morton Smith, *Freedom's Fetters: The Alien and Sedition Laws and American Civil Liberties* (1956).

Indians and African Americans

Douglas Egerton, *Gabriel's Rebellion: The Virginia Slave Conspiracies of 1800 and 1802* (1993); Dorothy Jones, *License for Empire: Colonization by Treaty in Early America* (1982); Theda Perdue, *Cherokee Women: Gender and Culture Change, 1700–1835* (1998); Francis Paul Prucha, *American Indian Policy in the Formative Years: The Indian Trade and Intercourse Acts, 1790–1834* (1962); James Sidbury, *Ploughshares into Swords: Race, Rebellion, and Identity in Gabriel's Virginia, 1730–1810* (1997); Mechal Sobel, *The World They Made Together: Black and White Values in Eighteenth-Century Virginia* (1987); Anthony F. C. Wallace, *The Death and Rebirth of the Seneca* (1969).

Chapter 9

General

Henry Adams, *History of the United States of America During the Administration of Thomas Jefferson and of James Madison,* 9 vols. (1889–1891); Noble E. Cunningham, Jr., *The United States in 1800: Henry Adams Revisited* (1988); Jean V. Matthews, *Toward a New Society: American Thought and Culture, 1800–1830* (1991); John Mayfield, *The New Nation, 1800–1845* (1981); Marshall Smelser, *The Democratic Republic, 1801–1815* (1968).

Party Politics

James M. Banner, *To the Hartford Convention: The Federalists and the Origins of Party Politics in the Early Republic, 1789–1815* (1967); Noble E. Cunningham, Jr., *The Jeffersonian Republicans in Power: Party Operations, 1801–1809* (1963); David Hackett Fischer, *The Revolution of American Conservatism: The Federalist Party in the Era of Jeffersonian Democracy* (1965); Linda K. Kerber, *Federalists in Dissent* (1970); Milton Lomask, *Aaron Burr,* 2 vols. (1979, 1983); Richard P. McCormick, *The Presidential Game: The Origins of American Presidential Politics* (1982); Drew McCoy, *The Elusive Republic* (1980); Arnold A. Rogow, *A Fatal Friendship: Alexander Hamilton and Aaron Burr* (1998); James Roger Sharp, *American Politics in the Early Republic: The New Nation in Crisis* (1993); James Sterling Young, *The Washington Community, 1800–1828* (1966).

Jefferson and Madison

Noble E. Cunningham, Jr., *In Pursuit of Reason: The Life of Thomas Jefferson* (1987); Noble E. Cunningham, Jr., *The Process of Government Under Jefferson* (1978); Joseph J. Ellis, *American Sphinx: The Character of Thomas Jefferson* (1996); Annette Gordon-Reed, *Thomas Jefferson and Sally Hemings: An American Controversy* (1997); Ralph Ketcham, *Presidents Above Party: The First American Presidency, 1789–1829* (1984); Drew R. McCoy, *The Last of the Fathers: James Madison and the Republican Legacy* (1989); Peter S. Onuf, ed., *Jeffersonian Legacies* (1993); Merrill D. Peterson, *Thomas Jefferson and the New Nation* (1970); Norman K. Risjord, *Thomas Jefferson* (1994); Robert Allen Rutland, *The Presidency of James Madison* (1990); Robert W. Tucker and David C. Hendrickson, *Empire of Liberty: The Statecraft of Thomas Jefferson* (1990).

The Supreme Court and the Law

Leonard Baker, *John Marshall: A Life in Law* (1974); Robert Lowry Clinton, *Marbury v. Madison and Judicial Review* (1989); Richard E. Ellis, *The Jeffersonian Crisis: Courts and Politics in the Young Republic* (1971); Morton J. Horowitz, *The Transformation of American Law, 1780–1860* (1977); Herbert A. Johnson, *The Chief Justiceship of John Marshall, 1801–1835* (1997); R. Kent Newmyer, *The Supreme Court Under Marshall and Taney* (1968); Thomas C. Shevory, *John Marshall's Law: Interpretation, Ideology, and Interest* (1994); Francis N. Stites, *John Marshall: Defender of the Constitution* (1981).

Louisiana and Lewis and Clark

Stephen E. Ambrose, *Undaunted Courage: Meriwether Lewis, Thomas Jefferson, and the Opening of the American West* (1996); Alexander De Conde, *This Affair of Louisiana* (1976); Donna J. Kessler, *The Making of Sacagawea: A Euro-American Legend* (1996); James P. Ronda, *Lewis and Clark Among the Indians* (1984); James P. Ronda, ed., *Thomas Jefferson and the Changing West* (1997); James P. Ronda, ed., *Voyage of Discovery: Essays on the Lewis and Clark Expedition* (1998).

Expansionism, the War of 1812, and Foreign Relations

Robert J. Allison, *The Crescent Obscured: The United States and the Muslim World, 1776–1815* (1995); Paul Baepler, ed., *White Slaves, African Masters: An Anthology of American Barbary Captivity Narratives* (1999); Roger H. Brown, *The Republic in Peril* (1964); R. David Edmunds, *Tecumseh and the Quest for Indian Leadership* (1984); R. David Edmunds, *The Shawnee Prophet* (1983); Clifford L. Egan, *Neither Peace nor War: Franco-American Relations, 1803–1812* (1983); Kenneth J. Hagan, *This People's Navy* (1991); Donald R. Hickey, *The War of 1812: A Short History* (1995); Frank Lawrence Owsley, Jr., and Gene A. Smith, *Filibusters and Expansionists: Jeffersonian Manifest Destiny, 1800–1821* (1997); Bradford Perkins, *The Creation of a Republican Empire, 1776–1865* (1993); Julius W. Pratt, *Expansionists of 1812* (1925); Robert V. Remini, *The Battle of New Orleans: Andrew Jackson and America's First Military Victory* (1999); J. C. A. Stagg, *Mr. Madison's War: Politics, Diplomacy, and Warfare in the Early Republic, 1783–1830* (1983); Anders Stephanson, *Manifest Destiny: American Expansionism and the Empire of Right* (1995); Steve Watts, *The Republic Reborn: War and the Making of a Liberal America, 1790–1820* (1987); David J. Weber, *The Spanish Frontier in North America* (1992); J. Leitch Wright, Jr., *Creeks and Seminoles* (1986).

Chapter 10

General

Jack Larkin, *The Reshaping of Everyday Life, 1790–1840* (1988); D. W. Meinig, *The Shaping of America: A Geographical Perspective on 500 Years of History*, vol. 2: *Contininental America, 1800–1867* (1993); Charles G. Sellers, Jr., *The Market Revolution: Jacksonian America, 1815–1840* (1991); Melvyn Stokes and Stephen Conway, eds., *The Market Revolution in America: Social, Political, and Religious Expressions, 1800–1860* (1996).

Postwar Nationalism

Harry Ammon, *James Monroe: The Quest for National Identity* (1971); Noble E. Cunningham, *The Presidency of James Monroe* (1996); Mary W. M. Hargreaves, *The Presidency of John Quincy Adams* (1985); Morton J. Horowitz, *The Transformation of American Law, 1780–1860* (1977); Ralph Ketcham, *Presidents Above Party: The First American Presidency, 1789–1829* (1984); Walter LaFeber, ed., *John Quincy Adams and American Continental Empire* (1965); Ernest R. May, *The Making of the Monroe Doctrine* (1976); Paul C. Nagel, *John Quincy Adams: A Public Life, a Private Life* (1997); R. Kent Newmyer, *The Supreme Court Under Marshall and Taney* (1968); Dexter Perkins, *Hands Off: A History of the Monroe Doctrine* (1941); Robert V. Remini, *Henry Clay: Statesman for the Union* (1991); Thomas C. Shevory, *John Marshall's Law: Interpretation, Ideology, and Interest* (1994); William Earl Weeks, *John Quincy Adams and American Global Empire* (1992).

The Market Economy, Manufacturing, and Commerce

Stuart Bruchey, *Enterprise: The Dynamic Economy of a Free People* (1990); Alfred D. Chandler, Jr., *The Visible Hand: Managerial Revolution in American Business* (1977); William Cronon, *Nature's Metropolis: Chicago and the Great West* (1991); Paul A. Gilje, ed., *Wages of Independence: Capitalism in the Early American Republic* (1997); Louis Hartz, *Economic Policy and Democratic Thought: Pennsylvania, 1776–1860* (1954); David A. Hounshell, *From the American System to Mass Production, 1800–1932: The Development of Manufacturing Technology in the United States* (1984); David J. Jeremy, *Transatlantic Industrial Revolution: The Diffusion of Textile Technologies Between Britain and America, 1790s–1830s* (1981); Herbert A. Johnson, *The Chief Justiceship of John Marshall, 1801–1835* (1997); David Klingaman and Richard Vedder, eds., *Essays in Nineteenth-Century History* (1975); Stanley I. Kutler, *Privilege and Creative Destruction: The Charles River Bridge Case* (1971); Walter Licht, *Industrializing America: The Nineteenth Century* (1995); Otto Mayr and Robert C. Post, eds., *Yankee Enterprise: The Rise of the American System of Manufacturers* (1981); Douglass C. North, *Economic Growth of the United States, 1790–1860* (1966); Theodore Steinberg, *Nature Incorporated: Industrialization and the Waters of New England* (1991).

Transportation

Albert Fishlow, *American Railroads and the Transformation of the Ante-Bellum Economy* (1965); Carter Goodrich, *Government Promotion of American Canals and Railroads, 1800–1890* (1960); Louis C. Hunter, *Steamboats on the Western Rivers* (1949); Richard R. John, *Spreading the News: The American Postal System from Franklin to Morse* (1995); Harry N. Scheiber, *Ohio Canal Era: A Case Study of Government and the Economy, 1820–1861* (1969); Ronald E. Shaw, *Canals for a Nation: The Canal Era in the United States, 1790–1860* (1990); Carol Sheriff, *The Artificial River: The Erie Canal and the Paradox of Progress, 1817–1862* (1996); George R. Taylor, *The Transportation Revolution, 1815–1860* (1951); James A. Ward, *Railroads and the Character of America, 1820–1887* (1986).

Commercial Farming

"American Agriculture, 1790–1840, A Symposium," *Agricultural History* 46 (January 1972); Jeremy Atack and Fred Bateman, *To Their Own Soil: Agriculture in the Antebellum North* (1987); Allen G. Bogue, *From Prairie to Corn Belt: Farming on the Illinois and Iowa Prairies in the Nineteenth Century* (1963); Christopher Clark, *The Roots of Rural Capitalism: Western Massachusetts, 1780–1860* (1990); Clarence Danhof, *Change in Agriculture: The Northern United States, 1820–1870* (1969); Paul W. Gates, *The Farmer's Age: Agriculture, 1815–1860* (1962); Benjamin H. Hibbard, *A History of Public Land Policies* (1939); Joan M. Jensen, *Loosening the Bonds: Mid-Atlantic Farm Women, 1750–1850* (1986); Robert Leslie Jones, *History of Agriculture in Ohio to 1880* (1983); Peter D. McClelland, *Sowing Modernity: America's First Agricultural Revolution* (1999); Sally McMurry, *Transforming Rural Life: Dairying Families and Agricultural Change, 1820–1885* (1995); Gavin Wright, *The Political Economy of the Cotton South* (1978).

Workers

Mary H. Blewett, *Men, Women, and Work: Class, Gender, and Protest in the New England Shoe Industry, 1780–1910* (1988); Jeanne Boydston, *Home and Work: Housework, Wages, and the Ideology of Labor in the Early Republic* (1990); Thomas Dublin, *Transforming Women's Work: New England Lives in the Industrial Revolution* (1994); Thomas Dublin, *Women at Work: The Transformation of Work and Community in Lowell, Massachusetts, 1826–1860* (1979); Bruce Laurie, *Artisans into Workers: Labor in Nineteenth-Century America* (1989); Howard B. Rock, Paul A. Gilje, and Robert Asher, eds., *American Artisans: Crafting Social Identity, 1750–1850* (1995); Sean Wilentz, *Chants Democratic: New York City and the Rise of the American Working Class, 1788–1850* (1984); David A. Zonderman, *Aspirations and Anxieties: New England Workers and the Mechanized Factory System, 1815–1850* (1992).

Americans on the Move

Joan Cashin, *A Family Venture: Men and Women on the Southern Frontier* (1991); James E. Davis, *Frontier America 1800–1840: A Comparative Demographic Analysis of the Frontier Process* (1977); Stewart Holbrook, *The Yankee Exodus: An Account of Migration from New England* (1950); Julie Roy Jeffrey, *Frontier Women: The Trans-Mississippi West, 1840–1880* (1979); Peter D. McClelland and Richard J. Zeckhauser, eds., *Demographic Dimensions of the New Republic* (1982); Virginia E. and Robert W. McCormick, *New Englanders on the Ohio Frontier* (1998); Gerald McFarland, *A Scattered People: An American Family Moves West* (1985); James Hebron Moore, *The Emergence of the Cotton Kingdom in the Old Southwest: Mississippi, 1770–1860* (1987); James Oakes, *The Ruling Race: A History of American Slaveholders* (1982); Malcom J. Rohrbough, *The Trans-Appalachian Frontier: People, Societies, and Institutions, 1775–1850* (1978); Russell Thornton, *American Indian Holocaust and Survival: A Population History Since 1492* (1987); David J. Weber, *The Spanish Frontier in North America* (1992); Richard White, *"It's Your Misfortune and None of My Own": A History of the American West* (1991).

Native American Resistance and Removal

Robert F. Berkhofer, Jr., *The White Man's Indian* (1978); Paul H. Carlson, *The Plains Indians* (1998); James W. Covington, *The Seminoles of Florida* (1993); Michael D. Green, *The Politics of Indian Removal: Creek Government and Society in Crisis* (1982); Stanley W. Hoig, *The Cherokees and Their Chiefs in the Wake of Empire* (1998); William G. McLoughlin, *Cherokee Renascence in the New Republic* (1986); Theda Perdue, *Slavery and the Evolution of Cherokee Society, 1540–1866* (1979); Ronald N. Satz, *American Indian Policy in the Jacksonian Era* (1975); Daniel H. Usner, Jr., *American Indians in the Lower Mississippi Valley* (1998); Anthony F. C. Wallace, *The Long, Bitter Trail: Andrew Jackson and the Indians* (1993); Richard White, *The Roots of Dependency: Subsistence, Environment, and Social Change Among the Choctaws, Pawnees, and Navajos* (1983); James Wilson, *The Earth Shall Weep: A History of Native America* (1998); J. Leitch Wright, Jr., *Creeks and Seminoles: The Destruction and Regeneration of the Muscogulge People* (1986).

Chapter 11

General

George Dangerfield, *The Awakening of American Nationalism, 1815–1828* (1965); Daniel Feller, *The Jacksonian Promise: America, 1815–1840* (1995); Jean V. Matthews, *Toward a New Society: American Thought and Culture, 1800–1830* (1991); John Mayfield, *The New Nation, 1800–1845* (1981); Charles Sellers, *The Market Revolution: Jacksonian America, 1815–1846* (1991).

Religion, Revivalism, and Reform

Robert H. Abzug, *Cosmos Crumbling: American Reform and the Religious Imagination* (1994); Michael Barkun, *Crucible of the Millennium: The Burned-over District of New York in the 1840s* (1986); Terry Bilhartz, *Urban Religion and the Second Great Awakening: Church and Society in Early National Baltimore* (1986); Paul K. Conkin, *The Uneasy Center: Reformed Christianity in Antebellum America* (1995); Clifford S. Griffen, *Their Brothers' Keepers: Moral Stewardship in the United States, 1800–1865* (1960); Keith J. Hardman, *Charles Grandison Finney, 1792–1875: Revivalist and Reformer* (1987); Nathan O. Hatch, *The Democratization of American Christianity* (1989); Christine Leigh Heyrman, *Southern Cross: The Beginnings of the Bible Belt* (1997); Curtis D. Johnson, *Islands of Holiness: Rural Religion in Upstate New York, 1790–1860* (1989); Paul E. Johnson, *A Shopkeeper's Millennium: Society and Revivals in Rochester, New York, 1815–1837* (1978); Steven Mintz, *Moralists and Modernizers: America's Pre–Civil War Reformers* (1995); Timothy L. Smith, *Revivalism and Social Reform in Mid-Nineteenth Century America* (1957); Alice Felt Tyler, *Freedom's Ferment* (1944); Ronald G. Walters, *American Reformers, 1815–1860*, rev. ed. (1997).

Temperance, Asylums, and Antimasonry

Thomas J. Brown, *Dorothea Dix: New England Reformer* (1998); David Gollaher, *Voice for the Mad: The Life of Dorothea Dix* (1995); Paul Goodman, *Towards a Christian Republic: Antimasonry and the Great Transition in New England, 1826–1836* (1988); Gerald N. Grob, *Mental Institutions in America: Social Policy to 1875* (1973); Kathleen Smith Kutolowski, "Antimasonry Reexamined: Social Bases of the Grass-Roots Party," *Journal of American History* 71 (September 1984): 269–293; W. J. Rorabaugh, *The Alcoholic Republic: An American Tradition* (1979); David J. Rothman, *The Discovery of the Asylum: Social Order and Disorder in the New Republic* (1971); Ian R. Tyrrell, *Sobering Up: From Temperance to Prohibition in Antebellum America, 1800–1860* (1979); William Preston Vaughn, *The Antimasonic Party in the United States, 1826–1843* (1983).

Women and Reform

Barbara J. Berg, *The Remembered Gate: Origins of American Feminism: The Woman and the City, 1800–1860* (1977); Ellen C. Du Bois, *Feminism and Suffrage: The Emergence of an Independent Woman's Movement in America, 1848–1869* (1978); Barbara Leslie Epstein, *The Politics of Domesticity: Women, Evangelism, and Temperance in Nineteenth-Century America* (1981); Lori D. Ginzberg, *Women and the Work of Benevolence: Morality, Politics, and Class in the Nineteenth-Century United States* (1990); Debra Gold Hansen, *Strained Sisterhood: Gender and Class in the Boston Female Anti-Slavery Society* (1993); Nancy A. Hewitt, *Women's Activism and Social Change: Rochester, New York, 1822–1872* (1984); Sylvia D. Hoffert, *When Hens Crow: The Woman's Rights Movement in*

Antebellum America (1995); Nancy Isenberg, *Sex and Citizenship in Antebellum America* (1998); Gerda Lerner, *The Grimké Sisters of South Carolina* (1967); Amanda Porterfield, *Mary Lyon and the Mount Holyoke Missionaries* (1997); Mary P. Ryan, *Cradle of the Middle Class: The Family in Oneida County, New York, 1790–1865* (1981); Mary P. Ryan, *Women in Public: Between Banners and Ballots, 1825–1880* (1990); Shirley J. Yee, *Black Women Abolitionists: A Study in Activism, 1828–1860* (1992); Jean Fagan Yellin, *Women & Sisters: The Antislavery Feminists in American Culture* (1989).

Antislavery and Abolitionism

James Brewer Stewart, *Holy Warriors: The Abolitionists and American Slavery*, rev. ed. (1996); David Brion Davis, *Slavery and Human Progress* (1984); Frederick Douglass, *Life and Times of Frederick Douglass* (1881); George M. Fredrickson, *The Black Image in the White Mind: The Debate on Afro-American Character and Destiny, 1817–1914* (1971); Lawrence J. Friedman, *Gregarious Saints: Self and Community in American Abolitionism, 1830–1870* (1982); Paul Goodman, *Of One Blood: Abolitionism and the Origins of Racial Equality* (1998); David Grimsted, *American Mobbing, 1828–1861* (1998); Aileen S. Kraditor, *Means and Ends in American Abolitionism: Garrison and His Critics on Strategy and Tactics* (1967); Henry Mayer, *All on Fire: William Lloyd Garrison and the Abolition of Slavery* (1998); William Lee Miller, *Arguing About Slavery: The Great Battle in the United States Congress* (1995); William H. Pease and Jane H. Pease, *They Who Would Be Free: Blacks' Search for Freedom, 1830–1861* (1974); Benjamin Quarles, *Black Abolitionists* (1969); John L. Thomas, *The Liberator: William Lloyd Garrison* (1963); Ronald G. Walters, *The Antislavery Appeal: American Abolitionism After 1830* (1976).

Politics and Diplomacy, 1816–1828

Harry Ammon, *James Monroe: The Quest for National Identity* (1971); Noble E. Cunningham, *The Presidency of James Monroe* (1996); Mary W. M. Hargreaves, *The Presidency of John Quincy Adams* (1985); Morton J. Horowitz, *The Transformation of American Law, 1780–1860* (1977); Ralph Ketcham, *Presidents Above Party: The First American Presidency, 1789–1829* (1984); Walter LaFeber, ed., *John Quincy Adams and American Continental Empire* (1965); Ernest R. May, *The Making of the Monroe Doctrine* (1976); Paul C. Nagel, *John Quincy Adams: A Public Life, a Private Life* (1997); R. Kent Newmyer, *The Supreme Court Under Marshall and Taney* (1968); Dexter Perkins, *Hands Off: A History of the Monroe Doctrine* (1941); Robert V. Remini, *Henry Clay: Statesman for the Union* (1991); Thomas C. Shevory, *John Marshall's Law: Interpretation, Ideology, and Interest* (1994); William Earl Weeks, *John Quincy Adams and American Global Empire* (1992).

Andrew Jackson and the Jacksonians

Donald B. Cole, *Martin Van Buren and the American Political System* (1984); Michael F. Holt, *Political Parties and American Political Development from the Age of Jackson to the Age of Lincoln* (1992); Richard B. Latner, *The Presidency of Andrew Jackson* (1979); John F. Marszalek, *The Petticoat Affair: Manners, Mutiny, and Sex in Andrew Jackson's White House* (1997); Marvin Meyers, *The Jacksonian Persuasion* (1960); John Niven, *Martin Van Buren* (1983); Edward Pessen, *Jacksonian America: Society, Personality, and Politics*, rev. ed. (1979); Robert V. Remini, *The Legacy of Andrew Jackson: Essays on Democracy, Indian Removal, and Slavery* (1988); Robert V. Remini, *The Life of Andrew Jackson* (1988); Harry L. Watson, *Liberty and Power: The Politics of Jacksonian America* (1990).

Democrats and Whigs

William J. Cooper, *The South and the Politics of Slavery, 1828–1856* (1978); Ronald P. Formisano, *The Transformation of Political Culture: Massachusetts Parties, 1790s–1840s* (1983); William W. Freehling, *Prelude to Civil War: The Nullification Controversy in South Carolina* (1966); Daniel Walker Howe, *The Political Culture of the American Whigs* (1979); Lawrence Frederick Kohl, *The Politics of Individualism: Parties and the American Character in the Jacksonian Era* (1989); Richard P. McCormick, *The Second American Party System: Party Formation in the Jacksonian Era* (1966); Merrill D. Peterson, *The Great Triumvirate: Webster, Clay, and Calhoun* (1987); Norman Lois Peterson, *The Presidencies of William Henry Harrison and John Tyler* (1989); James Roger Sharp, *The Jacksonians Versus the Banks: Politics in the States After the Panic of 1837* (1970).

Manifest Destiny and Foreign Policy

John M. Belohlavek, *"Let the Eagle Soar!" The Foreign Policy of Andrew Jackson* (1985); T. R. Fehrenbach, *Lone Star: A History of Texas and the Texans* (1968); Norman B. Graebner, ed., *Manifest Destiny* (1968); Thomas R. Hietala, *Manifest Destiny: Anxious Aggrandizement in Late Jacksonian America* (1985); Reginald Horsman, *Race and Manifest Destiny* (1981); Michael Hunt, *Ideology and U.S. Foreign Policy* (1987); Bradford Perkins, *The Creation of a Republican Empire, 1776–1865* (1993); David M. Pletcher, *The Diplomacy of Annexation: Texas, Oregon, and the Mexican War* (1973); Charles G. Sellers, Jr., *James K. Polk: Continentalist, 1843–1846* (1966); Anders Stephanson, *Manifest Destiny: American Expansionism and the Empire of Right* (1995); Paul A. Varg, *United States Foreign Relations, 1820–1860* (1979); David J. Weber, *The Spanish Frontier in North America* (1992); Albert K. Weinberg, *Manifest Destiny* (1935).

The Supreme Court and the Law

Leonard Baker, *John Marshall: A Life in Law* (1974); Francis N. Stites, *John Marshall: Defender of the Constitution* (1981).

Chapter 12

Rural and Utopian Communities

Leonard J. Arrington and Davis Bitton, *The Mormon Experience: A History of the Latterday Saints* (1979); Priscilla J. Brewer, *Shaker Communities, Shaker Lives* (1986); David B. Danbom, *Born in the Country: A History of Rural America* (1995); John Mack Faragher, *Sugar Creek: Life on the Illinois Prairie* (1986); Laurence Foster, *Religion and Sexuality: Three American Communal Experiments of the Nineteenth Century* (1981); Steven Hahn and Jonathan Prude, eds., *The Countryside in the Age of Capitalist Transformation* (1985); Joan M. Jensen, *Loosening the Bonds: Mid-Atlantic Farm Women, 1750–1850* (1986); Sally McMurry, *Families and Farmhouses in Nineteenth Century America: Vernacular Design and Social Change* (1988); Anthony F. C. Wallace, *Rockdale: The Growth of an American Village in the Early Industrial Revolution* (1978); Kenneth H. Winn, *Exiles in a Land of Liberty: Mormons in America, 1830–1846* (1989).

The West

John Mack Faragher, *Women and Men on the Overland Trail* (1979); Ramón A. Gutiérrez and Richard J. Orsi, eds., *Contested Eden: California Before the Gold Rush* (1998); Julie Roy Jeffrey, *Frontier Women: The Trans-Mississippi West, 1840–1880* (1979); Rudolph M. Lapp, *Blacks in Gold Rush California* (1977); Malcolm J. Rohrbough, *Days of Gold: The California Gold Rush and the American Nation* (1997); Quintard Taylor, *In Search of the Racial Frontier: African Americans in the American West, 1528–1990* (1998); John D. Unruh, Jr., *The Overland Emigrants and the Trans-Mississippi West, 1840–1860* (1979); David J. Weber, *The Spanish Frontier in North America* (1992); Richard White, *"It's Your Misfortune and None of My Own": A History of the American West* (1991).

Urban Communities

Melvin A. Adelman, *A Sporting Time: New York City and the Rise of Modern Athletics, 1820–1870* (1986); Stuart M. Blumin, *The Emergence of the Middle Class: Social Experience in the American City, 1760–1900* (1989); Edwin G. Burrows and Mike Wallace, *Gotham: A History of New York City to 1898* (1999); Susan G. Davis, *Parades and Power: Street Theater in Nineteenth-Century Philadelphia* (1986); Timothy J. Gilfoyle, *City of Eros: New York City, Prostitution, and the Commercialization of Sex, 1790–1920* (1992); Karen V. Hansen, *A Very Social Time: Crafting Community in Antebellum New England* (1994); Carl Kaestle, *Pillars of the Republic: Common Schools and American Society, 1780–1860* (1982); Jack Larkin, *The Reshaping of Everyday Life, 1790–1840* (1988); Timothy R. Mahoney, *Provincial Lives: Middle-Class Experience in the Antebellum Middle West* (1999); Edward Pessen, *Riches, Class and Power Before the Civil War* (1973); Christine Stansell, *City of Women: Sex and Class in New York, 1789–1860* (1986); Richard B. Stott, *Workers in the Metropolis: Class, Ethnicity, and Youth in Antebellum New York City* (1990); Alexis de Tocqueville, *Democracy in America*, 2 vols. (1835, 1840).

Women and American Families

Virginia K. Bartlett, *Keeping House: Women's Lives in Western Pennsylvania, 1790–1850* (1994); Janet Farrell Brodie, *Contraception and Abortion in Nineteenth-Century America* (1994); Lee Virginia Chambers-Schiller, *Liberty, A Better Husband: Single Women in America: The Generations of 1780–1840* (1984); Clifford Edward Clark, Jr., *The American Family Home, 1800–1960* (1986); Nancy F. Cott, *The Bonds of Womanhood: "Woman's Sphere" in New England, 1780–1835* (1977); Linda Gordon, *Woman's Body, Woman's Rights: A Social History of Birth Control in America* (1976); Joan Hoff, *Law, Gender and Injustice: A Legal History of U.S. Women* (1991); Suzanne Lebsock, *The Free Women of Petersburg: Status and Culture in a Southern Town, 1784–1860* (1984); Glenda Riley, *Divorce: An American Tradition* (1991); Mary P. Ryan, *Cradle of the Middle Class: The Family in Oneida County, New York, 1790–1865* (1981); Kathryn Kish Sklar, *Catharine Beecher: A Study in American Domesticity* (1973); Maris A. Vinovskis, *Fertility in Massachusetts from the Revolution to the Civil War* (1981); Robert V. Wells, *Revolutions in Americans' Lives* (1982); Barbara Welter, "The Cult of True Womanhood, 1820–1860," *American Quarterly* 18 (Summer 1966): 151–174.

Immigrants and Hispanics

Thomás Almaguer, *Racial Fault Lines: The Historical Origins of White Supremacy in California* (1994); Gunther Barth, *Bitter Strength: A History of Chinese in the United States, 1850–1870* (1964); Kathleen Neils Conzen, *Immigrant Milwaukee: 1836–1860* (1976); Arnoldo De León, *The Tejano Community, 1836–1900* (1982); Hasia R. Diner, *Erin's Daughters in America: Irish Immigrant Women in the Nineteenth Century* (1983); David A. Gerber, *The Making of an American Pluralism: Buffalo, New York, 1825–60* (1989); Noel Ignatiev, *How the Irish Became White* (1995); Matthew Frye Jacobson, *Whiteness of a Different Color: European Immigrants and the Alchemy of Race* (1998); Walter D. Kamphoefner, *The Westfalians: From Germany to Missouri* (1987); Walter D. Kamphoefner et al., eds., *News from the Land of Freedom: German Immigrants Write Home* (1991); Dale T. Knobel, *Paddy and the Republic: Ethnicity and Nationality in Antebellum America* (1986); Timothy M. Matovina, *Tejano Religion and Ethnicity: San Antonio, 1821–1860* (1995); Kerby A. Miller, *Emigrants and Exiles: Ireland and the Irish Exodus to North America* (1985); Stanley Nadel, *Little Germany: Ethnicity, Religion, and Class in New York City, 1845–80* (1990); David Roediger, *The Wages of Whiteness: Race and the Making of the Working Class* (1991); David J. Weber, *The Spanish Frontier in North America* (1992); Mark Wyman, *Immigrants in the Valley: Irish, Germans, and Americans in the Upper Mississippi, 1830–1860* (1984).

Free People of Color and Race

Ira Berlin, *Slaves Without Masters: The Free Negro in the Antebellum South* (1974); Dale Cockrell, *Demons of Disorder: Early Blackface Minstrels and Their World* (1997); Leonard P. Curry, *The Free Black in Urban America, 1800–1850* (1981); Thomas F. Gossett, *Race: The History of an Idea in America* (1963); James O. Horton and Lois E. Horton, *In Hope of Liberty: Culture, Community and Protest Among Northern Free Blacks, 1700–1860* (1996); Luther Porter Jackson, *Free Negro Labor and Property Holding in Virginia, 1830–1860* (1942); David M. Katzman, *Before the Ghetto: Black Detroit in the Nineteenth Century* (1973); W. T. Lhamon, Jr., *Raising Cain: Blackface Performance from Jim Crow to Hip Hop* (1998); Leon Litwack, *North of Slavery: The Negro in the Free States, 1790–1860* (1961); Eric Lott, *Love and Theft: Blackface Minstrelsy and the American Working Class* (1995); Joanne Pope Melish, *Disowning Slavery: Gradual Emancipation and "Race" in New England, 1780–1860* (1998); Floyd J. Miller, *The Search for a Black Nationality: Black Colonization and Emigration, 1787–1863* (1975); Gary B. Nash, *Forging Freedom: The Formation of Philadelphia's Black Community, 1720–1840* (1988); Quintard Taylor, *In Search of the Racial Frontier: African Americans in the American West, 1528–1990* (1998); Arthur Zilversmit, *The First Emancipation: The Abolition of Slavery in the North* (1967).

Chapter 13

The Peculiar South

Wilbur J. Cash, *The Mind of the South* (1939); Carl N. Degler, *Place Over Time* (1977); Drew G. Faust, "The Peculiar South Revisited," in John B. Boles and Evelyn T. Nolen, eds., *Interpreting Southern History* (1987); James Oakes, *Slavery and Freedom* (1990); C. Vann Woodward, *The Burden of Southern History* (1960).

Southern Society

Edward L. Ayers, *Vengeance and Justice* (1984); Bradley G. Bond, *Political Culture in the Nineteenth-Century South* (1995); Randolph B. Campbell, "Planters and Plain Folks," in John B. Boles and Evelyn T. Nolen, eds., *Interpreting Southern History* (1987); William J. Cooper, *The South and the Politics of Slavery, 1828–1856* (1978); Clement Eaton, *The Growth of Southern Civilization, 1790–1860* (1961); William W. Freehling, *Prelude to Civil War* (1965); Eugene D. Genovese, *The Political Economy of Slavery* (1965); Peter Kolchin, *Unfree Labor: American Slavery and Russian Serfdom* (1987); Donald G. Mathews, *Religion in the Old South* (1977); Christine L. Heyrman, *Southern Cross* (1997); James Hebron Moore, *The Emergence of the Cotton Kingdom in the Old Southwest: Mississippi, 1770–1860* (1987); Frederick Law Olmsted, *The Slave States*, ed. Harvey Wish (1959); Charles S. Sydnor, *The Development of Southern Sectionalism, 1819–1848* (1948); Larry E. Tise, *Proslavery* (1987); Ralph A. Wooster, *Politicians, Planters, and Plain Folk* (1975); Gavin Wright, *The Political Economy of the Cotton South* (1978); Bertram Wyatt-Brown, *Southern Honor* (1982).

Slaveholders and Nonslaveholders

Edward L. Ayers and John C. Willis, eds., *The Edge of the South* (1991); Bennet H. Barrow, *Plantation Life in the Florida Parishes of Louisiana*, ed. Edwin Adams Davis (1943); Ira Berlin, *Slaves Without Masters* (1974); Joan E. Cashin, *A Family Venture* (1991); Bill Cecil-Fronsman, *The Common Whites* (1992); Charles B. Dew, *Bond of Iron* (1995); Everett Dick, *The Dixie Frontier* (1948); Clement Eaton, *The Mind of the Old South* (1967); Paul D. Escott, ed., *North Carolina Yeoman* (1996); Drew Faust, *James Henry Hammond and the Old South* (1982); Drew Faust, *A Sacred Circle: The Dilemma of the Intellectual in the Old South* (1977); Drew Faust, ed., *The Ideology of Slavery* (1981); J. Wayne Flynt, *Dixie's Forgotten People* (1979); John Hope Franklin, *The Militant South, 1800–1861* (1956); John Inscoe, *Mountain Masters* (1989); Michael P. Johnson and James L. Roark, *Black Masters* (1984); Kenneth S. Greenberg, *Masters and Statesmen* (1985); Stephanie McCurry, *Masters of Small Worlds* (1995); Robert Manson Myers, ed., *The Children of Pride* (1972); James Oakes, *The Ruling Race* (1982); Frank L. Owsley, *Plain Folk of the Old South* (1949); Loren Schweninger, *Black Property Owners in the South, 1790–1915* (1990); J. Mills Thornton III, *Politics and Power in a Slave Society: Alabama, 1800–1860* (1978).

Southern Women

Carol Bleser, *In Joy and in Sorrow* (1990); Carol Bleser, ed., *Tokens of Affection* (1995); Victoria Bynum, *Unruly Women* (1992); Jane Turner Censer, *North Carolina Planters and Their Children, 1800–1860* (1984); Catherine Clinton, *The Plantation Mistress* (1982); Elizabeth Fox-Genovese, *Within the Plantation Household* (1988); Jean E. Friedman, *The Enclosed Garden* (1985); Harriet Jacobs, *Incidents in the Life of a Slave Girl*, ed. Jean Fagan Yellin (1987); Jacqueline Jones, *Labor of Love, Labor of Sorrow* (1985); Frances Anne Kemble, *Journal of a Residence on a Georgia Plantation in 1838–1839* (1863); Suzanne Lebsock, *Free Women of Petersburg* (1984); Sally McMillen, *Motherhood in the Old South* (1990); Patricia Morton, ed., *Discovering the Women in Slavery* (1995); Elisabeth Muhlenfeld, *Mary Boykin Chesnut* (1981); Mary D. Robertson, ed., *Lucy Breckinridge of Grove Hill* (1979); Deborah G. White, *Ar'n't I a Woman?* (1985); Virginia Ingraham Burr, ed., *The Secret Eye* (1990).

Conditions of Slavery

Larry E. Hudson, Jr., *To Have and to Hold* (1997); Kenneth F. Kiple and Virginia H. Kiple, "Black Tongue and Black Men," *Journal of Southern History* 43 (August 1977): 411–428; Wilma King, *Stolen Childhood* (1995); Peter Kolchin, *American Slavery, 1619–1877* (1993); Ronald L.

Lewis, *Coal, Iron, and Slaves* (1979); Randall M. Miller and John David Smith, eds., *Dictionary of Afro-American Slavery* (1997); Randall M. Miller, ed., *The Afro-American Slaves: Community or Chaos* (1981); Orlando Patterson, *Rituals of Blood* (1998); Todd L. Savitt, *Medicine and Slavery* (1978); Mark M. Smith, *Mastered by the Clock* (1997); Kenneth M. Stampp, *The Peculiar Institution* (1956); Robert S. Starobin, *Industrial Slavery in the Old South* (1970); Brenda E. Stevenson, *Life in Black and White: Family and Community in the Slave South* (1996); Michael Tadman, *Speculators and Slaves* (1989).

Slave Culture and Resistance

Herbert Aptheker, *American Negro Slave Revolts* (1943); William F. Allen, Charles P. Ware, and Lucy McKim, *Slave Songs of the United States* (1867); John W. Blassingame, *The Slave Community* (1979); John Blassingame, ed., *Slave Testimony* (1977); Judith Wragg Chase, *Afro-American Art and Craft* (1971); Frederick Douglass, *Narrative of the Life of Frederick Douglass*, ed. David W. Blight (1993); Dena J. Epstein, *Sinful Tunes and Spirituals* (1977); Paul D. Escott, *Slavery Remembered: A Record of Twentieth-Century Slave Narratives* (1979); Thomas Wentworth Higginson, "Negro Spirituals," *Atlantic Monthly* 19 (June, 1867); John Hope Franklin and Loren Schweninger, *Runaway Slaves* (1999); Eugene D. Genovese, *From Rebellion to Revolution* (1979); Eugene D. Genovese, *Roll, Jordan, Roll* (1974); Michael A. Gomez, *Exchanging Our Country Marks* (1998); Kenneth Greenberg, ed., *The Confessions of Nat Turner and Related Documents* (1996); Herbert G. Gutman, *The Black Family in Slavery and Freedom, 1750–1925* (1976); Vincent Harding, *There Is a River* (1981); Bruce Jackson, ed., *The Negro and His Folklore in Nineteenth Century Periodicals* (1967); Charles Joyner, *Down by the Riverside* (1984); Lawrence W. Levine, *Black Culture and Black Consciousness* (1977); Albert J. Raboteau, *Slave Religion* (1978); James Sidbury, *Plowshares into Swords: Gabriel's Virginia* (1997); Robert S. Starobin, *Denmark Vesey* (1970); Sterling Stuckey, *Slave Culture* (1987).

Chapter 14

General

Thomas B. Alexander, *Sectional Stress and Party Strength* (1967); Tyler Anbinder, *Nativism and Slavery* (1992); Maurice G. Baxter, *One and Inseparable: Daniel Webster and the Union* (1984); Paul Bergeron, *The Presidency of James K. Polk* (1987); Frederick J. Blue, *The Free Soilers: Third Party Politics, 1848–1854* (1973); Stanley W. Campbell, *The Slave Catchers* (1968); Richard J. Carwardine, *Evangelicals and Politics in Antebellum America* (1997); Don E. Fehrenbacher, *The Dred Scott Case* (1978); George M. Fredrickson, *The Black Image in the White Mind* (1971); William W. Freehling and Craig M. Simpson, eds., *Secession Debated* (1992); William W. Freehling, *The Road to Disunion* (1990); Holman Hamilton,

Prologue to Conflict: The Crisis and Compromise of 1850 (1964); Michael F. Holt, *Political Parties and American Political Development* (1992); Michael F. Holt, *The Political Crisis of the 1850s* (1978); Daniel Walker Howe, *The Political Culture of the American Whigs* (1979); Stephen E. Maizlish and John J. Kushma, eds., *Essays on American Antebellum Politics, 1840–1860* (1982); William Lee Miller, *Arguing About Slavery* (1996); Chaplain W. Morrison, *Democratic Politics and Sectionalism: The Wilmot Proviso Controversy* (1967); Paul D. Nagle, *One Nation Indivisible* (1964); Merrill D. Peterson, *The Great Triumvirate: Webster, Clay, and Calhoun* (1987); David M. Potter, *The Impending Crisis, 1848–1861* (1976); James A. Rawley, *Race and Politics* (1969); Robert V. Remini, *Henry Clay: Statesman for the Union* (1991); Richard H. Sewell, *A House Divided: Sectionalism and the Civil War, 1848–1865* (1988); Joel H. Silbey, *The Transformation of American Politics, 1840–1960* (1967); Joel H. Silbey, ed., *The American Party Battle*, 2 vols. (1999); Elbert B. Smith, *The Presidency of James Buchanan* (1975); Kenneth M. Stampp, *America in 1857* (1991); Kenneth M. Stampp, *And the War Came* (1950); Gerald W. Wolff, *The Kansas-Nebraska Bill* (1977).

The South and Slavery

William L. Barney, *The Secessionist Impulse* (1974); Malcolm Bell, Jr., *Major Butler's Legacy: Five Generations of a Slaveholding Family* (1987); Steven A. Channing, *A Crisis of Fear: Secession in South Carolina* (1970); William J. Cooper, Jr., *The South and the Politics of Slavery, 1828–1856* (1978); Avery O. Craven, *The Growth of Southern Nationalism, 1848–1861* (1953); Daniel W. Crofts, *Reluctant Confederates: Upper South Unionists in the Secession Crisis* (1989); Merton L. Dillon, *Slavery Attacked* (1991); Drew G. Faust, *The Ideology of Slavery* (1981); Drew G. Faust, *A Sacred Circle: The Dilemma of the Intellectual in the Old South* (1978); Lacy K. Ford, Jr., *Origins of Southern Radicalism* (1988); Eugene D. Genovese, *The World the Slaveholders Made* (1969); Eugene D. Genovese, *The Political Economy of Slavery* (1967); Michael P. Johnson, *Toward a Patriarchal Republic: The Secession of Georgia* (1977); John Niven, *John C. Calhoun and the Price of Union* (1988); James Oakes, *Slavery and Freedom* (1991); David M. Potter, *The South and the Sectional Conflict* (1968); Thomas E. Schott, *Alexander H. Stephens of Georgia* (1988); William R. Stanton, *The Leopard's Spots* (1960); J. Mills Thornton III, *Politics and Power in a Slave Society* (1978); Larry E. Tise, *Proslavery* (1987); Ralph Wooster, *The Secession Conventions of the South* (1962).

The North and Antislavery

Dale Baum, *The Civil War Party System* (1984); Eugene H. Berwanger, *The Frontier Against Slavery* (1967); Frederick J. Blue, *Salmon P. Chase* (1987); Gary Collison, *Shadrach Minkins: From Fugitive Slave to Citizen* (1997); David Donald, *Charles Sumner and the Coming of the Civil War* (1960); Paul

Finkelman, ed., *His Soul Goes Marching On: Responses to John Brown and the Harpers Ferry Raid* (1995); Eric Foner, *Free Soil, Free Labor, Free Men* (1970); Louis S. Gerteis, *Morality and Utility in American Antislavery Reform* (1987); William E. Gienapp, *The Origins of the Republican Party, 1852–1856* (1986); Joan D. Hedrick, *Harriet Beecher Stowe* (1994); James O. and Lois E. Horton, *In Hope of Liberty* (1997); James O. Horton, *Free People of Color* (1993); Henry V. Jaffa, *Crisis of the House Divided* (1959); Robert W. Johannsen, *Lincoln, the South, and Slavery* (1991); Robert W. Johannsen, *Stephen A. Douglas* (1973); Aileen S. Kraditor, *Means and Ends in American Abolitionism* (1969); Stephen B. Oates, *To Purge This Land with Blood*, 2d ed. (1984); Lewis Perry and Michael Fellman, eds., *Antislavery Reconsidered* (1979); Benjamin Quarles, *Black Abolitionists* (1969); C. Peter Ripley et al., ed., *Witness for Freedom: African American Voices on Race, Slavery and Freedom* (1993); Jeffrey Rossbach, *Ambivalent Conspirators* (1982); Richard Sewell, *Ballots for Freedom: Antislavery Politics in the United States, 1837–1860* (1976); Thomas P. Slaughter, *Bloody Dawn: The Cristiana Riot and Racial Violence* (1991); James B. Stewart, *Holy Warriors: The Abolitionists and American Slavery*, 2d ed. (1996); Albert J. Von Frank, *The Trials of Anthony Burns* (1998).

The War with Mexico and Foreign Policy

K. Jack Bauer, *Zachary Taylor* (1985); Gene M. Brack, *Mexico Views Manifest Destiny, 1821–1846* (1976); Richard Griswold del Castillo, *The Treaty of Guadalupe Hidalgo* (1990); Neal Harlow, *California Conquered* (1982); Reginald Horsman, *Race and Manifest Destiny* (1981); Robert W. Johannsen, *To the Halls of the Montezumas: The Mexican War and the American Imagination* (1985); Ernest M. Lander, Jr., *Reluctant Imperialists: Calhoun, the South Carolinians, and the Mexican War* (1980); Robert E. May, *The Southern Dream of a Caribbean Empire, 1854–1861* (1973); Frederick Merk, *The Monroe Doctrine and American Expansion, 1843–1849* (1966); Frederick Merk, *Manifest Destiny and Mission in American History* (1963); David M. Pletcher, *The Diplomacy of Annexation: Texas, Oregon, and the Mexican War* (1973); Dirk Raat, *Mexico and the United States* (1992); John H. Schroeder, *Mr. Polk's War: American Opposition and Dissent* (1973); Otis A. Singletary, *The Mexican War* (1960); Anders Stephanson, *Manifest Destiny* (1995); David J. Weber, *The Mexican Frontier, 1821–1846* (1982).

Chapter 15

The War and the South

Thomas B. Alexander and Richard E. Beringer, *The Anatomy of the Confederate Congress* (1972); Stephen Ash, *When the Yankees Came* (1995); Richard E. Beringer et al., *Why the South Lost the Civil War* (1986); William A. Blair, *Virginia's Private War: Feeding Body and Soul in the Confederacy* (1998);

Gabor S. Boritt, ed., *Why the Confederacy Lost* (1992); Richard N. Current, *Lincoln's Loyalists* (1992); William C. Davis, *Jefferson Davis* (1991); Robert F. Durden, *The Gray and the Black: The Confederate Debate on Emancipation* (1972); Paul D. Escott, *Many Excellent People* (1985); Paul D. Escott, *After Secession: Jefferson Davis and the Failure of Confederate Nationalism* (1978); Eli N. Evans, *Judah P. Benjamin* (1987); Drew Gilpin Faust, *The Creation of Confederate Nationalism* (1988); Mark Grimsley, *The Hard Hand of War* (1995); J. B. Jones, *A Rebel War Clerk's Diary*, 2 vols., ed. Howard Swiggett (1935); Ella Lonn, *Desertion During the Civil War* (1928); Mary Elizabeth Massey, *Refugee Life in the Confederacy* (1964); Larry E. Nelson, *Bullets, Ballots, and Rhetoric: Confederate Policy for the United States Presidential Contest of 1864* (1980); Alan T. Nolan, *Lee Considered* (1991); Harry P. Owens and James J. Cooke, eds., *The Old South in the Crucible of War* (1983); James L. Roark, *Masters Without Slaves* (1977); Daniel Sutherland, *Seasons of War* (1995); Emory M. Thomas, *The Confederate Nation* (1979); Emory M. Thomas, *The Confederacy as a Revolutionary Experience* (1971); William A. Tidwell, *April '65* (1995); Bell Irvin Wiley, *The Life of Johnny Reb* (1943); Bell Irvin Wiley, *The Plain People of the Confederacy* (1943); W. Buck Yearns, ed., *The Confederate Governors* (1985).

The War and the North

Ralph Andreano, ed., *The Economic Impact of the American Civil War* (1962); Iver Bernstein, *The New York City Draft Riots* (1990); Robert Cruden, *The War That Never Ended* (1973); David Donald, ed., *Why the North Won the Civil War* (1960); J. Matthew Gallman, *The North Fights the Civil War* (1994); James W. Geary, *We Need Men* (1991); Wood Gray, *The Hidden Civil War* (1942); Randall C. Jimerson, *The Private Civil War* (1988); Frank L. Klement, *The Copperheads in the Middle West* (1960); Susan Previant Lee and Peter Passell, *A New Economic View of American History* (1979); James M. McPherson, *Battle Cry of Freedom* (1988); James H. Moorhead, *American Apocalypse* (1978); Phillip S. Paludan, *"A People's Contest": The Union and the Civil War, 1861–1865* (1989); Robert Hunt Rhodes, ed., *All for the Union: The Civil War Diary and Letters of Elisha Hunt Rhodes* (1991); Anne C. Rose, *Victorian America and the Civil War* (1992); George Winston Smith and Charles Burnet Judah, *Life in the North During the Civil War* (1966); George Templeton Strong, *Diary*, 4 vols., ed. Allan Nevins and Milton Hasley Thomas (1952); Paul Studenski, *Financial History of the United States* (1952); Maris A. Vinovskis, ed., *Toward a Social History of the American Civil War* (1990); Bell Irvin Wiley, *The Life of Billy Yank* (1952).

Women

John Q. Anderson, ed., *Brokenburn: The Journal of Kate Stone* (1955); John R. Brumgardt, ed., *Civil War Nurse: The Diary and Letters of Hannah Ropes* (1980); Catherine Clinton and

Nina Silber, eds., *Divided Houses: Gender and the Civil War* (1992); Beth Gilbert Crabtree and James W. Patton, eds., *"Journal of a Secesh Lady": The Diary of Catherine Ann Devereux Edmondston, 1860–1866* (1979); Drew Gilpin Faust, *Mothers of Invention* (1996); Jacqueline Jones, *Labor of Love, Labor of Sorrow* (1985); Mary Elizabeth Massey, *Bonnet Brigades* (1966); George C. Rable, *Civil Wars: Women and the Crisis of Southern Nationalism* (1989); Mary D. Robertson, ed., *Lucy Breckinridge of Grove Hill: The Journal of a Virginia Girl, 1862–1864* (1979); Lee Ann Whites, *The Civil War as a Crisis in Gender* (1995); C. Vann Woodward and Elisabeth Muhlenfeld, eds., *Mary Chesnut's Civil War* (1981); Agatha Young, *Women and the Crisis* (1959).

African Americans

Virginia M. Adams, ed., *On the Altar of Freedom: A Black Soldier's Civil War Letters from the Front* (1991); Ira Berlin, ed., *Freedom: A Documentary History of Emancipation, 1861–1867*, Series I, *The Destruction of Slavery* (1979), and Series II, *The Black Military Experience* (1982); Richard M. Blackett, ed., *Thomas Morris Chester: Black Civil War Correspondent* (1989); David W. Blight, *Frederick Douglass' Civil War* (1989); Dudley Cornish, *The Sable Arm* (1956); Barbara Jeanne Fields, *Slavery and Freedom on the Middle Ground* (1985); Joseph T. Glatthaar, *Forged in Battle* (1990); James G. Hollandsworth, *The Louisiana Native Guards* (1995); Leon Litwack, *Been in the Storm So Long* (1979); James M. McPherson, *The Negro's Civil War* (1965); James M. McPherson, *The Struggle for Equality* (1964); Clarence L. Mohr, *On the Threshold of Freedom* (1986); Lynda J. Morgan, *Emancipation in Virginia's Tobacco Belt, 1850–1870* (1992); Benjamin Quarles, *The Negro in the Civil War* (1953); Edwin S. Redkey, ed., *A Grand Army of Black Men* (1992).

Military History

Nancy Scott Anderson and Dwight Anderson, *The Generals: Ulysses S. Grant and Robert E. Lee* (1987); David W. Blight, ed., *When This Cruel War Is Over: The Civil War Letters of Charles Harvey Brewster* (1992); Albert Castel, *Decision in the West* (1992); Bruce Catton, *Grant Takes Command* (1969); Bruce Catton, *A Stillness at Appomattox* (1953); Benjamin Franklin Cooling, *Forts Henry and Donelson* (1988); Peter Cozzens, *This Terrible Sound* (1992); William C. Davis, ed., *The Image of War*, multivolume (1983–1985); Michael Fellman, *Citizen Sherman* (1995); Shelby Foote, *The Civil War, a Narrative*, 3 vols. (1958–1974); Douglas Southall Freeman, *Lee's Lieutenants*, 3 vols. (1942–1944); Douglas Southall Freeman, *R. E. Lee*, 4 vols. (1934–1935); Gary W. Gallagher, *The Confederate War* (1997); Gary W. Gallagher, *Lee and His Generals in War and Memory* (1998); Joseph T. Glatthaar, *The March to the Sea and Beyond* (1985); Herman Hattaway and Archer Jones, *How the North Won* (1983); Laurence M. Hauptman, *Between Two Fires: American Indians in the Civil War* (1995); Archer Jones, *Civil War Command and Strategy*

(1992); Alvin M. Josephy, Jr., *The Civil War in the American West* (1991); Gerald F. Linderman, *Embattled Courage* (1989); Thomas L. Livermore, *Numbers and Losses in the Civil War in America* (1957); Grady McWhiney and Perry D. Jamieson, *Attack and Die* (1982); Reid Mitchell, *Civil War Soldiers* (1988); Reid Mitchell, *The Vacant Chair* (1993); Roy Morris, Jr., *Sheridan* (1992); Charles Royster, *The Destructive War* (1991); Stephen W. Sears, *To the Gates of Richmond* (1992); Stephen W. Sears, *George B. McClellan* (1988); Emory M. Thomas, *Robert E. Lee* (1995); Emory M. Thomas, *Bold Dragoon: The Life of J. E. B. Stuart* (1987); Noah Andre Trudeau, *The Last Citadel* (1991); Steven E. Woodworth, *Jefferson Davis and His Generals* (1990).

Foreign Relations

Stuart L. Bernath, *Squall Across the Atlantic: American Civil War Prize Cases and Diplomacy* (1970); Kinley J. Brauer, "The Slavery Problem in the Diplomacy of the American Civil War," *Pacific Historical Review* 46, no. 3 (1977): 439–469; David P. Crook, *The North, the South, and the Powers, 1861–1865* (1974); Charles P. Cullop, *Confederate Propaganda in Europe* (1969); Norman B. Ferris, *The Trent Affair* (1977); Howard Jones, *Union in Peril* (1992); Frank J. Merli, *Great Britain and the Confederate Navy* (1970); Frank L. Owsley and Harriet Owsley, *King Cotton Diplomacy* (1959); Gordon H. Warren, *Fountain of Discontent: The Trent Affair and Freedom of the Seas* (1981).

Abraham Lincoln and the Union Government

Allan G. Bogue, *The Earnest Men: Republicans of the Civil War Senate* (1981); Gabor S. Borit, ed., *The Historian's Lincoln* (1989); Fawn Brodie, *Thaddeus Stevens* (1959); Richard N. Current, *The Lincoln Nobody Knows* (1958); Leonard P. Curry, *Blueprint for Modern America: Non-Military Legislation of the First Civil War Congress* (1968); Christopher Dell, *Lincoln and the War Democrats* (1975); David Donald, *Charles Sumner and the Rights of Man* (1970); David Donald, *Lincoln* (1995); Ludwell H. Johnson, "Lincoln's Solution to the Problem of Peace Terms, 1864–1865," *Journal of Southern History* 34 (November 1968): 441–447; Peyton McCrary, *Abraham Lincoln and Reconstruction: The Louisiana Experiment* (1978); James M. McPherson, *Abraham Lincoln and the Second American Revolution* (1990); Mark Neely, *The Fate of Liberty* (1991); Stephen B. Oates, *With Malice Toward None* (1977); Philip S. Paludan, *The Presidency of Abraham Lincoln* (1994); Heather Cox Richardson, *The Greatest Nation of the Earth: Republican Economic Policies During the Civil War* (1997); Joel Silbey, *A Respectable Minority: The Democratic Party in the Civil War Era* (1977); Benjamin P. Thomas, *Abraham Lincoln* (1952); Hans L. Trefousse, *The Radical Republicans* (1969); Glyndon G. Van Deusen, *William Henry Seward* (1967); T. Harry Williams, *Lincoln and His Generals* (1952); T. Harry Williams, *Lincoln and the Radicals* (1941).

Chapter 16

National Policy, Politics, and Constitutional Law

Richard H. Abbott, *The Republican Party and the South, 1855–1877* (1986); Herman Belz, *Emancipation and Equal Rights* (1978); Herman Belz, *A New Birth of Freedom* (1976); Michael Les Benedict, *A Compromise of Principle: Congressional Republicans and Reconstruction, 1863–1869* (1974); Michael Les Benedict, *The Impeachment and Trial of Andrew Johnson* (1973); Charles S. Campbell, *The Transformation of American Foreign Relations, 1865–1900* (1976); Adrian Cook, *The Alabama Claims* (1975); Michael Kent Curtis, *No State Shall Abridge* (1987); David Donald, *Charles Sumner and the Rights of Man* (1970); Harold M. Hyman, *A More Perfect Union* (1973); Ronald J. Jensen, *The Alaska Purchase and Russian-American Relations* (1975); William S. McFeely, *Grant* (1981); William S. McFeely, *Yankee Stepfather: General O. O. Howard and the Freedmen* (1968); Eric L. McKitrick, *Andrew Johnson and Reconstruction* (1966); James M. McPherson, *The Abolitionist Legacy* (1975); Joel Silbey, *A Respectable Minority: The Democratic Party in the Civil War Era* (1977); Brooks D. Simpson, *Let Us Have Peace* (1991); Brooks D. Simpson, *The Reconstruction Presidents* (1998); Kenneth M. Stampp, *The Era of Reconstruction* (1965); Hans L. Trefousse, *Andrew Johnson* (1989).

The Freed Slaves

Roberta Sue Alexander, *North Carolina Faces the Freedmen* (1985); Ira Berlin, ed., *Freedom: A Documentary History of Emancipation, 1861–1867* (1984); Elizabeth R. Bethel, *Promiseland* (1981); Orville Vernon Burton, *In My Father's House Are Many Mansions* (1985); Edmund L. Drago, *Black Politicians and Reconstruction in Georgia* (1982); Paul D. Escott, *Slavery Remembered* (1979); Eric Foner, "Reconstruction and the Crisis of Free Labor," in *Politics and Ideology in the Age of the Civil War*, ed. Eric Foner (1980); Gerald Jaynes, *Branches Without Roots: The Genesis of the Black Working Class in the American South, 1862–1882* (1986); Leon Litwack, *Been in the Storm So Long* (1979); Edward Magdol, *A Right to the Land* (1977); Robert Morris, *Reading, 'Riting and Reconstruction* (1981); Howard Rabinowitz, ed., *Southern Black Leaders in Reconstruction* (1982); Emma Lou Thornbrough, ed., *Black Reconstructionists* (1972); Okon Uya, *From Slavery to Public Service* (1971); Clarence Walker, *A Rock in a Weary Land* (1982).

Politics and Reconstruction in the South

Robert W. Coakley, *The Role of Federal Military Forces in Domestic Disorders, 1789–1878* (1988); Richard N. Current, *Those Terrible Carpetbaggers* (1988); Jonathan Daniels, *Prince of Carpetbaggers* (1958); W. E. B. Du Bois, *Black Reconstruction* (1935); Paul D. Escott, *Many Excellent People: Power and Privilege in North Carolina, 1850–1900* (1985); W. McKee Evans, *Ballots and Fence Rails: Reconstruction on the Lower Cape Fear* (1966); Michael W. Fitzgerald, *The Union League Movement in the Deep South* (1989); Eric Foner, *Reconstruction: America's Unfinished Revolution, 1863–1877* (1988); Eric Foner, *Nothing but Freedom* (1983); William C. Harris, *The Day of the Carpetbagger* (1979); Thomas Holt, *Black over White: Negro Political Leadership in South Carolina During Reconstruction* (1977); J. Morgan Kousser and James M. McPherson, eds., *Region, Race and Reconstruction* (1982); Elizabeth Studley Nathans, *Losing the Peace* (1968); Michael Perman, *The Road to Redemption* (1984); Michael Perman, *Reunion Without Compromise* (1973); Lawrence N. Powell, *New Masters* (1980); George C. Rable, *But There Was No Peace* (1984); James Roark, *Masters Without Slaves* (1977); James Sefton, *The United States Army and Reconstruction, 1865–1877* (1967); Mark W. Summers, *Railroads, Reconstruction, and the Gospel of Prosperity* (1984); Allen Trelease, *White Terror* (1967); Ted Tunnell, *Carpetbagger from Vermont* (1989); Ted Tunnell, *Crucible of Reconstruction* (1984); Michael Wayne, *The Reshaping of Plantation Society* (1983); Sarah Woolfolk Wiggins, *The Scalawag in Alabama Politics, 1865–1881* (1977).

Women, Family, and Social History

Virginia I. Burr, ed., *The Secret Eye* (1990); Ellen Carol Dubois, *Feminism and Suffrage* (1978); Herbert G. Gutman, *The Black Family in Slavery and Freedom, 1750–1925* (1976); Elizabeth Jacoway, *Yankee Missionaries in the South* (1979); Jacqueline Jones, *Labor of Love, Labor of Sorrow* (1985); Jacqueline Jones, *Soldiers of Light and Love* (1980); Robert C. Kenzer, *Kinship and Neighborhood in a Southern Community* (1987); Mary P. Ryan, *Women in Public* (1990); Rebecca Scott, "The Battle over the Child," *Prologue* 10 (Summer 1978): 101–113.

The End of Reconstruction

Michael Les Benedict, "Southern Democrats in the Crisis of 1876–1877," *Journal of Southern History* 66 (November 1980): 489–524; William Gillette, *Retreat from Reconstruction, 1869–1879* (1980); William Gillette, *The Right to Vote* (1969); Keith Ian Polakoff, *The Politics of Inertia* (1973); John G. Sproat, *"The Best Men": Liberal Reformers in the Gilded Age* (1968); C. Vann Woodward, *Reunion and Reaction* (1951).

Reconstruction's Legacy for the South and the Nation

Robert G. Athearn, *In Search of Canaan* (1978); Edward L. Ayers, *The Promise of the New South* (1992); David W. Blight, *Race and Reunion: The Civil War in American Memory, 1863–1915* (2000); Norman L. Crockett, *The Black Towns* (1979); Stephen J. DeCanio, *Agriculture in the Postbellum South* (1974); Steven Hahn, *The Roots of Southern Populism* (1983); Jay R. Mandle, *The Roots of Black Poverty* (1978); Nell Irvin Painter, *Exodusters* (1976); Howard Rabinowitz, *Race Relations in the Urban South, 1865–1890* (1978); Roger L. Ransom and Richard Sutch, *One Kind of Freedom* (1977); Laurence Shore, *Southern Capitalists* (1986); Peter Wallenstein, *From Slave South to New South* (1987); Jonathan M. Wiener, *Social Origins of the New South* (1978); C. Vann Woodward, *Origins of the New South* (1951).

Historical Reference Books by Subject:
Encyclopedias, Dictionaries, Atlases, Chronologies, and Statistics

American History: General

Gorton Carruth, ed., *The Encyclopedia of American Facts and Dates* (1993); *Dictionary of American History* (1976) and Joan Hoff and Robert H. Ferrell, eds., *Supplement* (1996); John M. Farragher, ed., *The American Heritage Encyclopedia of American History* (1998); Eric Foner and John A. Garraty, eds., *The Reader's Companion to American History* (1991); Bernard Grun, *The Timetables of History* (1991); *International Encyclopedia of the Social Sciences* (1968–); Richard B. Morris and Jeffrey B. Morris, eds., *Encyclopedia of American History* (1996); Harry Ritter, *Dictionary of Concepts in History* (1986); Lawrence Urdang, ed., *The Timetables of American History* (1996); U.S. Bureau of the Census, *Historical Statistics of the United States* (1975).

American History: General, Twentieth Century

John D. Buenker and Edward R. Kantowicz, eds., *Historical Dictionary of the Progressive Era, 1890–1920* (1988); Robert H. Ferrell and John S. Bowman, eds., *The Twentieth Century: An Almanac* (1984); George H. Gallup, *The Gallup Poll: Public Opinion, 1935–1971* (1972), *1972–1977* (1978), and annual reports (1979–); Stanley Hochman, *The Penguin Dictionary of Contemporary American History* (1997); Stanley I. Kutler, ed., *Encyclopedia of the United States in the Twentieth Century* (1995); Peter B. Levy, *Encyclopedia of the Reagan-Bush Years* (1996); James S. Olson, *Historical Dictionary of the 1920s* (1988); Thomas Parker and Douglas Nelson, *Day by Day: The Sixties* (1983).

American History: General Atlases and Gazetteers

Geoffrey Barraclough, ed., *The Times Atlas of World History* (1994); Rodger Doyle, *Atlas of Contemporary America* (1994); Robert H. Ferrell and Richard Natkiel, *Atlas of American History* (1987); Edward W. Fox, *Atlas of American History* (1964); Archie Hobson, *The Cambridge Gazetteer of the United States and Canada* (1996); Eric Homberger, *The Penguin Historical Atlas of North America* (1995); Kenneth T. Jackson and James T. Adams, *Atlas of American History*

(1978); National Geographic Society, *Historical Atlas of the United States* (1994); U.S. Department of the Interior, *National Atlas of the United States* (1970). Other atlases are listed under specific categories.

American History: General Biographies

Lucian Boia, ed., *Great Historians of the Modern Age* (1991); John S. Bowman, *The Cambridge Dictionary of American Biography* (1995); *Current Biography* (1940–); *Dictionary of American Biography* (1928–); John A. Garraty and Mark C. Carnes, eds., *American National Biography* (1999); John Garraty and Jerome L. Sternstein, eds., *The Encyclopedia of American Biography* (1996); *National Cyclopedia of American Biography* (1898–). Other biographical works appear under specific categories.

African Americans

Molefi Asante and Mark T. Mattson, *Historical and Cultural Atlas of African-Americans* (1991); John N. Ingham, *African-American Business Leaders* (1993); Rayford W. Logan and Michael R. Winston, eds., *The Dictionary of American Negro Biography* (1983); Sharon Harley, *The Timetables of African-American History* (1995); Darlene C. Hine et al., eds., *Black Women in White America* (1994); Charles D. Lowery and John F. Marszalek, eds., *Encyclopedia of African-American Civil Rights* (1992); Larry G. Murphy et al., eds., *Encyclopedia of African American Religions* (1993); Jack Salzman et al., eds., *Encyclopedia of African-American Culture and History* (1996); Jessie Carney Smith, ed., *Notable Black American Women* (1992). See also "Slavery."

American Revolution and Colonies

Richard Blanco and Paul Sanborn, eds., *The American Revolution* (1993); Lester J. Cappon, ed., *Atlas of Early American History: The Revolutionary Era, 1760–1790* (1976); Jacob E. Cooke, ed., *Encyclopedia of the American Colonies* (1993); John M. Farragher, ed., *The Encyclopedia of Colonial and Revolutionary America* (1990); Jack P. Greene and J. R. Pole, eds., *The*

Blackwell Encyclopedia of the American Revolution (1991); Douglas W. Marshall and Howard H. Peckham, *Campaigns of the American Revolution* (1976); Gregory Palmer, ed., *Biographical Sketches of Loyalists of the American Revolution* (1984); John W. Raimo, ed., *Biographical Directory of American Colonial and Revolutionary Governors, 1607–1789* (1980); *Rand-McNally Atlas of the American Revolution* (1974); Seymour I. Schwartz, *The French and Indian War, 1754–1763* (1995).

Architecture

William D. Hunt, Jr., ed., *Encyclopedia of American Architecture* (1980).

Asian Americans

Hyung-Chan Kim, ed., *Dictionary of Asian American History* (1986); Brian Niiya, ed., *Japanese American History* (1993); Lynn Pan, ed., *The Encyclopedia of the Chinese Overseas* (1999). See also "Immigration and Ethnic Groups."

Business and the Economy

Christine Ammer and Dean S. Ammer, *Dictionary of Business and Economics* (1983); Douglas Auld and Graham Bannock, *The American Dictionary of Economics* (1983); Michael J. Freeman, *Atlas of World Economy* (1991); John N. Ingham, *Biographical Dictionary of American Business Leaders* (1983); John N. Ingham and Lynne B. Feldman, *Contemporary American Business Leaders* (1990); William H. Mulligan, Jr., ed., *A Historical Dictionary of American Industrial Language* (1988); Glenn G. Munn, *Encyclopedia of Banking and Finance* (1973); Paul Paskoff, ed., *Encyclopedia of American Business History and Biography* (1989); Glenn Porter, *Encyclopedia of American Economic History* (1980); Richard Robinson, *United States Business History, 1602–1988* (1990); Malcolm Warner, ed., *International Encyclopedia of Business and Management* (1996). See also "African Americans," "Native Americans and Indian Affairs," and "Transportation."

Cities and Towns

John L. Androit, ed., *Township Atlas of the United States* (1979); David J. Bodenhamer and Robert J. Barrows, eds., *The Encyclopedia of Indianapolis* (1994); Gary A. Goreham, ed., *Encyclopedia of Rural America* (1997); Melvin G. Holli and Peter d'A. Jones, eds., *Biographical Dictionary of American Mayors, 1820–1980: Big City Mayors* (1981); Kenneth T. Jackson, ed., *Encyclopedia of New York City* (1995); George T. Kurian, *World Encyclopedia of Cities* (1994); Ory M. Nergal, ed., *The Encyclopedia of American Cities* (1980); Neil Larry Shumsky, ed., *Encyclopedia of Urban America* (1998); David D. Van Tassel and John J. Grabowski, eds., *The Dictionary of Cleveland Biography* (1996); David D. Van Tassel and John J. Grabowski, eds., *The Encyclopedia of Cleveland History* (1987). See also "Politics and Government."

Civil War and Reconstruction

Mark M. Boatner III, *The Civil War Dictionary* (1988); Richard N. Current, ed., *Encyclopedia of the Confederacy* (1993); John T. Hubbell and James W. Geary, eds., *Biographical Dictionary of the Union* (1995); Kenneth C. Martis, *The Historical Atlas of the Congresses of the Confederate States of America: 1861–1865* (1994); James M. McPherson, ed., *The Atlas of the Civil War* (1994); Mark E. Neely, Jr., *The Abraham Lincoln Encyclopedia* (1982); Craig L. Symonds, *A Battlefield Atlas of the Civil War* (1983); Hans L. Trefousse, *Historical Dictionary of Reconstruction* (1991); U.S. War Department, *The Official Atlas of the Civil War* (1958); Jon L. Wakelyn, ed., *Biographical Dictionary of the Confederacy* (1977); Ezra J. Warner and W. Buck Yearns, *Biographical Register of the Confederate Congress* (1975); Steven E. Woodworth, ed., *The American Civil War* (1996). See also "South" and "Politics and Government."

The Cold War

Thomas S. Arms, *Encyclopedia of the Cold War* (1994); Michael Kort, *The Columbia Guide to the Cold War* (1998); Richard A. Schwartz, *Cold War Culture: The Media and the Arts* (1998). See also "Foreign Relations" and "Military and Wars."

Constitution, Supreme Court, and Judiciary

David Bradley and Shelly F. Fishkin, eds., *The Encyclopedia of Civil Rights* (1997); Congressional Quarterly, *The Supreme Court A to Z* (1994); Kermit L. Hall, ed., *The Oxford Companion to the Supreme Court of the United States* (1992); Kermit L. Hall, ed., *The Oxford Guide to United States Supreme Court Decisions* (1999); Richard F. Hixson, *Mass Media and the Constitution* (1989); Robert J. Janosik, ed., *Encyclopedia of the American Judicial System* (1987); John W. Johnson, ed., *Historic U.S. Court Cases, 1690–1990* (1992); Leonard W. Levy et al., eds., *Encyclopedia of the American Constitution* (1986); Fred R. Shapiro, *The Oxford Dictionary of American Legal Quotations* (1993); Melvin I. Urofsky, ed., *The Supreme Court Justices* (1994). See also "Politics and Government" and "Sexuality."

Crime, Violence, Police, and Prisons

William G. Bailey, *Encyclopedia of Police Science* (1994); Sanford H. Kadish, ed., *Encyclopedia of Crime and Justice* (1983); Marilyn D. McShane and Frank P. Williams III, eds., *Encyclopedia of American Prisons* (1995); Michael Newton and Judy Ann Newton, *Racial and Religious Violence in America* (1991); Michael Newton and Judy Newton, *The Ku Klux Klan* (1990); Carl Sifakis, *Encyclopedia of Assassinations* (1990); Carl Sifakis, *The Encyclopedia of American Crime* (1982).

Culture and Folklore

Hennig Cohen and Tristam Potter Coffin, eds., *The Folklore of American Holidays* (1987); Richard M. Dorson, ed., *Handbook of American Folklore* (1983); Robert L. Gale, *A Cultural Encyclopedia of the 1850s in America* (1993); Robert L. Gale, *The Gay Nineties in America* (1992); M. Thomas Inge, ed., *Handbook of American Popular Culture* (1979–1981); Wolfgang Mieder et al., eds., *A Dictionary of American Proverbs* (1992); J. F. Rooney, Jr., et al., eds., *This Remarkable Continent: An Atlas of United States and Canadian Society and Cultures* (1982); Jane Stern and Michael Stern, *Encyclopedia of Pop Culture* (1992); Justin Wintle, ed., *Makers of Nineteenth Century Culture, 1800–1914* (1982). See also "The Cold War," "Entertainment and the Arts," "Mass Media and Journalism," "Music," and "Sports."

Education and Libraries

Lee C. Deighton, ed., *The Encyclopedia of Education* (1971); Joseph C. Kiger, ed., *Research Institutions and Learned Societies* (1982); John F. Ohles, ed., *Biographical Dictionary of American Educators* (1978); Wayne A. Wiegard and Donald E. Davis, Jr., eds., *Encyclopedia of Library History* (1994).

Entertainment and the Arts

Tim Brooks and Earle Marsh, *The Complete Directory to Prime Time Network and Cable TV Shows, 1946–Present* (1995); Barbara N. Cohen-Stratyner, *Biographical Dictionary of Dance* (1982); John Dunning, *Tune in Yesterday* (radio) (1967); Larry Langman and Edgar Borg, *Encyclopedia of American War Films* (1989); Larry Langman and David Ebner, *Encyclopedia of American Spy Films* (1990); *Notable Names in the American Theater* (1976); Andrew Sarris, *The American Cinema: Directors and Directions, 1929–1968* (1968); Anthony Slide, *The American Film Industry* (1986); Anthony Slide, *The Encyclopedia of Vaudeville* (1994); Evelyn M. Truitt, *Who Was Who on Screen* (1977); Don B. Wilmeth and Tice L. Miller, eds., *The Cambridge Guide to American Theatre* (1993). See also "The Cold War," "Culture and Folklore," "Mass Media and Journalism," "Music," and "Sports."

Environment and Conservation

André R. Cooper, ed., *Cooper's Comprehensive Environmental Desk Reference* (1996); Forest History Society, *Encyclopedia of American Forest and Conservation History* (1983); Irene Franck and David Brownstone, *The Green Encyclopedia* (1992); Robert J. Mason and Mark T. Mattson, *Atlas of United States Environmental Issues* (1990); Robert Paehlke, ed., *Conservation and Environmentalism* (1995); World Resources Institute, *Environmental Almanac* (1992).

Exploration: From Columbus to Space

Silvio A. Bedini, ed., *The Christopher Columbus Encyclopedia* (1992); Michael Cassutt, *Who's Who in Space* (1987); W. P.

Cumming et al., *The Discovery of North America* (1972); William Goetzmann and Glyndwr Williams, *The Atlas of North American Exploration* (1992); Clive Holland, *Arctic Exploration and Development* (1993); Adrian Johnson, *America Explored* (1974); Kenneth Nebenzahl, *Atlas of Columbus and the Great Discoveries* (1990). See also "Science and Technology."

Foreign Relations

Gerard Chaliand and Jean-Pierre Rageau, *Strategic Atlas* (1990); Alexander DeConde, ed., *Encyclopedia of American Foreign Policy* (1978); Margaret B. Denning and J. K. Sweeney, *Handbook of American Diplomacy* (1992); Graham Evans and Jeffrey Newnham, eds., *The Dictionary of World Politics* (1990); John E. Findling, *Dictionary of American Diplomatic History* (1989); Chas. W. Freeman, Jr., *The Diplomat's Dictionary* (1997); Michael Kidron and Ronald Segal, *The State of the World Atlas* (1995); Bruce W. Jentleson and Thomas G. Paterson, eds., *Encyclopedia of U.S. Foreign Relations* (1997); Warren F. Kuehl, ed., *Biographical Dictionary of Internationalists* (1983); Edward Lawson, *Encyclopedia of Human Rights* (1991); Jack C. Plano and Roy Olton, eds., *The International Relations Dictionary* (1988). See also "The Cold War," "Peace Movements and Pacifism," "Politics and Government," "Military and Wars," and specific wars.

Immigration and Ethnic Groups

James P. Allen and Eugene J. Turner, *We the People: An Atlas of America's Ethnic Diversity* (1988); Gerald Chaliand and Jean-Pierre Rageau, *The Penguin Atlas of Diasporas* (1995); Francesco Cordasco, ed., *Dictionary of American Immigration History* (1990); David Levinson and Melvin Ember, eds., *American Immigrant Cultures* (1997); Judy B. Litoff and Judith McDonnell, eds., *European Immigrant Women in the United States* (1994); Sally M. Miller, ed., *The Ethnic Press in the United States* (1987); Stephan Thernstrom, ed., *Harvard Encyclopedia of American Ethnic Groups* (1980); Rudolph J. Vecoli et al., eds., *Gale Encyclopedia of Multicultural America* (1995). See also "Asian Americans," "Jewish Americans," and "Hispanics."

Jewish Americans

American Jewish Yearbook (1899–); Jack Fischel and Sanford Pinsker, eds., *Jewish-American History and Culture* (1992); Geoffrey Wigoder, *Dictionary of Jewish Biography* (1991). See also "Immigration and Ethnic Groups."

Labor

Ronald L. Filippelli, *Labor Conflict in the United States* (1990); Gary M. Fink, ed., *Biographical Dictionary of American Labor* (1984); Gary M. Fink, ed., *Labor Unions* (1977); Philip S. Foner, *First Facts of American Labor* (1984).

Hispanics

Nicolás Kanellos, ed., *The Hispanic-American Almanac* (1993); Nicolás Kanellos, ed., *Reference Library of Hispanic America* (1993); Francisco Lomelí, ed., *Handbook of Hispanic Cultures in the United States* (1993); Matt S. Meier, *Mexican-American Biographies* (1988); Matt S. Meier, *Notable Latino Americans* (1997); Matt S. Meier and Feliciano Rivera, *Dictionary of Mexican American History* (1981); Joseph C. Tardiff and L. Mpho Mabunda, eds., *Dictionary of Hispanic Biography* (1996). See also "Immigration and Ethnic Groups."

Literature

James T. Callow and Robert J. Reilly, *Guide to American Literature* (1976–1977); *Dictionary of Literary Biography* (1978–   ); Eugene Ehrlich and Gorton Carruth, *The Oxford Illustrated Literary Guide to the United States* (1982); Jon Tuska and Vicki Piekarski, *Encyclopedia of Frontier and Western Fiction* (1983). See also "Culture and Folklore," "The South," and "Women."

Mass Media and Journalism

Robert V. Hudson, *Mass Media* (1987); Joseph P. McKerns, ed., *Biographical Dictionary of American Journalism* (1989); William H. Taft, ed., *Encyclopedia of Twentieth-Century Journalists* (1986). See also "The Cold War," "Constitution, Supreme Court, and Judiciary," "Entertainment and the Arts," and "Immigration and Ethnic Groups."

Medicine and Nursing

Rima D. Apple, ed., *Women, Health, and Medicine in America* (1990); Vern L. Bullough et al., eds., *American Nursing: A Biographical Dictionary* (1988); Martin Kaufman et al., eds., *Dictionary of American Nursing Biography* (1988); Martin Kaufman et al., eds., *Dictionary of American Medical Biography* (1984); George L. Maddox, ed., *The Encyclopedia of Aging* (1995).

Military and Wars

William M. Arkin et al., *Encyclopedia of the U.S. Military* (1990); Charles D. Bright, ed., *Historical Dictionary of the U.S. Air Force* (1992); John W. Chambers, ed., *Oxford Companion to United States Military History* (2000); Andre Corvisier, ed., *A Dictionary of Military History* (1994); R. Ernest Dupuy and Trevor N. Dupuy, *The Harper Encyclopedia of Military History* (1993); David S. Frazier, ed., *The United States and Mexico at War* (1998); John E. Jessup, ed., *Encyclopedia of the American Military* (1994); Kenneth Macksey and William Woodhouse, *The Penguin Encyclopedia of Modern Warfare* (1992); Franklin D. Margiotta, ed., *Brassey's Encyclopedia of Naval Forces and Warfare* (1996); David F. Marley, *Pirates and Privateers of the Americas* (1994); James I. Matray, ed., *Historical Dictionary of the Korean War* (1991); Stanley Sandler, ed., *The Korean War* (1995); Roger J. Spiller and Joseph G. Dawson III, eds., *Dictionary of American Military Biography* (1984); Jerry K. Sweeney, ed., *A Handbook of American Military History* (1996); Peter G. Tsouras et al., *The United States Army* (1991); U.S. Military Academy, *The West Point Atlas of American Wars, 1689–1953* (1959); Bruce W. Watson et al., eds., *United States Intelligence* (1990); Bruce W. Watson and Susan M. Watson, *The United States Air Force* (1992); Bruce W. Watson and Susan M. Watson, *The United States Navy* (1991). See also "American Revolution and Colonies," "Civil War and Reconstruction," "The Cold War," "Vietnam War," and "World War II."

Music

John Chilton, *Who's Who of Jazz* (1972); Donald Clarke et al., eds., *The Penguin Encyclopedia of Popular Music* (1999); Edward Jablonski, *The Encyclopedia of American Music* (1981); Roger Lax and Frederick Smith, *The Great Song Thesaurus* (1984); Philip D. Morehead, *The New International Dictionary of Music* (1993); Austin Sonnier, Jr., *A Guide to the Blues* (1994). See also "Culture and Folklore" and "Entertainment and the Arts."

Native Americans and Indian Affairs

Gretchen M. Bataille, ed., *Native American Women* (1992); Michael Coe et al., *Atlas of Ancient America* (1986); Mary B. Davis, ed., *Native America in the Twentieth Century* (1994); Rayna Green, *The British Museum Encyclopedia of Native North America* (1999); *Handbook of North American Indians* (1978–); Sam D. Gill and Irene F. Sullivan, *Dictionary of Native American Mythology* (1992); J. Norman Heard et al., *Handbook of the American Frontier: Four Centuries of Indian–White Relationships* (1987–); Bruce E. Johansen, ed., *The Encyclopedia of Native American Economic History* (1999); Bruce E. Johansen, ed., *The Encyclopedia of Native American Legal Tradition* (1998); Bruce E. Johansen et al., eds., *The Encyclopedia of Native American Biography* (1997); Barry Klein, ed., *Reference Encyclopedia of the American Indian* (1993); Barry M. Plitzker, *Native Americans* (1998); Francis P. Prucha, *Atlas of American Indian Affairs* (1990); Paul Stuart, *Nation Within a Nation: Historical Statistics of American Indians* (1987); Helen H. Tanner, ed., *Atlas of Great Lakes Indian History* (1987); Carl Waldman, *Encyclopedia of Native American Tribes* (1988); Carl Waldman, *Atlas of the North American Indian* (1985).

The New Deal and Franklin D. Roosevelt

Otis L. Graham, Jr., and Meghan R. Wander, eds., *Franklin D. Roosevelt: His Life and Times* (1985); James S. Olson, ed., *Historical Dictionary of the New Deal* (1985). See also "Politics and Government."

Peace Movements and Pacifism

Harold Josephson et al., eds., *Biographical Dictionary of Modern Peace Leaders* (1985); Ervin Laszlo and Jong Y. Yoo, eds., *World Encyclopedia of Peace* (1986); Robert S. Meyer, *Peace Organizations Past and Present* (1988); Nancy L. Roberts, *American Peace Writers, Editors, and Periodicals* (1991). See also "Foreign Relations," "Military and Wars," and specific wars.

Politics and Government: General

Erik W. Austin and Jerome M. Clubb, *Political Facts of the United States Since 1789* (1986); *The Columbia Dictionary of Political Biography* (1991); Jack P. Greene, ed., *Encyclopedia of American Political History* (1984); Leon Hurwitz, *Historical Dictionary of Censorship in the United States* (1985); George T. Kurian, ed., *A Historical Guide to the U.S. Government* (1998); Philip Rees, *Biographical Dictionary of the Extreme Right Since 1890* (1991); Charles R. Ritter et al., *American Legislative Leaders, 1850–1910* (1989); William Safire, *Safire's Political Dictionary* (1993); Robert Scruton, *A Dictionary of Political Thought* (1982); Jay M. Shafritz, *The HarperCollins Dictionary of American Government and Politics* (1992). See also "Cities and Towns," "Constitution, Supreme Court, and Judiciary," "States," and the following sections.

Politics and Government: Congress

American Enterprise Institute, *Vital Statistics on Congress* (1980–); Donald C. Brown et al., eds., *The Encyclopedia of the United States Congress* (1995); Stephen G. Christianson, *Facts About the Congress* (1996); Congressional Quarterly, *Biographical Directory of the American Congress, 1774–1996* (1997); Congressional Quarterly, *Congress and the Nation* (1965–); Kenneth C. Martis, *Historical Atlas of Political Parties in the United States Congress, 1789–1989* (1989); Kenneth C. Martis, *Historical Atlas of United States Congressional Districts, 1789–1983* (1982); Joel H. Silbey, ed., *Encyclopedia of the American Legislative System* (1994).

Politics and Government: Election Statistics

Congressional Quarterly, *Guide to U.S. Elections* (1994); Congressional Quarterly, *Presidential Elections, 1789–1996* (1997); L. Sandy Maisel, ed., *Political Parties and Elections in the United States* (1991); Svend Petersen and Louis Filler, *A Statistical History of the American Presidential Elections* (1981); Richard M. Scammon et al., eds., *America Votes* (1956–); Harold W. Stanley and Richard G. Niemi, *Vital Statistics on American Politics* (1988–); Lyn Ragsdale, *Vital Statistics on the Presidency* (1998); G. Scott Thomas, *The Pursuit of the White House* (1987).

Politics and Government: Parties

Earl R. Kruschke, *Encyclopedia of Third Parties in the United States* (1991); George T. Kurian, ed., *The Encyclopedia of the Republican Party* and *The Encyclopedia of the Democratic Party* (1996); Edward L. Schapsmeier and Frederick H. Schapsmeier, eds., *Political Parties and Civic Action Groups* (1981). See also other listings for "Politics and Government."

Politics and Government: Presidency and Executive Branch

Alan Brinkley and Davis Dyer, eds., *The Reader's Companion to the Presidency* (2000); Henry F. Graff, *The Presidents* (1996); Bernard S. Katz and C. Daniel Vencill, eds., *Biographical Dictionary of the United States Secretaries of the Treasury, 1789–1995* (1996); Richard S. Kirkendall, ed., *The Harry S Truman Encyclopedia* (1989); Leonard W. Levy and Louis Fisher, eds., *Encyclopedia of the American Presidency* (1993); Merrill D. Peterson, ed., *Thomas Jefferson* (1986); Lyn Ragsdale, *Vital Statistics on the Presidency* (1998); Robert A. Rutland, ed., *James Madison and the American Nation* (1995); Robert Sobel, ed., *Biographical Directory of the United States Executive Branch, 1774–1977* (1977). See other categories for various presidents.

Politics and Government: Radicalism and the Left

Mari Jo Buhle et al., eds., *The American Radical* (1994); Mari Jo Buhle et al., eds., *Encyclopedia of the American Left* (1998); David DeLeon, ed., *Leaders of the 1960s* (1994); Bernard K. Johnpoll and Harvey Klehr, eds., *Biographical Dictionary of the American Left* (1986).

Religion and Cults

Henry Bowden, *Dictionary of American Religious Biography* (1993); S. Kent Brown et al., eds., *Historical Atlas of Mormonism* (1995); Edwin Gaustad and Philip L. Barlow, *New Historical Atlas of Religion in America* (1998); Michael Glazier and Thomas J. Shelley, eds., *The Encyclopedia of American Catholic History* (1997); Bill J. Leonard, *Dictionary of Baptists in America* (1994); Donald Lewis, ed., *A Dictionary of Evangelical Biography* (1995); Charles H. Lippy and Peter W. Williams, eds., *Encyclopedia of the American Religious Experience* (1988); J. Gordon Melton, *The Encyclopedia of American Religions* (1987); J. Gordon Melton, *The Encyclopedic Handbook of Cults in America* (1992); Mark A. Noll and Nathan O. Hatch, eds., *Eerdman's Handbook to Christianity in America* (1983); Stephen R. Prothero et al., *The Encyclopedia of American Religious History* (1996); Paul J. Weber and W. Landis Jones, *U.S. Religious Interest Groups* (1994). See also "African Americans."

Science and Technology

James W. Cortada, *Historical Dictionary of Data Processing* (1987); Clark A. Elliott, *Biographical Index to American Science: The Seventeenth Century to 1920* (1990); Charles C. Gillespie et al., eds., *Dictionary of Scientific Biography* (1970–); National Academy of Sciences, *Biographical Memoirs* (1877–);

Roy Porter, ed., *The Biographical Dictionary of Scientists* (1994). See also "Exploration."

Sexuality

Robert T. Francoeur, ed., *The International Encyclopedia of Sexuality* (1998); Wayne R. Dynes, ed., *Encyclopedia of Homosexuality* (1990); Steve Hogan and Lee Hudson, *Completely Queer: The Gay and Lesbian Encyclopedia* (1998); Arthur S. Leonard, ed., *Sexuality and the Law* (1993); Neil Schlager, ed., *Gay & Lesbian Almanac* (1998); Michael J. Tyrkus, ed., *Gay & Lesbian Biography* (1997); Bonnie Zimmerman and George Haggerty, eds., *Encyclopedia of Lesbian and Gay Histories and Cultures* (1999). See also "Social History and Reform."

Slavery

Seymour Drescher and Stanley L. Engerman, eds., *A Historical Guide to World Slavery* (1998); Paul Finkelman and Joseph C. Miller, eds., *Macmillan Encyclopedia of World Slavery* (1998); Randall M. Miller and John D. Smith, eds., *Dictionary of Afro-American Slavery* (1997); Junius P. Rodriguez, ed., *The Historical Encyclopedia of World Slavery* (1997). See also "African Americans."

Social History and Reform

Mary K. Cayton et al., eds., *Encyclopedia of American Social History* (1993); Louis Filler, *Dictionary of American Social Change* (1982); Robert S. Fogarty, *Dictionary of American Communal and Utopian History* (1980); Joseph M. Hawes and Elizabeth I. Nybakken, eds., *American Families* (1991); David Hey, ed., *The Oxford Companion to Local and Family History* (1996); Harold M. Keele and Joseph C. Kiger, eds., *Foundations* (1984); Mark E. Lender, *Dictionary of American Temperance Biography* (1984); Patricia M. Melvin, ed., *American Community Organizations* (1986); Randall M. Miller and Paul A. Cimbala, eds., *American Reform and Reformers* (1996); Roger S. Powers and William B. Vogele, eds., *Protest, Power, and Change* (1996); Alvin J. Schmidt, *Fraternal Organizations* (1980); Peter N. Stearns, ed., *Encyclopedia of Social History* (1993); Walter I. Trattner, *Biographical Dictionary of Social Welfare in America* (1986). See also "Crime, Violence, Police, and Prisons" and "Sexuality."

South

Edward L. Ayers and Brad Mittendorf, eds., *The Oxford Book of the American South* (1997); Robert Bain et al., eds., *Southern Writers* (1979); Kenneth Coleman and Charles S. Gurr, eds., *Dictionary of Georgia Biography* (1983); William S. Powell, ed., *Dictionary of North Carolina Biography* (1979–1996); David C. Roller and Robert W. Twyman, eds., *The Encyclopedia of Southern History* (1979); Walter P. Webb et al., eds., *The Handbook of Texas* (1952, 1976); Charles R. Wilson and William Ferris, eds., *Encyclopedia of Southern Culture* (1986).

See also "Civil War and Reconstruction," "Politics and Government," and "States."

Sports

Peter C. Bjarkman, ed., *Encyclopedia of Major League Baseball Team Histories* (1991); Ralph Hickok, *A Who's Who of Sports Champions* (1995); Ralph Hickok, *The Encyclopedia of North American Sports History* (1991); David Levinson and Karen Christensen, eds., *Encyclopedia of World Sport* (1996); Jonathan F. Light, *The Cultural Encyclopedia of Baseball* (1997); David L. Porter, *Biographical Dictionary of American Sports: Baseball* (2000), *Basketball and Other Indoor Sports* (1989), *Football* (1987), and *Outdoor Sports* (1988); Victoria Sherrow, *Encyclopedia of Women and Sports* (1996); David Wallechinsky, *The Complete Book of the Summer Olympics* (1996); David Wallechinsky, *The Complete Book of the Winter Olympics* (1993). See also "Culture and Folklore."

States

Gary Alampi, ed., *Gale State Rankings Reporter* (1994); Roy R. Glashan, comp., *American Governors and Gubernatorial Elections, 1775–1978* (1979); John Hoffmann, ed., *A Guide to the History of Illinois* (1991); Edith R. Hornor, *Almanac of the Fifty States* (1997); Joseph E. Kallenback and Jessamine S. Kallenback, *American State Governors, 1776–1976* (1977); Joseph N. Kane et al., eds., *Facts About the States* (1994); John E. Kleber et al., eds., *The Kentucky Encyclopedia* (1992); Thomas A. McMullin and Marie Mullaney, *Biographical Directory of the Governors of the United States, 1983–1987* (1988) and *1988–1993* (1994); Marie Mullaney, *Biographical Directory of the Governors of the United States, 1988–1994* (1994); Thomas J. Noel, *Historical Atlas of Colorado* (1994); John W. Raimo, ed., *Biographical Directory of the Governors of the United States, 1978–1983* (1985); James W. Scott and Ronald L. De Lorme, *Historical Atlas of Washington* (1988); Benjamin F. Shearer and Barbara S. Shearer, *State Names, Seals, Flags, and Symbols* (1994); Robert Sobel and John W. Raimo, eds., *Biographical Directory of the Governors of the United States, 1789–1978* (1978); Richard W. Wilkie and Jack Tager, eds., *Historical Atlas of Massachusetts* (1991). See also "Politics and Government," "South," and "West and Frontier."

Transportation

Keith L. Bryant, ed., *Railroads in the Age of Regulation, 1900–1980* (1988); Rene De La Pedraja, *A Historical Dictionary of the U.S. Merchant Marine and Shipping Industry* (1994); Robert L. Frey, ed., *Railroads in the Nineteenth Century* (1988). See also "Business and the Economy."

Vietnam War

John S. Bowman, ed., *The Vietnam War: An Almanac* (1986); Stanley I. Kutler, ed., *Encyclopedia of the Vietnam War* (1996); James S. Olson, ed., *Dictionary of the Vietnam War* (1988);

Harry G. Summers, Jr., *Vietnam War Almanac* (1985). Also see "Peace Movements and Pacifism" and "Military and Wars."

West and Frontier

William A. Beck and Ynez D. Haase, *Historical Atlas of the American West* (1989); Doris O. Dawdy, *Artists of the American West* (1974–1984); J. Norman Heard, *Handbook of the American Frontier* (1987); Howard R. Lamar, ed., *The New Encyclopedia of the American West* (1998); Clyde A. Milner III et al., eds., *The Oxford History of the American West* (1994); Jay Robert Nash, *Encyclopedia of Western Lawmen and Outlaws* (1992); Doyce B. Nunis, Jr., and Gloria R. Lothrop, eds., *A Guide to the History of California* (1989); Charles Phillips and Alan Axelrod, eds., *Encyclopedia of the American West* (1996); Dan L. Thrapp, *The Encyclopedia of Frontier Biography* (1988–1994); David Walker, *Biographical Directory of American Territorial Governors* (1984). See also "Cities and Towns," "Literature," and "Native Americans and Indian Affairs."

Women

Anne Gibson and Timothy Fast, *The Women's Atlas of the United States* (1986); Karen Greenspan, *The Timetables of Women's History* (1996); Maggie Humm, *The Dictionary of Feminist Theory* (1990); Edward T. James et al., *Notable American Women, 1607–1950* (1971); Lina Mainiero, ed., *American Women Writers* (1979–1982); Wilma Mankiller et al., *The Reader's Companion to U.S. Women's History* (1998); Kirstin Olsen, *Chronology of Women's History* (1994); Barbara G. Shortridge, *Atlas of American Women* (1987); Barbara Sicherman and Carol H. Green, eds., *Notable American Women, The Modern Period* (1980); Helen Tierney, ed., *Women's Studies Encyclopedia* (1991); James Trager, *The*

Women's Chronology (1994); Angela H. Zophy and Frances M. Kavenik, eds., *Handbook of American Women's History* (1990). See also "African Americans," "Immigration and Ethnic Groups," "Medicine and Nursing," "Native Americans and Indian Affairs," and "Sports."

World War I

David F. Burg and L. Edward Purcell, *Almanac of World War I* (1998); Martin Gilbert, *Atlas of World War I* (1994); Holger H. Herwig and Neil M. Heyman, *Biographical Dictionary of World War I* (1982); George T. Kurian, *Encyclopedia of the First World War* (1990); Stephen Pope and Elizabeth-Anne Wheal, *The Dictionary of the First World War* (1995); Anne C. Venzon, *The United States in the First World War* (1995). See also "Military and Wars."

World War II

Marcel Baudot et al., eds., *The Historical Encyclopedia of World War II* (1980); David G. Chandler and James Lawton Collins, Jr., eds., *The D-Day Encyclopedia* (1993); I. C. B. Dear and M. R. D. Foot, eds., *The Oxford Companion to World War II* (1995); Simon Goodenough, *War Maps: Great Land Battles of World War II* (1988); Robert Goralski, *World War II Almanac* (1981); John Keegan, ed., *The Times Atlas of the Second World War* (1989); George T. Kurian, *Encyclopedia of the Second World War* (1991); Norman Polmer and Thomas B. Allen, *World War II: America at War* (1991); Louis L. Snyder, *Louis L. Snyder's Historical Guide to World War II* (1982); U.S. Military Academy, *Campaign Atlas to the Second World War: Europe and the Mediterranean* (1980); Peter Young, ed., *The World Almanac Book of World War II* (1981). See also "Military and Wars."

Documents

DECLARATION OF INDEPENDENCE IN CONGRESS, JULY 4, 1776

When, in the course of human events, it becomes necessary for one people to dissolve the political bonds which have connected them with another, and to assume, among the powers of the earth, the separate and equal station to which the laws of nature and of nature's God entitle them, a decent respect to the opinions of mankind requires that they should declare the causes which impel them to the separation.

We hold these truths to be self-evident: That all men are created equal; that they are endowed by their Creator with certain unalienable rights; that among these are life, liberty, and the pursuit of happiness; that, to secure these rights, governments are instituted among men, deriving their just powers from the consent of the governed; that whenever any form of government becomes destructive of these ends, it is the right of the people to alter or to abolish it, and to institute new government, laying its foundation on such principles, and organizing its powers in such form, as to them shall seem most likely to effect their safety and happiness. Prudence, indeed, will dictate that governments long established should not be changed for light and transient causes; and accordingly all experience hath shown that mankind are more disposed to suffer, while evils are sufferable, than to right themselves by abolishing the forms to which they are accustomed. But when a long train of abuses and usurpations, pursuing invariably the same object, evinces a design to reduce them under absolute despotism, it is their right, it is their duty, to throw off such government, and to provide new guards for their future security. Such has been the patient sufferance of these colonies; and such is now the necessity which constrains them to alter their former systems of government. The history of the present King of Great Britain is a history of repeated injuries and usurpations, all having in direct object the establishment of an absolute tyranny over these states. To prove this, let facts be submitted to a candid world.

He has refused his assent to laws, the most wholesome and necessary for the public good.

He has forbidden his governors to pass laws of immediate and pressing importance, unless suspended in their operation till his assent should be obtained; and, when so suspended, he has utterly neglected to attend to them.

He has refused to pass other laws for the accommodation of large districts of people, unless those people would relinquish the right of representation in the legislature, a right inestimable to them, and formidable to tyrants only.

He has called together legislative bodies at places unusual, uncomfortable, and distant from the depository of their public records, for the sole purpose of fatiguing them into compliance with his measures.

He has dissolved representative houses repeatedly, for opposing, with manly firmness, his invasions on the rights of the people.

He has refused for a long time, after such dissolutions, to cause others to be elected; whereby the legislative powers, incapable of annihilation, have returned to the people at large for their exercise; the state remaining, in the mean time, exposed to all the dangers of invasions from without and convulsions within.

He has endeavored to prevent the population of these states; for that purpose obstructing the laws for naturalization of foreigners; refusing to pass others to encourage their migration hither, and raising the conditions of new appropriations of lands.

He has obstructed the administration of justice, by refusing his assent to laws for establishing judiciary powers.

He has made judges dependent on his will alone, for the tenure of their offices, and the amount and payment of their salaries.

He has erected a multitude of new offices, and sent hither swarms of officers to harass our people and eat out their substance.

He has kept among us, in times of peace, standing armies, without the consent of our legislatures.

He has affected to render the military independent of, and superior to, the civil power.

He has combined with others to subject us to a jurisdiction foreign to our constitution, and unacknowledged by our laws, giving his assent to their acts of pretended legislation:

For quartering large bodies of armed troops among us;

For protecting them, by a mock trial, from punishment for any murders which they should commit on the inhabitants of these states;

For cutting off our trade with all parts of the world;

For imposing taxes on us without our consent;

For depriving us, in many cases, of the benefits of trial by jury;

For transporting us beyond seas, to be tried for pretended offenses;

For abolishing the free system of English laws in a

neighboring province, establishing therein an arbitrary government, and enlarging its boundaries, so as to render it at once an example and fit instrument for introducing the same absolute rule into these colonies;

For taking away our charters, abolishing our most valuable laws, and altering fundamentally the forms of our governments;

For suspending our own legislatures, and declaring themselves invested with power to legislate for us in all cases whatsoever.

He has abdicated government here, by declaring us out of his protection and waging war against us.

He has plundered our seas, ravaged our coasts, burned our towns, and destroyed the lives of our people.

He is at this time transporting large armies of foreign mercenaries to complete the works of death, desolation, and tyranny already begun with circumstances of cruelty and perfidy scarcely paralleled in the most barbarous ages, and totally unworthy the head of a civilized nation.

He has constrained our fellow-citizens, taken captive on the high seas, to bear arms against their country, to become the executioners of their friends and brethren, or to fall themselves by their hands.

He has excited domestic insurrection among us, and has endeavored to bring on the inhabitants of our frontiers the merciless Indian savages, whose known rule of warfare is an undistinguished destruction of all ages, sexes, and conditions.

In every stage of these oppressions we have petitioned for redress in the most humble terms; our repeated petitions have been answered only by repeated injury. A prince, whose character is thus marked by every act which may define a tyrant, is unfit to be the ruler of a free people.

Nor have we been wanting in our attentions to our British brethren. We have warned them, from time to time, of attempts by their legislature to extend an unwarrantable jurisdiction over us. We have reminded them of the circumstances of our emigration and settlement here. We have appealed to their native justice and magnanimity; and we have conjured them, by the ties of our common kindred, to disavow these usurpations, which would inevitably interrupt our connections and correspondence. They, too, have been deaf to the voice of justice and of consanguinity. We must, therefore, acquiesce in the necessity which denounces our separation, and hold them, as we hold the rest of mankind, enemies in war, in peace friends.

We, therefore, the representatives of the United States of America, in General Congress assembled, appealing to the Supreme Judge of the world for the rectitude of our intentions, do, in the name and by the authority of the good people of these colonies, solemnly publish and declare, that these United Colonies are, and of right ought to be, FREE AND INDEPENDENT STATES; that they are absolved from all allegiance to the British crown, and that all political connection between them and the state of Great Britain is,

and ought to be, totally dissolved; and that, as free and independent states, they have full power to levy war, conclude peace, contract alliances, establish commerce, and do all other acts and things which independent states may of right do. And for the support of this declaration, with a firm reliance on the protection of Divine Providence, we mutually pledge to each other our lives, our fortunes, and our sacred honor.

ARTICLES OF CONFEDERATION

(The text of the Articles of Confederation can be found at http://college.hmco.com.)

CONSTITUTION OF THE UNITED STATES OF AMERICA AND AMENDMENTS*

Preamble

We the people of the United States, in order to form a more perfect union, establish justice, insure domestic tranquillity, provide for the common defense, promote the general welfare, and secure the blessings of liberty to ourselves and our posterity, do ordain and establish this Constitution for the United States of America.

Article I

Section 1 All legislative powers herein granted shall be vested in a Congress of the United States, which shall consist of a Senate and a House of Representatives.

Section 2 The House of Representatives shall be composed of members chosen every second year by the people of the several States, and the electors in each State shall have the qualifications requisite for electors of the most numerous branch of the State Legislature.

No person shall be a Representative who shall not have attained to the age of twenty-five years, and been seven years a citizen of the United States, and who shall not, when elected, be an inhabitant of that State in which he shall be chosen.

Representatives and direct taxes shall be apportioned among the several States which may be included within this Union, according to their respective numbers, *which shall be determined by adding to the whole number of free persons, including those bound to service for a term of years and excluding Indians not taxed, three-fifths of all other persons.* The actual enumeration shall be made within three years after the first meeting of the Congress of the United States, and within

*Passages no longer in effect are printed in italic type.

every subsequent term of ten years, in such manner as they shall by law direct. The number of Representatives shall not exceed one for every thirty thousand, but each State shall have at least one Representative; *and until such enumeration shall be made, the State of New Hampshire shall be entitled to choose three, Massachusetts eight, Rhode Island and Providence Plantations one, Connecticut five, New York six, New Jersey four, Pennsylvania eight, Delaware one, Maryland six, Virginia ten, North Carolina five, South Carolina five, and Georgia three.*

When vacancies happen in the representation from any State, the Executive authority thereof shall issue writs of election to fill such vacancies.

The House of Representatives shall choose their Speaker and other officers; and shall have the sole power of impeachment.

Section 3   The Senate of the United States shall be composed of two Senators from each State, *chosen by the legislature thereof,* for six years; and each Senator shall have one vote.

Immediately after they shall be assembled in consequence of the first election, they shall be divided as equally as may be into three classes. The seats of the Senators of the first class shall be vacated at the expiration of the second year, of the second class at the expiration of the fourth year, and of the third class at the expiration of the sixth year, so that one-third may be chosen every second year; and if vacancies happen by resignation or otherwise, during the recess of the legislature of any State, the Executive thereof may make temporary appointments until the next meeting of the legislature, which shall then fill such vacancies.

No person shall be a Senator who shall not have attained to the age of thirty years, and been nine years a citizen of the United States, and who shall not, when elected, be an inhabitant of that State for which he shall be chosen.

The Vice-President of the United States shall be President of the Senate, but shall have no vote, unless they be equally divided.

The Senate shall choose their other officers, and also a President *pro tempore*, in the absence of the Vice-President, or when he shall exercise the office of President of the United States.

The Senate shall have the sole power to try all impeachments. When sitting for that purpose, they shall be on oath or affirmation. When the President of the United States is tried, the Chief Justice shall preside: and no person shall be convicted without the concurrence of two-thirds of the members present.

Judgment in cases of impeachment shall not extend further than to removal from the office, and disqualification to hold and enjoy any office of honor, trust or profit under the United States: but the party convicted shall nevertheless be liable and subject to indictment, trial, judgment and punishment, according to law.

Section 4   The times, places and manner of holding elections for Senators and Representatives shall be prescribed in each State by the legislature thereof; but the Congress may at any time by law make or alter such regulations, except as to the places of choosing Senators.

The Congress shall assemble at least once in every year, and such meeting *shall be on the first Monday in December, unless they shall by law appoint a different day.*

Section 5   Each house shall be the judge of the elections, returns and qualifications of its own members, and a majority of each shall constitute a quorum to do business; but a smaller number may adjourn from day to day, and may be authorized to compel the attendance of absent members, in such manner, and under such penalties, as each house may provide.

Each house may determine the rules of its proceedings, punish its members for disorderly behavior, and with the concurrence of two-thirds, expel a member.

Each house shall keep a journal of its proceedings, and from time to time publish the same, excepting such parts as may in their judgment require secrecy; and the yeas and nays of the members of either house on any question shall, at the desire of one-fifth of those present, be entered on the journal.

Neither house, during the session of Congress, shall, without the consent of the other, adjourn for more than three days, nor to any other place than that in which the two houses shall be sitting.

Section 6   The Senators and Representatives shall receive a compensation for their services, to be ascertained by law and paid out of the treasury of the United States. They shall in all cases except treason, felony and breach of the peace, be privileged from arrest during their attendance at the session of their respective houses, and in going to and returning from the same; and for any speech or debate in either house, they shall not be questioned in any other place.

No Senator or Representative shall, during the time for which he was elected, be appointed to any civil office under the authority of the United States, which shall have been created, or the emoluments whereof shall have been increased, during such time; and no person holding any office under the United States shall be a member of either house during his continuance in office.

Section 7   All bills for raising revenue shall originate in the House of Representatives; but the Senate may propose or concur with amendments as on other bills.

Every bill which shall have passed the House of Representatives and the Senate, shall, before it become a law, be presented to the President of the United States; if he approve he shall sign it, but if not he shall return it with objections to that house in which it originated, who shall enter the objections at large on their journal, and proceed to reconsider it. If after such reconsideration two-thirds of that house shall agree to pass the bill, it shall be sent, together with the objections, to the other house, by which it shall likewise be reconsidered, and, if approved by two-thirds of that house, it shall become a law. But in all such cases the votes of both houses shall be determined by yeas and nays, and the names of the persons voting for and against the bill shall be entered on the journal of each house respectively. If any bill shall not be returned by the President within ten days (Sundays excepted) after it shall have been presented to him, the same shall be a law, in like manner as if he had signed it, unless the Congress by their adjournment prevent its return, in which case it shall not be a law.

Every order, resolution, or vote to which the concurrence of the Senate and House of Representatives may be necessary (except on a question of adjournment) shall be presented to the President of the United States; and before the same shall take effect, shall be approved by him, or being disapproved by him, shall be repassed by two-thirds of the Senate and House of Representatives, according to the rules and limitations prescribed in the case of a bill.

Section 8   The Congress shall have power

To lay and collect taxes, duties, imposts, and excises, to pay the debts and provide for the common defense and general welfare of the United States; but all duties, imposts and excises shall be uniform throughout the United States;

To borrow money on the credit of the United States;

To regulate commerce with foreign nations, and among the several States, and with the Indian tribes;

To establish an uniform rule of naturalization, and uniform laws on the subject of bankruptcies throughout the United States;

To coin money, regulate the value thereof, and of foreign coin, and fix the standard of weights and measures;

To provide for the punishment of counterfeiting the securities and current coin of the United States;

To establish post offices and post roads;

To promote the progress of science and useful arts by securing for limited times to authors and inventors the exclusive right to their respective writings and discoveries;

To constitute tribunals inferior to the Supreme Court;

To define and punish piracies and felonies committed on the high seas and offenses against the law of nations;

To declare war, grant letters of marque and reprisal, and make rules concerning captures on land and water;

To raise and support armies, but no appropriation of money to that use shall be for a longer term than two years;

To provide and maintain a navy;

To make rules for the government and regulation of the land and naval forces;

To provide for calling forth the militia to execute the laws of the Union, suppress insurrections, and repel invasions;

To provide for organizing, arming, and disciplining the militia, and for governing such part of them as may be employed in the service of the United States, reserving to the States respectively the appointment of the officers, and the authority of training the militia according to the discipline prescribed by Congress;

To exercise exclusive legislation in all cases whatsoever, over such district (not exceeding ten miles square) as may, by cession of particular States, and the acceptance of Congress, become the seat of government of the United States, and to exercise like authority over all places purchased by the consent of the legislature of the State, in which the same shall be, for erection of forts, magazines, arsenals, dockyards, and other needful buildings; —and

To make all laws which shall be necessary and proper for carrying into execution the foregoing powers, and all other powers vested by this Constitution in the government of the United States, or in any department or officer thereof.

Section 9   The migration or importation of such persons as any of the States now existing shall think proper to admit shall not be prohibited by the Congress prior to the year 1808; but a tax or duty may be imposed on such importation, not exceeding $10 for each person.

The privilege of the writ of habeas corpus shall not be suspended, unless when in cases of rebellion or invasion the public safety may require it.

No bill of attainder or ex post facto law shall be passed.

No capitation, or other direct, tax shall be laid, unless in proportion to the census or enumeration herein before directed to be taken.

No tax or duty shall be laid on articles exported from any State.

No preference shall be given by any regulation of commerce or revenue to the ports of one State over those of another; nor shall vessels bound to, or from, one State, be obliged to enter, clear, or pay duties in another.

No money shall be drawn from the treasury, but in consequence of appropriations made by law; and a regular statement and account of the receipts and expenditures of all public money shall be published from time to time.

No title of nobility shall be granted by the United States: and no person holding any office of profit or trust under them, shall, without the consent of the Congress, accept of any present, emolument, office, or title, of any kind whatever, from any king, prince, or foreign state.

Section 10   No State shall enter into any treaty, alliance, or confederation; grant letters of marque and reprisal; coin money; emit bills of credit; make anything but gold and silver coin a tender in payment of debts; pass any bill of attainder, ex post facto law, or law impairing the obligation of contracts, or grant any title of nobility.

No State shall, without the consent of Congress, lay any imposts or duties on imports or exports, except what may be absolutely necessary for executing its inspection laws: and the net produce of all duties and imposts, laid by any State on imports or exports, shall be for the use of the treasury of the United States; and all such laws shall be subject to the revision and control of the Congress.

No State shall, without the consent of Congress, lay any duty of tonnage, keep troops or ships of war in time of peace, enter into any agreement or compact with another State, or with a foreign power, or engage in war, unless actually invaded, or in such imminent danger as will not admit of delay.

Article II

Section 1   The executive power shall be vested in a President of the United States of America. He shall hold his office during the term of four years, and, together with the Vice-President, chosen for the same term, be elected as follows:

Each State shall appoint, in such manner as the legislature thereof may direct, a number of electors, equal to the whole number of Senators and Representatives to which the State may be entitled in the Congress; but no Senator or Representative, or person holding an office of trust or profit under the United States, shall be appointed an elector.

The electors shall meet in their respective States, and vote by ballot for two persons, of whom one at least shall not be an inhabitant of the same State with themselves. And they shall make a list of all the persons voted for, and of the number of votes for each; which list they shall sign and certify, and transmit sealed to the seat of government of the United States, directed to the President of the Senate. The President of the Senate shall, in the presence of the Senate and House of Representatives, open all the certificates, and the votes shall then be counted. The person having the greatest number of votes shall be the President, if such number be a majority of the whole number of electors appointed; and if there be more than one who have such majority, and have an equal number of votes, then the House of Representatives shall immediately choose by ballot one of them for President; and if no person have a majority, then from the five highest on the list said house shall in like manner choose the President. But in choosing the President the votes shall be taken by States, the representation from each State having one vote; a quorum for this purpose shall consist of a member or members from two-thirds of the States, and a majority of all the States shall be necessary to a choice. In every case, after the choice of the President, the person having the greatest number of votes of the electors shall be the Vice-President. But if there should remain two or more who have equal votes, the Senate shall choose from them by ballot the Vice-President.

The Congress may determine the time of choosing the electors and the day on which they shall give their votes; which day shall be the same throughout the United States.

No person except a natural-born citizen, *or a citizen of the United States at the time of the adoption of this Constitution,* shall be eligible to the office of President; neither shall any person be eligible to that office who shall not have attained to the age of thirty-five years, and been fourteen years a resident within the United States.

In cases of the removal of the President from office or of his death, resignation, or inability to discharge the powers and duties of the said office, the same shall devolve on the Vice-President, and the Congress may by law provide for the case of removal, death, resignation, or inability, both of the President and Vice-President, declaring what officer shall then act as President, and such officer shall act accordingly, until the disability be removed, or a President shall be elected.

The President shall, at stated times, receive for his services a compensation, which shall neither be increased nor diminished during the period for which he shall have been elected, and he shall not receive within that period any other emolument from the United States, or any of them.

Before he enter on the execution of his office, he shall take the following oath or affirmation:—"I do solemnly swear (or affirm) that I will faithfully execute the office of the President of the United States, and will to the best of my ability preserve, protect and defend the Constitution of the United States."

Section 2   The President shall be commander in chief of the army and navy of the United States, and of the militia of the several States, when called into the actual service of the United States; he may require the opinion, in writing, of the principal officer in each of the executive departments, upon any subject relating to the duties of their respective offices, and he shall have power to grant reprieves and pardons for offenses against the United States, except in cases of impeachment.

He shall have power, by and with the advice and consent of the Senate, to make treaties, provided two-thirds of the Senators present concur; and he shall nominate, and by and with the advice and consent of the Senate, shall appoint ambassadors, other public ministers and consuls, judges of the Supreme Court, and all other officers of the United States, whose appointments are not herein otherwise provided for, and which shall be established by law: but Congress may by law vest the appointment of such inferior officers, as they think proper, in the President alone, in the courts of law, or in the heads of departments.

The President shall have power to fill up all vacancies that may happen during the recess of the Senate, by granting commissions which shall expire at the end of their next session.

Section 3   He shall from time to time give to the Congress information of the state of the Union, and recommend to their consideration such measures as he shall judge necessary and expedient; he may, on extraordinary occasions, convene both houses, or either of them, and in case of disagreement between them, with respect to the time of adjournment, he may adjourn them to such time as he shall think proper; he shall receive ambassadors and other public ministers; he shall take care that the laws be faithfully executed, and shall commission all the officers of the United States.

Section 4   The President, Vice-President and all civil officers of the United States shall be removed from office on impeachment for, and on conviction of, treason, bribery, or other high crimes and misdemeanors.

Article III

Section 1 The judicial power of the United States shall be vested in one Supreme Court, and in such inferior courts as the Congress may from time to time ordain and establish. The judges, both of the Supreme and inferior courts, shall hold their offices during good behavior, and shall, at stated times, receive for their services a compensation which shall not be diminished during their continuance in office.

Section 2 The judicial power shall extend to all cases, in law and equity, arising under this Constitution, the laws of the United States, and treaties made, or which shall be made, under their authority;—to all cases affecting ambassadors, other public ministers and consuls;—to all cases of admiralty and maritime jurisdiction;—to controversies to which the United States shall be a party;—to controversies between two or more States;—*between a State and citizens of another State;*—between citizens of different States;—between citizens of the same State claiming lands under grants of different States, and between a State, or the citizens thereof, and foreign states, citizens or subjects.

In all cases affecting ambassadors, other public ministers and consuls, and those in which a State shall be party, the Supreme Court shall have original jurisdiction. In all the other cases before mentioned, the Supreme Court shall have appellate jurisdiction, both as to law and fact, with such exceptions, and under such regulations, as the Congress shall make.

The trial of all crimes, except in cases of impeachment, shall be by jury; and such trial shall be held in the State where said crimes shall have been committed; but when not committed within any State, the trial shall be at such place or places as the Congress may by law have directed.

Section 3 Treason against the United States shall consist only in levying war against them, or in adhering to their enemies, giving them aid and comfort. No person shall be convicted of treason unless on the testimony of two witnesses to the same overt act, or on confession in open court.

The Congress shall have power to declare the punishment of treason, but no attainder of treason shall work corruption of blood, or forfeiture except during the life of the person attainted.

Article IV

Section 1 Full faith and credit shall be given in each State to the public acts, records, and judicial proceedings of every other State. And the Congress may by general laws prescribe the manner in which such acts, records, and proceedings shall be proved, and the effect thereof.

Section 2 The citizens of each State shall be entitled to all privileges and immunities of citizens in the several States.

A person charged in any State with treason, felony, or other crime, who shall flee from justice, and be found in another State, shall on demand of the executive authority of the State from which he fled, be delivered up, to be removed to the State having jurisdiction of the crime.

No person held to service or labor in one State, under the laws thereof, escaping into another, shall, in consequence of any law or regulation therein, be discharged from such service or labor, but shall be delivered up on claim of the party to whom such service or labor may be due.

Section 3 New States may be admitted by the Congress into this Union; but no new State shall be formed or erected within the jurisdiction of any other State; nor any State be formed by the junction of two or more States, or parts of States, without the consent of the legislatures of the States concerned as well as of the Congress.

The Congress shall have power to dispose of and make all needful rules and regulations respecting the territory or other property belonging to the United States; and nothing in this Constitution shall be so construed as to prejudice any claims of the United States, or of any particular State.

Section 4 The United States shall guarantee to every State in this Union a republican form of government, and shall protect each of them against invasion; and on application of the legislature, or of the executive (when the legislature cannot be convened), against domestic violence.

Article V

The Congress, whenever two-thirds of both houses shall deem it necessary, shall propose amendments to this Constitution, or, on the application of the legislatures of two-thirds of the several States, shall call a convention for proposing amendments, which, in either case, shall be valid to all intents and purposes, as part of this Constitution, when ratified by the legislatures of three-fourths of the several States, or by conventions in three-fourths thereof, as the one or the other mode of ratification may be proposed by the Congress; provided *that no amendments which may be made prior to the year one thousand eight hundred and eight shall in any manner affect the first and fourth clauses in the ninth section of the first article;* and that no State, without its consent, shall be deprived of its equal suffrage in the Senate.

Article VI

All debts contracted and engagements entered into, before the adoption of this Constitution, shall be as valid against the United States under this Constitution, as under the Confederation.

This Constitution, and the laws of the United States which shall be made in pursuance thereof; and all treaties made, or which shall be made, under the authority of the United States, shall be the supreme law of the land; and the judges in every State shall be bound thereby, anything in the Constitution or laws of any State to the contrary notwithstanding.

The Senators and Representatives before mentioned, and the members of the several State legislatures, and all executive and judicial officers, both of the United States and of the several States, shall be bound by oath or affirmation to support this Constitution; but no religious test shall ever be required as a qualification to any office or public trust under the United States.

Article VII

The ratification of the conventions of nine States shall be sufficient for the establishment of this Constitution between the States so ratifying the same.

Done in Convention by the unanimous consent of the States present, the seventeenth day of September in the year of our Lord one thousand seven hundred and eighty-seven and of the Independence of the United States of America the twelfth. In witness whereof we have hereunto subscribed our names.

AMENDMENTS TO THE CONSTITUTION*

Amendment I

Congress shall make no law respecting an establishment of religion, or prohibiting the free exercise thereof; or abridging the freedom of speech, or of the press; or the right of the people peaceably to assemble, and to petition the government for a redress of grievances.

Amendment II

A well-regulated militia being necessary to the security of a free State, the right of the people to keep and bear arms shall not be infringed.

Amendment III

No soldier shall, in time of peace, be quartered in any house without the consent of the owner, nor in time of war, but in a manner to be prescribed by law.

Amendment IV

The right of the people to be secure in their persons, houses, papers, and effects, against unreasonable searches and seizures, shall not be violated, and no warrants shall issue but upon probable cause, supported by oath or affirmation, and particularly describing the place to be searched, and the persons or things to be seized.

Amendment V

No person shall be held to answer for a capital, or otherwise infamous crime, unless on a presentment or indictment of a grand jury, except in cases arising in the land or naval forces, or in the militia, when in actual service in time of war or public danger; nor shall any person be subject for the same offense to be twice put in jeopardy of life or limb; nor shall be compelled in any criminal case to be a witness against himself, nor be deprived of life, liberty, or property, without due process of law; nor shall private property be taken for public use without just compensation.

Amendment VI

In all criminal prosecutions, the accused shall enjoy the right to a speedy and public trial, by an impartial jury of the State and district wherein the crime shall have been committed, which district shall have been previously ascertained by law, and to be informed of the nature and cause of the accusation; to be confronted with the witnesses against him; to have compulsory process for obtaining witnesses in his favor, and to have the assistance of counsel for his defense.

Amendment VII

In suits at common law, where the value in controversy shall exceed twenty dollars, the right of trial by jury shall be preserved, and no fact tried by a jury shall be otherwise reexamined in any court of the United States, than according to the rules of the common law.

Amendment VIII

Excessive bail shall not be required, nor excessive fines imposed, nor cruel and unusual punishments inflicted.

Amendment IX

The enumeration in the Constitution, of certain rights, shall not be construed to deny or disparage others retained by the people.

Amendment X

The powers not delegated to the United States by the Constitution, nor prohibited by it to the States, are reserved to the States respectively, or to the people.

Amendment XI

[Adopted 1798]
The judicial power of the United States shall not be construed to extend to any suit in law or equity, commenced or prosecuted against one of the United States by citizens of another State, or by citizens or subjects of any foreign state.

Amendment XII

[Adopted 1804]

The electors shall meet in their respective States, and vote by ballot for President and Vice-President, one of whom, at least, shall not be an inhabitant of the same State with themselves; they shall name in their ballots the person voted for as President, and in distinct ballots the person voted for as Vice-

*The first ten Amendments (the Bill of Rights) were adopted in 1791.

President, and they shall make distinct lists of all persons voted for as President, and of all persons voted for as Vice-President, and of the number of votes for each, which lists they shall sign and certify, and transmit sealed to the seat of government of the United States, directed to the President of the Senate;—the President of the Senate shall, in the presence of the Senate and House of Representatives, open all the certificates and the votes shall then be counted;—the person having the greatest number of votes for President shall be the President, if such number be a majority of the whole number of electors appointed; and if no person have such majority, then from the persons having the highest numbers not exceeding three on the list of those voted for as President, the House of Representatives shall choose immediately, by ballot, the President. But in choosing the President, the votes shall be taken by States, the representation from each State having one vote; a quorum for this purpose shall consist of a member or members from two-thirds of the States, and a majority of all the States shall be necessary to a choice. And if the House of Representatives shall not choose a President whenever the right of choice shall devolve upon them, before *the fourth day of March* next following, then the Vice-President shall act as President, as in the case of the death or other constitutional disability of the President.

The person having the greatest number of votes as Vice-President shall be the Vice-President, if such number be a majority of the whole number of electors appointed; and if no person have a majority, then from the two highest numbers on the list the Senate shall choose the Vice-President; a quorum for the purpose shall consist of two-thirds of the whole number of Senators, and a majority of the whole number shall be necessary to a choice. But no person constitutionally ineligible to the office of President shall be eligible to that of Vice-President of the United States.

Amendment XIII

[Adopted 1865]

Section 1 Neither slavery nor involuntary servitude, except as a punishment for crime whereof the party shall have been duly convicted, shall exist within the United States, or any place subject to their jurisdiction.

Section 2 Congress shall have power to enforce this article by appropriate legislation.

Amendment XIV

[Adopted 1868]

Section 1 All persons born or naturalized in the United States, and subject to the jurisdiction thereof, are citizens of the United States and of the State wherein they reside. No State shall make or enforce any law which shall abridge the privileges or immunities of citizens of the United States; nor shall any State deprive any person of life, liberty, or property, without due process of law; nor deny to any person within its jurisdiction the equal protection of the laws.

Section 2 Representatives shall be apportioned among the several States according to their respective numbers, counting the whole number of persons in each State, excluding Indians not taxed. But when the right to vote at any election for the choice of Electors for President and Vice-President of the United States, Representatives in Congress, the executive and judicial officers of a State, or the members of the legislature thereof, is denied to any of the male inhabitants of such State, being twenty-one years of age and citizens of the United States, or in any way abridged, except for participation in rebellion, or other crime, the basis of representation therein shall be reduced in the proportion which the number of such male citizens shall bear to the whole number of male citizens twenty-one years of age in such State.

Section 3 No person shall be a Senator or Representative in Congress, or Elector of President and Vice-President, or hold any office, civil or military, under the United States, or under any State, who, having previously taken an oath, as a member of Congress, or as an officer of the United States, or as a member of any State legislature, or as an executive or judicial officer of any State, to support the Constitution of the United States, shall have engaged in insurrection or rebellion against the same, or given aid or comfort to the enemies thereof. Congress may, by a vote of two-thirds of each house, remove such disability.

Section 4 The validity of the public debt of the United States, authorized by law, including debts incurred for payment of pensions and bounties for services in suppressing insurrection or rebellion, shall not be questioned. But neither the United States nor any State shall assume or pay any debt or obligation incurred in aid of insurrection or rebellion against the United States, or any claim for the loss of emancipation of any slave; but all such debts, obligations, and claims shall be held illegal and void.

Section 5 The Congress shall have power to enforce, by appropriate legislation, the provisions of this article.

Amendment XV

[Adopted 1870]

Section 1 The right of citizens of the United States to vote shall not be denied or abridged by the United States or by any State on account of race, color, or previous condition of servitude.

Section 2 The Congress shall have power to enforce this article by appropriate legislation.

Amendment XVI

[Adopted 1913]

The Congress shall have power to lay and collect taxes on incomes, from whatever source derived, without apportionment among the several States, and without regard to any census or enumeration.

Amendment XVII

[Adopted 1913]

Section 1   The Senate of the United States shall be composed of two Senators from each State, elected by the people thereof, for six years; and each Senator shall have one vote. The electors in each State shall have the qualifications requisite for electors of [voters for] the most numerous branch of the State legislatures.

Section 2   When vacancies happen in the representation of any State in the Senate, the executive authority of such State shall issue writs of election to fill such vacancies: Provided, that the Legislature of any State may empower the executive thereof to make temporary appointments until the people fill the vacancies by election as the Legislature may direct.

Section 3   This amendment shall not be so construed as to affect the election or term of any Senator chosen before it becomes valid as part of the Constitution.

Amendment XVIII

[Adopted 1919; Repealed 1933]

Section 1   After one year from the ratification of this article the manufacture, sale, or transportation of intoxicating liquors within, the importation thereof into, or the exportation thereof from the United States and all territory subject to the jurisdiction thereof, for beverage purposes, is hereby prohibited.

Section 2   The Congress and the several States shall have concurrent power to enforce this article by appropriate legislation.

Section 3   This article shall be inoperative unless it shall have been ratified as an amendment to the Constitution by the legislatures of the several States, as provided by the Constitution, within seven years from the date of the submission thereof to the States by the Congress.

Amendment XIX

[Adopted 1920]

Section 1   The right of citizens of the United States to vote shall not be denied or abridged by the United States or by any State on account of sex.

Section 2   The Congress shall have power to enforce this article by appropriate legislation.

Amendment XX

[Adopted 1933]

Section 1   The terms of the President and Vice-President shall end at noon on the 20th day of January, and the terms of Senators and Representatives at noon on the 3rd day of January, of the years in which such terms would have ended if this article had not been ratified; and the terms of their successors shall then begin.

Section 2   The Congress shall assemble at least once in every year, and such meeting shall begin at noon on the 3d day of January, unless they shall by law appoint a different day.

Section 3   If, at the time fixed for the beginning of the term of the President, the President-elect shall have died, the Vice-President–elect shall become President. If a President shall not have been chosen before the time fixed for the beginning of his term, or if the President-elect shall have failed to qualify, then the Vice-President–elect shall act as President until a President shall have qualified; and the Congress may by law provide for the case wherein neither a President-elect nor a Vice-President–elect shall have qualified, declaring who shall then act as President, or the manner in which one who is to act shall be selected, and such persons shall act accordingly until a President or Vice-President shall have qualified.

Section 4   The Congress may by law provide for the case of the death of any of the persons from whom the House of Representatives may choose a President whenever the right of choice shall have devolved upon them, and for the case of the death of any of the persons from whom the Senate may choose a Vice-President whenever the right of choice shall have devolved upon them.

Section 5   Sections 1 and 2 shall take effect on the 15th day of October following the ratification of this article.

Section 6   This article shall be inoperative unless it shall have been ratified as an amendment to the Constitution by the Legislatures of three-fourths of the several States within seven years from the date of its submission.

Amendment XXI

[Adopted 1933]

Section 1   The eighteenth article of amendment to the Constitution of the United States is hereby repealed.

Section 2   The transportation or importation into any State, Territory, or Possession of the United States for delivery or use therein of intoxicating liquors, in violation of the laws thereof, is hereby prohibited.

Section 3   This article shall be inoperative unless it shall have been ratified as an amendment to the Constitution by conventions in the several States, as provided in the Constitution, within seven years from the date of submission thereof to the States by the Congress.

Amendment XXII

[Adopted 1951]

Section 1   No person shall be elected to the office of President more than twice, and no person who has held the office of President, or acted as President, for more than two years of a term to which some other person was elected President shall be elected to the office of President more than once. But this article shall not apply to any person holding the office of President when this article was proposed by the Congress, and shall not prevent any person who may be holding the office of President, or acting as President, during the term within which this article becomes operative from holding the office of President or acting as President during the remainder of such term.

Section 2 This article shall be inoperative unless it shall have been ratified as an amendment to the Constitution by the legislatures of three-fourths of the several States within seven years from the date of its submission to the States by the Congress.

Amendment XXIII

[Adopted 1961]

Section 1 The District constituting the seat of Government of the United States shall appoint in such manner as the Congress may direct:

A number of electors of President and Vice-President equal to the whole number of Senators and Representatives in Congress to which the District would be entitled if it were a State, but in no event more than the least populous State; they shall be in addition to those appointed by the States, but they shall be considered for the purposes of the election of President and Vice-President, to be electors appointed by a State; and they shall meet in the District and perform such duties as provided by the twelfth article of amendment.

Section 2 The Congress shall have the power to enforce this article by appropriate legislation.

Amendment XXIV

[Adopted 1964]

Section 1 The right of citizens of the United States to vote in any primary or other election for President or Vice-President, for electors for President or Vice-President, or for Senator or Representative in Congress, shall not be denied or abridged by the United States or any State by reason of failure to pay any poll tax or other tax.

Section 2 The Congress shall have the power to enforce this article by appropriate legislation.

Amendment XXV

[Adopted 1967]

Section 1 In case of the removal of the President from office or of his death or resignation, the Vice-President shall become President.

Section 2 Whenever there is a vacancy in the office of the Vice-President, the President shall nominate a Vice-President who shall take office upon confirmation by a majority vote of both Houses of Congress.

Section 3 Whenever the President transmits to the President pro tempore of the Senate and the Speaker of the House of Representatives his written declaration that he is unable to discharge the powers and duties of his office, and until he transmits to them a written declaration to the contrary, such powers and duties shall be discharged by the Vice-President as Acting President.

Section 4 Whenever the Vice-President and a majority of either the principal officers of the executive departments or of such other body as Congress may by law provide, transmit to the President pro tempore of the Senate and the Speaker of the House of Representatives their written declaration that the President is unable to discharge the powers and duties of his office, the Vice-President shall immediately assume the powers and duties of the office as Acting President.

Thereafter, when the President transmits to the President pro tempore of the Senate and the Speaker of the House of Representatives his written declaration that no inability exists, he shall resume the powers and duties of his office unless the Vice-President and a majority of either the principal officers of the executive department[s] or of such other body as Congress may by law provide, transmit within four days to the President pro tempore of the Senate and the Speaker of the House of Representatives their written declaration that the President is unable to discharge the powers and duties of his office. Thereupon Congress shall decide the issue, assembling within forty-eight hours for that purpose if not in session. If the Congress, within twenty-one days after receipt of the latter written declaration, or, if Congress is not in session, within twenty-one days after Congress is required to assemble, determines by two-thirds vote of both Houses that the President is unable to discharge the powers and duties of his office, the Vice-President shall continue to discharge the same as Acting President; otherwise, the President shall resume the powers and duties of his office.

Amendment XXVI

[Adopted 1971]

Section 1 The right of citizens of the United States, who are eighteen years of age or older, to vote shall not be denied or abridged by the United States or by any State on account of age.

Section 2 The Congress shall have power to enforce this article by appropriate legislation.

Amendment XXVII

[Adopted 1992]

No law, varying the compensation for the services of the Senators and Representatives, shall take effect, until an election of Representatives shall have intervened.

The American People and Nation: A Statistical Profile

Population of the United States

Year	Number of States	Population	Percent Increase	Population Per Square Mile	Percent Urban/ Rural	Percent Male/ Female	Percent White/ Non- white	Persons Per House- hold	Median Age
1790	13	3,929,214		4.5	5.1/94.9	NA/NA	80.7/19.3	5.79	NA
1800	16	5,308,483	35.1	6.1	6.1/93.9	NA/NA	81.1/18.9	NA	NA
1810	17	7,239,881	36.4	4.3	7.3/92.7	NA/NA	81.0/19.0	NA	NA
1820	23	9,638,453	33.1	5.5	7.2/92.8	50.8/49.2	81.6/18.4	NA	16.7
1830	24	12,866,020	33.5	7.4	8.8/91.2	50.8/49.2	81.9/18.1	NA	17.2
1840	26	17,069,453	32.7	9.8	10.8/89.2	50.9/49.1	83.2/16.8	NA	17.8
1850	31	23,191,876	35.9	7.9	15.3/84.7	51.0/49.0	84.3/15.7	5.55	18.9
1860	33	31,443,321	35.6	10.6	19.8/80.2	51.2/48.8	85.6/14.4	5.28	19.4
1870	37	39,818,449	26.6	13.4	25.7/74.3	50.6/49.4	86.2/13.8	5.09	20.2
1880	38	50,155,783	26.0	16.9	28.2/71.8	50.9/49.1	86.5/13.5	5.04	20.9
1890	44	62,947,714	25.5	21.2	35.1/64.9	51.2/48.8	87.5/12.5	4.93	22.0
1900	45	75,994,575	20.7	25.6	39.6/60.4	51.1/48.9	87.9/12.1	4.76	22.9
1910	46	91,972,266	21.0	31.0	45.6/54.4	51.5/48.5	88.9/11.1	4.54	24.1
1920	48	105,710,620	14.9	35.6	51.2/48.8	51.0/49.0	89.7/10.3	4.34	25.3
1930	48	122,775,046	16.1	41.2	56.1/43.9	50.6/49.4	89.8/10.2	4.11	26.4
1940	48	131,669,275	7.2	44.2	56.5/43.5	50.2/49.8	89.8/10.2	3.67	29.0
1950	48	150,697,361	14.5	50.7	64.0/36.0	49.7/50.3	89.5/10.5	3.37	30.2
1960	50	179,323,175	18.5	50.6	69.9/30.1	49.3/50.7	88.6/11.4	3.33	29.5
1970	50	203,302,031	13.4	57.4	73.6/26.4	48.7/51.3	87.6/12.4	3.14	28.0
1980	50	226,542,199	11.4	64.1	73.7/26.3	48.6/51.4	85.9/14.1	2.75	30.0
1990	50	248,718,301	9.8	70.3	75.2/24.8	48.7/51.3	83.9/16.1	2.63	32.8
1998	50	270,299,000	8.0	76.4	NA	48.9/51.1	82.5/17.5	2.62	35.2

NA = Not available.

Vital Statistics

| Year | Birth Rate* | Death Rate* | Life Expectancy in Years | | | | | Marriage Rate | Divorce Rate |
			Total Population	White Females	Nonwhite Females	White Males	Nonwhite Males		
1790	NA	NA	NA	NA	NA	NA	NA	NA	NA
1800	55.0	NA	NA	NA	NA	NA	NA	NA	NA
1810	54.3	NA	NA	NA	NA	NA	NA	NA	NA
1820	55.2	NA	NA	NA	NA	NA	NA	NA	NA
1830	51.4	NA	NA	NA	NA	NA	NA	NA	NA
1840	51.8	NA	NA	NA	NA	NA	NA	NA	NA
1850	43.3	NA	NA	NA	NA	NA	NA	NA	NA
1860	44.3	NA	NA	NA	NA	NA	NA	NA	NA
1870	38.3	NA	NA	NA	NA	NA	NA	NA	NA
1880	39.8	NA	NA	NA	NA	NA	NA	NA	NA
1890	31.5	NA	NA	NA	NA	NA	NA	NA	NA
1900	32.3	17.2	47.3	48.7	33.5	46.6	32.5	NA	NA
1910	30.1	14.7	50.0	52.0	37.5	48.6	33.8	NA	NA
1920	27.7	13.0	54.1	55.6	45.2	54.4	45.5	12.0	1.6
1930	21.3	11.3	59.7	63.5	49.2	59.7	47.3	9.2	1.6
1940	19.4	10.8	62.9	66.6	54.9	62.1	51.5	12.1	2.0
1950	24.1	9.6	68.2	72.2	62.9	66.5	59.1	11.1	2.6
1960	23.7	9.5	69.7	74.1	66.3	67.4	61.1	8.5	2.2
1970	18.4	9.5	70.8	75.6	69.4	68.0	61.3	10.6	3.5
1980	15.9	8.8	73.7	78.1	73.6	70.7	65.3	10.6	5.2
1990	16.6	8.6	75.4	79.4	75.2	72.7	67.0	9.8	4.7
1998	14.4	8.5	76.5[†]	73.9[†]	76.1[°]	74.3[†]	68.9[°]	8.9[†]	4.3

Note: Data per one thousand for Birth, Death, Marriage, and Divorce Rates.

NA = Not available. *Data for 1800, 1810, 1830, 1850, 1870, and 1890 for whites only. [†]Data for 1997. [°]Data for 1996.

Immigrants to the United States

| Immigration Totals by Decade | | | |
Years	Number	Years	Number
1820–1830	151,824	1911–1920	5,735,811
1831–1840	599,125	1921–1930	4,107,209
1841–1850	1,713,251	1931–1940	528,431
1851–1860	2,598,214	1941–1950	1,035,039
1861–1870	2,314,824	1951–1960	2,515,479
1871–1880	2,812,191	1961–1970	3,321,677
1881–1890	5,246,613	1971–1980	4,493,314
1891–1900	3,687,546	1981–1990	7,338,062
1901–1910	8,795,386	1991–1997	6,944,591
		Total	63,938,605

Major Sources of Immigrants by Country or Region (in thousands)

Period	Asia[a]	Germany	Mexico	Italy	Great Britain (UK)[b]	Ireland	Canada	Austria and Hungary	Soviet Union (Russia)	Caribbean	Central America and South America	Norway and Sweden
1820–1830	—	8	5	—	27	54	2	—	—	4	—	—
1831–1840	—	152	7	2	76	207	14	—	—	12	—	1
1841–1850	—	435	3	2	267	781	42	—	—	14	4	14
1851–1860	42	952	3	9	424	914	59	—	—	11	2	21
1861–1870	65	787	2	12	607	436	154	8	3	9	1	109
1871–1880	124	718	5	56	548	437	384	73	39	14	1	211
1881–1890	70	1,453	2[c]	307	807	655	393	354	213	29	3	568
1891–1900	75	505	1[c]	652	272	388	3	593	505	33	2	321
1901–1910	324	341	50	2,046	526	339	179	2,145	1,597	108	25	440
1911–1920	247	144	219	1,110	341	146	742	896	921	123	59	161
1921–1930	112	412	459	455	340	211	925	64	62	75	58	166
1931–1940	17	114	22	68	32	11	109	11	1	16	14	9
1941–1950	37	227	61	58	139	20	172	28	—	50	43	21
1951–1960	153	478	300	185	203	48	378	104	—	123	136	45
1961–1970	428	191	454	214	214	33	413	26	2	470	359	33
1971–1980	1,588	74	640	129	137	11	170	16	39	741	430	10
1981–1990	2,738	92	2,336	67	160	32	157	25	58	872	930	15
1991–1997	2,134	66	1,801	56	118	54	143	20	357	750	786	13
Total	8,153	7,149	5,689	5,429	5,238	4,779	4,439	4,363	3,801	3,453	2,856	2,159

Notes: Numbers for periods are rounded. Dash indicates less than 1,000. [a]Includes Middle East. [b]Since 1925, includes England, Scotland, Wales, and Northern Ireland data. [c]No data available for 1886–1894.

The American Worker

Year	Total Number of Workers	Males as Percent of Total Workers	Females as Percent of Total Workers	Married Women as Percent of Female Workers	Female Workers as Percent of Female Population	Percent of Labor Force Unemployed	Percent of Workers in Labor Unions
1870	12,506,000	85	15	NA	NA	NA	
1880	17,392,000	85	15	NA	NA	NA	
1890	23,318,000	83	17	14	19	4 (1894 = 18)	
1900	29,073,000	82	18	15	21	5	
1910	38,167,000	79	21	25	25	6	
1920	41,614,000	79	21	23	24	5 (1921 = 12)	
1930	48,830,000	78	22	29	25	9 (1933 = 25)	
1940	53,011,000	76	24	36	27	15 (1944 = 1)	
1950	62,208,000	72	28	52	31	5.3	
1960	69,628,000	67	33	55	38	5.5	
1970	82,771,000	62	38	59	43	4.9	
1980	106,940,000	58	42	55	52	7.1	
1990	125,840,000	55	45	54	58	5.6	
1998	137,673,000	54	46	53	60	4.5	

NA = Not available.

The American Economy

Year	Gross National Product (GNP) and Gross Domestic Product (GDP)[a] (in $ billions)	Steel Production (in tons)	Corn Production (millions of bushels)	Automobiles Registered	New Housing Starts	Foreign Trade (in $ millions) Exports	Imports
1790	NA	NA	NA	NA	NA	20	23
1800	NA	NA	NA	NA	NA	71	91
1810	NA	NA	NA	NA	NA	67	85
1820	NA	NA	NA	NA	NA	70	74
1830	NA	NA	NA	NA	NA	74	71
1840	NA	NA	NA	NA	NA	132	107
1850	NA	NA	592[d]	NA	NA	152	178
1860	NA	13,000	839[e]	NA	NA	400	362
1870	7.4[b]	77,000	1,125	NA	NA	451	462
1880	11.2[c]	1,397,000	1,707	NA	NA	853	761
1890	13.1	4,779,000	1,650	NA	328,000	910	823
1900	18.7	11,227,000	2,662	8,000	189,000	1,499	930
1910	35.3	28,330,000	2,853	458,300	387,000 (1918 = 118,000)	1,919	1,646
1920	91.5	46,183,000	3,071	8,131,500	247,000 (1925 = 937,000)	8,664	5,784
1930	90.7	44,591,000	2,080	23,034,700	330,000 (1933 = 93,000)	4,013	3,500
1940	100.0	66,983,000	2,457	27,465,800	603,000 (1944 = 142,000)	4,030	7,433
1950	286.5	96,836,000	3,075	40,339,000	1,952,000	9,997	8,954
1960	506.5	99,282,000	4,314	61,682,300	1,365,000	19,659	15,093
1970	1,016.0	131,514,000	4,200	89,279,800	1,434,000	42,681	40,356
1980	2,819.5	111,835,000	6,600	121,601,000	1,292,000	220,626	244,871
1990	5,764.9	98,906,000	7,933	143,550,000	1,193,000	394,030	485,453
1998	8,511.0	107,600,000	9,761	129,749,000[f]	1,617,000	682,100	911,900

[a] In December 1991 the Bureau of Economic Analysis of the U.S. government began featuring Gross Domestic Product rather than Gross National Product as the primary measure of U.S. production.

[b] Figure is average for 1869–1878.

[c] Figure is average for 1879–1888.

[d] Figure for 1849.

[e] Figure for 1859.

[f] Figure for 1997.

NA = Not available.

Federal Budget Outlays and Debt

Year	Defense[a]	Veterans Benefits[a]	Income Security[a]	Social Security[a]	Health and Medicare[a]	Education[a,d]	Net Interest Payments[a]	Federal Debt (dollars)
1790	14.9	4.1[b]	NA	NA	NA	NA	55.0	75,463,000[c]
1800	55.7	.6	NA	NA	NA	NA	31.3	82,976,000
1810	48.4 (1814: 79.7)	1.0	NA	NA	NA	NA	34.9	53,173,000
1820	38.4	17.6	NA	NA	NA	NA	28.1	91,016,000
1830	52.9	9.0	NA	NA	NA	NA	12.6	48,565,000
1840	54.3 (1847: 80.7)	10.7	NA	NA	NA	NA	.7	3,573,000
1850	43.8	4.7	NA	NA	NA	NA	1.0	63,453,000
1860	44.2 (1865: 88.9)	1.7	NA	NA	NA	NA	5.0	64,844,000
1870	25.7	9.2	NA	NA	NA	NA	41.7	2,436,453,000
1880	19.3	21.2	NA	NA	NA	NA	35.8	2,090,909,000
1890	20.9 (1899: 48.6)	33.6	NA	NA	NA	NA	11.4	1,222,397,000
1900	36.6	27.0	NA	NA	NA	NA	7.7	1,263,417,000
1910	45.1 (1919: 59.5)	23.2	NA	NA	NA	NA	3.1	1,146,940,000
1920	37.1	3.4	NA	NA	NA	NA	16.0	24,299,321,000
1930	25.3	6.6	NA	NA	NA	NA	19.9	16,185,310,000
1940	17.5 (1945: 89.4)	6.0	16.0	.3	.5	20.8	9.4	42,967,531,000
1950	32.2	20.3	9.6	1.8	.6	.6	11.3	256,853,000,000
1960	52.2	5.9	8.0	12.6	.9	1.0	7.5	290,525,000,000
1970	41.8	4.4	8.0	15.5	6.2	4.4	7.3	308,921,000,000
1980	22.7	3.6	14.6	20.1	9.4	5.4	8.9	909,050,000,000
1990	23.9	2.3	11.7	19.8	12.4	3.1	14.7	3,266,073,000,000
1998	16.2	2.5	14.1	22.9	19.6	3.3	14.7	5,555,565,000,000

[a]Figures represent percentage of total federal spending for each category. Not included are transportation, commerce, housing, and various other categories.

[b]1789–1791 figure.

[c]1791 figure.

[d]Includes training, employment, and social services.

NA = Not available.

The Fifty States, District of Columbia, and Puerto Rico

State	Date of Admission (with Rank)	Capital City	Population (1998) (with Rank)	Racial/Ethnic Distribution (1998)	Per Capita Personal Income (1998) (with Rank)	Total Area in Square Miles (with Rank)
Alabama (AL)	Dec. 14, 1819 (22)	Montgomery	4,352,000 (23)	White: 3,141,000; Black: 1,132,000; Hispanic: 36,000; Asian: 28,000; Native American: 15,000	$21,442 (40)	52,423 (30)
Alaska (AK)	Jan. 3, 1959 (49)	Juneau	614,000 (48)	White: 444,000; Black: 24,000; Hispanic: 19,000; Asian: 28,000; Native American: 100,000	$25,675 (20)	656,424 (1)
Arizona (AZ)	Feb. 14, 1912 (48)	Phoenix	4,669,000 (21)	White: 3,182,000; Black: 169,000; Hispanic: 963,000; Asian: 98,000; Native American: 256,000	$23,060 (35)	114,006 (6)
Arkansas (AR)	June 15, 1836 (25)	Little Rock	2,538,000 (33)	White: 2,055,000; Black: 408,000; Hispanic: 44,000; Asian: 19,000; Native American: 14,000	$20,346 (46)	53,182 (29)
California (CA)	Sept. 9, 1850 (31)	Sacramento	32,667,000 (1)	White: 16,511,000; Black: 2,456,000; Hispanic: 9,454,000; Asian: 3,938,000; Native American: 309,000	$27,503 (1)	163,707 (3)
Colorado (CO)	Aug. 1, 1876 (38)	Denver	3,971,000 (24)	White: 3,125,000; Black: 172,000; Hispanic: 541,000; Asian: 96,000; Native American: 37,000	$28,657 (18)	104,100 (8)
Connecticut (CT)	Jan. 9, 1788 (5)	Hartford	3,274,000 (29)	White: 3,125,000; Black: 172,000; Hispanic: 238,000; Asian: 96,000; Native American: 37,000	$37,598 (1)	5,544 (48)
Delaware (DE)	Dec. 7, 1787 (1)	Dover	744,000 (45)	White: 560,000; Black: 144,000; Hispanic: 22,000; Asian: 15,000; Native American: 2,000	$29,814 (6)	2,489 (49)
District of Columbia (DC)	U.S. Capital, Dec. 1, 1800	Washington (coextensive with DC)	523,000 (not ranked)	White: 149,000; Black: 326,000; Hispanic: 30,000; Asian: 16,000; Native American: 2,000	$33,433 (not ranked)	68 (not ranked)
Florida (FL)	Mar. 3, 1845 (27)	Tallahassee	14,916,000 (4)	White: 10,239,000; Black: 2,268,000; Hispanic: 2,080,000; Asian: 271,000; Native American: 58,000	$25,852 (19)	65,756 (22)
Georgia (GA)	Jan. 2, 1788 (4)	Atlanta	7,642,000 (10)	White: 5,100,000; Black: 2,181,000; Hispanic: 193,000; Asian: 149,000; Native American: 18,000	$25,020 (23)	59,441 (24)
Hawai'i (HI)	Aug. 21, 1959 (50)	Honolulu	1,193,000 (40)	White: 344,000; Black: 35,000; Hispanic: 51,000; Asian: 757,000; Native American: 7,000	$26,137 (17)	10,932 (43)
Idaho (ID)	July 3, 1890 (43)	Boise	1,229,000 (41)	White: 1,109,000; Black: 7,000; Hispanic: 82,000; Asian: 14,000; Native American: 17,000	$21,081 (43)	83,574 (14)
Illinois (IL)	Dec. 3, 1818 (21)	Springfield	12,045,000 (5)	White: 8,630,000; Black: 1,840,000; Hispanic: 1,145,000; Asian: 403,000; Native American: 27,000	$28,873 (8)	57,918 (25)
Indiana (IN)	Dec. 11, 1816 (19)	Indianapolis	5,899,000 (14)	White: 5,206,000; Black: 491,000; Hispanic: 132,000; Asian: 56,000; Native American: 15,000	$24,219 (29)	36,420 (38)

The Fifty States, District of Columbia, and Puerto Rico (continued)

State	Date of Admission (with Rank)	Capital City	Population (1998) (with Rank)	Racial/Ethnic Distribution (1998)	Per Capita Personal Income (1998) (with Rank)	Total Area in Square Miles (with Rank)
Iowa (IA)	Dec. 28, 1846 (29)	Des Moines	2,862,000 (30)	White: 2,709,000; Black: 57,000; Hispanic: 52,000; Asian: 36,000; Native American: 8,000	$23,925 (32)	56,276 (26)
Kansas (KS)	Jan. 29, 1861 (34)	Topeka	2,629,000 (32)	White: 2,278,000; Black: 155,000; Hispanic: 137,000; Asian: 46,000; Native American: 23,000	$24,981 (24)	82,282 (15)
Kentucky (KY)	June 1, 1792 (15)	Frankfort	3,936,000 (25)	White: 3,591,000; Black: 285,000; Hispanic: 28,000; Asian: 27,000; Native American: 6,000	$21,506 (39)	40,411 (37)
Louisiana (LA)	Apr. 30, 1812 (18)	Baton Rouge	4,369,000 (22)	White: 2,787,000; Black: 1,407,000; Hispanic: 100,000; Asian: 55,000; Native American: 19,000	$21,346 (41)	51,843 (31)
Maine (ME)	Mar. 15, 1820 (23)	Augusta	1,244,000 (39)	White: 1,215,000; Black: 6,000; Hispanic: 8,000; Asian: 9,000; Native American: 6,000	$22,952 (36)	35,387 (39)
Maryland (MD)	Apr. 28, 1788 (7)	Annapolis	5,135,000 (19)	White: 3,329,000; Black: 1,428,000; Hispanic: 158,000; Asian: 204,000; Native American: 16,000	$29,943 (5)	12,407 (42)
Massachusetts (MA)	Feb. 6, 1788 (6)	Boston	6,147,000 (13)	White: 5,217,000; Black: 395,000; Hispanic: 298,000; Asian: 223,000; Native American: 15,000	$32,797 (3)	10,555 (44)
Michigan (MI)	Jan. 26, 1837 (26)	Lansing	9,817,000 (8)	White: 7,961,000; Black: 1,405,000; Hispanic: 234,000; Asian: 158,000; Native American: 60,000	$25,857 (18)	96,705 (11)
Minnesota (MN)	May 11, 1858 (32)	Saint Paul	4,725,000 (20)	White: 4,328,000; Black: 141,000; Hispanic: 76,000; Asian: 124,000; Native American: 58,000	$27,510 (11)	86,943 (12)
Mississippi (MS)	Dec. 10, 1817 (20)	Jackson	2,752,000 (31)	White: 1,701,000; Black: 1,003,000; Hispanic: 18,000; Asian: 19,000; Native American: 10,000	$18,958 (50)	48,434 (32)
Missouri (MO)	Aug. 10, 1821 (24)	Jefferson City	5,439,000 (16)	White: 4,668,000; Black: 613,000; Hispanic: 77,000; Asian: 60,000; Native American: 21,000	$24,427 (28)	69,709 (21)
Montana (MT)	Nov. 8, 1889 (41)	Helena	880,000 (44)	White: 803,000; Black: 3,000; Hispanic: 13,000; Asian: 5,000; Native American: 56,000	$20,172 (47)	147,046 (4)
Nebraska (NE)	Mar. 1, 1867 (37)	Lincoln	1,663,000 (38)	White: 1,493,000; Black: 67,000; Hispanic: 66,000; Asian: 22,000; Native American: 15,000	$24,754 (27)	77,358 (16)
Nevada (NV)	Oct. 3, 1864 (36)	Carson City	1,747,000 (36)	White: 1,248,000; Black: 133,000; Hispanic: 253,000; Asian: 81,000; Native American: 31,000	$27,200 (14)	110,567 (7)
New Hampshire (NH)	June 21, 1788 (9)	Concord	1,185,000 (42)	White: 1,109,000; Black: 9,000; Hispanic: 16,000; Asian: 14,000; Native American: 2,000	$29,022 (7)	9,351 (46)
New Jersey (NJ)	Dec. 18, 1787 (3)	Trenton	8,115,000 (9)	White: 5,586,000; Black: 1,188,000; Hispanic: 866,000; Asian: 453,000; Native American: 22,000	$33,937 (2)	8,722 (47)
New Mexico (NM)	Jan. 6, 1912 (47)	Santa Fe	1,737,000 (37)	White: 834,000; Black: 45,000; Hispanic: 669,000; Asian: 26,000; Native American: 163,000	$19,936 (48)	121,598 (5)

The Fifty States, District of Columbia, and Puerto Rico (continued)

State	Date of Admission (with Rank)	Capital City	Population (1998) (with Rank)	Racial/Ethnic Distribution (1998)	Per Capita Personal Income (1998) (with Rank)	Total Area in Square Miles (with Rank)
New York (NY)	July 26, 1788 (11)	Albany	18,175,000 (3)	White: 11,895,000; Black: 3,220,000; Hispanic: 1,990,000; Asian: 995,000; Native American: 76,000	$31,734 (4)	54,471 (27)
North Carolina (NC)	Nov. 21, 1789 (12)	Raleigh	7,546,000 (11)	White: 5,545,000; Black: 1,665,000 Hispanic: 139,000; Asian: 100,000; Native American: 98,000	$24,036 (31)	53,821 (28)
North Dakota (ND)	Nov. 2, 1889 (39)	Bismarck	638,000 (47)	White: 593,000; Black: 4,000; Hispanic: 6,000; Asian: 5,000; Native American: 30,000	$21,675 (38)	70,704 (19)
Ohio (OH)	Mar. 1, 1803 (17)	Columbus	11,209,000 (7)	White: 9,610,000; Black: 1,290,000; Hispanic: 158,000; Asian: 129,000; Native American: 23,000	$25,134 (21)	44,828 (34)
Oklahoma (OK)	Nov. 16, 1907 (46)	Oklahoma City	3,347,000 (27)	White: 2,668,000; Black: 262,000; Hispanic: 109,000; Asian: 45,000; Native American: 263,000	$21,072 (44)	69,903 (20)
Oregon (OR)	Feb. 14, 1859 (33)	Salem	3,282,000 (28)	White: 2,888,000; Black: 61,000; Hispanic: 182,000; Asian: 106,000; Native American: 45,000	$24,766 (26)	98,386 (9)
Pennsylvania (PA)	Dec. 12, 1787 (2)	Harrisburg	12,001,000 (6)	White: 10,354,000; Black: 1,166,000; Hispanic: 265,000; Asian: 198,000; Native American: 18,000	$26,792 (16)	46,058 (33)
Puerto Rico (PR)	Ascession 1898; Commonwealth Status 1952	San Juan	3,860,000 (not ranked)	White: <1,000; Black: <1,000; Hispanic: 3,856,000; Asian: <1,000	$7,882* (not ranked)	3,427*
Rhode Island (RI)	May 29, 1790 (13)	Providence	988,000 (43)	White: 859,000; Black: 49,000; Hispanic: 52,000; Asian: 23,000; Native American: 5,000	$26,797 (15)	1,545 (50)
South Carolina (SC)	May 23, 1788 (8)	Columbia	3,836,000 (26)	White: 2,603,000; Black: 1,147,000; Hispanic: 42,000; Asian: 34,000; Native American: 9,000	$21,309 (42)	32,008 (40)
South Dakota (SD)	Nov. 2, 1889 (40)	Pierre	738,000 (46)	White: 662,000; Black: 5,000; Hispanic: 7,000; Asian: 5,000; Native American: 59,000	$22,114 (37)	77,121 (17)
Tennessee (TN)	June 1, 1796 (16)	Nashville	5,431,000 (17)	White: 4,413,000; Black: 900,000; Hispanic: 54,000; Asian: 53,000; Native American: 12,000	$23,559 (33)	42,149 (36)
Texas (TX)	Dec. 29, 1845 (28)	Austin	18,760,000 (2)	White: 11,038,000; Black: 2,430,000; Hispanic: 5,640,000; Asian: 556,000; Native American: 96,000	$24,957 (25)	268,601 (2)
Utah (UT)	Jan. 4, 1896 (45)	Salt Lake City	2,100,000 (32)	White: 1,866,000; Black: 19,000; Hispanic: 132,000; Asian: 53,000; Native American: 30,000	$21,019 (45)	84,904 (13)
Vermont (VT)	Mar. 4, 1791 (14)	Montpelier	591,000 (49)	White: 577,000; Black: 3,000; Hispanic: 5,000; Asian: 5,000; Native American: 2,000	$24,175 (30)	9,615 (45)
Virginia (VA)	June 25, 1788 (10)	Richmond	6,791,000 (12)	White: 4,943,000; Black: 1,363,000 Hispanic: 220,000; Asian: 247,000; Native American: 19,000	$27,385 (13)	42,777 (35)

The Fifty States, District of Columbia, and Puerto Rico (continued)

State	Date of Admission (with Rank)	Capital City	Population (1998) (with Rank)	Racial/Ethnic Distribution (1998)	Per Capita Personal Income (1998) (with Rank)	Total Area in Square Miles (with Rank)
Washington (WA)	Nov. 11, 1889 (42)	Olympia	5,689,000 (15)	White: 4,743,000; Black: 198,000; Hispanic: 315,000; Asian: 330,000; Native American: 103,000	$27,961 (11)	71,302 (18)
West Virginia (WV)	June 20, 1863 (35)	Charleston	1,811,000 (35)	White: 1,732,000; Black: 58,000; Hispanic: 9,000; Asian: 9,000; Native American: 3,000	$19,362 (49)	24,231 (41)
Wisconsin (WI)	May 29, 1848 (30)	Madison	5,224,000 (18)	White: 4,687,000; Black: 291,000; Hispanic: 120,000; Asian: 80,000; Native American: 56,000	$25,079 (22)	65,499 (23)
Wyoming (WY)	July 10, 1890 (44)	Cheyenne	481,000 (50)	White: 435,000; Black: 4,000; Hispanic: 27,000; Asian: 4,000; Native American: 11,000	$23,167 (34)	97,818 (10)

*1996 figure.

Presidential Elections

Year	Number of States	Candidates	Parties	Popular Vote	% of Popular Vote	Electoral Vote	% Voter Participation[a]
1789	10	**George Washington**	No party			69	
		John Adams	designations			34	
		Other candidates				35	
1792	15	**George Washington**	No party			132	
		John Adams	designations			77	
		George Clinton				50	
		Other candidates				5	
1796	16	**John Adams**	Federalist			71	
		Thomas Jefferson	Democratic-Republican			68	
		Thomas Pinckney	Federalist			59	
		Aaron Burr	Democratic-Republican			30	
		Other candidates				48	
1800	16	**Thomas Jefferson**	Democratic-Republican			73	
		Aaron Burr	Democratic-Republican			73	
		John Adams	Federalist			65	
		Charles C. Pinckney	Federalist			64	
		John Jay	Federalist			1	
1804	17	**Thomas Jefferson**	Democratic-Republican			162	
		Charles C. Pinckney	Federalist			14	
1808	17	**James Madison**	Democratic-Republican			122	
		Charles C. Pinckney	Federalist			47	
		George Clinton	Democratic-Republican			6	
1812	18	**James Madison**	Democratic-Republican			128	
		DeWitt Clinton	Federalist			89	
1816	19	**James Monroe**	Democratic-Republican			183	
		Rufus King	Federalist			34	
1820	24	**James Monroe**	Democratic-Republican			231	
		John Quincy Adams	Independent Republican			1	

Presidential Elections (continued)

Year	Number of States	Candidates	Parties	Popular Vote	% of Popular Vote	Electoral Vote	% Voter Participation[b]
1824	24	**John Quincy Adams**	Democratic-Republican	108,740	30.5	84	26.9
		Andrew Jackson	Democratic-Republican	153,544	43.1	99	
		Henry Clay	Democratic-Republican	47,136	13.2	37	
		William H. Crawford	Democratic-Republican	46,618	13.1	41	
1828	24	**Andrew Jackson**	Democratic	647,286	56.0	178	57.6
		John Quincy Adams	National Republican	508,064	44.0	83	
1832	24	**Andrew Jackson**	Democratic	701,780	54.2	219	55.4
		Henry Clay	National Republican	484,205	37.4	49	
		Other candidates		107,988	8.0	18	
1836	26	**Martin Van Buren**	Democratic	764,176	50.8	170	57.8
		William H. Harrison	Whig	550,816	36.6	73	
		Hugh L. White	Whig	146,107	9.7	26	
1840	26	**William H. Harrison**	Whig	1,274,624	53.1	234	80.2
		Martin Van Buren	Democratic	1,127,781	46.9	60	
1844	26	**James K. Polk**	Democratic	1,338,464	49.6	170	78.9
		Henry Clay	Whig	1,300,097	48.1	105	
		James G. Birney	Liberty	62,300	2.3		
1848	30	**Zachary Taylor**	Whig	1,360,967	47.4	163	72.7
		Lewis Cass	Democratic	1,222,342	42.5	127	
		Martin Van Buren	Free Soil	291,263	10.1		
1852	31	**Franklin Pierce**	Democratic	1,601,117	50.9	254	69.6
		Winfield Scott	Whig	1,385,453	44.1	42	
		John P. Hale	Free Soil	155,825	5.0		
1856	31	**James Buchanan**	Democratic	1,832,955	45.3	174	78.9
		John C. Frémont	Republican	1,339,932	33.1	114	
		Millard Fillmore	American	871,731	21.6	8	
1860	33	**Abraham Lincoln**	Republican	1,865,593	39.8	180	81.2
		Stephen A. Douglas	Democratic	1,382,713	29.5	12	
		John C. Breckinridge	Democratic	848,356	18.1	72	
		John Bell	Constitutional Union	592,906	12.6	39	
1864	36	**Abraham Lincoln**	Republican	2,206,938	55.0	212	73.8
		George B. McClellan	Democratic	1,803,787	45.0	21	
1868	37	**Ulysses S. Grant**	Republican	3,013,421	52.7	214	78.1
		Horatio Seymour	Democratic	2,706,829	47.3	80	

Presidential Elections (continued)

Year	Number of States	Candidates	Parties	Popular Vote	% of Popular Vote	Electoral Vote	% Voter Participation[b]
1872	37	**Ulysses S. Grant**	Republican	3,596,745	55.6	286	71.3
		Horace Greeley	Democratic	2,843,446	43.9	[b]	
1876	38	**Rutherford B. Hayes**	Republican	4,036,572	48.0	185	81.8
		Samuel J. Tilden	Democratic	4,284,020	51.0	184	
1880	38	**James A. Garfield**	Republican	4,453,295	48.5	214	79.4
		Winfield S. Hancock	Democratic	4,414,082	48.1	155	
		James B. Weaver	Greenback-Labor	308,578	3.4		
1884	38	**Grover Cleveland**	Democratic	4,879,507	48.5	219	77.5
		James G. Blaine	Republican	4,850,293	48.2	182	
		Benjamin F. Butler	Greenback-Labor	175,370	1.8		
		John P. St. John	Prohibition	150,369	1.5		
1888	38	**Benjamin Harrison**	Republican	5,447,129	47.9	233	79.3
		Grover Cleveland	Democratic	5,537,857	48.6	168	
		Clinton B. Fisk	Prohibition	249,506	2.2		
		Anson J. Streeter	Union Labor	146,935	1.3		
1892	44	**Grover Cleveland**	Democratic	5,555,426	46.1	277	74.7
		Benjamin Harrison	Republican	5,182,690	43.0	145	
		James B. Weaver	People's	1,029,846	8.5	22	
		John Bidwell	Prohibition	264,133	2.2		
1896	45	**William McKinley**	Republican	7,102,246	51.1	271	79.3
		William J. Bryan	Democratic	6,492,559	47.7	176	
1900	45	**William McKinley**	Republican	7,218,491	51.7	292	73.2
		William J. Bryan	Democratic; Populist	6,356,734	45.5	155	
		John C. Wooley	Prohibition	208,914	1.5		
1904	45	**Theodore Roosevelt**	Republican	7,628,461	57.4	336	65.2
		Alton B. Parker	Democratic	5,084,223	37.6	140	
		Eugene V. Debs	Socialist	402,283	3.0		
		Silas C. Swallow	Prohibition	258,536	1.9		
1908	46	**William H. Taft**	Republican	7,675,320	51.6	321	65.4
		William J. Bryan	Democratic	6,412,294	43.1	162	
		Eugene V. Debs	Socialist	420,793	2.8		
		Eugene W. Chafin	Prohibition	253,840	1.7		
1912	48	**Woodrow Wilson**	Democratic	6,296,547	41.9	435	58.8
		Theodore Roosevelt	Progressive	4,118,571	27.4	88	
		William H. Taft	Republican	3,486,720	23.2	8	
		Eugene V. Debs	Socialist	900,672	6.0		
		Eugene W. Chafin	Prohibition	206,275	1.4		
1916	48	**Woodrow Wilson**	Democratic	9,127,695	49.4	277	61.6
		Charles E. Hughes	Republican	8,533,507	46.2	254	

Presidential Elections (continued)

Year	Number of States	Candidates	Parties	Popular Vote	% of Popular Vote	Elec- toral Vote	% Voter Partici- pation[b]
		A. L. Benson	Socialist	585,113	3.2		
		J. Frank Hanly	Prohibition	220,506	1.2		
1920	48	**Warren G. Harding**	Republican	16,143,407	60.4	404	49.2
		James M. Cox	Democratic	9,130,328	34.2	127	
		Eugene V. Debs	Socialist	919,799	3.4		
		P. P. Christensen	Farmer-Labor	265,411	1.0		
1924	48	**Calvin Coolidge**	Republican	15,718,211	54.0	382	48.9
		John W. Davis	Democratic	8,385,283	28.8	136	
		Robert M. La Follette	Progressive	4,831,289	16.6	13	
1928	48	**Herbert C. Hoover**	Republican	21,391,993	58.2	444	56.9
		Alfred E. Smith	Democratic	15,016,169	40.9	87	
1932	48	**Franklin D. Roosevelt**	Democratic	22,809,638	57.4	472	56.9
		Herbert C. Hoover	Republican	15,758,901	39.7	59	
		Norman Thomas	Socialist	881,951	2.2		
1936	48	**Franklin D. Roosevelt**	Democratic	27,752,869	60.8	523	61.0
		Alfred M. Landon	Republican	16,674,665	36.5	8	
		William Lemke	Union	882,479	1.9		
1940	48	**Franklin D. Roosevelt**	Democratic	27,307,819	54.8	449	62.5
		Wendell L. Wilkie	Republican	22,321,018	44.8	82	
1944	48	**Franklin D. Roosevelt**	Democratic	25,606,585	53.5	432	55.9
		Thomas E. Dewey	Republican	22,014,745	46.0	99	
1948	48	**Harry S Truman**	Democratic	24,179,345	49.6	303	53.0
		Thomas E. Dewey	Republican	21,991,291	45.1	189	
		J. Strom Thurmond	States' Rights	1,176,125	2.4	39	
		Henry A. Wallace	Progressive	1,157,326	2.4		
1952	48	**Dwight D. Eisenhower**	Republican	33,936,234	55.1	442	63.3
		Adlai E. Stevenson	Democratic	27,314,992	44.4	89	
1956	48	**Dwight D. Eisenhower**	Republican	35,590,472	57.6	457	60.6
		Adlai E. Stevenson	Democratic	26,022,752	42.1	73	
1960	50	**John F. Kennedy**	Democratic	34,226,731	49.7	303	62.8
		Richard M. Nixon	Republican	34,108,157	49.5	219	
1964	50	**Lyndon B. Johnson**	Democratic	43,129,566	61.1	486	61.7
		Barry M. Goldwater	Republican	27,178,188	38.5	52	
1968	50	**Richard M. Nixon**	Republican	31,785,480	43.4	301	60.6
		Hubert H. Humphrey	Democratic	31,275,166	42.7	191	
		George C. Wallace	American Independent	9,906,473	13.5	46	
1972	50	**Richard M. Nixon**	Republican	47,169,911	60.7	520	55.2

Presidential Elections (continued)

Year	Number of States	Candidates	Parties	Popular Vote	% of Popular Vote	Electoral Vote	% Voter Participation[b]
		George S. McGovern	Democratic	29,170,383	37.5	17	
		John G. Schmitz	American	1,099,482	1.4		
1976	50	**James E. Carter**	Democratic	40,830,763	50.1	297	53.5
		Gerald R. Ford	Republican	39,147,793	48.0	240	
1980	50	**Ronald W. Reagan**	Republican	43,904,153	50.7	489	52.6
		James E. Carter	Democratic	35,483,883	41.0	49	
		John B. Anderson	Independent	5,720,060	6.6	0	
		Ed Clark	Libertarian	921,299	1.1	0	
1984	50	**Ronald W. Reagan**	Republican	54,455,075	58.8	525	53.3
		Walter F. Mondale	Democratic	37,577,185	40.6	13	
1988	50	**George H. W. Bush**	Republican	48,886,097	53.4	426	50.1
		Michael S. Dukakis	Democratic	41,809,074	45.6	111[c]	
1992	50	**William J. Clinton**	Democratic	44,909,326	43.0	370	55.2
		George H. W. Bush	Republican	39,103,882	37.4	168	
		H. Ross Perot	Independent	19,741,048	18.9	0	
1996	50	**William J. Clinton**	Democratic	47,402,357	49.2	379	49.1
		Robert J. Dole	Republican	39,196,755	40.7	159	
		H. Ross Perot	Reform	8,085,402	8.4	0	
		Ralph Nader	Green	684,902	0.7	0	

Candidates receiving less than 1 percent of the popular vote have been omitted. Thus the percentage of popular vote given for any election year may not total 100 percent.

Before the passage of the Twelfth Amendment in 1804, the Electoral College voted for two presidential candidates; the runner-up became vice president.

Before 1824, most presidential electors were chosen by state legislatures, not by popular vote.

[a]Percent of voting-age population casting ballots.

[b]Greeley died shortly after the election; the electors supporting him then divided their votes among minor candidates.

[c]One elector from West Virginia cast her Electoral College presidential ballot for Lloyd Bentsen, the Democratic Party's vice-presidential candidate.

Presidents and Vice Presidents

1. President	**George Washington**	1789–1797
Vice President	John Adams	1789–1797
2. President	**John Adams**	1797–1801
Vice President	Thomas Jefferson	1797–1801
3. President	**Thomas Jefferson**	1801–1809
Vice President	Aaron Burr	1801–1805
Vice President	George Clinton	1805–1809
4. President	**James Madison**	1809–1817
Vice President	George Clinton	1809–1813
Vice President	Elbridge Gerry	1813–1817
5. President	**James Monroe**	1817–1825
Vice President	Daniel Tompkins	1817–1825
6. President	**John Quincy Adams**	1825–1829
Vice President	John C. Calhoun	1825–1829
7. President	**Andrew Jackson**	1829–1837
Vice President	John C. Calhoun	1829–1833
Vice President	Martin Van Buren	1833–1837
8. President	**Martin Van Buren**	1837–1841
Vice President	Richard M. Johnson	1837–1841
9. President	**William H. Harrison**	1841
Vice President	John Tyler	1841
10. President	**John Tyler**	1841–1845
Vice President	None	
11. President	**James K. Polk**	1845–1849
Vice President	George M. Dallas	1845–1849
12. President	**Zachary Taylor**	1849–1850
Vice President	Millard Fillmore	1849–1850
13. President	**Millard Fillmore**	1850–1853
Vice President	None	
14. President	**Franklin Pierce**	1853–1857
Vice President	William R. King	1853–1857
15. President	**James Buchanan**	1857–1861
Vice President	John C. Breckinridge	1857–1861
16. President	**Abraham Lincoln**	1861–1865
Vice President	Hannibal Hamlin	1861–1865
Vice President	Andrew Johnson	1865
17. President	**Andrew Johnson**	1865–1869
Vice President	None	
18. President	**Ulysses S. Grant**	1869–1877
Vice President	Schuyler Colfax	1869–1873
Vice President	Henry Wilson	1873–1877
19. President	**Rutherford B. Hayes**	1877–1881
Vice President	William A. Wheeler	1877–1881
20. President	**James A. Garfield**	1881
Vice President	Chester A. Arthur	1881
21. President	**Chester A. Arthur**	1881–1885
Vice President	None	
22. President	**Grover Cleveland**	1885–1889
Vice President	Thomas A. Hendricks	1885–1889
23. President	**Benjamin Harrison**	1889–1893
Vice President	Levi P. Morton	1889–1893
24. President	**Grover Cleveland**	1893–1897
Vice President	Adlai E. Stevenson	1893–1897
25. President	**William McKinley**	1897–1901
Vice President	Garret A. Hobart	1897–1901
Vice President	Theodore Roosevelt	1901
26. President	**Theodore Roosevelt**	1901–1909
Vice President	Charles Fairbanks	1905–1909
27. President	**William H. Taft**	1909–1913
Vice President	James S. Sherman	1909–1913
28. President	**Woodrow Wilson**	1913–1921
Vice President	Thomas R. Marshall	1913–1921
29. President	**Warren G. Harding**	1921–1923
Vice President	Calvin Coolidge	1921–1923
30. President	**Calvin Coolidge**	1923–1929
Vice President	Charles G. Dawes	1925–1929
31. President	**Herbert C. Hoover**	1929–1933
Vice President	Charles Curtis	1929–1933
32. President	**Franklin D. Roosevelt**	1933–1945
Vice President	John N. Garner	1933–1941
Vice President	Henry A. Wallace	1941–1945
Vice President	Harry S Truman	1945
33. President	**Harry S Truman**	1945–1953
Vice President	Alben W. Barkley	1949–1953
34. President	**Dwight D. Eisenhower**	1953–1961
Vice President	Richard M. Nixon	1953–1961
35. President	**John F. Kennedy**	1961–1963
Vice President	Lyndon B. Johnson	1961–1963

Presidents and Vice Presidents (continued)

36. President	**Lyndon B. Johnson**	1963–1969		Vice President	Walter F. Mondale	1977–1981
	Vice President	Hubert H. Humphrey	1965–1969	40. President	**Ronald W. Reagan**	1981–1989
37. President	**Richard M. Nixon**	1969–1974		Vice President	George H. W. Bush	1981–1989
	Vice President	Spiro T. Agnew	1969–1973	41. President	**George H. W. Bush**	1989–1993
	Vice President	Gerald R. Ford	1973–1974		Vice President	J. Danforth Quayle	1989–1993
38. President	**Gerald R. Ford**	1974–1977	42. President	**William J. Clinton**	1993–2001
	Vice President	Nelson A. Rockefeller	1974–1977		Vice President	Albert Gore	1993–2001
39. President	**James E. Carter**	1977–1981				

For a complete list of Presidents, Vice Presidents, and Cabinet Members, go to http://college.hmco.com.

Party Strength in Congress

Period	Congress	House Majority Party		House Minority Party		House Others	Senate Majority Party		Senate Minority Party		Senate Others	Party of President	
1789–91	1st	Ad	38	Op	26		Ad	17	Op	9		F	Washington
1791–93	2nd	F	37	DR	33		F	16	DR	13		F	Washington
1793–95	3rd	DR	57	F	48		F	17	DR	13		F	Washington
1795–97	4th	F	54	DR	52		F	19	DR	13		F	Washington
1797–99	5th	F	58	DR	48		F	20	DR	12		F	J. Adams
1799–1801	6th	F	64	DR	42		F	19	DR	13		F	J. Adams
1801–03	7th	DR	69	F	36		DR	18	F	13		DR	Jefferson
1803–05	8th	DR	102	F	39		DR	25	F	9		DR	Jefferson
1805–07	9th	DR	116	F	25		DR	27	F	7		DR	Jefferson
1807–09	10th	DR	118	F	24		DR	28	F	6		DR	Jefferson
1809–11	11th	DR	94	F	48		DR	28	F	6		DR	Madison
1811–13	12th	DR	108	F	36		DR	30	F	6		DR	Madison
1813–15	13th	DR	112	F	68		DR	27	F	9		DR	Madison
1815–17	14th	DR	117	F	65		DR	25	F	11		DR	Madison
1817–19	15th	DR	141	F	42		DR	34	F	10		DR	Monroe
1819–21	16th	DR	156	F	27		DR	35	F	7		DR	Monroe
1821–23	17th	DR	158	F	25		DR	44	F	4		DR	Monroe
1823–25	18th	DR	187	F	26		DR	44	F	4		DR	Monroe
1825–27	19th	Ad	105	J	97		Ad	26	J	20		C	J. Q. Adams
1827–29	20th	J	119	Ad	94		J	28	Ad	20		C	J. Q. Adams
1829–31	21st	D	139	NR	74		D	26	NR	22		D	Jackson
1831–33	22nd	D	141	NR	58	14	D	25	NR	21	2	D	Jackson
1833–35	23rd	D	147	AM	53	60	D	20	NR	20	8	D	Jackson
1835–37	24th	D	145	W	98		D	27	W	25		D	Jackson
1837–39	25th	D	108	W	107	24	D	30	W	18	4	D	Van Buren
1839–41	26th	D	124	W	118		D	28	W	22		D	Van Buren
1841–43	27th	W	133	D	102	6	W	28	D	22	2	W	W. Harrison
												W	Tyler
1843–45	28th	D	142	W	79	1	W	28	D	25	1	W	Tyler
1845–47	29th	D	143	W	77	6	D	31	W	25		D	Polk
1847–49	30th	W	115	D	108	4	D	36	W	21	1	D	Polk
1849–51	31st	D	112	W	109	9	D	35	W	25	2	W	Taylor
												W	Fillmore
1851–53	32nd	D	140	W	88	5	D	35	W	24	3	W	Fillmore
1853–55	33rd	D	159	W	71	4	D	38	W	22	2	D	Pierce
1855–57	34th	R	108	D	83	43	D	40	R	15	5	D	Pierce
1857–59	35th	D	118	R	92	26	D	36	R	20	8	D	Buchanan
1859–61	36th	R	114	D	92	31	D	36	R	26	4	D	Buchanan
1861–63	37th	R	105	D	43	30	R	31	D	10	8	R	Lincoln
1863–65	38th	R	102	D	75	9	R	36	D	9	5	R	Lincoln

Party Strength in Congress (continued)

Period	Congress	House Majority Party		House Minority Party		Others	Senate Majority Party		Senate Minority Party		Others	Party of President	
1865–67	39th	U	149	D	42		U	42	D	10		R	Lincoln
												R	A. Johnson
1867–69	40th	R	143	D	49		R	42	D	11		R	A. Johnson
1869–71	41st	R	149	D	63		R	56	D	11		R	Grant
1871–73	42nd	R	134	D	104	5	R	52	D	17	5	R	Grant
1873–75	43rd	R	194	D	92	14	R	49	D	19	5	R	Grant
1875–77	44th	D	169	R	109	14	R	45	D	29	2	R	Grant
1877–79	45th	D	153	R	140		R	39	D	36	1	R	Hayes
1879–81	46th	D	149	R	130	14	D	42	R	33	1	R	Hayes
1881–83	47th	D	147	R	135	11	R	37	D	37	1	R	Garfield
												R	Arthur
1883–85	48th	D	197	R	118	10	R	38	D	36	2	R	Arthur
1885–87	49th	D	183	R	140	2	R	43	D	34		D	Cleveland
1887–89	50th	D	169	R	152	4	R	39	D	37		D	Cleveland
1889–91	51st	R	166	D	159		R	39	D	37		R	B. Harrison
1891–93	52nd	D	235	R	88	9	R	47	D	39	2	R	B. Harrison
1893–95	53rd	D	218	R	127	11	D	44	R	38	3	D	Cleveland
1895–97	54th	R	244	D	105	7	R	43	D	39	6	D	Cleveland
1897–99	55th	R	204	D	113	40	R	47	D	34	7	R	McKinley
1899–1901	56th	R	185	D	163	9	R	53	D	26	8	R	McKinley
1901–03	57th	R	197	D	151	9	R	55	D	31	4	R	McKinley
												R	T. Roosevelt
1903–05	58th	R	208	D	178		R	57	D	33		R	T. Roosevelt
1905–07	59th	R	250	D	136		R	57	D	33		R	T. Roosevelt
1907–09	60th	R	222	D	164		R	61	D	31		R	T. Roosevelt
1909–11	61st	R	219	D	172		R	61	D	32		R	Taft
1911–13	62nd	D	228	R	161	1	R	51	D	41		R	Taft
1913–15	63rd	D	291	R	127	17	D	51	R	44	1	D	Wilson
1915–17	64th	D	230	R	196	9	D	56	R	40		D	Wilson
1917–19	65th	D	216	R	210	6	D	53	R	42		D	Wilson
1919–21	66th	R	240	D	190	3	R	49	D	47		D	Wilson
1921–23	67th	R	301	D	131	1	R	59	D	37		R	Harding
1923–25	68th	R	225	D	205	5	R	51	D	43	2	R	Coolidge
1925–27	69th	R	247	D	183	4	R	56	D	39	1	R	Coolidge
1927–29	70th	R	237	D	195	3	R	49	D	46	1	R	Coolidge
1929–31	71st	R	267	D	167	1	R	56	D	39	1	R	Hoover
1931–33	72nd	D	220	R	214	1	R	48	D	47	1	R	Hoover
1933–35	73rd	D	310	R	117	5	D	60	R	35	1	D	F. Roosevelt
1935–37	74th	D	319	R	103	10	D	69	R	25	2	D	F. Roosevelt
1937–39	75th	D	331	R	89	13	D	76	R	16	4	D	F. Roosevelt
1939–41	76th	D	261	R	164	4	D	69	R	23	4	D	F. Roosevelt
1941–43	77th	D	268	R	162	5	D	66	R	28	2	D	F. Roosevelt

Party Strength in Congress (continued)

Period	Congress	House Majority Party		House Minority Party		Others	Senate Majority Party		Senate Minority Party		Others	Party of President	
1943–45	78th	D	218	R	208	4	D	58	R	37	1	D	F. Roosevelt
1945–47	79th	D	242	R	190	2	D	56	R	38	1	D	Truman
1947–49	80th	R	245	D	188	1	R	51	D	45		D	Truman
1949–51	81st	D	263	R	171	1	D	54	R	42		D	Truman
1951–53	82nd	D	234	R	199	1	D	49	R	47		D	Truman
1953–55	83rd	R	221	D	211	1	R	48	D	47	1	R	Eisenhower
1955–57	84th	D	232	R	203		D	48	R	47	1	R	Eisenhower
1957–59	85th	D	233	R	200		D	49	R	47		R	Eisenhower
1959–61	86th	D	284	R	153		D	65	R	35		R	Eisenhower
1961–63	87th	D	263	R	174		D	65	R	35		D	Kennedy
1963–65	88th	D	258	R	117		D	67	R	33		D	Kennedy
												D	L. Johnson
1965–67	89th	D	295	R	140		D	68	R	32		D	L. Johnson
1967–69	90th	D	246	R	187		D	64	R	36		D	L. Johnson
1969–71	91st	D	245	R	189		D	57	R	43		R	Nixon
1971–73	92nd	D	254	R	180		D	54	R	44	2	R	Nixon
1973–75	93rd	D	239	R	192	1	D	56	R	42	2	R	Nixon
1975–77	94th	D	291	R	144		D	60	R	37	3	R	Ford
1977–79	95th	D	292	R	143		D	61	R	38	1	D	Carter
1979–81	96th	D	276	R	157		D	58	R	41	1	D	Carter
1981–83	97th	D	243	R	192		R	53	D	46	1	R	Reagan
1983–85	98th	D	269	R	166		R	54	D	46		R	Reagan
1985–87	99th	D	253	R	182		R	53	D	47		R	Reagan
1987–89	100th	D	258	R	177		D	55	R	45		R	Reagan
1989–91	101st	D	259	R	174		D	55	R	45		R	Bush
1991–93	102nd	D	267	R	167	1	D	56	R	44		R	Bush
1993–95	103rd	D	258	R	176	1	D	57	R	43		D	Clinton
1995–97	104th	R	230	D	204	1	R	52	D	48		D	Clinton
1997–99	105th	R	227	D	207	1	R	55	D	45		D	Clinton
1999–2001	106th	R	223	D	211	1	R	55	D	45		D	Clinton

AD = Administration; AM = Anti-Masonic; C = Coalition; D = Democratic; DR = Democratic-Republican; F = Federalist; J = Jacksonian; NR = National Republican; Op = Opposition; R = Republican; U = Unionist; W = Whig. Figures are for the beginning of the first session of each Congress, except the 93rd, which are for the beginning of the second session.

Justices of the Supreme Court

	Term of Service	Years of Service	Life Span
John Jay	1789–1795	5	1745–1829
John Rutledge	1789–1791	1	1739–1800
William Cushing	1789–1810	20	1732–1810
James Wilson	1789–1798	8	1742–1798
John Blair	1789–1796	6	1732–1800
Robert H. Harrison	1789–1790	—	1745–1790
James Iredell	1790–1799	9	1951–1799
Thomas Johnson	1791–1793	1	1732–1819
William Paterson	1793–1806	13	1745–1806
*John Rutledge**	1795	—	1739–1800
Samuel Chase	1796–1811	15	1741–1811
Oliver Ellsworth	1796–1800	4	1745–1807
Bushrod Washington	1798–1829	31	1762–1829
Alfred Moore	1799–1804	4	1755–1810
John Marshall	1801–1835	34	1755–1835
William Johnson	1804–1834	30	1771–1834
H. Brockholst Livingston	1806–1823	16	1757–1823
Thomas Todd	1807–1826	18	1765–1826
Joseph Story	1811–1845	33	1779–1845
Gabriel Duval	1811–1835	24	1752–1844
Smith Thompson	1823–1843	20	1768–1843
Robert Trimble	1826–1828	2	1777–1828
John McLean	1829–1861	32	1785–1861
Henry Baldwin	1830–1844	14	1780–1844
James M. Wayne	1835–1867	32	1790–1867
Roger B. Taney	1836–1864	28	1777–1864
Philip P. Barbour	1836–1841	4	1783–1841
John Catron	1837–1865	28	1786–1865
John McKinley	1837–1852	15	1780–1852
Peter V. Daniel	1841–1860	19	1784–1860
Samuel Nelson	1845–1872	27	1792–1873
Levi Woodbury	1845–1851	5	1789–1851
Robert C. Grier	1846–1870	23	1794–1870
Benjamin R. Curtis	1851–1857	6	1809–1874
John A. Campbell	1853–1861	8	1811–1889
Nathan Clifford	1858–1881	23	1803–1881
Noah H. Swayne	1862–1881	18	1804–1884
Samuel F. Miller	1862–1890	28	1816–1890
David Davis	1862–1877	14	1815–1886
Stephen J. Field	1863–1897	34	1816–1899
Salmon P. Chase	1864–1873	8	1808–1873
William Strong	1870–1880	10	1808–1895
Joseph P. Bradley	1870–1892	22	1813–1892
Ward Hunt	1873–1882	9	1810–1886
Morrison R. Waite	1874–1888	14	1816–1888
John M. Harlan	1877–1911	34	1833–1911
William B. Woods	1880–1887	7	1824–1887
Stanley Mathews	1881–1889	7	1824–1889
Horace Gray	1882–1902	20	1828–1902
Samuel Blatchford	1882–1893	11	1820–1893
Lucius Q. C. Lamar	1888–1893	5	1825–1893
Melville W. Fuller	1888–1910	21	1833–1910
David J. Brewer	1890–1910	20	1837–1910
Henry B. Brown	1890–1906	16	1836–1913
George Shiras, Jr.	1892–1903	10	1832–1924
Howell E. Jackson	1893–1895	2	1832–1895
Edward D. White	1894–1910	16	1845–1921
Rufus W. Peckham	1895–1909	14	1838–1909
Joseph McKenna	1898–1925	26	1843–1926
Oliver W. Holmes	1902–1932	30	1841–1935
William D. Day	1903–1922	19	1849–1923
William H. Moody	1906–1910	3	1853–1917
Horace H. Lurton	1910–1914	4	1844–1914
Charles E. Hughes	1910–1916	5	1862–1948
Willis Van Devanter	1911–1937	26	1859–1941
Joseph R. Lamar	1911–1916	5	1857–1916
Edward D. White	1910–1921	11	1845–1921
Mahlon Pitney	1912–1922	10	1858–1924
James C. McReynolds	1914–1941	26	1862–1946
Louis D. Brandeis	1916–1939	22	1856–1941
John H. Clarke	1916–1922	6	1857–1945
William H. Taft	1921–1930	8	1857–1930
George Sutherland	1922–1938	15	1862–1942
Pierce Butler	1922–1939	16	1866–1939
Edward T. Sanford	1923–1930	7	1865–1930
Harlan F. Stone	1925–1941	16	1872–1946
Charles E. Hughes	1930–1941	11	1862–1948
Owen J. Roberts	1930–1945	15	1875–1955
Benjamin N. Cardozo	1932–1938	6	1870–1938
Hugo L. Black	1937–1971	34	1886–1971
Stanley F. Reed	1938–1957	19	1884–1980
Felix Frankfurter	1939–1962	23	1882–1965
William O. Douglas	1939–1975	36	1898–1980
Frank Murphy	1940–1949	9	1890–1949
Harlan F. Stone	1941–1946	5	1872–1946
James F. Byrnes	1941–1942	1	1879–1972

Justices of the Supreme Court (continued)

	Term of Service	Years of Service	Life Span		Term of Service	Years of Service	Life Span
Robert H. Jackson	1941–1954	13	1892–1954	Thurgood Marshall	1967–1991	24	1908–1993
Wiley B. Rutledge	1943–1949	6	1894–1949	*Warren C. Burger*	1969–1986	17	1907–1995
Harold H. Burton	1945–1958	13	1888–1964	Harry A. Blackmun	1970–1994	24	1908–1998
Fred M. Vinson	1946–1953	7	1890–1953	Lewis F. Powell, Jr.	1972–1987	15	1907–1998
Tom C. Clark	1949–1967	18	1899–1977	*William H. Rehnquist*	1972–	—	1924–
Sherman Minton	1949–1956	7	1890–1965	John P. Stevens III	1975–	—	1920–
Earl Warren	1953–1969	16	1891–1974	Sandra Day O'Connor	1981–	—	1930–
John Marshall Harlan	1955–1971	16	1899–1971	Antonin Scalia	1986–	—	1936–
William J. Brennan, Jr.	1956–1990	34	1906–1977	Anthony M. Kennedy	1988–	—	1936–
Charles E. Whittaker	1957–1962	5	1901–1973	David H. Souter	1990–	—	1939–
Potter Stewart	1958–1981	23	1915–1985	Clarence Thomas	1991–	—	1948–
Byron R. White	1962–1993	31	1917–	Ruth Bader Ginsburg	1993–	—	1933–
Arthur J. Goldberg	1962–1965	3	1908–1990	Stephen Breyer	1994–	—	1938–
Abe Fortas	1965–1969	4	1910–1982				

Note: Chief justices are in italics.

*Appointed and served one term, but not confirmed by the Senate.

INDEX

A PEOPLE & A NATION

Complete Edition (ISBN 0-618-00550-1)
Volume One: To 1877 (ISBN 0-618-00551-X)
Volume Two: Since 1865 (ISBN 0-618-00552-8)

Since its first edition was published in 1982, *A People and a Natio*
has been a leader among textbooks for its innovative coverage and
spirited narrative. The Sixth Edition represents a groundbreaking
revision, introducing as coauthor David Blight, who revised chapte
on the South, the Civil War, and Reconstruction. A new feature,
"Legacy for a People and a Nation," demonstrates history's relevar
to current society, politics, and culture. In addition, Volume One
presents a reorganization of the antebellum period for heightened
chronology; an inviting new design; and new coverage of the South
slavery, culture, the Civil War, and regional interconnections in the
antebellum market economy.

John Neagle, *Pat Lyon at the Forge*, 1829

A People and a Nation is supported by a cutting-edge supplements package:

❖ Web site for *A People and a Nation*, Sixth Edition, with an online Instructor's Resource Manual,
   PowerPoint lecture slides, online Legacy activities, primary sources with activities, annotated web
   links, and the APAN community page
❖ Study Guide, Volumes One and Two
❖ Rand McNally American History Atlas available free to students
❖ Printed Test Bank
❖ Computerized Test Bank for Macintosh and Windows
❖ Map Transparencies
❖ *@history* CD-ROM for *A People and a Nation* (Instructor and Student versions)
❖ *American History GeoQuest* CD-ROM

**For a look at A PEOPLE AND A NATION's online resources
and for further information about Houghton Mifflin's history offerings,
please visit our web site: http://college.hmco.com.**

HOUGHTON MIFFLIN

New Ways to Know ®